MCA

T0268947

Microsoft 365® Certified Associate Modern Desktop Administrator

Complete Study Guide

Exam MD-100 and Exam MD-101

Second Edition

MCA
Microsoft 365® Certified Associate Modern Desktop Administrator

Complete Study Guide

Exam MD-100 and Exam MD-101
Second Edition

William Panek

SYBEX®
A Wiley Brand

Published by John Wiley & Sons, Inc., Hoboken, New Jersey.
Published simultaneously in Canada and the United Kingdom.

ISBN: 978-1-119-98464-1
ISBN: 978-1-119-98466-5 (ebk.)
ISBN: 978-1-119-98465-8 (ebk.)

For general information on our other products and services or for technical support, please contact our Customer Care Department within the United States at (800) 762-2974, outside the United States at (317) 572-3993 or fax (317) 572-4002.

Wiley also publishes its books in a variety of electronic formats. Some content that appears in print may not be available in electronic formats. For more information about Wiley products, visit our web site at www.wiley.com.

Library of Congress Control Number: 2022949492

Cover image: © Getty Images Inc./Jeremy Woodhouse
Cover design: Wiley

SKY10057547_101323

This book is dedicated to the three ladies of my life: Crystal, Alexandria, and Paige.

Acknowledgments

I would like to thank my wife and best friend, Crystal. She is always the light at the end of my tunnel. I want to thank my two daughters, Alexandria and Paige, for all of their love and support during the writing of all my books. The three of them are my support system and I couldn't do any of this without them.

I want to thank my family, and especially my brothers, Rick, Gary, and Rob. They have always been there for me. I want to thank my father, Richard, who helped me become the man I am today, and my mother, Maggie, for all of her love and support.

I would like to thank all of my friends and co-workers at StormWind Studios (www .stormwindstudios.com). Thanks to all of you for everything that you do. I would not have been able to complete this book without all of your help and support.

I want to thank everyone on my Sybex team, especially my development editor, Kim Wimpsett, who helped me make this the best book possible, and Doug Holland, who is the technical editor and an outstanding resource on this book. It's always good to have the very best technical person backing you up. I want to thank Saravanan Dakshinamurthy, who was my production editor, and Elizabeth Welch, the copyeditor.

Special thanks to my acquisitions editor, Kenyon Brown, who was the lead for the entire book. Finally, I want to thank everyone else behind the scenes who helped make this book possible. It's truly an amazing thing to have so many people work on my books to help make them the very best. I can't thank you all enough for your hard work.

About the Author

William Panek   holds the following certifications: MCP, MCP+I, MCSA, MCSA+ Security and Messaging, MCSE-NT (3.51 and 4.0), MCSE (2000, 2003, 2012/2012 R2), MCSE+Security and Messaging, MCDBA, MCT, MCTS, MCITP, CCNA, CCDA, and CHFI. Will is also a five-time and current Microsoft MVP winner.

After many successful years in the computer industry, Will decided that he could better use his talents and his personality as an instructor. He began teaching for schools such as Boston University and the University of Maryland, just to name a few. He has done consulting and training for some of the biggest government and corporate companies in the world, including the United States Secret Service, Cisco, United States Air Force, and United States Army.

In 2015, Will became a Sr. Microsoft Instructor for StormWind Studios (www .stormwindstudios.com). He currently lives in New Hampshire with his wife and two daughters. Will was also a Representative in the New Hampshire House of Representatives from 2010 to 2012. In his spare time, he likes to do blacksmithing, shooting (trap and skeet), snowmobiling, playing racquetball, and riding his Harley. Will is also a commercially rated helicopter pilot.

About the Technical Editor

Doug Holland is a software architect at Microsoft and a former Microsoft MVP and Intel Black Belt Developer. Based in Northern California, Doug works with Microsoft's partners, assisting them in the development of solutions based on Microsoft Azure and emerging technologies.

Contents at a Glance

Introduction   *xxix*

Assessment Tests   *xliii*

Part I   **Exam MD-100**   **1**

Chapter   1   Windows Client Installation   3

Chapter   2   Configuring Users   93

Chapter   3   Managing Data   197

Chapter   4   Managing the Windows Client Environment   239

Chapter   5   Configuring Security and Devices   335

Chapter   6   Configuring Network Connectivity   419

Chapter   7   Configuring Recovery   485

Part II   **Exam MD-101**   **539**

Chapter   8   Deploy Windows Client   541

Chapter   9   Managing Identity and Access   585

Chapter   10   Planning and Managing Microsoft Intune   655

Chapter   11   Managing Devices   719

Chapter   12   Managing Security   747

Chapter   13   Monitoring Devices   797

Appendix   Answers to Review Questions   827

Index   *873*

Contents

Introduction   *xxix*

Assessment Test – MD-100   *xliii*

Assessment Test – MD-101   *xlix*

Answers to Assessment Test – MD-100   *lv*

Answers to Assessment Test – MD-101   *lviii*

Part I   **Exam MD-100**   **1**

Chapter   1   **Windows Client Installation**   **3**

Understanding the Basics   4
   Windows 10/11 Features   9
Windows 10 vs. Windows 11   11
What Has Been Changed in Windows 11?   12
Windows 10 and 11 Architecture   13
Preparing to Install Windows   14
   Windows Home   15
   Windows Pro   15
   Windows Enterprise   16
   Windows 10 Enterprise E3 and E5   17
   Windows Client Requirements   18
   New Installation or Upgrade?   20
   Disk Partitioning   24
   Language and Region Pack   25
Installing Windows 10   25
   Performing a Clean Installation of Windows 10   26
   Performing an Upgrade to Windows 10 from
      Windows 8.1   36
Installing Windows 11   41
   Performing a Clean Installation of Windows 11   42
   Performing an Upgrade to Windows 11
      from Windows 10   43
   Troubleshooting Installation Problems   43
   Supporting Multiple-Boot Options   45
   Using Windows Activation   47
Understanding Automated Deployment Options   48
   An Overview of the Microsoft Deployment Toolkit   48
   An Overview of Unattended Installation   54

An Overview of Windows Deployment Services   56
An Overview of the System Preparation Tool and Disk
   Imaging   59
Overview of the Windows Assessment and
   Deployment Kit   63
Windows Configuration Designer   64
Summary of Windows Client Deployment Options   64
Deploying Unattended Installations   66
Using the System Preparation Tool to Prepare
   an Installation for Imaging   67
Using Windows Configuration Designer to Create a
   Disk Image   69
Using the Deployment Image Servicing and
   Management Tool   71
Using Windows System Image Manager to
   Create Answer Files   73
Windows Update   74
The Update Process   75
Using Windows Update   76
Using Windows Update for Business   78
Delivery Optimization   81
Using Command-Line Options   83
Installing Microsoft Store Updates   83
Summary   85
Exam Essentials   86
Video Resources   87
Review Questions   88

Chapter 2   Configuring Users   93

Understanding User Accounts   94
Account Types   95
Built-In Accounts   96
Local and Domain User Accounts   97
Working with User Accounts   98
Using the Local Users and Groups Utility   98
Using the User Accounts Option in Control Panel   101
Creating New Users   102
Disabling User Accounts   107
Deleting User Accounts   108
Renaming User Accounts   109
Changing a User's Password   110
Using Windows Hello, Pictures, and Biometrics   111
Using Device Guard   112
Understanding Windows Defender Credential Guard   114
Configuring Device Health Attestation   116
Managing User Properties   117

Managing User Group Membership   117
Setting Up User Profiles, Logon Scripts, and
   Home Folders   119
Troubleshooting User Account Authentication   126
Managing and Creating Groups   127
   Using Built-In Groups   127
   Creating Groups   131
   Managing Group Membership   133
   Deleting Groups   135
Managing Security Using GPOs and LGPOs   135
   Understanding the GPO and LGPO Basics   135
   Using the Group Policy Result Tool   137
   Managing and Applying LGPOs   138
   Configuring Local Security Policies   140
   Using Account Policies   141
   Using Local Policies   147
Configuring User Account Control   155
   Privilege Elevation   156
   Managing Credentials by Using Credential Manager   157
   Local Administrator Password Solutions (LAPS)   159
   Registry and File Virtualization   165
Understanding Smart Cards   165
Configuring Remote Management   167
   Remote Assistance   168
   Easy Connect   168
   Remote Desktop   173
   Quick Assist   176
   Windows Admin Center   180
   Enabling PowerShell Remoting   182
   Configuring a VPN Connection   182
   Transparent Caching   185
   Broadband Tethering   185
Using PowerShell   186
Summary   189
Exam Essentials   189
Video Resources   190
Review Questions   191

Chapter   3   **Managing Data**   **197**

Managing File and Folder Security   198
   Folder Options/File Explorer Options   199
   Understanding Dynamic Access Control   203
   Securing Access to Files and Folders   204
   Determining and Viewing Effective Permissions for NTFS   208
   Determining NTFS Permissions for Copied or
      Moved Files   211

Managing Network Access   211
  Creating and Managing Shared Folders   211
  Configuring Share Permissions   213
  Cloud-Based Storage   214
  Configuring OneDrive   215
Understanding Hardware Security   220
  Using BitLocker Drive Encryption   221
  Features of BitLocker   222
  Windows 7 vs. Windows 10/11   224
  Using the BitLocker Administration and
    Monitoring Utility   227
  Use Configuration Manager to Manage
    BitLocker Drive Encryption (BDE)   228
  Understanding Smart Cards   229
Summary   230
Exam Essentials   231
Video Resources   231
Review Questions   232

Chapter 4   Managing the Windows Client Environment   239

Managing Windows   240
  Manipulating the Desktop Environment   241
  Configuring Personalization   251
  Using Control Panel   259
  Using the Microsoft Management Console   270
  Using the System Settings   272
  Understanding the Settings Window   273
  Using PowerShell   277
Configuring Mobility Options   279
  Configuring Offline Files and Synchronization   279
  Configuring Power Policies   281
Managing Windows 10/11 Services   288
Configuring Internet Browsers   291
  Cortana   291
  Browser Controls   293
  Pinning Sites to the Taskbar   293
  Searchable Address Bar   293
  Security and Privacy Enhancements   293
  Using the Browser's Compatibility Mode   294
  Using Enhanced Security Mode in Edge   295
  Using InPrivate Browsing   297
  Configuring Internet Options   297
Manage and Use Hyper-V on Windows Client   303
  Hyper-V System Requirements   304

Enabling the Hyper-V Role   304
Opening the Hyper-V Manager   305
Changing Configuration on an Existing Virtual Machine   311
Deleting Virtual Machines   313
Manage Virtual Switches   314
Managing Virtual Hard Disks   316
PowerShell Commands   322
Windows Sandbox   325
Summary   328
Exam Essentials   329
Video Resources   329
Review Questions   330

Chapter   5   Configuring Security and Devices   335

Configuring Disk Storage   336
Basic Storage   337
Dynamic Storage   337
GUID Partition Table   339
Using the Disk Management Utility   340
Understanding the Disk Management Utility   340
Managing Storage   355
Managing Dynamic Storage   355
Understanding Filesystems   358
Filesystem Selection   358
Filesystem Conversion   361
Configuring NTFS   361
Configuring Hardware   365
Understanding Devices   365
Using Device Manager   366
Installing and Updating Device Drivers   370
Driver Signing   379
Managing I/O Devices   381
Configuring Removable Storage Devices   381
Managing Printers   385
Configuring Windows Defender Firewall   401
Understanding the Windows Defender Firewall Basics   401
Windows Defender Firewall with Advanced Security   403
Managing Windows Security   408
Windows Security Center   408
Summary   411
Exam Essentials   412
Video Resources   412
Review Questions   413

Chapter 6   Configuring Network Connectivity   419

Understanding the Basics   420
    Peer-to-Peer Networks   420
    On-Site Active Directory Networks   422
    Cloud-Based Azure Active Directory   424
    Other Microsoft Networking Terms and Roles   424
Configuring NIC Devices   427
    Configuring a Network Adapter   428
    Troubleshooting a Network Adapter   434
    Configuring Wireless NIC Devices   434
    Configuring Wi-Fi Direct   442
Understanding TCP/IP   445
    Benefits and Features of TCP/IP   446
    Basics of IP Addressing and Configuration   448
    Using IPv6 Addresses   452
    Configuring TCP/IP on Windows 10   463
    Testing Your IP Configuration   467
    Configuring Windows Client on a Network   468
Configure VPN Clients   470
    Create a VPN Profile   471
    Configure and Manage Certificates on Client Devices   475
Summary   478
Exam Essentials   479
Video Resources   479
Review Questions   480

Chapter 7   Configuring Recovery   485

Understanding Recovery   487
Knowing the Startup/Boot Options   488
    Starting in Safe Mode   489
    Enabling Boot Logging   492
    Using Other Startup Setting Options   494
    Understanding System Restore   495
    Using the System Image Recovery   497
    Using the Startup Repair Tool   498
Maintaining Windows 10/11 with Backup and Restore   498
    Creating a Backup   499
    Restoring Files from a Backup   500
    Recovering Files from OneDrive   501
    Using the WBAdmin Command Utility   502
    Using Advanced Backup Options   503
Using System Protection   505
    Creating Restore Points   506
    Restoring Restore Points   507

Cleaning Up Old Restore Points   507
Storage Sense   508
Using the Recycle Bin   510
Monitoring Windows   511
Introducing Performance Monitor   511
Using Other Performance-Monitoring Tools   521
Manage the Registry   531
Summary   532
Exam Essentials   533
Video Resources   533
Review Questions   534

Part II   Exam MD-101   539

Chapter   8   Deploy Windows Client   541

Plan a Windows Client Deployment   542
Microsoft Endpoint Manager (MEM) Overview   542
Endpoint Analytics   544
Deploying with Windows Autopilot   551
Windows Autopilot Requirements   552
Configure Device Registration for Autopilot   557
Windows Autopilot Profiles   559
Provision Windows Devices by Using Autopilot   563
Troubleshoot an Autopilot Deployment   564
Using Microsoft Deployment Toolkit (MDT)   567
Planning MDT Deployments   567
MDT Configuration Options   568
Plan and Implement PXE Boot by Using Windows
  Deployment Services (WDS)   569
Summary   576
Exam Essentials   576
Video Resources   577
Review Questions   578

Chapter   9   Managing Identity and Access   585

Active Directory vs. Azure Active Directory   586
Understanding Active Directory   586
Understanding Azure Active Directory   597
Managing Hybrid Networks   625
Password Hash Synchronization with Azure AD   625
Azure Active Directory Pass-Through Authentication   626
Federation with Azure AD   627
Common Identity Scenarios   630
Azure AD Connect   631

	Configure Enterprise State Roaming in Azure AD	638
	Requirements of Enterprise State Roaming	638
	Enable Enterprise State Roaming	639
	Plan and Implement Conditional Access Policies	639
	Create a Conditional Access Policy	642
	Troubleshooting Conditional Access	643
	Using PowerShell Commands	645
	Summary	647
	Exam Essentials	648
	Video Resources	649
	Review Questions	650
Chapter 10	**Planning and Managing Microsoft Intune**	**655**
	Managing Devices with Microsoft Intune	656
	Understanding Microsoft Intune Benefits	658
	Configuring Intune Subscriptions	658
	Provisioning User Accounts	665
	Setting Administrator Accounts	665
	Supporting Applications	687
	Deploying Applications Using Intune	687
	Supporting Broadband Connectivity	694
	Understanding Data Synchronization	695
	Using Mobile Application Management	697
	Understanding Updates	699
	Deploying Software Updates Using Intune	699
	Using Intune Compliance Reports	705
	Using Intune Reports	705
	Implement App Protection and App Configuration Policies	706
	PowerShell Commands	710
	Summary	711
	Exam Essentials	711
	Video Resources	712
	Review Questions	713
Chapter 11	**Managing Devices**	**719**
	Compliance Policies	721
	Conditional Access	721
	Plan Device Compliance Policies	723
	Device Configuration Profiles	728
	Summary	740
	Exam Essentials	741
	Video Resources	741
	Review Questions	742

Chapter	**12**	**Managing Security**	**747**
		Windows Security	748
		Planning and Implementing Endpoint Protection	749
		Endpoint Security	751
		Managing Endpoint Security in Microsoft Intune	752
		Implementing Microsoft Defender for Endpoint	759
		Understanding Microsoft Defender Application Guard	771
		Understanding Microsoft Defender Credential Guard	780
		Implementing and Managing Microsoft Defender Exploit Guard	783
		Using Windows Defender Application Control	787
		Summary	788
		Exam Essentials	789
		Video Resources	790
		Review Questions	791
Chapter	**13**	**Monitoring Devices**	**797**
		Monitoring Windows	799
		Monitor Cloud-Based Tools	799
		Monitor Azure Device Security	809
		Monitor Devices by Using Endpoint Manager Admin Center	813
		Monitoring Devices by Using Endpoint Analytics	818
		Summary	820
		Exam Essentials	820
		Video Resources	820
		Review Questions	821
Appendix		**Answers to Review Questions**	**827**
		Chapter 1: Windows Client Installation	828
		Chapter 2: Configuring Users	830
		Chapter 3: Managing Data	833
		Chapter 4: Managing the Windows Client Environment	836
		Chapter 5: Configuring Security and Devices	840
		Chapter 6: Configuring Network Connectivity	843
		Chapter 7: Configuring Recovery	846
		Chapter 8: Deploy Windows Client	850
		Chapter 9: Managing Identity and Access	855
		Chapter 10: Planning and Managing Microsoft Intune	858
		Chapter 11: Managing Devices	862
		Chapter 12: Managing Security	865
		Chapter 13: Monitoring Devices	869
		Index	*873*

Table of Exercises

Exercise	1.1	Performing a Clean Installation of Windows 10	27
Exercise	1.2	Upgrading Windows 8.1 to Windows 10	37
Exercise	1.3	Configuring Locales	41
Exercise	1.4	Troubleshooting Failed Installations with Setup Logs	45
Exercise	1.5	Downloading and Installing MDT	50
Exercise	1.6	Configuring MDT	52
Exercise	1.7	Prepare a System for Imaging by Using the System Preparation Tool	69
Exercise	2.1	Adding the Local Users and Groups Snap-In	99
Exercise	2.2	Accessing Local Users and Groups via the Computer Management Utility	100
Exercise	2.3	Creating New Users via the MMC	105
Exercise	2.4	Disabling User Accounts	107
Exercise	2.5	Deleting a User Account	109
Exercise	2.6	Renaming a User Account	110
Exercise	2.7	Changing a User's Password	111
Exercise	2.8	Adding a User to an Existing Group	119
Exercise	2.9	Setting Up User Profiles	120
Exercise	2.10	Assigning Home Folders	125
Exercise	2.11	Creating Local Groups	133
Exercise	2.12	Adding Accounts to Groups	134
Exercise	2.13	Adding the Local Computer Policy Snap-In	139
Exercise	2.14	Accessing an LGPO	140
Exercise	2.15	Configuring Password Policy	144
Exercise	2.16	Configuring Account-Lockout Policies	146
Exercise	2.17	Configuring Audit Policies	150
Exercise	2.18	Applying a User Rights Policy	155
Exercise	2.19	Seeing How UAC Affects Accounts	157
Exercise	2.20	Enabling Remote Desktop on Windows 10	175
Exercise	2.21	Setting Up a VPN Connection on Windows 10	184
Exercise	3.1	Managing NTFS Permissions	207
Exercise	3.2	Logging into OneDrive	217
Exercise	3.3	Using BitLocker in Windows 10	226
Exercise	4.1	Configuring Windows 10 Desktop Options	258

Exercise   **4.2**   Installing New Features. 267

Exercise   **4.3**   Changing the Computer Name on a Windows 10/11 Computer 276

Exercise   **4.4**   Changing the System's Virtual Memory on a Windows 10/11 Computer . 277

Exercise   **4.5**   Configuring a Power Plan. 285

Exercise   **4.6**   Configuring the Power Button for Hibernate Mode 286

Exercise   **4.7**   Configuring Services. 290

Exercise   **4.8**   Creating a New Virtual Machine. 306

Exercise   **4.9**   Creating an Internal Virtual Network 315

Exercise   **4.10**   Creating a Differencing Hard Disk 318

Exercise   **5.1**   Creating a New Volume. 349

Exercise   **5.2**   Converting a Basic Disk to a GPT Disk. 352

Exercise   **5.3**   Converting a Basic Disk to a Dynamic Disk. 353

Exercise   **5.4**   Editing a Drive Letter. 354

Exercise   **5.5**   Deleting a Partition 355

Exercise   **5.6**   Creating an Extended Volume 356

Exercise   **5.7**   Opening Devices 366

Exercise   **5.8**   Viewing Devices Using Device Manager. 367

Exercise   **5.9**   Configuring Network Adapter Advanced Properties. 370

Exercise   **5.10**   Viewing Driver Details. 374

Exercise   **5.11**   Updating a Driver 374

Exercise   **5.12**   Rolling Back a Driver. 375

Exercise   **5.13**   Disabling and Enabling a Device in Device Manager. 376

Exercise   **5.14**   Uninstalling and Reinstalling a Device Driver. 377

Exercise   **5.15**   Verifying Signed Drivers. 381

Exercise   **5.16**   Configuring an Input/Output Device 385

Exercise   **5.17**   Installing a Printer 389

Exercise   **5.18**   Installing a Shared Network Print Device 390

Exercise   **5.19**   Managing Documents in the Local Queue in Windows 10 395

Exercise   **5.20**   Removing a Printer from Printers & Scanners in Windows 10 397

Exercise   **5.21**   Using the Print Migration Tools 399

Exercise   **5.22**   Creating a New Inbound Rule. 406

Exercise   **5.23**   Running an Advanced Scan 410

Exercise   **6.1**   Viewing the Network Connection Details in Windows 10 437

Exercise   **6.2**   Viewing Wireless Network Connection Properties 438

Exercise   **6.3**   Accessing the Windows Client Wireless Properties 440

Exercise **6.4** Configure a Static TCP/IP Address in Windows 10 463

Exercise **6.5** Using DHCP in Windows 10/11 465

Exercise **6.6** Connecting a Windows Client Machine to the Domain 469

Exercise **7.1** Booting Your Windows 10/11 Computer to Safe Mode from
the Sign-In Screen 491

Exercise **7.2** Viewing the Boot Log File 493

Exercise **7.3** Backing Up Files 500

Exercise **7.4** Restoring Files 501

Exercise **7.5** Configuring OneDrive 502

Exercise **7.6** Creating a System Image 503

Exercise **7.7** Creating a Restore Point 506

Exercise **7.8** Restoring a Restore Point 507

Exercise **7.9** Using the Recycle Bin 511

Exercise **9.1** Setting Up an On-Site Domain Controller 591

Exercise **9.2** Creating an Azure AD User Account 616

Exercise **9.3** Creating an Azure AD Group Account 618

Exercise **9.4** Setting Up Self-Service Password Reset 619

Exercise **9.5** Testing the Self-Service Password Reset 621

Exercise **9.6** Adding Azure AD Identity Protection 622

Exercise **9.7** Installing Azure AD Connect 632

Exercise **9.8** Creating the Site-to-Site VPN Connection 634

Exercise **9.9** Creating the Local Network Gateway 636

Exercise **10.1** Setting Up an Intune Account 660

Exercise **10.2** Adding Users to Intune 668

Exercise **10.3** Creating a New Group 669

Exercise **10.4** Confirming the Windows Version 677

Exercise **10.5** Enrolling Windows 10 Desktop Version 1607 or Higher 679

Exercise **12.1** Installing Microsoft Defender Application Guard 772

Exercise **12.2** Using Microsoft Defender Application Guard 775

Exercise **12.3** Microsoft Defender Application Guard Enterprise 777

Exercise **12.4** Enabling Microsoft Defender Credential Guard Using a GPO 781

Exercise **12.5** Enabling Microsoft Defender Exploit Guard Using Intune 784

Introduction

This book was written from over 25 years of IT experience. I have taken that experience and translated it into a Windows 10/11 book that will help you not only prepare for the Microsoft 365 Certified: Modern Desktop Administrator Associate exams but also develop a clear understanding of how to install and configure Windows 10/11 while avoiding all the possible configuration pitfalls.

Many Microsoft books just explain the Windows operating system, but with *MCA Microsoft 365® Certified Associate Modern Desktop Administrator Complete Study Guide: Exam MD-100 and Exam MD-101, Second Edition,* I will go a step further, providing many in-depth, step-by-step procedures to support my explanations of how the operating system performs at its best.

The exams MD-100 and MD-101 cover aspects from both Windows 10 and Windows 11. Hence, I will refer to them collectively as Microsoft Windows 10/11. These are Microsoft's client operating system software. Windows 11 is the newest version of the operating system launched by Microsoft.

Windows 10/11 eliminates many of the problems that plagued the previous versions of Windows clients, and it includes a much faster boot time and shutdown. It is also easier to install and configure, and it barely stops to ask the user any questions during installation. In this book, I will show you what features are installed during the automated installation and where you can make changes if you need to be more in charge of your operating system and its features.

This book takes you through all the ins and outs of Windows 10/11, including installation, configuration, online Microsoft subscriptions, auditing, backups, and so much more.

Windows 10/11 has improved on Microsoft's desktop environment and made networking easier, working with Microsoft Azure, enhanced search ability, improved performance—and that's only scratching the surface.

When all is said and done, this is a technical book for IT professionals who want to take Windows 10/11 to the next step and get certified. With this book, you will not only learn Windows 10/11 and hopefully pass the exams, you will also become a Windows client expert.

The Microsoft Certification Program

Since the inception of its certification program, Microsoft has certified more than 2 million people. As the computer network industry continues to increase in both size and complexity, this number is sure to grow—and the need for proven ability will also increase. Certifications can help companies verify the skills of prospective employees and contractors.

The Microsoft certification track for Windows includes the following certification:

Microsoft 365 Certified: Modern Desktop Administrator Associate   The Microsoft 365 Certified: Modern Desktop Administrator Associate is now the highest-level certification you can achieve with Microsoft in relation to Windows 10/11. It requires passing exams MD-100 and MD-101. This book assists in your preparation for both exams.

How Do You Become Certified on Windows 10/11?

Attaining Microsoft certification has always been a challenge. In the past, students have been able to acquire detailed exam information—even most of the exam questions—from online "brain dumps" and third-party "cram" books or software products. For the new generation of exams, this is simply not the case.

Microsoft has taken strong steps to protect the security and integrity of its new certification tracks. Now prospective candidates must complete a course of study that develops detailed knowledge about a wide range of topics. It supplies them with the true skills needed, derived from working with the technology being tested.

The new generations of Microsoft certification programs are heavily weighted toward hands-on skills and experience. It is recommended that candidates have troubleshooting skills acquired through hands-on experience and working knowledge.

Fortunately, if you are willing to dedicate the time and effort to learn Windows 10/11, you can prepare yourself well for the exam by using the proper tools. By working through this book, you can successfully meet the requirements to pass the Windows 10/11 exams.

Microsoft 365 Certified: Modern Desktop Administrator Associate Exam Requirements

Candidates for MCA certification on Windows 10/11 must pass two Windows 10 MCSA tests:

- **MD-100:** Windows Client
- **MD-101:** Managing Modern Desktops

Microsoft provides exam objectives to give you a general overview of possible areas of coverage on the Microsoft exams. Keep in mind, however, that exam objectives are subject to change at any time without prior notice and at Microsoft's sole discretion. Please visit the Microsoft Learning website (www.microsoft.com/learning) for the most current listing of exam objectives.

For a more detailed description of the Microsoft certification programs, including a list of all the exams, visit the Microsoft Learning website at www.microsoft.com/learning.

Like all exams, the MCA certification from Microsoft is updated periodically and may eventually be retired or replaced. At some point after Microsoft is no longer offering this exam, the old editions of our books and online tools will be retired. If you have purchased this book after the exam was retired, or are attempting to register in the Sybex online learning environment after the exam was retired, please know that we make no guarantees that this exam's online Sybex tools will be available once the exam is no longer available.

Types of Exam Questions

In an effort to both refine the testing process and protect the quality of its certifications, Microsoft has focused its latest certification exams on real experience and hands-on proficiency. There is a greater emphasis on your past working environments and responsibilities and less emphasis on how well you can memorize. In fact, Microsoft says that certification candidates should have hands-on experience before attempting to pass any certification exams.

 Microsoft will accomplish its goal of protecting the exams' integrity by regularly adding and removing exam questions, limiting the number of questions that any individual sees in a beta exam, limiting the number of questions delivered to an individual by using adaptive testing, and adding new exam elements.

Exam questions may be in a variety of formats. Depending on which exam you take you may see multiple-choice questions as well as select-and-place and prioritize-a-list questions. Simulations and case study–based formats are included as well. Let's take a look at the types of exam questions, so you'll be prepared for all of the possibilities.

Multiple-Choice Questions

Multiple-choice questions come in two main forms. One is a straightforward question followed by several possible answers of which one or more is correct. The other type of multiple-choice question is more complex and based on a specific scenario. The scenario may focus on several areas or objectives.

Select-and-Place Questions

Select-and-place exam questions involve graphical elements that you must manipulate to successfully answer the question. For example, you might see a diagram of a computer network.

A typical diagram will show computers and other components next to boxes that contain the text "Place here." The labels for the boxes represent various computer roles on a network, such as a print server and a file server. Based on information given for each computer, you are asked to select each label and place it in the correct box. You need to place *all* of the labels correctly. No credit is given for the question if you correctly label only some of the boxes.

In another select-and-place problem, you might be asked to put a series of steps in order by dragging items from boxes on the left to boxes on the right and placing them in the correct order. One other type requires that you drag an item from the left and place it under an item in a column on the right.

 For more information on the various exam question types, go to https://docs.microsoft.com/en-us/certifications/exam-duration-question-types.

Simulations

Simulations are the kinds of questions that most closely represent actual situations and test the skills you use while working with Microsoft software interfaces. These exam questions include a mock interface on which you are asked to perform certain actions according to a given scenario. The simulated interfaces look nearly identical to what you see in the actual product.

Because of the number of possible errors that can be made on simulations, be sure to consider the following recommendations from Microsoft:

- Do not change any simulation settings that don't pertain to the solution directly.

- When related information has not been provided, assume that the default settings are used.

- Make sure that your entries are spelled correctly.

- Close all the simulation application windows after completing the set of tasks in the simulation.

The best way to prepare for simulation questions is to spend time working with the graphical interface of the product on which you will be tested.

Case Study–Based Questions

Case study–based questions first appeared in the MCSD program. These questions present a scenario with a range of requirements. Based on the information provided, you answer a series of multiple-choice and select-and-place questions. The interface for case study–based questions have a number of tabs, each of which contains information about the scenario. At present, this type of question appears only in most of the Design exams.

Tips for Taking the Windows Client Exams

Here are some general tips for achieving success on your certification exam:

- Arrive early at the exam center so that you can relax and review your study materials. During this final review, you can look over tables and lists of exam-related information.

- Read the questions carefully. Do not be tempted to jump to an early conclusion. Make sure that you know *exactly* what the question is asking.

- Answer all questions. If you are unsure about a question, mark it for review and come back to it at a later time.

- On simulations, do not change settings that are not directly related to the question. Also, assume default settings if the question does not specify or imply which settings are used.

- For questions that you're not sure about, use a process of elimination to get rid of the obviously incorrect answers first. This improves your odds of selecting the correct answer when you need to make an educated guess.

Exam Registration

At the time this book was released, Microsoft exams are given using more than 1,000 Authorized VUE Testing Centers around the world. For the location of a testing center near you, go to VUE's website at www.vue.com. If you are outside the United States and Canada, contact your local VUE registration center.

Find out the number of the exam you want to take, and then register with the VUE registration center nearest to you. At this point, you will be asked for advance payment for the exam. The exams are $165 each and you must take them within one year of payment. You can schedule exams up to six weeks in advance or as late as one working day prior to the date of the exam. You can cancel or reschedule your exam if you contact the center at least two working days prior to the exam. Same-day registration is available in some locations, subject to space availability. Where same-day registration is available, you must register a minimum of two hours before test time.

When you schedule the exam, you will be provided with instructions regarding appointment and cancellation procedures, ID requirements, and information about the testing center location. In addition, you will receive a registration and payment confirmation letter from VUE.

Microsoft requires certification candidates to accept the terms of a nondisclosure agreement before taking certification exams.

Exam policies can change from time to time. We highly recommend that you check both the Microsoft and Pearson VUE sites for the most up-to-date information when you begin your preparing, when you register, and again a few days before your scheduled exam date.

Who Should Read This Book?

This book is intended for individuals who want to earn their Microsoft 365 Certified: Modern Desktop Administrator Associate certification.

Not only will this book help anyone who is looking to pass the Microsoft exams, it will also help anyone who wants to learn the real ins and outs of the Windows client operating system.

What's Inside?

Here is a glance at what's in each chapter.

Part I: MD-100

Chapter 1: Windows Client Installation   In the first chapter, I explain the requirements and steps to install and configure Windows client. I will also show you the different versions of Windows 10/11. This chapter also shows you how to configure automated installation of Windows 10/11.

Chapter 2: Configuring Users   This chapter shows you how to configure user authorization and authentication. Understanding how users authenticate onto your network and knowing how to secure your network and users is one of the most important tasks that administrators must perform. I will also show you how to manage local groups, manage local users, configure remote connectivity, configure remote management, and configure devices by using local policies.

Chapter 3: Managing Data   I show you how to configure disks, volumes, and filesystem options using Disk Management and Windows PowerShell. I will also discuss how to configure removable devices and how to create and configure storage spaces. Finally, I will show you how to troubleshoot storage and removable device issues.

Chapter 4: Managing the Windows Client Environment   This chapter takes you through the different ways to configure the Windows 10/11 environment, including performing post-installation configuration, configuring Edge, configuring mobility settings, configuring sign-in options, and customizing the Windows desktop.

Chapter 5: Configuring Security and Devices   This chapter takes you through the different ways to configure Windows client devices, including configuring Windows Defender Firewall and implementing encryption.

Chapter 6: Configuring Network Connectivity   This chapter will show you how to implement and configure Windows networking, including workgroups and domains. I will also talk about how to configure TCP/IP.

Chapter 7: Configuring Recovery   This chapter will explain to you how to implement and configure Windows backups and recovery points. I will show you how to use cloud-based backups and how to recover the Windows client system using advanced boot options.

Part II: MD-101

Chapter 8: Deploy Windows Client   This chapter shows you how to configure automated installation of Windows 10/11.

Chapter 9: Managing Identity and Access   This chapter shows you how to configure user authorization and authentication. Understanding how users authenticate onto your network and Azure is one of the most important tasks that administrators must perform. I will also teach you how to manage user profiles.

Chapter 10: Planning and Managing Microsoft Intune   This chapter takes you through the different ways to manage Intune device enrollment and inventory. I will also show you how to deploy and update your applications. Finally, I will talk about implementing Mobile Application Management.

Chapter 11: Managing Devices   I show you how to implement conditional access and compliance policies for devices. I will show you how to configure device profiles and also how to plan and implement co-management between your on-site network with your Azure-based network.

Chapter 12: Managing Security   This chapter teaches you how to configure and manage Windows Defender. I will show you how to use Windows Defender Credential Guard, Windows Defender Exploit Guard, Windows Defender Advanced Threat Protection, Windows Defender Application Guard, and Windows Defender Antivirus.

Chapter 13: Monitoring Devices   This chapter will show you how to monitor your different devices using Azure Monitor, Endpoint Manager Admin Center, and using Endpoint Analytics.

What's Included with the Book

There are many helpful items intended to prepare you for the Microsoft 365 Certified: Modern Desktop Administrator Associate certification included in this book:

Assessment Test   There is an assessment test at the conclusion of the introduction that can be used to quickly evaluate where you are with Windows 10/11. This test should be taken prior to beginning your work in this book and should help you identify areas in which you are either strong or weak. Note that these questions are purposely more simplistic than the types of questions you may see on the exams.

Opening List of Objectives   Each chapter includes a list of the exam objectives that are covered in that chapter.

Helpful Exercises   Throughout the book, I have included step-by-step exercises of some of the more important tasks you should be able to perform. Some of these exercises have corresponding videos that can be downloaded from the book's website. Also, later in this introduction you'll find a recommended home lab setup that will be helpful in completing these tasks.

Video Resources   After each chapter summary, if the chapter includes exercises with corresponding videos, a list or description of the exercises with video resources will be provided. The videos can be accessed at www.wiley.com/go/Sybextestprep.

Exam Essentials   The end of each chapter also includes a listing of exam essentials. These are essentially repeats of the objectives, but remember that any objective on the exam blueprint could show up on the exam.

Chapter Review Questions   Each chapter includes review questions. These are used to assess your understanding of the chapter and are taken directly from the chapter. These questions are based on the exam objectives and are similar in difficulty to items you might encounter on the Microsoft 365 Certified: Modern Desktop Administrator Associate exams.

The Sybex Interactive Online Test Bank, flashcards, videos, and glossary can be accessed at www.wiley.com/go/Sybextestprep.

Interactive Online Learning Environment and Test Bank

The interactive online learning environment that accompanies *MCA Microsoft 365® Certified Associate Modern Desktop Administrator Complete Study Guide, Exam MD-100 and Exam MD-101* provides a test bank with study tools to help you prepare for the certification exams and increase your chances of passing the exam the very first time! The test bank includes the following elements:

Sample Tests   All of the questions in this book are provided, including the assessment test, which you'll find at the end of this introduction, and the chapter tests that include the review questions at the end of each chapter. In addition, there are practice exams. Use these questions to test your knowledge of the study guide material. The online test bank runs on multiple devices.

Electronic Flashcards   The flashcards are included for quick reference and are great tools for learning quick facts. You can even consider them additional simple practice questions, which is essentially what they are.

Videos   Some of the exercises include corresponding videos. These videos show you how I do the exercises. There is also a video that shows you how to set up virtualization so that you can complete the exercises within a virtualized environment. I also have videos to help you on the Microsoft exams at www.youtube.com/c/williampanek.

PDF of Glossary of Terms   There is a glossary included that covers the key terms used in this book.

Recommended Home Lab Setup

To get the most out of this book, you will want to make sure that you complete the exercises throughout the chapters. To complete the exercises, you will need one of two setups. First, you can set up a machine with Windows 10/11 and complete the labs using a regular Windows client machine.

The second way to set up Windows 10/11 is by using virtualization. I set up Windows 10/11 as a virtual hard disk (VHD) and I did all the labs this way. The advantages of using virtualization are that you can always just wipe out the system and start over without losing a real server. Plus, you can set up multiple virtual servers and create a full lab environment on one machine.

I created a video for this book showing you how to set up a virtual machine and how to install Windows 10 onto that virtual machine. This video can be seen at www.youtube.com/c/williampanek.

How to Contact Sybex or the Author

Sybex strives to keep you supplied with the latest tools and information you need for your work. Please check the website at www.wiley.com/go/Sybextestprep, where I'll post additional content and updates that supplement this book should the need arise.

You can contact me by going to my website at www.willpanek.com. I also have videos and test prep information at www.youtube.com/c/williampanek. I also have a Twitter account, @AuthorWillPanek.

Objective Mapping

Table I.1 contains an objective map to show you at a glance where you can find each objective covered.

TABLE I.1   MD-100 Objective Map

Objective	Chapter
Install and configure Windows (20–25%)	
Install Windows client	**Chapter 1**
▪ Select the appropriate Windows edition; prepare hardware for installation; perform a manual clean installation; plan and implement an upgrade from a previous version of Windows; customize a Windows client installation by using the Windows ADK; configure activation and troubleshoot activation issues.	
Manage and use Hyper-V on Windows client	**Chapter 4**
▪ Create and configure virtual machines by using Hyper-V; manage virtual hard drives; manage virtual networks; configure Hyper-V settings; configure and manage checkpoints; enable and use Windows Sandbox.	
Configure Windows settings	**Chapters 4, 7**
▪ Configure system settings; manage user interface in Windows 10 and Windows 11; configure Microsoft Edge; configure language and region; configure and troubleshoot connections to printers and other devices; configure Windows client by using provisioning packages; configure startup options; configure and manage services; install and configure optional features.	
Configure and manage connectivity and storage (15–20%)	
Configure networking and access	**Chapter 6**
▪ Configure client IP settings; configure mobile networking; configure VPN client by using built-in tools or Connection Manager Administration Kit (CMAK); configure and manage certificates on client devices; troubleshoot client connectivity.	
Configure and manage storage	**Chapters 3, 5, 7**
▪ Configure local storage; configure OneDrive on Windows client; optimize local drives by using Disk cleanup or Storage Sense; configure file and folder permissions.	
Maintain Windows (30–35%)	

Objective	Chapter
Perform system and data recovery	**Chapter 7**

- Troubleshoot boot and startup processes; recover Windows client; recover files; create and manage restore points; restore from restore points.

Manage Windows updates	**Chapter 1**

- Configure updates; configure Windows delivery optimization; control updates by using group policy settings; configure updates by using Windows Update for Business; troubleshoot updates.

Configure remote management	**Chapter 2**

- Configure Remote Desktop; configure Windows Admin Center; configure PowerShell remoting and Windows Remote Management; configure remote assistance tools including Remote Assist and Quick Assist.

Monitor and manage Windows	**Chapter 7**

- Configure and analyze event logs; monitor and manage performance and reliability; configure scheduled tasks; manage Registry.

Protect devices and data (25–30%)

Manage users, groups, and computer objects	**Chapter 2**

- Manage local users; manage local user profiles; manage local groups; manage Microsoft accounts on Windows client; enable users and groups from Active Directory to access Windows client; join computers to Active Directory; configure sign-in options; manage credentials by using Credential Manager; configure user account control (UAC); implement and manage Local Administrator Password Solutions (LAPS).

Configure and manage local and group policies	**Chapter 2**

- Troubleshoot local policies and domain group policies on Windows client; configure and manage local and group policies, including security policy, user rights; assignment, and audit policy; configure Windows client settings by using group policy.

TABLE I.1   MD-100 Objective Map *(continued)*

Objective	Chapter
Manage security settings on Windows client	**Chapter 3, 4 & 5**
▪ Implement BitLocker; configure and manage Windows client firewall; manage virus and threat protection; manage application and browser control settings.	

TABLE I.2   MD-101 Objective Map

Objective	Chapter
Deploy Windows client (25–30%)	
Plan a Windows client deployment	**Chapter 8**
▪ Assess infrastructure readiness by using Endpoint Analytics; select a deployment tool based on requirements; choose between migrate and rebuild; choose an imaging and/or provisioning strategy; plan and implement changes to Windows edition by using subscription activation or MAK license management.	
Plan and implement Windows client provisioning by using Windows Autopilot	**Chapter 8**
▪ Choose an Autopilot deployment method based on requirements, including user-driven mode, self-deploying mode, autopilot reset, and pre-provisioning; configure device registration for Autopilot; create, validate, and assign deployment profiles; provision Windows devices by using Autopilot; troubleshoot an Autopilot deployment.	
Plan and implement Windows client deployment by using Microsoft Deployment Toolkit (MDT)	**Chapter 8**
▪ Plan and implement an MDT deployment infrastructure; choose configuration options based on requirements, such as boot images, OS images, upgrade packages, task sequences, and drivers; create, manage, and deploy images; plan and implement PXE boot by using Windows Deployment Services (WDS); create and use task sequences; manage application and driver deployment; customize an MDT deployment by using customsettings.ini and bootstrap.ini; monitor and troubleshoot deployment; plan and configure user state migration.	

Objective	Chapter

Manage identity and access (10–15%)

Manage identity   **Chapter 9**

- Enable users and groups from Azure Active Directory to access Windows client; register devices in and join devices to Azure Active Directory; manage AD DS and Azure AD groups; manage AD DS and Azure AD users; configure Enterprise State Roaming in Azure AD.

Plan and implement conditional access policies   **Chapter 9**

- Plan conditional access; set up conditional access policies; determine which users are affected by a conditional access policy; troubleshoot conditional access.

Manage compliance policies and configuration profiles (10–15%)

Implement device compliance policies   **Chapter 11**

- Plan device compliance policies; implement device compliance policies; manage notifications for device compliance policies; monitor device compliance; troubleshoot device compliance policies.

Plan and implement device configuration profiles   **Chapter 11**

- Plan device configuration profiles; implement device configuration profiles; monitor and troubleshoot device configuration profiles; configure and implement assigned access on public devices, including kiosks and dedicated devices.

Manage, maintain, and protect devices (25–30%)

Manage device lifecycle   **Chapter 10**

- Configure enrollment settings in Intune; configure automatic and bulk enrollment in Intune; configure policy sets; restart, retire, or wipe devices.

Monitor devices   **Chapter 13**

- Monitor devices by using Azure Monitor; monitor device hardware and software inventory by using Endpoint Manager Admin Center; monitor devices by using Endpoint Analytics.

TABLE I.2   MD-101 Objective Map *(continued)*

Objective	Chapter
Manage device updates	**Chapter 10**
■ Plan for device updates; create and manage quality update policies by using Intune; create and manage feature update policies by using Intune; create and manage iOS/iPadOS update policies by using Intune; manage Android updates by using device configuration profiles; monitor updates; troubleshoot updates in Intune; configure Windows client delivery optimization by using Intune; create and manage update rings by using Intune.	
Plan and implement endpoint protection	**Chapter 12**
■ Plan endpoint security; implement and manage security baselines in Intune; create and manage configuration policies for Endpoint Security including antivirus, encryption, firewall, endpoint detection and response, and attack surface reduction; onboard devices into Microsoft Defender for Endpoint; monitor Microsoft Defender for Endpoint; investigate and respond to threats.	
Manage apps (10–15%)	
Deploy and update applications	**Chapter 10**
■ Deploy apps by using Intune; configure Microsoft 365 Apps deployment by using Office Deployment Toolkit or Office; Customization Tool; manage Microsoft 365 Apps by using Microsoft 365 Apps Admin Center; deploy Microsoft 365 Apps by using Intune; manage Office app settings by using group policy or Intune; deploy apps by using Microsoft Store for Business, Apple store, and Google store.	
Implement app protection and app configuration policies	**Chapter 10**
■ Plan app protection policies; plan app configuration policies for iOS and Android; implement app protection policies; implement app configuration policies for iOS and Android; manage app protection policies; manage app configuration policies.	

How to Contact the Publisher

If you believe you have found a mistake in this book, please bring it to our attention. At John Wiley & Sons, we understand how important it is to provide our customers with accurate content, but even with our best efforts an error may occur.

In order to submit your possible errata, please email it to our Customer Service Team at wileysupport@wiley.com with the subject line "Possible Book Errata Submission."

Assessment Test – MD-100

1. You want to create roaming profiles for users in the Sales department. They frequently log on at computers in a central area. The profiles should be configured as mandatory and roaming profiles. Which users are able to manage mandatory profiles on Windows 10/11 computers?

   A. The user who uses the profile

   B. Server operators

   C. Power users

   D. Administrators

2. What filename extension is applied by default to custom consoles that are created for the MMC?

   A. .mmc

   B. .msc

   C. .con

   D. .mcn

3. You are the IT administrator for a large computer-training company that uses laptops for all its employees. Currently the users have to connect to the wireless network through the wireless network adapter. Windows 10/11 includes this built in as which feature?

   A. Available Network Finder (ANF)

   B. View Networks (VN)

   C. Network Availability Viewer (NAV)

   D. View Available Networks (VAN)

4. If you wanted to require that a user enter an Administrator password to perform administrative tasks, what type of user account should you create for the user?

   A. Administrator user account

   B. Standard user account

   C. Power user account

   D. Authenticated user account

5. You have installed a clean installation of Windows 10/11 on your computer. You want to create an image of the new installation to use as a basis for remote installs. What Windows utility should you use to accomplish this?

   A. WDS

   B. Windows SIM

   C. ImageX

   D. Sysprep

6. You are the administrator in charge of a computer that runs both Windows 7 and Windows 10. Windows 10 is installed on a different partition from Windows 7. You have to make sure that the computer always starts Windows 10 by default. What action should you perform?

   A. Run Bcdedit.exe and the /default parameter.

   B. Run Bcdedit.exe and the /bootcd parameter.

   C. Create a Boot.ini file in the root of the Windows 10 partition.

   D. Create a Boot.ini file in the root of the Windows 7 partition.

7. You have a user with limited vision. Which accessibility utility is used to read aloud screen text, such as the text in dialog boxes, menus, and buttons?

   A. Read-Aloud

   B. Orator

   C. Dialog Manager

   D. Narrator

8. You have just purchased a new computer that has Windows 10 preinstalled. You want to migrate existing users from a previous computer that was running Windows XP Professional. Which two files would you use to manage this process through the User State Migration Tool?

   A. usmt.exe

   B. ScanState.exe

   C. LoadState.exe

   D. Windows7Migrate.exe

9. You are using Windows 10 Home and you want to update your video drivers. How do you accomplish this?

   A. Install new drivers using Driver Manager.

   B. Upgrade the drivers using Device Manager.

   C. Upgrade the drivers using Driver Manager.

   D. Install new drivers using Device Manager.

10. You are the network administrator for a large organization. You have a Windows client machine that is working fine, but you downloaded and installed a newer version of the network adapter driver. After you load the driver, the network device stops working properly. Which tool should you use to help you fix the problem?

   A. Driver rollback

   B. Driver Repair utility

   C. Reverse Driver application

   D. Windows Driver Compatibility tool

11. You are the network administrator for your organization. Your organization has been using Windows 10/11 Enterprise. You need to run the Print Management tools from the command prompt. What command do you run?

 A. `Printmgmt.exe`

 B. `PrintMig.exe`

 C. `Prtmgmt.exe`

 D. `Printbrm.exe`

12. You are configuring power settings on your laptop. You configure the laptop to enter Sleep mode after a specified period of inactivity. Which of the following will occur when the computer enters Sleep mode?

 A. The computer will be shut down gracefully.

 B. Data will be saved to the hard disk.

 C. The monitor and hard disk will be turned off, but the computer will remain in a fully active state.

 D. The user session will not be available when you resume activity on the computer.

13. You are the administrator for a large organization that is moving to Windows 10. You need to set up a way that you can run multiple storage commands from a scripting tool. How can you set this up?

 A. Use SCCM for scripting.

 B. Use PowerShell for scripting.

 C. Use AD FS for scripting.

 D. Use Disk Administrator scripting.

14. What is the CIDR equivalent for 255.255.255.224?

 A. /24

 B. /25

 C. /26

 D. /27

15. You have compressed a 4 MB file into 2 MB. You are copying the file to another computer that has a FAT32 partition. How can you ensure that the file will remain compressed?

 A. When you copy the file, use the XCOPY command with the /Comp switch.

 B. When you copy the file, use the Windows Explorer utility and specify the option Keep Existing Attributes.

 C. On the destination folder, make sure that you set the option Compress Contents To Save Disk Space in the folder's properties.

 D. You can't maintain disk compression on a non-NTFS partition.

16. You are the network administrator for your company. Your network consists of 200 Windows client computers, and you want to assign static IP addresses rather than use a DHCP server. You want to configure the computers to reside on the 192.168.10.0 network. What subnet mask should you use with this network address?

    A. 255.0.0.0

    B. 255.255.0.0

    C. 255.255.255.0

    D. 255.255.255.255

17. You are using a laptop running Windows 10 Home. You want to synchronize files between your laptop and a network folder. Which of the following actions must you perform first in order to enable synchronization to occur between your laptop and the network folder?

    A. Upgrade your laptop to Windows 10 Enterprise.

    B. Enable one-way synchronization between the laptop and the network folder.

    C. Enable two-way synchronization between the laptop and the network folder.

    D. Configure the files on your laptop as read-only.

18. You have a DNS server that contains corrupted information. You fix the problem with the DNS server, but one of your users is complaining that they are still unable to access Internet resources. You verify that everything works on another computer on the same subnet. Which command can you use to fix the problem?

    A. `ipconfig /flush`

    B. `ipconfig /flushdns`

    C. `ping /flush`

    D. `DNS /flushdns`

19. You are the network administrator for a medium-sized company. Rick was the head of HR and recently resigned. John has been hired to replace Rick and has been given Rick's laptop. You want John to have access to all of the resources to which Rick had access. What is the easiest way to manage the transition?

    A. Rename Rick's account to John.

    B. Copy Rick's account and call the copied account John.

    C. Go into the Registry and do a search and replace to replace all of Rick's entries with John's name.

    D. Take ownership of all of Rick's resources and assign John Full Control to the resources.

20. Which of the following statements are true regarding the creation of a group in Windows 10/11? (Choose two.)

    A. Only members of the Administrators group can create users on a Windows client computer.

    B. Group names can be up to 64 characters.

    C. Group names can contain spaces.

    D. Group names can be the same as usernames but not the same as other group names on the computer.

21. You need to expand the disk space on your Windows client computer. You are considering using spanned volumes. Which of the following statements are true concerning spanned volumes? (Choose all that apply.)

    A. Spanned volumes can contain space from 2 to 32 physical drives.

    B. Spanned volumes can contain space from 2 to 24 physical drives.

    C. Spanned volumes can be formatted as FAT32 or NTFS partitions.

    D. Spanned volumes can be formatted only as NTFS partitions.

22. You have a network folder that resides on an NTFS partition on a Windows client computer. NTFS permissions and share permissions have been applied. Which of the following statements best describes how share permissions and NTFS permissions work together if they have been applied to the same folder?

    A. The NTFS permissions will always take precedence.

    B. The share permissions will always take precedence.

    C. The system will look at the cumulative share permissions and the cumulative NTFS permissions. Whichever set is less restrictive will be applied.

    D. The system will look at the cumulative share permissions and the cumulative NTFS permissions. Whichever set is more restrictive will be applied.

23. Your home computer network is protected by a firewall. You have configured your Windows client home computer to use Exchange. After you configure your email accounts, you discover that you are unable to send email messages. Your email provider uses POP3 and SMTP. What port should you open on the firewall?

    A. 25

    B. 110

    C. 443

    D. 995

24. You need Windows 10 to be the primary operating system on a dual-boot machine. Which file do you configure for this?

    A. `boot.ini`

    B. `bcdedit`

    C. `bcboot.ini`

    D. `bcdboot`

25. Which of the following versions of Windows can be upgraded to Windows 10 Enterprise edition? (Choose all that apply.)

    A. Windows 8 Home

    B. Windows 8 Professional

    C. Windows 8 Home Premium

    D. Windows 8 Enterprise

26. You are configuring a Windows client computer that is going to be used by your children. You are configuring access restrictions using the Parental Controls feature of Windows 10/11. Which of the following can be configured by setting Parental Controls? (Choose all that apply.)

    A. When your children can access the computer

    B. Which websites your children can view

    C. Which programs your children can access

    D. Which other computers on your home network your children can access

27. How do you access the Advanced Boot Options menu in Windows 10/11 during the boot process?

    A. Hold the Shift key down and choose the Restart option.

    B. Press F6.

    C. Press F8.

    D. Press F10.

28. You have a computer that runs Windows 10. Your computer has two volumes, C: and D:. Both volumes are formatted by using the NTFS filesystem. You need to disable previous versions on the D: volume. What should you do?

    A. From System Properties, modify the System Protection settings.

    B. From the properties of the D: volume, modify the Quota settings.

    C. From the properties of the D: volume, modify the Sharing settings.

    D. From the Disk Management snap-in, convert the hard disk drive that contains the D: volume to Dynamic.

29. Which utility is used to upgrade a FAT32 partition to NTFS?

    A. UPFS

    B. UPGRADE

    C. Disk Manager

    D. Convert

30. Your work computer network is protected by a firewall. You have configured your Windows client computer to use HTTPS. What port should you open on the firewall?

    A. 25

    B. 110

    C. 443

    D. 995

Assessment Test – MD-101

1. You need to automatically register all the existing computers to the Azure AD network and also enroll all of the computers in Intune. What should you use?

   A. Use a DNS Autodiscover address record.

   B. Use a Windows Autopilot deployment profile.

   C. Use an Autodiscover service connection point (SCP).

   D. Set up a Group Policy Object (GPO).

2. You need to create a new Azure Active Directory policy for your users. What PowerShell command would you use to accomplish this task?

   A. `New-AzurePolicy`

   B. `New-AzureActiveDirectoryPolicy`

   C. `Set-AzurePolicy`

   D. `New-AzureADPolicy`

3. You have a computer that runs Windows 10/11 Pro. The computer is joined to Azure Active Directory (Azure AD) and enrolled in Microsoft Intune. You need to upgrade the computer to Windows 10/11 Enterprise for another user. What should you configure in Intune?

   A. Windows Autopilot device profile

   B. A device enrollment policy

   C. A device cleanup rule

   D. A device compliance policy

4. You decide to install Windows Deployment Services (WDS). You are using a Windows Server 2022 domain and have verified that your network meets the requirements for using WDS. What command-line utility can you use to configure the WDS server?

   A. `dism.exe`

   B. `wdsutil.exe`

   C. `setup.exe`

   D. The WDS icon in Control Panel

5. You are the network administrator for your company's Azure AD network. You need to view an Azure Active Directory policy for your users. What PowerShell command would you use to accomplish this task?

   A. `Get-AzureADPolicy`

   B. `Get-AzurePolicy`

   C. `View-AzurePolicy`

   D. `View-AzureADPolicy`

6. You are the administrator for your organization. Your company wants to set up a way to integrate its on-site AD with Azure AD. What tool can you use to do this?

   A. Site-to-Site VPN Gateway Connectors

   B. Azure AD Connect

   C. Azure AD Replication

   D. Active Directory Replicator

7. An administrator wants to look at an Azure Active Directory application policy for your users' applications. What PowerShell command would you use to accomplish this task?

   A. `Add-AzureADPolicy`

   B. `Add-AzureADApplicationPolicy`

   C. `Create-AzurePolicy`

   D. `Install-AzureADPolicy`

8. Your boss has asked you about Azure security and making sure that user logins are secure. What feature can you explain to your boss to ease their concerns?

   A. Azure AD User Security

   B. Azure AD Identity Protection

   C. Azure AD Security add-on

   D. Azure Identity Protection

9. An administrator wants to change an Azure Active Directory policy for one of their users. What PowerShell command would you use to accomplish this task?

   A. `New-AzureADPolicy`

   B. `Edit-AzureADPolicy`

   C. `New-AzurePolicy`

   D. `Set-AzureADPolicy`

10. An administrator wants to view their Azure AD directory settings for the company's Azure AD subscription. What PowerShell command would you use to accomplish this task?

    A. `View-AzureADDirectorySetting`

    B. `Get-AzureADDirectorySetting`

    C. `Add-AzureADDirectorySetting`

    D. `Set-AzureADDirectorySetting`

11. You need to upgrade 100 Windows 10 Pro computers to Windows 10 Enterprise. What should you configure in Intune?

    A. A device enrollment policy

    B. A device cleanup rule

    C. A device compliance policy

    D. A device configuration profile

12. An administrator needs to create a device configuration profile in Microsoft Intune. You need to implement an ADMX-backed policy. Which profile type should you use?

A. Identity protection

B. Custom

C. Device restrictions

D. System restrictions

13. You need to set up a Windows client system in a break room where all employees can use it. Which device configuration profile type should you use?

A. Kiosk

B. Endpoint protection

C. Identity protection

D. Device restrictions

14. You are the IT manager of a large company. Sales personnel use their Windows client computers while on the road. All devices are enrolled into the Intune network for application and data maintenance. One of your salespeople reports that their Windows device was just stolen. You need to make sure no one can gain access to the company data. What action can you take to protect the device?

A. Prevent the computer from connecting to the corporate wireless network.

B. Remove the computer from the management infrastructure.

C. Lock the device remotely.

D. Do a remote wipe on the user's device.

15. What is Microsoft Intune?

A. Computer-based software

B. A cloud-based service

C. Third party non-Microsoft software

D. A set of programs that are designed to prevent, search for, detect, and remove software viruses

16. When your users get added to Intune and get licensed, how many devices can each user use by default?

A. 14

B. 15

C. 16

D. 17

17. How do you allow your tablets to connect to your cell phones for Internet access?

A. Configure the broadband connection as a metered network.

B. Turn on cellular tethering.

C. Enable tablet tethering.

D. Enable tablet metering in the tablets' settings.

18. An administrator needs to secure some of the Microsoft operating system's loopholes that hackers use. What type of updates would you need to install to help solve this problem?

A. Security updates

B. Definition updates

C. Critical updates

D. Software updates

19. You want to enable self-service password reset on the sign-in screen. Which settings should you configure from the Microsoft Intune blade?

A. Device configuration

B. Device compliance

C. Device enrollment

D. Conditional access

20. What do you need to do to be sure that all iOS devices can be managed by the Intune Administrators?

A. Add an Employee Portal app from the Apple App Store.

B. Create a device enrollment manager account.

C. Configure an Intune Service Connector for Exchange.

D. Import an Apple Push Notification service (APNs) certificate.

21. You are the new Azure AD Global administrator for your organization. Your company has an Azure AD domain name of `WillPanek.onmicrosoft.com`. Your bosses want you to change the default domain name to `Panek.onmicrosoft.com`. How can you change the initial domain name?

A. Use the Custom Domain Names section of Azure AD and change the name.

B. In Azure AD, go to Default Directories and change the domain name.

C. Use PowerShell to change the default domain name.

D. This can't be done.

22. You are the new Azure AD Global administrator for your organization. Your company has an Azure AD domain name of `WillPanek.onmicrosoft.com`. Your bosses want you to add a new domain name for `Panek.onmicrosoft.com`. How can you add the new domain name to your existing domain?

A. Use the Custom Domain Names section of Azure AD and change the name.

B. In Azure AD, go to Default Directories and add the domain name.

C. Use the Azure Administrative Center to add the new domain name.

D. This can't be done.

23. Your company is using Microsoft Azure Active Directory and all computers are enrolled in Microsoft Intune. The administrator needs to make sure that only approved applications are allowed to run on all of these computers. What should you implement to ensure this?

A. Microsoft Defender Credential Guard

B. Microsoft Defender Exploit Guard

C. Microsoft Defender Application Guard

D. Microsoft Defender Antivirus

24. You have a Microsoft 365 subscription. All computers are enrolled in Microsoft Intune. You have business requirements for securing your Windows client devices. You need to lock any device that has a high Microsoft Defender for Endpoint risk score. Which device configuration profile type should you use?

A. Kiosk

B. Endpoint Protection

C. Identity Protection

D. Device Restrictions

25. You have a Windows client machine that has a virus that was caused by a malicious font. You need to stop this type of threat from affecting your corporate computers in the future. What should you use?

A. Microsoft Defender Exploit Guard

B. Microsoft Defender Application Guard

C. Microsoft Defender Credential Guard

D. Microsoft Defender System Guard

26. You have been asked by your boss to set up a device configuration profile in Microsoft Intune to allow your users to be able to reset their own passwords. Which device configuration profile option should you configure in Intune?

A. Kiosk

B. Endpoint protection

C. Identity protection

D. Custom

27. You are the network administrator for your company. Your company is using Microsoft Intune to manage all of their devices. The company uses conditional access to restrict access to Microsoft 365 services for devices that do not comply with the company's security policies. You want to view which devices will be prevented from accessing the services. What should you use?

A. The Device Health solution in Windows Analytics.

B. Use the Windows Defender Security Center.

C. Device Compliance in the Microsoft Endpoint Manager admin center.

D. The Conditional access blade in the Azure Active Directory admin center.

28. You need to use a Microsoft Azure monitoring tool to monitor devices and change settings. Which of the following tools can you use?

  A. Performance Monitor

  B. Microsoft Azure IoT Central Application

  C. Azure Performance Center

  D. Intune Performance Center

29. You are the administrator of a company that has bought an application where everyone needs access to the application. You have decided that you want to install the application to all employees by using the Microsoft Store. How do you do that?

  A. Sideloading

  B. WS Installations

  C. BranchCache

  D. Image Installation

30. You have a computer named Portable1. You need to view the events collected from Portable1. Which query would an administrator run in Log Analytics?

  A. `Eventview | where SourceSystem = = " Portable1"`

  B. `Eventview | where Computer = = " Portable1"`

  C. `Event | where SourceSystem = = " Portable1"`

  D. `Event | where Computer = = " Portable1"`

Answers to Assessment Test – MD-100

1. D. Only members of the Administrators group can manage mandatory profiles. See Chapter 2 for more information.

2. B. When you create a custom console for the MMC, the `.msc` filename extension is automatically applied. See Chapter 2 for more information.

3. D. The feature the question is referring to is View Available Networks (VAN). Before Windows 10, when you used a wireless network adapter you would choose the wireless network that you wanted to connect to by using the wireless network adapter properties. In Windows 10/11, this is built into the operating system. See Chapter 1 for more information.

4. B. You would create a standard user account for the user. Standard users must provide the credentials of an administrator account when prompted by User Account Control (UAC) in order to perform administrative tasks. See Chapter 2 for more information.

5. C. You can use the ImageX utility to create an image of a Windows 10/11 installation. After the image has been created, you can prepare the image with a utility such as the System Preparation Tool (Sysprep). The image can then be used for remote installations of Windows client. See Chapter 1 for more information.

6. A. The Boot Configuration Data (BCD) store contains boot information parameters that were previously found in `Boot.ini` in older versions of Windows. To edit the boot options in the BCD store, use the `bcdedit` utility, which can be launched only from a command prompt. See Chapter 1 for more information.

7. D. The Narrator utility uses a sound output device to read onscreen text. See Chapter 4 for more information.

8. B, C. Windows 10 ships with a utility called the User State Migration Tool (USMT) that is used by administrators to migrate users from one computer to another via a command-line utility. The USMT consists of two executable files: `ScanState.exe` and `LoadState.exe`. See Chapter 8 for more information.

9. B. To get the latest drivers for any piece of hardware, you need to use the Upgrade Drivers button in Device Manager. After the upgrade button is chosen, you can use downloaded drivers or drivers from a new DVD. See Chapter 5 for more information.

10. A. Driver rollback allows you to replace a newly installed driver with the previous driver. You can do the driver rollback using the Device Manager utility. See Chapter 5 for more information.

11. D. The `Printbrm.exe` command should be run from a command prompt with administrative permission. This command is the command-line version of the Print Management tool. See Chapter 5 for more information.

12. B. Sleep mode is a combination of Standby mode and Hibernate mode. When Sleep mode is configured, the user's session is quickly accessible on wakeup, but the data is saved to the hard disk. Sleep mode is the preferred power-saving mode in Windows 10/11. See Chapter 4 for more information.

13. B. PowerShell commands allow you to run multiple configurations by using scripts or even by using individual commands. See Chapter 4 for more information.

14. D. A subnet mask of 255.255.255.224 equals a CIDR of /27. CIDR is the number of on bits. See Chapter 6 for more information.

15. D. Windows client data compression is supported only on NTFS partitions. If you move the file to a FAT32 partition, then it will be stored as uncompressed. See Chapter 5 for more information.

16. C. You should use the subnet mask 255.255.255.0 on your network in this scenario. The IP network address 192.168.10.0 is a Class C address. Class C addresses, by default, use the subnet mask 255.255.255.0. The network portion of the address is 192.168.10, and the host portion of the address can be 1 to 254. See Chapter 6 for more information.

17. A. To enable synchronization of files between your laptop and a network folder, you must first upgrade your laptop to a version of Windows 10 that supports synchronization with network folders, such as Windows 10 Enterprise. Windows Sync Center also supports synchronization of files between computers and mobile devices. See Chapter 4 for more information.

18. B. The `ipconfig /flushdns` command is used to purge the DNS Resolver cache. The `ipconfig` command displays a computer's IP configuration. See Chapter 6 for more information.

19. A. The easiest way is to simply rename Rick's account to John. When you rename Rick's account to John, John will automatically have all of the rights and permissions to any resource that Rick had access to. See Chapter 2 for more information.

20. A, C. Only administrators can create new groups on a Windows 10/11 computer. Group names can contain up to 256 characters and can contain spaces. Group names must be unique to the computer, different from all the other usernames and group names that have been specified on that computer. See Chapter 2 for more information.

21. A, C. You can create a spanned volume from free space that exists on a minimum of 2 to a maximum of 32 physical drives. When the spanned volume is initially created in Windows 10/11, it can be formatted with FAT32 or NTFS. If you extend a volume that already contains data, however, the partition must be NTFS. See Chapter 5 for more information.

22. D. When both NTFS and share permissions have been applied, the system looks at the effective rights for NTFS and share permissions and then applies the most restrictive of the cumulative permissions. If a resource has been shared and you access it from the local computer where the resource resides, then you will be governed only by the NTFS permission. See Chapter 3 for more information.

23. A. Port 25 should be opened on the firewall. SMTP is used for outbound mail and uses port 25. POP3, which is used for receiving inbound mail, uses port 110. See Chapter 5 for more information.

24. B. You should configure the `bcdedit` utility to configure your boot order. See Chapter 1 for more information.

25. B, D. You can upgrade Windows 8 Professional and Windows 8 Enterprise to Windows 10 Enterprise edition. See Chapter 1 for more information.

26. A, B, C. Using Parental Controls, you can configure which websites your children can access, when they can use the computer, which games they can play, and which programs they can run, and you can view reports regarding their activity. See Chapter 2 for more information.

27. A. Hold the Shift key down and choose the Restart option to access the Advanced Boot Options menu. You can do this within the Windows client operating system or at the sign-in screen. See Chapter 7 for more information.

28. A. If you need to disable previous versions on the D: volume, this needs to be done from the System Protection settings from the computer system properties. See Chapter 7 for more information.

29. D. The Convert utility is used to convert a FAT32 partition to NTFS. See Chapter 5 for more information.

30. C. Port 443 should be opened on the firewall. SMTP is used for outbound mail and uses port 25. POP3, which is used for receiving inbound mail, uses port 110. See Chapter 5 for more information.

Answers to Assessment Test – MD-101

1. B. Windows Autopilot profiles allow an administrator to choose how the Windows 10/11 system will be set up and configured on Azure AD and Intune. See Chapter 8 for more information.

2. D. Administrators can use the `New-AzureADPolicy` command to create a new Azure AD policy. See Chapter 9 for more information.

3. A. Windows Autopilot profiles allow an administrator to choose how the Windows 10/11 system will be set up and configured on Azure AD and Intune. See Chapter 8 for more information.

4. B. `wdsutil.exe` is a command-line utility that can be used to configure the WDS server. Several other configuration options need to be specified on the WDS server, and you can set them using `wdsutil.exe`. See Chapter 8 for more information.

5. A. The `Get-AzureADPolicy` command allows an Azure admin to view an Azure AD policy. See Chapter 9 for more information.

6. B. Azure AD Connect is a Microsoft utility that allows you to set up a hybrid design between Azure AD and your on-site AD. Azure AD Connect allows both versions of AD to connect to each other. See Chapter 9 for more information.

7. B. Administrators can use the `Add-AzureADApplicationPolicy` command to add an application policy. See Chapter 9 for more information.

8. B. Azure AD Identity Protection allows an Azure administrator to use the same type of protection that Microsoft uses to protect and secure users' identities. See Chapter 9 for more information.

9. D. Administrators can use the `Set-AzureADPolicy` command to update an Azure AD policy. See Chapter 9 for more information.

10. B. Administrators can use the `Get-AzureADDirectorySetting` command to view their directory settings. See Chapter 9 for more information.

11. D. You can upgrade your devices by using a device configuration profile. The option that you want to configure is Edition Upgrade. Edition Upgrade allows you to upgrade Windows 10 (and later) devices to a newer version of Windows. See Chapter 11 for more information.

12. B. One of the options you have in device configuration profiles is the ability to set up custom profiles. Custom profile settings allow an Intune administrator to configure options that are not automatically included with Intune. See Chapter 11 for more information.

13. A. Kiosk systems are normally designed in a location where many people can use the same device and that device will only run limited applications. See Chapter 11 for more information.

14. D. Administrators can use the remote wipe feature to delete all of the data on the company devices. See Chapter 11 for more information.

15. B. Microsoft Intune is a cloud-based service that focuses on Mobile Device Management (MDM) and Mobile Application Management (MAM). You can determine how your organization's devices (mobile phones, tablets, and laptops) are used. You can also configure specific policies to control applications. See Chapter 10 for more information.

16. B. By default, licensed users can add up to 15 devices to their accounts. Device Administrators have the ability to add devices to Intune, but users do have the ability to enroll 15 devices on their own. See Chapter 11 for more information.

17. B. Tethering means that users can connect one device to another for Internet services. See Chapter 11 for more information.

18. A. Security updates are updates that need to be applied to fix a security issue. These security issues are used by hackers to either hack into a device or software. See Chapter 11 for more information.

19. A. You will want to configure device configuration settings. To do this, sign into the Azure portal and click Intune. Create a new device configuration profile by going to Device Configuration ➤ Profiles ➤ Create Profile. See Chapter 11 for more information.

20. D. An Apple Push Notification service (APNs) certificate must be imported from Apple so that the company can manage iOS devices. See Chapter 10 for more information.

21. D. Administrators can't change or delete the initial domain name that is created, but Azure Administrators do have the ability to add your organization's new or existing domain names to the list of supported names. See Chapter 9 for more information.

22. A. You can use the Custom Domain Names section of Azure AD to create your organization's new or existing domain names to the list of supported names. See Chapter 9 for more information.

23. C. Administrators can use Microsoft Defender Application Guard to ensure that only applications that you explicitly allow can run on the Windows client computers. See Chapter 12 for more information.

24. B. Endpoint Protection allows you to set Windows 10 (and above) options for BitLocker and Microsoft Defender settings. For example, you can set Microsoft Defender for a threat score setting. If a user with a High threat score rating attempts to access cloud-based resources, you can stop this device from accessing your resources. See Chapter 12 for more information.

25. A. Microsoft Defender Exploit Guard helps protect your system from common malware hacks that use executable files and scripts to attack applications like Microsoft Office. See Chapter 12 for more information.

26. D. One of the options that you can set in device configuration profiles is the ability to set up custom profiles. Custom profile settings allow an Intune Administrator to configure options that are not automatically included with Intune. For example, an administrator can set a custom profile that allows you to create an ADMX-backed policy or even enable self-service password resets. See Chapter 11 for more information.

27. C. One of the advantages to using Azure is the ability to protect the corporate data by ensuring that users and devices meet certain requirements. When using Intune, this is referred to as compliance policies. Compliance policies are rules and settings that your users and their devices must follow in order to connect and access Intune. See Chapter 11 for more information.

28. B. Use Microsoft Azure Internet of Things (IoT) Central Application to monitor devices and change settings. Azure IoT Central Applications are hosted by Microsoft, which reduces the administrative overhead of managing applications. See Chapter 13 for more information.

29. A. Sideloading an application means that you are loading an application that you already own or one that your company created into a delivery system (i.e., Intune, Microsoft Store, or images). See Chapter 10 for more information.

30. D. An Administrator can view the events collected from a specific computer in Azure by running the query `Event | where Computer = = "Portable1"` in Logs Analytics. See Chapter 13 for more information.

Exam MD-100

Chapter

1

Windows Client Installation

MICROSOFT EXAM OBJECTIVES COVERED IN THIS CHAPTER:

✓ **Install Windows Client**

- Select the appropriate Windows edition; prepare hardware for installation; perform a manual clean installation; plan and implement an upgrade from a previous version of Windows; customize a Windows client installation by using the Windows ADK; configure activation and troubleshoot activation issues.

✓ **Manage Windows updates**

- Check for updates, configure updates; validate and test updates; select the appropriate servicing channel; configure Windows update options; configure Windows delivery optimization; control updates by using group policy settings; configure updates using Windows Update for Business; troubleshoot updates.

This section of the book is for Exam MD-100, which is the first of two Windows Client exams (MD-100 and MD-101) for the Microsoft 365 Certified: Modern Desktop Administrator Associate. Let me be the first to welcome you to Windows Client and the beginning of a new journey. Both the MD-100 and the MD-101 have recently been updated to include Windows 11. So, these updates will be included in this book. This update consists mainly of adding Windows 11 and changing the name to reflect that addition. The name of the updated MD-100 is "Windows Client," and it covers both Windows 10 and 11. This book will feature both Windows 10 and Windows 11. There are a few differences between the two operating systems. Windows 11 is the next client operating system, and it's built on the same foundation as Windows 10.

But as with the start of any journey, we must take our first steps. The first step for this exam is to learn about the installation process. It is important that you understand the different versions of Windows clients and which one is right for you and your organization.

In this chapter, I will show you the many different features of Windows 10/11, and then I will describe each edition. I will then show you how to install Windows clients and also how to do an upgrade from a previous version.

Before you can perform an installation, you must first be sure your hardware meets the minimum requirements and is supported by the operating system. After we install the Windows client operating system, I will show you how to get updates.

Understanding the Basics

Microsoft Windows 11 is the latest version of Microsoft's client operating system software. Both Windows 11 and Windows 10 combine the best of Windows 7 and Windows 8, and they also make it much easier to work within the cloud.

Microsoft has released many different versions of the Windows 10 and Windows 11 operating systems. The following lists just a few of the most popular versions:

- Windows 10 Editions
  - Windows 10 Home
  - Windows 10 Pro
  - Windows 10 Pro for Workstation
  - Windows 10 Enterprise

- Windows 10 Enterprise E3
- Windows 10 Enterprise E5
- Windows 10 Education
- Windows 11 Editions
  - Windows 11 Home
  - Windows 11 Pro
  - Windows 11 Pro for Workstation
  - Windows 11 Enterprise
  - Windows 11 Education
  - Windows 11 Pro Education
  - Windows 11 Mixed Reality

One major difference between Windows 10 and Windows 11 is basically the look. Windows 11 provides an interface with pastel colors and rounded corners for all windows. Another difference between the two is that the Start Menu has been moved to the center of the taskbar. But it can be moved back to the left side, as it was in Windows 10, if the user prefers. Other than the appearance, Windows 11 functions pretty much the same as Windows 10 with a few minor differences.

Microsoft also offers some of these operating systems as slimmed-down versions called "Windows 10 IoT Core." This version is one of the previously listed Windows 10 versions that doesn't require a monitor or system. For example, say you are building a toy robot and you want to load Windows 10 into your core computer. You can use the IoT (which stands for Internet of Things) versions to run the robot's functionality.

Windows 10 and 11 have been improved in many of the weak areas that plagued Windows 8. They have a much faster boot time and shutdown compared to Windows 8. They also bring back the previous Start button that we are all so familiar with from previous editions. In Windows 10 the Start button is on the left side of the taskbar and in Windows 11 it's in the center of the taskbar.

The Windows 10 and 11 operating system functions are also faster than their previous counterparts. The processes for opening, moving, extracting, compressing, and installing files and folders are more efficient than they were in previous versions of Microsoft's client operating systems.

Let's take a look at some of the features of each Windows 10 edition (this is just an overview of some of the benefits to using Windows 10). Table 1.1 and Table 1.2 show each edition and what some of the features are for those editions.

 The information in Table 1.1 and Table 1.2 was taken directly from Microsoft's website and documentation.

TABLE 1.1 Windows 10 security and protection

Description	Home	Pro	Pro for Workstation	E3	E5
Integrity enforcement of operating system boot-up process	☐	☐	☐	☐	■
Integrity enforcement of sensitive operating system components	☐	☐	☐	☐	■
Advanced vulnerability and zero-day exploit mitigations	☐	☐	☐	☐	■
Reputation-based network protection for Microsoft Edge, Internet Explorer, and Chrome	☐	☐	☐	☐	■
Host-based firewall	☐	☐	☐	☐	■
Ransomware mitigations	☐	☐	☐	☐	■
Pre-execution emulation executables and scripts	☐	☐	☐	☐	■
Runtime behavior monitoring	☐	☐	☐	☐	■
In-memory anomaly and behavior monitoring	☐	☐	☐	☐	■
Machine learning and AI-based protection from viruses and malware threats	☐	☐	☐	☐	■
Cloud protection for fastest responses to new/unknown web-based threats	☐	☐	☐	☐	■
Protection from fileless-based attacks	☐	☐	☐	☐	■
Industry standards–based multifactor authentication	☐	☐	☐	☐	■
Support for biometrics (Facial and Fingerprints)	☐	☐	☐	☐	■
Support for Microsoft Authenticator	☐	☐	☐	☐	■
Support for Microsoft-compatible security devices	☐	☐	☐	☐	■
Automatic encryption on capable devices	☐	☐	☐	☐	■
Advanced encryption configuration options		☐	☐	☐	■
Removable storage protection		☐	☐	☐	■
Supports for Active Directory and Azure Active Directory		☐	☐	☐	■

Description	Home	Pro	Pro for Workstation	E3	E5
Hardware-based isolation for Microsoft Edge		□	□	□	■
Application control powered by the Intelligent Security Graph		□	□	□	■
Device Control (e.g., USB)		□	□	□	■
Personal and business data separation		□	□	□	■
Application access control		□	□	□	■
Copy and paste protection		□	□	□	■
Removable storage protection		□	□	□	■
Integration with Microsoft Information Protection		□	□	□	■
Network protection for web-based threats				□	■
Enterprise management of hardware-based isolation for Microsoft Edge				□	■
Hardware isolation of single sign-in tokens				□	■
Direct Access & Always On VPN Device Tunnel				□	■
Centralized configuration management, analytics, reporting, and security operations					■
Centralized management, analytics, reporting, and operations					■
Customizable network protection for web-based threats					■
Host intrusion prevention rules					■
Device-based conditional access					■
Tamper protection of operating system					■
Advanced monitoring, analytics, and reporting for attack surface					■
Advanced machine learning and AI-based protection for Apex-level viruses and malware threats					■

TABLE 1.1   Windows 10 security and protection *(Continued)*

Description	Home	Pro	Pro for Workstation	E3	E5
Advanced cloud protection that includes deep inspection and detonation					■
Emergency outbreak protection from the Intelligent Security Graph					■
ISO 27001 compliance					■
Geolocation and sovereignty of sample data					■
Sample data retention policy					■
Monitoring, analytics, and reporting for Next Generation Protection capabilities					■

TABLE 1.2   Windows 10 updates

Description	Home	Pro	Pro for Workstation	E3	E5
In-place upgrades	☐	☐	☐	☐	■
Express updates	☐	☐	☐	☐	■
Delivery optimization	☐	☐	☐	☐	■
Windows Analytics Upgrade Readiness		☐	☐	☐	■
Windows Analytics Update Compliance		☐	☐	☐	■
Windows Update for Business		☐	☐	☐	■
Windows Analytics Device Health				☐	■
30 months of support for September targeted releases				☐	■
Windows 10 LTSC Access				☐	■

Windows 10/11 Features

Now that you have seen which editions contain which features, let's take a look at some of the features in greater detail. This section describes only a few of these features, but all features will be explained throughout this book.

Cortana Integration   Windows 10/11 comes with Cortana integration. Cortana is your very own personal assistant. You can type in or ask Cortana a question and Cortana will seek out the best possible answer based on your question.

Secure Boot   Windows 10/11 provides the ability for securely booting the operating system. Secure Boot validates all drivers and operating system components before they are loaded against the signature database.

Virtual Smart Cards   Windows 10/11 has started offering a new way to do two-factor authentication with virtual smart cards. Virtual smart cards help an IT department that doesn't want to invest in extra hardware and smart cards. Virtual smart cards use Trusted Platform Module (TPM) devices that allow for the same capabilities as physical smart cards with the physical hardware.

Miracast   Windows 10/11 allows you to project your laptop or mobile device to a projector or television. Miracast allows you to connect to an external device through the use of your mobile wireless display (WiDi) adapter.

Hyper-V   Windows 10/11 (except the Home version) come with Hyper-V built into the operating system. Hyper-V is Microsoft's version of a virtual server.

Enterprise Data Protection   Windows 10/11 Enterprise Data Protection (EDP) helps protect corporate data in a world that is increasingly becoming a Bring Your Own Device (BYOD) environment. Since many organizations are allowing employees to connect their own devices to their network, the possibility of corporate data being compromised because of noncorporate programs running on these personnel devices is increasing. For example, many third-party apps may put corporate data at risk by accidently disclosing corporate information through the application.

Enterprise Data Protection helps protect information by separating corporate applications and corporate data from being disclosed by personal devices and personal applications.

Device Guard   Because employees can use multiple types of Windows 10/11 devices (Surface Pros, Intel and ARM-based devices, and Windows 10/11 computer systems), Device Guard is a feature that helps guarantee that only trusted applications will run on any of these devices.

Device Guard uses both hardware and software security features to lock down a device so that it can run only trusted and approved applications. This also helps prevent hackers from running malicious software on these devices.

Microsoft Passport/Windows Hello   Microsoft has introduced two security features for Windows 10/11 called Windows Hello and Microsoft Passport. Windows Hello is a biometrics system integrated into Windows 10/11 and is a piece of the user's authentication experience. Microsoft Passport allows users to use a two-factor authentication system that combines a PIN or biometrics with an encrypted key from a user's device to provide two-factor authentication.

Start Menu   Windows 10 brought back the Start Menu that users are familiar with. The Start Menu combines the best of both Windows 7 and Windows 8. So, the Start Menu gives you a menu that we were familiar with in Windows 7 as well as the Live Tiles that users liked in Windows 8. However, in Windows 11 the Start Menu is now in the center of the taskbar.

Microsoft Edge and Internet Explorer 11   Windows 10 has introduced a new way to surf the Internet with Microsoft Edge. But Windows 10 also still comes with Internet Explorer 11 in the event that you need to run ActiveX controls or run backward-compatible web services or sites. However, Windows 11 only comes with Microsoft Edge.

Microsoft Edge allows users to start using many new Microsoft features, including Web Note (allows you to annotate, highlight, and call things out directly on web pages), Reading View (allows you to print and save as a PDF for easy reading), and Cortana (personal assistant).

Domain Join and Group Policy   Depending on the version of Windows 10 or Windows 11 that you are using, administrators have the ability to join Windows 10/11 clients to either a corporate version of Active Directory or a cloud-based version of Azure Active Directory.

Microsoft Store for Business   Microsoft Store has included many applications that allow users to get better functionality and productivity out of their Windows 10/11 devices. One advantage for corporations is that they can create their own applications and load them into the Microsoft Store for users to download (called *sideloading*).

Mobile Device Management   Mobile Device Management (MDM) allows administrators to set up Windows 10/11 policies that can integrate many corporate scenarios, including the ability to control users' access to the Microsoft Store and the ability to use the corporate VPN. MDM also allows administrators to manage multiple users who have accounts set up on Microsoft Azure Active Directory (Azure AD). Windows 10/11 MDM support is based on the Open Mobile Alliance (OMA) Device Management (DM) protocol 1.2.1 specification.

Windows 10 vs. Windows 11

Here are the differences between Windows 10 and Windows 11.

 The information in Table 1.3 was taken directly from Microsoft's website and documentation.

TABLE 1.3   Comparison between Windows 10 and Windows 11

Feature and description	Windows 10	Windows 11
Auto HDR – Produces a wider, more vivid range of colors for a truly captivating visual experience.		■
Chat from Microsoft Teams – Reach anyone however you prefer (call, chat, text, video) right from your taskbar.		■
Desktop Groups – Switch between desktops for greater organization of open windows.		■
DirectStorage – Get faster load times and more detailed game worlds.		■
Microsoft Store – Find the apps, movies, and shows you love faster and select from a wider variety of apps.	□	■
Microsoft Teams – Call, chat, and make plans come to life all in one app.	□	■
New Emojis – Express every statement you write with faces, people, and celebration emojis.		■
Photos app – The updated Photos app makes editing and viewing much easier.	□	■
Seamless Redocking – Continue right where you left off when you plug/unplug from your external monitor.		■
Snap Assist – Features Layouts and Groups; helps you arrange your open windows into perfect grids.	□	
Touchscreen – New gestures make navigating with touch much more intuitive.	□	■

TABLE 1.3 Comparison between Windows 10 and Windows 11 *(continued)*

Feature and description	Windows 10	Windows 11
Updates – Faster reduction in download size for updates in Windows 11.		■
Widgets – Photos. News. To-dos. Weather. Widgets help you find content that matters to you.		■
Windows on ARM – Devices with thin and light designs and amazing battery lift that run the apps you care about.	☐	■

What Has Been Changed in Windows 11?

When you're upgrading to Windows 11 from Windows 10 or when installing an update to Windows 11, some features may be removed or deprecated. Here are what will change:

- **Cortana:** Will no longer be included in the first boot experience or pinned to the taskbar.
- **Desktop wallpaper:** Cannot be roamed to or from device when signed in with a Microsoft account.
- **Internet Explorer:** Microsoft Edge with IE mode replaces the Internet Explorer 11 desktop application in Windows 11.
- **Management capabilities:** Organizations that want to deliver customized Start and Taskbar experiences are limited:
    - Start supports the ability for organizations to override the Start layout, but does not support locking down the layout from user modification.
    - Taskbar pins and ordering can be controlled by organizations.
- **Math Input Panel:** Has been removed. Math Recognizer will install on demand and includes the math input control and recognizer. Math inking in apps like OneNote are not impacted by this change.
- **Multi-App Kiosk Mode:** Is not available. Windows 11 only supports the use of a single app in Kiosk Mode.
- **News & Interests:** Has evolved. New functionality has been added, which can be found by clicking the Widgets icon on the taskbar.
- **Quick Status:** From the Lock screen and associated settings have been removed.
- **S Mode:** Is only available now for Windows 11 Home edition.

- **Search Results from the Internet:** Windows 11 does not support disabling the return of Internet Search results via `Registry` Key. The related Group Policy setting is not impacted by this change.

- **Snipping Tool and Snip and Sketch:** Have been merged into a single experience, keeping the familiar Snipping Tool name.

- **Start:** Has changed in Windows 11; changes include the following key deprecations and removals:
  - Named groups and folders of apps are no longer supported and the layout is not currently resizable.
  - Pinned apps and sites will not migrate when upgrading from Windows 10.
  - Live Tiles are no longer available.

- **Tablet Mode:** Has been removed and new functionality and capability is now included for keyboard attach and detach postures.

- **Taskbar:** Changes include:
  - People is no longer present on the taskbar.
  - Some icons may no longer appear in the System Tray (systray) for upgraded devices, including previous customizations.
  - Alignment to the bottom of the screen is the only location allowed.
  - Apps can no longer customize areas of the taskbar.

- **Timeline:** Has been removed. Some similar functionality is available in Microsoft Edge.

- **Touch Keyboard:** Will no longer dock and undock keyboard layouts onscreen sizes 18 inches and larger.

- **Wallet:** Has been removed.

- **Windows Deployment Services:** Is being partially deprecated.

- **Windows Store for Business and Windows Store for Education:** No longer include the Private Store tab.

Windows 10 and 11 Architecture

Windows 10 and 11 have limited the number of files that load at system startup to help with the core performance of the operating system, thus allowing for better performance.

Microsoft offers both a 32-bit version and a 64-bit version of Windows 10. But Windows 11 uses a 64-bit architecture only. The terms *32-bit* and *64-bit* refer to the CPU, or processor. The number represents how the data is processed. It is processed either as 2^{32} or 2^{64}. The larger the number, the larger the amount of data that can be processed at any one time.

To get an idea of how 32-bit and 64-bit processors operate, think of a large highway with 32 lanes. Vehicles can travel on those 32 lanes only, so when traffic gets backed up, the result is delays. Now think of how many more vehicles can travel on a 64-lane highway. The problem here is that a 32-lane highway can't handle the number of vehicles a 64-lane highway can. You need to have the infrastructure to allow for that volume of vehicles. The same is true for computers. Your computer has to be configured to allow you to run a 64-bit processor.

So, what does all of this mean to the common user or administrator? It's all about random access memory, or RAM. A 32-bit operating system can handle up to 4 GB of RAM, and a 64-bit processor can handle up to 16 exabytes (EB) of RAM. None of this is new. Although 64-bit processors are just starting to get accepted with Windows systems, other operating systems, such as Apple, have been using 64-bit processors for many years.

Computer processors are typically rated by speed. The speed of the processor, or central processing unit (CPU), is rated by the number of clock cycles that can be performed in 1 second. This measurement is typically expressed in gigahertz (GHz). One GHz is one billion cycles per second. Keep in mind that processor architecture must also be taken into account when considering processor speed. A processor with a more efficient pipeline will be faster than a processor with a less efficient pipeline at the same CPU speed.

Now that you have seen the new features of Windows 10 and 11, let's look at how to prepare the machine to install Windows.

Preparing to Install Windows

Installing Windows can be relatively simple because of the installation wizard. The installation wizard will walk you through the entire installation of the operating system.

The most difficult part of installing Windows is preparing and planning for the installation. One thing I often say to IT pros is, "An hour of planning will save you days of work." Planning a Windows rollout is one of the hardest and most important tasks that you will perform when installing Windows. Since Windows 11 is built on the same foundation as Windows 10, you can use the same deployment capabilities, scenarios, and tools. You can also use the same basic deployment strategies that are used for Windows 10. So, when I'm mentioning Windows 10 in this book, it implies the same for Windows 11.

There are many decisions that should be made before you install Windows. The first decision is which version of Windows you want to install. As mentioned previously, Microsoft has several different versions of the Windows operating system. This allows an administrator to custom-fit a user's hardware and job function to the appropriate version and edition of Windows. Many times, Microsoft releases multiple editions of the operating system contained within the same Windows media disk. You can choose to unlock the one you want based on the product key you have. Let's take a closer look at the different versions of Windows that are offered with both Windows 10 and Windows 11.

In this book, we will not talk much about Windows 10 Education or Windows 11 Education. Windows Education is the counterpart to Windows Enterprise, but it is a volume-licensed version of Windows that is specifically priced for educational institutions. Educational institutions receive the same Enterprise functionality, but they pay much less than a corporation.

Windows Home

Windows Home is the main operating system for home users. Windows Home offers many features, including these:

- Broad application and device compatibility with unlimited concurrent applications
- A safe, reliable, and supported operating system
- Microsoft Passport/Windows Hello
- HomeGroup, which allows a user to easily share media, documents, and printers across multiple PCs in homes or offices without the need of a domain
- Improved taskbar and jump lists (the Jump Lists feature in Windows 10 and 11 allows you to quickly access files that you have been working on)
- Live thumbnail previews and an enhanced visual experience
- Advanced networking support (ad hoc wireless networks and Internet connection sharing)
- View Available Networks (VAN) (Windows by default has the ability, when you use a wireless network adapter, to choose the wireless network that you want to connect to by using the wireless network adapter properties)
- Device encryption
- Easy networking and sharing across all your PCs and devices
- Windows Update
- Multitouch
- Improved handwriting recognition

Windows Pro

Windows Pro is designed for small-business owners. Microsoft designed Windows Pro for users to get more done and safeguard their data. Pro offers the following features:

- Broad application and device compatibility with unlimited concurrent applications
- A safe, reliable, and supported operating system
- Microsoft Passport/Windows Hello
- Domain Join, which enables simple and secure server networking

- Improved taskbar and jump lists
- Enterprise Mode Internet Explorer (EMIE)
- Advanced networking support (ad hoc wireless networks and Internet connection sharing)
- View Available Networks (VAN) (Windows by default has the ability, when you use a wireless network adapter, to choose the wireless network that you want to connect to by using the wireless network adapter properties)
- Mobility Center
- Action Center, which makes it easier to resolve many IT issues yourself
- Easy networking and sharing across all your PCs and devices
- Group Policy Management
- Windows Update and Windows Update for Business
- Multitouch
- Improved handwriting recognition
- Domain Join, which enables simple and secure server networking
- BitLocker, which protects data on removable devices
- Device encryption
- Encrypting File System, which protects data
- Client Hyper-V
- Location-Aware Printing, which helps find the right printer when moving between the office and home
- Start Menu that includes Live Tiles

Windows Enterprise

Windows Enterprise is the version designed for midsize and large organizations. This operating system has the most features and security options of all Windows 10 and 11 versions. Here are some of its features:

- Broad application and device compatibility with unlimited concurrent applications
- A safe, reliable, and supported operating system
- Microsoft Passport/Windows Hello
- Enterprise Mode Internet Explorer (EMIE) (not available in Windows 11)
- Group Policy Management
- Windows Update and Windows Update for Business
- Advanced networking support (ad hoc wireless networks and Internet connection sharing)

- View Available Networks (VAN) (Windows by default has the ability, when you use a wireless network adapter, to choose the wireless network that you want to connect to by using the wireless network adapter properties)
- Mobility Center
- Easy networking and sharing across all your PCs and devices
- Multitouch
- Start Menu that includes Live Tiles (not available in Windows 11)
- Improved handwriting recognition
- Domain Join, which enables simple and secure server networking
- Device encryption
- Encrypting File System, which protects data
- Location-Aware Printing, which helps find the right printer when you are moving between the office and home
- Client Hyper-V
- Credential Guard
- Device Guard
- BitLocker, which protects data on removable devices
- DirectAccess, which links users to corporate resources from the road without a virtual private network (VPN)
- BranchCache, which makes it faster to open files and web pages from a branch office
- AppLocker, which restricts unauthorized software and also enables greater security hardware requirements

Windows 10 Enterprise E3 and E5

Microsoft has released a new cloud-based way to deploy Windows 10 Enterprise with the introduction of Windows 10 Enterprise E3 and E5. Windows 10 Enterprise E3 and E5 are subscription-based versions of Windows 10 for organizations that like to work with Microsoft 365.

When Microsoft released Windows 10 version 1703, it included a Windows 10 Enterprise E3 and E5 benefit for Microsoft customers with either Enterprise Agreements (EAs) or Microsoft Products & Services Agreements (MPSAs).

One of the advantages of using the subscription-based service for Windows 10 E3 and E5 is that the users can activate the Windows 10 subscription on up to five devices. Users can then download the corporate version of Windows 10 onto their work systems, personal systems, and other devices.

As you can see from Table 1.1 and Table 1.2, by purchasing the Windows 10 E3 and E5 subscriptions, you get many additional features, including enterprise-level security and control. Some of the E3 and E5 components are available if you would like to purchase them separately.

Windows Client Requirements

Before you can install the operating system, you must make sure the machine's hardware can handle the operating system.

To install the Windows client successfully, your system must meet or exceed certain hardware requirements. Table 1.4 lists the minimum requirements for a Windows client–capable PC.

TABLE 1.4   Hardware requirements

Component	Windows 10 requirements	Windows 11 requirements
CPU (processor)	1 GHz or faster processor or system-on-a-chip (SoC)	1 GHz or faster with 2 or more cores on a compatible 64-bit processor or system-on-a-chip (SoC)
Memory (RAM)	1 GB for 32-bit or 2 GB for 64-bit	4 GB
Hard disk	32GB or larger hard disk	64 GB or larger storage device
Video adapter	DirectX 9 or later with WDDM 1.0 driver	DirectX 12 or later with WDDM 2.0 driver
Internet Connection	Internet connectivity is necessary to perform updates and to download and take advantage of some features.	For all Windows 11 editions, Internet access is required to perform updates and to download and take advantage of some features.

The hardware requirements listed in Table 1.4 are those specified at the time this book was written. Always check the Microsoft website for the most current information.

The Windows client–capable PC must meet or exceed the basic requirements to deliver the core functionality of the Windows operating system. These requirements are based on the assumption that you are installing only the operating system, without any premium functionality. For example, you may be able to get by with the minimum requirements if you are installing the operating system just to learn the basics of the software. Remember, the better the hardware, the better the performance.

Real World Scenario

Deciding on Minimum Hardware Requirements

The company you work for has decided that everyone will have their own laptop running Windows 10. You need to decide on the new computers' specifications for processor, memory, and disk space.

The first step is to determine which applications will be used. Typically, most users will work with an email program, a word processor, a spreadsheet, presentation software, and maybe a drawing or graphics program. Additionally, an antivirus application will probably be used. Under these demands, a 1 GHz Celeron processor and 1 GB of RAM will make for a very slow-running machine. So, for this usage, you can assume that the minimum baseline configuration would be higher than a 1 GHz processor with at least 2 GB of RAM.

Based on your choice of baseline configuration, you should then fit a test computer with the applications that will be used on it and test the configuration in a lab environment simulating normal use. This will give you an idea of whether the RAM and processor calculations you have made for your environment are going to provide a suitable response.

Today's disk drives have become capable of much larger capacity while dropping drastically in price. So, for disk space, the rule of thumb is to buy whatever is the current standard. At the time this book was written, 500 GB drives were commonplace, which is sufficient for most users. If users plan to store substantial graphics or video files, you may need to consider buying larger-than-standard drives.

Also consider what the business requirements will be over the next 12 to 18 months. If you will be implementing applications that are memory or processor intensive, you may want to spec out the computers with hardware sufficient to support upcoming needs to avoid costly upgrades in the near future.

The requirements for the graphics card depend on the resolution at which you want to run. The required amount of memory is as follows:

- 64 MB is required for a single monitor at a resolution of 1,310,720 pixels or less, which is equivalent to a 1280×1024 resolution.

- 128 MB is required for a single monitor at a resolution of 2,304,000 pixels or less, which is equivalent to a 1920×1200 resolution.

- 256 MB is required for a single monitor at a resolution larger than 2,304,000 pixels.

Measurement Used for Disk Space and Memory

Storage, such as hard disks and solid-state drives, are commonly rated by capacity. The following measurements are used for disk space and memory capacity:

- 1 MB (megabyte) = 1,024 KB (kilobytes)

- 1 GB (gigabyte) = 1,024 MB

- 1 TB (terabyte) = 1,024 GB

- 1 PB (petabyte) = 1,024 TB

- 1 EB (exabyte) = 1,024 PB

If you are not sure if your machine meets the minimum requirements, Microsoft includes some tools that can help you determine if a machine is Windows 10 or 11 compatible, which we will look at in the following sections.

BIOS Compatibility

Before you install Windows, you should verify that your computer has the most current BIOS. This is especially important if your current BIOS does not include support for Advanced Configuration and Power Interface (ACPI) functionality. ACPI functionality is required for Windows to function properly. Check the computer vendor's website for the latest BIOS version information.

Driver Requirements

To successfully install Windows 10 or 11, you must have the critical device drivers for your computer, such as the hard drive device driver. The Windows media comes with an extensive list of drivers. If your computer's device drivers are not on the Windows installation media, you should check the device manufacturer's website.

New Installation or Upgrade?

Once you've determined that your hardware meets the minimum requirements, you need to decide whether you want to do an upgrade or a clean installation. An upgrade allows you to retain your existing operating system's applications, settings, and files.

The bad news is that if you are moving from Windows Vista, Windows XP, or earlier versions of Windows to Windows 10 or 11, you must perform a clean installation. You can perform an upgrade to Windows 10 or 11 if the following conditions are true:

- You are running Windows 7 or Windows 8.

- You want to keep your existing applications and preferences.

- You want to preserve any local users and groups you've created.

You must perform a clean installation if any of the following conditions are true:

- There is no operating system currently installed.

- You have an operating system installed that does not support an in-place upgrade (such as DOS, Windows 9x, Windows NT, Windows Me, Windows 2000 Pro, Windows Vista, or Windows XP).

- You want to start from scratch, without keeping any existing preferences.

- You want to be able to dual-boot between Windows 10 or 11 and your previous operating system.

Table 1.5 shows each operating system that can be upgraded and the edition of Windows 10 to which it should be upgraded.

TABLE 1.5   Windows 7 and Windows 8 upgrade options

From current edition	Windows 10 edition
Windows 7 Starter	Windows 10 Home
Windows 7 Home Basic	Windows 10 Home
Windows 7 Home Premium	Windows 10 Home
Windows 7 Pro	Windows 10 Pro
Windows 7 Ultimate	Windows 10 Pro
Windows 7 Enterprise	Windows 10 Enterprise
Windows 8.1 Home	Windows 10 Home
Windows 8.1 Pro	Windows 10 Pro
Windows 8.1 Enterprise	Windows 10 Enterprise
Windows 8.1 Pro for Students	Windows 10 Pro

Upgrade Considerations

Almost all Windows 7 and Windows 8 applications should run with the Windows 10 operating system. However, possible exceptions to this statement include the following:

- Applications that use filesystem filters, such as antivirus software, may not be compatible.

- Custom power-management tools may not be supported.

Before upgrading to Windows 10 or 11, be sure to stop any antivirus scanners, network services, or other client software. These software packages may see the installation as a virus and cause issues.

Windows 7 and 8 cannot be upgraded to Windows 11. If you are looking to upgrade to Windows 11, then your device must be running Windows 10, version 2004 or later. At the time of this writing, Microsoft is offering free updates to Windows 11. They are currently available through Windows Update in Settings ➤ Update and Security.

If you are performing a clean installation to the same partition as an existing version of Windows, the contents of the existing Users (or Documents and Settings), Program Files, and Windows directories will be placed in a directory named Windows.old, and the old operating system will no longer be available.

Hardware Compatibility Issues

You need to ensure that you have the device drivers for the hardware for the version of Windows you are installing. If you have a video driver without a compatible driver, the upgrade will install the Standard VGA driver, which will display the video with an 800×600 resolution. Once you get the appropriate driver for your video, you can install it and adjust video properties accordingly.

Application Compatibility Issues

Not all applications that were written for earlier versions of Windows will work with Windows 10 or Windows 11. After the upgrade, if you have application problems, you can address the problems in any of the following ways:

- If the application is compatible with Windows 10 or 11, reinstall the application after the upgrade is complete.

- If the application uses dynamic-link libraries (DLLs) and there are migration DLLs for the application, apply the migration DLLs.

- Use the Microsoft Application Compatibility Toolkit (ACT) to determine the compatibility of your current applications with Windows. ACT will determine which applications are installed, identify any applications that may be affected by Windows updates, and identify any potential compatibility problems with User Account Control and Internet Explorer. Reports can be exported for detailed analysis.

- If applications were written for earlier versions of Windows but are incompatible with Windows 10, use the Windows 10 Program Compatibility Wizard. From the Control Panel, click the Programs icon, and then click the Run Programs From Previous Versions link to start the Program Compatibility Wizard. If the application is not compatible with Windows 10, upgrade your application to a Windows 10–compliant version.

An Upgrade Checklist for Upgrading from Windows 7 or Windows 8/8.1 to Windows 10

Once you have made the decision to upgrade, you should develop a plan of attack. The following upgrade checklist (valid for upgrading from Windows 7 or Windows 8/8.1) will help you plan and implement a successful upgrade strategy:

- Verify that your computer meets the minimum hardware requirements for Windows 10.

- Make sure you have the Windows 10 drivers for the hardware. You can verify this with the hardware manufacturer.

- To audit the current configuration and status of your computer, run the Get Windows 10 App tool from the Microsoft website, which also includes documentation on using the utility. It will generate a report of any known hardware or software compatibility issues based on your configuration. You should resolve any reported issues before you upgrade to Windows 10.

- Make sure your BIOS is current. Windows 10 requires that your computer has the most current BIOS. If it does not, it may not be able to use advanced power-management features or device-configuration features. In addition, your computer may cease to function during or after the upgrade. Use caution when performing BIOS updates because installing the incorrect BIOS can cause your computer to fail to boot.

- Take an inventory of your current configuration. This inventory should include documentation of your current network configuration, the applications that are installed, the hardware items and their configuration, the services that are running, and any profile and policy settings.

- Back up your data and configuration files. Before you make any major changes to your computer's configuration, you should back up your data and configuration files and then verify that you can successfully restore your backup. Chances are, if you have a valid backup, you won't have any problems. Likewise, if you don't have a valid backup, you will likely have problems.

- Delete any unnecessary files or applications, and clean up any program groups or program items you don't use. Theoretically, you want to delete all the junk on your computer before you upgrade. Think of this as the spring-cleaning step.

- Verify that there are no existing problems with your hard drive prior to the upgrade. Perform a disk scan, a current virus scan, and defragmentation. These too are spring-cleaning chores. This step just prepares your hard drive for the upgrade.

- Perform the upgrade. In this step, you upgrade from the Windows 7 or Windows 8/8.1 operating system to Windows 10.

- Verify your configuration. After Windows 10 has been installed, use the inventory to compare and test each element that was inventoried prior to the upgrade to verify that the upgrade was successful.

Handling an Upgrade Failure

Before you upgrade, you should have a contingency plan in place. Your plan should assume the worst-case scenario. For example, what happens if you upgrade and the computer doesn't work anymore? It is possible that, after checking your upgrade list and verifying that everything should work, your attempt at the actual upgrade may not work. If this happens, you may want to return your computer to the original, working configuration.

Indeed, I have made these plans, created my backups (two, just in case), verified them, and then had a failed upgrade anyway—only to discover that I had no clue where to find the original operating system CD. A day later, with the missing CD located, I was able to get up and running again. My problem was an older BIOS, and the manufacturer of my computer did not have an updated BIOS. Thankfully, nowadays, it is also possible to download a Windows ISO image and create a bootable CD or USB device.

Disk Partitioning

Disk partitioning is the act of taking the physical hard drive and creating logical partitions. A logical drive is how space is allocated to the drive's primary and logical partitions. For example, if you have a 500 GB hard drive, you might partition it into three logical drives:

- C: drive, which might be 200 GB
- D: drive, which might be 150 GB
- E: drive, which might be 150 GB

The following items detail some of the major considerations for disk partitioning:

Partition Size   One important consideration in your disk-partitioning scheme is determining the partition size. You need to consider the amount of space taken up by your operating system, the applications that will be installed, and the amount of stored data. It is also important to consider the amount of space required in the future.

For Windows 10, Microsoft recommends that if you are installing the 32-bit version you will need at least 16 GB, while the 64-bit version will require 20 GB of free space. However, if you are installing Windows 11, Microsoft recommends 64 GB of free space. This allows room for the operating system files and for future growth in terms of upgrades and installation files that are placed with the operating system files.

System and Boot Partitions   When you install the Windows operating system, files will be stored in two locations: the system partition and the boot partition. The system partition and the boot partition can be the same partition.

The system partition contains the files needed to boot the operating system. The system partition contains the Master Boot Record (MBR) and boot sector of the active drive partition. It is often the first physical hard drive in the computer and normally contains the necessary files to boot the computer. The files stored on the system partition do not take any significant disk space. The active partition is the system partition that is used to start your computer. The C: drive is usually the active partition.

The boot partition contains the Windows operating system files. By default, the Windows operating system files are located in a folder named Windows.

Disk Partition Configuration Utilities   If you are partitioning your disk prior to installation, you can use several utilities, such as the DiskPart utility or a third-party utility such as Partition Magic. You can also configure the disks during the installation of the Windows operating system.

You might want to create only the first partition where Windows will be installed. You can then use the Disk Management utility to create any other partitions you need. The Disk Management utility is covered in Chapter 5, "Configuring Security and Devices."

Language and Region Pack

In this chapter, we will briefly discuss the language and region settings. These will determine the language the computer will use. Windows supports many languages for the operating system interface and utilities. We will cover this in greater detail later in this book.

Regional settings are for configuring the format for items such as numbers, currencies, times, and dates. For example, English for the United States specifies a short date as mm/dd/yyyy (month/day/year), while English for South Africa specifies a short date as yyyy/mm/dd (year/month/day).

It is very important to only choose the locales that this machine will need to use. The reason for this is that your system will get updates for every locale you choose and set up.

Installing Windows 10

This section will discuss how to install Windows 10. The first step to installing Windows 10 is to know what type of media you need to install the Windows 10 operating system. Windows 10 gives you multiple ways to do an installation.

You can install Windows 10 either from the bootable DVD or through a network installation using files that have been copied to a network share point or USB device. You can also install Windows 10 by using a virtual hard drive (VHD). This option will be discussed in Chapter 2, "Configuring Users." You can also launch the setup.exe file from within the Windows 10 operating system to upgrade your operating system.

To start the installation, you simply restart your computer and connect to either a USB thumb drive or boot to the DVD. The installation process will begin automatically. You will walk through the steps of performing a clean installation of Windows 10 from the DVD in Exercise 1.1.

If you are installing Windows 10 from the network, you need a distribution server and a computer with a network connection. A distribution server is a server that has the Windows 10 distribution files copied to a shared folder. The following steps are used to install Windows 10 over the network:

1. Boot the target computer.

2. Attach to the distribution server and access the share that has the files copied to it.

3. Launch `setup.exe`.

4. Complete the Windows 10 installation using either the clean installation method or the upgrade method. These methods are discussed in detail in the following sections.

Performing a Clean Installation of Windows 10

On any installation of Windows 10, there are three stages.

Collecting Information   During the collection phase, Windows 10 gathers the information necessary to complete the installation. This is where Windows 10 gathers your local time, location, keyboard, license agreement, installation type, and installation disk partition information.

Installing Windows   This phase is where your Windows 10 files are copied to the hard disk and the installation is completed. This phase takes the longest because the files are installed.

Setting Up Windows   In this phase, you set up a username, computer name, and password; enter the product key; configure the security settings; and review the date and time. Once this is finished, your installation will be complete.

As explained earlier, you can run the installation from the optical media, from a USB, or over a network. The only difference in the installation procedure is your starting point: from your optical drive or USB or a network share. The steps in Exercise 1.1 and Exercise 1.2 assume you are using the Windows 10 DVD to install Windows 10.

Setting Up Your Computer for Hands-On Exercises

Before beginning Exercise 1.1, verify that your computer meets the requirements for installing Windows 10, as listed earlier in Table 1.4. For Exercise 1.1, it is assumed you are not currently running a previous version of Windows that will be upgraded.

The exercises in this book are based on your computer being configured in a specific manner. Your computer should have at least a 50 GB hard drive (this exceeds the basic minimums) that is configured with the minimum space requirements and partitions.

When you boot to the Windows 10 installation media, the Setup program will automatically start the Windows 10 installation. In Exercise 1.1, you will perform a clean installation of Windows 10. This exercise assumes that you have access to Windows 10 Enterprise; other editions may vary slightly. You can also download an evaluation version of Windows 10 from the Microsoft website.

Also, I may list steps that you may not see or I may not list steps that you see—this is because my version of Windows may be different. For example, the version of Windows 10 Enterprise I am installing, I am not required to enter a license number during installation. A normal version bought from a vendor may ask for the license during the actual installation.

 I am loading Windows 10 Enterprise into a VMware Workstation virtual machine. Again, this may make your installation a little different than the steps listed in Exercise 1.1. Plus, depending on your version and license model, not all screens may appear.

EXERCISE 1.1

Performing a Clean Installation of Windows 10

1. Insert the Windows 10 DVD, USB thumb drive, or ISO image in the machine or virtual machine with no operating system and start the computer.

2. If you are directed to "Hit any key" to start the DVD, press Enter.

3. The first screen will ask you to enter your language, time and currency format, and keyboard or input method (see Figure 1.1). After filling in these fields, click Next.

FIGURE 1.1 Windows Setup screen

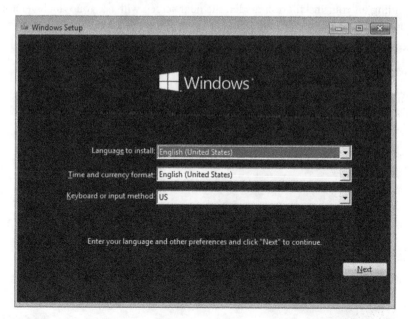

4. On the next screen, click the Install Now button (see Figure 1.2).

FIGURE 1.2 Windows install screen

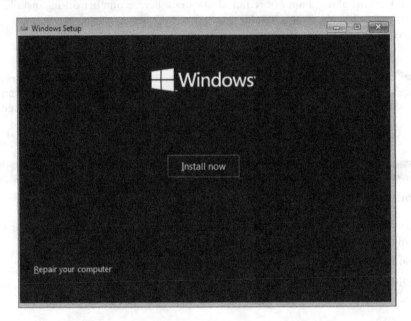

5. Depending on your installation media, the next screen will ask you which version of Windows 10 you want to install. I am choosing Windows 10 Enterprise (see Figure 1.3).

6. A message appears to tell you that the setup is starting. The licensing screen will be first. Read the license agreement and then select the I Accept The License Terms check box. Click Next.

7. When asked which type of installation you want, click Custom (Advanced) as shown in Figure 1.4.

FIGURE 1.3   Windows Version screen

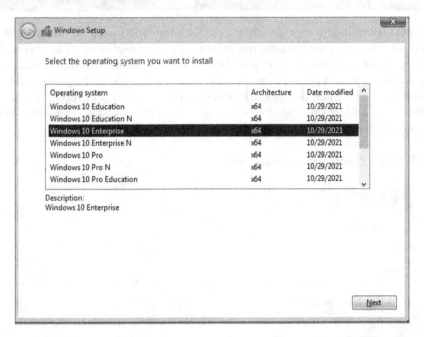

FIGURE 1.4   Type of installation screen

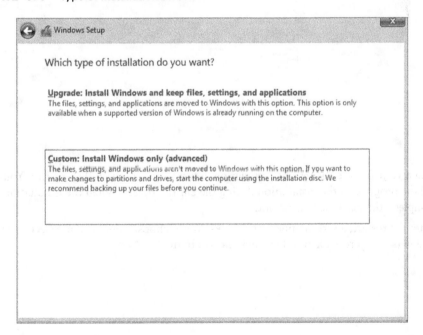

8. The next screen asks you to identify the disk to which you would like to install Windows 10. Choose an unformatted free space or a partition (partition will be erased) with at least 50 GB available. You can also click the Drive Options (Advanced) link to create and format your own partition, as shown in Figure 1.5. Click the New link and click Apply to create the new partition for Windows 10. A message will appear stating that Windows 10 will set some partitions for system files. Just click the OK button. After you choose your partition, click Next.

FIGURE 1.5   Windows disk setup screen

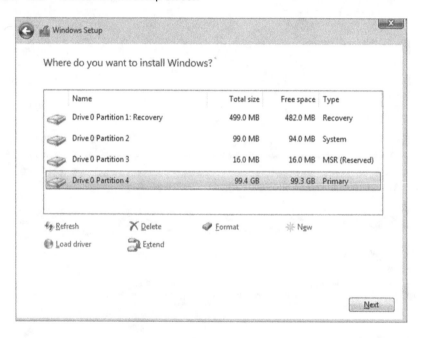

9. When your partition is set, the installation will start (as shown in Figure 1.6). You will see the progress of the installation during the entire process. When the installation is complete, the machine will reboot.

10. After the restart, a screen appears that asks you to choose your region. Select your region (see Figure 1.7), and then click the Yes button.

FIGURE 1.6   Windows installation status screen

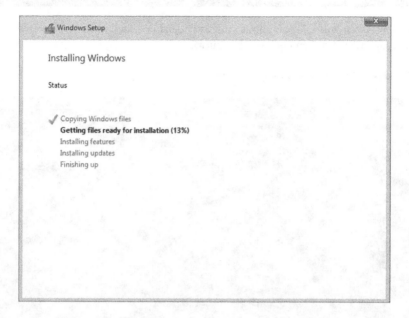

FIGURE 1.7   Choose your Region screen.

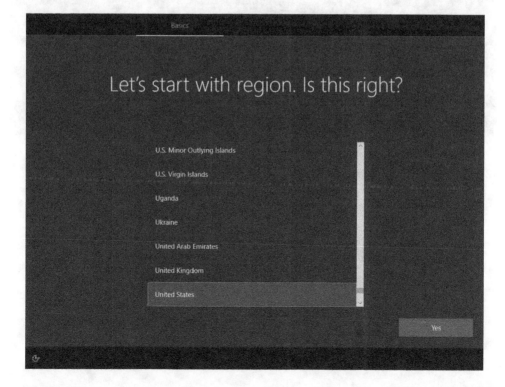

11. The next screen will ask you about your keyboard layout. Choose your keyboard layout (see Figure 1.8) and then click the Yes button.

FIGURE 1.8   Choosing your keyboard layout

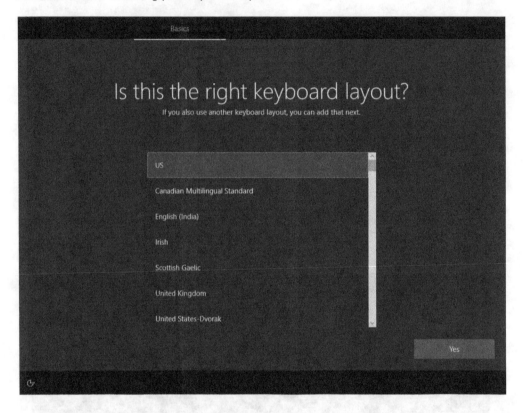

12. The next screen will ask you if you have a second keyboard. If you do, click the Add Layout button. If not, click the Skip button (as seen in Figure 1.9).

FIGURE 1.9   Adding a Second Keyboard

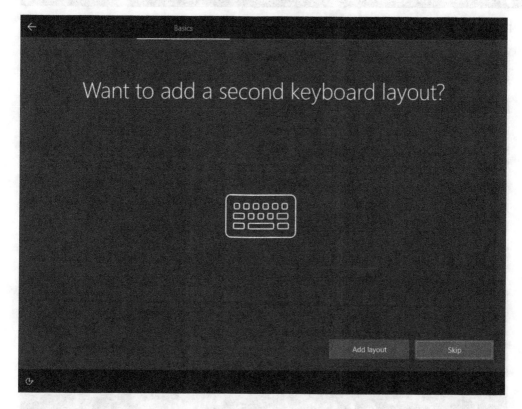

13. At the Sign In With Microsoft screen, choose the Domain Join Instead link. It will ask you who is going to use this PC. Enter your username and click the Next button.

14. Next it's going to ask you to enter a super memorable password (as shown in Figure 1.10). Type in your password and click the Next button.

15. You will be asked to reenter your password. Enter your password again and click the Next button.

FIGURE 1.10 Windows 10 screen

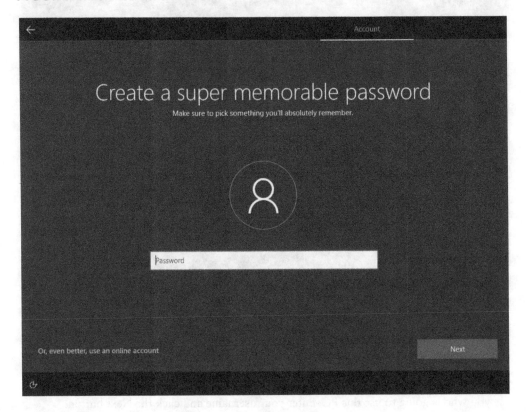

16. Depending on your version, you may be asked to create three security questions. If your edition asks this, put in your security questions and click the Next button for each security question. After the third question, click the Next button to move on.

17. The next screen will ask if you want to make Cortana your personal assistant. You can either accept or decline this. I am going to choose Decline.

18. The next screen will ask if you want Microsoft to save your activity history. If you accept this, you will send Microsoft information about all activities that you are doing. This allows you to continue to finish these activities from any other device. Since this is a corporate machine, I will choose not to send Microsoft my activity history by clicking the No button (see Figure 1.11).

FIGURE 1.11 Windows activity screen

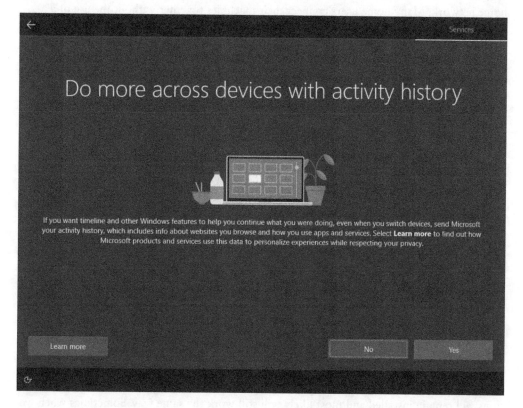

19. The next screen will be the privacy settings screen. Disable any of the privacy settings that you want disabled (all will be enabled by default). Once you're finished, click the Accept button.

20. A different screen will appear letting you know that the system is being set up. This may take a few minutes. Be sure not to turn off the machine during this process. Once this is all completed, the system may ask you to log in. Put in your password and click the right arrow next to the password box. Your installation is now complete.

Before we talk about the Windows 10 upgrade procedure, I want to quickly explain something that you saw during the Windows 10 installation. In step 13, I had you choose Domain Join Instead rather than using a Microsoft password. We will explore both of the choices in greater detail, but I wanted to quickly explain why we chose one over the other.

Microsoft offers two main networks: workgroup-based or domain-based. *Workgroups* (also referred to as peer-to-peer networks) are when you just connect your computers together directly to each other. A perfect example for most of us is what you do in your home network. Many home users connect their machines together without the use of a main server.

Corporations normally do things a bit differently than that. *Domains* are networks that are controlled by servers called *domain controllers*. Domain controllers are Windows servers that have a copy of a database called Active Directory (AD). Recently Microsoft took domain-based networks a step further by allowing companies to set up a cloud-based version of an Active Directory domain (Azure AD). This means that companies no longer need to maintain and manage their own domain controllers. Since most people don't have a cloud-based version of Azure AD, I had you choose the option Join A Domain so that we could finish the Windows 10 installation.

We will go over all of these options in greater detail throughout this book, but I wanted to introduce you to these two Windows 10 options.

Performing an Upgrade to Windows 10 from Windows 8.1

This section describes how to perform an upgrade to Windows 10 from Windows 8.1. Similar to a clean installation, you can run the process from the installation DVD, from a USB, or over a network. The only difference in the procedure is your starting point: from your optical or USB drive or from a network share. For the steps in the following sections, it is assumed that you are using the Windows 10 DVD to install the Windows 10 operating system.

Upgrading a Windows 7 or Windows 8/8.1 system to Windows 10 will save you a lot of time and trouble. Because we are upgrading the system, all of the user's data and applications will remain installed and most likely will still work the same way. Sometimes when we upgrade a system, we run into problems with applications. But many times that is caused by a driver or a needed software update that will most likely solve the issue.

The three main steps in the Windows 10 upgrade process are very similar to the ones for a clean installation. The three steps of upgrading to Windows 10 are as follows:

1. Collecting information
2. Installing Windows
3. Setting up Windows

In Exercise 1.2, you will go through the process of installing Windows 10 by upgrading Windows 8.1. I have a Windows 8.1 Enterprise system that I will update to Windows 10 Enterprise.

Upgrading Windows 8.1 to Windows 10

1. Insert the Windows 10 DVD. (We are upgrading Windows 8.1 Enterprise to Windows 10 Enterprise.)

2. If Autorun does not start, navigate to the DVD drive and click `setup.exe`. Once the setup starts (via either `setup.exe` or Autorun), click Run Setup.exe, as shown in Figure 1.12.

FIGURE 1.12   DVD setup screen

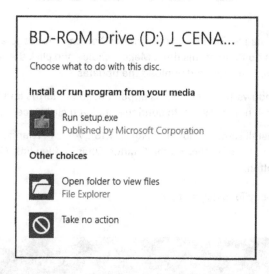

3. If a pop-up box appears for User Account Control, click the Yes button (see Figure 1.13).

FIGURE 1.13   User Account Control screen

EXERCISE 1.2 *(continued)*

You should then see a message appear stating that Windows is preparing the system, as shown in Figure 1.14.

FIGURE 1.14   Preparing screen

4.   You may be prompted to Get Important Updates. You can choose to either download the updates or not do them at this time. Make a choice and click the Next button. (During my installation, I decided to download the updates.)

5.   The Microsoft Windows 10 license terms appear. Read the terms and then click Accept. (The installation will not allow you to continue until you click Accept.)

6.   At the Ready To Install screen (shown in Figure 1.15), you can change what files and/ or apps you want to keep by clicking the Change What To Keep link. Once you're ready, click the Install button.

FIGURE 1.15   Ready To Install screen

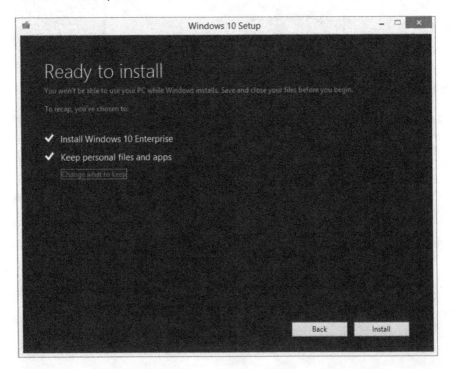

7. Windows 10 will begin to install (as shown in Figure 1.16). Your computer may restart multiple times. This is normal. As the upgrade status screen states, "Sit back and relax."

8. After the upgrade has completed, a welcome screen will be displayed, similar to the one shown in Figure 1.17. Click Next.

FIGURE 1.16   Installing Status screen

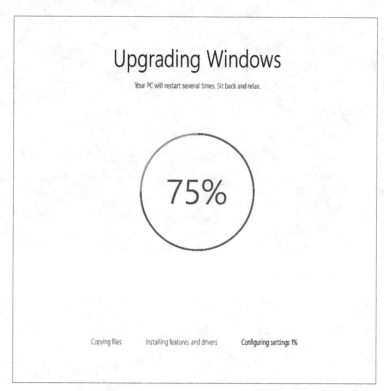

9. At the Get Going Fast screen, click the Use Express Settings button.

10. At the New Apps screen, just click Next.

And that's it—Windows 10 is installed (see Figure 1.18). Congrats.

FIGURE 1.17   Welcome screen

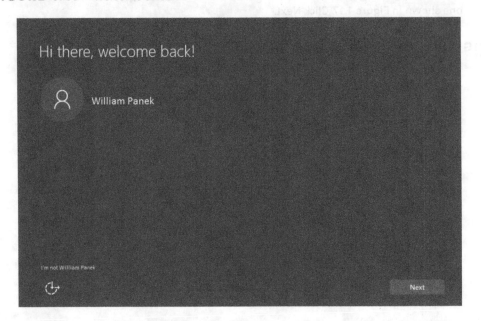

FIGURE 1.18   Windows 10 screen

Now that we have installed the Windows 10 operating system, let's take a look at how to change your system's locales. Earlier I explained that the locale settings help you with the system's language format, settings, and region-specific details.

In Exercise 1.3, I will show you how to change your current locale. This helps when you take your Windows 10 laptop, tablet, or phone to another part of the world.

EXERCISE 1.3

Configuring Locales

1. Click the Start button and choose Settings.

2. Once on the Settings screen, choose Time And Language.

3. This should place you on the Date & Time screen. Make sure your time zone is set correctly. If it's not, pull down the time zone options and choose your time zone.

4. Scroll down and make sure the date and time formats are set the way you want. If they are not, click the Change Date And Time Formats link. Change the formats to the way you want them set.

5. Click the Region And Language link on the left-hand side.

6. Make sure the country or region is set properly. If you want to add a second language to this Windows 10 system, click the Add A Language link. Choose the language you want.

7. Once completed, close the Settings screen.

Installing Windows 11

This section will discuss how to install Windows 11. The method of installing Windows 11 is the same as installing Windows 10. The first step to is to know what type of media you need to install the operating system. Windows 11 gives you multiple ways to perform an installation.

You can install Windows 11 either from the bootable DVD or through a network installation using files that have been copied to a network share point or USB device. You can also install Windows 11 by using a virtual hard drive (VHD). This option will be discussed in Chapter 2. You can also launch the setup.exe file from within the Windows 11 operating system to upgrade your operating system.

To start the installation, you simply restart your computer and boot to the DVD. The installation process will begin automatically.

If you are installing Windows 11 from the network, you need a distribution server and a computer with a network connection. A distribution server is a server that has the Windows

11 distribution files copied to a shared folder. Use the following steps to install Windows 11 over the network:

1. Boot the target computer.

2. Attach to the distribution server and access the share that has the files copied to it.

3. Launch `setup.exe`.

4. Complete the Windows 11 installation using either the clean installation method or the upgrade method. These methods are discussed in detail in the following sections.

Performing a Clean Installation of Windows 11

On any installation of Windows 11, you have the same three stages listed earlier in the section "Performing a Clean Installation of Windows 10." The stages include collecting information, installing Windows, and setting up Windows.

As explained earlier, you can run the installation from the optical media, from a USB, or over a network. The only difference in the installation procedure is your starting point: from your optical drive or USB or a network share.

I am going to discuss how to create a Windows 11 USB with the Media Creation Tool to install Windows 11. To create an installation media using this tool, connect a USB flash drive with at least 8 GB of space and perform the following:

1. Go to the Microsoft Windows 11 download page at `www.microsoft.com/en-gb/software-download/windows11`.

2. Under Create Windows 11 Installation Media, click the Download Now button to save the file on the device.

3. Double-click the `MediaCreationToolW11.exe` file to launch the tool.

4. Click the Accept button to agree to the terms.

5. Clear the Use The Recommended Options For This PC (Optional) option.

6. Select the correct language and edition of Windows 11.

7. Click Next.

8. Select the USB Flash Drive option.

9. Click Next.

10. Select the USB flash drive.

11. Click Next.

12. Click Finish.

After you finish these steps, the files will be downloaded and will create the installation media. You can then use this USB to boot the device and proceed with a fresh copy of Windows 11.

Performing an Upgrade to Windows 11 from Windows 10

This section describes how to perform an upgrade to Windows 11 from Windows 10. Remember, if you are looking to upgrade to Windows 11, then your device must be running Windows 10, version 2004 or later.

If your computer meets the minimum system requirements to run Windows 11, as shown in Table 1.4 earlier, and you are running Windows 10, version 2004 or later, then typically you should expect to receive an offer from Microsoft to upgrade to Windows 11. If you don't receive the offer to upgrade to Windows 11, then you can also go to Microsoft's website at `www.microsoft.com/en-us/windows/get-windows-11` for more information.

You can also check and see if the Windows 11 upgrade is ready for your machine by going to your Windows Update settings page. Click the Start button and type **Settings**, then press Enter to get to the Settings app. From there, select Update & Security and then Windows Update, then click the Check For Updates button.

If your upgrade is ready, the option to download and install should show up. You can download it and install it, then follow the onscreen prompts.

Troubleshooting Installation Problems

The Windows installation process is designed to be as simple as possible. The chances for installation errors are greatly minimized through the use of wizards and the step-by-step process. However, it is possible that errors will occur.

Identifying Common Installation Problems

As most of you are aware, errors sometimes do occur during installations. You might encounter some of the following installation errors:

Media Errors   Media errors are caused by defective or damaged DVDs. To check the disc, put it into another computer and see if you can read it. Also check your disc for scratches or dirt—it may just need to be cleaned.

Insufficient Disk Space   Both Windows 10 and 11 have minimum requirements needed for the amount of disk required. Please refer to Table 1.4 from earlier in this chapter or check out Microsoft's website for updated requirements. If the Setup program cannot verify that this space exists, the program will not let you continue.

Not Enough Memory   Make sure your computer has the minimum amount of memory required. Having insufficient memory may cause the installation to fail or blue-screen errors to occur after installation.

Not Enough Processing Power   Make sure your computer has the minimum processing power required. Having insufficient processing power may cause the installation to fail or blue-screen errors to occur after installation.

Hardware That Is Not on the HCL   If your hardware is not listed on the hardware compatibility list (HCL), Windows may not recognize the hardware or the device may not work properly.

Hardware with No Driver Support   Windows will not recognize hardware without driver support.

Hardware That Is Not Configured Properly   If your hardware is Plug and Play (PnP) compatible, Windows should configure it automatically. If your hardware is not Plug and Play compatible, you will need to manually configure the hardware per the manufacturer's instructions.

Incorrect Product Key   Without a valid product key, the installation will not go past the Product Key screen. Make sure you have not typed in an incorrect key (check your Windows installation folder or your computer case for this key).

Failure to Access TCP/IP Network Resources   If you install Windows with typical settings, the computer is configured as a DHCP client. If there is no DHCP server to provide IP configuration information, the client will still generate an autoconfigured IP address but be unable to access network resources through TCP/IP if the other network clients are using DHCP addresses.

Installing Nonsupported Hard Drives   If your computer is using a hard disk that does not have a driver included on the Windows media, you will receive an error message stating that the hard drive cannot be found. You should verify that the hard drive is properly connected and functional. You will need to obtain a disk driver for the version of Windows you are installing from the manufacturer and then specify the driver location by selecting the Load Driver option during partition selection.

Troubleshooting with Installation Log Files

When you install Windows 10 or 11, the Setup program creates several log files. You can view these logs to check for any problems during the installation process. Two log files are particularly useful for troubleshooting:

- The action log includes all the actions that were performed during the setup process and a description of each action. These actions are listed in chronological order. The action log is stored as \Windows\setupact.log.

- The error log includes any errors that occurred during the installation. For each error, there is a description and an indication of the severity of the error. This error log is stored as \Windows\setuperr.log.

In Exercise 1.4, you will view the Windows Setup logs to determine whether there were any problems with your Windows installation.

EXERCISE 1.4

Troubleshooting Failed Installations with Setup Logs

1. Select Start ➤ Computer.

2. Double-click Local Disk (C:).

3. Double-click Windows.

4. In the Windows folder, double-click the Setupact.log file to view your action log in Notepad. When you are finished viewing this file, close Notepad.

5. Double-click the Setuperr.log file to view your error file in Notepad. If no errors occurred during installation, this file will be empty. When you are finished viewing this file, close Notepad.

6. Close the directory window.

Supporting Multiple-Boot Options

You may want to install Windows 10 or 11 and still be able to run other operating systems. *Dual-booting* or multibooting allows your computer to boot multiple operating systems. Your computer will be automatically configured for dual-booting if there was a dual-boot–supported operating system on your computer prior to the Windows installation, you didn't upgrade from that operating system, and you installed Windows 10 or 11 into a different partition.

One reason for dual-booting is to test various systems. If you have a limited number of computers in your test lab and you want to be able to test multiple configurations, you should dual-boot. For example, you might configure one computer to dual-boot with Windows 7, Windows 8/8.1, and Windows 10.

Here are some keys to successful dual-boot configurations:

-   Make sure you have plenty of disk space.

-   Windows 10 or 11 must be installed on a separate partition in order to dual-boot with other operating systems.

-   Install older operating systems before installing newer operating systems. If you want to support dual-booting with Windows 7 and Windows 10, Windows 7 must be installed first. If you install Windows 10 first, you cannot install Windows 7 without ruining your Windows 10 configuration; this applies to Windows 11 also.

-   Do not install Windows 10 or 11 on a compressed volume unless the volume was compressed using NTFS compression.

Once you have installed each operating system, you can choose the operating system that you will boot to during the boot process. You will see a boot-selection screen that asks you to choose which operating system you want to boot.

The Boot Configuration Data (BCD) store contains boot information parameters that were previously found in boot.ini in older versions of Windows. To edit the boot options in the BCD store, use the bcdedit utility, which can be launched only from a command prompt. To open a command prompt window, you can do the following:

1. Launch \Windows\system32\cmd.exe.

2. Open the Run command by pressing the [Windows] key + R and then entering **cmd**.

3. Type **cmd.exe** in the Search Programs And Files box and press Enter.

Once the command-prompt window is open, type **bcdedit** to launch the bcdedit utility. You can also type **bcdedit/?** to see all the different bcdedit commands. A few bcdedit commands may be needed when dual-booting a machine. Table 1.6 shows some of the bcdedit commands that may be needed when dual-booting.

TABLE 1.6   bcdedit commands for dual-booting

Command	Explanation
/createstore	Creates a new empty Boot Configuration Data store
/default	Allows you to specify which operating system will start when the timeout expires
/deletevalue	Allows you to delete a specified element from a boot entry
/displayorder	Shows the display order that the boot manager uses when showing the display order to the user
/export	Allows you to export the contents of the system store into a file
/import	Restores the system store by using the data file previously generated by using the /export option
/set	Allows you to set an entry option value
/store	Specifies the store to be used
/timeout	Specifies the amount of time used before the system boots into the default operating system

Using Windows Activation

Windows Activation is Microsoft's way of reducing software piracy. Unless you have a corporate license for Windows 10 or Windows 11, then you will need to perform post-installation activation. This can be done online or through a telephone call. Windows will attempt automatic activation three days after you log onto it for the first time. There is a grace period when you will be able to use the operating system without activation. After the grace period expires, a permanent watermark is displayed. Until the activation key is entered, certain personalization settings are not configurable until Windows is activated. When the grace period runs out, the Windows Activation Wizard will automatically start; it will walk you through the activation process.

To access the Windows Activation screen, click the Start button and choose Settings (the spoke icon). Scroll down to Update And Security and click that link. On the left side, you will see a link for Activation. When you click Activation, you will see the Activation screen (shown in Figure 1.19). Scroll down to the Activate Windows Now section. You may need to click the Change Product Key button and put in the license number that came with your Windows 10 or 11 copy. Once Windows 10 is activated, it will show that you are activated.

FIGURE 1.19   The Windows Activation Wizard screen

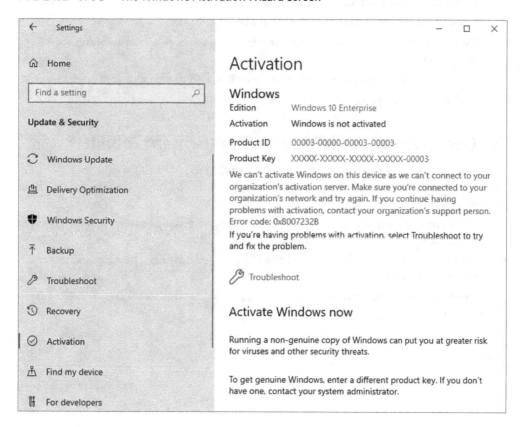

Understanding Automated Deployment Options

If you need to install Windows 10 or 11 on multiple computers, you could manually install the operating system on each computer. However, automating the deployment process will make your job easier, more efficient, and more cost effective if you have a large number of client computers on which to install Windows.

Windows 10 and 11 come with several utilities that can be used for deploying and automating the Windows installation. With access to multiple utilities with different functionality, administrators have increased flexibility in determining how to best deploy Windows within a large corporate environment.

The following sections contain overviews of the automated deployment options, which will help you choose which solution is best for your requirements and environment. Each utility will then be covered in more detail throughout this chapter. The options for automated deployment of Windows 10 or 11 are as follows:

- Microsoft Deployment Toolkit (MDT)
- Unattended installation, or unattended setup, which uses `Setup.exe`
- Windows Automated Installation Kit (Windows AIK)
- Windows Deployment Services (WDS) server, which requires Windows Server for deployment
- System Preparation Tool (`Sysprep.exe`), which is used to create images or clones
- Windows Assessment and Deployment Kit (ADK)

An Overview of the Microsoft Deployment Toolkit

Microsoft includes a deployment assistance toolset called the *Microsoft Deployment Toolkit (MDT)*. It is used to automate desktop and server deployment. The MDT provides an administrator with the following benefits:

- Administrative tools that allow for the deployment of desktops and servers through the use of a common console (see Figure 1.20)
- Quicker deployments and the capabilities of having standardized desktop and server images and security
- Zero-touch deployments of Windows 11, Windows 10, Windows Server, and Windows 7 / 8 / 8.1

FIGURE 1.20   Microsoft Deployment Toolkit console

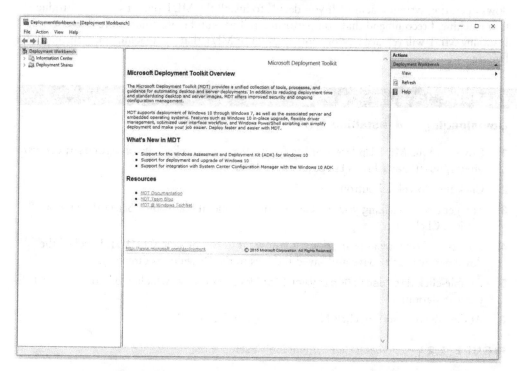

To install the MDT package onto your computer (regardless of the operating system being deployed), you must first meet the minimum requirements of MDT. These components need to be installed only on the computer where MDT is being installed:

- Windows 11, Windows 10, Windows 7, Windows 8, Windows 8.1, or Windows Server.

- The Windows Assessment and Deployment Kit (ADK) for Windows 10 or 11 is required for all deployment scenarios.

- System Center 2012 R2 Configuration Manager Service Pack 1 with the Windows ADK for Windows 10 or 11 is required for zero-touch installation (ZTI) and user-driven installation (UDI) scenarios.

- If you are using ZTI and/or UDI, you are allowed to add the MDT SQL database to any version of System Center Configuration Manager with SQL Technology; if you are using LTI, you must use a separately licensed SQL Server product to host your MDT SQL database.

You can install MDT without installing Windows (ADK) first, but you will not be able to use the package fully until Windows (ADK) is installed.

In Exercise 1.5, you will download and install MDT. You can install MDT on the Windows operating system machine. If you decide to install the MDT onto a server or production machine, I recommend that you perform a full backup before completing Exercise 1.5. Installing MDT will replace any previous version of MDT that the machine may currently be using.

Downloading and Installing MDT

1. Download the MDT Update 1 utility from Microsoft's website (www.microsoft.com/en-us/download/details.aspx?id=54259).

2. Click the Download button.

3. You get a screen asking you to "Choose the download you want." Select the x64 or x86 version. Click Next.

4. A message box may appear asking if you want to run or save the MDT. I clicked the down arrow next to Save and saved the files to the Downloads directory.

5. Double-click MicrosoftDeploymentToolkit_xxx.exe, which you choose to start the installation.

6. At the Welcome screen, click Next, as shown in Figure 1.21.

FIGURE 1.21   Microsoft Deployment Toolkit setup screen

7. At the License screen, click the I Accept The Terms In The License Agreement radio button and click Next.

8. At the Custom Setup screen, click the down arrow next to Microsoft Deployment Toolkit and choose Entire Feature Will Be Installed On Local Hard Drive. Click Next, as shown on Figure 1.22.

FIGURE 1.22   Microsoft Deployment Toolkit Custom Setup screen

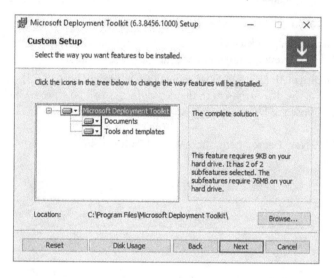

9. At the Customer Experience Improvement Program screen, choose if you want to participate or not and click Next.

10. At the Ready To Install screen, click the Install button.

11. If a User Account Control dialog box appears, click Yes.

12. When the installation completes, click Finish.

Now that you have installed MDT, you are going to configure the package. In Exercise 1.6, you will configure MDT and set up a distribution share and database. I am creating the MDT on a Windows Server machine so that we can distribute Windows 10. Make sure the Windows Assessment and Deployment Kit (ADK) for Windows 10 is installed because it is required for this deployment scenario. If installing Windows 11 you will want to be sure to install the ADK for Windows 11. The steps will be the same.

Configuring MDT

1. Create a shared folder on your network called Distribution, and give the Everyone group Full Control to the folder for this exercise.

2. Open the MDT workbench by choosing Start ➢ Microsoft Development Toolkit ➢ Deployment Workbench.

3. If the User Account Control box appears, click Yes.

4. In the left-hand pane, click Deployment Shares, and then right-click the deployment shares and choose New Deployment Share.

5. The New Deployment Share Wizard begins (as shown in Figure 1.23). At the first screen, you will choose the directory where the deployments will be stored. Click the Browse button and choose the Distribution share that you created in step 1. Then click Next.

FIGURE 1.23   New Deployment Share Wizard Path screen

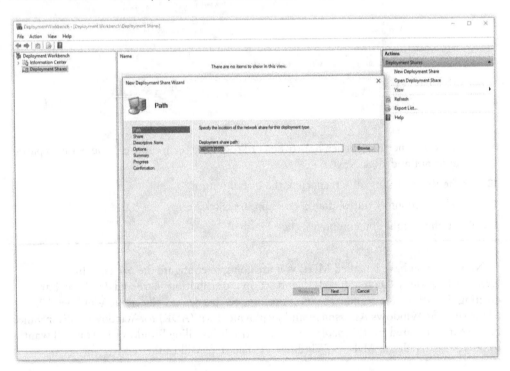

6. At the Share Name screen, accept the default, Distribution. Click Next.

7. At the Deployment Share Description screen, accept the default description name (as shown in Figure 1.24) and click Next.

FIGURE 1.24   New Deployment Share Wizard Deployment Share Description screen

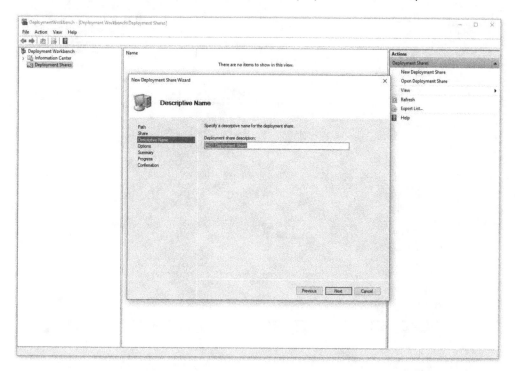

8. At the Options screen, make sure all check boxes are selected, as shown in Figure 1.25.

9. At the Summary screen, look over the options and click Next.

10. The Installation Will Progress screen will show you how the installation is performing. Once it's finished, click Finish.

FIGURE 1.25   New Deployment Share Wizard Options screen

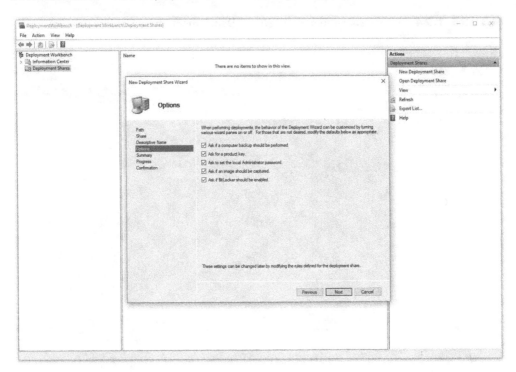

11. The new Deployment share is set up and ready to start deploying. Now an operating system needs to be set up in the MDT for deployment.

12. Close the MDT workbench.

Now that you have seen how to install the MDT utility, let's take a look at some other ways to automatically install Windows 10 or 11.

An Overview of Unattended Installation

Unattended installation is a practical method of automating deployments when you have a large number of clients to install and the computers require different hardware and software configurations. Unattended installations allow you to create customized installations that are specific to your environment. Custom installations can support custom hardware and software installations.

Unattended installations utilize an answer file called `Autounattend.xml` to provide configuration information during the installation process. Think about the Windows installation from earlier in this chapter. You are asked for your locale, type of installation, and so on. The answer file allows these questions to be answered without user interaction. In addition to providing standard Windows configuration information, the answer file can provide installation instructions for applications, additional language support, service packs, and device drivers.

With an unattended installation, you can use a distribution share to install Windows 10/11 on the target computers. You can also use a Windows DVD with an answer file located on the root of the DVD, or on a universal flash device (UFD), such as an external USB flash drive.

Unattended installations allow you to create customized installations that are specific to your environment. Custom installations can support custom hardware and software installations. Since the answer file for Windows 10/11 is in XML format, all custom configuration information can be contained within the `Autounattend.xml` file. This is different from past versions of Windows, where creating automated installation routines for custom installations required multiple files to be used.

If you use a distribution share, it should contain the Windows operating system image and the answer file to respond to installation configuration queries. The target computer must be able to connect to the distribution share over the network. After the distribution share and target computers are connected, you can initiate the installation process. Figure 1.26 illustrates the unattended installation process.

FIGURE 1.26   Unattended installation with distribution share and a target computer

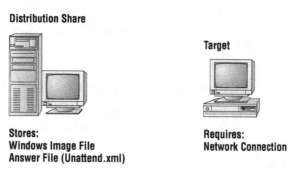

Advantages of Unattended Installation

In a midsize or large organization, it just makes sense to use automated setups. As stated earlier, it is nearly impossible to install Windows 10/11 one at a time on hundreds of machines.

But there are many advantages to using unattended installations as a method for automating Windows:

- Unattended installation saves time and money because users do not have to interactively respond to each installation query.

- It can be configured to provide automated query responses while still selectively allowing users to provide specified input during installations.

- It can be used to install clean copies of Windows 10/11 or upgrade an existing operating system (providing it is on the list of permitted operating systems) to Windows.

- It can be expanded to include installation instructions for applications, additional language support, service packs, and device drivers.

- The physical media for Windows 10/11 does not need to be distributed to all computers on which it will be installed.

Disadvantages of Unattended Installation

As stated earlier, a manual installation is not practical for mass installations. But one of the biggest disadvantages to performing an unattended installation is that an administrator does not physically walk through the installation. A client operating system is one of the most important items that you will install onto a machine. As an IT manager and consultant, I have always felt better physically installing a client operating system. This way, if there are any glitches, I can see and deal with them immediately. If something happens during an unattended installation, you may never know it, but the end user may experience small issues throughout the lifetime of the machine.

Two other disadvantages of using unattended installations as a method for automating Windows 10/11 installations are listed here:

- They require more initial setup than a standard installation of Windows 10/11.

- Someone must have access to each client computer and must initiate the unattended installation process on the client side.

An Overview of Windows Deployment Services

Windows Deployment Services (WDS) is an updated version of Remote Installation Services (RIS). WDS is a suite of components that allows you to remotely install Windows on client computers.

A WDS server installs Windows 10 on the client computers, as illustrated in Figure 1.27. The WDS server must be configured with the Preboot Execution Environment (PXE) boot files, the images to be deployed to the client computers, and the answer file. WDS client computers must be PXE-capable. PXE is a technology that is used to boot to the network when no operating system or network configuration has been installed and configured on a client computer.

FIGURE 1.27   Windows Deployment Services (WDS) uses a WDS server and WDS clients.

WDS Server

WDS Client

Stores:
PXE Boot Files and Boot Images
Windows Boot Images
Answer File(s)

Requires:
PXE-Compatible Boot

The WDS clients access the network with the help of a Dynamic Host Configuration Protocol (DHCP) server. This allows the WDS client to remotely install the operating system from the WDS server. The network environment must be configured with a DHCP server, a Domain Name System (DNS) server, NTFS volumes, and Active Directory to connect to the WDS server. No other client software is required to connect to the WDS server. Remote installation is a good choice for automatic deployment when you need to deploy to large numbers of computers and the client computers are PXE-compliant.

Starting with Windows 11, the operating system deployment functionality of WDS is being partially deprecated. Workflows that rely on boot.wim from installation media or on running Windows Setup in WDS mode will no longer be supported and will be blocked. When you PXE-boot from a WDS server that uses the boot.wim file from installation media as its boot image, Windows Setup will automatically launch in WDS mode. According to Microsoft, alternatives to WDS, such as Microsoft Endpoint Configuration Manager and Microsoft Deployment Toolkit (MDT), provide a better, more flexible experience for deploying Windows images. WDS PXE boot is not affected by this change, and you can still use WDS to PXE-boot devices with custom boot images, but you cannot use boot.wim as the boot image and run Windows Setup in WDS mode.

Advantages of WDS

The advantages of using WDS as a method for automating Windows 10/11 installations are as follows:

- Allows an IT department to remotely install Windows operating systems through the network. This advantage helps reduce the difficulty and IT labor cost compared to a manual installation.

- Allows an IT department to deploy multiple images for mixed environments, including Windows 7, Windows 8/8.1, Windows 10, Windows 11, and Windows Server.

- For Windows 10, allows IT departments to use Windows setups, including Windows Preinstallation Environment (Windows PE), WIM files, and image-based setups.

- WDS uses multicasting to allow the transmitting and image data to communicate with each other.

- An IT department can create reference images using the Image Capture Wizard, which is an alternative to the ImageX tool.

- Allows an IT administrator to install a driver package to the server and configure the drivers to be deployed to client computers at the same time the image is installed.

- Allows IT departments to standardize Windows 10/11 installations throughout a group or organization.

- The physical media does not need to be distributed to all computers that will be installed.

- End-user installation deployment can be controlled through the Group Policy utility. For example, you can configure what choices a user can access or that are automatically specified through the end-user Setup Wizard.

Disadvantages of WDS

The disadvantages of using WDS as a method for automating Windows 10/11 installations include the following:

- WDS can be used only if your network is running Windows Server 2008 and above with Active Directory installed.

- The clients that use WDS must be PXE-capable.

You can configure WDS on a Windows Server computer by using the Windows Deployment Services Configuration Wizard or by using the WDSUTIL command-line utility. Table 1.7 describes the WDSUTIL command-line options.

TABLE 1.7   WDSUTIL command-line options

WDSUTIL option	Description
/initialize-server	Initializes the configuration of the WDS server
/uninitialized-server	Undoes any changes made during the initialization of the WDS server
/add	Adds images and devices to the WDS server
/convert-ripimage	Converts Remote Installation Preparation (RIPrep) images to WIM images
/remove	Removes images from the server
/set	Sets information in images, image groups, WDS servers, and WDS devices

WDSUTIL option	Description
/get	Gets information from images, image groups, WDS servers, and WDS devices
/new	Creates new capture images or discover images
/copy-image	Copies images from the image store
/export-image	Exports to WIM files images contained within the image store
/start	Starts WDS services
/stop	Stops WDS services
/disable	Disables WDS services
/enable	Enables WDS services
/approve-autoadddevices	Approves Auto-Add devices
/reject-autoadddevices	Rejects Auto-Add devices
/delete-autoadddevices	Deletes records from the Auto-Add database
/update	Uses a known-good resource to update a server resource

An Overview of the System Preparation Tool and Disk Imaging

The *System Preparation Tool,* or *Sysprep* (Sysprep.exe), is used to prepare a computer for disk imaging, and the disk image can then be captured using Image Capture Wizard (an imaging-management tool included with Windows 10/11) or third-party imaging software. Sysprep is a free utility that comes on all Windows operating systems. By default, the Sysprep utility can be found on Windows Server and Windows operating systems in the \Windows\ system32\sysprep directory.

Disk *imaging* is the process of taking a checkpoint of a computer and then using that checkpoint to create new computers, thus allowing for automated deployments. The reference, or source, computer has Windows 10/11 installed and is configured with the settings and applications that should be installed on the target computers. The image (checkpoints) is then created and can be transferred to other computers, thus installing the operating system, settings, and applications that were defined on the reference computer.

Using Imaging Software

Using the System Preparation Tool and disk imaging is a good choice (and the one most commonly used in the real world) for automatic deployment when you have a large number of computers with similar configuration requirements or machines that need to be rebuilt frequently.

For example, StormWind Studios, an online computer education company, reinstalls the same software every few weeks for new classes. Imaging is a fast and easy way to simplify the deployment process.

Most organizations use images to create new machines quickly and easily, but they also use them to reimage end users' machines that crash.

In most companies, end users will have space on a server (home folders) to allow them to store data. We give our end users space on the server because this way we need to back up only the servers at night and not the end users' machines. If your end users place all of their important documents on the server, that information gets backed up.

Now, if we are also using images in our company and an end user's machine crashes, we just reload the image and they are backed up and running in minutes. Since their documents are being saved on the server, they do not lose any of their information.

Many organizations use third-party imaging software (such as Ghost) instead of using Sysprep.exe and the Image Capture Wizard. This is another good way of imaging your Windows machines. Just make sure your third-party software supports the Windows 10/11 operating system.

To perform an unattended installation, the System Preparation Tool prepares the reference computer by stripping away any computer-specific data, such as the Security Identifier (SID), which is used to uniquely identify each computer on the network; any event logs; and any other unique system information. The System Preparation Tool also detects any Plug and Play devices that are installed and can adjust dynamically for any computers that have different hardware installed.

When the client computer starts an installation using a disk image, you can customize what is displayed on the Windows Welcome screen and the options that are displayed through the setup process. You can also fully automate when and how the Windows Welcome screen is displayed during the installation process by using the /oobe option with the System Preparation Tool and an answer file named Oobe.xml.

Sysprep is a utility that is good only for setting up a new machine. You do not use Sysprep to image a computer for upgrading a current machine. There are a few switches that you can use in conjunction with Sysprep to configure the Sysprep utility for your specific needs. Table 1.8 shows you the important Sysprep switches and what they will do for you when used.

TABLE 1.8   Sysprep switches

Switch	Explanation
/pnp	Forces a mini-setup wizard to start at reboot so that all Plug and Play devices can be recognized.
/generalize	This allows Sysprep to remove all system-specific data from the Sysprep image. If you're running the GUI version of Sysprep, this is a check box option.
/oobe	Initiates the Windows Welcome screen at the next reboot.
/audit	Initiates Sysprep in audit mode.
/nosidgen	Sysprep does not generate a new SID on the computer restart. It forces a mini-setup on restart.
/reboot	Stops and restarts the computer system.
/quiet	Runs without any confirmation dialog box messages being displayed.
/mini	Tells Sysprep to run the mini-setup on the next reboot.

 **Real World Scenario**

The SID Problem with Deployment Software

For many years, when you had to create a number of machines that each had a Microsoft operating system on it, you would have to use files to help deploy the multiple systems.

Then, multiple third-party companies came out with software that allowed you to take a picture of the Microsoft operating system, and you could deploy that picture to other machines. One advantage was that all the software that was installed on the system could also be part of that picture. This was a great way to copy all the software on a machine over to another machine.

There was one major problem for years—*Security Identifier (SID)* numbers. All computers get assigned a unique SID that represents them on a domain network. The problem for a long time was that when you copied a machine to another machine, the SID number was also copied.

Microsoft released Sysprep many years ago, and that helped solve this problem. Sysprep would allow you to remove the SID number so that a third-party software package could image it to another machine. Many third-party image software products now also remove the SID numbers, but Sysprep was one of the first utilities to help solve this problem.

When you decide to use Sysprep to set up your images, there are a few rules that you must follow for Sysprep to work properly:

- You can use images to restart the Windows activation clock. The Windows activation clock starts to decrease as soon as Windows starts for the first time. You can restart the Windows activation clock only three times using Sysprep.

- The computer on which you're running Sysprep has to be a member of a workgroup. The machine can't be part of a domain. If the computer is a member of the domain, when you run Sysprep, the computer will automatically be removed from the domain.

- When installing the image, the system will prompt you for a product key. During the installation, you can use an answer file, which in turn will have all the information needed for the installation, and you will not be prompted for any information.

- A third-party utility or the Image Capture Wizard is required to deploy the image that is created from Sysprep.

- If you are using Sysprep to capture an NTFS partition, any files or folders that are encrypted will become corrupt and unreadable.

One advantage to Sysprep and Windows 10/11 is that you can use Sysprep to prepare a new machine for duplication. You can use Sysprep to image a Windows machine. The following steps are necessary to image a new machine:

1. Install the Windows 10/11 operating system.

2. Install all components on the OS.

3. Run Sysprep /generalize to create the image.

When you image a computer using the Windows Sysprep utility, a Windows image (WIM) file is created. Most third-party imaging software products can work with the Windows image file.

Advantages of the System Preparation Tool

The following are advantages of using the System Preparation Tool as a method for automating Windows 10/11 installations:

- For large numbers of computers with similar hardware, it greatly reduces deployment time by copying the operating system, applications, and desktop settings from a reference computer to an image, which can then be deployed to multiple computers.

- Using disk imaging facilitates the standardization of desktops, administrative policies, and restrictions throughout an organization.

- Reference images can be copied across a network connection or through DVDs that are physically distributed to client computers.

Disadvantages of the System Preparation Tool

There are some disadvantages of using the System Preparation Tool as a method for automating Windows 10/11 installations:

- The Image Capture Wizard, third-party imaging software, or hardware disk-duplication devices must be used for an image-based setup.

- The version of the System Preparation Tool that shipped with Windows must be used. An older version of Sysprep cannot be used on a Windows 10/11 image.

- The System Preparation Tool will not detect any hardware that is not Plug and Play compliant.

Overview of the Windows Assessment and Deployment Kit

Another way to install Windows 10/11 is to use the *Windows Assessment and Deployment Kit (ADK)*. The Windows ADK is a set of utilities and documentation that allows an administrator to configure and deploy Windows operating systems. An administrator can use the Windows ADK to do the following:

- Windows Configuration Designer
- Windows Assessment Toolkit
- Windows Performance Toolkit

The Windows ADK can be installed and configured on the following operating systems:

- Windows 11
- Windows 10
- Windows 7 with SP1
- Windows 8 / 8.1
- Windows Server 2019
- Windows Server 2016
- Windows Server 2012 R2
- Windows Server 2012
- Windows Server 2008
- Windows Server 2008 R2

The Windows ADK is a good solution for organizations that need to customize the Windows deployment environments. The Windows ADK allows an administrator to have the flexibility needed for mass deployments of Windows operating systems. Since every organization's needs are different, the Windows ADK allows you to use all or just some of the deployment tools available.

You want to choose the right ADK to meet your needs. If possible, use the ADK version that matches the Windows version that you are working with. If your environment uses a mix of Windows versions, then use the ADK version that matches the latest operating system in your environment.

ADK allows you to manage deployments by using some additional tools:

Windows Configuration Designer   The tools included with this part of the Windows ADK will allow an administrator to easily deploy and configure Windows operating systems and images.

Windows Assessment Toolkit   When new Windows operating systems are installed, applications that ran on the previous version of Windows may not work properly. The Windows Assessment Toolkit allows an administrator to help solve these issues before they occur.

Windows Performance Toolkit   The Windows Performance Toolkit is a utility that will locate computers on a network and then perform a thorough inventory of them. This inventory can then be used to determine which machines can have Windows 10/11 installed.

Windows Configuration Designer

The Windows Configuration Designer allows an administrator to work with images. The Windows Configuration Designer allows an IT department to do the following;

- View and configure all of the settings and policies for a Windows 10/11 image or provisioning package.
- Create Windows provisioning answer files.
- Allow an answer file to add third-party drivers, apps, or other assets.
- Create variants and specify the settings that apply to each variant.
- Build and flash a Windows image.
- Build a provisioning package.

The Windows Configuration Designer gives an IT department many options for deploying and setting up Windows 10/11 clients. The following are some of the tools included with the Windows Configuration Designer:

- Configure and edit images by using the Deployment Image Servicing and Management (DISM) utility.
- Create Windows Preinstallation Environment (Windows PE) images.
- Migrate user data and profiles using the User State Migration Tool (USMT).
- Windows Configuration Designer (Windows Configuration Designer).

Summary of Windows Client Deployment Options

Table 1.9 summarizes the installation tools and files that are used with unattended, automated installations of Windows 10/11, the associated installation method, and a description of each tool.

TABLE 1.9   Summary of Windows 10/11 unattended deployment utilities

Tool or file	Automated installation option	Description
Setup.exe	Unattended installation	Program used to initiate the installation process
Autounattend.xml	Unattended installation	Answer file used to customize installation queries
Windows System Image Manager	Unattended installation	Program used to create answer files to be used for unattended installations
DISM.exe	DISM	Command-line utility that works in conjunction with Sysprep to create and manage Windows image files for deployment
Sysprep.exe	Sysprep	System Preparation Tool, which prepares a source reference computer that will be used in conjunction with a distribution share or with disk duplication through the Image Capture Wizard, third-party software, or hardware disk-duplication devices

The Windows 10/11 installation utilities and resources relating to automated deployment are found in a variety of locations. Table 1.10 provides a quick reference for each utility or resource and its location.

TABLE 1.10   Location of Windows 10/11 deployment utilities and resources

Utility	Location
DISM.exe	Included with Windows 10/11; installed to %WINDIR%\system32\DISM
Sysprep.exe	Included with Windows 10/11; installed to %WINDIR%\system32\sysprep
Image Capture Wizard.exe	Installed with the WAIK; installed to C:\ProgramFiles\Windows AIK\Tools\x86\Image Capture Wizard.exe
Windows System Image Manager	Installed with WAIK; installed to C:\ProgramFiles\Windows AIK\Tools\Image Manager\ImgMgr.exe

Deploying Unattended Installations

You can deploy Windows 10/11 installations or upgrades through a Windows distribution DVD or through a distribution server that contains Windows 10/11 images and associated files, such as `Autounattend.xml` for unattended installations. Using a DVD can be advantageous if the computer on which you want to install Windows is not connected to the network or is connected via a low-bandwidth network. It is also typically faster to install a Windows 10/11 image from DVD than to use a network connection.

Unattended installations rely on options configured in an answer file that is deployed with the Windows image. Answer files are XML files that contain the settings that are typically supplied by the installer during attended installations of Windows 10/11. Answer files can also contain instructions for how programs and applications should be run.

The Windows Setup program is run to install or upgrade to Windows from computers that are running compatible versions of Windows. In fact, Windows Setup is the basis for the other types of installation procedures, including unattended installations, WDS, and image-based installations.

The Windows Setup program (`Setup.exe`) replaces `Winnt32.exe` and `Winnt.exe`, which are the setup programs used in versions of Windows prior to Windows 7. Although it's a graphical tool, Windows Setup can be run from the command line. For example, you can use the following command to initiate an unattended installation of Windows 10/11:

```
setup.exe /unattend:answerfile
```

The Windows Setup program has several command-line options that can be applied. Table 1.11 describes the `Setup.exe` command-line options.

TABLE 1.11   `Setup.exe` command-line options and descriptions

`Setup.exe` **Option**	**Description**
`/1394debug: ` *`channel`* `[baudrate:`*`baudrate`*`]`	Enables kernel debugging over a FireWire (IEEE 1394) port for troubleshooting purposes. The [baudrate] optional parameter specifies the baud rate for data transfer during the debugging process.
`/debug:`*`port`*`[baudrate:`*`baudrate`*`]`	Enables kernel debugging over the specified port for troubleshooting purposes. The [baudrate] optional parameter specifies the baud rate for data transfer during the debugging process.
`/DynamicUpdate {enable	disable}`	Used to prevent a dynamic update from running during the installation process.
`/emsport:{com1|com2|usebiossettings |off}[/emsbaudrate:`*`baudrate`*`]`	Configures EMS to be enabled or disabled. The [baudrate] optional parameter specifies the baud rate for data transfer during the debugging process.

Setup.exe **Option**	**Description**
/m:*folder_name*	Used with Setup to specify that replacement files should be copied from the specified location. If the files are not present, Setup will use the default location.
/noreboot	Normally, when the down-level phase of Setup.exe is complete, the computer restarts. This option specifies that the computer should not restart so that you can execute another command prior to the restart.
/tempdrive:*drive letter*	Specifies the location that will be used to store the temporary files for Windows 10/11 and the installation partition.
/unattend:[*answerfile*]	Specifies that you will be using an unattended installation for Windows 10/11. The *answerfile* variable points to the custom answer file you will use for installation.

Next, we'll look at the System Preparation Tool (Sysprep); using it is one of many ways to install Windows 10/11 automatically.

Using the System Preparation Tool to Prepare an Installation for Imaging

You can use disk images to install Windows 10 or Windows 11 on computers that have similar hardware configurations. Also, if a computer is having technical difficulties, you can use a disk image to quickly restore it to a baseline configuration.

To create a disk image, you install Windows 10/11 on the source computer with the configuration that you want to copy and use the System Preparation Tool to prepare the installation for imaging. The source computer's configuration should also include any applications that should be installed on target computers.

Once you have prepared the installation for imaging, you can use imaging software such as the Image Capture Wizard to create an image of the installation.

The System Preparation Tool (Sysprep.exe) is included with Windows 10/11, in the %WINDIR%\system32\sysprep directory. When you run this utility on the source computer, it strips out information that is unique for each computer, such as the SID. Table 1.12 defines the command options that you can use to customize the Sysprep.exe operation.

TABLE 1.12   System Preparation Tool command-line options

Switch	Description
/audit	Configures the computer to restart into audit mode, which allows you to add drivers and applications to Windows or test the installation prior to deployment
/generalize	Removes any unique system information from the image, including the SID and log information
/oobe	Specifies that the Windows Welcome screen should be displayed when the computer reboots
/quiet	Runs the installation with no user interaction
/quit	Specifies that the System Preparation Tool should quit after the specified operations have been completed
/reboot	Restarts the target computer after the System Preparation Tool completes
/shutdown	Specifies that the computer should shut down after the specified operations have been completed
/unattend	Indicates the name and location of the answer file to use

In the following sections, you will learn how to create a disk image and how to copy and install from it.

Preparing a Windows 10/11 Installation

To run the System Preparation Tool and prepare an installation for imaging, take the following steps:

1. Install Windows 10 or Windows 11 on a source computer. The computer's hardware configuration should be similar to that of the destination computer(s). The source computer should not be a member of a domain.

2. Log onto the source computer as Administrator and, if desired, install and configure any applications, files (such as newer versions of Plug and Play drivers), or custom settings (for example, a custom desktop) that will be applied to the target computer(s).

3. Verify that your image meets the specified configuration criteria and that all applications are properly installed and working.

4. Select Start ➢ Computer, and navigate to C:\%WINDIR%\System32\sysprep. Double-click the Sysprep application icon.

5. The Windows System Preparation Tool dialog box appears. Select the appropriate options for your configuration.

6. If configured to do so, Windows 10/11 will be rebooted into setup mode, and you will be prompted to enter the appropriate setup information.

7. You will now be able to use imaging software to create an image of the computer to deploy to other computers.

In Exercise 1.7, you will use the System Preparation Tool to prepare the computer for disk imaging. The Sysprep utility must be run on a machine with a clean version of Windows 10/11. If you upgraded a Windows 7/8/8.1 machine to Windows 10, you will not be able to run the Sysprep utility.

EXERCISE 1.7

Prepare a System for Imaging by Using the System Preparation Tool

1. Log onto the source computer as Administrator, and if desired, install and configure any applications that should also be installed on the target computer.

2. Select Start ➤ Computer, and navigate to `C:\%WINDIR%\System32\sysprep`. Double-click the Sysprep application icon.

3. In the System Preparation Tool dialog box, select Enter System Out-Of-Box Experience (OOBE) in the System Cleanup Action.

4. Under the shutdown options, depending on the options selected, the System Preparation Tool will quit, the computer will shut down, or the computer will be rebooted into setup mode, where you will need to configure the setup options. Choose the Reboot option. Click OK.

5. Configure the Sysprep utility and name the image **image.wim**.

After creating the Sysprep image, you need to use some type of third-party software to capture it. Windows includes a utility called Image Capture Wizard for just that purpose.

Using Windows Configuration Designer to Create a Disk Image

After you've run the System Preparation Tool on the source computer, you can create an image from the installation, and you can then install the image on target computers. To create an image, you can use the Image Capture Wizard, which is a utility that can be used to create and manage Windows image (WIM) files.

To run the Image Capture Wizard utility to create a disk image of a Windows 10/11 installation, follow these steps:

1. Open Windows Configuration Designer.

2. Select your desired option on the Start page (see Figure 1.28).

FIGURE 1.28   Windows Configuration Designer Start page

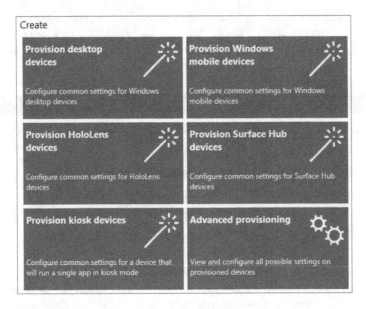

3. Name your project and click Finish. The pages for desktop provisioning will walk you through the following steps:

    1. Set up device (this includes device name and Product Key number).

    2. Set up network settings.

    3. Set up Account Management (this includes adding the machine to a domain or Azure domain and inputting the username and password).

    4. Add applications.

    5. Add any needed certificates.

    6. Finish the configuration.

There is also a command-line version of the Windows Configuration Designer tool that you can use called the Windows Configuration Designer command-line interface (CLI). The Microsoft exams have started using a lot of command-line utilities on their tests. So let's take a look at the Windows Configuration Designer CLI.

Table 1.13 shows you the Windows Configuration Designer CLI switches that you can use to configure the images.

TABLE 1.13   Windows Configuration Designer command-line interface (CLI) switches

Switch	Description
/CustomizationXML	This command identifies the location of the Windows provisioning XML file. This file holds the information for customization assets and settings.
/PackagePath	Identifies the location and the built provisioning package name where the package will be saved.
/StoreFile	This command allows IT administrators to use their own settings store instead of the default store used by Windows Configuration Designer. If an IT administrator does not determine their own store, then a default store that's common to all Windows editions will be loaded by Windows Configuration Designer.
/Variables	Identifies a macro pair that is separated by semicolon <name> and <value>. The format for the argument must be <name>=<value>.
Encrypted	Indicates whether or not the provisioning package should be created with encryption. Windows Configuration Designer will then automatically generate a decryption password that is included with the output.
Overwrite	Indicates whether or not to overwrite the existing provisioning package.
/?	This command is used to access the Windows Configuration Designer help. The help lists the switches and their descriptions for the Windows Configuration Designer command-line tool.

Using the Deployment Image Servicing and Management Tool

Deployment Image Servicing and Management (DISM.exe) is a command-line utility that allows you to manipulate a Windows image. DISM also allows you to prepare a Windows PE image. DISM replaces multiple programs that were included with Windows 7/8/8.1. These programs include Package Manager (Pkgmgr.exe), PEimg, and Intlcfg. These tools have been consolidated into one tool (DISM.exe), and new functionality has been added to improve the experience for offline servicing.

When DISM was first released, it was primarily used for servicing and managing Windows images. But now DISM has become even more powerful, including capturing images and deploying images.

DISM provides additional functionality when used with Windows 10/11 and Windows Server. You can use DISM to do the following:

- Capture Windows images.
- Copy and move Windows images.
- Install Windows images.
- Add, remove, and enumerate packages.
- Add, remove, and enumerate drivers.
- Enable or disable Windows features.
- Apply changes to an Unattend.xml answer file.
- Configure international settings.
- Upgrade a Windows image to a different edition.
- Prepare a Windows PE 3.0 image.
- Work with all platforms (32-bit, 64-bit, and Itanium).
- Use Package Manager scripts.

Table 1.14 shows the different commands that can be used with DISM.exe.

TABLE 1.14   DISM.exe command-line commands

Command	Description
/Add-Driver	Adds third-party driver packages to an offline Windows image.
/Get-CurrentEdition	Displays the edition of the specified image.
/Get-Drivers	Displays basic information about driver packages in the online or offline image. By default, only third-party drivers will be listed.
/Get-DriverInfo	Displays detailed information about a specific driver package.
/Get-Help /?	Displays information about the option and the arguments.
/Get-TargetEditions	Displays a list of Windows editions that an image can be changed to.
/Remove-Driver	Removes third-party drivers from an offline image.

Command	Description
`/Set-ProductKey:<productKey>`	Can only be used to enter the product key for the current edition in an offline Windows image.
`/Online /Enable-Feature /All / FeatureName:Microsoft-Hyper-V`	This command allows you to install Hyper-V into a Windows image while it's an actual image.

Using Windows System Image Manager to Create Answer Files

Answer files are automated installation scripts used to answer the questions that appear during a normal Windows 10/11 installation. You can use answer files with Windows 10/11 unattended installations, disk image installations, or WDS installations. Setting up answer files allows you to easily deploy Windows 10 or Windows 11 to computers that may not be configured in the same manner, with little or no user intervention. Because answer files are associated with image files, you can validate the settings within an answer file against the image file.

You can create answer files by using the Windows System Image Manager (Windows SIM) utility. There are several advantages to using Windows SIM to create answer files:

- You can easily create and edit answer files through a graphical interface, which reduces syntax errors.

- It simplifies the addition of user-specific or computer-specific configuration information.

- You can validate existing answer files against newly created images.

- You can include additional application and device drivers in the answer file.

In the following sections, you will learn about options that can be configured through Windows SIM, how to create answer files with Windows SIM, how to format an answer file, and how to manually edit answer files.

Configuring Components through Windows System Image Manager

You can use Windows SIM to configure a wide variety of installation options. The following list defines which components can be configured through Windows SIM and gives a short description of each component:

auditSystem Adds additional device drivers, specifies firewall settings, and applies a name to the system when the image is booted into audit mode. Audit mode is initiated by using the `sysprep/audit` command.

auditUser   Executes RunSynchronous or RunAsynchronous commands when the image is booted into audit mode. Audit mode is initiated by using the sysprep/audit command.

generalize   Removes system-specific information from an image so that the image can be used as a reference image. The settings specified in the generalize component will be applied only if the sysprep/generalize command is used.

offlineServicing   Specifies the language packs and packages to apply to an image prior to the image being extracted to the hard disk.

oobeSystem   Specifies the settings to apply to the computer the first time the computer is booted into the Windows Welcome screen, which is also known as the Out-Of-Box Experience (OOBE). To boot to the Welcome screen, the sysprep/oobe command should be used.

specialize   Configures the specific settings for the target computer, such as network settings and domain information. This configuration pass is used in conjunction with the generalize configuration pass.

Windows PE   Sets the Windows PE specific configuration settings as well as several Windows Setup settings, such as partitioning and formatting the hard disk, selecting an image, and applying a product key.

Windows Update

Windows Update is a utility that connects to the Microsoft website or to a local update server called a Windows Server Update Services (WSUS) server to ensure that the Windows 10/11 operating system (along with other Microsoft products) has the most up-to-date versions of Microsoft operating system files or software.

Some of the common update categories associated with Windows Update are as follows:

- Security updates
- Critical updates
- Service packs
- Drivers
- Product/software updates
- Windows Store

So, let's begin by looking at how Windows 10/11 updates get created by Microsoft.

The Update Process

To truly understand updates, you need to understand how the update process works with Microsoft. Microsoft normally releases updates to their products on Tuesdays (this is why we use the term *Patch Tuesdays*). But before that update gets released to the public, it has already been tested at Microsoft.

It all starts with the Windows engineering team adding new features and functionality to Windows using product cycles. These product cycles consist of three phases; development, testing, and release.

After the new Windows 10/11 features or functionality are developed, Microsoft employees test these updates out themselves on their own Windows machines. This is referred to as "self-host testing."

After the updates get tested at Microsoft, they then get released to the public. With Windows 10, Microsoft has introduced new ways to service updates. Microsoft's new servicing options are referred to as Semi-Annual Channel, Long-Term Servicing Branch (LTSB), and Windows Insider. Table 1.15 (taken directly from Microsoft's website) shows the different servicing options and the benefits of those options.

TABLE 1.15 Servicing options

From this channel	To this channel	You need to
Windows Insider Program	Semi-Annual Channel (Targeted)	Wait for the final Semi-Annual Channel release.
	Semi-Annual Channel	Not directly possible, because Windows Insider Program devices are automatically upgraded to the Semi-Annual Channel (Targeted) release at the end of the development cycle.
	Long-Term Servicing Channel	Not directly possible (requires wipe-and-load).
Semi-Annual Channel (Targeted)	Insider	Use the Settings app to enroll the device in the Windows Insider Program.
	Semi-Annual Channel	Select the Defer Upgrade setting, or move the PC to a target group or flight that will not receive the next upgrade until it is business ready. Note that this change will not have any immediate impact; it only prevents the installation of the next Semi-Annual Channel release.
	Long-Term Servicing Channel	Not directly possible (requires wipe-and-load).

TABLE 1.15   Servicing options *(Continued)*

From this channel	To this channel	You need to
Semi-Annual Channel	Insider	Use the Settings app to enroll the device in the Windows Insider Program.
	Semi-Annual Channel (Targeted)	Disable the Defer Upgrade setting, or move the device to a target group or flight that will receive the latest Current Semi-Annual Channel release.
	Long-Term Servicing Channel	Not directly possible (requires wipe-and-load).
Long-Term Servicing Channel	Insider	Use media to upgrade to the latest Windows Insider Program build.
	Semi-Annual Channel (Targeted)	Use media to upgrade. Note that the Semi-Annual Channel build must be a later build.
	Semi-Annual Channel	Use media to upgrade. Note that the Semi-Annual Channel build must be a later build.

Using Windows Update

There are multiple ways a user can receive updates: directly from Microsoft or by using Microsoft Windows Server Update Services (WSUS). WSUS runs on a Windows server, and that server goes out to the Microsoft website and downloads the updates for your Windows clients. This allows client machines to receive their updates from a local server.

When it comes to company-based updates, there are better options. Administrators can set up either Group Policy Objects (GPOs) or Azure MDM solutions (such as Microsoft Intune) to configure the Windows Update for Business settings that control how and when Windows 10 devices are updated and which updates get accepted by the IT department. Windows Update for Business updates are updates that you receive from your Microsoft cloud-based services (MDM and Intune).

One advantage to using WSUS is that administrators can approve the updates before they get deployed to the client machines. Another advantage is that your clients only need to download updates locally, without using your Internet bandwidth.

 WSUS is discussed in detail in *MCSA Windows Server 2016 Complete Study Guide: Exam 70-740, Exam 70-741, Exam 70-742, and Exam 70-743, 2nd Edition,* by William Panek (Wiley, 2018).

If you want the Windows 10/11 clients to access and get their own updates follow these steps to configure Windows Update:

1. Select Start ➤ Settings.

   - From Settings, select Update And Security.

2. Configure the options you want to use for Windows Update by clicking the Advanced Options link. You can access the following options from Windows Update:

   - Give Me Updates For Other Microsoft Products.
     - This setting allows you to get updates for other Microsoft products like Microsoft Office.
   - Choose When Updates Are Installed.
   - Pause Updates.
   - Delivery Optimization.
     - Windows Update Delivery Optimization provides you with Windows and Store app updates and other Microsoft products quickly and reliably.
     - Allow updates from other PCs.
   - Privacy Settings.
     - This option allows you to set all of your system's privacy settings.

Check For Updates

When you click Check For Updates, Windows Update will retrieve a list of available updates from the Internet. You can then click View Available Updates to see what updates are available. Updates are marked as Important, Recommended, or Optional. Figure 1.29 shows the Check For Updates button.

FIGURE 1.29   Check For Updates button

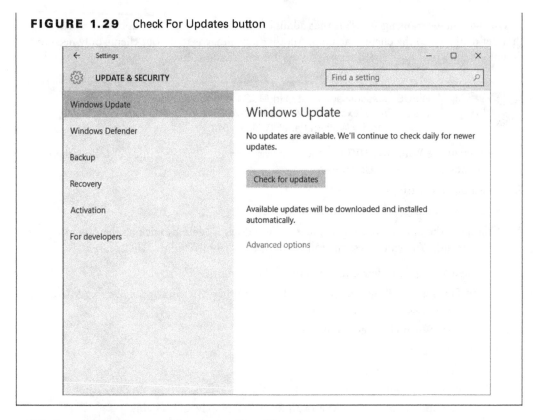

Using Windows Update for Business

Windows Update for Business allows an IT administrator to keep their organization's Windows 10/11 devices up-to-date with the latest Microsoft security defenses and Windows features by using Microsoft Azure. Windows Update for Business allows your Windows systems to connect to Microsoft's Windows Update service.

Administrators have the ability to configure Windows Update for Business by using Group Policies or MDM solutions to configure the Windows Update for Business settings. These settings will control how and when Windows devices are updated.

So, what does this mean for your organization? Administrators have total control over how updates are delivered and which updates will be delivered. Administrators can do this best by doing reliability and performance testing on a small group of systems (including just a single system for testing) before allowing updates to roll out to all of the computers in their organization. By testing updates, administrators can determine which updates will work best for their company.

Windows Update for Business Update Types

Windows Update for Business allows an organization to choose which updates an organization wants delivered to their Windows 10/11 systems. Administrators can do this by setting up management policies to help choose which updates they want delivered to their users. The following are different types of updates that administrators can deploy to their Windows devices:

Feature Updates   These updates were previously referred to as upgrades. Feature Updates not only contain security updates and revisions, but also include major feature additions and changes. Feature Updates are released semi-annually in the spring and in the fall.

Quality Updates   Quality Updates are normally operating system updates that are usually released the second Tuesday of each month. Sometimes these updates, depending on their importance, can be released at any time. Quality Updates include security updates, critical updates, and driver updates.

Windows Update for Business also deploys non-Windows operating system updates (for example, Visual Studio) as part of the Quality Updates deployment.

Driver Updates   Driver Updates are updates for third-party devices that apply to your Windows 10/11 systems. For example, you may be using a printer that Microsoft Windows 10 has a driver for; these drivers get updated as part of the Driver Updates process. Administrators have the ability to enable or disable Driver Updates by using Windows Update for Business policies.

Microsoft Product Updates   Microsoft Product Updates are updates for Microsoft application or software products like Office. Administrators have the ability to enable or disable Microsoft Product Updates by using Windows Update for Business policies.

Deferring Updates

Windows Update for Business allows administrators to defer updates from being installed for a specific period of time. Administrators can defer the installation of both Feature Updates and Quality Updates for a specific period of time, but that specific period of time starts as soon as those updates are first made available through the Windows Update service.

Administrators can use this time to test and validate the updates before they are pushed to all of your Windows client devices. The way deferrals work is by allowing administrators to specify the amount of time after an update is released before it is offered to your Windows 10 devices.

For example, if an administrator decides to defer Feature Updates for 365 days, the Windows devices will not install any Feature Update before the 365 days expire. Administrators can defer Feature Updates by using the Select When Preview Builds And Feature Updates Are Received policy.

Table 1.16 shows the different updates that can be deferred and the maximum time that they can be deferred for.

TABLE 1.16 Maximum update deferral

Update	Maximum deferral
Feature Updates	365 days
Quality Updates	30 days
Nondeferrable	None

Pausing an Update

Administrators also have the ability to pause an update if they discover an issue while they are deploying Feature Updates or Quality Updates. Administrators can choose to pause the update for up to 35 days. This helps prevent other Windows devices from experiencing the same issues.

If the administrator pauses the installation of a Feature Update, then Quality Updates are still deployed, and vice versa. When an administrator sets a pause time period for an update, the pause time is calculated from the start date that the administrator sets.

To pause a Feature Update, the administrator uses the Select When Preview Builds And Feature Updates Are Received policy. To pause a Quality Update, the administrator uses the Select When Quality Updates Are Received policy.

Selecting Branch Readiness Level for Feature Updates

Windows Update for Business allows administrators to choose which channel of Feature Updates they want to receive. Currently Microsoft offers branch readiness level options to organizations for prerelease and released updates. The following options are included:

- Windows Insider Program for Business prerelease updates. These updates include Windows Insider Fast, Windows Insider Slow, and Windows Insider Release Preview.
- Semi-Annual Channel for released updates.

Prior to version 1903 of Windows 10, there were only two channels for released updates: Semi-Annual Channel and Semi-Annual Channel (Targeted). Versions of Windows 10 released after version 1903 get a single release channel: Semi-Annual Channel.

Administrators have the ability to configure the branch readiness level by configuring the Select When Preview Builds And Feature Updates Are Received policy. But if an administrator wants to manage prerelease builds, they need to enable preview builds by configuring the Manage Preview Builds policy.

Monitoring Windows Updates

Administrators have the ability to monitor which Windows computers are receiving their updates by using the Update Compliance utility. The Update Compliance utility lets administrators see a complete view of Windows 10/11 operating system updates. Administrators can view which operating systems are meeting compliance, how the update deployments are progressing, and any errors that may have occurred on the Windows devices.

The Update Compliance utility uses multiple factors to show you a complete view of the update process. These factors include diagnostic data from the installation progress, Windows Update configuration settings, and additional data (for example, Windows Defender Antivirus diagnostic data). This service is included free with your Azure subscription, and there is no need to set up any additional infrastructure requirements.

Update Compliance Prerequisites

To use the Update Compliance utility, your organization must meet some prerequisites:

- Only Windows 10/11 Professional, Education, and Enterprise editions can be used with the Update Compliance utility. Update Compliance only gathers data for the standard desktop Windows version. The Update Compliance utility is not currently compatible with other operating systems like Windows Server, Surface Hub, or IoT.

- Windows 10/11 devices must be on the Semi-Annual Channel and the Long-Term Servicing Channel. The Update Compliance utility will show you Windows Insider Preview devices. But currently Windows Insider Preview devices will not have any detailed deployment information.

- The Update Compliance utility requires at the minimum the Basic level of diagnostic data and a Commercial ID to be enabled on the Windows device.

- You must opt in to the Windows Analytics to see device names for versions of Windows 10 version 1803 or higher.

- If you want to use the Windows Defender Status, Windows devices must be E3 licensed and have Cloud Protection enabled. E5-licensed devices should use Windows Defender ATP instead.

- You must add the Update Compliance utility to your Azure subscription. To do this, you must log in to the Azure portal and select + Create A Resource. At the Search For window, type **Update Compliance**. At the bottom of the screen, click the Create button to add the Update Compliance utility to your Azure subscription.

Delivery Optimization

Delivery Optimization is a cloud-managed solution that allows users to download packages from alternate sources. Delivery Optimization works by allowing you to obtain Windows updates and Microsoft Store apps from other sources such as other computers on the local network or computers on the Internet.

You can use Delivery Optimization with:

- Windows Update
- Windows Server Update Services (WSUS)
- Windows Update for Business
- Microsoft Endpoint Manager (when Express Updates is enabled)

Both access to the Internet and the Delivery Optimization cloud services are required in order to utilize Deliver Optimization. Depending on your settings, when Windows downloads an update or app using Delivery Optimization, it looks for other computers on your local network or on the Internet that have already downloaded that update or app. Delivery Optimization creates a local cache and then stores the downloaded files into that cache for a short period of time.

In Windows client Enterprise, Professional, and Education editions, Delivery Optimization is enabled by default for peer-to-peer sharing on the local network.

You can use Group Policy or an MDM solution such as Intune to configure Delivery Optimization.

You will find the Delivery Optimization settings in Group Policy under `Computer Configuration\Administrative Templates\Windows Components\ Delivery Optimization`.

Controlling Windows Update Delivery Optimization in Windows 10

To stop downloading updates and apps from or sending updates and apps to other Windows 10 devices on the Internet, follow these steps:

1. Select Start, then select Settings ➤ Update & Security ➤ Windows Update ➤ Advanced Options.
2. Select Delivery Optimization (or choose how updates are delivered in earlier versions of Windows 10).
3. Select PCs On My Local Network.

To stop downloading from or uploading to other computers on the local network:

1. Select Start, then select Settings ➤ Update & Security ➤ Windows Update ➤ Advanced Options.
2. Select Delivery Optimization.
3. Make sure that the Allow Downloads From Other PCs option is turned Off. You will now only obtain updates and apps directly from Windows Update and from Microsoft Store.

Controlling Windows Update Delivery Optimization in Windows 11

To stop downloading updates and apps from or sending updates and apps to other Windows 11 devices on the Internet, follow these steps:

1. Select Start, then select Settings ➤ Windows Update ➤ Advanced Options.
2. Select Delivery Optimization. Under Allow Downloads From Other PCs, select Devices On My Local Network.

To stop downloading from or uploading to other computers on the local network:

1. Select Start, then select Settings ➤ Windows Update ➤ Advanced Options.

2. Select Delivery Optimization.

3. Make sure Allow Downloads From Other PCs is turned Off. You will now only obtain updates and apps directly from Windows Update and from Microsoft Store.

Using Command-Line Options

Command-line options are becoming more and more popular among administrators and users. Windows Update has a few command-line options that can be used to help configure and maintain it. First, to start Windows Update from a command prompt, you can type **wuapp.exe**. Another command-line option that works with Windows Update is called Windows Update Automatic Update Client (wuauclt.exe), which offers the following options:

detectnow   When working with WSUS, waiting for detection to start can become very time-consuming. So, Microsoft has added an option to allow you to initiate the process of detecting available updates right away. To run the detectnow option, type the following command at the command prompt: **wuauclt.exe /detectnow**.

reportnow   This command allows you to send all queued reporting events to the server asynchronously. To execute this command, type **wuauclt.exe /reportnow** at the command prompt.

resetauthorization   WSUS uses a cookie on Windows 10/11 client computers to store different types of information. By default, an hour after the cookie is created, it expires. If you need the cookie to expire now, you can use the resetauthorization option along with the detectnow option. Using these options will expire the cookie, initiate detection, and have WSUS update computer group membership. To execute this command, type **wuauclt.exe /resetauthorization /detectnow** at the command prompt.

Installing Microsoft Store Updates

Besides getting updates for the Windows 10/11 operating system and the different Microsoft products, you may also need to get updates for any of the applications, games, music, videos, and software that you downloaded from the Microsoft Store. To receive Microsoft Store updates, you need to go to the Microsoft Store (see Figure 1.30). To get updates, perform the following steps:

1. Select Start ➤ Microsoft Store.

2. After you've opened the Microsoft Store app, select Library ➤ Get Updates (as shown in Figure 1.31).

3. If there are updates, select Update All or choose which apps you want to update. This will allow you to download and install any Microsoft Store updates.

FIGURE 1.30   Microsoft Store

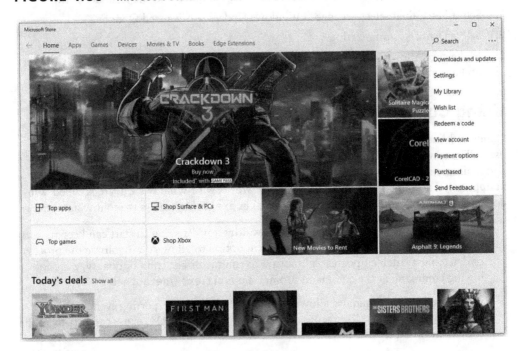

FIGURE 1.31   Get Updates button

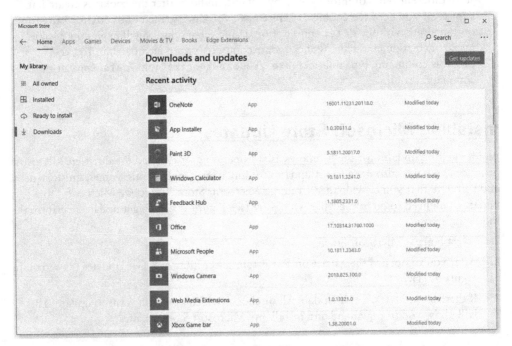

Summary

This chapter started with a discussion of the features included with Windows 10/11. We also took a look at the difference between 64-bit and 32-bit operating systems and explored some of the advantages that 64-bit entails, such as greater RAM and processor speed.

Then you learned about installing Windows 10 and Windows 11. Installation is an easy process, but you must first make sure the machine is compatible with the Windows operating system.

There are two main ways to install Windows 10/11. You can either upgrade or perform a clean installation. You can upgrade a Windows 7 or Windows 8/8.1 machine to Windows 10. You can't upgrade Windows XP to Windows 10.

We discussed automated installation of Windows 10/11. Installing Windows 10/11 through an automated process is an effective way to install the Windows operating system on multiple computers.

There are several methods for automated installation: unattended installations, Windows Deployment Services (WDS), Windows Assessment and Deployment Kit (ADK), third-party applications, unattended installations, and using the System Preparation Tool along with the Image Capture Wizard.

Windows Deployment Services (WDS) is a suite of components that allows you to remotely install Windows 10/11 on client computers.

The Windows ADK is a set of utilities and documentation that allows you to configure and deploy Windows operating systems.

You can use unattended answer files to automatically respond to the queries that are generated during the normal installation process.

You can also prepare an installation for imaging by using the System Preparation Tool (Sysprep.exe) and creating a disk image by using the Image Capture Wizard utility or a third-party utility.

Microsoft Deployment Toolkit (MDT) is a way of automating desktop and server deployment. With the MDT, you can deploy desktops and servers through the use of a common console, which allows for quicker deployments; having standardized desktop and server images and security; and zero-touch deployments of Windows 11, Windows 10, Windows 8, Windows 7, and Windows Server.

After the Windows 10/11 installation is complete, you'll want to make sure all updates and service packs are installed. You can use Windows Update to complete that task. Finally, I explained how to set up and configure cloud-based updates by using Windows Update for Business. I talked about how you can use the Update Compliance utility to get reporting data on how updates are being delivered to your Windows 10/11 devices.

Exam Essentials

Understand the Windows 10 and Windows 11 hardware requirements. The minimum hardware requirements to run Windows 10 properly are a 1 GHz or faster processor or SoC, 1 GB of RAM for 32-bit or 2 GB for 64-bit of RAM, 32 GB or larger hard drive space, DirectX 9 or later with a WDDM 1.0 video driver, and an Internet connection in order to perform updates and to download and take advantage of some features. The minimum hardware requirements to run Windows 11 properly are 1 GHz or faster with two or more cores on a compatible 64-bit processor or SoC, 4 GB of RAM, 64 GB or larger storage device, DirectX 12 or later with a WDDM 2.0 driver, and for all Windows 11 editions, Internet access is required to perform updates and to download and take advantage of some features.

Understand how to complete a clean installation. If your machine meets the minimum hardware requirements, you can install Windows 10/11. There are a few different ways to install Windows clients onto a computer. You can use the installation disk or USB, install it over a network, or install it from an image.

Understand how to complete an upgrade. You can't upgrade a Windows Vista machine to Windows 10. To complete an upgrade on a Windows 7 or Windows 8/8.1 machine, insert the Windows 10 DVD into the Windows machine or connect to the Windows 10 files over the network and complete an upgrade on the computer.

You can't upgrade a Windows XP machine directly to Windows 10. If the machine is running Windows XP, you have to use a migration tool to migrate all the user data from Windows XP to a Windows 10 machine.

If you are looking to upgrade to Windows 11, then your device must be running Windows 10, version 2004 or later.

Know the difference between the various unattended installation methods. Understand the various options available for unattended installations of Windows 10/11 and when it is appropriate to use each installation method.

Understand the features and uses of WDS. Know when it is appropriate to use WDS to manage unattended installations. Be able to list the requirements for setting up WDS servers and WDS clients. Be able to complete an unattended installation using WDS.

Be able to use disk images for unattended installations. Know how to perform unattended installations of Windows 10/11 using the System Preparation Tool and disk images.

Understand the Microsoft Deployment Toolkit (MDT). Know that the MDT is a way of automating desktop and server deployment. Understand that the MDT allows an administrator to deploy desktops and servers through the use of a common console.

Understand how to receive updates. You need to understand how to set up and receive Microsoft updates for Windows 10/11, Microsoft products, and the Microsoft Store. Make sure you know the different settings for configuring update advanced options.

Understand Windows Update for Business.   You need to understand how to set up and receive Microsoft updates for Windows 10/11 using Windows Update for Business in Azure. Make sure you know the different settings for configuring Windows Update for Business options.

Video Resources

There are videos available for the following exercises:

1.1

1.2

1.7

You can access the videos at www.wiley.com/go/sybextestprep.

Review Questions

1. You are the administrator in charge of a computer that runs both Windows 7 and Windows 10. Windows 10 is installed on a different partition from Windows 7. You have to make sure that the computer always starts Windows 7 by default. What action should you perform?

    A. Run Bcdedit.exe and the /default parameter.

    B. Run Bcdedit.exe and the /bootcd parameter.

    C. Create a Boot.ini file in the root of the Windows 10 partition.

    D. Create a Boot.ini file in the root of the Windows 7 partition.

2. You are the administrator for a Windows 10 computer. You have decided to use Windows Update, but you want to be able to change the settings manually. What should you do?

    A. Log onto Windows 10 as a member of the Administrators group.

    B. From the local Group Policy, modify the Windows Update settings.

    C. Right-click Windows Update and select Run As Administrator.

    D. Right-click the command prompt, select Run As Administrator, and then run Wuapp.exe.

3. You want to initiate a new installation of Windows 10 from the command line. You plan to accomplish this by using the Setup.exe command-line setup utility. You want to use an answer file with this command. Which command-line option should you use?

    A. /unattend

    B. /apply

    C. /noreboot

    D. /generalize

4. You are the network administrator for your organization. You have a reference computer that runs Windows 10. You need to create and deploy an image of the Windows 10 computer. You create an answer file named answer.xml. You have to make sure that the installation applies the answer file after you deploy the image. Which command should you run before you capture the image?

    A. DISM.exe /append answer.xml /check

    B. DISM.exe /mount answer.xml /verify

    C. Sysprep.exe /reboot /audit /unattend:answer.xml

    D. Sysprep.exe /generalize /oobe /unattend:answer.xml

5. You have a Windows 10 Windows Image (WIM) that is mounted. You need to view the list of third-party drivers installed on the WIM. What should you do?

    A. Run DISM and specify the /get-drivers parameter.

    B. Run Driverquery.exe and use the /si parameter.

    C. From Device Manager, view all hidden drivers.

    D. From Windows Explorer, open the mount folder.

6. You are planning on deploying 1,000 new Windows 10 computers throughout your company. Each new computer has the same configuration. You want to create a reference image that will then be applied to the remaining images. Which of the following utilities should you use?

   A. WDSUTIL

   B. Setup.exe

   C. Windows SIM

   D. DISM.exe

7. You are the network administrator for a large organization. You are in charge of developing a plan to install 200 Windows 10 computers in your company's data center. You decide to use WDS. You are using a Windows Server 2012 R2 domain and have verified that your network meets the requirements for using WDS. What command-line utility should you use to configure the WDS server?

   A. DISM

   B. WDSUTIL

   C. Setup.exe

   D. The WDS icon in Control Panel

8. Will is the network manager for a large company. He has been tasked with creating a deployment plan to automate installations for 100 computers that need to have Windows 10 installed. Will wants to use WDS for the installations. To fully automate the installations, he needs to create an answer file. Will does not want to create the answer files with a text editor. What other program can he use to create unattended answer files via a GUI interface?

   A. DISM

   B. Answer Manager

   C. Windows System Image Manager

   D. System Preparation Tool

9. You are using WDS to install 20 Windows 10 computers. When the clients attempt to use WDS, they are not able to complete the unattended installation. You suspect that the WDS server has not been configured to respond to client requests. Which one of the following utilities would you use to configure the WDS server to respond to client requests?

   A. Active Directory Users and Computers

   B. Active Directory Users and Groups

   C. WDS MMC Snap-in

   D. WDSMAN

10. You want to install a group of 25 computers using disk images created in conjunction with the System Preparation Tool. Your plan is to create an image from a reference computer and then copy the image to all the machines. You do not want to create an SID on the destination computer when you use the image. Which `Sysprep.exe` command-line option should you use to set this up?

   A. `/specialize`

   B. `/generalize`

   C. `/oobe`

   D. `/quiet`

11. You are the network administrator for a large communications company. You have 25 computers that currently run Windows 7. These computers have the following configurations:

   ▪ A single MBR disk

   ▪ A disabled TPM chip

   ▪ Disabled hardware virtualization

   ▪ UEFI firmware running in BIOS mode

   ▪ Enabled Data Execution Prevention (DEP)

   You plan to upgrade the computers to Windows 10. You need to ensure that the computers can use Secure Boot. Which two actions should you perform? (Choose two.)

   A. Convert the MBR disk to a GPT disk.

   B. Enable the TPM chip.

   C. Disable DEP.

   D. Enable hardware virtualization.

   E. Convert the firmware from BIOS to UEFI.

12. You are the administrator for your company network. You have a large number of computers running Windows 10 in a workgroup. These computers have low-bandwidth metered Internet connections. What should you configure if you need to reduce the amount of Internet bandwidth that is being consumed when updates are being downloaded?

   A. Use Background Intelligent Transfer Service (BITS).

   B. Use Delivery Optimization.

   C. Use distributed cache mode in BranchCache.

   D. Use hosted mode in BranchCache.

13. You are the network administrator for a large company. You have two computers that run Windows 7. Computer 1 has a 32-bit CPU that runs Windows 7 Enterprise. Computer 2 has a 64-bit CPU that runs Windows 7 Enterprise. You plan to perform an in-place upgrade to the 64-bit version of Windows 10. Which computers can you upgrade to the 64-bit version of Windows 10?

   A. Computer 1 only

   B. Computer 2 only

   C. Computer 1 and Computer 2

   D. Neither

14. You have recently just installed Windows client on a user's device and you want to review the action log that was generated during the installation process. What is the name of this log file, and where is it stored?

   A. `C:\Windows\setupact.log`

   B. `C:\Windows\setuperr.log`

   C. `C:\Windows\error.log`

   D. `C:\Windows\setuperror.log`

15. You and a colleague are discussing Windows Update and where you would need to go to configure it. To configure Windows Updates where should you go?

   A. Personalization

   B. Restore Hidden Updates

   C. Settings

   D. View Update History

16. You are the administrator for your company network. You have a Windows 10 computer with a microphone attached. You want a hands-free way to ask your system a question. You want to use Microsoft's digital assistant. What is the name of this application?

   A. Alexa

   B. Cortana

   C. Google Assistant

   D. Siri

17. You have two computers on your Windows domain named Computer1 and Computer2. You are currently sitting at Computer1, and you want to see what devices and drivers are installed. What should you run?

   A. `Driverquery.exe`

   B. `Get-OdbcDriver`

   C. `Get-PnpDevice`

   D. `Get-WindowsDriver`

18. If you decide to perform a clean installation of Windows client to the same partition as an existing Windows installation, the contents of the original Windows directory will be placed in which directory?

   A. `C:\Windows`

   B. `C:\Windows.old`

   C. `C:\Windows\old`

   D. `C:\WindowsOS`

19. You and a colleague are discussing Microsoft updates and how/when they become available to the public. Updates are usually released on a particular day of the week. What is the nickname of this day called?

    A. Maintenance Mondays

    B. Patch Tuesdays

    C. Update Wednesdays

    D. Fixed Fridays

20. You have a Windows client computer that you use to test new Windows features. You want this computer to receive preview builds as soon as they become available. What should you configure in the Settings ➢ Update & Security section to set this up?

    A. Delivery Optimization

    B. For Developers

    C. Windows Insider Program

    D. Windows Update

Chapter 2

Configuring Users

MICROSOFT EXAM OBJECTIVES COVERED IN THIS CHAPTER:

✓ **Manage users, groups, and computer objects**

- Manage local users; manage local user profiles; manage local groups; manage Microsoft account on Windows client; enable users and groups from Active Directory to access Windows client; join computers to Active Directory; manage credentials by using Credential Manager, configure user account control (UAC); implement and manage Local Administrator Password Solutions (LAPS).

✓ **Configure remote management**

- Configure Remote Desktop; configure Windows Admin Center; configure PowerShell Remoting and Windows Remote Management; configure remote assistance tools including Remote Assist and Quick Assist.

✓ **Configure and manage local and group policies**

- Troubleshoot local policies and domain group policies on Widows client; configure and manage local and group policies, including security policy, user rights assignment, and audit policy; configure Windows client settings by using group policy.

Now that we have discussed installing Windows 10/11, we need to look at one of the most important topics in this book: authorization and authentication.

Understanding how users authenticate onto your network and knowing some of the tricks on how to secure your network and users is one of the most important tasks that administrators must perform.

One administrative job that we need to perform is creating user and group accounts. Without a user account, a user cannot log onto a computer, server, or network. When users log on, they supply a username and password. Then their user accounts are validated by a security mechanism. In Windows 10/11, users can log onto a computer locally, or if the machine is a member of an Active Directory domain, the user can authenticate against a local copy of Active Directory or a cloud-based copy of Active Directory.

Groups are used to ease network administration by grouping users who have similar permission requirements. Groups are an important part of network management. Many administrators are able to accomplish the majority of their management tasks through the use of groups; they rarely assign permissions to individual users. Windows 10 and Windows 11 include built-in local groups, such as Administrators and Backup Operators.

You create and manage local groups through the Local Users and Groups utility. With this utility, you can add groups, change group membership, rename groups, and delete groups.

Windows 10/11 also offers a wide variety of security options. If the Windows client computer is a part of a domain, you can apply security through Group Policy Objects using the Group Policy Management Console. If the Windows client computer is not a part of a domain, then you can use Local Group Policy Objects to manage local security.

Understanding User Accounts

When you install Windows 10/11, several user accounts are created automatically. Additionally, you can create new user accounts. As you already know, user accounts allow a user to log onto machines and access resources.

You can create local user accounts, which reside locally on the Windows client machine. Such accounts cannot be utilized to gain access to any resources hosted on the network. If you have installed Active Directory either in the cloud (Azure Active Directory) or on a network that has a Windows Server domain controller, your network can have domain user accounts as well.

In the following sections, you will learn about the different account types: the default user accounts that are created by Windows 10/11 and the difference between local and domain user accounts.

Account Types

Windows 10/11 supports two basic types of user accounts: administrator and standard user (see Figure 2.1). Each of these accounts is used for specific reasons.

FIGURE 2.1   Choosing an account type

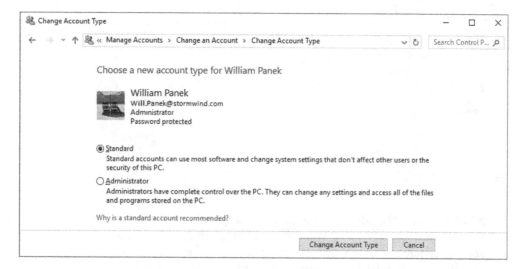

Administrator   The administrator account type provides unrestricted access for performing administrative tasks. As a result, administrator accounts should be used only for performing administrative tasks and should not be used for normal computing tasks.

Only administrator accounts can change the Registry. This is important to know because when most software is installed onto a Windows client machine, the Registry gets changed. This is why you need administrator rights to install most software.

Standard User   The standard user account type should be assigned to every user of the computer. Standard user accounts can perform most day-to-day tasks, such as running Microsoft Word, accessing email, using a browser, and so on. Running as a standard user increases security by limiting the possibility of a virus or other malicious code from infecting the computer. Standard user accounts are unable to make systemwide changes, which also helps to increase security.

When you install Windows 10/11, by default there are premade accounts called built-in accounts. Let's take a look at them.

Built-In Accounts

When installed into a workgroup environment, Windows 10/11 has four built-in accounts, which are created automatically at the time you install the operating system (see Figure 2.2). Figure 2.2 also shows the accounts that I created while writing this book.

FIGURE 2.2   The four built-in accounts

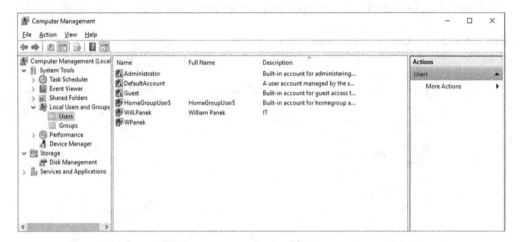

Administrator   The Administrator account is a special account that has Full Control over the computer. The Administrator account can perform all tasks, such as creating users and groups, managing the filesystem, installing applications, and setting up printing. Note that the Administrator account is disabled by default.

DefaultAccount   This is a user account created by the system and used by the system. This account is a member of the System Managed Accounts group.

Guest   The Guest account allows users to access the computer even if a person does not have a unique username and password. Because of the inherent security risks associated with this type of user, the Guest account is disabled by default. When this account is enabled, it is usually given very limited privileges.

Initial User   The Initial User account uses the name of the registered user. By default, the initial user is a member of the Administrators group.

By default, the name Administrator is given to a user account that is a member of the Administrators group. However, in Windows 10/11, this user account is disabled by default. You can increase the computer's security by leaving this account disabled and assigning other users to the Administrators group. This way, a malicious user will be unable to log onto the computer using the Administrator user account.

All four of these users are considered local users, and their permissions are contained to the Windows client machine. If the user's account needs to access resources on machines other than their own, you can have a user log into the Windows client computer as a remote user (a user who is not in front of the machine they're logging onto), and this would be considered a domain user's account. Let's take a look at the difference between these account types.

Local and Domain User Accounts

Windows 10/11 supports two kinds of users: local users and domain users. Local users get set up on each Windows 10/11 client system. The Windows client system can be part of a workgroup or it can be a stand-alone system. A computer that is running Windows 10/11 has the ability to store its own user accounts database. The user accounts stored at the local computer are known as *local user accounts*.

Workgroups are networks that have user databases on each individual Windows client machine. However, you can share resources on the workgroup network.

Domains

Domains are networks where there is a centralized security database (Active Directory), and you can control all of your users and groups from one central location.

Active Directory is a directory service that stores information in a central database, which allows users to have a single user account for the network. The user accounts stored in Active Directory's central database are called *domain user accounts*. Active Directory is available in two different models. There is a cloud-based Active Directory called Azure Active Directory (Azure AD) and a server-based version that runs on Windows Server platforms.

Workgroups

You can log on locally to a Windows client computer using a locally stored user account, or you can log onto a domain using an Active Directory account. When you install Windows 10/11 on a computer, you specify that the computer will be a part of a workgroup, which implies a local logon, or that it will be a part of a domain, which implies a domain logon.

On all Windows versions except domain controllers, you can create local users through the Local Users and Groups utility, as described in the section "Working with User Accounts" later in this chapter. On Windows Server domain controllers (Windows Server 2000 and above), you manage users with the Microsoft Active Directory Users and Computers MMC.

NOTE   Active Directory is covered in detail in *MCSA Windows Server 2016 Complete Study Guide: Exam 70-740, Exam 70-741, Exam 70-742 and Composite Upgrade Exam 70-743, 2nd Edition* by William Panek (Wiley, 2018).

Workplace Join

There may be times when you need someone to gain access to a domain resource but that person doesn't have a domain account. That's where Workplace Join can help. Workplace Join is a Windows tool that you can download and use on your domain.

Workplace Join allows an end user to use a corporate email address and password to connect a Windows device to a domain. The email address and password are then sent to an Active Directory server to be verified. The server can be set to then send a message to the device to confirm that the device should be given access to the domain. After the verification is done, Workplace Join creates a new device object in Active Directory and installs a certificate onto the Windows device.

Logging Off

No matter what type of network you have, you will eventually need to log off the Windows client system. When users are ready to stop working, they should either log off or shut down the system by clicking the power icon on the Start Menu. This will provide you with options on how you would like to shut your system down. Some of the options are Sleep, Shut Down, or Restart.

Working with User Accounts

To set up and manage your local user accounts, you will want to use the Computer Management console. From here you can create, disable, delete, and rename user accounts as well as change user passwords.

Windows 10/11 includes User Account Control (UAC), which provides an additional level of security by limiting the level of access that users have when performing normal, everyday tasks. When needed, users can gain elevated access for specific administrative tasks.

Using the Local Users and Groups Utility

There are two common methods for accessing the Local Users and Groups utility:

- Load Local Users and Groups as a Microsoft Management Console (MMC) Snap-in.
- Access the Local Users and Groups utility through the Computer Management utility.

If your computer doesn't have a custom MMC configured, the quickest way to access the Local Users and Groups utility is through the Computer Management utility.

In Exercise 2.1, you will add the Local Users and Groups Snap-in MMC to the Desktop. You can also access the Local Users and Groups MMC by right-clicking Start and choosing Computer Management. This exercise needs to be completed in order to complete other exercises in this chapter.

EXERCISE 2.1

Adding the Local Users and Groups Snap-In

1. In the Search box, type **MMC** and press Enter.

2. If a warning box appears, click Yes.

3. Select File ➤ Add/Remove Snap-in.

4. Scroll down the list and highlight Local Users And Groups, and then click the Add button (shown in Figure 2.3).

FIGURE 2.3   MMC Snap-ins

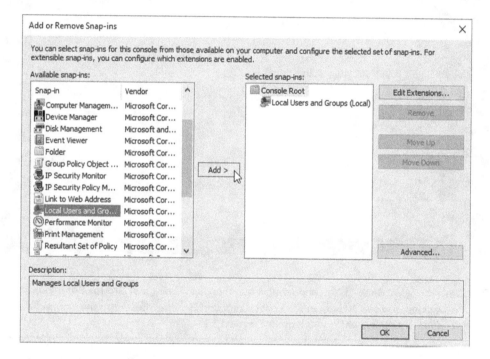

5. In the Choose Target Machine dialog box, click the Finish button to accept the default selection of Local Computer.

6. Click OK in the Add Or Remove Snap-Ins dialog box.

7. In the MMC window, right-click the Local Users And Groups folder and choose New Window From Here. You will see that Local Users and Groups is now the main window.

8. Click File ➤ Save As. Name the console **Local Users and Groups** and choose Desktop under the Save In pull-down box. Click the Save button. This is creating the shortcut shown in Figure 2.4 for you to use in exercises throughout this chapter.

FIGURE 2.4   Local Users and Groups MMC

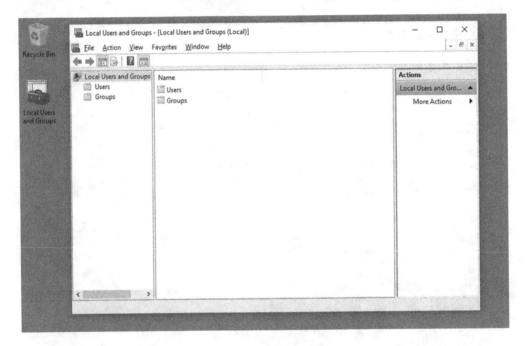

9. Close the MMC Snap-in. You should now see the Local Users and Groups Snap-in on the Desktop. You can also open the Local Users and Groups MMC from the Computer Management utility, which you'll do in Exercise 2.2.

Accessing Local Users and Groups via the Computer Management Utility

1. Right-click the Start button and then choose Computer Management.

2. In the Computer Management window, expand the System Tools folder and then the Local Users and Groups folder.

Using the User Accounts Option in Control Panel

Now let's look at an alternative way to configure local users and groups, through the *User Accounts Control (UAC)* Control Panel option, which provides the ability to manage user accounts in addition to configuring parental controls. To access the User Accounts Control Panel option, click Start ➢ Windows Systems ➢ Control Panel ➢ User Accounts. Table 2.1 briefly describes the configurable options in the User Accounts option in Control Panel.

TABLE 2.1   Configurable user-account options in Control Panel

Option	Explanation
Change Your Password	Allows you to change a user's password.
Change Your Account Name	Allows you to rename the account.
Change Your Account Type	Allows you to change your account type between the standard user and administrator account type.
Manage Another Account	Allows you to configure other accounts on the Windows client machine.
Change User Account Control Settings	Allows you to set the level of notification displayed through pop-up messages when changes are made to your computer. These notifications can prevent potentially hazardous programs from being loaded onto the operating system.
Manage Your Credentials	Allows you to set up credentials so you can easily connect to websites that require usernames and passwords or computers that require certificates.
Manage Your File Encryption Certificates	Allows you to manage your file-encryption certificates.
Configure Advanced User Profile Properties	Takes you directly to the User's Profile dialog box in Control Panel ➢ System ➢ Advanced ➢ System Settings.
Change My Environment Variables	Allows you to access the Environment Variables dialog box directly.

Creating New Users

You can create an offline account, also called a local user account, for anyone who may use a computer often. However, Microsoft recommends that everyone should have a Microsoft account that they can use to access apps, files, and Microsoft services across devices.

To create a local user account on a Windows client computer, you must be logged on as a user with permission to create a new user, which means your account must be a member of the Administrators group.

When you create a new user, there are many options that you have to configure. Table 2.2 describes all the options available in the New User dialog box. (You access this dialog box through the MMC, which is detailed in Exercise 2.3 later in this chapter.)

TABLE 2.2   User account options available in the New User dialog box

Option	Description
User Name	Defines the username for the new account. Choose a name that is consistent with your naming convention (e.g., WPanek). This is the only required field. Usernames are not case sensitive.
Full Name	Allows you to provide more detailed name information. This typically consists of the user's first and last names (e.g., Will Panek). By default, this field contains the same name as the User Name field.
Description	Typically used to specify a title and/or location (e.g., Sales-Nashville) for the account, but it can be used to provide any additional information about the user.
Password	Assigns the initial password for the user. For security purposes, avoid using readily available information about the user. Passwords are case sensitive.
Confirm Password	Confirms that you typed the password the same way two times to verify that you entered the password correctly.
User Must Change Password At Next Logon	If enabled, forces the user to change the password the first time they log on. This is done to increase security. By default, this option is selected.
User Cannot Change Password	If enabled, prevents a user from changing their password. This is useful for accounts such as Guest and accounts that are shared by more than one user. By default, this option is not selected.

Option	Description
Password Never Expires	If enabled, specifies that the password will never expire, even if a password policy has been specified. For example, you might enable this option if this is a service account and you do not want the administrative overhead of managing password changes. By default, this option is not selected.
Account Is Disabled	If enabled, specifies that this account cannot be used for logon purposes. For example, you might select this option for template accounts or if an account is not currently being used. It helps keep inactive accounts from posing security threats. By default, this option is not selected.

In the following sections, you will learn about username rules and conventions and Security Identifiers.

Username Rules and Conventions

The only real requirement for creating a new user is that you provide a valid username. To be valid, the name must follow the Windows client rules for usernames. However, it's also a good idea to have your own rules for usernames, which form your naming convention.

The following are the Windows client rules for usernames:

- A username must be from 1 to 20 characters.

- The username must be unique among all the other user and group names stored on the computer.

- The username cannot contain any of the following characters:

  / \ [ ] : ; | = , + ? < > " @

- A username cannot consist exclusively of periods or spaces.

Keeping the Windows client rules in mind, you should choose a naming convention (a consistent naming format) for your company. For example, your naming convention might be to use the last name and first initial, so for a user named William Panek, the username would be WillP or WilliamP. Another naming convention might use the first initial and last name, for the username WPanek. This is the naming convention followed by many mid-sized and larger organizations. You could base usernames on the naming convention your company has defined for email names so that the logon name and the name in the email address match.

You should also provide a mechanism that will accommodate duplicate names. For example, if you have a user named Jane Smith and a user named John Smith, you might use a middle initial for usernames, such as JDSmith and JRSmith. It is also a good practice to come up with a naming convention for groups, printers, and computers.

Real World Scenario

Naming Convention Considerations

As an IT manager, I don't recommend using first name, first initial of last name (WilliamP) as a naming convention. In a midsized-to-large company, there is the possibility of having two WilliamPs, but the odds that you will have two WPaneks are rare.

If you choose to use the first name, first initial of last name option, it can be a lot of work to go back and change this format later if the company grows. Choose a naming convention that can grow with the company.

When creating users, it's important to make sure your usernames and passwords are as strong as possible. The reason you want strong security is because when a user logs into a system, the user's credentials are placed into the computer's Local Security Authority Sub-system Service (LSASS) process memory. This is done so that the credentials can be used by the account during a session connection.

Credentials will also get stored on the Windows 10/11 authoritative databases, such as the SAM database and in the database that is used by Active Directory Domain Services (AD DS). Therefore, it's important to make your usernames and passwords strong so that no one can easily hack into a system and steal these cached credentials.

Now let's take a look at how user accounts get security ID numbers associated with them and how those numbers affect your accounts.

Security Identifiers

When you create a new user account, a *Security Identifier (SID)* is automatically created for the user account. The username is a property of the SID. For example, a user SID might look like this:

```
S-1-5-21-823518204-746137067-120266-629-500
```

It's apparent that using SIDs for user identification would make administration a nightmare. Fortunately, for your administrative tasks, you see and use the username instead of the SID.

SIDs have several advantages. Because Windows 10/11 uses the SID as the user object, you can easily rename a user while retaining all the user's properties. All security settings get associated with the SID, not the user account. Every time you create a new user, a unique SID gets associated. This ensures that if you delete and re-create a user account with the same username, the new user account will not have any of the properties of the old account because it is based on a new, unique SID. Even if the username is the same as a previously deleted account, the system still sees the account as a new user.

Because every user account gets a unique SID number, it is a good practice to disable rather than delete accounts for users who leave the company or have an extended absence. If you ever need to access the disabled account again, you have the ability to do so.

Secure Channel

Another part of authentication and encrypted communications between a client and a server is a mechanism called *Secure Channel*. Secure Channel, also known as Schannel, is a set of security protocols that help offer secure encrypted communications and authentication between a client and a server.

Schannel is a security package that uses the following protocols on the Windows platforms:

- Transport Layer Security (TLS 1.1)
- Transport Layer Security (TLS 1.2)
- Transport Layer Security (TLS 1.3)
- Secure Sockets Layer (SSL 3.0)

To create a Schannel connection, the clients and servers are both required to obtain Schannel credentials and create a security session. Once the client and server connection is obtained, the security credentials become available. If a connection is lost for any reason, the client and server can automatically renegotiate the connection and finish all communications.

Creating a New Local User Account

Complete Exercise 2.3 to create a new local user account. Before you complete the following steps, make sure you are logged on as a user with permissions to create new user accounts and have already added the Local Users and Groups Snap-in to the MMC (Exercise 2.1). I created bogus usernames; you can change these to whatever names you want to use, but I refer to the ones I created in other exercises.

EXERCISE 2.3

Creating New Users via the MMC

1. Open the Local Users and Groups MMC Desktop shortcut that you created in Exercise 2.1, and expand the Local Users and Groups Snap-in. If a dialog box appears, click Yes.

2. Highlight the Users folder and select Action ➢ New User. The New User dialog box appears, as shown in Figure 2.5.

FIGURE 2.5   New User dialog box

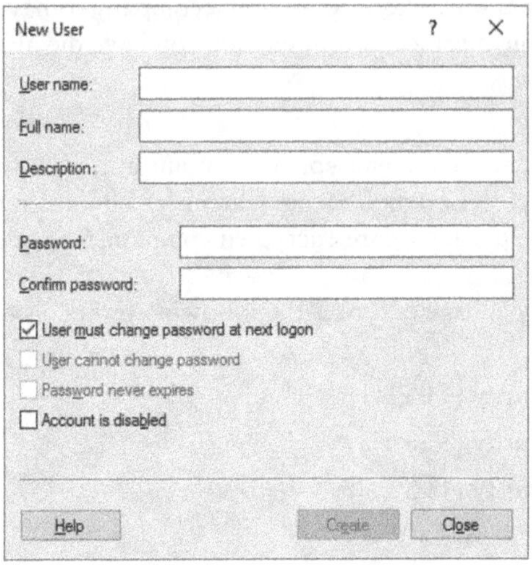

New User dialog box showing fields: User name, Full name, Description, Password, Confirm password, with checkboxes: User must change password at next logon (checked), User cannot change password, Password never expires, Account is disabled. Buttons: Help, Create, Close.

3. In the User Name text box, type **APanek**.

4. In the Full Name text box, type **Alexandria Panek**.

5. In the Description text box, type **Operations Manager**.

6. Leave the Password and Confirm Password text boxes empty. Make sure you deselect the User Must Change Password At Next Logon option, and accept the defaults for the remaining check boxes. Click the Create button to add the user.

7. Use the New User dialog box to create four more users, filling out the fields as follows:

    User Name: **PPanek**; Full Name: **Paige Panek**

    User Name: **GWashington**; Full Name: **George Washington**

    User Name: **JAdams**; Full Name: **John Adams**

    User Name: **ALincoln**; Full Name: **Abe Lincoln**

8. After you've finished creating all the users, click the Close button to exit the New User dialog box.

You can also create users through the command-line utility NET USER. For more information about this command, type **NET USER /?** at the command prompt.

Disabling User Accounts

When a user account is no longer needed, the account should be disabled or deleted. After you've disabled an account, you can later reenable it to restore it with all of its associated user properties. An account that is deleted, however, can never be recovered unless you complete a restore from a backup.

You might disable an account because a user will not be using it for a period of time, perhaps because that employee is going on vacation or taking a leave of absence. Another reason to disable an account is that you're planning to put another user in that same function and would like to reuse the account.

For example, suppose that Gary, the engineering manager, quits. If you disable his account, when your company hires a new engineering manager, you can simply rename Gary's user account (to the username for the new manager), enable it, and reset the password. This ensures that the user who takes over Gary's position will have all the same user properties and own all the same resources.

Disabling accounts also provides a security mechanism for special situations. For example, if your company is laying off a group of people, as a security measure you could disable their accounts at the same time the layoff notices are given out. This prevents those users from inflicting any damage to the company's files after they receive their layoff notice. (Note, however, that this won't affect users who are already logged in.)

In Exercise 2.4, you will disable a user account. Before you complete this exercise, you should have created new users in Exercise 2.3.

EXERCISE 2.4

Disabling User Accounts

1. Open the Local Users and Groups MMC Desktop shortcut that you created in Exercise 2.1 and expand the Local Users and Groups Snap-in.

2. Open the Users folder (C:\Users). Double-click user PPanek to open her Properties dialog box.

3. In the General tab, select the Account Is Disabled check box. Click OK.

4. Close the Local Users and Groups MMC.

5. Log off and attempt to log on as PPanek. This should fail because the account is now disabled.

6. Log back on using your user account.

NOTE   You can also access a user's properties by highlighting the user, right-clicking, and selecting Properties.

When a user has left the company for a long period of time and you know you no longer need the user account, you can delete it. Let's take a look at how to delete user accounts.

Deleting User Accounts

As noted in the preceding section, you should disable a user account if you are not sure whether the account will ever be needed again. But if the account has been disabled and you know that the user account will never need to be accessed again, you should delete the account.

To delete a user, open the Local Users and Groups utility, highlight the user account you wish to delete, click Action to bring up the menu shown in Figure 2.6, and then select Delete. You can also delete an account by clicking the account and pressing the Delete key on the keyboard.

FIGURE 2.6   Deleting a user account

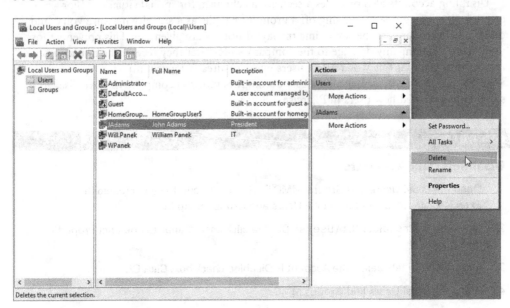

Because deleting an account is a permanent action, you will see the dialog box shown in Figure 2.7, asking you to confirm that you really wish to delete the account. After you click the Yes button here, you will not be able to re-create or re-access the account (unless you restore your local user accounts database from a backup).

Complete Exercise 2.5 to delete a user account. These steps assume you have completed Exercises 2.2, 2.3, and 2.4.

FIGURE 2.7 Confirming account deletion

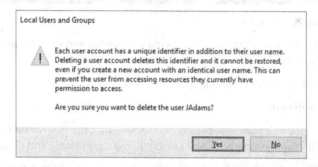

Local Users and Groups

⚠ Each user account has a unique identifier in addition to their user name. Deleting a user account deletes this identifier and it cannot be restored, even if you create a new account with an identical user name. This can prevent the user from accessing resources they currently have permission to access.

Are you sure you want to delete the user JAdams?

Yes   No

EXERCISE 2.5

Deleting a User Account

1. Open the Local Users and Groups MMC Desktop shortcut and expand the Local Users and Groups Snap-in.

2. Expand the Users folder and single-click user JAdams to select his user account.

3. Select Action ➢ Delete. The dialog box for confirming user deletion appears.

4. Click the Yes button to confirm that you wish to delete this user.

5. Close the Local Users and Groups MMC.

Now that you have disabled and deleted accounts, let's take a look at how to rename a user's account.

Renaming User Accounts

Once an account has been created, you can rename it at any time. Renaming a user account allows the account to retain all the associated user properties such as group memberships and assigned permissions even though the username is being changed.

You might want to rename a user account because the user's name has changed (for example, the user gets married) or because the name was spelled incorrectly. Also, as explained in the section "Disabling User Accounts," you can rename an existing user's account for a new user, such as someone hired to take an ex-employee's position, when you want the new user to have the same properties.

Complete Exercise 2.6 to rename a user account. These steps assume you have completed Exercises 2.2 through 2.5.

EXERCISE 2.6

Renaming a User Account

1. Open the Local Users and Groups MMC Desktop shortcut and expand the Local Users and Groups Snap-in.

2. Open the Users folder and highlight user ALincoln.

3. Select Action ➤ Rename.

4. Type the username **RReagan** and press Enter. Notice that the Full Name field retains the original Full Name property of Abe Lincoln in the Local Users and Groups utility.

5. Double-click RReagan to open the properties and change the user's full name to Ronald Reagan.

6. Click the User Must Change Password At Next Logon check box.

7. Click OK.

8. Close the Local Users and Groups MMC.

Renaming a user does not change any hard-coded names, such as the name of the user's home folder. If you want to change these names as well, you need to modify them manually—for example, through Windows Explorer. (Note that there is a small possibility that you'll have to change the Registry to point to the new name.)

Another very common task that we must deal with is changing the user's password. Let's take a look at how to do that.

Changing a User's Password

What should you do if a user forgets their password and can't log on? As the administrator, you can change the user's password, which they can then use.

It is very important as IT managers and IT administrators that we teach our users proper security measures that go along with password protection. As you have all probably seen before, the users who tape their password to their monitors or under the keyboards are not following correct security precautions. It's our job as IT professionals to teach our users proper security, and it always amazes me when I do consulting how many IT departments don't teach their users properly.

Complete Exercise 2.7 to change a user's password. This exercise assumes you have completed Exercise 2.2.

EXERCISE 2.7

Changing a User's Password

1. Open the Local Users and Groups MMC Desktop shortcut and expand the Local Users and Groups Snap-in.

2. Open the Users folder and highlight user APanek.

3. Select Action ➤ Set Password. The Set Password dialog box appears.

4. A warning appears, indicating the risks involved in changing the password. Select Proceed.

5. Type the new password and then confirm the password. Click OK.

6. Close the Local Users and Groups MMC.

Using Windows Hello, Pictures, and Biometrics

Now that we have looked at how to set up and manage local and domain accounts, let's look at how you can use other options to help you log into your system or network.

Those of us who have been certified for a long time are quite familiar with using a Microsoft account to log into the Microsoft websites. Now we can use this same account to log into our computer and networks.

Windows Hello is a Microsoft authentication technology that you can use to authenticate to a domain, to a cloud-based domain, or to a computer. To do this, you need to link your Microsoft account to your Windows 10/11 system.

Linking your Windows client system is an easy two-step verification process with Windows Hello enrollment. When you set up Windows Hello on the device, you can set up the system to use Windows Hello or a personal identification number (PIN).

Windows Hello allows you to sign in to your Windows client devices with just a look or a touch. Windows Hello can be set up so that you can use biometrics, face recognition, or even an iris scan. To configure Windows Hello options, click the Start Menu and choose Settings. Once you're in the settings, choose Accounts.

You also have the ability to set up Windows Hello to use a PIN. This is a secure number that you input instead of a username and password. You may be thinking to yourself that a PIN doesn't seem as secure as a username and password, but actually that is not true.

PINs can be very complex and include special characters and letters, both uppercase and lowercase. So that means that you can have a PIN of 1234 or a PIN of 1234Wi!!Panek1001. Also, PINs are tied directly to a machine and not to an account, so when you set up a PIN, it's good for that machine only. Because of this, PINs are actually better than a password that can be used anywhere on the network. If someone steals your password, they can access your account from anywhere. This is not the case with a PIN, because anyone trying to use it would also need access to your machine.

Using Device Guard

So far, we have been discussing how to secure your computer or network based on username, passwords, biometrics, and Windows Hello, but there are other ways to help lock your Windows 10/11 systems down. One of those ways is Device Guard.

Device Guard is an enterprise set of hardware and software security features that when used together can lock a system down so that only trusted applications can run on the operating system. As an administrator, you have the ability to define policies, and it is these policies that help Windows clients lock down applications that do not adhere to the policies that your organization has defined.

If you created a policy and an application does not meet the criteria of the defined policy, the application will not run. This is very useful when it comes to unauthorized people trying to access your network. Even if a hacker gets into the Windows 10/11 operating system and takes control of the kernel, because of the policies that you have created, it is almost impossible that any unauthorized software will be able to run.

As long as you are using Windows 10/11 Enterprise or Education, Device Guard can be used with virtualization-based security policies. This is possible because Device Guard works in conjunction with the Hyper-V hypervisor. Because of this, Device Guard can help protect applications and operating systems that run within the Hyper-V application.

The advantage to Device Guard is that it works on two levels: the kernel mode code integrity (KMCI) and user mode code integrity (UMCI). Because Device Guard works at both levels, it helps protect against hardware and software-based threats.

Understanding Device Guard Protection

Table 2.3 shows some of the different features available that can help protect against multiple types of threats.

TABLE 2.3   Device Guard features

Security threat	Device Guard feature
Boot attacks	To help protect against attacks at system startup, Device Guard includes a feature called Universal Extensible Firmware Interface (UEFI) Secure Boot. This feature protects the system from hacks during the boot process and also from malicious firmware installations. Because of the Device Guard security features, the UEFI is locked down (boot order, boot entries, Secure Boot, virtualization extensions, IOMMU, Microsoft UEFI CA) and changes can't be made to compromise the system.
Control of kernel	To help protect against kernel invasions, Device Guard uses virtualization-based security (VBS). VBS helps guard the Hyper-V hypervisor, which in turn protects the kernel and the operating system. After an administrator enable VBS, VBS tightens the default kernel-mode code integrity policy (which helps protect system files or bad drivers from being deployed) or the configurable code integrity policy.

Security threat	Device Guard feature
Direct Memory Access (DMA)-based attacks	With this policy, virtualization-based security (VBS) uses input/output memory management units (IOMMUs) to evaluate memory usage. This policy helps determine whether the memory access is accepted or denied.
New malware	This policy helps protect against kernel invasions by protecting against code integrity policies. Administrators have the ability to control a white list of software that is allowed to run. This way, if a hacker tries to run a malicious piece of code that has not been white-listed, it will not run.
Unassigned code	When hackers build malicious code, the one advantage we have in IT is that the code is not signed by an authorized vendor. Because of this, Administrators can set up code integrity policies with catalog files. This policy will immediately help protect against many known and unknown threats. The one drawback to this policy is that many organizations use unsigned line-of-business (LOB) applications.

Managing Device Guard

There are many different ways that an administrator can configure Device Guard. Let's take a look at some of the different options available for managing and configuring Device Guard.

Group Policy

One of the ways that you can configure Device Guard is through the use of a Group Policy object (GPO). You can configure the GPOs using the Windows Server 2022/2019/2016 Group Policy Management console or directly through a local GPO within Windows client.

GPOs provide a template that allows an administrator to manage and configure the hardware-based security features in Device Guard that you would like to enable and deploy. You can manage Device Guard settings and your other network settings within the same GPO.

Microsoft System Center Configuration Manager

Administrators also have the ability to use System Center Configuration Manager to easily deploy and manage catalog files, code integrity policies, and hardware-based security features.

Windows PowerShell

You can use Windows PowerShell to create and service code integrity policies. Table 2.4 shows Windows PowerShell commands for managing Device Guard.

TABLE 2.4 Device Guard PowerShell commands

PowerShell command	Description
Add-SignerRule	Allows an administrator to create a signer rule and add that rule to a policy.
ConvertFrom-CIPolicy	Allows an administrator to convert an XML file into binary format. These files contain code integrity policies.
Get-CIPolicy	Allows an administrator to view the rules in a code integrity policy.
Get-CIPolicyIdInfo	Allows an administrator to view code Integrity policy information.
Get-SystemDriver	Administrators can view the drivers on a system.
Merge-CIPolicy	Allows an administrator to merge the rules of several code Integrity policy files.
New-CIPolicy	Allows an administrator to create a Code Integrity policy as an XML file.
New-CIPolicyRule	Administrators can create code Integrity policy rules for drivers.
Set-CIPolicyIdInfo	Allows an administrator to modify the name and ID of a code Integrity policy.
Set-CIPolicyVersion	Allows an administrator to modify the version number of a policy.
Set-HVCIOptions	Administrators can change hypervisor code integrity options for a specific policy.
Set-RuleOption	Allows an administrator to modify the rule options in a code Integrity policy.

Understanding Windows Defender Credential Guard

Another security feature that was introduced with Windows 10 Enterprise and Windows Server 2016 is Windows Defender Credential Guard. Credential Guard relies on Hyper-V–based security measures to help operating systems run only software with the appropriate security privileges. Credential Guard helps stop unauthorized access to credentials, thus stopping many types of security threats.

When a user sends a username and password to a domain controller, after the domain controller authenticates the user and the Windows client system, a domain token (sometimes referred to as a Kerberos ticket) is issued to the user. Credential Guard helps protect against attacks that specifically target this authentication process.

Credential Guard Protection

One of the advantages of Credential Guard is that hardware can be secured. Credential Guard can help secure your hardware by using virtualization-based security and a feature called Secure Boot. By securing the Windows client hardware, you can also secure the Windows client operating system.

One of the nicest advantages of using Credential Guard is that it's easy to manage and deploy. Credential Guard can be configured by using a GPO, from a Windows 10/11 command prompt, or by using Windows PowerShell. But before we look at managing Credential Guard, let's take a look at each security measure.

Virtualization-Based Security

One of the greatest advantages of virtualization is that each guest operating system runs independently of every other guest operating system. So, basically that means that each operating system works as if it's on its own physical piece of hardware. Credential Guard uses a security feature that works in much the same way. The Windows services that manage domain authentication credentials are separated into their own special environment that is separated from the Windows client operating system.

It is because of this separation that you get added protection for your Windows environment. Virtualization-based security protects against credential theft attack techniques that are used in most credential attacks. Many types of attacks that run in the Windows operating system run using administrative privileges. Because virtualization-based security separates authentication credentials into their own special environment, it protects system credentials from being extracted by the hackers or malware programs that are running on the operating system.

Secure Boot

Secure Boot is another way that Windows 10/11 can help protect your hardware because it verifies that only manufacturer-trusted firmware gets used by the system. It can protect your system from hackers and hacks that attack the system's firmware. But, as with any good thing, there could also be issues. Secure Boot may possibly cause issues with things like hardware (high-end graphics cards) or operating systems such as Linux or previous versions of Windows.

So, one thing that you may need to know is how to disable Secure Boot in the event that it does conflict with some hardware. There are normally two ways that you can do so:

through the BIOS or through the Windows 10/11 bootup process. If you need to disable Secure Boot, complete the following steps:

1. Open the PC BIOS menu, or from the Windows client operating system, hold the Shift key while selecting Restart. Then choose Troubleshoot ➤ Advanced Options: UEFI Firmware Settings.

2. Locate the Secure Boot setting (normally on the Security or the Boot tab) and set it to Disabled.

3. Save the changes and reboot the system.

To reenable Secure Boot, follow the same procedure except choose Enabled for the Secure Boot option.

Configuring Device Health Attestation

In today's Bring Your Own Device (BYOD) world, many companies allow users to bring their own personal devices into the workplace. The issue with this is that you have no idea what security measures they have on their machines. Something new with Windows 10/11 is the ability to check the health of your computers and make sure they meet certain system requirements. This is where Device Health Attestation comes into play.

As an administrator, you can use the Configuration Manager console in Device Health Attestation to view the status of Windows client machines on your network and make sure that they meet the minimum requirements that your organization sets.

Administrators can now view the computer systems that are on-site or managed through the cloud using Microsoft Intune. Administrators have the ability to determine whether reporting is done through the on-site infrastructure or through the cloud. The advantage of being able to work with both cloud-based and internal computers is that if your company loses Internet access, you can still use the Device Health Attestation utility.

Device Health Attestation allows an administrator to verify that client systems have TPM enabled and have proper BIOS configurations and that boot security measures are enabled.

Device Health Attestation Requirements

If you want to use Device Health Attestation on your network or in the cloud, your systems must meet some minimum requirements:

- Client devices running a supported version of Windows 10 or Windows Server 2016 or later, with Device Health Attestation enabled.

- Client devices running a supported version of Windows 10 or Windows Server 2016 or later, with Device Health Attestation enabled.

- TPM 1.2 or TPM 2–enabled devices.

- Internet communication needs to be established between your Configuration Manager client agent and has.spserv.microsoft.com (port 443) Health Attestation service.

After you have met the minimum requirements for your systems, you have to configure your systems to run Device Health Attestation:

1. In the Configuration Manager console, select Administration ➤ Overview ➤ Client Settings. Select the Computer Agent tab.

2. In the Default Settings dialog box, choose Computer Agent and then scroll down to Enable Communication With Health Attestation Service and choose Yes. Click OK.

You may also need to enable on-premises the Health Attestation service:

1. In the Configuration Manager console, navigate to Administration ➤ Overview ➤ Client Settings. You will then need to set Use On-Premises Healthy Attestation Service to Yes.

2. Specify the On-Premise Health Attestation Service URL and then click OK.

Managing User Properties

For more control over user accounts, you can configure user properties. Through the user's Properties dialog box, you can change the original password options, add the user to existing groups, and specify user profile information.

To open a user's Properties dialog box, access the Local Users and Groups utility, open the Users folder, and double-click the user account. The user's Properties dialog box has tabs for the three main categories of properties: General, Member Of, and Profile.

The General tab contains the information you supplied when you set up the new user account, including the full name and a description, the password options you selected, and whether the account is disabled. If you want to modify any of these properties after you've created the user, simply open the user's Properties dialog box and make the changes on the General tab (Figure 2.8).

You can use the Member Of tab to manage the user's membership in groups, and the Profile tab lets you set properties to customize the user's environment. The following sections discuss the Member Of and Profile tabs in detail.

Managing User Group Membership

The Member Of tab of the user's Properties dialog box displays all the groups that the user belongs to, as shown in Figure 2.9. From this tab, you can add the user to an existing group or remove the user from a group. To add a user to a group, click the Add button and select the group that the user should belong to. If you want to remove the user from a group, highlight the group and click the Remove button.

Complete Exercise 2.8 to add a user to an existing group. These steps assume you have completed Exercise 2.2.

FIGURE 2.8   General tab of the user's Properties dialog box

FIGURE 2.9   The Member Of tab of the user's Properties dialog box

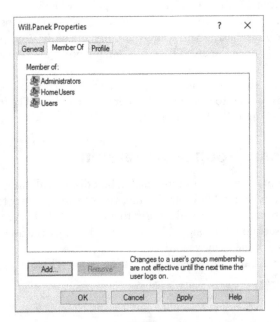

Adding a User to an Existing Group

1. Open the Local Users and Groups MMC Desktop Snap-in that you created previously.

2. Open the Users (C:\Users) folder and double-click user APanek. The APanek Properties dialog box appears.

3. Select the Member Of tab and click the Add button. The Select Groups dialog box appears.

4. Under Enter The Object Names To Select, type **Backup Operators**, and click the Check Names button. After the name is confirmed, click OK.

5. Click OK to close the APanek Properties dialog box.

Now let's take a look at the Profile tab and what options can be configured there.

Setting Up User Profiles, Logon Scripts, and Home Folders

The Profile tab of the user's Properties dialog box, shown in Figure 2.10, allows you to customize the user's environment. Here, you can specify the following items for the user:

- User profile path
- Logon script
- Home folder

FIGURE 2.10   The Profile tab of the user's Properties dialog box

The following sections describe how these properties work and when you might want to use them.

Setting a User's Profile Path

User profiles contain information about the Windows 10/11 environment for a specific user. For example, profile settings include the desktop arrangement, program groups, and screen colors that users see when they log on.

Each time you log onto a Windows client computer, the system checks to see if you have a local user profile in the Users folder, which was created on the boot partition when you installed Windows 10/11. The first-time users log on they receive a default user profile. A folder that matches the user's logon name is created for the user in the Users folder. The user profile folder that is created holds a file called NTUSER.DAT as well as subfolders that contain directory links to the user's desktop items (as shown previously in Figure 2.10).

In Exercise 2.9, you'll create two new users and set up local user profiles.

EXERCISE 2.9

Setting Up User Profiles

1. Using the Local Users and Groups utility, create two new users: WPanek and CPanek. Deselect the User Must Change Password At Next Logon option for each user.

2. Right-click the Start button and choose File Explorer. Click This PC and then double-click Local Disk (C:). Then, double-click the Users folder. Notice that the Users folder does not contain user profile folders for the new users.

3. Log off and log on as WPanek.

4. Right-click an open area on the desktop and select Personalize. In the Personalization dialog box, select a picture under Choose Your Picture, and then close the Settings app.

5. Right-click an open area on the desktop and select New ≻ Shortcut. In the Create Shortcut dialog box, type **CALC** to open the Calculator program. Accept CALC as the name for the shortcut and click Finish.

6. Log off as WPanek and log on as CPanek. Notice that user PPanek sees the Desktop configuration stored in the default user profile.

7. Log off as CPanek and log on as WPanek. Notice that WPanek sees the Desktop configuration you set up in steps 4, and 5.

8. Log off as WPanek and log on as your user account. Right-click the Start button and choose File Explorer. Click This PC and then double-click Local Disk (C:). Finally, double-click the Users folder. Notice that this folder now contains user profile folders for WPanek and CPanek.

The drawback of local user profiles is that they are available only on the computer where they were created. For example, suppose all of your Windows 10/11 computers are a part of a domain and you use only local user profiles. User Rick logs on at Computer A and creates a customized user profile. When he logs on to Computer B for the first time, he will receive the default user profile rather than the customized user profile he created on Computer A. To enable users to access their user profile from any computer they log onto, you need to use roaming profiles; however, these require the use of a network server because they can't be stored on a local Windows 10/11 computer.

In the next sections, you will learn how roaming profiles and mandatory profiles can be used. To have a roaming profile or a mandatory profile, your computer must be a part of a network with server access.

Using Roaming Profiles

A *roaming profile* is stored on a network server and allows a user to access their user profile regardless of the client computer to which they're logged on. Roaming profiles provide a consistent desktop for users who move around, no matter which computer they access. Even if the server that stores the roaming profile is unavailable, the user can still log on using a local profile.

If you are using roaming profiles, the contents of the user's `systemdrive:\Users\UserName` folder will be copied to the local computer each time the roaming profile is accessed. If you have stored large files in any subfolders of your user profile folder, you may notice a significant delay when accessing your profile remotely as opposed to locally. If this problem occurs, you can reduce the amount of time the roaming profile takes to load by moving the subfolder to another location, such as the user's home directory, or you can use GPOs within Active Directory to specify that specific folders should be excluded when the roaming profile is loaded.

Using Mandatory Profiles

A *mandatory profile* is a profile that can't be modified by the user. Only members of the Administrators group can manage mandatory profiles. You can create mandatory profiles for a single user or a group of users. You might consider creating mandatory profiles for users who should maintain consistent desktops.

For example, suppose you have a group of 20 salespeople who know enough about system configuration to make changes but not enough to fix any problems they create. For ease of support, you could use mandatory profiles. This way, all of the salespeople will always have the same profile, which they will not be able to change.

The mandatory profile is stored in a file named `NTUSER.MAN`. To create a mandatory profile, you just change the user's profile extension from `.dat` to `.man` and the profile will become mandatory. A user with a mandatory profile can set different desktop preferences while logged on, but those settings will not be saved when the user logs off.

There are two folders where the profiles are stored. They are *Username* and *Username* `.v2` (*Username* will be replaced with the user's name). The difference is that if you are using

Windows XP, the profile gets placed in the *Username* folder. If the users are using Windows Vista, Windows 7/8/8.1, Windows 10/11, or Windows Server, the user profile gets placed in the *Username*.v# folder. The # will depend on the version of Windows that is getting used. For example, Windows 7 was v2. Table 2.5 was taken directly from Microsoft's website (at the time this book was written) and it shows what version number goes with each Microsoft operating system version.

To see current version numbers, please check out Microsoft's website at

docs.microsoft.com/en-us/windows/client-management/
mandatory-user-profile

TABLE 2.5   User profile version numbers

Operating system	Profile version number
Windows Vista, Windows 7, and Windows Server 2008/2008 R2	*<username>*.V2
Windows 8 and Windows Server 2012	*<username>*.V2 (before the software update and Registry key are applied) *<username>*.V3 (after the software update and Registry key are applied)
Windows 8.1 and Windows Server 2012 R2	*<username>*.V2 (before the software update and Registry key are applied) *<username>*.V4 (after the software update and Registry key are applied)
Windows 10 versions 1507 to 1511	*<username>*.V5
Windows 10, versions 1607, 1703, 1709, 1803, 1809, 1903, and 1909 and Windows Server 2016/2019	*<username>*.V6

You can use only roaming profiles as mandatory profiles. Mandatory profiles do not work for local user profiles.

Now let's look at a second type of mandatory profile called super-mandatory profile.

Using Super-Mandatory Profiles

A *super-mandatory profile* is a mandatory user profile with an additional layer of security. With mandatory profiles, a temporary profile is created if the mandatory profile is not available when a user logs on. However, when super-mandatory profiles are configured, temporary profiles are not created if the mandatory profile is not available over the network, and the user is unable to log onto the computer.

The process for creating super-mandatory profiles is similar to that for creating mandatory profiles, except that instead of renaming the user folder *Username*.v2 as you would for a mandatory profile, you name the folder *Username*.man. User profiles become *super-mandatory* when the folder name of the profile path ends in .man, as in, for example, \\server\share\APanek.man\. Only system administrators can make changes to mandatory user profiles.

 Real World Scenario

Copying User Profiles

Within your company, you have a user, Paige, who logs in with two different user accounts. One account is a regular user account, and the other is an administrator account used for administration tasks only.

When Paige established all her desktop preferences and installed the computer's applications, they were installed with the administrator account. Now, when she logs in with the regular user account, she can't access the desktop and profile settings that were created for her as an administrative user.

To solve this problem, you can copy a local user profile from one user to another (for example, from Paige's administrative account to her regular user account) by choosing Start ➤ Windows System ➤ Control Panel ➤ System ➤ Advanced System Settings ➤ User Profiles Settings. When you copy a user profile, the following items are copied: favorites, cookies, documents, Start Menu items, and other unique user Registry settings.

Using Logon Scripts

Another configurable element within the Profile tab of the user's properties is logon scripts—files that run every time a user logs on to the network. They are usually batch files, but they can be any type of executable file. Logon scripts are either created by the admin or just grabbed off the Internet. Creating these scripts is beyond the scope of this book.

You might use logon scripts to set up drive mappings or to run a specific executable file each time a user logs on to the computer. For example, you could run an inventory-management file that collects information about the computer's configuration and sends that data to a central management database. Logon scripts are also useful for compatibility with non–Windows client operating systems for users who want to log on but still maintain consistent settings with their native operating system.

To run a logon script for a user, enter the script name in the Logon Script text box on the Profile tab of the user's Properties dialog box.

Setting Up Home Folders

Users usually store their personal files and information in a private folder called a *home folder*. On the Profile tab of the user's Properties dialog box, you can specify the location of a home folder as a local folder or a network folder. The main reason you give your users a home folder on the server is because the servers are usually the only machines that get backed up. Most companies do not back up individual users' machines. If your users place all their important documents in the home folder location on the network, those documents will get backed up as part of the nightly backup.

To specify a local folder, choose the Local Path option and type the path in the text box next to that option. To specify a network path for a folder, select the Connect option and specify a network path using a Universal Naming Convention (UNC) path. A UNC name consists of the computer name and the share that has been created on the computer. When you are connecting to a UNC name, the network folder you are connecting to should already be created and shared. For example, if you wanted to connect to a folder called \Users\ Will on a server called SALES, you'd choose the Connect option, select a drive letter that would be mapped to the home directory, and then type **\\SALES\Users\Will** in the To box.

If the home folder you are specifying does not exist, Windows 10/11 will attempt to create the folder for you. You can also use the variable %username% in place of a specific user's name. The %username% will automatically change to the name of the user you are currently working on.

WARNING   Be careful when you're specifying your home folder. If you make a mistake when typing in the path for the directory, Windows will create a bogus-named folder for you.

Complete Exercise 2.10 to assign a home folder to a user. These steps assume you have completed Exercise 2.2 onward.

EXERCISE 2.10

Assigning Home Folders

1. Open the Local Users and Groups MMC Desktop shortcut and expand the Local Users and Groups Snap-in.

2. Open the Users folder and double-click user GWashington. The GWashington Properties dialog box appears.

3. Select the Profile tab and click the Local Path radio button to select it.

4. Specify the home folder path by typing **C:\HomeFolders\GWashington** in the text box for the Local Path option. Then click OK.

5. Use Windows Explorer to verify that this folder was created.

6. Close the Local Users and Groups MMC.

 Real World Scenario

Using Home Folders to Keep Files Backed Up

As an administrator for a large network, one of my primary responsibilities is to make sure all data is backed up daily. This has become difficult because daily backup of each user's local hard drive is impractical. You can also have problems with employees deleting important corporate information as they are leaving the company.

After examining the contents of a typical user's local drive, you will realize that most of the local disk space is taken by the operating system and the user's stored applications. This information does not change and does not need to be backed up. What you are primarily concerned with is backing up the user's data.

To more effectively manage this data and accommodate the necessary backup, you should create home folders for each user and store them on a network share. This allows the data to be backed up daily, to be readily accessible should a local computer fail, and to be easily retrieved if the user leaves the company.

Here are the steps to create a home folder that resides on the network:

1. Decide which server will store the users' home folders.

2. Create a directory structure that will store the home folders efficiently (for example, C:\HOME).

3. Create a single share to the user's home folder. (You can do this by right-clicking the home folder and choosing Properties.)

4. Use NTFS and share permissions to ensure that only the specified user has permissions to their home folder.

5. Specify the location of the home folder through the Profile tab of the user's Properties dialog box.

Troubleshooting User Account Authentication

When a user attempts to log on through Windows 10/11 and is unable to be authenticated, you will need to track down the reason for the problem.

If a local user is having trouble logging on, the problem may be with the username, the password, or the user account itself. The following are some common causes of local logon errors:

> Because many of these same issues happen when logging on to a domain from a Windows 10 machine, these approaches can be used for both local logons and domain logons.

Incorrect Username   You can verify that the username is correct by checking the Local Users and Groups utility. Verify that the name was spelled correctly.

Incorrect Password   Remember that passwords are case sensitive. Is the Caps Lock key on? If you see any messages relating to an expired password or locked-out account, the reason for the problem is obvious. If necessary, you can assign a new password through the Local Users and Groups utility.

Prohibitive User Rights   Does the user have permission to log on locally at the computer? By default, the Log On Locally user right is granted to the Users group so that all users can log onto Windows client computers.

However, if this user right was modified, you will see an error message stating that the local policy of this computer does not allow interactive logon. The terms *interactive logon* and *local logon* are synonymous and mean that the user is logging on at the computer where the user account is stored on the computer's local database.

A Disabled or Deleted Account   You can verify whether an account has been disabled by checking the account properties through the Local Users and Groups utility. If the account is no longer in the database, then it has most likely been deleted.

A Domain Account Logon at the Local Computer   If a computer is a part of a domain, the logon dialog box has options for logging on to the domain or to the local computer. Make sure the user has chosen the correct option.

Managing and Creating Groups

Groups are an important part of network management. Many administrators are able to accomplish the majority of their management tasks through the use of groups; they rarely assign permissions to individual users.

Windows 10/11 includes built-in local groups (such as Administrators and Backup Operators) that already have all the permissions needed to accomplish specific tasks. Windows 10/11 also uses built-in special groups in which users are placed automatically when they meet certain criteria.

You can create and manage local groups (but not special groups) through the Local Users and Groups utility. With this utility, you can add groups, change group membership, rename groups, and delete groups.

One misconception about groups is that they have to work with Group Policy Objects (GPOs). This is not correct. Group Policy Objects are sets of rules that allow you to set computer-configuration and user-configuration options that apply to users or computers. Group Policies, on the other hand, are typically used with Active Directory and are applied as Group Policy Objects.

Using Built-In Groups

On a Windows 10/11 computer, built-in local groups have already been created and assigned all necessary permissions to accomplish basic tasks. In addition, there are built-in special groups that the Windows 10/11 system handles automatically. These groups are described in the following sections.

Built-In Local Groups

A local group is a group that is stored on the local computer's accounts database. You can add users to these groups and can manage the groups directly on a Windows client computer. By default, some of the following local groups are created on Windows 10/11 computers:

- Administrators
- Backup Operators
- Cryptographic Operators

- Distributed COM Users
- Event Log Readers
- Guests
- IIS_IUSRS
- Network Configuration Operators
- Performance Log Users
- Performance Monitor Users
- Power Users
- Remote Desktop Users
- Replicator
- Users

I will briefly describe each group, its default permissions, and the users assigned to the group by default.

> If possible, you should add users to the built-in local groups rather than creating new groups from scratch. This simplifies administration because the built-in groups already have the appropriate permissions. All you need to do is add the users you want to be members of the group.

Administrators   The Administrators group has full permissions and privileges. Its members can grant themselves any permissions they do not have by default to manage all the objects on the computer. (Objects include the filesystem, printers, and account management.) By default, the Administrator account, which is disabled by default, and the Initial User account are members of the Administrators local group.

> Assign users to the Administrators group with caution since they will have full permissions to manage the computer.

Members of the Administrators group can perform the following tasks:

- Install the operating system.
- Install and configure hardware device drivers.
- Install system services.
- Install service packs, hotfixes, and Windows updates.
- Upgrade the operating system.
- Repair the operating system.
- Install applications that modify the Windows system files.
- Configure password policies.

- Configure audit policies.
- Manage security logs.
- Create administrative shares.
- Create administrative accounts.
- Modify groups and accounts that have been created by other users.
- Remotely access the Registry.
- Stop or start any service.
- Configure services.
- Increase and manage disk quotas.
- Increase and manage execution priorities.
- Remotely shut down the system.
- Assign and manage user rights.
- Reenable locked-out and disabled accounts.
- Manage disk properties, including formatting hard drives.
- Modify systemwide environment variables.
- Access any data on the computer.
- Back up and restore all data.

Backup Operators   Members of the Backup Operators group have permissions to back up and restore the filesystem, even if the filesystem is NTFS and they have not been assigned permissions to access the filesystem. However, the members of Backup Operators can access the filesystem only through the Backup utility. To access the filesystem directly, Backup Operators must have explicit permissions assigned. There are no default members of the Backup Operators local group.

Cryptographic Operators   The Cryptographic Operators group has access to perform cryptographic operations on the computer. There are no default members of the Cryptographic Operators local group.

Distributed COM Users   The Distributed COM Users group has the ability to launch and run Distributed COM objects on the computer. There are no default members of the Distributed COM Users local group.

Event Log Readers   The Event Log Readers group has access to read the event log on the local computer. There are no default members of the Event Log Readers local group.

Guests   The Guests group has limited access to the computer. This group is provided so that you can allow people who are not regular users to access specific network resources. As a general rule, most administrators do not allow Guest access because it poses a potential security risk. By default, the Guest user account is a member of the Guests local group.

IIS_IUSRS   The IIS_IUSRS group is used by Internet Information Services (IIS). The NT AUTHORITY\IUSR user account (premade for IIS) is a member of the IIS_IUSRS group by default.

Network Configuration Operators   Members of the Network Configuration Operators group have some administrative rights to manage the computer's network configuration, for example, editing the computer's TCP/IP settings.

Performance Log Users   The Performance Log Users group has the ability to access and schedule logging of performance counters and can create and manage trace counters on the computer. There are no default members of this group.

Performance Monitor Users   The Performance Monitor Users group has the ability to access and view performance counter information on the computer. Users who are members of this group can access performance counters both locally and remotely. There are no default members of this group.

Power Users   The Power Users group is included in Windows 10/11 for backward compatibility. The Power Users group primarily provides backward compatibility for running legacy programs. Otherwise, the Power Users group has limited administrative rights. There are no default members of this group.

Remote Desktop Users   The Remote Desktop Users group allows members of the group to log on remotely for the purpose of using the Remote Desktop service. There are no default members of this group.

Replicator   The Replicator group is intended to support directory replication, which is a feature used by domain servers. Only domain users who will start the replication service should be assigned to this group. The Replicator local group has no default members.

Users   The Users group is intended for end users who should have very limited system access. If you have installed a fresh copy of Windows 10/11, the default settings for the Users group prohibit its members from compromising the operating system or program files. By default, all users who have been created on the computer, except Guest, are members of the Users local group.

Special Groups

Special groups are premade groups that can be used by the system or by administrators. Membership in special groups is automatic if certain criteria are met. You cannot manage special groups through the Local Users and Groups utility, but an administrator can add special groups to resources. The following describes the special groups that are built into Windows 10/11:

Anonymous Logon   This group includes users who access the computer through anonymous logons. When users gain access through special accounts created for anonymous access to Windows 10/11 services, they become members of the Anonymous Logon group.

Authenticated Users   This group includes users who access the Windows 10/11 operating system through a valid username and password. Users who can log on belong to the Authenticated Users group.

Batch   This group includes users who log on as a user account that is used only to run a batch job.

Creator Owner   This is the account that created or took ownership of an object. This is typically a user account. Each object (files, folders, printers, and print jobs) has an owner. Members of the Creator Owner group have special permissions to resources. For example, if you are a regular user who has submitted 12 print jobs to a printer, you can manipulate your print jobs as Creator Owner, but you can't manage any print jobs submitted by other users.

Dialup   This group includes users who log onto the network from a dial-up connection.

Everyone   This group includes anyone who could possibly access the computer—all users who have been defined on the computer (including Guest), plus (if your computer is a part of a domain) all users within the domain. If the domain has trust relationships with other domains, all users in the trusted domains are part of the Everyone group as well. The exception to automatic group membership with the Everyone group is that members of the Anonymous Logon group are not included as a part of the Everyone group.

Interactive   This group includes all users who use the computer's resources locally.

Network   This group includes users who access the computer's resources over a network connection.

Service   This group includes users who log on as a user account that is used only to run a service. You can configure the use of user accounts for logon through the Services program.

System   There are times when the Windows 10/11 operating system will access functions within the system. When the operating system accesses these functions, it does it as a system user. When the system accesses specific functions as a user, that process becomes a member of the System group.

Terminal Server User   This group includes users who log on through Terminal Services.

Creating Groups

To create a group, you must be logged on as a member of the Administrators group. The Administrators group has full permissions to manage users and groups.

Keep your naming conventions in mind when assigning names to groups, just as you do when choosing usernames. Consider the following guidelines:

- The group name should be descriptive; for example, Accounting Data Users.

- The group name must be unique to the computer and different from all other group names and usernames that exist on that computer.

- Group names can be up to 256 characters. It is best to use alphanumeric characters for ease of administration. The backslash (\) character is not allowed.

Creating groups is similar to creating users, and it is a fairly easy process. After you've added the Local Users and Groups MMC or used Local Users and Groups through the Computer Management utility, expand it to see the Users and Groups folders. Right-click the Groups folder and select New Group from the context menu. This brings up the New Group dialog box, shown in Figure 2.11.

FIGURE 2.11   The New Group dialog box

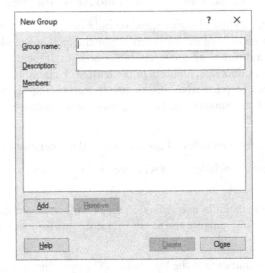

The only required entry in the New Group dialog box is the group name. If appropriate, you can enter a description for the group, and you can add (or remove) group members. When you're ready to create the new group, click the Create button.

Complete Exercise 2.11 to create two new local groups. (Creating domain groups is beyond the scope of this book.)

Creating Local Groups

1. Open the Admin Console MMC Desktop shortcut you created and expand the Local Users and Groups Snap-in.

2. Right-click the Groups folder and select New Group.

3. In the New Group dialog box, type **Data Users** in the Group Name text box. Click the Create button.

4. Repeat step 3, but type **Application Users** in the Group Name text box.

After the groups are created, you will have to manage the groups and their membership. In the next section, we will look at managing groups.

Managing Group Membership

After you've created a group, you can add members to it. As mentioned earlier, you can put the same user in multiple groups. You can easily add and remove users through a group's Properties dialog box, shown in Figure 2.12. To access a group's Properties dialog box from the Groups folder in the Local Users and Groups utility, double-click the name of the group you want to manage.

FIGURE 2.12   IT Group's Properties dialog box

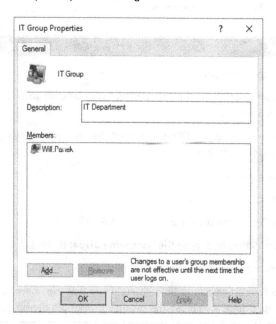

From the group's Properties dialog box, you can change the group's description and add or remove group members. When you click the Add button to add members, the Select Users dialog box appears (Figure 2.13).

FIGURE 2.13   The Select Users dialog box

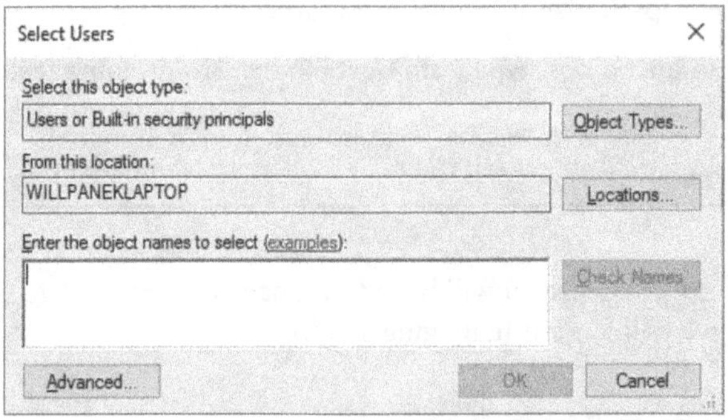

In the Select Users dialog box, you enter the object names of the users you want to add. You can use the Check Names button to validate the users against the database. Select the user accounts you wish to add and click Add. Click OK to add the selected users to the group.

To remove a member from the group, select the member in the Members list of the Properties dialog box and click the Remove button.

In Exercise 2.12, you'll create new user accounts and then add these users to one of the groups you created in the previous exercises.

EXERCISE 2.12

Adding Accounts to Groups

1.   Open the Local Users and Groups MMC shortcut you created and expand the Local Users and Groups Snap-in.

2.   Create two new users: JDoe and DDoe. Deselect the User Must Change Password At Next Logon option for each user.

3.   Expand the Groups folder.

4.   Double-click the Data Users group.

5.   In the Data Users Properties dialog box, click the Add button.

6.   In the Select Users dialog box, type the username **JDoe**; then click OK.

7.   Click Add and type the username **DDoe**; then click OK.

8.   In the Data Users Properties dialog box, you will see that the users have both been added to the group. Click OK to close the group's Properties dialog box.

There may come a point when a specific group is no longer needed. In the next section, we will look at how to delete a group from the Local Users and Groups utility.

Deleting Groups

If you are sure that you will never again want to use a particular group, you can delete it. Once a group is deleted, you lose all permissions assignments that have been specified for the group.

To delete a group, right-click the group name and choose Delete from the context menu. You will see a warning that once a group is deleted, it is gone for good. Click the Yes button if you're sure you want to delete the group.

If you delete a group and give another group the same name, the new group won't be created with the same properties as the deleted group because, like users, groups get unique SIDs assigned at the time of creation.

Creating users and groups is one of the most important tasks that we as IT members can do. On a Windows client machine, creating users and groups is an easy and straightforward process.

Now that you understand how to create users and groups, you need to know how to manage Windows 10/11 security using GPOs and LGPOs. We'll look at that next.

Managing Security Using GPOs and LGPOs

Windows 10/11 offers a wide variety of security options. If the Windows client computer is a part of a domain, then you can apply security through a Group Policy Object using the Group Policy Management Console. If the Windows client computer is not a part of a domain, then you use Local Group Policy Objects to manage local security.

Additionally, you can use policies to help manage user accounts. Account policies control the logon environment for the computer, such as password and logon restrictions. Local policies specify what users can do once they log on and include auditing, user rights, and security options. You can also manage critical security features through the Windows Security Center.

Understanding the GPO and LGPO Basics

The tools you use to manage Windows 10/11 computer security configurations depend on whether the Windows 10/11 computer is a part of a Windows Server domain environment.

If the Windows 10/11 client is not a part of a domain, then you apply security settings through *Local Group Policy Objects (LGPOs)*. LGPOs are sets of security configuration settings that are applied to users and computers. LGPOs are created and stored locally on the Windows client computer.

If your Windows client computer is a part of a domain, which uses the services of Active Directory, then you typically manage and configure security through *Group Policy Objects (GPOs)*. Active Directory is the database that contains all your domain user and group accounts along with all other domain objects.

Group Policy Objects are policies that can be applied to either users or computers in the domain. The Group Policy Management Console (GPMC) is a Microsoft Management Console (MMC) Snap-in that is used to configure and manage GPOs for users and computers via Active Directory. You can access the LGPO console by typing **gpedit.msc** in the Windows 10/11 Search box.

Windows client computers that are part of a domain still have LGPOs, and you can use LGPOs in conjunction with the Active Directory group policies (GPOs).

Usage of Group Policy Objects for domains is covered in greater detail in my book *MCSA Windows Server 2016 Complete Study Guide: Exam 70-740, Exam 70-741, Exam 70-742 and Composite Upgrade Exam 70-743 2nd Edition* (Wiley, 2018).

The settings you can apply through the Group Policy utility within Active Directory are more comprehensive than the settings you can apply through LGPOs. Table 2.6 lists some of the options that can be set for GPOs within Active Directory and which of those options can be applied through LGPOs.

TABLE 2.6   Group Policy and LGPO setting options

Group Policy setting	Available for LGPO?
Software installation	No
Remote Installation Services	Yes
Scripts	Yes
Printers	Yes
Security settings	Yes
Policy-based QOS	Yes
Administrative templates	Yes
Folder redirection	No
Internet Explorer configuration	Yes
Windows Update settings	Yes

Now that we have looked at LGPOs, let's explore some of the tools available for creating and managing them.

Using the Group Policy Result Tool

When a user logs on to a computer or domain, a resulting set of policies to be applied is generated based on the LGPOs, site GPOs, domain GPOs, and OU GPOs. The overlapping nature of Group Policies can make it difficult to determine what Group Policies will actually be applied to a computer or user.

To help determine what policies will actually be applied, Windows 10/11 includes the Group Policy Result Tool, also known as the *Resultant Set of Policy (RSoP)*. You can access this tool through the GPResult command-line utility. The gpresult command displays the set of policies that were enforced on the computer and the specified user during the logon process.

The gpresult command will display the RSoP for the computer and the user who is currently logged in. Several switches that can be used with the gpresult command are listed in Table 2.7.

TABLE 2.7   gpresult switches

Switch	Explanation
/F	Forces gpresult to override the filename specified in the /X or /H command
/H	Saves the report in an HTML format
/P	Specifies the password for a given user context
/R	Displays RSoP summary data
/S	Specifies the remote system to connect to
/U	Specifies the user context under which the command should be executed
/V	Specifies that verbose information should be displayed
/X	Saves the report in XML format
/Z	Specifies that the super-verbose information should be displayed
/?	Shows all the gpresult command switches
/scope	Specifies whether the user or the computer settings need to be displayed
/User	Specifies the username for which the RSoP data is to be displayed

In the next section, we will look at how to create and apply Local Group Policy Objects to the Windows client machine.

Managing and Applying LGPOs

Policies that have been linked through Active Directory will, by default, take precedence over any established local Group Policies. Local Group Policies are typically applied to computers that are not part of a network or are in a network that does not have a domain controller and thus does not use Active Directory.

Pre-Vista versions of Windows contained only one Local Group Policy Object that applied to all of the computer's users unless NTFS permissions were applied to the LGPO. However, Windows Vista and Windows 10/11 changed that with the addition of *Multiple Local Group Policy Objects (MLGPOs)*. MLGPOs are applied in the following hierarchical order:

1. Local Computer Policy

2. Administrators and Non-Administrators Local Group Policy

3. User-Specific Group Policy

The Local Computer Policy is the only LGPO that includes computer and user settings; the other LGPOs contain only user settings. Settings applied here will apply to all users of the computer.

The Administrators LGPO is applied to users who are members of the built-in local Administrators group. As you might guess, the Non-Administrators LGPO is applied to users who are not members of the local Administrators group. Because each user of a computer can be classified as an administrator or a non-administrator, either one policy or the other will apply.

User-Specific LGPOs are also included with Windows 10/11. These LGPOs make it possible for specific policy settings to apply to a single user.

As with Active Directory GPOs, any GPO settings applied lower in the hierarchy will override GPO settings applied higher in the hierarchy by default. For example, any User-Specific GPO settings will override any conflicting Administrator/Non-Administrator GPO settings or Local Computer Policy settings. And, of course, any AD GPO settings will still override any conflicting LGPO settings.

> Domain administrators can disable LGPOs on Windows 10/11 computers by selecting the Turn Off Local Group Policy Objects Processing Domain GPO setting under `Computer Configuration\ Administrative Templates\System\Group Policy`.

You apply an LGPO to a Windows client computer through the Group Policy Object Editor Snap-in within the MMC. Figure 2.14 shows the Local Computer Policy for a Windows client computer.

Complete Exercise 2.13 to add the Local Computer Policy Snap-in to the MMC.

FIGURE 2.14   Local Computer Policy

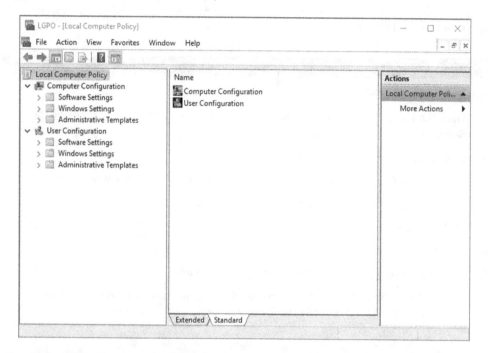

Adding the Local Computer Policy Snap-In

1. Open the Local Users and Groups MMC shortcut by typing **MMC** in the Search Programs And Files box.

2. A User Account Control dialog box appears. Click Yes.

3. Select File ➤ Add/Remove Snap-in.

4. Highlight the Group Policy Object Editor Snap-in and click the Add button.

5. The Group Policy Object specifies Local Computer by default. Click the Finish button.

6. In the Add Or Remove Snap-Ins dialog box, click OK.

7. In the left pane, right-click the Local Computer Policy and choose New Windows From Here.

8. Choose File ➤ Save As and name the console **LGPO**. Make sure you save it to the Desktop. Click Save.

9. Close the Local Users and Groups MMC.

Now we will look at how to open an LGPO for a specific user account on a Windows client machine. Complete Exercise 2.14 to access the Administrators, Non-Administrators, and User-Specific LGPOs.

EXERCISE 2.14

Accessing an LGPO

1. Open the Local Users and Groups MMC shortcut by typing **MMC** in the Windows 10/11 Search box.

2. Select File ➤ Add/Remove Snap-in.

3. Highlight the Group Policy Object Editor Snap-in and click the Add button.

4. Click Browse so that you can browse for a different GPO.

5. Click the Users tab.

6. Select the user you want to access and click OK.

7. In the Select Group Policy Object dialog box, click Finish.

8. In the Add Or Remove Snap-Ins dialog box, click OK. You may close the console when you have finished looking at the LGPO settings for the user you chose.

Notice that the Administrators, Non-Administrators, and User-Specific LGPOs contain only User Configuration settings, not Computer Configuration settings.

Now let's examine the security settings that can be configured in the LGPO.

Configuring Local Security Policies

Through the use of the Local Computer Policy, you can set a wide range of security options under Computer Configuration\Windows Settings\Security Settings.

This portion of the Local Computer Policy is also known as the Local Security Policy. The following list describes in detail how to apply security settings through LGPOs. The main areas of security configuration of the LGPO are as follows:

Account Policies Account policies are used to configure password and account lockout features. Some of these settings include password history, maximum password age, minimum password age, minimum password length, password complexity, account lockout duration, account lockout threshold, and whether to reset the account lockout counter afterward.

Local Policies   Local policies are used to configure auditing, user rights, and security options.

Windows Firewall with Advanced Security   Windows Firewall with Advanced Security provides network security for Windows computers. Through this LGPO, you can set domain, private, and public profiles. You can also set this LGPO to authenticate communications between computers and inbound/outbound rules.

Network List Manager Policies   This section allows you to set the network name, icon, and location Group Policies. Administrators can set Unidentified Networks, Identifying Networks, and All Networks.

Public Key Policies   Use the Public Key Policies settings to specify how to manage certificates and certificate life cycles.

Software Restriction Policies   The settings under Software Restriction Policies allow you to identify malicious software and control that software's ability to run on the Windows client machine. These policies allow an administrator to protect the Microsoft Windows 10/11 operating system against security threats such as viruses and Trojan horse programs.

Application Control Policies   This section allows you to set up AppLocker. You can use AppLocker to configure a Denied list and an Accepted list for applications. Applications that are configured on the Denied list will not run on the system, and applications on the Accepted list will operate properly.

IP Security Policies on Local Computer   This section allows you to configure the IPsec policies. IPsec is a way to secure data packets at the IP level of the message.

Advanced Audit Policy Configuration   Advanced Audit Policy Configuration settings can be used to provide detailed control over audit policies. This section also allows you to configure auditing to help show administrators either successful or unsuccessful attacks on their network.

You can also access the Local Security Policy by running secpol.msc or by opening Control Panel and selecting Administrative Tools ➤ Local Security Policy.

Now that you have seen all the options in the security section of the LGPO, let's take a look at account policies and local policies in more detail.

Using Account Policies

Account policies are used to specify the user account properties that relate to the logon process. They allow you to configure computer security settings for passwords and account-lockout specifications.

If security is not an issue—perhaps because you are using your Windows client computer at home—then you don't need to bother with account policies. If, on the other hand, security is important—for example, because your computer provides access to payroll information—then you should set very restrictive account policies.

> Account policies at the LGPO level apply only to local user accounts, not domain accounts. To ensure that user account security is configured for domain user accounts, you need to configure these policies at the domain GPO level.

To access the `Account Policies` folder from the MMC, follow this path: Local Computer Policy ➢ Computer Configuration ➢ Windows Settings ➢ Security Settings ➢ Account Policies. In the following sections, you will learn about the password policies and account-lockout policies that define how security is applied to account policies.

Setting Password Policies

Password policies ensure that security requirements are enforced on the computer. It is important to understand that password policies are set on a per-computer basis; they cannot be configured for specific users. Figure 2.15 shows the password policies, which are described in Table 2.8.

FIGURE 2.15 The password policies

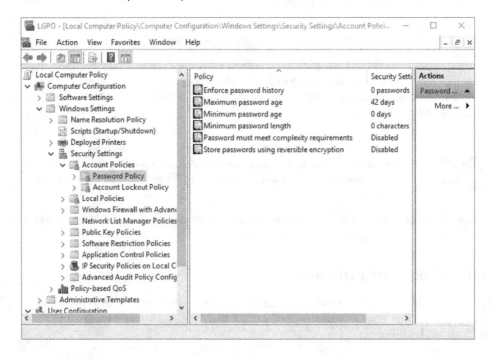

TABLE 2.8   Password policy options

Policy	Description	Default	Minimum	Maximum
Enforce Password History	Keeps track of user's password history	Remember 0 passwords	Same as default	Remember 24 passwords
Maximum Password Age	Determines maximum number of days user can keep valid password	Keep password for 42 days	Keep password for 1 day	Keep password for up to 999 days
Minimum Password Age	Specifies how long password must be kept before it can be changed	0 days (Password can be changed immediately.)	Same as default	998 days
Minimum Password Length	Specifies minimum number of characters password must contain	0 characters (No password required.)	Same as default	14 characters
Password Must Meet Complexity Requirements	Requires that passwords meet minimum levels of complexity	Disabled	No minimum	No maximum
Store Passwords Using Reversible Encryption	Specifies higher level of encryption for stored user passwords	Disabled	No minimum	No maximum

You can use the password policies in Table 2.8 as follows:

Enforce Password History   Prevents users from repeatedly using the same passwords. Users must create a new password when their password expires or is changed.

Maximum Password Age   Forces users to change their passwords after the maximum password age is exceeded. Setting this value to 0 will specify that the password will never expire.

Minimum Password Age   Prevents users from changing their passwords several times in rapid succession in order to defeat the purpose of the Enforce Password History policy.

Minimum Password Length   Ensures that a user creates a password and specifies the length requirement for that password. If this option isn't set, users are not required to create a password at all.

Password Must Meet Complexity Requirements   Passwords must be six characters or longer and cannot contain the user's account name or any part of the user's full name. In addition, passwords must contain three of the following four different character types:

- English uppercase characters (A through Z)
- English lowercase characters (a through z)
- Decimal digits (0 through 9)
- Symbols (such as !, @, #, $, and %)

Store Passwords Using Reversible Encryption   Provides a higher level of security for user passwords. This is required for Challenge Handshake Authentication Protocol (CHAP) authentication through remote access or Network Policy Server and for Digest Authentication with Internet Information Services (IIS).

Complete Exercise 2.15 to configure password policies for your computer. These steps assume that you have added the Local Computer Policy Snap-in to the MMC in Exercise 2.1.

EXERCISE 2.15

Configuring Password Policy

1. Open the LGPO MMC shortcut that you created earlier.

2. Expand the Local Computer Policy Snap-in.

3. Expand the folders as follows: Computer Configuration ➤ Windows Settings ➤ Security Settings ➤ Account Policies ➤ Password Policy.

4. Open the Enforce Password History policy. On the Local Security Setting tab, specify that five passwords will be remembered. Click OK.

5. Open the Maximum Password Age policy. On the Local Security Setting tab, specify that the password expires in 60 days. Click OK.

Let's now look at how to set and manage the policies in the Account Lockout Policies section.

Setting Account-Lockout Policies

The account-lockout policies specify how many invalid logon attempts should be tolerated. You configure the account-lockout policies so that after x number of unsuccessful logon attempts within y number of minutes, the account will be locked for a specified amount of time or until the administrator unlocks it.

Account-lockout policies are similar to a bank's arrangements for ATM access-code security. You have a certain number of chances to enter the correct PIN. That way, anyone who steals your card can't just keep guessing your access code until they get it right. Typically, after three unsuccessful attempts, the ATM takes the card. Then you need to request a new card from the bank. Figure 2.16 shows the account-lockout policies, which are described in Table 2.9.

TABLE 2.9 Account-lockout policy options

Policy	Description	Default	Minimum	Maximum
Account Lockout Duration	Specifies how long account will remain locked if the account lockout threshold is reached	Disabled (If Account Lockout Threshold is enabled, 30 minutes.)	Same as default	99,999 minutes
Account Lockout Threshold	Specifies number of invalid attempts allowed before account is locked out	0 (Disabled; account will not be locked out.)	Same as default	999 attempts
Reset Account Lockout Counter After	Specifies how long counter will remember unsuccessful logon attempts	Disabled (If Account Lockout Threshold is enabled, 30 minutes.)	Same as default; if enabled, must be equal to or less than the Account Lockout Duration value	99,999 minutes

The Account Lockout Duration and Reset Account Lockout Counter After policies will be disabled until a value is specified for the Account Lockout Threshold policy. After the Account Lockout Threshold policy is set, the Account Lockout Duration and Reset Account Lockout Counter After policies will be set to 30 minutes. If you set Account Lockout Duration to 0, the account will remain locked out until an administrator unlocks it.

The Reset Account Lockout Counter After value must be equal to or less than the Account Lockout Duration value.

Complete Exercise 2.16 to configure account-lockout policies and test their effects.

FIGURE 2.16   Account-lockout policies

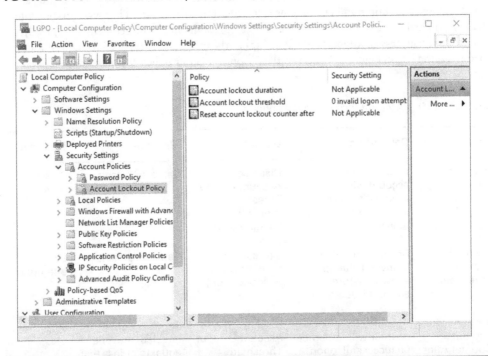

EXERCISE 2.16

Configuring Account-Lockout Policies

1. Open the LGPO MMC shortcut.

2. Expand the Local Computer Policy Snap-in.

3. Expand the folders as follows: Computer Configuration ➤ Windows Settings ➤ Security Settings ➤ Account Policies ➤ Password Policy.

4. Open the Account Lockout Threshold policy. On the Local Security Setting tab, specify that the account will lock after three invalid logon attempts. Click OK.

5. Accept the suggested value changes for the Account Lockout Duration and Reset Account Lockout Counter After policies by clicking OK.

6. Open the Account Lockout Duration policy. On the Local Security Setting tab, specify that the account will remain locked for 5 minutes. Click OK.

7. Accept the suggested value changes for the Reset Account Lockout Counter After policy by clicking OK.

8. Log off your Administrator account. Try to log on as one of the accounts that have been created on this Windows client machine and enter an incorrect password four times.

9. After you see the error message stating that the referenced account has been locked out, log on as an administrator.

10. To unlock the account, open the Local Users and Groups Snap-in in the MMC, expand the Users folder, and double-click the user.

11. On the General tab of the user's Properties dialog box, deselect the Account Is Locked Out check box. Then click OK.

Using Local Policies

As you learned in the preceding section, account policies are used to control logon procedures. When you want to control what a user can do after logging on, you use local policies. With local policies, you can implement auditing, specify user rights, and set security options.

To use local policies, first add the Local Computer Policy Snap-in to the MMC. Then, from the MMC, follow this path to access the Local Policies folders: Local Computer Policy ➢ Computer Configuration ➢ Windows Settings ➢ Security Settings ➢ Local Policies. Figure 2.17 shows the three Local Policies folders: Audit Policy, User Rights Assignment, and Security Options. We will look at Audit Policy and User Rights Assignment in the following sections.

FIGURE 2.17   Accessing the Local Policies folders

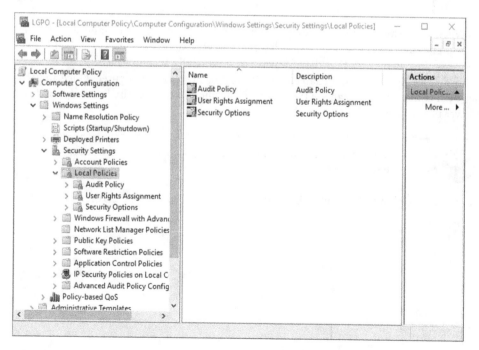

Setting Audit Policies

Audit policies can be implemented to track the success or failure of specified user actions. You audit events that pertain to user management through the audit policies. By tracking certain events, you can create a history of specific tasks, such as user creation and successful or unsuccessful logon attempts. You can also identify security violations that arise when users attempt to access system management tasks for which they do not have permission.

Real World Scenario

Auditing Failed Attempts

As an IT manager, you have to make sure that you monitor failed attempts to access resources. A failed attempt to access a resource usually means that someone tried to access the resource and was denied because of insufficient privileges.

Users who try to go to areas for which they do not have permission usually fall into two categories: hackers and people who are just curious to see what they can get away with. Both are very dangerous.

If a user is trying to access an area in which they do not belong, make sure to warn the user. This is very common on a network and needs to be nipped in the bud.

When you define an audit policy, you can choose to audit success or failure of specific events. The success of an event means that the task was successfully accomplished. The failure of an event means that the task was not successfully accomplished.

By default, auditing is not enabled, and it must be manually configured. Once auditing has been configured, you can see the results of the audit in the security log using the Event Viewer utility.

Only members of the Administrators group can view the security log in Event Viewer.

Figure 2.18 shows the audit policies, which are described in Table 2.10.

FIGURE 2.18 Audit policies

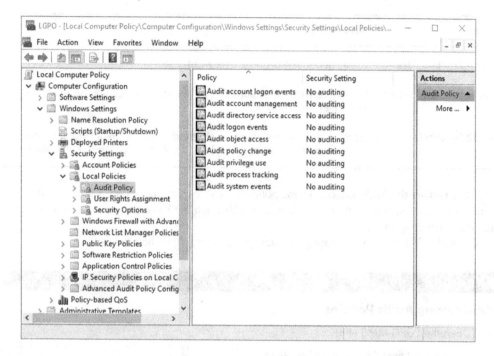

TABLE 2.10 Audit-policy options

Policy	Description
Audit Account Logon Events	Tracks when a user logs on or logs off either their local machine or the domain (if domain auditing is enabled)
Audit Account Management	Tracks user and group account creation, deletion, and management actions, such as password changes
Audit Directory Service Access	Tracks directory service accesses
Audit Logon Events	Audits events related to logon, such as running a logon script, accessing a roaming profile, and accessing a server
Audit Object Access	Enables auditing of access to files, folders, and printers.
Audit Policy Change	Tracks any changes to the audit policies, trust policies, or user rights assignment policies

TABLE 2.10   Audit-policy options *(continued)*

Policy	Description
Audit Privilege Use	Tracks users exercising a user right
Audit Process Tracking	Tracks events such as activating a program, accessing an object, and exiting a process
Audit System Events	Tracks system events such as shutting down or restarting the computer as well as events that relate to the security log in Event Viewer

After you set the Audit Object Access policy to enable auditing of object access in the object's properties, you must enable file auditing through NTFS security or print auditing through printer security.

Complete Exercise 2.17 to configure audit policies and view their results.

EXERCISE 2.17

Configuring Audit Policies

1. Open the LGPO MMC shortcut.

2. Expand the Local Computer Policy Snap-in.

3. Expand the folders as follows: Computer Configuration ➢ Windows Settings ➢ Security Settings ➢ Local Policies ➢ Audit Policy.

4. Open the Audit Account Logon Events policy. Select the Success and Failure check boxes. Click OK.

5. Open the Audit Account Management policy. Select the Success and Failure check boxes. Click OK.

6. Log off of your Administrator account. Attempt to log back on to your Administrator account using an incorrect password. The logon should fail (because the password is incorrect).

7. Log on as an administrator.

8. Select Start, right-click Computer, and choose Manage to open Event Viewer.

9. From Event Viewer, open the security log by selecting Windows Logs ➢ Security. You should see the audited events listed with a Task Category of Credential Validation.

Assigning User Rights

The user rights policies determine what rights a user or group has on the computer. User rights, also called privileges, apply to the system. They are not the same as permissions, which apply to a specific object. An example of a user right is Back Up Files And Directories. This right allows a user to back up files and folders even if the user does not have permissions that have been defined through NTFS filesystem permissions. The other user rights are similar because they deal with system access as opposed to resource access.

Figure 2.19 shows the first several user rights policies; all of the policies are described in Table 2.11.

FIGURE 2.19   User rights policies

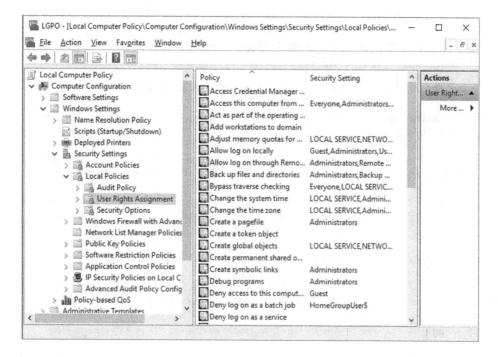

In Exercise 2.18, you'll apply a user rights policy.

TABLE 2.11   User Rights Assignment policy options

Right	Description
Access Credential Manager As A Trusted Caller	Used to back up and restore Credential Manager.
Access This Computer From The Network	Allows a user to access the computer from the network.
Act As Part Of The Operating System	Allows low-level authentication services to authenticate as any user.
Add Workstations To Domain	Allows a user to create a computer account on the domain.
Adjust Memory Quotas For A Process	Allows you to configure how much memory can be used by a specific process.
Allow Log On Locally	Allows a user to log on at the physical computer.
Allow Log On Through Remote Desktop Services	Gives a user permission to log on through Remote Desktop Services.
Back Up Files And Directories	Allows a user to back up all files and directories regardless of how the file and directory permissions have been set.
Bypass Traverse Checking	Allows a user to pass through and traverse the directory structure, even if that user does not have permissions to list the contents of the directory.
Change The System Time	Allows a user to change the internal time and date on the computer.
Change The Time Zone	Allows a user to change the time zone.
Create A Pagefile	Allows a user to create or change the size of a page file.
Create A Token Object	Allows a process to create a token if the process uses an internal API to create the token.
Create Global Objects	Allows a user to create global objects when connected using Terminal Server.
Create Permanent Shared Objects	Allows a process to create directory objects through Object Manager.

Right	Description
Create Symbolic Links	Allows a user to create a symbolic link.
Debug Programs	Allows a user to attach a debugging program to any process.
Deny Access To This Computer From The Network	Allows you to deny specific users or groups access to this computer from the network. Overrides the Access This Computer From The Network policy for accounts present in both policies.
Deny Log On As A Batch Job	Allows you to prevent specific users or groups from logging on as a batch file. Overrides the Log On As A Batch Job policy for accounts present in both policies.
Deny Log On As A Service	Allows you to prevent specific users or groups from logging on as a service. Overrides the Log On As A Service policy for accounts present in both policies.
Deny Log On Locally	Allows you to deny specific users or groups access to the computer locally. Overrides the Log On Locally policy for accounts present in both policies.
Deny Log On Through Terminal Services	Specifies that a user is not able to log on through Terminal Services.
Enable Computer And User Accounts To Be Trusted For Delegation	Allows a user or group to set the Trusted For Delegation setting for a user or computer object. A user or computer that is trusted for delegation can access resources on another computer using delegated credentials of a client.
Force Shutdown From A Remote System	Allows the system to be shut down by a user at a remote location on the network.
Generate Security Audits	Allows a user, group, or process to make entries in the security log.
Impersonate A Client After Authentication	Enables programs running on behalf of a user to impersonate a client.
Increase A Process Working Set	The working set of a process is the current set of pages in the virtual address space of the process that resides in physical memory. This setting allows you to increase the size of the process working set.
Increase Scheduling Priority	Specifies that a process can increase or decrease the priority that is assigned to another process.

TABLE 2.11 User Rights Assignment policy options *(continued)*

Right	Description
Load And Unload Device Drivers	Allows a user to dynamically unload and load device drivers. This right does not apply to Plug and Play drivers.
Lock Pages In Memory	Allows an account to create a process that runs only in physical RAM, preventing it from being paged.
Log On As A Batch Job	Allows a process to log onto the system and run a file that contains one or more operating system commands.
Log On As A Service	Allows a service to log on in order to run.
Manage Auditing And Security Log	Allows a user to enable object access auditing for files and other Active Directory objects. This right does not allow a user to enable general object access auditing in the Local Security Policy.
Modify An Object Label	Allows a user to change the integrity level of files, folders, or other objects.
Modify Firmware Environment Variables	Allows a user to install or upgrade Windows. It also allows a user or process to modify the firmware environment variables stored in NVRAM of non-x86-based computers. This right does *not* affect the modification of system environment variables or user environment variables.
Perform Volume Mainte- nance Tasks	Allows a user to perform volume maintenance tasks such as defragmentation and error checking.
Profile Single Process	Allows a user to monitor non-system processes through performance-monitoring tools.
Profile System Performance	Allows a user to monitor system processes through performance-monitoring tools.
Remove Computer From Docking Station	Allows a user to undock a laptop through the Windows 10 user interface.
Replace A Process Level Token	Allows a process, such as Task Scheduler, to call an API to start another service.
Restore Files And Directories	Allows a user to restore files and directories regardless of file and directory permissions.

Right	Description
Shut Down The System	Allows a user to shut down the Windows client computer locally.
Synchronize Directory Service Data	Allows a user to synchronize Active Directory data.
Take Ownership Of Files Or Other Objects	Allows a user to take ownership of system objects, such as files, folders, printers, and processes.

EXERCISE 2.18

Applying a User Rights Policy

1. Open the LGPO MMC shortcut.

2. Expand the Local Computer Policy Snap-in.

3. Expand the folders as follows: Computer Configuration ➤ Windows Settings ➤ Security Settings ➤ Local Policies ➤ User Rights Assignment.

4. Open the Log On As A Service user right.

5. Click the Add User Or Group button. The Select Users Or Groups dialog box appears.

6. Click the Advanced button, and then select Find Now.

7. Select a user. Click OK.

8. Click OK in the Select Users Or Groups dialog box.

9. In the Log On As A Service Properties dialog box, click OK.

Configuring User Account Control

Most administrators have had to wrestle with the balance between security and enabling applications to run correctly. In the past, some applications simply would not run correctly under Windows unless the user running the application was a local administrator.

Unfortunately, granting local administrator permissions to a user also allows the user to install software and hardware, change configuration settings, modify local user accounts, and delete critical files. Even more troubling is the fact that malware that infects a computer while an administrator is logged in is able to perform administrative functions.

The problem is that many applications require that users have permissions to write to protected folders and to the Registry. Windows 10/11's solution is *User Account Control (UAC)*. When any standard user tries to run an application that requires an administrator access token, the UAC requires that the user provide valid administrator credentials.

Privilege Elevation

UAC protects computers by requiring privilege elevation for all users, even users who are members of the local Administrators group. As you have no doubt seen by now, UAC will prompt you for permission when performing a task that requires privilege elevation. This prevents malware from silently launching processes without your knowledge.

Privilege elevation is required for any feature that contains the security shield. For example, the small shield shown on the Change Date And Time button in the Date And Time dialog box indicates an action that requires privilege elevation.

Now let's take a look at how to elevate privileges for users and executables.

Elevated Privileges for Users

By default, local administrators are logged on as standard users. When administrators attempt to perform a task that requires privilege escalation, they are prompted for confirmation by default. This can require administrators to authenticate when performing a task that requires privilege escalation by changing the User Account Control: Behavior Of The Elevation Prompt For Administrators In Admin Approval Mode policy setting to Prompt For Credentials. On the other hand, if you don't want UAC to prompt administrators for confirmation when elevating privileges, you can change the policy setting to Elevate Without Prompting.

Non-administrator accounts are called standard users. When standard users attempt to perform a task that requires privilege elevation, they are prompted for a password of a user account that has administrative privileges. You cannot configure UAC to automatically allow standard users to perform administrative tasks, nor can you configure UAC to prompt a standard user for confirmation before performing administrative tasks. The UAC does this automatically. If you do not want standard users to be prompted at all for credentials when attempting to perform administrative tasks, you change the User Account Control: Behavior Of The Elevation Prompt For Standard Users policy setting to Automatically Deny Elevation Requests.

The built-in Administrator account, though disabled by default, is not affected by UAC. UAC will not prompt the built-in Administrator account for elevation of privileges. Thus, it is important to use a normal user account whenever possible and use the built-in Administrator account only when absolutely necessary.

With the Default UAC setting enabled, a user's desktop will be dimmed when they are notified of a change to the computer. The administrator or user must either approve or deny the request in the UAC dialog box before the user can do anything else on that computer. This is known as the *secure desktop*. You have the ability to turn off the secure desktop by modifying either the Local Security Policy or the Registry.

Complete Exercise 2.19 to see how UAC affects administrator and non-administrator accounts differently.

Seeing How UAC Affects Accounts

1. Log onto Windows 10/11 as a non-administrator account.

2. Click Start ➤ Windows System ➤ Control Panel ➤ Large Icons View ➤ Windows Firewall.

3. Click the Turn Windows Firewall On Or Off link on the left side. The UAC box should prompt you for permission to continue. Click Yes. You should be denied access to the Windows Firewall Settings dialog box.

4. In the Users and Groups MMC, enable the Administrator account and also reset the Administrator's password.

5. Log off and log on as the Administrator account.

6. Click Start ➤ Windows System ➤ Control Panel ➤ *Large Icons View* ➤ Windows Firewall.

7. Click the Turn Windows Firewall On Or Off link.

8. You should automatically be taken to the Windows Firewall screen. Close the Windows Firewall screen.

Let's now see how to elevate privileges for executable applications.

Elevated Privileges for Executables

You can also enable an executable file to run with elevated privileges. To do so, you can right-click a shortcut or executable and select Run As Administrator. The elevation applies to that session only.

But what if you need to configure an application to always run with elevated privileges for a user? To do so, log in as an administrator, right-click a shortcut or executable, and select Properties. On the Compatibility tab, select the Run This Program As An Administrator check box. If the Run This Program As An Administrator check box is unavailable, that means the program is blocked from permanently running as an administrator because the program doesn't need administrative privileges or you are not logged on as an administrator.

Managing Credentials by Using Credential Manager

Credential Manager is a feature in Windows 10/11 that allows users to manage their web and Windows login credentials. It allows users to add, edit, delete, backup and restore their credentials. It is essentially a digital library that stores saved login credentials. Credential Manager contains two categories:

- Web Credentials
- Windows Credentials

Web credentials consist of website login information that is stored in Windows, Edge, Internet Explorer, Skype, and other web-based apps. Windows Credentials consists of login information that is used by Windows services and applications to automatically log you in.

One way to open Credential Manager is to type **credential manager** in the search box on the taskbar and then select Credential Manager Control Panel (see Figure 2.20).

FIGURE 2.20   Credential Manager

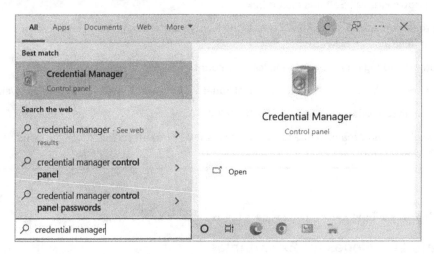

Then, select the type of credentials you'd like to manage (see Figure 2.21).

FIGURE 2.21   Credential Manager options

Adding New Credentials Using Credential Manager

Once thing that you can do with Credential Manager is to add new login information. The process of adding new login information is the same whether the login information is a Web or Windows credential. Click the type of credential you want to add. For example, if you want to add new login information for Windows Credentials, on the right-hand side of the window, there are blue links that say, "Add a Windows credential," "Add a certificate-based credential," or "Add a generic credential." Select the type of credential you'd like to add. This will open a window with text entries for the type of credential you want to add; fill it out with the appropriate information and click OK. The new credentials will be saved.

Editing or Deleting Credentials Using Credential Manager

Editing login information can be helpful when you've had a password change and you'd like to update it. Within Windows Credentials, you will see a list of all Windows Credentials that are saved to Credential Manager.

Simply click the credential you want to edit. This will expand the credential to show you the saved information. Under the information, on the left-hand side, you will have two options: Edit and Remove. To edit the information, select Edit, then replace the old credentials with the new credentials and click OK. The new credentials will be saved.

To delete credentials, click the credentials you'd like to delete and then click Remove. This will remove the selected credentials from your system.

Backing Up or Restoring Credentials Using Credential Manager

Credential Manager allows you to back up Windows Credentials only. To back up the Windows Credentials, click Windows Credentials. You will see two blue options: Back Up Credentials and Restore Credentials. To back up the credentials, select Back Up Credentials. You will then see a window asking you where you want to back up the stored login credentials. Click Browse and navigate to where you'd like to save them, name the backup file, click Save, and then click Next. The backup file will be saved as a CRD file.

To restore the credentials, click Restore Credentials. Then, click Browse in the next window, locate the CRD file you created previously, select the file, click Open, and then click Next. The credentials will be restored.

Local Administrator Password Solutions (LAPS)

One thing that an administrator might do is set the same password for all local administrator accounts to make it easier for admins to log in across the network. However, this can be one of the most harmful misconfigurations on your Windows network. If you use the same password across your network, it can cause a lot of issues if that password happens to get stolen. Then, your entire network may be at risk. Local Administrator Password Solutions (LAPS) solves this issue by setting a different, random password for the local administrator account on every computer in the domain. So, basically, LAPS is a password management feature that randomizes administrator passwords across a single domain and stores the new password and share permissions in Active Directory (AD).

For domain-joined computers, LAPS provides management of local administrator account passwords. The passwords are randomized and stored in Active Directory (AD) and protected by access control lists (ACLs) so that only authorized users can read them or request a reset. The domain administrator will determine which users, such as helpdesk admins, are authorized to read the passwords.

Microsoft recommends using LAPS and it's offered for free. You can download it from the Microsoft Download Center: www.microsoft.com/en-us/download/details.aspx?id=46899.

LAPS provides the following features:

- Regularly randomizes the local administrator passwords
- Centrally stores the passwords in the existing infrastructure AD
- Controls access using AD ACL permissions
- Transmits the encrypted passwords from the client to AD by using Kerberos encryption by default

The components of LAPS include:

- Agent - Group Policy client-side extension (CSE), which is installed with an MSI file. The agent provides:
  - Event logging
  - Random password generation
- A PowerShell module for configuration
- Centralize control using Active Directory that allows:
  - An audit trail in the security log of the domain controller
  - Computer object, confidential attribute

LAPS is built on the Active Directory infrastructure and does not require other supporting technologies. It uses a Group Policy CSE that you install on managed computers to perform all management tasks.

Requirements for installing LAPS

At the time this book was written, these are the minimum system requirements needed to run LAPS:

- Supported operating system:
  - Windows Server 2022, Windows Server 2019, Windows Server 2016, Windows Server 2012 R2, Windows Server 2012, Windows Server 2008 R2, Windows Server 2008, Windows Server 2003, Windows 11, Windows 10, Windows 8.1, Windows 8, Windows 7, Windows Vista
- Active Directory (requires AD schema extension):
  - Windows 2003 SP1 or later

- Managed machines:
  - Windows Server 2003 SP2 or later, or Windows Server 2003 x64 Edition SP2 or later
- Management tools:
  - .NET Framework 4.0
  - PowerShell 2.0 or later

How LAPS Works

The core of the LAPS solution is a GPO CSE, which performs the following tasks during a GPO update:

- Checks to see if the password of the local Administrator account has expired
- Generates a new password when the old password has either expired or is required to be changed prior to the upcoming expiration
- Validates the new password against the password policy
- Reports the password to AD, storing it with a confidential attribute with the computer account in AD
- Reports the next expiration time for the password to AD, storing it with an attribute with the computer account in AD
- Changes the password of the Administrator account

The password can then be read from AD by users who are allowed to do so. Eligible users can request a password change for a computer.

Installing LAPS

Start by downloading the MSI installation file directly from Microsoft by going to www .microsoft.com/en-us/download/details.aspx?id=46899. LAPS does not need to be installed on a specific server; you can install it on either a server built specifically for LAPS or on a shared server.

1. Log onto the target server using the local admin rights and double-click the downloaded MSI file. This will initiate the installation wizard.
2. Click Next on the Welcome screen.
3. Accept the licenses agreement and click Next.
4. In the next window, select the components you want to install (see Figure 2.22).
5. On the next page, click Install to start the installation.
6. Once the installation is complete, click Finish.

FIGURE 2.22 LAPS components

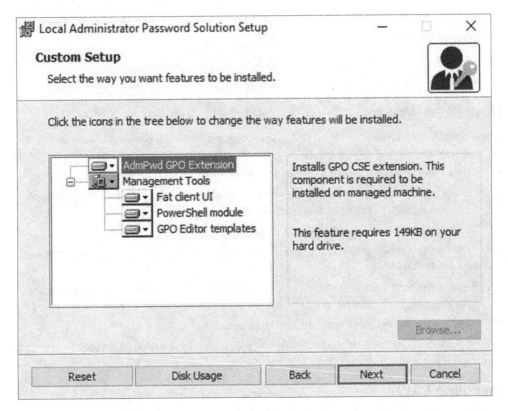

Once the installation is complete, you must complete a few other steps:

- Update the Active Directory schema.
- Change Computer object permissions.
- Assign permissions to the group for password access.
- Install CSE in Computers.
- Create GPOs for LAPS settings.

Update Active Directory Schema

LAPS uses two new attributes in Computer objects:

- `ms-Mcs-AdmPwd`, which saves the administrator password in Cleartext
- `ms-Mcs-AdmPwdExpirationTime`, which saves the timestamp of password expiration

To extend the AD schema:

1. Launch PowerShell as Active Directory Schema Administrator.

2. Import the PowerShell module by typing **Import-module AdmPwd.PS**.

3. Once the module is imported successfully, update the schema by typing **Update-AdmPwdADSchema**.

Once the schema updates, you will see the two new attributes in the Computer object.

Change Computer Object Permissions

The Computer object needs to have permission to write values to ms-Mcs-AdmPwd and ms-Mcs-AdmPwdExpirationTime attributes, so you need to grant permission to the SELF built-in account. To do this:

1. Launch PowerShell as a Domain Administrator.

2. Run the command **Set-AdmPwdComputerSelfPermission -OrgUnit [OUNAME]**.

Assign Permissions to a Group for Password Access

Next, you will want to assign the appropriate permissions to the group that requires access. Before assigning permissions, you can use PowerShell to see who has passwords by default and then grant permission:

1. Launch PowerShell as a Domain Administrator.

2. Import the PowerShell module by typing **Import-module AdmPwd.PS**.

3. To view the users/groups with extended rights, run the following command: **Find-AdmPwdExtendedRights -Identity "[OUNAME]"**.

4. If you need to grant permission to a specific group, run the following command:
   Set-AdmPwdReadPasswordPermission -Identity "[OUNAME]" -AllowedPrincipals "[GROUP]".

Install Client-Side Extension (CSE) in Computers

LAPS requires CSE to be installed on each device. There are several different ways to install the agent onto a computer, but for this book, we are going to use a GPO to publish and install the agent on computers.

1. Log into your domain controller and launch the Group Policy Management Console (GPMC).

2. Create New Group Policy under the [OUNAME] OU.

3. Right-click the Group Policy and click Edit.

4. Go to Computer Configuration | Policies | Software Settings | Software Installations.

5. Right-click it and select New | Package.

6. This will open up a new window. Browse to the network share that has the LAPS MSI file.

7. Specify the deployment method as Assigned.

Create a GPO for LAPS Settings

The last step is to set up a new GPO with the LAPS settings. To do this, perform the following steps:

1. Log into the domain controller and launch the GPMC.

2. Create a New Group Policy under the [OUNAME] OU.

3. Right-click the Group Policy and then click Edit.

4. In the new window, navigate to Computer Configuration | Administrative Templates | LAPS. You can now see the four LAPS settings, as shown in Figure 2.23.

FIGURE 2.23 LAPS GPO settings

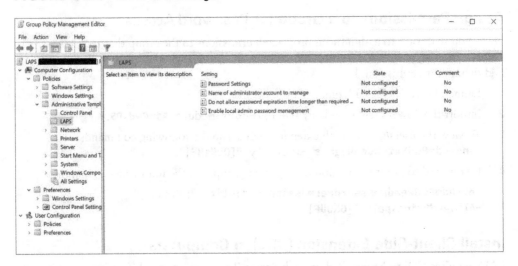

5. To enable the password management feature, double-click Enable Local Admin Password Management; then click Enable and click OK to apply the settings.

6. Double-click Password Settings; this is where you can set the password complexity settings and password age. Once you're done, click OK.

7. If you want to make changes to the other settings, just double-click the settings and then modify them to suit your needs.

Registry and File Virtualization

Many applications that are installed on a Windows 10/11 machine need to have access to the Registry. By default, Windows 10/11 protects the Registry from non-administrator accounts, but a feature called Registry and File Virtualization enables non-administrator users to run applications that previously required administrative privileges to run correctly. As discussed earlier, some applications write to the Registry and to protected folders, such as C:\Windows and C:\Program Files. For non-administrator users, Windows 10/11 redirects any attempts to write to protected locations to a per-user location. By doing so, Windows 10/11 enables users to use the application successfully while it protects critical areas of the system.

Understanding Smart Cards

Another way to help secure Windows 10/11 is by using smart cards. *Smart cards* are plastic cards (the size of a credit card) that can be used in combination with other methods of authentication. This process of using a smart card along with another authentication method is called two-factor authentication or *multifactor authentication*. Authentication is the process of using user credentials to log onto either the local Windows client machine or the domain.

Multifactor authentication support allows you to increase the security of many critical functions of your company, including client authentication, interactive logon, and document signing.

Multifactor authentication (using smart cards) is now easier than ever to use and deploy because of the new features included with all versions of Windows 10/11:

Enhanced Support for Smart Card–Related Plug and Play and the Personal Identity Verification (PIV) Standard   This allows users of Windows 10/11 to use smart cards from vendors who publish their drivers through Windows Update, allowing Windows 10/11 to use the smart card without special middleware. These drivers are downloaded in the same way as drivers for other Windows devices. When a smart card that is PIV-compliant is placed into a smart card reader, Windows 10/11 will try to download a current driver from Windows Update. If a driver is not available, the PIV-compliant mini-driver that is included with Windows 10/11 is used for the smart card.

Encrypting Drives with BitLocker   If your users are using Windows 10/11 Enterprise or Professional, the users can choose to encrypt their removable media by turning on Bit-Locker and then choosing the smart card option to unlock the drive. Windows will then retrieve the correct mini-driver for the smart card and allow the operation to complete.

Smart Card Domain Logon   When using Windows 10/11, the correct mini-driver for a smart card is automatically retrieved. This allows a new smart card to authenticate with the domain controller without requiring the user to install or configure additional middleware.

Document and Email Signing   Windows 10/11 users can use smart cards to sign an email or document. XML Paper Specification (XPS) documents can also be signed without additional software.

Use with Line-of-Business Applications   Using Windows 10/11 smart cards allows applications that use Cryptography Next Generation (CNG) or CryptoAPI to retrieve the correct mini-driver at runtime. This eliminates the need for middleware.

When you decide to use multifactor authentication, you are deciding to use a process that will require certificate authorities (CAs). CAs are servers that are running the certificate services on them. When you move forward with the decision to use smart cards, you will then need to install and configure CAs to make all of the components work together.

CAs are built on Windows Server operating systems, and if your Windows 10/11 users are having issues logging into the Windows 10/11 operating systems using smart cards, then you must check the server CAs to make sure that they are configured and running properly.

 Certificate servers are covered in greater detail in *MCSA Windows Server 2016 Complete Study Guide: Exam 70-740, Exam 70-741, Exam 70-742 and Composite Upgrade Exam 70-743 2nd Edition* by William Panek (Wiley, 2018).

There are two types of smart cards: physical and virtual. Physical smart cards are cards that look like ATM cards. Most of them have either a magnetic strip or a chip built into the physical card. To use a physical smart card, you need a smart card reader. This is a device that either connects to a computer or is built into a computer and you place the physical smart card into the reader. You then enter a PIN into the system and the machine is unlocked or logged onto the network.

There is a downside to using physical smart cards: they can get lost or misplaced. When I implemented a smart card system into a previous company, we ended up replacing one-fourth of all cards in the first month due to loss or damage.

This is where virtual smart cards can be an advantage. Virtual smart cards use a cryptographic key technology that is stored on the actual Windows client computer, as long as that computer has a Trusted Platform Module (TPM) installed on the motherboard.

Virtual smart cards offer the security benefits of two-factor authentication without the price of physical cards and readers. This is possible because of the TPM technology. TPM devices allow us to use cryptographic capabilities, the same as physical smart cards do, but without the cards. Virtual smart cards give us the same benefits as physical cards, including non-exportability, anti-hammering, and isolated cryptography:

Non-Exportability   TPM technology is built to be tamperproof. When a system uses TPM encryption, the TPM encryption is specific to the machine that installed it. Because of this, you can't take a virtual smart card from one system and use it on another.

Anti-Hammering (Lockout) Smart cards use PINs to unlock the system. If a PIN is entered incorrectly, the TPM uses an anti-hammering technology that locks the system from further attempts for a specific amount of time.

Isolated Cryptography TPM is the only mechanism on a Windows 10/11 system that loads a copy of the private keys. These keys are not loaded into the system's memory, and because only TPM has the keys, the keys stay isolated and inaccessible to anything or anyone.

Virtual smart cards function the same way as physical smart cards that are continuously inserted into a system. The machine gets the same benefits and results. To set up virtual smart cards, you need to build a certificate authority (CA) server in your organization, and all of your Windows clients need to be Windows 8 or higher.

After the CA is built, you then need to build a certificate template for the virtual smart cards to use. Then, to create the TPM virtual smart card for a Windows 10/11 system, open a command prompt with administrative credentials on a Windows 10/11 domain computer and type the following command:

```
tpmvscmgr.exe create /name tpmvsc /pin default /adminkey random /generate
```

After you run this command, you will create a virtual smart card with the name `tpmvsc`. The system will then prompt you for a PIN. You will need to enter and confirm a PIN of at least eight characters. After a few seconds, the process will complete. The TPM application (`tpmvscmgr.exe`) will then provide you with the device instance ID for the virtual smart card. You may want to store this ID in case you will need it to manage or remove the virtual smart card later.

Finally, you will need to enroll the certificate into the CA by requesting a new certificate and then selecting the TPM Virtual Smart Card Logon check box. When you are prompted for a device, select the Microsoft virtual smart card that you created earlier.

Configuring Remote Management

End-user support is a major concern and a time-consuming endeavor for most IT departments. Anything you can do to provide a more efficient solution to user issues is a major benefit. Basic telephone or chat support works in many cases, but what if you could see what the end user sees or even interface with their machine? By using Remote Assistance and Remote Desktop, you can.

Remote Assistance in Windows provides many enhancements over previous versions, including improvements in security, performance, and usability. Windows 10/11 goes even further by adding a technology integrated with Remote Assistance called Easy Connect. This makes it even easier for novice users to request help from expert users. Group Policy support has been increased. There is command-line functionality (meaning you can add scripting), bandwidth optimization, logging, and even more.

Remote Desktop is a tool that allows you to take control of a remote computer's keyboard, video, and mouse. This tool does not require someone collaborating with you on the remote computer. Remote Desktop is used to access remote machines' applications and troubleshoot issues as well as meet end-user needs where you want complete control of the remote machine. Let's start the discussion with Remote Assistance.

In the following sections, we will also look at how to use virtual private networks (VPNs). You'll learn how to configure VPNs and the protocols that work with VPNs.

Remote Assistance

Remote Assistance provides a method for inviting help by instant message, email, or a file. To use Remote Assistance, the computer requesting help and the computer providing help must have Remote Assistance capabilities and the feature enabled, and both computers must have network connectivity (they have to be able to talk to each other).

Remote Assistance is designed to have an expert user (the assistor) provide assistance to a novice user (assistee). When assisting a novice user, the expert can use text-based chat built into Remote Assistance. The expert can also take control of a novice user's desktop (with permission, of course). Here are two common examples of when you would use Remote Assistance:

- Diagnosing problems that are difficult to explain or reproduce. Remote Assistance can allow an expert to remotely view the computer, and the novice user can show the expert an error or problem.

- Guiding a novice user to perform a complex set of actions. The expert can also take control of the computer and complete the tasks if necessary.

Easy Connect

Easy Connect is a technology integrated with Remote Assistance and it's a method for getting remote assistance that is integrated with Windows 10/11. Easy Connect uses Peer Name Resolution Protocol (PNRP) to set up direct peer-to-peer transfer using a central machine on the Internet to establish the connection. PNRP uses IPv6 and Teredo tunneling to register a machine as globally unique. You're not using IPv6? You are with PNRP; Windows 10/11 (as well as Windows 7/8/8.1 and Windows Server) has IPv6 turned on natively as well as the currently used standard of IPv4. We'll discuss IPv6 in more detail in a later chapter, but to give you an idea, you can see the structure of the PNRP Teredo IPv6 packet in Figure 2.24.

To establish a Remote Assistance session with a user, the novice should open the Windows Remote Assistance screen by typing **msra** in the integrated search box next to the Start Menu.

FIGURE 2.24   Teredo and IPv6 PNRP structure

Time	Source	Destination	Protocol	Info
88 15.301866	2001:0:4137:9e50:2810	2001:0:4137:9e50:1864	IPv6	IPv6 no next header
89 15.310901	2001:0:4137:9e50:2810	2002:d093:467d::d093:	ICMPv6	Echo request
90 15.321489	192.168.1.124	70.41.124.129	UDP	Source port: 59021 Des
91 15.321832	2001:0:4137:9e50:2810	2001:0:4137:9e50:205c	IPv6	IPv6 no next header
92 15.330986	65.55.129.172	192.168.1.124	UDP	Source port: pnrp-port
93 15.331173	65.55.129.172	192.168.1.124	UDP	Source port: pnrp-port

⊞ User Datagram Protocol, Src Port: 59021 (59021), Dst Port: teredo (3544)
   Teredo IPv6 over UDP tunneling

Remote Assistance can also be incorporated in Group Policy in an enterprise environment by having the expert user configured as a Helper for users in the enterprise (by domain or OU). Once configured as a Helper, the expert can initiate a Remote Assistance session by issuing the command msra /offerra. This will bring up the Who Do You Want To Help? Remote Assistance screen.

The expert can also include the novice user's IP address or computer name as an option to the offerRA switch to initiate the Remote Assistance session in one step (e.g., msra / offerra ipaddress | computername).

There are several msra.exe switches available to further control the establishment of the Remote Assistance session for both the novice and the expert user. Table 2.12 highlights many of the switches.

TABLE 2.12   MSRA command-line switches

Switch	OS availability	Functionality
/?	Vista and above	Displays the help options.
/novice	Vista and above	Starts Remote Assistance at the Invite screen.
/expert	Vista and above	Starts Remote Assistance at the Help Someone screen.
/offerRA ip | computer	Vista and above	Starts Remote Assistance at the Expert Initiated screen or with the options, by automatically initiating with the novice user (used with Group Policy configured in an enterprise environment).

TABLE 2.12 MSRA command-line switches *(continued)*

Switch	OS availability	Functionality
/email *password*	Vista and above	Creates an email invitation to be sent to an expert user to request assistance using the novice's default email program; a random password will be generated and needs to be conveyed to the expert, or alternatively a password can be specified with the password option and conveyed to the expert.
/saveasfile *path password*	Vista and above	Creates a file invitation to be given to an expert user to request assistance; a random password will be generated, or optionally a password can be specified with the *password* option and conveyed to the expert.
/openfile *path*	Vista and above	Used to open the invitation file sent to the expert; can be local or on a shared network drive; the expert will enter the password given to the user when the session was initiated.
/geteasyhelp	Windows 7 and above	Starts a novice user's Remote Assistance session using Easy Connect; presents the novice with the password to convey to the expert user.
/offereasyhelp	Windows 7 and above	Starts an expert user's Remote Assistance session using Easy Connect; presents the expert user with the screen to enter the password from the novice user.
/getcontacthelp *address*	Windows 7 and above	Reestablishes a Remote Assistance session from a novice user's machine to the address from the previous session. The address is in the RAContactHistory .xml file as a 20-byte hexadecimal string with an .RAContact extension.
/offercontacthelp *address*	Windows 7 and above	Reestablishes a Remote Assistance session from an expert user's machine to the address from the previous session. The address is in the RAContactHistory .xml file as a 20-byte hexadecimal string with an .RAContact extension.

Whichever way the novice or the expert launches the feature, the Windows Remote Assistance screen will become available (see Figure 2.25). To start using Easy Connect, the novice user will select Invite Someone You Trust To Help You.

FIGURE 2.25   Remote Assistance initial screen

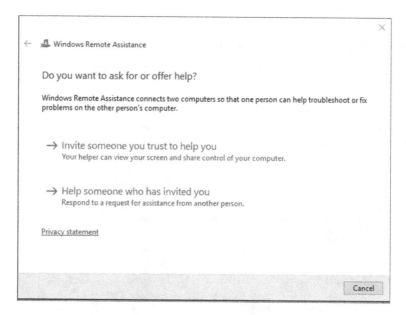

One nice feature of Easy Connect is that if the novice user has established an Easy Connect session previously with an expert user, the screen after selecting Use Easy Connect will offer the novice the ability to connect to the same expert. The novice user can also choose to invite someone new and/or delete the old contact. The expert user will have the same option after choosing Use Easy Connect from the machine used for a previous Easy Connect session.

After the Use Easy Connect option is selected, Windows 10/11 will verify network connectivity briefly. This is the point at which the PNRP actions take place and the novice user's information is added to a cloud on the Internet. The cloud is the group of machines holding little pieces of information—the identifiers of users needing connectivity, set up in a peer-to-peer sharing environment. PNRP uses this distributed infrastructure for its peer-to-peer name resolution. The novice user's contact information is entered into the PNRP cloud, and an associated password is created and displayed to the novice user.

The novice user will now relay the password to the expert by text message, telephone, or any convenient conversation method. The novice will simply have to wait for the expert to initiate their part. The novice user will still have to accept the connection once the expert starts the remote assistance session.

The expert user needs to start a Remote Assistance session the same way the novice did in Figure 2.25, but the expert will choose Help Someone Who Has Invited You from the Windows Remote Assistance screen.

The expert user will be presented with a dialog box to Use an invitation file and then after you choose the file, you will be prompted to enter the password (Figure 2.26) to connect to the Remote Assistance session.

FIGURE 2.26   Remote Assistance screen

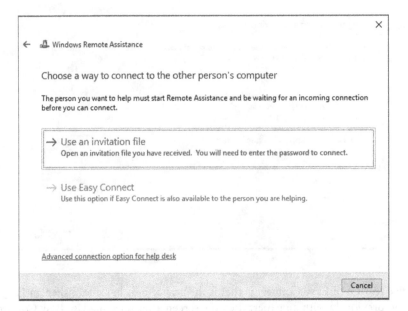

After a few moments of querying the PNRP cloud and finding the connection information that provides the path back to the novice user, Remote Assistance presents the novice user with a confirmation box verifying that the user wants to allow help from the expert.

The novice user will then have a control bar on their screen indicating that the Remote Assistance session is active. From this control bar, the novice can initiate a chat session with the expert and modify some general session settings (bandwidth, logging, contact information exchange, and sharing control).

The expert user will be shown the novice user's Desktop within a separate Remote Assistance window. The expert user will also have some general configuration-setting capabilities as well as an option to request control of the novice user's desktop. The novice user will, of course, be allowed to accept or reject the expert's request.

The expert and novice user can now have an interactive session in which the necessary assistance can be provided. This method of help really takes out the "can you tell me what you see on your screen" issues between two users. The Easy Connect feature takes one more problem out of the equation, getting a novice user to send an invitation to another user. The one caveat here is that both users must be using Windows 10/11 for Easy Connect to be an option.

Now what if the user is not available to send you the invitation? You can still connect to a user's computer using Remote Desktop, which I will discuss in the next section.

Remote Desktop

Remote Desktop is a tool in Windows 10/11 that allows you to take control of a remote computer's keyboard, video, and mouse. This tool does not require someone to be available to collaborate with you on the remote computer. While the remote computer is being accessed, locally it remains locked and any actions that are performed remotely will not be visible to the monitor that is attached to the remote computer.

Windows 10/11 Remote Desktop is, again, an enhanced version of the remote desktop functionality that has been with us for many of the previous versions of Windows, both client and server operating systems. Remote Desktop uses Remote Desktop Protocol (RDP) to provide the data between a host and a client machine. Windows 10/11 Remote Desktop features are as follows:

- RDP core performance enhancements.
- True multimonitor support.
- Direct 2D and Direct 3D 10.1 application support.
- Bi-directional audio support.
- Multimedia and Media Foundation support.
- Remote FX has a few end-user enhancements for RDP. These enhancements allow for an enhanced desktop environment within your corporate network.

There are many uses for Remote Desktop, but the most common use is that of the administrator attempting to perform a task on an end user's machine (or on a server).

Another use is the end user connecting to a machine from their home or on the road. If you have noticed the enhancements of Remote Desktop (which are enhancements to RDP), you can see that one of the main goals of enhancing Remote Desktop is to make the user experience as comfortable and seamless as possible.

Real World Scenario

Using Remote Desktop Functionality

I have mentioned many times using Remote Desktop for troubleshooting client computers. As an administrator, I like to just take control of an end-user machine and fix it. Although this can be done in Remote Assistance, the end user is required to allow us to have access and then can watch what we do. In Remote Desktop, we just take control and close the interactive session at the remote machine (yes, the remote end user can block us or take over the session, but not if they want their problem solved).

But there are other uses as well. We provide servers with resources to our clients, and that server may need to be changed or updated on a regular basis (sometimes a couple of changes in a day). Remote Desktop allows us to maintain our servers from wherever we are without impacting the clients or other administrators.

Remote Desktop Connection Options

When connecting to a Remote Desktop host machine, you have several options to enhance the client user session. The options allow configuration for general settings, display options, local resource access, programs to be executed on startup, the user experience, and advanced options for security and Remote Desktop gateway access. The options become available by clicking the Options button in the lower-left area of the initial Remote Desktop Connection screen. Figure 2.27 shows the options window displayed.

FIGURE 2.27   Remote Desktop Connection options

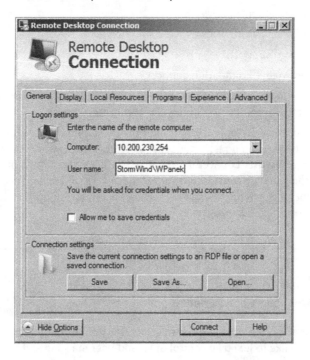

From the General tab, you can select the target remote computer and username. You can save the user credentials from this tab as well. You can save the connection settings to a file or open an existing RDP file from the General tab.

On the Display tab you can choose the size of the display screen. This is also where you select the option to use multiple monitors. The color depth (color quality) is also selected in the Display tab. The option to display the connection bar when using full-screen display is available here as well.

On the Local Resources tab, you can configure remote audio settings, keyboard settings, and local device and resource access.

The Programs tab for Remote Desktop options allows you to select a program to run at connection startup. The program name and path are specified, as is a startup folder if necessary.

The end-user experience is important to the overall success of using Remote Desktop in the user environment. Remote Desktop can be used to provide a user with the ability to connect to their machine and "remote in." The most seamless environment from the user to the remote location is desirable, but that will be dependent on the bandwidth available. The more bandwidth, the more high-end features can be made available to the end user.

This is also nice for the administrator who is working on an end-user machine. The Experience tab allows the configuration of the end-user experience.

Controlling the behavior of the Remote Desktop connection with regard to security is configured on the Advanced tab of the Remote Desktop options dialog box. The Advanced tab also supports the configuration of a Remote Desktop gateway to allow Remote Desktop connections to be established from any Internet location through SSL. The user must still be authorized and the Remote Desktop client must still be available.

In Exercise 2.20, you will enable the Windows client machine to allow Remote Desktop connections. It is up to the company to decide whether all user machines are to be configured this way when you install Windows 10/11 or whether you should do this only when it becomes necessary for a given computer.

EXERCISE 2.20

Enabling Remote Desktop on Windows 10

1. Set up the computer you want to connect to so it allows remote connections:

- Select Start ➤ Settings ➤ System ➤ Remote Desktop, and turn on Enable Remote Desktop toggle switch.

- Make note of the name of this computer under How To Connect To This PC.

2. Use Remote Desktop to connect to the PC you set up:

- On your local Windows computer: In the search box on the taskbar, type **Remote Desktop Connection**, and then select Remote Desktop Connection. In Remote Desktop Connection, type the name of the computer you want to connect to (from step 1), and then select Connect.

- On your Windows, Android, or iOS device: Open the Remote Desktop app (available for free from Microsoft Store, Google Play, and the Mac App Store), and add the name of the computer that you want to connect to (from step 1). Select the remote computer name that you added, and then wait for the connection to complete.

To enable Remote Desktop on Windows 11 the steps are similar; however, to enable Remote Desktop you will need to go to Start ➤ Settings ➤ System, select Remote Desktop, set the Remote Desktop option to On, and then select Confirm. The remaining steps are the same as with Windows 10.

Quick Assist

Quick Assist is another remote management tool that has been around since Windows 10. This is another tool that allows you to remotely control another user's Windows 10/11 system. This tool is similar to the Windows Remote Assistance tool that we discussed earlier in this chapter. Both tools are available with Windows 10/11 client machines.

Quick Assist enables a person to share their device with another person over a remote connection. All that's required is an Internet connection, and the helper must have a Microsoft account.

Quick Assist provides some options that are not available with Windows Remote Assistance, these options include the ability to use the keyboard layout of the helper and a pause button for the help session.

Quick Assist has also moved to a new location with the introduction of Windows 11, so the best way to locate it is by using the Search option from the Start Menu. Either the support staff or a user can start a Quick Assist session. There are a couple ways to open Quick Assist:

- Type **Quick Assist** in the search box and press Enter.
- From the Start Menu, select Windows Accessories, and then select Quick Assist.
- Press Ctrl + [Windows] key + Q.

Quick Assist communicates using port 443 (HTTPS) and connects to the Remote Assistance Service by using the Remote Desktop Protocol (RDP). The traffic is encrypted with TLS 1.2. Both the helper and the sharer must be able to reach these endpoints over port 443.

So, how does Quick Assist work?

1. Both the helper and the sharer start Quick Assist. If you are the sharer, you want to make sure you trust the person assisting you, and you may want to shut down any non-essential applications.

2. The helper selects Assist Another Person. Quick Assist on the helper's side contacts the Remote Assistance Service to obtain a session code. A remote call control (RCC) chat session is established and the helper's Quick Assist instance joins it. The helper then provides the code to the sharer.

3. After the sharer enters the code in their Quick Assist app, Quick Assist uses that code to contact the Remote Assistance Service and join that specific session. The sharer's Quick Assist instance joins the RCC chat session.

4. The helper is prompted to select View Only or Full Control.

5. The sharer is prompted to confirm allowing the helper to share their desktop with the helper.

6. Quick Assist starts RDP control and connects to the RDP Relay service.

7. RDP shares the video to the helper over HTTPS (port 443) through the RDP relay service to the helper's RDP control. Input is shared from the helper to the sharer through the RDP relay service.

How to Use Quick Assist in Windows 10/11

1. Open Quick Assist. Both the helper (you) and the sharer start Quick Assist. Use the Search option from the Start Menu, and type **quick assist** (see Figure 2.28).

FIGURE 2.28   Opening Quick Assist

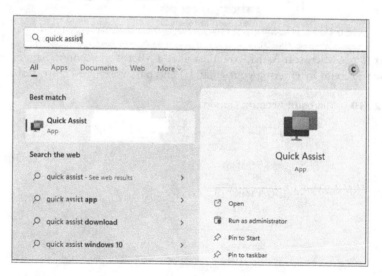

2. Once you open the app, click the Assist Another Person button (see Figure 2.29).

FIGURE 2.29 Quick Assist options

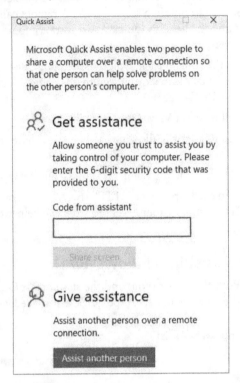

3. In order to use Microsoft Assist, you must have a Microsoft account. Sign in to your Microsoft account by entering your email ID and password (see Figure 2.30).

FIGURE 2.30 Microsoft Account sign-in

4. Once you're signed in, a security code will appear on the screen that will then need to be shared with the person you are helping. If you click Provide Instructions, Quick Assist will provide a brief set of instructions that you can send to the other person so they can do the things they need to on their end (see Figure 2.31).

FIGURE 2.31   Share Security Code screen

Share security code

The person you are helping needs a security code to let you connect to their device.

Security code: 902740
Code expires in **05:45**

How do you want to deliver this info?

Copy to clipboard

Provide instructions

Cancel and start over

5. They will then enter the code in the Code From Assistant text box. The code expires in 10 minutes, so it's best to make sure the person is ready to be assisted before generating the code. Once the code has been entered, it may take a moment to establish the connection.

6. Then, as the helper, you decide the sharing option by clicking the radio button. You can choose either Take Full Control or View Screen. If you choose Take Full Control, the person you are assisting will receive a permission request to allow you to take full control. When they select Allow, you will have full control over their system (see Figure 2.32).

7. The Remote Assist toolbar will appear at the top of your screen with options to conduct the session. In addition to having full control of the cursor, the toolbar presents options such as selecting a monitor, making annotations, viewing full screen, opening the Task Manager, restarting or pausing the session, and ending the session (see Figure 2.33).

8. Once you have finished the assistance session, you can end the session.

FIGURE 2.32   Quick Assist sharing options

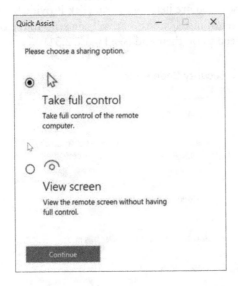

FIGURE 2.33   Quick Assist helper toolbar

Windows Admin Center

The Windows Admin Center runs in a web browser and manages Windows Server 2022, Windows Server 2019, Windows Server 2016, Windows Server 2012 R2, Windows Server 2012, Windows 11, Windows 10, Azure Stack HCI, and more through the Windows Admin Center gateway that is installed on Windows Server or a domain-joined Windows 10/11 machine, or by using your Azure portal. It is a free product and can be downloaded from the Microsoft Evaluation Center at www.microsoft.com/en-us/evalcenter/ evaluate-windows-admin-center.

It should be noted that the Windows Admin Center complements System Center and should not be used as a replacement. The gateway manages the servers by using Remote PowerShell and WMI over WinRM. The gateway is included with the Windows Admin Center download.

There are a few benefits to using the Windows Admin Center:

Simplifies Server Management   It allows you to manage your servers and clusters with current versions of familiar tools such as Server Manager.

Works with Hybrid Solutions   It integrates with Azure to help you connect your on-premises servers to cloud services.

Streamlines Hyperconverged Management   Windows Admin Center can streamline the management of Azure Stack HCI or Windows Server hyperconverged clusters. It allows you to use simplified workloads to create and manage VMs, Storage Spaces Direct volumes, software-defined networking, and more.

The Windows Admin Center will operate only on Google Chrome and Microsoft Edge browsers. While the Windows Admin Center runs in a browser, it does not require Internet access to operate.

The Windows Admin Center dashboard shows the performance of a cluster and resource utilization on a server. It can run Remote Desktop, Event Viewer, and File Explorer, as well as handle a variety of administrative tasks, such as:

- Certificate management

- Firewall administration

- Local user and group setups

- Network setting monitoring

- Process management

- Registry edits

- Roles and features control

- Storage handling

- Virtual switch and Hyper-V VM administration

- Windows services management

- Windows Update management

At the time of writing this book, the Windows Admin Center cannot manage certain roles, such as Active Directory (AD), Dynamic Host Configuration Protocol (DHCP), Domain Name System (DNS), and Internet Information Services (IIS).

The Windows Admin Center also comes with a PowerShell console that allows you to run scripts.

The Windows Admin Center uses role-based access control to restrict features from certain users. Windows Admin Center supports three roles:

Administrator   This role allows the user to access most of the Windows Admin Center tools without the need for PowerShell or Remote Desktop access.

Hyper-V Administrators   This role allows the user to only adjust Hyper-V VMs and switches.

Readers   This role only allows users to see server settings and information, without making any changes.

Enabling PowerShell Remoting

PowerShell is one way to remotely configure and maintain Windows 10/11. It is becoming more and more popular as newer versions of Windows get released. You need to make sure that your Windows systems (including Windows 10/11) can accept remote PowerShell commands. If this feature is not already enabled on your system, you can enable it by running the **Enable-PSRemoting** cmdlet. To enable remote PowerShell commands, you must be an administrator when running the cmdlet. After PowerShell is enabled, you can then enter a PowerShell session on the Windows 10/11 system by using **New-PSSession**. To exit the PowerShell session when completed, run the **Exit-PSSession** cmdlet.

Many PowerShell commands do not require an active PowerShell session when running commands remotely (as long as remote commands are enabled). If you are running a PowerShell command that has the computer name in the command, you can specify the Windows client machine in the command. For example, the following PowerShell command shows the computer name (our Windows client systems are named Computer01 and Computer02):

```
Restart-Computer -ComputerName "Computer01," "Computer02," "localhost"
```

Now that you can connect and run commands on a remote Windows client system, you can also run scripts on Windows 10/11. After you write a PowerShell script (a file that ends in .ps1) for Windows 10/11, you can then run that command remotely by using the **Invoke-Command** cmdlet. The following example is running a PowerShell script on a Windows client machine named Computer01:

```
Invoke-Command -ComputerName Computer01 -FilePath c:\Scripts\DataCollect.ps1
```

PowerShell Remoting

If you would like to see additional commands and information about PowerShell remote connections, visit Microsoft's website:

```
docs.microsoft.com/en-us/powershell/scripting/learn/remoting/
running-remote-commands?view=powershell-6
```

Configuring a VPN Connection

A virtual private network (VPN) is a way to establish a connection between a client machine (VPN client) and server machine (VPN server). A VPN gives you the ability to connect (called *tunneling*) to a server through the use of the Internet or a dial-up connection (hopefully not dial-up), typically with the intention of accessing resources that are available on the network where the VPN server is connected. The VPN server acts as a bridge for the external user connecting from the Internet or other external connections points to the internal network. In a nutshell, a VPN allows you to connect to a private network from a public network.

VPN connections can be secured using various protocols. The following list shows you some of the tunneling protocols that can be used when connecting a Windows 10/11 machine to a remote server:

Internet Key Exchange Version 2 (IKEv2)   Windows 10/11 can connect to a Windows Server VPN using the *Internet Key Exchange version 2 (IKEv2)* VPN tunneling protocol. The IKEv2 VPN protocol is the newest VPN protocol out of all of the following protocols and can be used with Windows Server 2012 and above. The main advantage of using the IKEv2 VPN protocol is that it allows for the interruptions of the network connection. IKEv2 will then automatically restore the VPN connection after the network connection is restored. This feature is referred to as VPN Reconnect, and it is automatically built into the IKEv2 protocol.

Secure Socket Tunneling Protocol   *Secure Socket Tunneling Protocol (SSTP)* was released with Windows Server 2008 and is one of the tunneling protocols available with a Windows Server 2008/2008 R2 server and Windows 7 machines and later. SSTP works by allowing encapsulated Point-to-Point Protocol (PPP) packets to be transmitted over an HTTPS connection. Because of this, firewalls or Network Address Translation (NAT) devices allow SSTP VPN connections to be more easily established. SSTP is the best choice for securing a VPN connection.

Point-to-Point Tunneling Protocol   *Point-to-Point Tunneling Protocol (PPTP)* is one of the predecessors to SSTP, and it also allows point-to-point packets to have encryption for secure connections. PPTP uses TCP/IP for the encryption. PPTP encapsulates PPP frames in IP and uses the TCP for the management side of PPTP.

Layer 2 Tunneling Protocol   *Layer 2 Tunneling Protocol (L2TP)* is a tunneling protocol that has no encryption included in the protocol. L2TP uses the IP Security protocol (IPSec) to make L2TP secure. L2TP with IPSec is a much more secure tunneling option than PPTP.

Before you can connect to a VPN, you must have a VPN profile on the computer. You can either create a VPN profile on your own or set up a work account to get a VPN profile from your company.

Before you start, if it's work related, check for VPN settings or a VPN app on your company's intranet site or contact your company's IT support. If it's for a VPN service you subscribe to for personal use, then visit the Microsoft Store to see if there's an app for that service, then go to the VPN service's website to see if the VPN connection settings you need to use are listed there.

In Exercise 2.21, you will set up a new VPN connection on Windows 10.

EXERCISE 2.21

Setting Up a VPN Connection on Windows 10

1. Select Start ➤ Settings ➤ Network & Internet ➤ VPN ➤ Add A VPN Connection.

2. In the Add A VPN Connection window, do the following:

- For VPN Provider, choose Windows (Built-in).

- In the Connection Name box, enter a VPN connection name.

- In the Server Name Or Address box, enter the address for the VPN server.

- For VPN Type, choose the type of VPN connection you want to create.

- For Type Of Sign-In Info, choose the type of sign-in information (or credentials) you want to use. Enter your username and password in the respective boxes (if required).

3. Click Save.

4. If you need to edit the VPN connection info or specify additional settings, such as proxy settings, select the VPN connection and then select Advanced Options.

Now, that you have a VPN profile, you are ready to connect:

1. On the far right of the taskbar, click the Network icon.

2. Select the VPN connection you want to use, then do either of the following depending on what happens when you select the VPN connection:

- If the Connect button displays under the VPN connection, click Connect.

- If the VPN section in Settings opens, select the VPN connection there, then click Connect.

3. If prompted, enter your username and password or other sign-in info. Once connected, the VPN connection name will display Connected underneath it. To see if you're connected to the VPN, click the Network icon on the taskbar, then see if the VPN connection says Connected.

If using Windows 11, the steps to create a VPN profile are the same, but the steps to connect are a bit different. To connect to a VPN on Windows 11, select Start ➤ Settings ➤ Network & Internet ➤ VPN. Then, next to the VPN connection you want to use, click Connect. Then, if prompted, enter your username and password or other sign-in credentials. Once connected, the VPN connection name will show Connected underneath it. To see if you are connected to the VPN, hover your mouse pointer over the Network icon on the taskbar to see the VPN connection.

Transparent Caching

Windows 10/11 has a feature called *transparent caching* to help reduce the time needed for retrieving shared files and folders. Transparent caching reduces the time required to access files for the second and subsequent times across a slow network.

In previous versions of Windows, to access a file across a slower network, client computers had to retrieve the file from the server computer. But now with Windows 10/11 transparent caching, computers can cache these remote files, thus reducing the number of times a computer might retrieve the same data.

When a user opens a file for the first time, Windows 10/11 accesses the file from the server and then stores the file in the cache of the local disk. From that point on, the user reads the same cached file instead of reading it from the server computer.

To make sure the file is accurate, the Windows 10/11 client always contacts the server to ensure the cached copy is up-to-date. The file would not be accessible if the server is unavailable. Transparent caching is not enabled by default on fast networks. Transparent caching can be enabled through the use of a Group Policy.

Broadband Tethering

One nice advantage to Windows 10/11 and mobility is Broadband Tethering. Let's all pretend that we are at a large Microsoft conference and only one of us in our group can get onto the Internet. Windows 10/11 Broadband Tethering allows at least 10 devices to connect to your Internet connection and use your Internet for their access. As long as their devices have broadband-enabled capabilities, they will be able to connect to your system and use the Internet.

When you set up Broadband Tethering, you can set up a connection name and password for all of the other users in your group to connect to your system.

All you need to do is go to your Windows 10/11 mobile device (see Figure 2.34—I'm using a Windows 10 Surface Pro) and you just need to open your Internet connection by sharing the connection.

As you can see in Figure 2.35, once you open the connection, you need to specify a password (at least 8 characters) and then you can share that password with the other members of your group who you want to allow your Internet to be shared with.

FIGURE 2.34   Manage Wi-Fi Settings

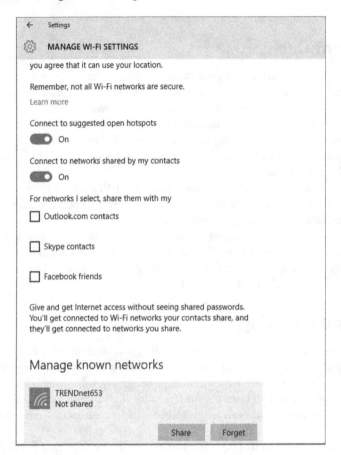

Using PowerShell

PowerShell commands are becoming more important when managing and maintaining Windows devices. Table 2.13 shows some of the common PowerShell commands for user management and remote access.

FIGURE 2.35   Manage Wi-Fi Settings password

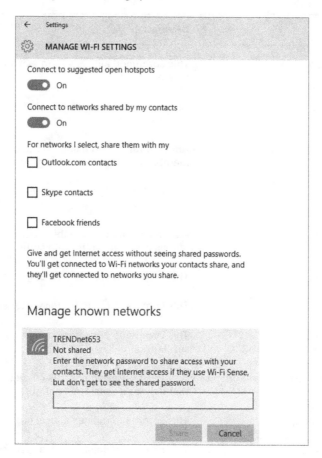

TABLE 2.13   Common PowerShell commands for Windows 10/11

Command	Description
Add-LocalGroupMember	This command adds members to a local group.
Disable-LocalUser	Administrators can use this cmdlet to disable a local user account.
Disconnect-PSSession	Administrators can use this cmdlet to disconnect from a remote PowerShell session.
Enable-LocalUser	Administrators can use this cmdlet to enable a local user account.
Enable-PSRemoting	This command enables remote PowerShell commands on a Windows computer.

TABLE 2.13 Common PowerShell commands for Windows 10/11 *(continued)*

Command	Description
Exit-PSSession	This command allows you to exit a PowerShell session.
Get-LocalGroup	Administrators can use this cmdlet to view a local security group.
Get-LocalGroupMember	Administrators can use this cmdlet to view the members of a local security group.
Get-LocalUser	Administrators can use this cmdlet to view a local user account.
Invoke-Command	Administrators can use this cmdlet to run commands on local and remote computers.
New-LocalGroup	This command creates a local group.
New-LocalUser	This command creates a local user account.
New-PSSession	This command allows you to start a PowerShell session.
New-PSSessionConfigurationFile	Administrators can use this cmdlet to create a file that defines a session's configuration.
Remove-LocalGroup	This command deletes a local group.
Remove-LocalUser	This command deletes a local user account.
Rename-LocalGroup	Administrators can use this cmdlet to rename a local group.
Rename-LocalUser	Administrators can use this cmdlet to rename a local user account.
Set-LocalUser	This command allows an administrator to modify a local user account.

Summary

In this chapter, you learned how to create and manage user and group accounts. We looked at the different tools that can be used to create users in Windows 10/11.

We also looked at Windows client security. We reviewed the difference between LGPOs, which are applied at the local computer level, and GPOs, which are applied through a Windows domain, and how they are applied.

We looked at account policies, which control the logon process. The two types of account policies are password and account lockout policies. We also looked at local policies, which control what a user can do at the computer. The three types of local policies are audit, user rights, and security options policies.

Finally, we looked at how administrators can do remote administration and many of the different utilities that we can use to make sure that our hardware and boot up process is secure.

Exam Essentials

Be able to create and manage user accounts.   When creating user accounts, be aware of the requirements for doing so. Be familiar with User Account Control. Know how to rename and delete user accounts. Be able to manage all user properties.

Know how to configure and manage local user authentication.   Understand the options that can be configured to manage local user authentication and when these options would be used to create a more secure environment. Be able to specify where local user authentication options are configured.

Know how to manage local groups.   Understand the local groups that are created on Windows 10/11 computers by default, and be familiar with the rights each group has. Know how to create and manage new groups.

Know how to set local Group Policies.   Understand the purpose of account policies and local policies. Know the purpose and implementation of account policies for managing password policies and account lockout policies. Understand the purpose and implementation of local policies and how they can be applied to users and groups for audit policies, user rights assignments, and security options.

Understand User Account Control.   Understand the purpose and features of User Account Control. Be familiar with Registry and file virtualization. Understand privilege escalation. Know the basics of the new UAC Group Policy settings.

Understand remote management.   Understand the tools for remote management to assist end users. End-user support is a major concern and a time-consuming endeavor for most IT departments, and these tools can ease administration.

Video Resources

There are videos available for the following exercises:

2.1

2.3

2.4

You can access the videos at www.wiley.com/go/sybextestprep.

Review Questions

1. You are the network administrator for a Fortune 500 company. The Accounting department has recently purchased a custom application for running financial models. To run properly, the application requires that you make some changes to the computer policy. You decide to deploy the changes through a Local Group Policy setting. You suspect that the policy is not being applied properly because of a conflict somewhere with another Local Group Policy setting. What command should you run to see a list of how the Group Policies have been applied to the computer and the user?

   A. gpresult

   B. gporesult

   C. gpaudit

   D. gpinfo

2. You have a Windows 10/11 computer that is located in an unsecured area. You want to track usage of the computer by recording user logon and logoff events. To do this, which of the following auditing policies must be enabled?

   A. Audit Account Logon Events

   B. Audit Account Management

   C. Audit Process Tracking

   D. Audit System Events

3. You are the administrator for a printing company. After you configure the Password Must Meet Complexity Requirements policy, several users have problems when changing their passwords. Which of the following passwords meet the minimum complexity requirements? (Choose all that apply.)

   A. aBc-1

   B. Abcde!

   C. 1247445Np

   D. !@#$%^&*(-[]

4. You are the administrator for StormWind Studios. You want to configure some Local Group Policy Objects (LGPOs) on your Windows 10/11 machines. Which of the following is not configurable through an LGPO on Windows 10/11?

   A. Administrative templates

   B. Folder redirection

   C. Internet Explorer settings

   D. Windows Update settings

5. You are the administrator of a large company. You believe that your network's security has been compromised. You do not want hackers to be able to repeatedly attempt user logon with different passwords. What Local Security Policy box should you define?

   A. Password Policy

   B. Audit Policy

   C. Security Options

   D. Account Lockout Policy

6. You have recently hired Will as an assistant for network administration. You have not decided how much responsibility you want Will to have. In the meantime, you want Will to be able to restore files on Windows client computers in your network, but you do not want Will to be able to run the backups. What is the minimum assignment that will allow Will to complete this task?

   A. Add Will to the Administrators group.

   B. Grant Will the Read right to the root of each volume he will back up.

   C. Add Will to the Backup Operators group.

   D. Grant Will the user right Restore Files and Directories.

7. You are the network administrator of a medium-size company. Your company requires a fair degree of security, and you have been tasked with defining and implementing a security policy. You have configured password policies so that users must change their passwords every 30 days. Which password policy would you implement if you want to prevent users from reusing passwords they have used recently?

   A. Passwords Must Be Advanced.

   B. Enforce Password History.

   C. Passwords Must Be Unique.

   D. Passwords Must Meet Complexity Requirements.

8. You are the administrator for your company network. You and a colleague are discussing a Windows 10/11 feature that, when configured, will lock a device down so that it can only run trusted applications that are defined in your code integrity policies. What is this feature called?

   A. Credential Guard

   B. Device Guard

   C. Local Security Authority (LSA)

   D. Virtualization-Based Security (VBS)

9. You have been asked to create a new local user on a Windows client by using Windows PowerShell. Which of the following PowerShell commands allow you to create a new local user?

   A. `Add-LocalUser`

   B. `New-WindowsUser`

   C. `New-LocalUser`

   D. `Add-WindowsUser`

10. You are the administrator for your company network. You have a Windows client computer that is part of a workgroup. You run the following command on the computer:

```
New-LocalUser -Name NewUser -NoPassword
Add-LocalGroupMember User -Member NewUser
```

What does this do to the computer configuration?

A. NewUser appears on the sign-in screen and can log in without a password.

B. NewUser appears on the sign-in screen but must set a new password on the first login attempt.

C. NewUser is prevented from logging in until an administrator manually sets a password for the user.

D. NewUser is prevented from logging in until the user is assigned additional user rights.

11. You are the administrator for your company network. You have a Windows client computer. You need to configure User Account Control (UAC) to prompt you for your credentials. Which setting should you modify so you will be prompted for your credentials?

A. You should modify the Administrators Properties in Local Users and Groups.

B. You should modify the Security options in Local Group Policy Editor.

C. You should modify the User Account Control settings in Control Panel.

D. You should modify the User Rights Assignment in Local Group Policy Editor.

12. You are the administrator for your company network. What port should you open on your firewall if you want to use Device Health Attestation on your network or in the cloud?

A. You should open port 25.

B. You should open port 110.

C. You should open port 443.

D. You should open port 995.

13. You are the administrator for your company network. You have a Windows client computer, named Computer1, which has a service named App1 that is configured to log on as an account named Service1. You find out that a user has used the Service1 account to sign into the computer and delete some files. You need to ensure that the account that is used by App1 cannot be used by a user to sign into the computer. Using the principle of least privilege, what should you do?

A. On Computer1, configure App1 to sign in as a Local System account and then select the Allow Service To Interact With Desktop check box. Then, you should delete the Service1 account.

B. On Computer1, assign the Service1 account the deny log on locally user right.

C. On Computer1, assign the Service1 account the deny log on as a service user right.

D. On Computer1, configure App1 to sign in as a Guest account and then select the Allow Service To Interact With Desktop check box. Then, you should delete the Service1 account.

14. You are the administrator for your company network. You have a Window client computer that contains a folder named MyFolder. Which action(s) should you take to log any users who take ownership of the files within the folder? (Choose all that apply.)

    A. Configure the Audit File System setting from a Group Policy object (GPO).

    B. Configure the Audit Sensitive Privilege Use setting from a Group Policy object (GPO).

    C. Install the Remote Server Administration Tools (RSAT).

    D. In MyFolder, modify the Advanced Security Settings.

    E. In MyFolder, modify the folder attributes.

15. You are the administrator for your company network. You have several Windows client computers that are part of a workgroup. You want to prevent the employees from using Microsoft Store apps on their computers. How should you achieve this task?

    A. Configure the Security Options from Security Settings in the Local Group Policy.

    B. Configure the Software Restriction Policies from Security Settings in the Local Group Policy.

    C. Configure the Store settings from Administrative Templates in the Local Group Policy.

    D. Configure the Store Restriction Policies from Security Settings in the Local Group Policy.

16. You are the administrator for your company network. You have about 25 Windows client computers. You have configured the computers to forward all events to a computer named Computer1. When you log into Computer1, you do not see any of the security events from the other computers. What should you do to ensure that the security events are forwarded to Computer1?

    A. Add the account of Computer1 to the Event Log Readers group on Computer1.

    B. Add the Network Service account to the Event Log Readers group on each computer.

    C. Run wecutil ac /q on each computer.

    D. Run winrm qc -q on each computer.

17. You are the administrator for your company network. You have several Windows 10/11 Enterprise desktop computers that are members of an Active Directory domain. The standard domain user accounts are configured with mandatory user profiles. What should you do if you have several users who have been transferred into a different department and you need to modify their profiles?

    A. Change the extension of the NTUSER.MAN file in the user profile directory to NTUSER.DAT.

    B. Configure the user's document library to include folders from network shares.

    C. Remove the .man extension from the user profile name.

    D. Use Group Policy to configure folder redirection.

18. You are the administrator for your company network. Your network contains an Active Directory domain and Windows client computers. Which group would you add a user to if you wanted them to be able to remotely create and modify the shares on the computers?

   A. You would add the user to the Administrators group.

   B. You would add the user to the Network Configuration Operators group.

   C. You would add the user to the Power Users group.

   D. You would add the user to the Remote Management Users group.

19. You are the administrator for your company network. You recently had an employee resign and another user has been hired to take over their position. This new user has been assigned the old user's laptop. You want the new user to have access to all of the same resources as the old employee. What is the easiest way to handle the new employee's transition into the position?

   A. Copy the old employee's account and name the new copied account the name of the new hire.

   B. Do a search in the Registry and replace all of the old employee's entries with the new hire's name.

   C. Rename the old employee's account to the new hire's name.

   D. Take ownership of all of the old employee's resources and assign the new hire Full Control to the resources.

20. You are the administrator for your company network. A new corporate policy has been initiated where the company wants to start using virtual smart cards on the Windows client laptops and tablets. Before you implement any changes, you want to ensure that the systems can support the virtual smart cards. What should you do to verify that the systems can support the virtual smart cards?

   A. Ensure that BitLocker Drive Encryption is enabled on a system drive.

   B. Ensure that the laptops and tablets are running Windows 10/11 Enterprise Edition.

   C. Ensure that each laptop and tablet can read a physical smart card.

   D. Ensure that each laptop and tablet have a Trusted Platform Module (TPM) chip.

Chapter

3

Managing Data

MICROSOFT EXAM OBJECTIVES COVERED IN THIS CHAPTER:

✓ **Configure and manage storage**

- Configure file and folder permissions; configure OneDrive on Windows client.

✓ **Manage security settings on Windows client**

- Implement BitLocker.

One of the most fundamental tasks in network management is setting up users' rights and permissions. This is by far one of the most important tasks that we as IT members face every day. Too much access and your users can cause issues. Not enough access and your users can't do their job.

One way to help make sure your users don't have more permissions or security than they need is to use groups. Groups are used to ease network administration by grouping users together who have similar permission requirements. Groups are an important part of network management.

When setting up network data, one of the most important topics that you need to understand are how NTFS and shared resources work together and how to secure the network hardware. So that's where this chapter comes into play.

In this chapter I will also talk about users accessing resources on a network. If you think about it, that's one of the main reasons we set up networks: to share resources. If we didn't have resources that users needed access to, why even bother setting up a network? So, I will talk about sharing resources and assigning permissions to those shares.

You will then learn about NTFS security and share permissions and how they work independently and together. Finally, I will introduce you to some of the Windows 10/11 security options, including BitLocker. So, let's start exploring ways to make your data more secure.

Managing File and Folder Security

Setting up proper file and folder security is one of the most important tasks that an IT professional can perform. If permissions and security are not properly configured, users will be able to access resources that they shouldn't. File and folder security defines what access a user has to local resources. You can limit access by applying security for files and folders. You should know what NTFS security permissions are and how they are applied.

A powerful feature of networking is the ability to allow network access to local folders. In Windows 10/11, it is very easy to share folders. You can also apply security to shared folders in a manner that is similar to applying NTFS permissions. Once you share a folder, users with appropriate access rights can access the folders through a variety of methods.

When a user is created on a local Windows client system or if the user is created on an Active Directory domain, the user gets a Security Identifier (SID) number. It is important to remember that when you assign rights to a user, those rights and permissions get associated to the user's SID number and not the username. It's because of this that we can rename user accounts without any issues.

Before diving into the security nitty-gritty, you need to know about the folder options. So, let's start with that discussion.

Folder Options/File Explorer Options

The Windows 10/11 Folder Options/File Explorer Options dialog box allows you to configure many properties associated with files and folders, such as what you see when you access folders and how Windows searches through files and folders.

With the introduction of Windows 11, the File Explorer has been updated with a new look and removed the ribbon-style menu and replaced them with a new command bar that has icons that include Cut, Copy, Paste, Rename, Share, and Delete. In Windows 11, Folder Options is now referred to as File Explorer Options, but for this section, I will still refer to it as Folder Options, as they are one and the same.

There are a number of ways to get to Folder Options. To open Folder Options using File Explorer in Windows 11, press the [Windows] key + E, click the three-dot menu in File Explorer, and select Options. To open the Folder Options dialog box in Windows 10, click Start ➤ File Explorer, select View, and then click Options. You can also access Folder Options in Windows 10 by choosing Start ➤ Windows System ➤ Control Panel ➤ Large Icons View ➤ File Explorer Options.

Regardless of what version of Windows you are using, the three tabs available in Folder Options are the same. You will see the General, View, and Search tabs. The options on each of these tabs are described in the following sections.

Folder General Options

The General tab, shown in Figure 3.1, includes the following options:

- Whether folders are opened all in the same window when a user is browsing folders or each folder is opened in a separate window

- Whether a user opens items with a single mouse click or a double-click

- Whether to have the navigation pane show all folders and automatically expand to the current folder

Folder View Options

The View tab of the Folder Options dialog box, shown in Figure 3.2, is used to configure what users see when they open files and folders. For example, you can change the default setting so that hidden files and folders are displayed. Table 3.1 describes the View tab options.

FIGURE 3.1   The General tab of the Folder Options dialog box

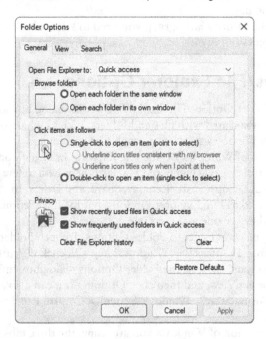

FIGURE 3.2   The View tab of the Folder Options dialog box

TABLE 3.1   Folder view options

Option	Description	Default
Always Show Icons, Never Thumbnails	Shows icons for files instead of thumbnail previews.	Not selected
Always Show Menus	Shows the File, Edit, View, Tools, and Help menus when you're browsing for files.	Not selected
Decrease Space Between Items (Compact View)	On Windows 11, spacing between items has increased. This option allows you to decrease the spacing between items.	Not selected
Display File Icon On Thumbnails	Displays the file icon on thumbnails.	Selected
Display File Size Information In Folder Tips	Specifies whether the file size is automatically displayed when you hover your mouse over a folder.	Selected
Display The Full Path In The Title Bar	Specifies whether the title bar shows an abbreviated path of your location. Selecting this option displays the full path as opposed to showing an abbreviated path.	Not selected
Hidden Files And Folders	Specifies whether files and folders with the Hidden attribute are listed. Choosing Show Hidden Files, Folders, Or Drives displays these items.	Don't Show Hidden Files, Folders, Or Drives
Hide Empty Drives	Prevents drives that are empty from being displayed.	Selected
Hide Extensions For Known File Types	By default, filename extensions, which identify known file types (such as .doc for Word files and .xls for Excel files) are not shown. Disabling this option displays all filename extensions.	Selected
Hide Folder Merge Conflicts	When this box is selected, if you move a folder from one directory to another and that folder already exists, folders will be merged without any warning.	Selected
Hide Protected Operating System Files (Recommended)	By default, operating system files are not shown, which protects operating system files from being modified or deleted by a user. Deselecting this option displays the operating system files.	Selected
Launch Folder Windows In A Separate Process	By default, when you open a folder, it shares memory with the previous folders that were opened. Selecting this option opens folders in separate parts of memory, which increases the stability of Windows 10/11 but can slightly decrease the performance of the computer.	Not selected

TABLE 3.1   Folder view options *(continued)*

Option	Description	Default
Show Drive Letters	Specifies whether drive letters are shown in the folder. When disabled, only the name of the disk or device will be shown.	Selected
Show Encrypted Or Compressed NTFS Files In Color	Displays encrypted or compressed files in an alternate color when they are displayed in a folder window.	Selected
Show Pop-up Description For Folder And Desktop Items	Displays whether a pop-up tooltip is displayed when you hover your mouse over files and folders.	Selected
Show Preview Handlers In Preview Pane	Shows the contents of files in the preview pane.	Selected
Use Check Boxes To Select Items	Adds a check box next to each file and folder so that one or more of them may be selected. Actions can then be performed on selected items.	Not selected
Use Sharing Wizard (Recommended)	Allows you to share a folder using a simplified sharing method.	Selected
When Typing Into List View	Selects whether text is automatically typed into the search box or whether the typed item is selected in the view.	Select The Typed Item In The View

Search Options

The Search tab of the Folder Options dialog box, shown in Figure 3.3, is used to configure how your Windows client searches for files. You can choose to search by filename only, by filenames and contents, or by a combination of the two, depending on whether indexing is enabled. You can also select from the following options:

- Don't Use The Index When Searching In File Folders For System Files
- Include System Directories
- Include Compressed Files (Zip, Cab, . . .)
- Always Search File Names And Contents (This Might Take Several Minutes)

FIGURE 3.3   The Search tab of the Folder Options dialog box

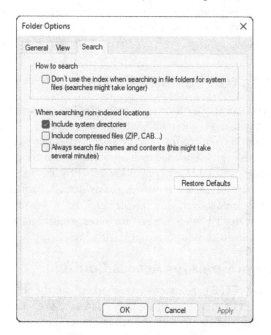

There are several different ways to search for files and folders. In Windows 10, just click Start ➤ Search and type your query in the search box. In Windows 11, there is a dedicated taskbar icon for Windows Search; just click the magnifying glass icon to begin a search.

Understanding Dynamic Access Control

One of the advantages of Windows Server and Windows 10/11 is the ability to apply data governance to your file server. This will help control who has access to information and auditing. We get these advantages through the use of Dynamic Access Control (DAC). Dynamic Access Control allows you to identify data by using data classifications (both automatic and manual) and then control access to these files based on these classifications.

DAC also gives you the ability to control file access by using a central access policy. A central access policy will also allow you to set up audit access to files for reporting and forensic investigation.

DAC can be configured to automatically encrypt Microsoft Office documents with Active Directory Rights Management Service (AD RMS) based on these classifications. For example, you can set up encryption for any documents that contain financial information.

DAC gives you the flexibility to configure file access and auditing to domain-based file servers. To do this, DAC uses the claims of the user for controlling access to the resource.

You have the ability to give users access to files and folders based on Active Directory attributes. For example, a user named Dana is given access to the file server share because in the user's Active Directory (department attribute) properties, the value contains the value Sales.

Securing Access to Files and Folders

On NTFS partitions, you can specify the access each user has to specific folders or files on the partition based on the user's logon name and group associations. Access control consists of rights (which pertain to operations on the system) and permissions (which pertain to operations on specific objects). The owner of an object or any user who has the necessary rights to modify permissions can apply permissions to NTFS objects. If permissions are not explicitly granted within NTFS, then they are implicitly denied. Permissions can also be explicitly denied; explicit denials override explicitly granted permissions.

The following sections describe design goals for access control as well as how to apply NTFS permissions and some techniques for optimizing local access.

Considering Design Goals for Access Control

Before you start applying NTFS permissions to resources, you should develop design goals for access control as a part of your overall security strategy. Basic security strategy suggests that you provide each user and group with the minimum level of permissions needed for job functionality. The following list includes some of the considerations when planning access control:

- Defining the resources that are included within your network—in this case, the files and folders residing on the filesystem

- Defining which resources will put your organization at risk, including defining the resources and defining the risk of damage if a resource is compromised

- Developing security strategies that address possible threats and minimize security risks

- Defining groups that security can be applied to based on users within the group membership who have common access requirements, and applying permissions to groups as opposed to users

- Applying additional security settings through Group Policy if your Windows 10 clients are part of an Active Directory network

- Using additional security features, such as Encrypted File System (EFS), to provide additional levels of security or file auditing to track access to critical files and folders

After you have decided what your design goals are, you can start applying your NTFS permissions.

Applying NTFS Permissions

NTFS permissions control access to NTFS files and folders. Ultimately, the person who owns an object has complete control over the object. The owner or administrator can configure access by allowing or denying NTFS permissions to users and groups.

Normally, NTFS permissions are cumulative, based on group memberships. The user gets the highest level of security from all the different groups they belong to. However, if the user had been denied access through user or group membership, those deny permissions override the allowed permissions. Windows 10/11 offers seven levels of NTFS permissions, plus special permissions:

Full Control   This permission allows the following rights:

- Traverse folders and execute files (programs) in the folders. The ability to traverse folders allows you to access files and folders in lower subdirectories, even if you do not have permissions to access specific portions of the directory path.

- List the contents of a folder and read the data in a folder's files.

- See the attributes of a folder or file.

- Change the attributes of a folder or file.

- Create new files and write data to the files.

- Create new folders and append data to the files.

- Delete subfolders and files.

- Delete files.

- Compress files.

- Change permissions for files and folders.

- Take ownership of files and folders.

If you select the Full Control permission, all permissions will be selected by default and can't be deselected.

Any user with Full Control access can manage the security of a folder. However, to access folders, a user must have physical access to the computer as well as a valid logon name and password. By default, regular users can't access folders over the network unless the folders have been shared.

Modify   This permission allows the following rights:

- Traverse folders and execute files in the folders.

- List the contents of a folder and read the data in a folder's files.

- See the attributes of a folder or file.

- Change the attributes of a folder or file.
- Create new files and write data to the files.
- Create new folders and append data to the files.
- Delete files.

If you select the Modify permission, the Read & Execute, List Folder Contents, Read, and Write permissions will be selected by default and can't be deselected.

Read & Execute   This permission allows the following rights:

- Traverse folders and execute files in the folders.
- List the contents of a folder and read the data in a folder's files.
- See the attributes of a folder or file.

If you select the Read & Execute permission, the List Folder Contents and Read permissions will be selected by default and can't be deselected.

List Folder Contents   This permission allows the following rights:

- Traverse folders.
- List the contents of a folder.
- See the attributes of a folder or file.

Read   This permission allows the following rights:

- List the contents of a folder and read the data in a folder's files.
- See the attributes of a folder or file.
- View ownership.

Write   This permission allows the following rights:

- Overwrite a file.
- View file ownership and permissions.
- Change the attributes of a file or folder.
- Create new files and write data to the files.
- Create new folders and append data to the files.

Special Permissions   This allows you to configure any permission beyond the normal permissions, such as auditing, and to take ownership. To apply NTFS permissions, right-click the file or folder to which you want to control access, select Properties from the context menu, and then select the Security tab. The Security tab lists the users and groups who have been assigned permissions to the file or folder. When you click a user or group in the top half of the dialog box, you see the permissions that have been allowed or denied for that user or group in the bottom half (see Figure 3.4).

Exercise 3.1 walks you through assigning NTFS permissions.

FIGURE 3.4   The object's Security tab

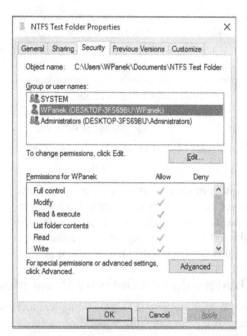

EXERCISE 3.1

Managing NTFS Permissions

1. Right-click the file or folder to which you want to control access, select Properties from the context menu, and click the Security tab.

2. Click the Edit button to modify permissions.

3. Click the Add button to open the Select Users Or Groups dialog box. You can select users from the computer's local database or from the domain you are in (or trusted domains) by typing the user or group name in the Enter The Object Names To Select portion of the dialog box and clicking OK.

    By clicking the Advanced button on the Security tab, you can configure more granular NTFS permissions, such as Traverse Folder and Read Attributes permissions.

4. You return to the Security tab of the folder Properties dialog box. Highlight a user or group in the top list box, and in the Permissions list, specify the NTFS permissions to be allowed or denied. When you have finished, click OK. To remove the NTFS permissions for a user, computer, or group, highlight that entity in the Security tab and click the Remove button. Be careful when you remove NTFS permissions. You won't be asked to confirm their removal as you are when deleting most other types of items in Windows 10/11.

Controlling Permission Inheritance

Normally, the directory structure is organized in a hierarchical manner. This means you are likely to have subfolders in the folders to which you apply permissions. In Windows clients, by default, the parent folder's permissions are applied to any files or subfolders in that folder as well as any subsequently created objects. These are called inherited permissions.

You can specify how permissions are inherited by subfolders and files by clicking the Advanced button on the Security tab of a folder's Properties dialog box. This calls up the Permissions tab of the Advanced Security Settings dialog box. To edit these options, click the Disable Inheritance button. You can edit the following options:

- Convert Inherited Permissions Into Explicit Permissions On This Object
- Remove All Inherited Permissions From This Object

If an Allow or a Deny item in the Permissions list on the Security tab has a shaded check mark, this indicates that the permission was inherited from an upper-level folder. If a check mark is not shaded, it means the permission was applied at the selected folder. This is known as an explicitly assigned permission. Knowing which permissions are inherited and which are explicitly assigned is useful when you need to troubleshoot permissions.

Understanding Ownership and Security Descriptors

When an object is initially created on an NTFS partition, an associated security descriptor is created. A security descriptor contains the following information:

- The user or group who owns the object
- The users and groups who are allowed or denied access to the object
- The users and groups whose access to the object will be audited

After an object is created, the owner of the object has full permissions to change the information in the security descriptor, even for members of the Administrators group. You can view the owner of an object from the Security tab of the specified folder's Properties dialog box by clicking the Advanced button.

Although the owner of an object can set the permissions of an object so that the administrator can't access the object, the administrator or any member of the Administrators group can take ownership of an object and thus manage the object's permissions. When you take ownership of an object, you can specify whether you want to replace the owner on subdirectories and subobjects of the object. If you would like to see who owns a directory from the command prompt, type **dir /q**.

Determining and Viewing Effective Permissions for NTFS

To determine a user's effective permissions (the aggregate permissions the user has to a file or folder), add all of the permissions that have been allowed through the user's assignments based on that user's username and group associations. After you determine what the user is allowed, you subtract any permissions that have been denied the user through the username or group associations.

As an example, suppose that user Marilyn is a member of both the Accounting and Execs groups. The following assignments have been made to the Accounting group permissions:

Permission	Allow	Deny
Full Control		
Modify	X	
Read & Execute	X	
List Folder Contents		
Read		
Write		

The following assignments have been made to the Execs group permissions:

Permission	Allow	Deny
Full Control		
Modify		
Read & Execute		
List Folder Contents		
Read	X	
Write		

To determine Marilyn's effective rights, you combine the permissions that have been assigned. The result is that Marilyn's effective rights are Modify, Read & Execute, and Read, so she effectively has Modify (the highest right).

As another example, suppose that user Dan is a member of both the Sales and Temps groups. The following assignments have been made to the Sales group permissions:

Permission	Allow	Deny
Full Control		
Modify	X	
Read & Execute	X	
List Folder Contents	X	

(continued)

Permission	Allow	Deny
Read	X	
Write	X	

The following assignments have been made to the Temps group permissions:

Permission	Allow	Deny
Full Control		
Modify		X
Read & Execute		
List Folder Contents		
Read		
Write		X

To determine Dan's effective rights, you start by seeing what Dan has been allowed: Modify, Read & Execute, List Folder Contents, Read, and Write permissions. You then remove anything that he is denied: Modify and Write permissions. In this case, Dan's effective rights are Read & Execute, List Folder Contents, and Read.

If permissions have been applied at the user and group levels and inheritance is involved, it can sometimes be confusing to determine what the effective permissions are. To help identify which effective permissions will actually be applied, you can view them from the Effective Access tab of Advanced Security Settings, or you can use the icacls command.

To see what the effective permissions are for a user or group, you click the Select button and then type in the user or group name. Then click OK. If a box is selected and not shaded, then explicit permissions have been applied at that level. If the box is shaded, then the permissions to that object were inherited.

The icacls command can also be used to display or modify user access permissions. The options associated with the icacls command are as follows:

- /grant grants permissions.
- /remove revokes permissions.
- /deny denies permissions.
- /setintegritylevel sets an integrity level of Low, Medium, or High.

One issue that IT people run into is what happens to the security when you move or copy a file or folder. Let's take a look at NTFS permissions when they are moved or copied.

Determining NTFS Permissions for Copied or Moved Files

When you copy or move NTFS files, the permissions that have been set for those files might change. The following are guidelines to predict what will happen:

- If you move a file from one folder to another folder on the same volume, the file will retain the original NTFS permissions.

- If you move a file from one folder to another folder between different NTFS volumes, the file is treated as a copy and will have the same permissions as the destination folder.

- If you copy a file from one folder to another folder on the same volume or on a different volume, the file will have the same permissions as the destination folder.

- If you copy or move a file or folder to a FAT partition, it will not retain any NTFS permissions.

Managing Network Access

In every network, there are resources to which the users need to gain access. As IT professionals, we share these resources so that our users can do their jobs.

Sharing is the process of allowing network users access to a resource located on a computer. A network share provides a single location to manage shared data used by many users. Sharing also allows you to install an application once, as opposed to installing it locally at each computer, and to manage the application from a single location.

The following sections describe how to create and manage shared folders and configure share permissions.

Creating and Managing Shared Folders

In Windows 10/11, you can share a folder in two ways. To use the Sharing Wizard, right-click a folder and select Share. If the Sharing Wizard feature is enabled, you will see the File Sharing screen, where you can add local users. Alternatively, you can access the wizard by right-clicking a folder and then selecting Properties ➤ Sharing tab ➤ Share button.

However, you cannot use the Sharing Wizard to share resources with domain users. To share a folder with domain users, right-click the folder and select Properties; then select the Sharing tab, shown in Figure 3.5.

The Share button will take you to the Sharing Wizard. To configure Advanced Sharing, click the Advanced Sharing button, which will open up the Advanced Sharing dialog box.

When you share a folder, you can configure the options listed in Table 3.2.

FIGURE 3.5 The Sharing tab of a folder's Properties dialog box

TABLE 3.2 Shared folder options

Option	Description
Share This Folder	Makes the folder available through local access and network access.
Share Name	A descriptive name by which users will access the folder.
Comments	Additional descriptive information about the share (optional).
Limit The Number Of Simultaneous Users To	The maximum number of connections to the share at any one time (no more than 20 users can simultaneously access a share on a Windows client computer).
Permissions	How users will access the folder over the network.
Caching	How folders are cached when the folder is offline.

If you share a folder and then decide that you do not want to share it, just deselect the Share This Folder check box. You can easily tell that a folder has been shared by the group icon located at the bottom left of the folder icon.

Keep in mind the following regarding sharing:

- Only folders, not files, can be shared.
- Share permissions can be applied only to folders and not to files.
- If a folder is shared over the network and a user is accessing it locally, then share permissions will not apply to the local user; only NTFS permissions will apply.
- If a shared folder is copied, the original folder will still be shared but not the copy.
- If a shared folder is moved, the folder will no longer be shared.
- If the shared folder will be accessed by a mixed environment of clients, including some that do not support long filenames, you should use the 8.3 naming format for files.
- Folders can be shared through the Net Share command-line utility.

Now let's take a look at configuring share permissions for your users.

Configuring Share Permissions

You can control users' access to shared folders from the network by assigning share permissions. Share permissions are less complex than NTFS permissions and can be applied only to folders (unlike NTFS permissions, which can be applied to files and folders).

To assign share permissions, click the Permissions button in the Advanced Sharing dialog box. This brings up the Share Permissions dialog box, shown in Figure 3.6.

FIGURE 3.6   The Share Permissions dialog box

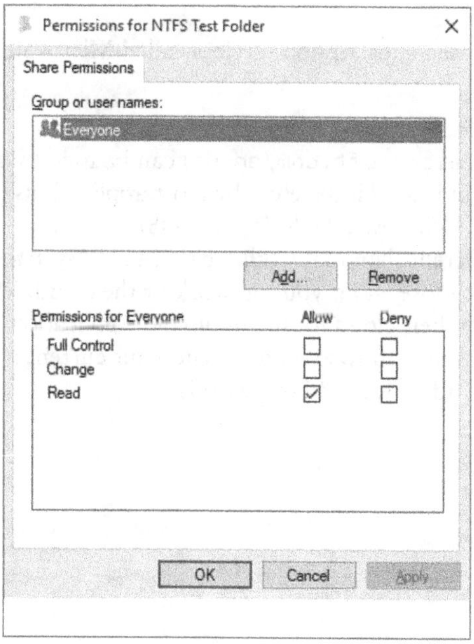

You can assign three types of share permissions:

Full Control   Allows full access to the shared folder.

Change   Allows users to change data within a file or to delete files.

Read   Allows a user to view and execute files in the shared folder. Read is the default permission on shared folders for the Everyone group.

Shared folders do not use the same concept of inheritance as NTFS folders. If you share a folder, there is no way to block access to lower-level resources through share permissions. One thing that is the same between shared and NTFS is that all shared permissions are additive if you belong to multiple groups. This means that you add up all the permissions of the groups and get the highest permission.

When applying conflicting share and NTFS permissions, the most restrictive permissions win. Remember that share and NTFS permissions are both applied only when a user is accessing a shared resource over a network. Only NTFS permissions apply to a user accessing a resource locally. So, for example, if a user's NTFS security setting on a resource is Read and the share permission on the same resource is Full Control, the user would have only Read permission when they connect to the shared resource. The most restrictive set of permissions wins.

Cloud-Based Storage

One of the fastest growing parts of the IT world is cloud-based services. From cloud-based user storage to cloud-based corporate data storage, it seems like the cloud is all we hear about anymore.

Microsoft has cloud-based subscription services called Microsoft Azure and OneDrive.

Microsoft Azure

Microsoft Azure (azure.microsoft.com/en-us) can be used by almost any operating system on the market (Windows, Linux, etc.), by most applications (Java, .NET, PHP, etc.), and by most device types (Windows, Android, and iOS).

Microsoft Azure is different than many other cloud-based systems because Microsoft Azure doesn't make you choose either your network or the cloud. Many cloud-based service providers want you to use their cloud to run all of your applications and/or storage from their location. Microsoft Azure allows you to extend your current network infrastructure into the cloud to take full advantage of both worlds.

This way you can still have a full IT server room with full-time IT employees but get the benefits of storing data both locally and also in a cloud environment, which is then available from anywhere in the world.

One advantage to using Azure is that you only pay for what you need. The more cloud-based storage you need, the more you pay for and the less you need means less money. Table 3.3 shows you the maximum amount of data that can be stored on Azure.

TABLE 3.3   Microsoft Azure data size availability

Operating system	Maximum size of data source
Windows Server 2012 or above	54,400 GB
Windows 8 or above	54,400 GB
Windows Server 2008, Windows Server 2008 R2	1,700 GB
Windows 7	1,700 GB

If you decide that you want your company to use Azure for some of its cloud-based storage or all of its cloud-based storage, please go to azure.microsoft.com/en-us to get the current subscription rates.

Configuring OneDrive

Windows 10/11 includes Microsoft OneDrive with the operating system. OneDrive is a cloud-based storage system where corporate users or home users can store their data in the cloud. It allows users to use up to 5 GB of cloud storage for free without a subscription. Users have the ability to get more cloud-based storage by purchasing a higher subscription. Microsoft's professional version of OneDrive is called OneDrive for Business and is available to companies with a Microsoft 365 subscription.

To set up a corporate user or home user with OneDrive, you must first have a Microsoft account. You can create a Microsoft account at the time you are accessing OneDrive, as shown in Figure 3.7.

Once you have a Microsoft account, you then sign into the OneDrive system. where you can begin uploading data. Figure 3.8 shows OneDrive from the Internet browser. Using the Internet browser, you can control the files that are located in the cloud.

In Exercise 3.2, I will show you how to sign into your Microsoft OneDrive application.

FIGURE 3.7 Microsoft OneDrive Sign-in screen

FIGURE 3.8 Microsoft OneDrive

EXERCISE 3.2

Logging into OneDrive

1. Click the Start button and click the OneDrive tile, as shown in Figure 3.9.

FIGURE 3.9 OneDrive tile

2. A dialog box will prompt you for your email address, where you will enter your email address for your Microsoft account. If Microsoft does not recognize the email address associated with a Microsoft account, you can click Sign Up For A New Account.

   Depending on your setup, you may need to use Microsoft Authenticator to verify the new account.

3. If a Microsoft account is associated with your email, the next screen will prompt you for your Microsoft account and password, as shown in Figure 3.10.

4. The next screen will allow you to start using OneDrive (shown in Figure 3.11).

EXERCISE 3.2 *(continued)*

FIGURE 3.10 OneDrive login

FIGURE 3.11 Start using OneDrive

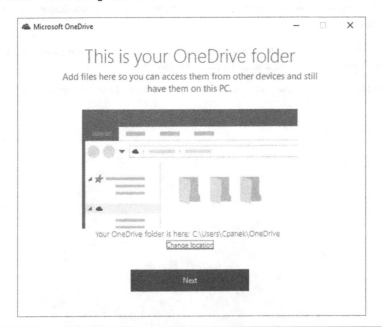

At this point you can start using OneDrive to create and upload files to the OneDrive cloud. You can modify OneDrive settings by clicking the icon for OneDrive (cloud) in the notification tray, clicking the three dots (More), and then choosing Settings. You can choose which folders are synchronized to OneDrive by clicking the Choose Folders button on the Account tab. You can then select which folders you want to synchronize, as shown in Figure 3.12.

FIGURE 3.12   Changing the OneDrive settings

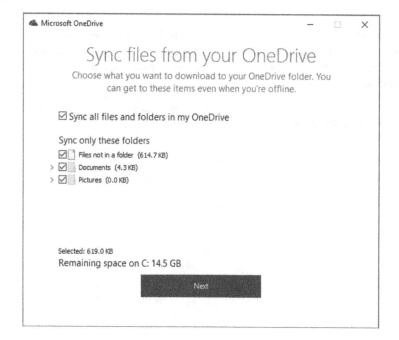

This screen gives you the ability to change how much bandwidth will be used to sync with the cloud, which accounts will be associated to this OneDrive, and many other options. The OneDrive cloud-based storage is a good way to back up some documents for protection of data loss.

With Windows 11, you can now configure OneDrive as the default folder in File Explorer. If you want to use this feature, follow these steps:

1. Open File Explorer ➤ Folder options.

2. Under Open File Explorer, select OneDrive.

3. Click OK.

Now, when you launch File Explorer you can get to the OneDrive folder quickly (see Figure 3.13).

FIGURE 3.13   Getting to OneDrive from File Explorer

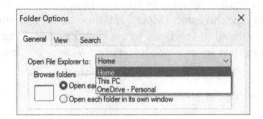

Another OneDrive feature in Windows 11 is a OneDrive icon (see Figure 3.14), which appears in the top-right corner of File Explorer. When you click this icon, a drop-down menu opens that displays the user's OneDrive status, including how much storage capacity remains and file syncing progress.

FIGURE 3.14   The OneDrive icon in File Explorer

Understanding Hardware Security

One issue that we have to face is the protection of not only our data but the hardware that the data resides on. You may remember a case a few years back when an individual stole some hard drives from a VA office. Well, let's take a look at a security measure that will help you protect your data drives from physically being taken.

We must make sure that if anyone steals hardware from our corporation or from our server rooms that the data that they are stealing is secured and can't be used. This is where BitLocker can help.

Using BitLocker Drive Encryption

To prevent individuals from stealing your computer and viewing personal and sensitive data found on your hard disk, some editions of Windows come with a feature called *BitLocker Drive Encryption*. BitLocker encrypts the entire system drive. New files added to this drive are encrypted automatically, and files moved from this drive to another drive or computers are decrypted automatically.

BitLocker is available on:

- Windows Vista & Windows 7 – Ultimate and Enterprise editions
- Windows 8 and 8.1 – Pro and Enterprise editions
- Windows 10 and 11 – Pro, Enterprise, and Education editions
- Windows Server 2008 and later

Only the operating system drive (usually C:) or internal hard drives can be encrypted with BitLocker. Files on other types of drives must be encrypted using BitLocker To Go. BitLocker To Go allows you to put BitLocker on removable media such as external hard disks or USB drives.

On supported devices running Windows 10 or newer, BitLocker is automatically turned on the first time you log into a personal Microsoft account or a work or school account. Bit-Locker is not automatically turned on with local accounts, but you can manually turn it on in Manage BitLocker.

BitLocker uses a Trusted Platform Module (TPM) version 1.2 or higher to store the security key. A TPM is a chip that is found in newer computers. If you do not have a computer with a TPM, you can store the key on a removable USB drive. If you don't have a system with TPM, you will need to turn off the TPM setting in local computer settings, as shown in Figure 3.15. The USB drive will be required each time you start the computer so that the system drive can be decrypted.

If the TPM discovers a potential security risk, such as a disk error or changes made to BIOS, hardware, system files, or startup components, the system drive will not be unlocked until you enter the 48-digit BitLocker recovery password or use a USB drive with a recovery key as a recovery agent.

BitLocker must be set up either within the Local Group Policy editor or through the Bit-Locker icon in Control Panel.

BitLocker Recovery Password/Key

When you set up BitLocker, you have the option to use a recovery key or password. The BitLocker recovery password/key is very important. Do not lose it or you may not be able to unlock the drive. Even if you do not have a TPM, be sure to keep your recovery password in case your USB drive becomes lost or corrupted.

FIGURE 3.15   Changing the TPM settings

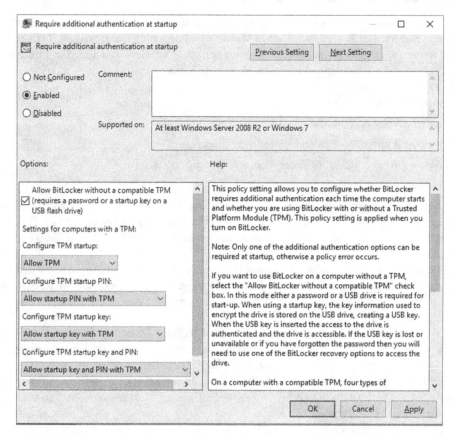

BitLocker requires that you have a hard disk with at least two partitions, both formatted with NTFS. One partition will be the system partition that will be encrypted. The other partition will be the active partition that is used to start the computer. This partition will remain unencrypted.

Features of BitLocker

As with any version of Windows, Microsoft continues to improve on technologies for Windows Server and Windows 10/11. The following sections cover some of the features of BitLocker.

BitLocker Provisioning

In previous versions of BitLocker (Windows 7) the BitLocker provisioning (system and data volumes) was completed during the post-installation of the BitLocker utility. The BitLocker provisioning was done either through the command-line interface (CLI) or Control Panel. In the Windows 8, Windows 10/11, and Windows Server (2012 and above) of BitLocker, you can choose to provision BitLocker before the operating system is even installed.

You have the ability to enable BitLocker, prior to the operating system deployment, from the Windows Preinstallation Environment (WinPE). BitLocker is applied to the formatted volume and encrypts the volume prior to running the Windows setup process.

If you want to check the status of BitLocker on a particular volume, you can view the status of the drive in either the BitLocker Control Panel applet or Windows Explorer.

Used Disk Space–Only Encryption

Windows 10/11 BitLocker has a requirement that all data and free space on the drive has to be encrypted. Because of this, the encryption process can take a very long time on larger volumes. In Windows 10/11 BitLocker, you have the ability to encrypt either the entire volume or just the space being used. When you choose the Used Disk Space Only encryption option, only the section of the drive that has data will be encrypted. Because of this, encryption is completed much faster.

Standard User PIN and Password Change

One issue that BitLocker has had is that you need to be an administrator to configure Bit-Locker on operating system drives. This can be an issue in a large organization due to the fact deploying the Trusted Platform Module (TPM) + PIN to a large number of computers can be very challenging.

Even with the new operating system changes, administrative privileges are still needed to configure BitLocker, but now your users have the ability to change the BitLocker PIN for the operating system or change the password on the data volumes.

When a user gets to choose their own PIN and password, they normally choose something that has meaning and is something easy for them to remember. That is a good thing and a bad thing. It's good because when your users choose their own PIN and password, normally they don't need to write it down—they just know it. It's bad because if anyone knows the user well, they can have an easier time figuring out the person's PIN and password. Even when you allow your users to choose their own PIN and password, make sure you set a GPO to require password complexity.

Network Unlock

One of the features of BitLocker is called Network Unlock. *Network Unlock* allows you to easily manage desktop and servers that are configured to use BitLocker. Network Unlock allows you to configure BitLocker to unlock automatically an encrypted hard drive during a system reboot when that hard drive is connected to your trusted corporate environment. For this to function properly on a machine, there has to be a DHCP driver implementation in the system's firmware.

If your operating system volume is also protected by the TPM + PIN protection, you have to be sure to enter the PIN at the time of the reboot. This protection can actually make using Network Unlock more difficult to use.

Support for Encrypted Hard Drives for Windows

One of the advantages of using BitLocker is *full volume encryption (FVE)*. BitLocker provides built-in encryption for Windows data files and Windows operating system files. The advantage of this type of encryption is that encrypted hard drives that use *full disk encryption (FDE)* get each block of the physical disk space encrypted. Because each physical block gets encrypted, it offers much better encryption. The only downside is the fact that because each physical block is encrypted, it adds some degradation to the hard drive speed. So, as an administrator, you have to decide if you want better speeds or better security on your hard disk.

Windows 7 vs. Windows 10/11

Table 3.4 covers the specific data-protection concerns and how Windows 10/11 and Windows 7 address the issues.

TABLE 3.4   Data protection in Windows 7 and Windows 10/11

Windows 7	Windows 10/11
When BitLocker is used with a PIN to protect startup, computers such as kiosks cannot be restarted remotely.	Modern Windows devices are more likely to be protected with BitLocker Device Encryption out of the box; single sign-on is supported to protect the BitLocker encryption keys from cold-boot attacks.
	Network Unlock allows computers to start automatically when connected to the internal network.
When BitLocker is enabled, the provisioning process may take several hours.	On new computers, BitLocker pre-provisioning, encrypting hard drives, and Used Space Only encryption allow you to enable BitLocker quickly.
There is no support for using Bit-Locker with self-encrypting drives (SEDs).	BitLocker supports offloading encryption to encrypted hard drives.
You have to use separate tools to manage encrypted hard drives.	BitLocker supports encrypted hard drives with onboard encryption hardware built in, which allows you to use the familiar BitLocker administrative tools to manage them.
Encrypting a new flash drive may take more than 20 minutes.	Used Space Only encryption in BitLocker To Go allows users to encrypt removable data drives in seconds.

Windows 7	Windows 10/11
BitLocker could require users to enter a recovery key when system configuration changes occur.	BitLocker requires the user to enter a recovery key only when disk corruption occurs or when the user loses the PIN or password.
Users have to enter a PIN to start the computer and then enter their password to sign into Windows.	Modern Windows devices are more likely to be protected with BitLocker Device Encryption out of the box; single sign-on is supported to protect the BitLocker encryption keys from cold-boot attacks.

There are a number of ways to turn on device encryption and to turn on standard BitLocker encryption. Next, we will discuss a few of those methods.

To Turn On Device Encryption: Windows 10

1. Sign into the Windows device with an administrator account.
2. Select the Start button, then select Settings ➤ Update & Security ➤ Device Encryption. If Device Encryption doesn't appear, that means it isn't available. You may then be able to turn on standard BitLocker encryption instead (see the next subsection).
3. If Device Encryption is turned off, select Turn On.

Turn On Standard BitLocker Encryption: Windows 10

1. Sign into the Windows device with an administrator account.
2. In the search box on the taskbar, type **Manage BitLocker** and then select it from the list of results. Or, click the Start button, and then under Windows System, select Control Panel. In Control Panel, select System And Security, and then under BitLocker Drive Encryption, select Manage BitLocker.
3. Select Turn On BitLocker and then follow the instructions.

To Turn On Device Encryption: Windows 11

1. Sign into the Windows device with an administrator account.
2. Select Start ➤ Settings ➤ Privacy & Security ➤ Device Encryption. If Device Encryption doesn't appear, that means it isn't available. You may then be able to turn on standard BitLocker encryption instead (see the next subsection).
3. If Device Encryption is turned off, select Turn On.

Turn On Standard BitLocker Encryption: Windows 11

1. Sign into the Windows device with an administrator account.

2. In the search box on the taskbar, type **Manage BitLocker** and then select it from the list of results. Or, select Start ➢ Settings ➢ Privacy & Security ➢ Device Encryption ➢ Bit-Locker Drive Encryption.

3. Select Turn On BitLocker and then follow the instructions.

In Exercise 3.3, we will use another method to enable BitLocker on a Windows 10 system. At the time this book was written, BitLocker is controlled using Control Panel. Microsoft has been phasing the Control Panel out, and you may need to eventually use the Windows Settings to configure Bitlocker.

EXERCISE 3.3

Using BitLocker in Windows 10

1. Open Control Panel by typing **Control Panel** in the Windows Search box.

2. Change the View By: Category option to Large Icons by using the pull-down options in the upper-right corner of the window.

3. Click the BitLocker Drive Encryption option, as shown in Figure 3.16.

4. Click the Turn On BitLocker link.

FIGURE 3.16   Clicking the BitLocker option

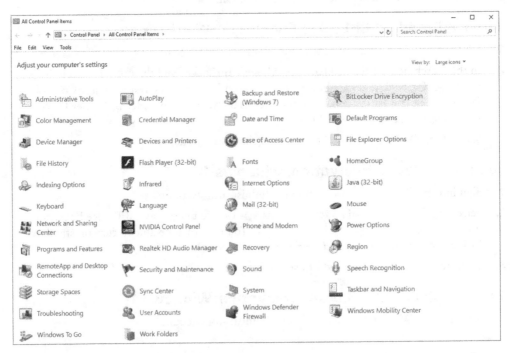

5. On the Choose How To Unlock The Drive screen, click the Enter A Password link.

6. Enter a password, then reenter the password and click Next.

7. On the How Do You Want To Save The Recovery Key? screen, pick one of the options, and after you configure the option, click Next.

8. At the Choose How Much You Want To Encrypt screen, choose to encrypt used disk space or the entire drive. I am choosing the entire drive.

9. At the Are You Ready To Encrypt The Drive? screen, click Continue.

10. The drive will be encrypted. You can unencrypt the drive at any time by choosing Unencrypt Drive from the BitLocker option in Control Panel.

Using the BitLocker Administration and Monitoring Utility

Microsoft BitLocker Administration and Monitoring (MBAM) will allow the IT department to use enterprise-based utilities for managing and maintaining BitLocker and BitLocker To Go. As mentioned earlier, one of the hardest components of BitLocker is managing and maintaining BitLocker deployment and key recovery. This is where MBAM comes into play.

MBAM helps IT departments simplify BitLocker deployment and key recovery while also providing centralized compliance monitoring and reporting. MBAM also helps reduce costs for provisioning and supporting encrypted BitLocker drives.

BitLocker helps protect against the theft of hardware, and MBAM helps an IT department administer BitLocker in an easy-to-use administrative Microsoft Management Console (MMC) interface.

Overview of MBAM

At the time this book was written, Microsoft's latest version of Microsoft Administration and Monitoring is MBAM 2.5 with Service Pack 1.

Microsoft BitLocker Administration and Monitoring (MBAM) mainstream support ended on July 2019 and is currently in extended support until April 2026. Going forward, the functionality of MBAM will be incorporated into Microsoft Endpoint Manager Config Manager (MEMCM). Customers not using Config Manager can utilize the built-in features of Azure AD and Microsoft Endpoint Manager Microsoft Intune (MEMMI) for administration and monitoring.

MBAM helps you handle and administer BitLocker and BitLocker To Go. MBAM offers many of the following features:

- Allows you to automatically set up client computers to use encrypted volumes across the entire enterprise.

- Allows corporate security personnel to rapidly determine if the corporate compliances have been met; also allows them to check the state of individual computers throughout the network.

- You can use Microsoft System Center Configuration Manager as a centralized reporting and hardware management utility that works with MBAM.

- Helps you rapidly assist end users with BitLocker PIN and recovery key requests.

- Allows corporate users to recover their own encrypted devices by using the MBAM Self-Service Portal.

- Give you peace of mind that your users can work anywhere in the world with the knowledge that corporate data is being protected.

MBAM is a downloadable Microsoft utility, but your network must meet certain requirements (MBAM requires the Microsoft Desktop Optimization Pack [MDOP]). Many of these requirements include server installations and are beyond the scope of this book. To learn more about MBAM, go to Microsoft's website to see all of the requirements:

```
http://docs.microsoft.com/en-us/
microsoft-desktop-optimization-pack/mbam-v25
```

Use Configuration Manager to Manage BitLocker Drive Encryption (BDE)

Since support for MBAM will eventually be changing, I thought I'd share a section on Configuration Manager, which is part of the Microsoft Endpoint Manager, to manage BitLocker Drive Encryption. For on-premises Windows clients that are joined to Active Directory, you can use Configuration Manager to manage BitLocker Drive Encryption (BDE).

Configuration Manager provides the following management capabilities for BDE:

- Client deployment:
  - Deploy the BitLocker client to managed Windows devices running Windows 8.1, Windows 10, or Windows 11.
  - For on-premises and Internet-based clients, manage BitLocker policies and escrow recovery keys.

- Manage encryption policies:
  - Select the drive encryption and cipher strength, configure user exemption policy, fixed data drive encryption settings.
  - Determine the algorithms to encrypt the device and the disks that you target for encryption.
  - Force users to get compliant with new security policies prior to using the device.
  - Customize the organization's security profile on a per-device basis.
  - When a user unlocks the OS drive, specify whether to unlock only an OS drive or all attached drives.
- Compliance reports—providing built-in reports for:
  - Encryption status per volume or per device
  - The primary user of the device
  - Compliance status
  - Reasons for noncompliance
- Administration and monitoring website—Allow other personnel (i.e., help desk administrators) outside of the Configuration Manager console to help with key recovery, including key rotation and other BitLocker-related support.
- User self-service portal—Allow users to help themselves with a single-use key for unlocking a BitLocker-encrypted device. Once the key is used, it will generate a new key for the device.

For a BitLocker deployment comparison chart, check out Microsoft's website at `http://docs.microsoft.com/en-us/windows/security/information-protection/bitlocker/bitlocker-deployment-comparison`.

Understanding Smart Cards

Another way to help secure Windows clients is by using smart cards. *Smart cards* are plastic cards (the size of a credit card) that can be used in combination with other methods of authentication. This process of using a smart card along with another authentication method is called two-factor authentication or *multifactor authentication*. Authentication is the process of using user credentials to log onto either the local Windows client machine or the domain.

Smart card support allows you to increase the security of many critical functions of your company, including client authentication, interactive logon, and document signing.

Smart cards are now easier than ever to use and deploy because of the features included with all versions of Windows 10/11:

Enhanced Support for Smart Card–Related Plug and Play and the Personal Identity Verification (PIV) Standard This feature allows users of Windows 10/11 to use smart cards from vendors who publish their drivers through Windows Update, allowing Windows clients to use the smart card without special middleware. These drivers are downloaded in the same way as drivers for other Windows devices. When a smart card that is PIV-compliant is placed into a smart-card reader, Windows 10/11 will try to download a current driver from Windows Update. If a driver is not available, the PIV-compliant mini-driver that is included with Windows 10/11 is used for the smart card.

Encrypting Drives with BitLocker   If your users are using Windows 10/11 Enterprise or Professional, the users can choose to encrypt their removable media by turning on Bit-Locker and then choosing the smart-card option to unlock the drive. Windows will then retrieve the correct mini-driver for the smart card and allow the operation to complete.

Smart-Card Domain Logon   When using Windows 10/11, the correct mini-driver for a smart card is automatically retrieved. This allows a new smart card to authenticate with the domain controller without requiring the user to install or configure additional middleware.

Document and Email Signing   Windows 10/11 users can use smart cards to sign an email or document. XML Paper Specification (XPS) documents can also be signed without additional software.

Use with Line-of-Business Applications   Using Windows 10/11 smart cards allows applications that use Cryptography Next Generation (CNG) or CryptoAPI to retrieve the correct mini-driver at runtime. This eliminates the need for middleware.

Summary

In this chapter, we started looking at how to set up and configure folders on Windows 10/11 and Windows Server systems. You learned about sharing those folders and how to grant access to those folders by using NTFS and shared permissions.

The chapter also covered Dynamic Access Control (DAC) and how it allows you to identify data by using data classifications and then control access to these files based on these classifications.

DAC also gives you the ability to control file access by using a central access policy. This central access policy will also allow you to set up audit access to files for reporting and forensic investigation.

You also learned about BitLocker and BitLocker To Go, including Data Recovery Agent and Microsoft BitLocker Administration and Monitoring (MBAM). The chapter ended with a discussion of two-factor authentication using smart cards.

Exam Essentials

Understand folder options.   Understand the purpose and features of using folders and files. Properly configuring folders and folder access is one of the most important tasks that we do on a daily basis.

Understand NTFS and share permissions.   Be able to configure security permissions and know the difference between NTFS and share permissions.

Know how to use BitLocker Drive Encryption.   Understand the purpose and requirements of BitLocker Drive Encryption. Know which editions of Windows 10/11 (Enterprise, Education, and Professional) include BitLocker.

Know Microsoft BitLocker Administration and Monitoring (MBAM).   Understand the purpose and requirements of MBAM. MBAM allows an IT department to manage all your BitLocker settings through the use of one application.

Understand smart cards.   You need to understand smart cards and two-factor authentication. The reason it is called two-factor authentication is because you need the smart cards and the PIN number (two factors).

Video Resources

There are videos available for the following exercises:

3.1

3.3

You can access the videos at www.wiley.com/go/sybextestprep.

Review Questions

1. You are the IT manager for your company. You have been asked to give the Sales group the rights to read and change documents in the StormWind Documents folder. The following table shows the current permissions on the StormWind Documents shared folder:

Group/User	NTFS	Shared
Sales	Read	Read
Marketing	Modify	Change

What do you need to do to give the Sales group the rights to do their job? (Choose all that apply.)

   A. Give Sales Change to shared permissions.

   B. Give Sales Modify to NTFS security.

   C. Give Marketing Change to shared permissions.

   D. Give Sales Full Control to NTFS security.

2. You are the network administrator for a large organization. You have a Windows 10 machine that needs to prevent data from being accessed if the hard drive is stolen. How do you accomplish this task?

   A. In the System window in Control Panel, set the BitLocker Drive Encryption.

   B. In the Hardware window in Control Panel, select BitLocker Drive Encryption.

   C. In the Device Manager window in Control Panel, select BitLocker Drive Encryption.

   D. In a Local Group Policy, specify BitLocker Drive Encryption.

3. In which editions of Windows 10/11 can you enable BitLocker? (Choose all that apply.)

   A. Windows 10/11 Education Edition

   B. Windows 10/11 Basic Edition

   C. Windows 10/11 Professional Edition

   D. Windows 10/11 Enterprise Edition

4. You have a network folder that resides on an NTFS partition on a Windows client computer. NTFS permissions and share permissions have been applied. Which of the following statements best describes how share permissions and NTFS permissions work together if they have been applied to the same folder?

   A. The NTFS permissions will always take precedence.

   B. The share permissions will always take precedence.

   C. The system will look at the cumulative share permissions and the cumulative NTFS permissions. Whichever set is less restrictive will be applied.

   D. The system will look at the cumulative share permissions and the cumulative NTFS permissions. Whichever set is more restrictive will be applied.

5. You are the network administrator for a medium-sized company. Rick was the head of HR and recently resigned. John has been hired to replace Rick and has been given Rick's laptop. You want John to have access to all of the resources to which Rick had access. What is the easiest way to manage the transition?

   A. Rename Rick's account to John.

   B. Copy Rick's account and call the copied account John.

   C. Go into the Registry and do a search and replace to replace all of Rick's entries with John's name.

   D. Take ownership of all of Rick's resources and assign John Full Control to the resources.

6. Jeff, the IT manager for StormWind, has been asked to give Tom the rights to read and change documents in the StormWind Documents folder. The following table shows the current permissions on the shared folder:

Group/User	NTFS	Shared
Sales	Read	Change
Marketing	Modify	Change
R&D	Deny	Full Control
Finance	Read	Read
Tom	Read	Change

   Tom is a member of the Sales and Finance groups. When Tom accesses the StormWind Documents folder, he can read all the files, but the system won't let him change or delete files. What do you need to do to give Tom the minimum amount of rights to do his job?

   A. Give Sales Full Control to shared permissions.

   B. Give Tom Full Control to NTFS security.

   C. Give Finance Change to shared permissions.

   D. Give Finance Modify to NTFS security.

   E. Give Tom Modify to NTFS security.

7. You are the IT manager for your company. You have been asked to give the Admin group the rights to read, change, and assign permissions to documents in the StormWind Documents folder. The following table shows the current permissions on the StormWind Documents shared folder:

Group/User	NTFS	Shared
Sales	Read	Change
Marketing	Modify	Change
R&D	Deny	Full Control
Finance	Read	Read
Admin	Change	Change

What do you need to do to give the Admin group the rights to do their job? (Choose all that apply.)

A.   Give Sales Full Control to shared permissions.

B.   Give Full Control to NTFS security.

C.   Give Admin Full Control to shared permissions.

D.   Give Finance Modify to NTFS security.

E.   Give Admin Full Control to NTFS security.

8.   Vincent is an instructor for StormWind and he is talking to Paige, the company IT manager. Vince asks Paige to implement some type of two-factor authentication. What can Paige install to complete this request?

A.   Passwords and usernames

B.   Retina scanners

C.   Fingerprint scanners

D.   Smart cards

9.   You are using a Windows 10/11 client and you have created a file called "my text," and it was created in Notepad and has a `.txt` extension type. You need to change the extension type from `.txt` to `.vbx`. What setting do you need to change on the folder so that you can see the extension types?

A.   Deselect Hide Extensions For Known File Types.

B.   Select Unhide Extensions For Files.

C.   Select Show Extensions For Files.

D.   Deselect Hide All File Types.

10.   You are the administrator for your company network. You have a Windows client computer on your network that has classified, sensitive data stored on it. You need to prevent users from copying files from this machine to any removable disk. What should you do to ensure that files cannot be copied to a USB device?

A.   This can't be done; the files can still be copied onto a USB device.

B.   Set the BitLocker Drive Encryption option using the Hardware window in Control Panel.

C.   Set the BitLocker Drive Encryption option using the Device Manager window in Control Panel.

D.   Set the BitLocker Drive Encryption option using a Local Group Policy.

11.   You are the administrator for your company network. You have decided to take advantage of the security provided by shared permissions. The default shared permission for administrators on new folders is which of the following?

A.   Change

B.   Full Control

C.   Read

D.   Write

12. You are the administrator for your company network. You have a Windows client computer that has a network folder, which resides on an NTFS partition. Both NTFS permissions and share permissions have been applied. Which statement best describes how NTFS permissions and share permissions work together when applied to the same folder?

    A. NTFS permissions will always take priority over the share permissions.

    B. Share permissions will always take priority over the NTFS permissions.

    C. The system will look at the combined share permissions and the combined NTFS permissions. Whichever set is least restrictive will be applied.

    D. The system will look at the combined share permissions and the combined NTFS permissions. Whichever set is most restrictive will be applied.

13. You are the administrator for your company network. You have a Windows client computer that needs to have security, so that if the drive is stolen, the data will be prevented from being accessed. What should you to do prevent the data from being accessed from a stolen hard drive?

    A. Set the BitLocker Drive Encryption option using the Device Manager window in Control Panel.

    B. Set the BitLocker Drive Encryption option using the Hardware window in Control Panel.

    C. Set the BitLocker Drive Encryption option using a Local Group Policy.

    D. Set the BitLocker Drive Encryption option using the System window in Control Panel.

14. You are the administrator for your company network. You have been tasked to implement a form of two-factor authentication. What should you implement to meet this request?

    A. Implement and install fingerprint scanners.

    B. Implement and install retina scanners.

    C. Implement passwords and usernames.

    D. Implement smart cards.

15. You are the administrator for your company network. You and a colleague are discussing NTFS. What is an advantage to using NTFS?

    A. Compression

    B. Encryption

    C. Quotas

    D. Security

    E. All of the above

16. You are the administrator for your company network. You have a Windows 10/11 computer named Computer1. On this computer, you create an NTFS folder and assign it Full Control to Everyone. You share this folder as Share1 and assign permissions. You assign User1 Full Control and you assign User2 Change. Given the assigned permissions to the share, what can be performed by User1 and not by User2?

    A. User1 can copy a file created by another user to a subfolder.

    B. User1 can delete a file created by another user.

    C. User1 can rename a file created by another user.

    D. User1 can set the permissions for a file and take ownership of files.

17. You are the administrator for your company network. Your network contains an Active Directory domain that contains a group called Group1. All of the computers in this domain are running Windows 10/11. Every computer has a folder named `C:\Documents` that has the default NTFS permissions assigned. You add a folder named `Templates` to the `C:\Documents` directory on all of the computers. You have to configure the NTFS permissions to meet the requirements for a new company policy, which states that all domain users must be able to open the files within the `Templates` folder, but that only the members of Group1 can edit the files within it. How should you configure the NTFS settings on the `Templates` folder with regard to inheritance?

    A. You should disable inheritance and copy explicit permissions.

    B. You should disable inheritance and remove permissions.

    C. You should enable inheritance.

    D. You should enable inheritance and remove permissions.

18. You and a colleague are discussing using BitLocker. You know that there is a requirement for the number of partitions that are needed. What is the minimum number of partitions that are needed to use BitLocker?

    A. One

    B. Two

    C. Three

    D. Four

19. You are the administrator for your company network. You and a colleague are discussing shared folder permissions. Which of the following are true regarding shared folder permissions? (Choose all that apply.)

    A. Shared folder permissions apply to files.

    B. Shared folder permissions apply to folders.

    C. Shared folder permissions apply locally to the data.

    D. Shared folder permissions apply remotely to the data.

20. You are the administrator for your company network. You and a colleague are discussing whether you want to implement BitLocker onto your corporate network. Which of the following statement is true regarding BitLocker?

   A. BitLocker uses Remote Lock and Wipe.

   B. BitLocker uses Network Unlock.

   C. BitLocker can't protect against a stolen server drive.

   D. BitLocker has to be associated with a corporate SAN.

Chapter

4

Managing the Windows Client Environment

MICROSOFT EXAM OBJECTIVES COVERED IN THIS CHAPTER:

✓ **Configure Windows settings**

  ▪ Configure system settings; configure Microsoft Edge; configure Windows client by using provisioning packages; configure language and region; configure and manage services; install and configure optional features.

✓ **Manage security settings on Windows client**

  ▪ Manage application and browser control settings.

✓ **Manage and use Hyper-V on Windows client**

  ▪ Create and configure virtual machines by using Hyper-V; manage virtual hard drives; manage virtual networks; configure Hyper-V settings; configure and manage checkpoints; enable and use Windows Sandbox.

Now that Windows 10/11 is installed, it's time to start setting up some of the configuration options that we have. In this chapter, we will look at performing post-installation tasks like setting up and configuring the Start Menu, Device Manager, and Cortana.

Another tool that we use in IT to configure the Windows client operating systems is Control Panel. Control Panel is one of the most important configuration tools for Windows 10/11. It includes many icons that can help you optimize, maintain, and personalize the operating system. One of the most important icons in Control Panel is the System icon. The System icon not only has operating-system information, but it also allows you to configure devices, remote settings, and system protection.

All of the same configuration settings that you can set in Control Panel can also be set in the Settings section of Windows 10/11. Microsoft has been slowly moving options from Control Panel to the Settings section. You can still use Control Panel in Windows 10/11 while getting used to the newer Settings section.

Next, we will talk about laptop users. If you use Windows client on a laptop computer, it is important to properly configure your power and mobility options. Configuring these options on a laptop will allow you to get the most out of your laptop and Windows 10/11. There are many different mobility options that you can choose from to help customize the laptop to each individual user.

We will examine how services operate and how to configure your services to start manually or automatically. We will examine how to configure services in the event of a service error.

I will then discuss managing and using Hyper-V on a Windows client machine from how to enable Hyper-V to creating a virtual machine.

Managing Windows

Once you've installed the operating system, the next step is to manage the operating system. If Windows 10/11 is not properly configured, it may cause your IT department issues for a long time.

When you are the IT administrator for a company, you need to make sure that the Windows client systems are configured properly and, in most cases, the same.

There are many ways to do this, such as individually configuring the Windows client systems to use Group Policy Objects (GPOs). Most companies are going to set Windows 10/11 configurations through the use of Windows Server and GPOs, but you still need to understand each component and what it does so that you can configure the proper settings.

The following sections describe many of the configuration options for customizing Windows clients for each user's needs. We will start with configuring the Windows client desktop environment.

Manipulating the Desktop Environment

As I stated earlier in this book, there are a few differences between Windows 10 and 11. Windows 11 is the next client operating system and is built on the same foundation as Windows 10. Windows 11 features a new look, with the Start Menu and taskbar centered along the bottom of the screen, and rounded corners and pastel shades. The Windows 10/11 desktop is the interface that appears when a user logs into the operating system. The desktop includes the wallpaper, Start Menu, tiles, and icons (as shown in Figure 4.1 and Figure 4.2).

FIGURE 4.1   The default Windows 10 Desktop

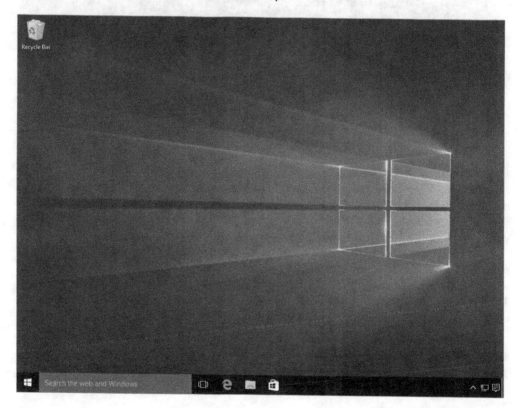

As I mentioned earlier, the Windows 10 Start Menu is located at the bottom left of the desktop by default and includes the default All Apps section as shown in Figure 4.3. The Windows 11 Start Menu is located in the center of the desktop by default, as shown in Figure 4.4.

FIGURE 4.2   The default Windows 11 Desktop

The default desktop appears after a user has logged onto a Windows client computer for the first time. When you install a new instance of Windows client, you will notice that the desktop is clean except for the Recycle Bin. You may also have a message displayed on the desktop that states that the Windows client system has not been activated; an example of what that looks like on a Windows 10 desktop is shown in Figure 4.5.

Users can then configure their desktop to suit their personal preferences and to work more efficiently. The following list describes some of the common default options that appear on the Start Menu, in the Most Used section, Control Panel, and All Apps section. This list includes some of the more commonly used applications and shortcuts; it's not a complete list of every application available to you.

Depending on which version of Windows 10/11 you are using, these options may vary a bit. Also, many options are unavailable for configuration until you activate your Windows client.

FIGURE 4.3   The Windows 10 All Apps section

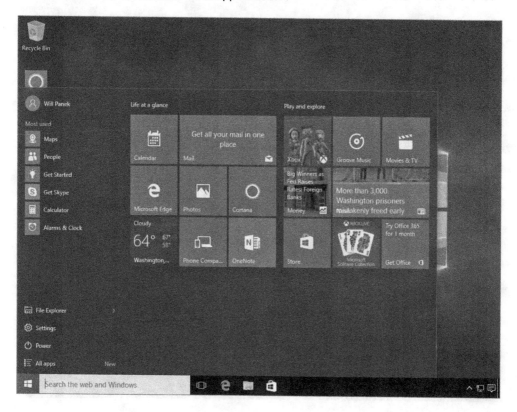

FIGURE 4.4   The Windows 11 All Apps section

FIGURE 4.5 The Windows 10 desktop with an activation notice

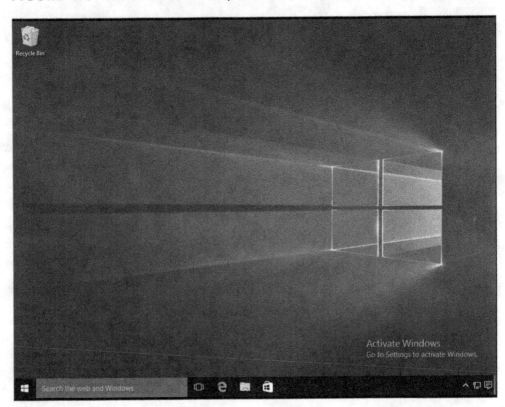

Windows 10/11 Applications

The following are some of the applications for Windows clients. These are not all of the applications installed by default on Windows 10/11, but just a few to get you started:

Calculator This shortcut starts the Calculator program. The Calculator works like any other store-bought calculator, and it can even be changed from a Standard calculator to a Scientific, Programmer, Converter, Volume, Length, Weight & Mass, or Temperature calculator.

Cortana With this application, you can speak or type into the Windows 10/11 system and your personal assistant, Cortana, will try to find answers to queries you may have.

Maps This app allows you to see the current location and area of the Windows 10/11 system. You can use Maps to search for locations and services (food, gas, directions, etc.), as shown in Figure 4.6.

FIGURE 4.6   Maps

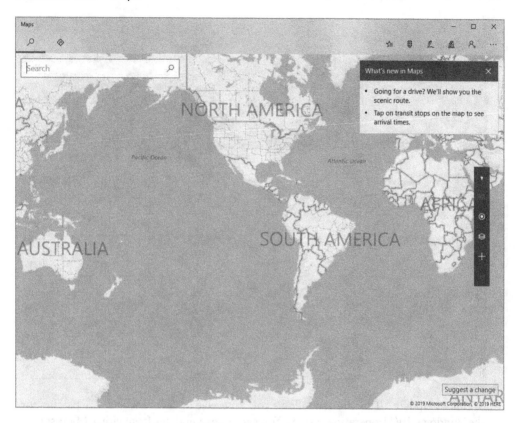

Microsoft Edge   This shortcut starts the built-in web browser. When used with an Internet connection, Microsoft Edge provides an interface for accessing the Internet or a local intranet.

OneDrive   This application allows you to connect with the Microsoft OneDrive cloud-based utility. You can use this application to share documents between the Windows 10/11 system and the OneDrive cloud-based subscription.

People   This application, in Windows 10, allows you to look up and work with your contacts. It enables you to use social media to connect to people and contacts. This app is not available in Windows 11.

Tips   The Tips app in Windows 10/11 allows a user to see Windows client tips and tricks that help any user get the most out of Windows 10/11. Every tip has a button in it that allows you to try the tip out with a single click. An example of what the Tips app looks like in Windows 10 is shown in Figure 4.7.

FIGURE 4.7   Tips app on Windows 10

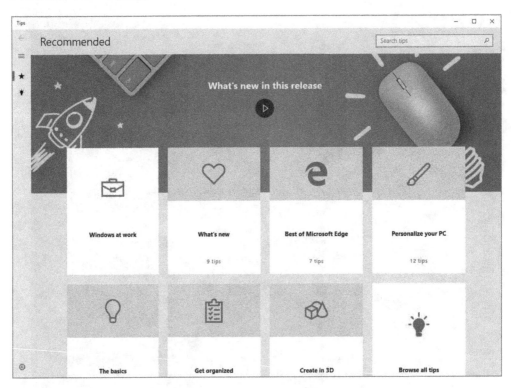

Windows Update   This shortcut allows you to receive updates and security patches for the Windows 10/11 operating system. You can receive updates from either Microsoft's web server or a Windows Server Update Services (WSUS) machine.

XPS Viewer   This application allows you to view Microsoft XML Paper Specification (XPS) files. The XPS viewer also allows you to print these files. Depending on your version release, the XPS viewer may be installed by default. However, in newer versions of Windows 10/11, they have stopped installing the XPS viewer by default and you may need to install it manually if you need the application. To install the application, on Windows 10 clients, open Settings ➤ Apps ➤ Apps & Features ➤ Manage Optional Features ➤ Add A Feature ➤ XPS Viewer.

If you wish to install the XPS Viewer on a Windows 11 client, perform the following:

1. Click Start, then go to Settings.
2. In Settings, select Apps from the list of options on the left.
3. Select the Optional Features tile in the right panel.
4. Click the View Features button.

5. You will see a new Add An Optional Feature window. In the search bar, type **XPS Viewer**.

6. Select XPS Viewer and then click Next.

7. Click Install.

Windows 10/11 Accessories

Windows Accessories are some basic tools that are included with Windows 10/11 to help you do tasks from surfing the Internet to playing DVDs.

Microsoft Edge   This shortcut starts the default built-in web browser. When used with an Internet connection, Microsoft Edge provides an interface for accessing the Internet or a local intranet. Microsoft Edge provides new ways to find pages and read and write on the web, plus get help from Cortana when you need it.

Microsoft Store   This app allows you to download and purchase applications from the Microsoft Store. The Microsoft Store has thousands of business and personal applications that you can use on Windows 10/11.

Notepad   This app allows you to create text files. This is a great way to store notes on the Windows client system without using a full word processing application like Word.

Paint   This shortcut starts the Paint program. The Paint program is an application that allows you to change or manipulate graphics files.

Remote Desktop Connection   This program allows a user to connect remotely to another machine. For you to connect to another computer, Remote Desktop Connection must be enabled on the receiving computer.

Snipping Tool   This tool allows a user to capture an item on the desktop (see Figure 4.8). The user clicks the Snipping Tool and drags the cursor around an area that will then be captured. The captured area can then be drawn on, highlighted, or saved as a file.

FIGURE 4.8   Snipping Tool

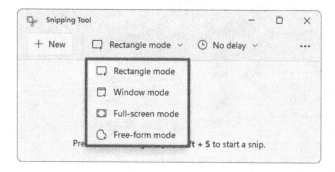

Sticky Notes   This app places a sticky note on the desktop, as shown in Figure 4.9. You can then type a message or reminder into the sticky note. It will remain on the desktop until you delete it.

FIGURE 4.9   Sticky Notes app

Settings   This app opens the Settings window. In the Settings window, you can configure options in the following areas: System, Devices, Phone, Network & Internet, Personalization, Apps, Accounts, Time & Language, Gaming, Ease Of Access, Search, Privacy, and Update & Security. I will be discussing the Settings app in greater detail later in this chapter.

Windows Fax And Scan   This allows you to create and manage scans and faxes. Windows Fax And Scan allows users to send or receive faxes from their workstation.

Windows Media Player   With this app, you can play all your media files, including videos, music, pictures, and recorded TV.

Windows Ease of Access Tools/Accessibility Settings

The Windows Ease of Access Tools on a Windows 10 system helps individuals who have difficulty seeing the screen. The Ease Of Access tools can be accessed via Start ➤ All Apps ➤ Ease Of Access and include a magnifier, narrator, onscreen keyboard, and Windows Speech Recognition, as shown in Figure 4.10.

FIGURE 4.10   Ease of Access tools in Windows 10

In Windows 11, Microsoft has rebranded the Ease of Access Tools and the feature is now called Accessibility. It has also been moved to the Settings section. The redesign is meant to make it easier to find and utilize all the different accessibility features. The new look can be seen in Figure 4.11.

FIGURE 4.11   Windows 11 Accessibility window

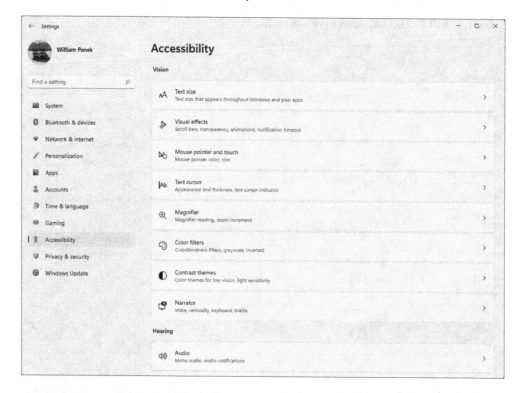

Windows System Utilities

The following utilities can help you manage and control Windows 10/11 systems and applications:

Command Prompt   The command prompt is one of the most useful utilities to an IT administrator. You can run commands through the command prompt and program the Windows client system using system commands.

Control Panel   Control Panel holds many utilities and tools that allow you to configure your computer. It is discussed in greater detail later in this chapter.

Default Apps   When you choose Default Apps (as shown in Figure 4.12), four different configuration items can be accessed: Choose Your Default Apps, Choose Default Apps By File Type, Choose Default Apps By Protocols, and Set Defaults By App.

Devices   This shortcut opens the Devices section, where you can add or configure any of your hardware devices.

FIGURE 4.12   Default Apps in Windows 10

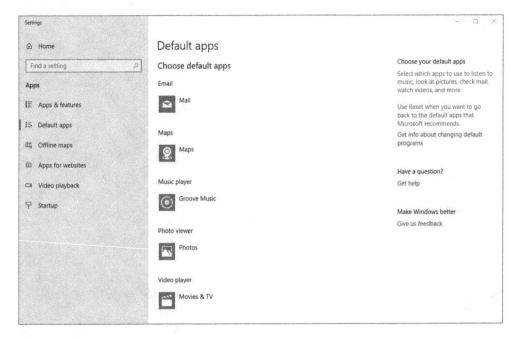

File Explorer   By default, this application shows all the folders and files that are on the Windows 10/11 system. You can use this application to look at all of the files located on the Windows client system.

Run   You can either put in commands or run applications from the Run box.

Task Manager   This is one of the few applications that I used as an IT director on a daily basis. The Task Manager allows you to see what applications are running on the Windows systems (including servers). The Task Manager also allows you to stop applications from running on a system. This utility will be explained in greater detail throughout this book.

This PC   This shortcut allows you to centrally manage your computer's files, hard drives, and devices with removable storage. It also allows you to manage system tasks and to view details about your computer.

Windows User's Tools

The Windows User's tools are the utilities we use to store and access users' data and documents. These are the applications and folders that we use to keep user data.

Desktop   This folder shows all of the app that are located on the desktop.

Documents   By default, this folder stores the documents that are created. Each user has a unique `Documents` folder, so even if a computer is shared, each user will have their own personal folder.

Downloads   This folder allows you to store all the apps and files that you download. By storing downloaded apps and files in this folder, you can always use these files to reinstall apps or files when needed. In many instances, when you download files from the Internet, they are placed into this folder by default. Some downloads allow you to choose a file location, but many downloads are placed in the `Downloads` folder automatically.

Pictures   This app shows any pictures that are in the user's `Pictures` folder.

Music   This shortcut will show any music that is in the user's `Music` folder.

Videos   This shortcut shows you all the videos that are stored on this Windows client system.

Shut Down Or Restart   There is an arrow next to this button that you can click and choose whether to restart the machine or shut down the system.

The desktop also includes the Recycle Bin. The Recycle Bin holds the files and folders that have been deleted, assuming that your hard drive has enough free space to hold the deleted files. You can restore or permanently delete a file by opening the Recycle Bin and right-clicking that file.

When configuring the desktop, you have the ability to decide between configuring a background of your choice as your desktop backdrop or choosing one of the built-in desktop themes. Desktop themes are a preset package containing graphical appearance details used to customize the look and feel of an operating system.

Backgrounds are the graphics that you decide to set as your wallpaper. To switch between different themes, right-click an area of open space on the desktop and select Personalize. In the Theme Settings dialog box, you can select the theme you want to use. You can also configure the desktop by customizing the taskbar and Start Menu, by adding shortcuts, and by setting display properties.

Configuring Personalization

To configure the Windows Desktop in Windows 10/11 and to change how your desktop works, you can go to Start ➤ Settings ➤ Personalization, or you can right-click the desktop and select Personalize. When you choose to personalize the desktop, you have several different settings that you can configure (as shown in Figure 4.13). The only difference between the Windows 10 and Windows 11 Personalization is basically just the look of the screens; the functionality is all the same.

FIGURE 4.13 Windows 11 Personalization screen

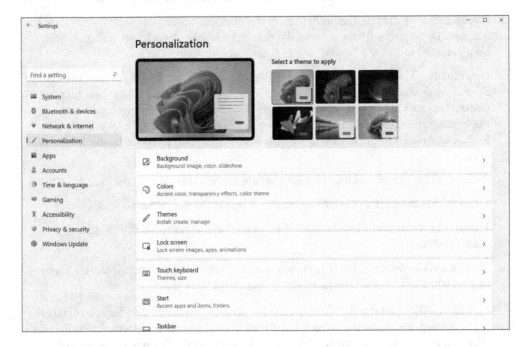

Background

This setting lets you pick your desktop background, which uses a picture or an HTML document as wallpaper. Setting up a desktop background can be as easy as picking a solid color and placing a picture of your favorite sports team or pet on top of it.

Windows 10/11 comes with some pictures already in the system, but you can basically turn any picture into your background desktop picture. As you can see in Figure 4.14, you can click the Browse button and choose the pictures that you want in your background.

Colors

This setting allows you to fine-tune the color and style of your windows' background. As shown in Figure 4.15, you can pick an accent color for your background.

Windows 10/11 users also have the ability to choose their own background colors. You can show colors on the Start screen, taskbar, and Action Center. You can also make the Start screen, taskbar, and Action Center transparent.

FIGURE 4.14   Windows 11 Background screen

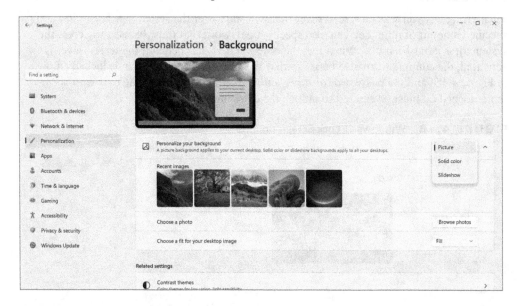

FIGURE 4.15   Windows 11 Colors screen

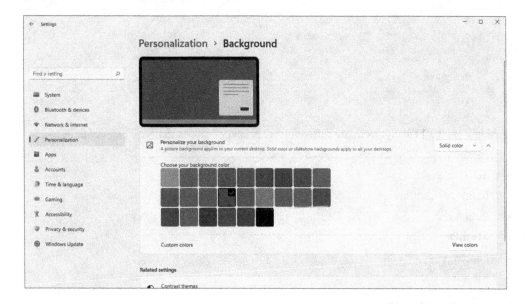

Lock Screen

This setting lets you select a screen saver that will start after the system has been idle for a specified amount of time. You can also specify a password that must be used to access the system after it has been idle. When the idle time has been reached and the screen saver is activated, the computer can also be set so that the Windows 10/11 system is locked (shown in Figure 4.16) and the password (or other authentication method) of the user who is currently logged on must be entered to unlock the computer again.

FIGURE 4.16   Windows 11 Lock Screen options

Windows 10/11 includes many different screen saver options that you can configure:

- None
- 3D Text
- Blank
- Bubbles
- Mystify
- Photos
- Ribbons

Personalization Themes

This screen allows you to set the different themes that you can have for your desktop. Themes allow you to change the color pattern for the desktop and all applications in one setting. The Themes screen (as shown in Figure 4.17 and Figure 4.18) also allows you to change the advanced sound settings, desktop icon settings, and mouse pointer settings.

FIGURE 4.17   Windows 10 Themes screen

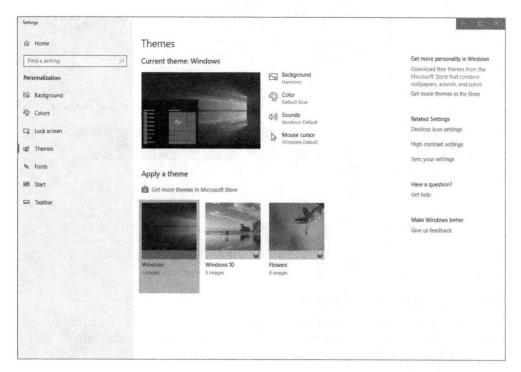

Advanced Sound Settings   These settings let you choose the sounds that will be played based on the action taken. Each action can have its own sound. The Sound options also allow you to set up the external or internal speakers and microphones that you want to use. You can also calibrate different pieces of hardware.

Desktop Icon Settings   These settings let you to customize the desktop icons. You also have the ability to change shortcut icons. Some of the icons that you can add to the desktop are the Computer icon, User's Files icon, Network icon, Recycle Bin icon, and Control Panel icon. You also have the ability to change icons at the screen.

Mouse Cursor Settings   These settings let you to customize the appearance of the mouse pointers. You can go from the traditional pointer to a Help Select, Busy, and Precision Select pointer, to name just a few. You can also change the Button options, Pointer options, Wheel options, and Hardware options.

FIGURE 4.18   Windows 11 Themes screen

Personalization Start Screen

The Start section allows you to configure what you are going to see on your Start Menu and which folders appear on the Start Menu. Figure 4.19 shows you the options that you have available in Windows 10:

- Show more tiles on Start.
- Show app list in Start Menu.
- Show recently added apps.
- Show most used apps.
- Show suggestions occasionally in Start.
- Use Start full screen.
- Show recently opened items in Jump Lists on Start or the taskbar.

The Start section in Windows 11 is a bit different, as you can see in Figure 4.20. You can choose to show the recently added apps, most used apps, and recently opened items in Start, Jump Lists, and File Explorer. You can also choose the folders you wish to show on the Start Menu.

FIGURE 4.19   Windows 10 Start options

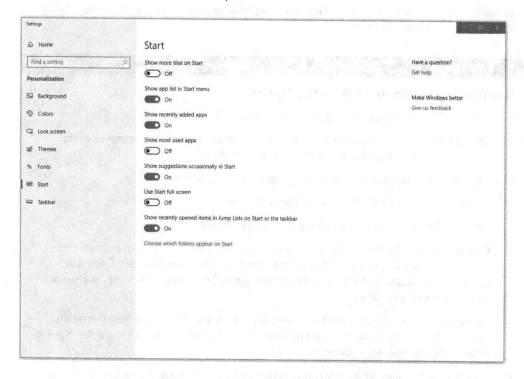

FIGURE 4.20   Windows 11 Personalization - Start options

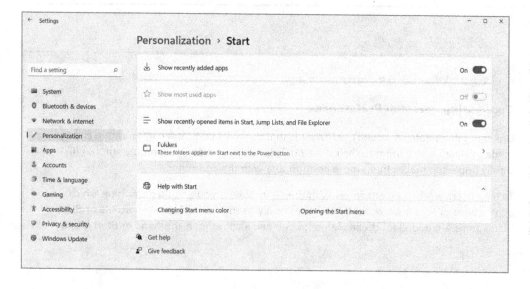

Now that we have looked at how to configure the Windows 10/11 desktop, let's practice doing just that. Exercise 4.1 will walk you through the process of configuring your theme and choosing additional options.

EXERCISE 4.1

Configuring Windows 10 Desktop Options

1. Right-click an open area of the desktop and choose Personalize.

2. On the Background screen, either select a new picture or open the pull-down menu under Background and choose Solid Color or Slideshow.

3. After you have set your new desktop, go to the Lock Screen page.

4. Scroll down and click the link Screen Saver Settings.

5. From the Screen Saver pull-down menu, choose 3D Text.

6. Click the Settings button. Make sure the radio button is set for Custom Text and enter the text you would like to see. Change the font or size or rotation speed. Once that's completed, click OK. At the Screen Saver Settings screen, change the Wait Time value to 15 minutes and then click OK.

7. Select the Themes screen. Click the Theme Settings link and choose a new theme that you like. You can also keep the current theme if you like that one. Click the upper-right X to close the window once you're finished.

8. Click the Start screen. Make any changes that you want for your Start Menu. Once you are finished, close the Personalization window.

 **Real World Scenario**

Configuring Personal Preferences

One thing that I noticed as an IT manager is that the most common configuration change made by users is to configure their desktop. This lets them use the computer more efficiently and often makes them more comfortable with the computer.

To help users work more efficiently with their computers, you should determine which applications or files are frequently and commonly used and verify that shortcuts or Start Menu items are added for those elements. You can also remove shortcuts or Start Menu items for elements that are seldom used or not used at all, helping to make the work area less cluttered and confusing.

Less experienced users will feel more comfortable with their computer if they have a desktop that has been personalized to their preferences. This might include their choice of a desktop theme and screen saver.

Windows 10/11 includes several utilities for managing various aspects of the operating system configuration. In the following sections, you will learn how to configure your operating system using Control Panel and the Registry Editor.

We will start with Control Panel and the different utilities included within it.

Using Control Panel

Control Panel is a set of GUI utilities that allow you to configure Registry settings without having to use the Registry Editor. The Registry is a database used by the operating system to store configuration information.

You can configure the system by using the Registry Editor (REGEDIT or REGEDT32). Windows 10/11 only uses the REGEDIT command. If you type **REGEDT32**, it just opens the REGEDIT command utility.

If you don't want to open the Registry directly but you still want to make some Registry changes, you can just use Control Panel. Control Panel is still an option with Windows 10/11; however, Microsoft is slowly transitioning users away from using Control Panel. On Windows 11, some of the options available in the Windows 10 Control Panel have moved to the Settings app. The icons still appear in Control Panel; however, they now redirect to the appropriate pages in Settings. A few changes in the Windows 11 Control Panel are that the Programs & Features section will now open in the Settings ➤ Installed Apps section and the Uninstall Updates option will open in the Settings ➤ Windows Update and Update History sections. Also, the Network Discovery, File and Printer Sharing, and Public Folder sharing sections will now open in the Settings ➤ Advanced Network Settings section.

So, let's take a closer look at the utilities that are available through Control Panel. I have set Control Panel to Large Icons view, but you can set it to Small Icons view if you prefer (see Figure 4.21 and Figure 4.22).

If you keep the Control Panel view set to Category, you will not be able to follow along and see all the different items I am going to cover. The Category view has all of these settings, but they are in different sections. I feel it's easier to understand each item using the Large Icons view.

FIGURE 4.21   Control Panel in Windows 10

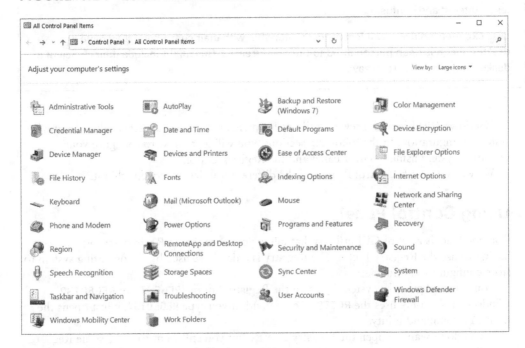

FIGURE 4.22   Control Panel in Windows 11

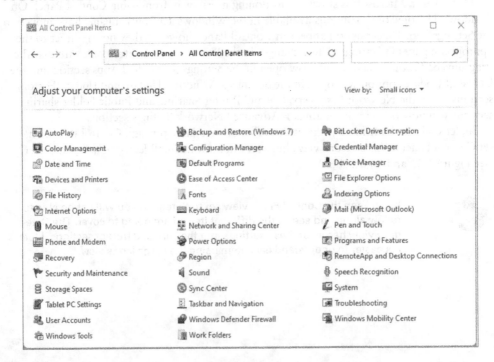

Administrative Tools/Windows Tools   Administrative Tools is the option in the Windows 10 Control Panel while it's called Windows Tools in the Windows 11 Control Panel. These can be seen in Figure 4.21 and Figure 4.22 earlier. These folders contain tools for system administrators and advanced users. These icons have multiple administrative tools that can help you configure and monitor the Windows 10/11 operating system. The following tools are included:

- Component Services
- Computer Management
- Defragment and Optimize Drives
- Disk Cleanup
- Event Viewer
- iSCSI Initiator
- Local Security Policy
- ODBC Data Sources (32-bit)
- ODBC Data Sources (64-bit)
- Performance Monitor
- Print Management
- Recovery Drive
- Resource Monitor
- Services
- System Configuration
- System Information
- Task Scheduler
- Windows Firewall with Advanced Security
- Windows Memory Diagnostics

AutoPlay   This option lets you configure media discs and will AutoPlay the discs when inserted into the Media Player (see Figure 4.23). Each media type has different configuration settings, but the basic choices are as follows:

- Use AutoPlay For All Media And Devices
- Removable Drive
- Camera Storage
- DVDs
- Blue-Ray Discs
- CDs
- Software
- Devices

FIGURE 4.23 AutoPlay options on Windows 10

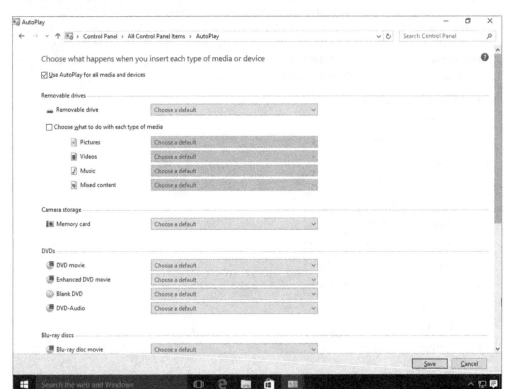

Backup And Restore (Windows 7)   The Backup And Restore option allows you to configure your backup media. Users can make copies of all important data on their machine to avoid losing it in the event of a hardware failure or disaster. Backups will be discussed in greater detail in Chapter 7, "Configuring Recovery."

BitLocker Drive Encryption   BitLocker Drive Encryption helps prevent unauthorized users from accessing files stored on hard drives by encrypting the drive in its entirety. The user is able to use the computer as they normally would, but unauthorized users cannot read or use any of their files if the hard drive is stolen from the original machine.

Color Management   The Color Management feature allows you to configure some of the video adapter's settings. You can configure the Windows color system defaults, the ICC Rendering Intent to WCS Gamut Mapping settings, and the display calibration. You can also change the system defaults to indicate how these items should be handled.

Credential Manager   Users can use the Credential Manager to store credentials such as usernames and passwords. These usernames and passwords get stored in vaults so that you can easily log onto computers or websites.

There are two sections in the Credential Manager: Web Credentials and Windows Credentials. You can add credentials by clicking the link next to each of the two credential sections.

Date And Time   The Date And Time setting allows you to configure your local date and time for the Windows 10/11 machine. You also have the ability to synchronize your clock with the Internet, as shown in Figure 4.24. Be aware that if your computer is a member of a domain, you will not see this screen and you will not be able to synchronize your time with an Internet time server.

FIGURE 4.24   Time synchronization in Windows 10

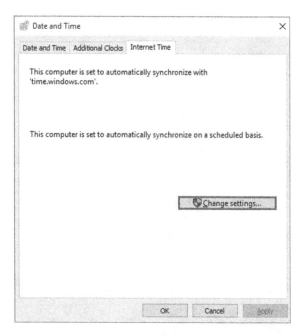

Default Programs   The Default Programs icon allows you to choose the programs that Windows will use by default. In Windows 11, this icon will link you to Settings ➤ Apps.

Device Manager   Device Manager allows you to configure the devices on your Windows 10/11 machine. You can configure such devices as disk drives, display adapters, DVD/CD-ROM drives, monitors, and network adapters.

Devices And Printers   The Devices And Printers option lets you add or configure the devices on your machine and your printers. This is where you add the printers that you have on your network.

Ease of Access Center   The Ease of Access Center allows you to set up your accessibility options. These are settings that you can set for people with vision issues. The Ease of Access Center allows you to configure voice narration (a computer voice tells you what you're mousing over) and an onscreen keyboard or to start the magnifier (which allows you to see everything magnified).

File Explorer Options   The Folder Options feature lets you configure how you view folders on the Windows client machine by default. You have the ability to set up how you browse and navigate folders, which files and folders you can view (see Figure 4.25), and how folders are searched.

FIGURE 4.25   File Explorer Options settings in Windows 10

File History   File History allows users to save copies of their files so that they can get them back in the event of a file being lost or damaged. You have the ability to restore personal files, select drives, exclude folders, and even set advanced settings on the File History settings.

Flash Player (32-Bit)   The Flash Player application allows you to set up how your Flash Player is going to operate and which applications the Flash Player will be associated with.

Fonts This option displays a screen where you can install, preview, delete, show, hide, and configure the fonts that the applications on your Windows 10/11 operating system can use. It enables you to get fonts online, adjust cleartext, find a character, and change font size.

Indexing Options Windows uses indexing to perform very fast searches of common files on your computer. The Indexing Options feature gives you the ability to configure which files and applications get indexed.

Infrared If a device allows infrared transfers, the Infrared option allows you to send and receive files and images to your Windows client computer. Many digital cameras today allow you to use infrared to transfer images to your Windows 10/11 computer.

Internet Options The Internet Options feature (see Figure 4.26) lets you configure your home page, browsing history, tabs, security, privacy, content, connections, and programs.

FIGURE 4.26 Windows 10 Internet Properties dialog box

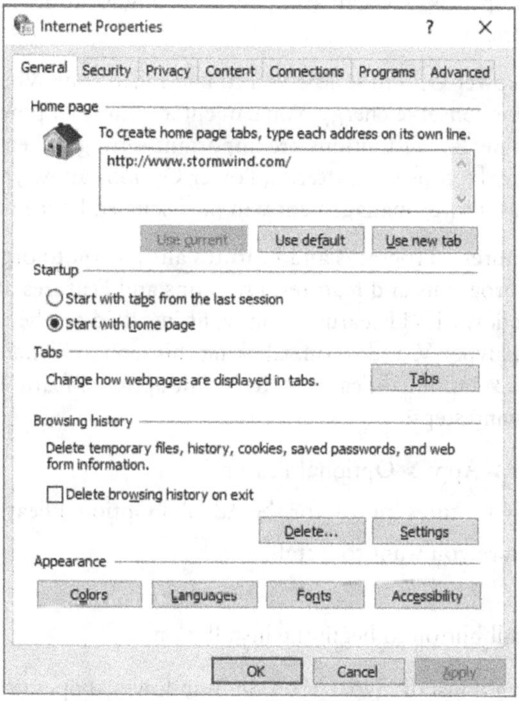

Keyboard The Keyboard properties allow you to configure how the keyboard will react when used. You can set the character repeat speed (how fast the keyboard will repeat what you are typing) and the cursor speed. You can also use these properties to configure the keyboard drivers.

Mouse   Mouse properties let you configure how the mouse will operate. You can configure the buttons, click speed, ClickLock, pointer type, pointer options, center wheel, and hardware properties.

Mail   You may or may not have this Mail application in Control Panel. If you have a mail client, such as Outlook, then the Mail application icon will be in Control Panel. If you don't have a mail client, then this icon will be missing from Control Panel.

When you configure the Mail properties, you set up your client-side mail settings. In the Mail properties, you can set up different user profiles (mailboxes) and the local mail servers or Internet mail servers to which they connect.

Network and Sharing Center   Use the Network and Sharing Center properties to configure your Windows 10/11 machine to connect to a local network or the Internet. You can configure TCP/IP, set up a new network, connect to a network, choose a homegroup, and configure the network adapter.

Phone and Modem   Use the Phone and Modem properties to set up local dialing properties and modem options. You can set up your dialing location, modem properties, and telephony providers.

Power Options   Power Options allow you to maximize your Windows 10/11 machine's performance and/or conserve energy. You can enter your own power restrictions to customize your machine. Power Options are important settings when you are dealing with laptops. Since many laptops use batteries, Power Options allow you to get the most time from their batteries. Power management will be discussed later in this chapter.

Programs and Features   Programs and Features allows you to organize, uninstall, change, or repair programs and features. Programs and Features also allows you to choose which Windows 10/11 features you want installed on the machine, such as Indexing Services, Hyper-V, and so on. Clicking this icon in Windows 11 will take you to Settings ➤ Apps ➤ Optional Features. To install optional features on Windows 11, perform the following steps:

1. Open Settings ➤ Apps ➤ Optional Features.
2. Click the View Features button for the Add An Optional Feature setting.
3. Select the feature you want to install.
4. Click Next.
5. Click the Install button to begin the installation.

In Exercise 4.2, you'll install Hyper-V on the Windows 10 operating system. If you are using a virtual version of Windows 10 (for example, Windows 10 loaded onto a Hyper-V server), you will not be able to install Hyper-V onto the virtual version of Windows 10. But you can still follow the steps and choose a different application to install.

EXERCISE 4.2

Installing New Features

1. Open the Programs And Features tool by clicking Start ≻ Windows System ≻ Control Panel ≻ Programs And Features.

2. Click the Turn Windows Features On Or Off link in the upper-left corner. Scroll down the features list and check the Hyper-V check box (shown in Figure 4.27).

3. Click OK.

FIGURE 4.27   Hyper-V check box on Windows 10

Recovery   The Recovery feature allows you to recover the Windows client system to a previously captured restore point. System Restore is one of the first recovery options that should be considered when your Windows 10/11 system is experiencing problems. Unlike previous versions of Windows, System Restore is not enabled by default on Windows 11. Before you can start using this feature in Windows 11, you need to manually enable it. To do that, perform the following steps:

1. Open Start.

2. Search for **Create a restore point** and click the top result to open the System Properties page.

3. In the Protection Settings section, select the main System drive.

4. Click the Configure button.

5. Select the Turn On System Protection option.

6. Use the Max Usage slider to select how much space you want to reserve for the restore points.

7. Click Apply.

8. Click OK.

Once you enable System Restore, Windows 11 will automatically create a restore point when applying system updates or when you make specific system changes.

Region   The Region tool allows you to configure your local regional settings as well as configure date and time formats. In Windows 11, clicking this icon redirects the user to Settings ➤ Time & Language ➤ Language & Region.

RemoteApp and Desktop Connections   RemoteApp and Desktop Connections allows you to access programs and desktops on your network. To connect to these resources (remote applications and desktops), you must have the proper permission.

With RemoteApp and Desktop Connections, you can connect to either a remote computer or a virtual computer. To create a new connection, use the Set Up A New Connection Wizard on the RemoteApp and Desktop Connections menu.

Security and Maintenance   The Security and Maintenance utility has two configurable sections: Security and Maintenance. The Security section allows you to configure:

- Network firewall
- Virus protection
- Internet security settings
- User Access Control

The Maintenance section allows you to:

- Install already downloaded device software
- View reliability history
- Start maintenance/change maintenance settings
- Show drive status
- Show device software status

Sound   The Sound option allows you to configure your machine's audio. You can configure output (speakers and audio drivers) and your input devices (microphones).

Speech Recognition   The Speech Recognition tool lets you configure your speech properties. Speech Recognition allows you to speak into the computer and have that speech be displayed on the system. Many programs, including Microsoft Office, can display the words onscreen as you speak them into the system. You can complete the following actions via the Speech Recognition tool:

- Start Speech Recognition.
- Set up a microphone.
- Take speech tutorials.
- Train your computer to better understand you.
- Open the Speech Reference Card, which allows you to view and print a list of common commands.

Storage Spaces   Storage Spaces in Windows 10/11 is another way to give your users data redundancy. You have the ability to group hard drives together into storage pools. Windows 10/11 users can then use these storage pool capacities to turn the pools into individual Storage Spaces. You can configure your Storage Pools in this application.

Sync Center   The Sync Center lets you configure synchronization between a Windows 10/11 machine and a network server. The Sync Center also allows you to see when synchronization occurred, if the synchronization was successful, and if there were any errors.

System   The System feature is one of the most important in Control Panel. Clicking this icon will now redirect you to the Settings app. The System feature allows you to view which operating system your machine is using, view installed system resources (processor, RAM), change the computer name/domain/workgroup, and activate Windows 10/11. You can also configure the following settings:

- BitLocker settings
- Device Manager
- Remote desktop
- System protection
- Advanced system settings

Taskbar and Navigation   The Taskbar and Navigation tool allows you to configure how the taskbar, Start Menu, and toolbars will operate.

Troubleshooting   The Troubleshooting feature in Control Panel allows you to troubleshoot common Windows 10/11 problems in the following categories:

- Programs
- Hardware and Sound
- Network and Internet
- System and Security

User Accounts   User Accounts allows you to create and modify local user accounts. You can perform the following tasks:

- Change user passwords.
- Remove passwords.
- Change the account picture.
- Change the account name.
- Change the account type.
- Manage user accounts.
- Change user account control settings.

Windows Defender Firewall   Windows Defender Firewall helps prevent unauthorized users or hackers from accessing your Windows 10/11 machine from the Internet or the local network.

Windows Mobility Center   The Windows Mobility Center allows a laptop or other mobile user to quickly access the most common mobile features. Depending on the hardware and the computer manufacturer, there may be more or fewer tiles displayed. Some of the tiles that may be displayed are:

- Display brightness
- Volume
- Battery Status
- Screen Orientation
- External Display
- Wireless Network
- Sync Center

Work Folders   Work Folders allows you to make data files available on all of the devices that they use. You can access that data even when the devices are offline.

Using the Microsoft Management Console

One really cool advantage of using Windows is the ability to create your own windows. All of the command windows that we have talked about run through the Microsoft Management Console (MMC).

The MMC is the console framework for application management. The MMC provides a common environment for snap-ins. Snap-ins are administrative tools developed by Microsoft or third-party vendors. Some of the MMC snap-ins that you may use are Computer Management, Active Directory Users and Computers, Active Directory Sites and Services, Active Directory Domains and Trusts, and DNS Management.

Knowing how to use and configure the MMC snap-ins will allow you to customize your work environment. For example, if you are in charge of Active Directory Users and Computers and DNS, you can add both of these snap-ins into the same window. This would then allow you to open just one application to configure all your tasks. The MMC offers many other benefits:

- The MMC is highly customizable—you add only the snap-ins you need.

- Snap-ins use a standard, intuitive interface, so they are easier to use than previous versions of administrative utilities.

- You can save customized MMCs and share them with other administrators.

- You can configure permissions so that the MMC runs in authoring mode, which you can manage, or in user mode, which limits what users can access.

- You can use most snap-ins for remote computer management.

By default, the MMC contains three panes: a console tree on the left, a Details pane in the middle, and an optional Actions pane on the right. The console tree lists the hierarchical structure of all snap-ins that have been loaded into the console. The Details pane contains a list of properties or other items that are part of the snap-in that is highlighted in the console tree. The Actions pane provides a list of actions that the user can access depending on the item selected in the Details pane.

On a Windows client computer, to open the MMC click the Start button and type **MMC** in the Search box. When you first open the MMC, it contains only the `Console Root` folder. The MMC does not have any default administrative functionality. It is simply a framework used to organize administrative tools through the addition of snap-in utilities.

Configuring MMC Modes

You can configure the MMC to run in author mode for full access to the MMC functions or in one of three user modes, which have more limited access to the MMC functions. To set a console mode, while in the MMC editor, select File ➤ Options to open the Options dialog box. In this dialog box, you can select from the console modes listed in Table 4.1.

TABLE 4.1   MMC modes

Console mode	Description
Author mode	Allows use of all the MMC functions.
User mode—full access	Gives users full access to window management commands, but they cannot add or remove snap-ins or change console properties.
User mode—limited access, multiple window	Allows users to create new windows but not close any existing windows. Users can access only the areas of the console tree that were visible when the console was last saved.
User mode—limited access, single window	Allows users to access only the areas of the console tree that were visible when the console was last saved, and they cannot create new windows.

After you decide which administrative role you are going to run, it's time to start configuring your MMC snap-ins.

Adding Snap-Ins

The biggest advantage of using the MMC is to configure snap-ins the way your organization needs them. Adding snap-ins is a simple and quick procedure. To add a snap-in to the MMC and save it, perform the following steps:

1. To start the MMC editor, click Start, type **MMC** in the search box, and press Enter.

2. From the main console window, select File ➤ Add/Remove Snap-In to open the Add Or Remove Snap-Ins dialog box.

3. Highlight the snap-in you want to add and click the Add button.

4. If prompted, specify whether the snap-in will be used to manage the local computer or a remote computer. After you choose the MMCs you want in your custom snap-in, click Finish.

5. When you have finished adding snap-ins, click OK.

6. After you have added snap-ins to create a console, you can save it by selecting File ➤ Save As and entering a name for your console. Place the console on the desktop.

You can save the console to a variety of locations, including a program group or the Desktop. By default, custom consoles have an .msc filename extension.

Many applications that are MMC snap-ins, including Disk Management, are already configured for you under the Administrative Tools section of Windows 10/11.

Using the System Settings

When you click the System icon in Control Panel in Windows 10/11, you are redirected to the Settings ➤ System ➤ About section of the Settings app. As I mentioned before, Microsoft is slowly transitioning the Control Panel items to the Settings app. The System icon in Control Panel is a gateway to a very useful set of utilities and tasks that can enable you to specify remote settings, device settings, system protection, and the computer name, among other things. A majority of the Settings app has already been discussed in greater detail earlier in this chapter.

The About section will give you information regarding your Windows Security, device specifications (with a button that allows you to rename your computer), Windows specifications that shows the specifics of what you are currently running, support information, and links to related settings.

Let's look at a few of the utilities and tasks that you can configure on the About page:

Device Specifications   The Device Specifications section shows the following information about the system hardware:

- Device Name
- Processor

- Installed RAM
- Device ID
- Product ID
- System Type
- Pen And Touch

There are two buttons, one that allows you to copy the information in the Device Specification section and another button that allows you to rename the PC.

Windows Specifications   The Windows Specifications section shows the following information about the system operating system:

- Edition
- Version
- Installed On
- OS Build
- Experience

There is also a button that allows you to copy the information in the Windows Specifications section. There are also links that allow you to change the product key, upgrade your edition of Windows, read the Microsoft Services Agreement that applies to your services, and read the Microsoft Software License Terms.

Support   The Support section shows you the manufacturer of the device and a website link.

Related Settings   The Related Settings section provides you with links to some of the following tasks:

- BitLocker Settings
- Device Manager
- Remote Desktop
- System Protection
- Advance System Settings
- Rename This PC (Advanced)

Understanding the Settings Window

As stated earlier in the book, Microsoft took the best of both Windows 7 and Windows 8 and created Windows 10/11. When you click the Start Menu, you will see an option called Settings (see Figure 4.28). Also, as I mentioned previously, Microsoft is slowly transitioning the Control Panel items to this Settings app.

FIGURE 4.28   Windows 10 Settings option

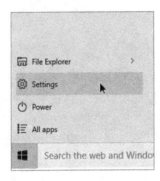

The Settings screen is a way to configure different parts of the Windows 10/11 system. When you select the Settings option from the Start Menu, you will see the Settings screen appear. The Windows 10 Settings window can be seen in Figure 4.29. In Windows 11, the look of the Settings window has changed and shows how a user navigates and provides descriptive thumbnails on almost every page that indicates what the page is all about. The Windows 11 Settings window can be seen in Figure 4.30.

FIGURE 4.29   Windows 10 Settings window

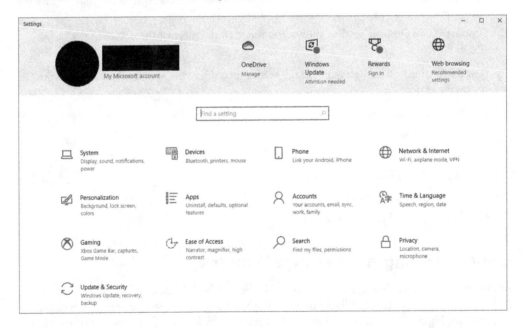

FIGURE 4.30 Windows 11 Settings window

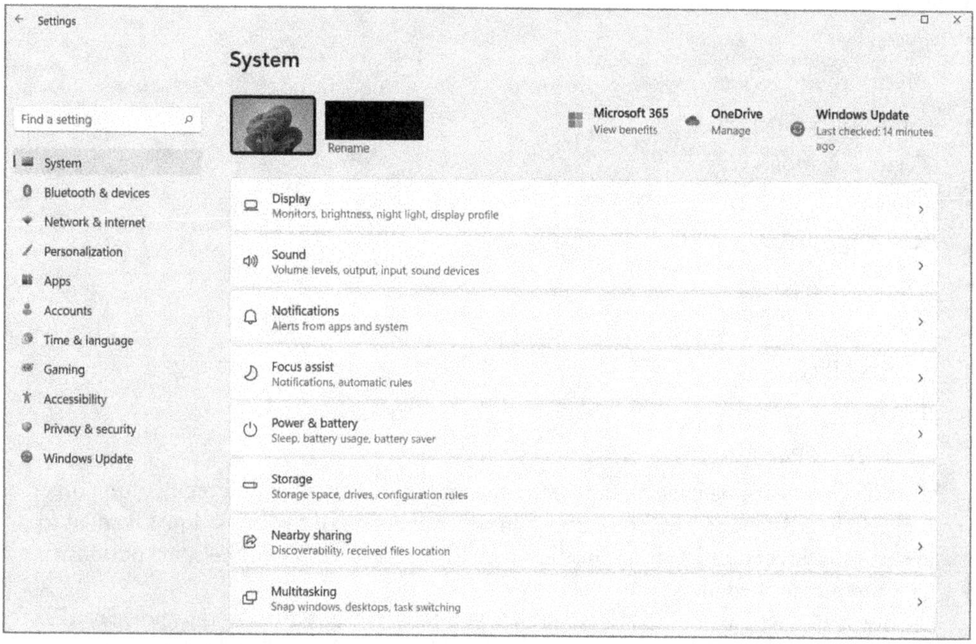

As you can see in Figure 4.29 and Figure 4.30, the Settings window has multiple sections of Windows 10/11 that you can configure. The following areas are settings that can be configured using the Settings screen in Windows 10:

- System
- Devices
- Phone
- Network & Internet
- Personalization
- Apps
- Accounts
- Time & Language
- Gaming
- Ease Of Access
- Search
- Privacy
- Updates & Security

The following areas are settings that can be configured using the Settings screen in Windows 11:

- System
- Bluetooth & Devices
- Network & Internet
- Personalization
- Apps
- Accounts
- Time & Language
- Gaming
- Accessibility
- Privacy & Security
- Windows Update

Most of these sections have already been covered in this chapter, and many of the other sections (such as Accounts) will be covered in other chapters of the book. I just wanted to make sure you understand that it's another way to configure many of the same options that we have already looked at.

The one area that I would recommend that you look at right away is the choice for Privacy. Microsoft has turned on many features that Microsoft and other third-party vendors can use to access data on your system and also get information on how you use your Windows 10/11 system. Take a few minutes to look through the Privacy section and make sure nothing you don't want turned on is on by default.

Now that we've looked at the Settings app, let's take a look at how to configure some of the System options in the About section of Settings. Complete Exercise 4.3 to change the computer name. There are a number of ways to change a computer name on a Windows 10/11 device. This is just one way.

EXERCISE 4.3

Changing the Computer Name on a Windows 10/11 Computer

1. Select Start ➤ Settings ➤ System ➤ About.

2. Select Rename This PC.

3. Enter a new name and click Next. You may be asked to sign in.

4. Select Restart Now or Restart Later.

Now that you have renamed the computer, Exercise 4.4 shows how to configure performance options. Complete the exercise to manipulate your system's virtual memory.

EXERCISE 4.4

Changing the System's Virtual Memory on a Windows 10/11 Computer

1. Select Start ➤ Settings ➤ System ➤ About.

2. In the Related Settings section, click the Advanced System Settings option.

3. The System Properties box will open; select the Advanced tab.

4. In the Performance section, click the Settings button.

5. The Performance Options box will open; select the Advanced tab.

6. In the Virtual Memory section, click the Change button.

7. Deselect the Automatically Manage Paging File Size For All Drives check box.

8. Click the Custom Size radio button.

9. Set the Minimum and Maximum settings to two times the size of your RAM. For example, if your RAM is 4,096 MB, set them to 8,192 MB.

10. Click the Set button.

11. Click OK. Then click OK again on the Performance Options screen.

12. Close the System Properties window.

13. Restart the device.

 Microsoft Windows 10/11 handles the virtual memory requirements by default, but I recommend increasing the virtual memory on your machine if hard drive space is available. I use the rule of thumb of one and a half to two times the size of RAM.

Using PowerShell

Another way to configure Control Panel and its apps is to use PowerShell commands. So, let's take a look at how to use PowerShell for configuration.

The first PowerShell command you need to understand is the `Get-ControlPanelItem` command. This command allows you to find Control Panel items on a local computer by name, category, or description. For example, here is the `Get-ControlPanelItem` command you would use to configure the Windows Firewall:

```
PS C:\> Get-ControlPanelItem -Name "Windows Defender Firewall" |
Show-ControlPanelItem
```

Table 4.2 includes some of the PowerShell configuration commands that you would use to help manage and configure the Windows client system.

TABLE 4.2   PowerShell configuration commands

Command	Description
Clear-EventLog	Allows you to delete all entries from the event logs on a local or remote computer
Debug-Process	Debugs processes running on a local computer
Get-ComputerInfo	Returns the computer's system information
Get-EventLog	Finds an event in a specific event log
Get-Service	Finds a service on a Windows client system
Get-TimeZone	Gets the systems time zone
New-EventLog	Creates a new event log
New-Service	Allows you to create a new service
Remove-EventLog	Deletes an event log
Rename-Computer	Allows you to rename a computer
Restart-Computer	Reboots your system
Restart-Service	Restarts a service
Resume-Service	Resumes a service
Set-TimeZone	Sets the system's time zone
Start-Process	Starts a process
Start-Service	Starts a service

Command	Description
Stop-Computer	Shuts down a system
Stop-Service	Stops a service
Test-Connection	Sends a ping to test NIC adapter settings
Write-EventLog	Writes an event to an event log

Now that we have looked at how to configure Windows 10/11, I'll show you how Windows client mobility works.

Configuring Mobility Options

So far in this chapter, you have learned about using Control Panel options and working with the Settings app. Now we need to dive into a few of these settings in greater detail. The ones that we are going to discuss all have to deal with Windows 10/11 mobility.

Windows 10/11 is designed to be mobile, and it has many features that revolve around that. The mobility issues that are covered in the following sections are how to configure offline file policies and sync options using the Sync Center and power policies.

Configuring Offline Files and Synchronization

One of the advantages of Windows 10/11 is how the operating system works and synchronizes with other systems and data.

The term *synchronization* could mean different things to different people. We could be talking about synchronization of offline files and data, or we could be talking about synchronization between two systems like a Windows 10/11 system and cloud-based Azure or OneNote.

In this section, we will talk about both. We will address synchronization between offline and online files, and we will discuss synchronization between Windows client and cloud-based services.

The Offline Files feature allows network files to be available to clients even when a network connection to the server is unavailable or slow. When a user is accessing a server that is unavailable or when the network connection is slower than a configurable threshold, files are then retrieved from the Offline Files folders.

Offline Files is enabled by default on the following client computer operating systems: Windows 10/11 Professional, Windows 10/11 Enterprise, and Windows Education. This feature is turned off by default on Windows Server operating systems.

Because in many organizations Windows 10/11 will be loaded onto a laptop computer, offline file access can be an important part of how Windows clients stay current even while off the network.

When you decide to turn synchronization on, Windows will automatically keep track of your synchronization choices for you on all of your Windows 10/11 devices (as long as you are logged onto all of the Windows devices using the same account or have set up synchronization with the other accounts and your Microsoft account).

Users have the ability to choose what items that they want to synchronize. For example, users can synchronize passwords, web browser settings, File Explorer settings, and even notifications.

To truly have synchronization work the way that Microsoft has intended, you need to link all of your devices together using your Microsoft account or have your other accounts linked to your Microsoft account. This includes having your school or work accounts all tied into one Microsoft account.

As an IT director for many years, I feel a bit uneasy about this idea. I truly believe that linking your personal accounts together to synchronize all of your personal data is a good way to go, but for obvious security reasons, I don't agree with corporate users linking into their personal accounts.

So how do we go about synchronizing everything in Windows 10/11 easily? There are a number of ways to open the Sync Center, but the best method is to use the Sync Center in Control Panel (just click Start ➤ Windows System ➤ Control Panel ➤ Sync Center).

The Sync Center is built into Windows 10/11, and it's a one-stop shop for all of your synchronization needs, including working with offline files (see Figure 4.31).

FIGURE 4.31   The Sync Center

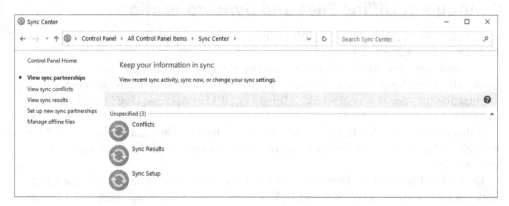

As you can see in Figure 4.31, you can set up synchronization between other devices and partnerships. You can also manage offline files. To do so, you have to enable that feature on the Windows client system (done through the Sync Center) and then also configure offline folder access with the Windows servers that you have at your company.

When you click the Manage Offline Files link and enable offline folder access, you will see four tabs that can help you set up offline folder access properly:

General   The General tab will let you see whether or not offline files are enabled. If not, you can click Enable Offline Files and click OK, then restart your computer. This tab also allows you to disable offline files, provides a button to open the Sync Center, and lets you view your offline files.

Disk Usage   The Disk Usage tab will show you how much disk space is currently being reserved on the Windows 10/11 system for keeping offline files. You can change the amount of space that is set for the Windows 10/11 system by clicking the Change Limits button.

Encryption   To make sure the offline files are encrypted while on the system, click the Encryption button. The files will get encrypted based on your user's Security Identifier (SID) number. When you log into the Windows 10/11 account using the account with the matching SID number, the files will become automatically decrypted when they are opened. If someone with a different user ID (SID) number tries to access these files, they will be denied access.

Network   The Network tab allows you to set a time interval (such as 5 minutes), and when that interval is hit, the Windows 10/11 system will automatically check the network connection to make sure that the connection is not on a slow connection. For example, when you are at home and you don't have direct access to your network, the Windows system will automatically revert to using the offline files due to the connection being slow or not available.

Configuring Power Policies

Power Options allow a user or administrator to maximize their Windows 10/11 machine's performance and/or conserve energy.

As an administrator or user, you have the ability to enter your own power restrictions to customize your machine. Power Options are important settings when you are dealing with laptops. Since many laptops use batteries, Power Options allow you to get the most time from their batteries.

Now here is the kicker! Depending on what type of system you are on, you will see different power plan options. For example, Figure 4.32 shows the power plan options for a desktop system. You can tell that the only real options you have is what happens when you choose when to turn off the display or change your power consumption options.

FIGURE 4.32   Desktop power plan options

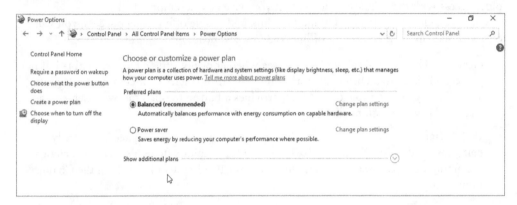

However, if you look at Figure 4.33, you can see that you have additional options based on whether your laptop or tablet is plugged in. You will not have those options on a desktop, because most desktops can't work when unplugged (unless you have a magical desktop).

FIGURE 4.33   Laptop power plan options

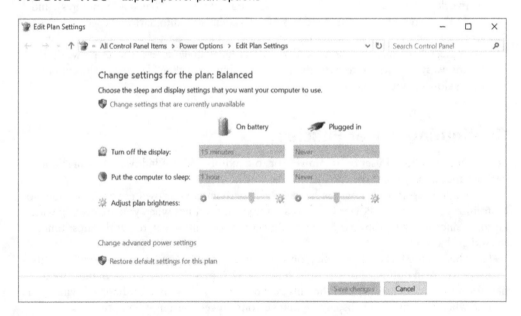

So, setting up your Power Options depends on what type of machine or tablet you're using. But some of the settings are the same no matter which one you use. The following are just some of the options that are the same no matter what type of Windows 10/11 system you're on:

- Require a password on wakeup.
- Choose what the power button does.
- Create a power plan.

Laptops will have additional choices, such as what happens when you close the lid of the laptop. No matter what type of system you are on, you can choose to go into Advanced options and set specific options on what system components would do while the system was running or while the system was idle.

For example, you can tell the system when the network card or hard drive can go into a Sleep mode based on idle time (amount of time when no one is working on the system). So, if you want to configure each individual component and how it should work while active or idle, you can go into the Advanced options and configure each component separately.

Managing Power States

In Windows 10/11, the Advanced Configuration and Power Interface (ACPI) specifies different levels of power states:

- Working
- Sleep (Modern Standby)
- Sleep
- Hibernate
- Soft Off
- Mechanical Off

The Sleep power option allows your computer to use very little power (while you're away from the computer), but it also allows your computer to start up faster and you will be instantly back to the spot where you left off. Users won't have to be concerned that they will lose their work because their battery drains while they are away from the computer. Sleep allows Windows to automatically save all your work and turn off the computer if the battery gets too low. Using the Sleep option is good for when you're going to be away from your computer for just a short amount of time.

Hibernate mode, which falls short of a complete shutdown of the computer, may not be available on all Windows 10/11 computers (depending on if you are working on a laptop or a desktop). With hibernation, the computer saves your desktop state as well as any open files to the hard drive. To use the computer again, you need to press the power button. The computer should start more quickly than from a complete shutdown because it does not have to go through the complete startup process. You will have to again log onto the computer. Similar to when the computer is put into Sleep mode, all the documents that were open when the computer went into hibernation are still available. With hibernate, you can easily resume work where you left off. You can configure your computer to hibernate through Power Options or by choosing Start and then clicking the arrow and selecting Hibernate from the drop-down menu. This option will appear only if hibernation has been enabled through Power Options.

As stated earlier, the Hibernate mode may not be available on your Windows 10/11 laptop machine by default. You must make sure your firmware can support hibernation before attempting to enable it. Now let's take a look at the different types of Power Options that you can configure.

Managing Power Options

You configure Power Options through the Power Options Properties dialog box. You can get to the Power Options through Control Panel or by selecting Start ➤ Settings ➤ System ➤ Power & Sleep ➤ Additional Power Settings. The Power Options dialog box provides the ability to manage power plans and to control Power Options, such as when the display is turned off, when the computer sleeps, and what the power button does.

Configuring Power Plans

Windows 10/11 includes three configurable power plans: Balanced, Power Saver, and High Performance. Power plans control the trade-off between quick access to an existing computer session and energy savings. In Windows 10/11, each power plan contains default options that can be customized to meet the needs of various scenarios.

The Balanced power plan, as its name suggests, provides a balance between power savings and performance. By default, this plan is configured to turn off the display after 20 minutes and to put the computer to sleep after 1 hour of idle time. You can modify these times as needed. Other Power Options that you can modify include Wireless Adapter settings and Multimedia settings. Wireless adapters can be configured for maximum power savings or maximum performance. By default, the Balanced power plan configures wireless adapters for maximum performance. Additionally, you can configure the Multimedia settings so that the computer will not be put into Sleep mode when sharing media. For example, if the computer is acting as a Media Center device, then you can configure the computer to remain on by setting the Prevent Idling To Sleep option so that other computers can connect to it and stream media from it even when the computer is not being used for other purposes.

The Power Saver power plan is optimized for power savings. By default, the display is configured to be turned off after 20 minutes of inactivity, and the computer will be put into Sleep mode after 1 hour of inactivity. Additionally, this power plan configures hard disks to be turned off after 20 minutes of inactivity.

The High Performance power plan is configured to provide the maximum performance for portable computers. By default, the computer will never enter Sleep mode, but the display will be turned off after 20 minutes. When this setting is configured, by default the Multimedia settings are configured with the new Allow The Computer To Enter Away Mode option. Away mode configures the computer to look like it's off to users but remain accessible for media sharing. For example, the computer can record television shows when in Away mode. You can modify the existing power plans to suit your needs by clicking Change Plan Settings, or you can use the preconfigured power plans listed in Table 4.3.

TABLE 4.3 Windows 10/11 power plans

Power Plan	Turn Off Display	Put Computer To Sleep	Turn Hard Disks Off
Balanced	After 20 minutes	1 hour	
Power Saver	After 20 minutes	1 hour	After 20 minutes
High Performance	After 20 minutes	Never	

In Exercise 4.5, I will show you how to configure a power plan for your computer.

EXERCISE 4.5

Configuring a Power Plan

1. Click Start ➤ Windows System ➤ Control Panel ➤ Power Options.

2. Select a power plan to modify from the Preferred Plans list, and click Change Plan Settings.

3. Configure the power plan options for your computer based on your personal preferences. Click Change Advanced Power Settings to modify the Advanced power settings. When all changes have been made, click Save Changes.

4. Close Control Panel.

Other desktop options you can use are the power button and switching users. Let's take a look at these features.

Configuring the Power Button

Unless you decide to run your computer 24 hours a day, you will eventually want to shut it down. By default, the Start Menu has a power button. When you click this button, your machine will power off. But the power button does not have to be set to the Shut Down option. You can configure this button to Switch User, Logoff, Lock, Restart, or Shut Down.

You may have a machine that is shared by multiple users, and it may be better for you to have the Switch User button instead of the Shut Down button on the Start Menu. Configuring the Switch User option would make it easier on your users.

In Exercise 4.6, you will configure the power button to use the Hibernate mode.

EXERCISE 4.6

Configuring the Power Button for Hibernate Mode

1. Click Start ➤ Windows System ➤ Control Panel ➤ Power Options.

2. On the left side, click Choose What The Power Button Does.

3. From the Power Button Settings drop-down menu, choose Hibernate.

4. Click OK.

5. Click the power button and see if the system goes into the Hibernate mode. Once the system is brought out of the Hibernate mode, redo this exercise and choose Shut Down in step 3 to return the system to normal (if it was set to turn off).

After you decide how the power button is going to be used, you may want to configure some of the advanced Power Options. In the next section, we will look at Power Options.

Configuring Advanced Power Settings

Each power plan contains advanced settings that can be configured, such as when the hard disks will be turned off and whether a password is required on wakeup. To configure these advanced settings, click Start ➤ Windows System ➤ Control Panel ➤ Power Options and select the power plan you want to use. Then click Change Advanced Power Settings to open the Advanced Settings tab of the Power Options dialog box and modify the settings as desired (or restore the plan defaults).

For example, one option that you might want to change if you are using a mobile computer is the Power Buttons And Lid option, which configures what happens when you press the power button or close the lid of the mobile computer. When either of these actions occurs, the computer can be configured to do nothing, shut down, go into Sleep mode, or go into Hibernate mode.

Configuring Hibernation

Although sleep is the preferred power-saving mode in Windows 10/11, hibernate is still available for use. Hibernate for a computer means that anything stored in memory is written to your hard disk. This ensures that when your computer is shut down, you do not lose any of the information that is stored in memory. When you take your computer out of hibernation, it returns to its previous state by loading the hibernation reserved area of hard disk back into memory. To configure your computer to hibernate, complete the same steps as you did previously in Exercise 4.6.

Command-Line Configuration

Microsoft gives you the ability to configure and manage your power settings through the use of the command line. The Powercfg.exe tool allows you to control power settings and configure computers to default to Hibernate or Standby mode. The `Powercfg.exe` tool is installed with Windows 10/11 by default. The `powercfg` command has a few switches that provide you with better functionality. Table 4.4 describes some of these switches.

TABLE 4.4 powercfg command switches

Switch	Description
-batteryreport	Generates a report of battery usage.
-change	Changes a setting in the current power scheme.
-changename	Changes the name of a power scheme. Also gives you the ability to change the description.
-delete	Deletes the power scheme of the GUID specified.
-deletesetting	Deletes a power setting.
-energy	Looks for common energy-efficiency and battery-life issues and displays these issues in an HTML format. This switch is used to identify problems with the power scheme.
-list	Shows all the power schemes in the current user's environment.
-query	Shows the content of a power scheme.
-qh	Displays the content (including hidden content) of the power scheme.
-waketimers	Enumerates the wake timers. If this is enabled, when the wake timer expires, the system will wake from hibernation or sleep state.

 For a complete list of `powercfg` switches, visit the Microsoft website here:

docs.microsoft.com/en-us/windows-hardware/design/
device-experiences/powercfg-command-line-options

There is a useful tool when you're using a laptop on battery power that allows you to see how much time you have left until the battery dies. Let's take a look at the battery meter.

Managing Power Consumption Using the Battery Meter

Windows 10/11 includes a battery meter that you can use to monitor the battery-power consumption on your mobile computer (laptop or tablet). The battery meter also provides notification as to what power plan is being used.

In Windows 10, the battery meter appears in the notification area of the Windows taskbar and indicates the status of the battery, including the percentage of battery charge. As the battery charge gets lower, the battery meter provides a visual indication of the amount of charge left. For example, when the battery charge reaches the low-battery level, a red circle with a white *X* is displayed.

The battery meter also provides a quick method for changing the power plan in use on the computer. By clicking the battery-meter icon, you can select among the preferred power plans available with Windows 10.

In Windows 11, however, the battery meter is no longer displayed on the taskbar. In order to see battery percentage in Windows 11, you will need to utilize the Settings app. To check the estimated amount of time remaining on Windows 11, select Start ➤ Settings ➤ System ➤ Power And Battery. At the top of the Power & Battery menu, you'll see Estimated Time Remaining under the percentage figure.

Managing Windows 10/11 Services

A *service* is a program, routine, or process that performs a specific function within the Windows 10/11 operating system. You can manage services through the Services window, which can be accessed in a variety of ways.

One way to access Services in Window 10 is to go through Control Panel and select Administrative Tools ➤ Services.

In Windows 11, Microsoft decided to combine system utilities into a single Windows Tools folder. To access Services in Windows 11, you can go to Start ➤ All Apps ➤ Windows Tools; then in the new window, scroll down and click Services.

The Services window lists the name of each service, a short description, the status, the startup type, and the logon account that is used to start it. To configure the properties of a service, double-click it to open its Properties dialog box, shown in Figure 4.34. This dialog box contains four tabs of options for services:

General   This tab allows you to view and configure the following options:

- The service name
- The display name
- A description of the service
- The path to the service executable
- The startup type, which can be automatic, manual, or disabled
- The current service status
- Start parameters that can be applied when the service is started

FIGURE 4.34   The Properties dialog box for a service

In addition, the buttons across the lower part of the dialog box allow you to change the service state to start, stop, and pause, and if paused, you can also resume the service.

Log On   The Log On tab allows you to configure the logon account that will be used to start the service. Choose the local system account or specify another logon account.

Recovery   The Recovery tab allows you to designate what action will be taken if the service fails to load. For the first, second, and subsequent failures, you can select an action from the following list:

- Take No Action
- Restart The Service
- Run A Program
- Restart The Computer

If you choose Run A Program, specify it along with any command-line parameters. If you choose Restart The Computer, you can configure a message that will be sent to users who are connected to the computer before it is restarted. You can also specify how long until a machine is restarted if an error occurs.

Dependencies   The Dependencies tab lists any services that must be running in order for the specified service to start. If a service fails to start, you can use this information to examine the dependencies and then make sure each one is running. In the bottom panel, you can verify whether any other services depend on this service before you decide to stop it.

In Exercise 4.7, you will complete the steps needed to configure services in Windows 10.

EXERCISE 4.7

Configuring Services

1. Depending on what client you are utilizing:

   ▪ In Window 10, select Start ➤ Windows System ➤ Control Panel ➤ Administrative Tools ➤ Services.

   ▪ In Windows 11, select Start ➤ All Apps ➤ Windows Tools ➤ Services.

2. Scroll down the list and double-click Remote Desktop Configuration.

3. Under Startup Type, choose Automatic.

4. On the Logon tab, click the This Account radio button.

5. Click the Browse button and choose the local administrator account. Click OK.

6. In the Password boxes, type and verify the administrator password.

7. On the Recovery tab, make sure the following settings are configured:

   Action: Response

   First Failure: Restart The Service

   Second Failure: Restart The Service

   Subsequent Failures: Take No Action

   Reset Fail Count After: 1 Day

   Restart Service After: 10 Minutes

8. Click OK.

9. Close the Computer Management MMC.

Using services is just another troubleshooting and configuring tool that is part of your arsenal of troubleshooting techniques. Just remember that when your services are working properly, your Windows 10/11 operating system will be working properly.

Configuring Internet Browsers

Windows 10/11 comes with Microsoft Edge by default and is the Microsoft-recommended browser.

With the explosion of Internet use—even for the inexperienced end user browsing the Internet for personal reasons as well as for those who use it for work-related tasks—enhancing the user interface (UI) while providing better levels of security (which include privacy) has been the focus in the development of Microsoft Edge.

Microsoft Edge is loaded with user features to provide end users with a simple way to get the information they desire from their browsing experience.

The features in Edge are designed to give end users an easy way to browse the Internet for the information they're looking for while providing a secure environment for networks by recognizing potentially bad sites (those attempting to sneak viruses or Trojan horses into the network), phishing sites (those that attempt to steal private information about the user), or invasive sites that users may go to either on purpose or inadvertently.

Edge has taken browsing a step further with the implementation of Cortana. Cortana can assist you while working with Edge.

Cortana

Cortana is a powerful search and help utility. If your system has a microphone, you can ask Cortana questions and Cortana will help find an answer. If you don't have a microphone, you can type in your questions and Cortana will try to help find an answer.

Cortana is available for both Windows 10 and Windows 11; however, by default, on Windows 11, Cortana is no longer pinned to the taskbar and is not activated. You can still add the Cortana app to the taskbar as you would any other app. In addition, the keyboard shortcut that launched Cortana ([Windows] key + C) no longer opens Cortana.

There is no longer a Cortana icon on the Windows 11 taskbar, so the easiest way to find Cortana is by doing a search. Click the Search icon on the taskbar and type **cortana** into the search box. Press the Enter key and select the Cortana app from the search results (see Figure 4.35). Another way to get to the Cortana app is by going to Start ➤ Settings ➤ Apps ➤ Apps & Features and then type **Cortana** in the search apps box.

Before you can start using Cortana, you need to sign in with a Microsoft account. If you already use one for logging into Windows, click Sign In, select your account, and click Continue. Cortana may need access to some of your personal information to work. Click Accept and continue. Cortana is now ready to be used. You can type questions and press Enter, or you can click the Microphone button in the bottom right of the Cortana window and ask Cortana questions using speech.

With Cortana in Windows 10, you could add appointments to your calendar, set reminders, and send emails, but unfortunately, Cortana cannot do those tasks anymore in Windows 11. According to Microsoft:

We've spent a lot of time thinking through this transition and understand that these changes may be disruptive to some of our customers. We look forward to continuing to innovate on ways Cortana can help you navigate the modern workplace so you can save time and focus on the things that matter most in your day.

FIGURE 4.35 Searching for Cortana on Windows 11

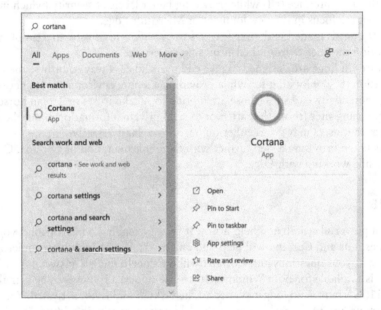

To modify the Cortana options, click the three dots in the upper-left corner of the Cortana app (see Figure 4.36).

FIGURE 4.36 Changing settings on the Cortana app

Browser Controls

When you open Edge, one of the first things that will catch your attention is the simplified design. The most common controls, like tools and favorite buttons, are just a click away. You also have the ability to customize how the browser will look and which tools that you can use with the browser.

Pinning Sites to the Taskbar

Pinning sites to your taskbar allows you to access websites by clicking the pinned site at the bottom of the taskbar. Pinning a site is a very easy process. Just drag the tab of the website to the taskbar. An icon for the website will stay pinned until you remove it. When you click the pinned icon, the website will open within the Internet browser. Another option is, while in Microsoft Edge, navigate to the website you want, click the three vertical dots to go to More Tools, then click Pin To Taskbar. Select a name for your website and then click Pin. You will now see the desired website pinned to the taskbar.

Searchable Address Bar

You can search the Internet directly from the Address bar. You still have the ability to enter a website's address and go directly to the website. But now you can enter a search term or incomplete address, thus launching a search using your currently selected search engine. You can choose which search engine you want to use by clicking the Address bar and choosing the search engine from the listed icons or adding a new search engine.

Security and Privacy Enhancements

Edge includes many security and privacy enhancements, including the following:

- ActiveX Filtering allows you to block ActiveX controls for any sites. You can turn them back on for the sites that you trust.

- Domain highlighting allows you to see the real web address of a website you are visiting. This allows you to avoid websites that use misleading web addresses.

- SmartScreen Filter helps protect you from online phishing attacks, fraud, and spoofed or malicious websites.

- You can use a 128-bit Secure Sockets Layer (SSL) connection with secure websites.

- InPrivate Browsing allows you to use the web without saving any data from the websites you visit while the browser is in this mode.

Using the Browser's Compatibility Mode

Microsoft Edge is Microsoft's default web browser and some websites may not be updated to use the new features or display their content correctly. Problems may exist, displaying misaligned images or text. When you use Compatibility mode, the browsers will display a web page the way it would have been displayed in previous versions, which should correct any display issues.

To enable Compatibility mode/Internet Explorer (IE) mode in Microsoft Edge, perform the following steps:

1. Open the Edge browser and click the Settings And More icon (three dots) at the top-right corner.

2. Choose Settings from the drop-down menu.

3. From the left sidebar on the Settings page, click Default Browser (see Figure 4.37).

4. Under the Internet Explorer Compatibility section, click the drop-down menu next to Allow Sites To Be Reloaded In Internet Explorer Mode, and select the Allow option.

5. Click the Restart button for this setting change to take effect.

FIGURE 4.37   Edge settings for Compatibility mode

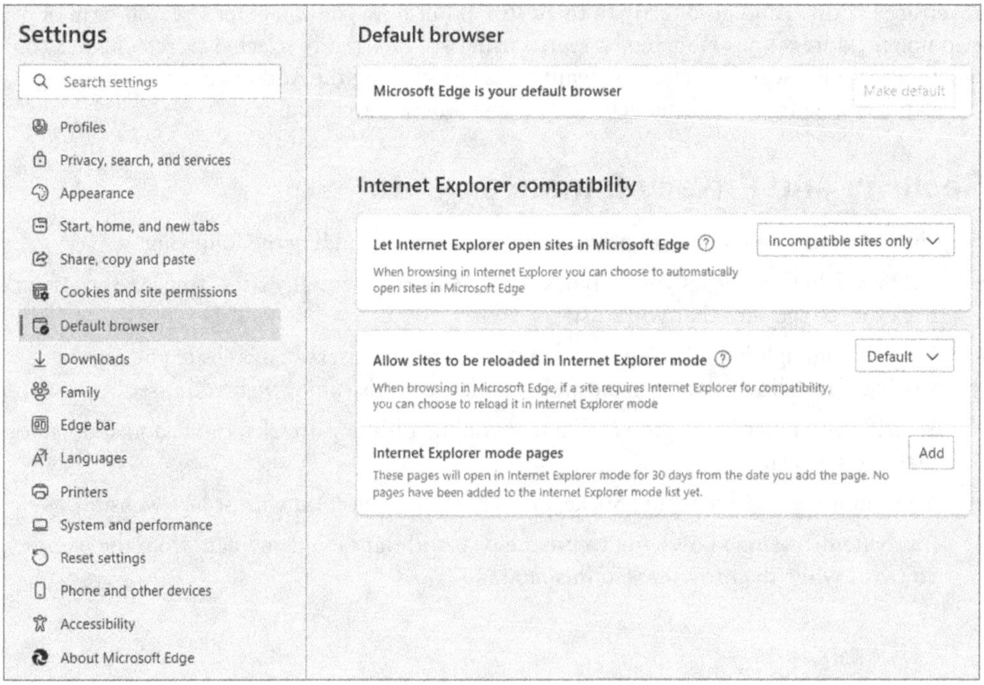

To open a website in IE Compatibility Mode, you need to browse to the website, then right-click the opened tab and choose Reload Tab In Internet Explorer Mode from the drop-down menu. You will see an Internet Explorer icon on the left navigation bar, which indicates that the web page is now opened in the Compatibility Mode or IE mode. When the pop-up window opens, click the Done button. If you want to open the specific web page always in IE Compatibility Mode, turn on the toggle switch next to Open This Page In Internet Explorer Mode Next Time. When you want to exit the Compatibility mode for a website, again right-click the tab and choose Exit Tab From Internet Explorer Mode.

When a web page loads in IE mode, the IE logo indicator displays on the left side of the navigation bar. You can click the IE logo indicator to display additional information, as shown in Figure 4.38.

FIGURE 4.38 Internet Explorer mode

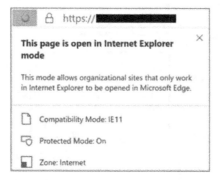

There is also a setting that allows you to manage the sites currently set to be viewed in Compatibility mode/IE mode. This can be seen in Figure 4.37 under the Internet Explorer mode pages. You have the option to also add sites by URL as well.

Using Enhanced Security Mode in Edge

The Enhanced Security mode is a browsing mode in Microsoft Edge where the security of your browser takes precedence and provides an extra layer of protection when you're surfing the web. You will want to turn on this mode if you want to browse the web more securely and help protect your browser from malware. There are two levels you can select from (see Figure 4.39):

- **Balanced – (Recommended):** Add Security Mitigations For Sites You Don't Visit Frequently, Most Sites Work As Expected, Blocks Security Threats

- **Strict:** Adds Security Mitigations For All Sites, Parts Of Sites Might Not Work, Blocks Security Threats

FIGURE 4.39   Enhanced Security mode

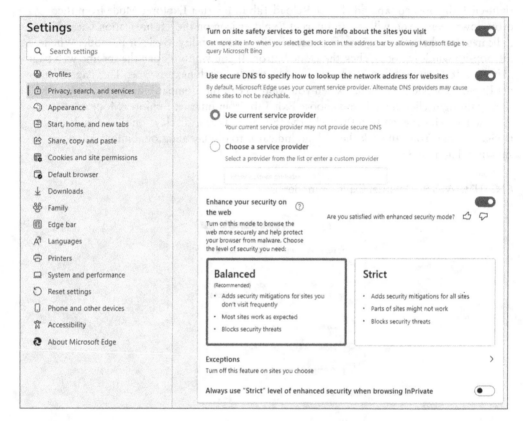

To enable Enhanced Security mode in Edge, follow these steps:

1. Open the Microsoft Edge browser on your computer.
2. Click the three-dotted icon and select Settings.
3. Select Privacy, Search, And Services from the menu on the left-hand side.
4. Scroll down to find the Enhance Your Security On The Web option.
5. Toggle the switch to turn it on.
6. Select your desired security level.

If you want to turn off Enhanced Security mode, just go back into the settings and turn off the toggle switch.

Using InPrivate Browsing

InPrivate Browsing provides some level of privacy to users using Microsoft Edge. The privacy maintained with InPrivate Browsing relates to a current browser where an InPrivate session has been enabled. The InPrivate session prevents the browsing history from being recorded and prevents temporary Internet files from being retained. Cookies, usernames, passwords, and form data will not remain in Edge following the closing of the InPrivate session, nor will there be any footprints or data pertaining to the InPrivate Browsing session.

InPrivate Browsing keeps information from being saved to the local machine while the session is active, but don't get lulled into a false sense of security; malware, phishing, and other methods that send data out of the local machine are still valid and can provide personal information to a cybercriminal. In addition, employees visiting forbidden sites from work, for instance, could still be detected via forensics.

InPrivate Browsing is a good method of protecting user data if you are not surfing from your own machine or are surfing from a public location (always a bad place to leave personal information). InPrivate Browsing can also be used if you don't want anyone to be able to see data from your Internet browsing session.

There are several ways to launch an Edge InPrivate Browsing session:

- Select and hold (right-click) the Microsoft Edge logo in the taskbar and select New InPrivate Window.

- In Microsoft Edge, select and hold (right-click) a link and select Open Link In InPrivate Window.

- In Microsoft Edge, select Settings And More (. . .)➢ New InPrivate Window.

Configuring Internet Options

In addition to security and usability options that you can configure in Edge, you can configure other options for managing the browser. Many of the configurations we have discussed in this chapter and have used to quickly change individual parameters are also available for modification within the Internet Options dialog box. The general parameters, security parameters, privacy configurations, content controls, connection settings, program options, and advanced settings available within Internet Options are discussed in the following sections.

You can open the Internet Properties dialog box by going to Control Panel and selecting Internet Options or by typing **Internet options** in the search box.

General Parameters

The General tab (Figure 4.40) allows you to change the default home page that appears when Microsoft Edge is launched. An interesting feature here is that you can have more than one default home page. When you enter more than one page in the Home Page text box, each time Edge is launched, all pages will open in their own tab.

FIGURE 4.40   General tab of Edge's Internet Properties

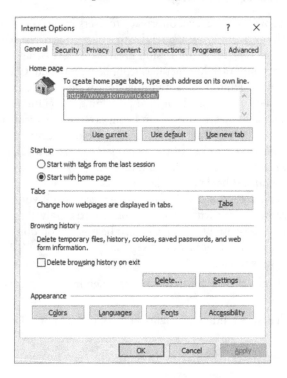

The General tab also allows you to control your Browsing History, Search, Tabs, and Appearance (including accessibility options) settings for the Edge interface.

Security Parameters

The Security tab (Figure 4.41) of Edge's Internet Properties dialog box not only gives you access to control Protected mode as discussed earlier in this section, it also gives you the ability to set security settings on the specific zones you may browse to as understood by Edge. The zones are Internet, Local Intranet, Trusted Sites, and Restricted Sites. You can set the behavior of Edge individually for each zone and even individual sites within each zone. For example, if you add a website to the Local Intranet settings, you will not be asked to authenticate your credentials when connecting to the website.

Privacy Configurations

The Privacy (Figure 4.42) tab of Edge's Internet Properties allows the management of privacy settings for the Internet zone; this is the cookie management for specific sites. You can also control the settings for the pop-up blocker and your InPrivate Filtering and InPrivate Browsing here.

FIGURE 4.41   Security tab of Edge's Internet Properties

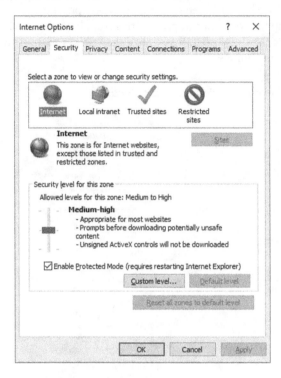

FIGURE 4.42   Privacy tab of Edge's Internet Properties

The pop-up blocker allows you to prevent unwanted Internet pop-ups from appearing while you are online. We have all been on websites where pop-up windows start appearing. With the Edge pop-up blocker, you can prevent this from happening. Make sure the check box under Pop-up Blocker is selected. If you click the Settings button, you can customize exceptions, as shown in Figure 4.43.

FIGURE 4.43   Privacy tab – Pop-up Blocker Settings

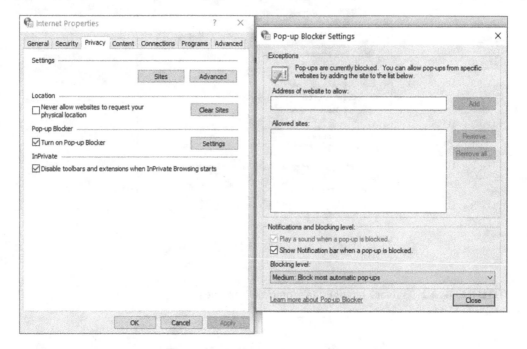

You can also block pop-ups by following these steps:

1. In Microsoft Edge, go to Settings And More (. . .)➤ Settings ➤ Cookies And Site Permissions.

2. Select Pop-ups And Redirects.

3. Turn the Block (Recommended) toggle to On.

   You can also block cookies by following these steps:

1. In Microsoft Edge, go to Settings And More (. . .)➤ Settings ➤ Cookies And Site Permissions.

2. Select Manage And Delete Cookies And Site Data.

3. Turn the Block Third-Party Cookies toggle to On.

Content Control

Figure 4.44 shows the Content tab of Internet Properties. Certificate management for secure browsing is managed through the Content tab. You have the ability to manage AutoComplete functionality as well as RSS feeds and Web Slice data from the Content tab.

The AutoComplete functionality allows Edge to automatically fill in fields as you complete forms on the Internet. It uses previously entered data to complete the fields on the form.

The Feeds And Web Slices section allows you to fill in what subscription feeds you belong to on the Internet and specify how often those feeds and slices will be updated along with other configuration options (i.e., playing a sound when the feed or slice is updated).

FIGURE 4.44   Content tab of the Internet Options dialog box

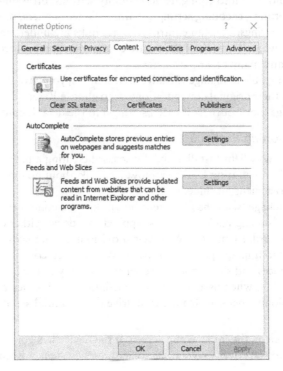

Connection Settings

The Connections tab of Edge's Internet Properties dialog box allows you to manage the way Edge gains access to the network. You can initiate the Connect To The Internet Wizard from this tab as well as set up a virtual private network (VPN). If you are using dial-up networking, this connection is also configured from the Connections tab. Local area network

(LAN) general settings, which include specifying a proxy server if you need to use one (this is typical across many corporate sites, to provide a better level of anonymity for Internet surfing), are configured here as well.

Program Options

The Programs tab of the Edge's Internet Properties dialog box allows you to establish a default web browser. You can manage add-ons specific to Edge here as well. Additionally, you can set up an application to allow for HTML editing and set up default programs to be used for Internet services such as email.

Advanced Options

The Advanced tab allows you to configure accessibility settings, browsing settings, international browsing settings, encoding settings, multimedia parameters, printing parameters, and general security settings. You can control whether links are underlined, whether pictures should be displayed, which versions of the secure communication protocols or SSL are used, background colors, and many other parameters.

In addition to being able to change the advanced settings, you have the option to restore advanced settings to their original configurations or to choose Reset Edge Settings, which resets all Edge settings (not just the advanced settings) to the default configuration.

Applying a Provisioning Package

In Chapter 1, "Windows Client Installation," I discussed creating a provisioning package by using the Windows Configuration Designer. Now, let's talk about how to install the provisioning package onto a client machine.

A provisioning package (with the file extension .ppkg) is a container for a set of configuration settings. Provisioning packages can be applied to a device either during the initial OOBE setup or afterward. Remember, Windows provisioning can make it easier for you to configure devices without imaging. You can specify your desired configuration and settings in order to enroll devices and then apply those settings quickly to the targeted devices. Provisioning packages are best when used for small to medium-sized businesses.

To apply a provisioning package from a USB drive during initial setup, perform the following steps:

1. Start with a device on the initial setup screen. If the device has gone past this screen, reset the device to start over. To reset, go to Settings ➢ System ➢ Recovery ➢ Reset This PC.

2. Insert the USB drive. If nothing happens when you insert the USB drive, press the [Windows] key five times.

   ▪ If there is only one provisioning package on the USB drive, the provisioning package is applied. If this is the case, move to step 5.

   ▪ If there is more than one provisioning package on the USB drive, Windows Setup will recognize the drive and will ask how you want to provision the device. Select Install Provisioning Package and click Next.

3. Select the provisioning package that you want to apply, and click Yes.

   Windows installs the selected provisioning package and applies it to the device.

4. Wait for the device to load and begin applying the provisioning package. Once you see "You can remove your removable media now!" remove your USB drive. Windows will continue provisioning the device.

Provisioning packages can also be applied after the initial setup by going through the Windows Settings or by double-clicking a provisioning package. To apply a provisioning package using Windows Settings, perform the following:

1. Insert the USB drive, then navigate to Settings ➤ Accounts ➤ Access Work Or School ➤ Add Or Remove A Provisioning Package ➤ Add A Package.

2. Choose the method you want to use, such as Removable Media.

3. Select the provisioning package that you want to apply, and click Add.

4. Provisioning packages require administrator privileges because they can modify system policies and run scripts at the system level. Ensure that you trust the package you are installing before accepting the UAC prompt. Click Yes.

5. The provisioning runtime will ask if the package is from a source you trust. Verify that you are applying the correct package and that it is trusted. Click Yes, Add It.

Another option is to apply the provisioning package directly, such as from a USB drive, folder, network, or SharePoint site. To do this perform the following:

1. Navigate to the provisioning package and double-click it to begin the installation.

2. Provisioning packages require administrator privileges because they can modify system policies and run scripts at the system level. Ensure that you trust the package you are installing before accepting the UAC prompt. Click Yes.

3. The provisioning runtime will ask if the package is from a source you trust. Verify that you are applying the correct package and that it is trusted. Click Yes, Add It.

You can also utilize PowerShell to install a provisioning package. You will use the PowerShell cmdlet `Install-ProvisioningPackage`. This cmdlet is used to install PPKG files that are generated and exported by the Windows Configuration Designer tool. The `Install-ProvisioningPackage` cmdlet is supported on Windows 11 client operating systems only. For a complete list of parameters, check out Microsoft's website at `docs .microsoft.com/en-us/powershell/module/provisioning/ install-provisioningpackage`.

Manage and Use Hyper-V on Windows Client

Microsoft's hardware virtualization product is known as Hyper-V. Hyper-V is a built-in Windows feature that allows you to create a virtualized environment on a physical device known as a host machine. Using Hyper-V, you can create and run a software version of a computer, called a virtual machine (VM). A VM acts like a complete computer that runs an operating system and programs. One nice thing is that a Windows client can have multiple VMs.

Hyper-V provides hardware virtualization, which means that each VM runs on virtual hardware. Hyper-V allows you to create virtual hard drives, virtual switches, and a number of other virtual devices, all of which can be added to virtual machines.

There are a number of reasons why you might want to set up Hyper-V. Some of those reasons are:

- You can run software that requires an older version of Windows or non-Windows operating systems.

- You can experiment with other operating systems.

- You can test software on multiple operating systems using multiple virtual machines.

Hyper-V System Requirements

There are a few system requirements when setting up Hyper-V. These are:

- Windows 10/11 Enterprise, Pro, Workstation, or Education

- 64-bit Processor with Second Level Address Translation (SLAT)

- CPU support for VM Monitor Mode Extension (VT-c on Intel CPUs)

- Minimum of 4 GB of memory

The Hyper-V role cannot be installed on Windows 10/11 Home edition.

Enabling the Hyper-V Role

Hyper-V is the built-in tool for creating and using virtual machines on Windows 10/11. You do not need additional software to create a virtual machine, but Hyper-V isn't enabled by default, so to use Hyper-V virtualization, you need to enable it first.

There are several ways to enable the Hyper-V role on a Windows 10/11 client machine. Here is how you enable the Hyper-V role by using Settings:

1. Right-click the Start button and select Apps And Features.

2. Select Programs And Features on the right under Related Settings.

3. Select Turn Windows Features On Or Off (on the left-hand side).

4. Select Hyper-V and click OK (as shown in Figure 4.45).

5. When the installation is complete, you will be prompted to restart the computer.

You can also enable Hyper-V by using PowerShell. If you prefer, you can perform the following steps:

1. Open a PowerShell console as an administrator.

2. Run the following command:

```
Enable-WindowsOptionalFeature -Online -FeatureName Microsoft-
Hyper-V -All.
```

3. When the installation is complete, you will be prompted to restart the computer.

FIGURE 4.45   Enabling Hyper-V in the Windows Features dialog box

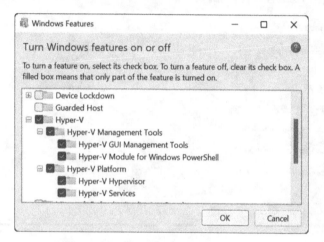

Opening the Hyper-V Manager

Once the device reboots, you can start using the Hyper-V Manager. Hyper-V Manager is the central management console for configuring your server and creating and managing your virtual machines, virtual networks, and virtual hard disks. Hyper-V Manager is managed through a Microsoft Management Console (MMC) snap-in. Whether you are using Windows 10 or Windows 11, the Hyper-V Manager is the same tool. The only difference between the two is that Hyper-V Manager on Windows 11 has rounded corners.

There are several different ways to launch the Hyper-V Manager, one way is to click Start and search for Hyper-V Manager by typing **hyper-v manager** in the search bar. When it appears as the best match result, click Run As Administrator on the right, as shown in Figure 4.46.

Virtual machines define the child partitions in which you run operating system instances. Each VM is separate and can communicate with the others only by using a virtual network. You can assign hard drives, virtual networks, DVD drives, and other system components to it. A VM is similar to an existing physical server, but it no longer runs on dedicated hardware—it shares the hardware of the host system with the other VMs that run on the host.

FIGURE 4.46   Launching the Hyper-V Manager

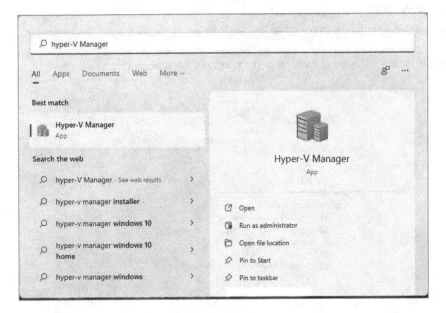

Exercise 4.8 shows you how to create a new VM. Before completing this exercise, download an evaluation copy of Windows from Microsoft's website (www.microsoft.com/downloads). Make sure the file downloaded is an image file (with the extension .iso). You will use this image to install the operating system into the virtual machine, and it will be used for demonstration purposes.

EXERCISE 4.8

Creating a New Virtual Machine

1. Open Hyper-V Manager (as shown in Figure 4.46 earlier).

2. In Hyper-V Manager, in the Actions pane, choose New ➤ Virtual Machine (see Figure 4.47).

3. In the New Virtual Machine Wizard, click Next on the Before You Begin page (see Figure 4.48).

FIGURE 4.47   Creating a new virtual machine in Hyper-V Manager

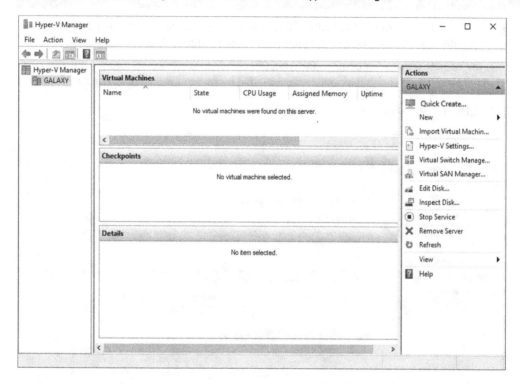

FIGURE 4.48   New Virtual Machine Wizard

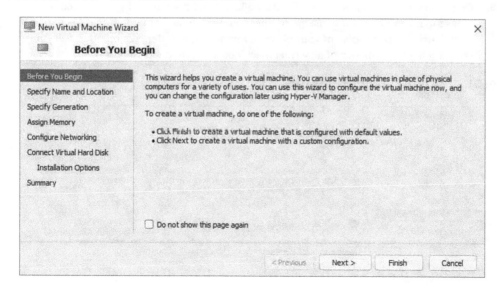

4. On the Specify Name And Location page, give your virtual machine a name and change the default location of the virtual machine configuration files. Click Next to continue.

5. The Specify Generation page opens next. Choose Generation 2 (see Figure 4.49) and click Next. Generation types will be discussed in more detail later in this chapter.

FIGURE 4.49   Specify Generation page

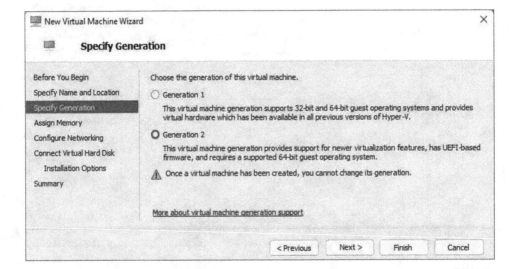

6. On the Assign Memory page (see Figure 4.50), define how much of your host computer's memory you want to assign to this virtual machine. Remember that once your virtual machine uses up all of your physical memory, it will start swapping to disk, thus reducing the performance of all virtual machines. Click Next to continue.

FIGURE 4.50   Assign Memory page

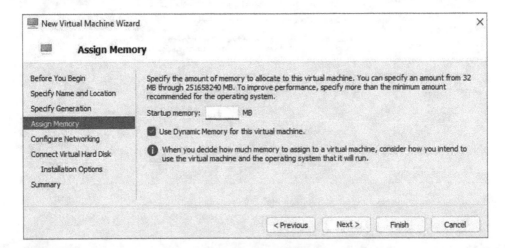

7. On the Configure Networking page (see Figure 4.51), select the virtual network that you previously configured using Virtual Network Manager. Click Next to continue.

FIGURE 4.51   Networking page

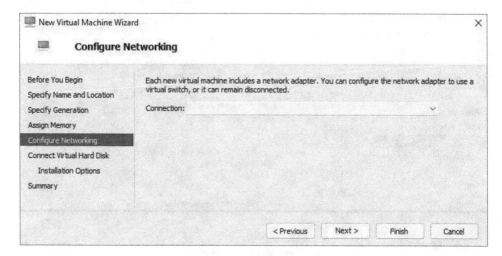

8. On the next page, you configure your virtual hard disk (see Figure 4.52). You can create a new virtual hard disk, select an existing disk, or choose to attach the hard disk later. Be aware that you can create only a dynamically expanding virtual disk on this page; you cannot create a differencing, physical, or fixed virtual hard disk here. However, if you created the virtual hard disk already, you can, of course, select it. Click Next to continue.

9. On the Installation Options page (see Figure 4.53), you can select how you want to install your operating system. You have the option to install an operating system later, install the operating system from a boot CD/DVD-ROM where you can select a physical device or an image file (ISO file), install an operating system from a floppy disk image (VFD file, or a virtual boot floppy disk), or install an operating system from a network-based installation server. The last option will install a legacy network adapter to your virtual machine so that you can boot from the network adapter. Select Install An Operating System From A Bootable CD/DVD-ROM and choose Image File (.iso). Then click Next.

EXERCISE 4.8 *(continued)*

FIGURE 4.52 Connect Virtual Hard Disk page

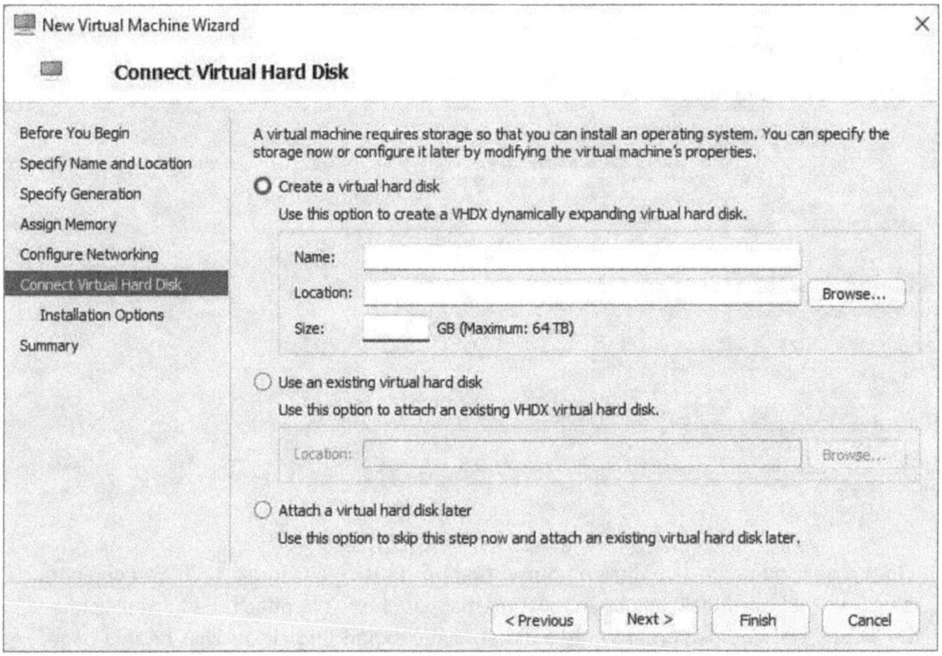

FIGURE 4.53 Installation Options page

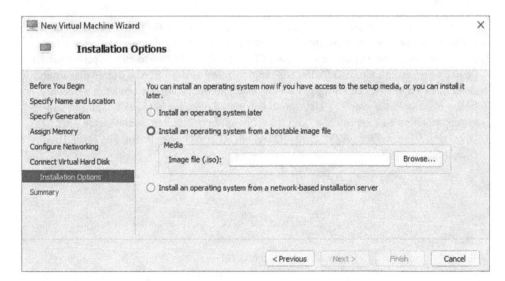

10. On the Completing the New Virtual Machine Wizard Summary page, verify that all settings are correct. You also have the option to start the virtual machine immediately after creation. Click Next to create the virtual machine.

11. Repeat this process and create a few more virtual machines.

After completing Exercise 4.8, you will have a VM available in Hyper-V Manager. Initially, the state of the VM will be Off. Virtual machines can have the following states: Off, Starting, Running, Paused, and Saved. You can change the state of a VM in the Virtual Machines pane by right-clicking the virtual machine's name or by using the Virtual Machine Connection window.

Here is a list of some of the state options (when the VM is running) available for a virtual machine:

Start   Turn on the virtual machine. This is similar to pressing the power button when the machine is turned off. This option is available when your VM is Off or in Saved state.

Turn Off   Turn off the virtual machine. This is similar to pressing the power-off button on the computer. This option is available when your virtual machine is in Running, Saved, or Paused state.

Shut Down   This option shuts down your operating system. You need to have the Hyper-V Integration Components installed on the operating system; otherwise, Hyper-V will not be able to shut down the system.

Save   The virtual machine is saved to disk in its current state. This option is available when your virtual machine is in Running or Paused state.

Pause   Pause the current virtual machine, but do not save the state to disk. You can use this option to release processor utilization quickly from this virtual machine to the host system.

Reset   Reset the virtual machine. This is like pressing the reset button on your computer. You will lose the current state and any unsaved data in the virtual machine. This option is available when your VM is in the Running or the Paused state.

Resume   When your virtual machine is paused, you can resume it and bring it online again.

Changing Configuration on an Existing Virtual Machine

To change the configuration settings on an existing virtual machine, right-click the virtual machine's name in the Virtual Machines pane in Hyper-V Manager and choose Settings.

You can change settings such as memory allocation and hard drive configuration. All items that you can configure are described in the following list:

Add Hardware   Add devices to your virtual machine, namely, a SCSI controller, a network adapter, or a legacy network adapter. A legacy network adapter is required if you want to perform a network-based installation of an operating system.

Firmware   This is the replacement of the virtual machine's BIOS. Because you can no longer enter the BIOS during startup, you need to configure it with this setting. You can turn Num Lock on or off and change the basic startup order of the devices.

Security   This is where you have the option to enable Secure Boot, set up encryption support using Trusted Platform Module (TPM), and set up a security policy by enabling shielding.

Memory   Change the amount of RAM allocated to the virtual machine.

Processor   Change the number of logical processors this VM can use and define resource control to balance resources among virtual machines by using a relative weight.

IDE Controller   Add/change and remove devices from the IDE controller. You can have hard drives or DVD drives as devices. Every IDE controller can have up to two devices attached, and by default, you have two IDE controllers available.

Hard Drive   Select a controller to attach to this device as well as specify the media to use with your virtual hard disk. The available options are Virtual Hard Disk File (with additional buttons labeled New, Edit, Inspect, and Browse) and Physical Hard Disk. You can also remove the device here.

DVD Drive   Select a controller to attach to this device and specify the media to use with your virtual CD/DVD drive. The available options are None, Image File (ISO Image), and Physical CD/DVD Drive Connected To The Host Computer. You also can remove the device here.

SCSI Controller   Configure all hard drives that are connected to the SCSI controller. You can add up to 63 hard drives to each SCSI controller, and you can have multiple SCSI controllers available.

Network Adapter   Specify the configuration of the network adapter or remove it. You can also configure the virtual network and MAC address for each adapter and enable virtual LAN identification. The Network Adapter section also allows you to control Bandwidth Management.

Bandwidth Management allows you to specify how the network adapter will utilize network bandwidth. You have the ability to set a minimum network bandwidth that a network adapter can use and a maximum bandwidth. This gives you greater control over how much bandwidth a virtual network adapter can use.

Diskette   Specify a virtual floppy disk file to use.

Name   Edit the name of the VM and provide some notes about it.

Integration Services   Define what integration services are available to your virtual machine. Options are Operating System Shutdown, Time Synchronization, Data Exchange, Heartbeat, and Backup (Volume Snapshot).

Checkpoints   Define the default file location of your checkpoint files. Checkpoints will be discussed in greater detail later in this chapter.

Smart Paging File Location   This area allows you to set up a paging file for your virtual machine. If you have a VM that has a smaller amount of memory than what it needs for startup memory, when the VM gets restarted, Hyper-V then needs additional memory to restart it. Smart Paging is used to bridge the memory gap between minimum memory and startup memory. This allows your virtual machines to restart properly.

Automatic Start   Define what this VM will do when the physical computer starts. Options are Nothing, Automatically Start If The Service Was Running, and Always Start This Virtual Machine. You also can define a start delay here.

Automatic Stop   Define what this virtual machine will do when the physical computer shuts down. Options are Save State, Turn Off, and Shut Down.

Please be aware that only some settings can be changed when the virtual machine's state is Running. It is best practice to shut down the virtual machine before you modify any setting.

Deleting Virtual Machines

You can also delete virtual machines using Hyper-V Manager. Doing so deletes all of the configuration files, as shown in Figure 4.54.

FIGURE 4.54   Delete Selected Virtual Machines warning window

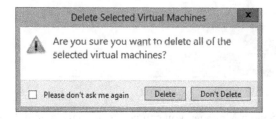

Make sure you manually delete any virtual disks that were part of the virtual machines to free up disk space. Virtual disks are *not* deleted when you delete a virtual machine.

Manage Virtual Switches

A *virtual network* provides the virtual links between nodes in either a virtual or a physical network. Virtual networking in Hyper-V is provided in a secure and dynamic way because you can granularly define virtual network switches for their required usage. For example, you can define a private or internal virtual network if you don't want to allow your virtual machines to send packages to the physical network.

To allow your virtual machines to communicate with each other, you need virtual networks. Just like normal networks, virtual networks exist only on the host computer and allow you to configure how virtual machines communicate with each other, with the host, and with the network or the Internet. You manage virtual networks in Hyper-V using the Virtual Switch Manager, as shown in Figure 4.55.

FIGURE 4.55   Virtual Switch Manager

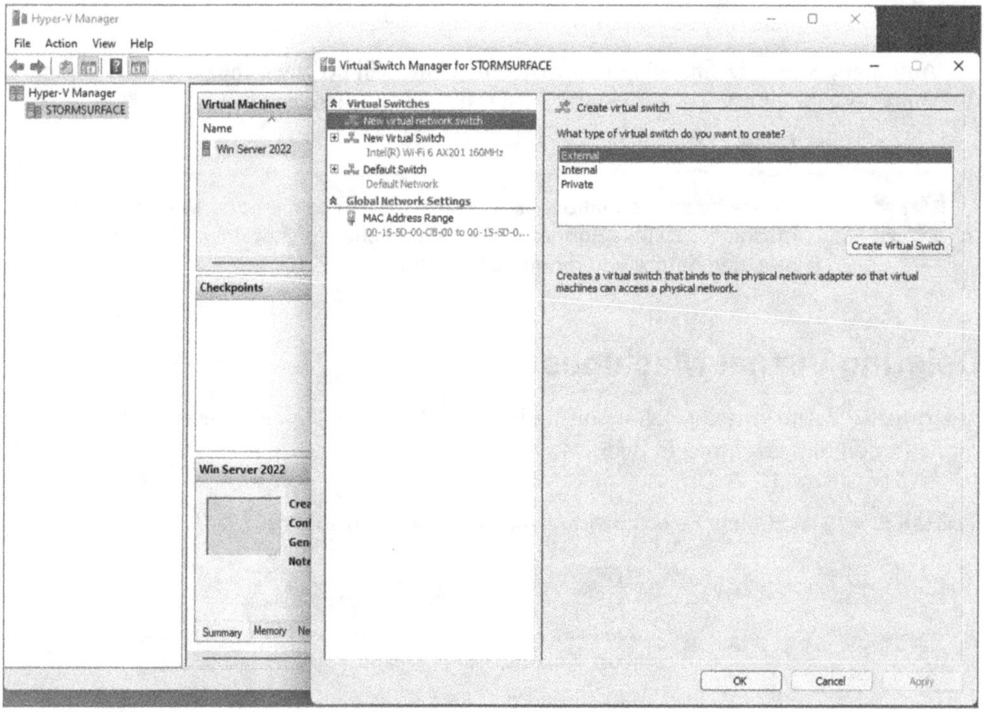

Using the Virtual Switch Manager, you can create, manage, and delete virtual switches. You can define the network type as external, internal only, or private:

External   Any virtual machine connected to this virtual switch can access the physical network. You would use this option if you want to allow your virtual machines to access—for example, other servers on the network or the Internet. This option is used in production environments where your clients connect directly to the virtual machines.

Internal This option allows virtual machines to communicate with each other as well as the host system but not with the physical network. When you create an internal network, it also creates a local area connection in Network Connections that allows the host machine to communicate with the virtual machines. You can use this if you want to separate your host's network from your virtual networks.

Private When you use this option, virtual machines can communicate with each other but not with the host system or the physical network; thus, no network packets are hitting the wire. You can use this to define internal virtual networks for test environments or labs, for example.

On the external and internal-only virtual networks, you also can enable virtual LAN (VLAN) identification. You can use VLANs to partition your network into multiple subnets using a VLAN ID. When you enable virtual LAN identification, the NIC that is connected to the switch will never see packets tagged with VLAN IDs. Instead, all packets traveling from the NIC to the switch will be tagged with the access mode VLAN ID as they leave the switch port. All packets traveling from the switch port to the NIC will have their VLAN tags removed. You can use this if you are already logically segmenting your physical machines and also use it for your virtual ones.

Exercise 4.9 explains how to create an internal-only virtual switch.

EXERCISE 4.9

Creating an Internal Virtual Network

1. Open the Hyper-V Manager.

2. In Hyper-V Manager, in the Actions pane, choose Virtual Switch Manager.

3. On the Virtual Switch page, select Private and click the Create Virtual Switch button.

4. On the New Virtual Switch page, enter **Private Virtual Network** in the Name field.

5. Click OK.

Now that you have created an internal switch, it appears under Virtual Switches in the Virtual Switch Manager, as shown in Figure 4.56.

This is also the case when you create an external virtual network because it will replace the physical network card of the host machine to give the parent partition a virtual network card that is also used in the child partitions.

FIGURE 4.56 Virtual Switch Manager with new internal switch

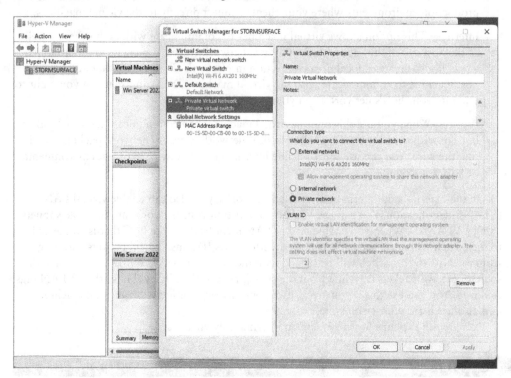

Hyper-V binds the virtual network service to a physical network adapter only when an external virtual network is created. The benefit of this is that the performance is better if you do not use the external virtual network option. The downside, however, is that there will be a network disruption when you create or delete an external virtual network.

> Communication between the virtual machine and the local host computer is not configured automatically. Once you install a VM, you need to make sure that the TCP/IP settings are in agreement with the settings you define in the virtual network card. Start with a ping from your host machine to the virtual machines to verify that communication is working.

Managing Virtual Hard Disks

In addition to virtual networks, you need to manage virtual hard disks (VHDs) that you attach to your virtual machines. A virtual hard disk in Hyper-V is a VHD or VHDX file that basically simulates a hard drive on your virtual machine.

VHD is a file format that represents a virtual hard disk drive (HDD). A VHD may contain the same components that are found on a physical HDD, such as disk partitions and a filesystem. It is typically used as the hard disk of a virtual machine.

VHDX is a Hyper-V virtual hard disk file format. VHDX has a larger storage capacity of 64 TB and provides data corruption protection in the event of a power failure. It prevents performance degradation on new, large-sector physical disks by optimizing structural alignments of dynamic and differencing disks.

The following sections will first show you what types of virtual hard disks are available and then show you how to create them. You will also learn about what options are available to manage virtual hard disks.

Types of Hard Disks

Depending on how you want to use the disk, Hyper-V offers various types, as described in Table 4.5.

TABLE 4.5 Virtual hard disks in Hyper-V

Type of disk	Description	When to use it
Dynamically expanding	This disk starts with a small VHD file and expands it on demand once an installation takes place. It can grow to the maximum size you defined during creation. You can use this type of disk to clone a local hard drive during creation.	This option is effective when you don't know the exact space needed on the disk and when you want to preserve hard disk space on the host machine. Unfortunately, it is the slowest disk type.
Fixed size	The size of the VHD file is fixed to the size specified when the disk is created. This option is faster than a dynamically expanding disk. However, a fixed-size disk uses up the maximum defined space immediately. This type is ideal for cloning a local hard drive.	A fixed-size disk provides faster access than dynamically expanding or differencing disks, but it is slower than a physical disk.
Differencing	This type of disk is associated in a parent-child relationship with another disk. The differencing disk is the child, and the associated virtual disk is the parent. Differencing disks include only the differences to the parent disk. By using this type, you can save a lot of disk space in similar virtual machines. This option is suitable if you have multiple virtual machines with similar operating systems.	Differencing disks are most commonly found in test environments and should not be used in production environments.

Creating Virtual Hard Disks

There are a number of ways that you can create a new VHD or VHDX in Windows 10/11. These include using Disk Management, Hyper-V Manager, PowerShell, and the command prompt. We are going to be using Hyper-V Manager to help you gain practice in creating virtual hard disks. Exercise 4.10 will teach you how to create a differencing virtual hard disk.

EXERCISE 4.10

Creating a Differencing Hard Disk

1. Open Hyper-V Manager.

2. In Hyper-V Manager, on the Actions pane, choose New ≻ Hard Disk.

3. In the New Virtual Hard Disk Wizard, click Next on the Before You Begin page.

4. On the Choose Disk Format screen, choose VHDX and click Next. The size of your VHDs depends on which format you choose. If you're going to have a VHD larger than 2,040 GB, use VHDX. If your VHD is less than 2,040 GB, then you should use VHD.

5. On the Choose Disk Type page, select Differencing and click Next.

6. On the Specify Name And Location page, enter the new name of the child disk (for example, **newvirtualharddisk.vhdx**). You can also modify the default location of the new VHD file if you want. Click Next.

7. On the Configure Disk page, specify the size of the VHD file. Choose a size based on your hard disk and then click Next. I used 60 GB as our test size.

8. On the Completing the New Virtual Hard Disk Wizard page, verify that all settings are correct and click Finish to create the hard disk.

Managing Virtual Hard Disks

Hyper-V also provides two tools to manage virtual hard disks: Inspect Disk and Edit Disk. These tools are available on the Actions pane in Hyper-V Manager:

Inspect Disk   This provides you with information about the virtual hard disk. It shows you not only the type of the disk but also information such as the maximum size for dynamically expanding disks and the parent VHD for differencing disks.

Edit Disk   This provides you with the Edit Virtual Hard Disk Wizard, which you can use to compact, convert, expand, merge, or reconnect hard disks. Figure 4.57 shows you the Edit Virtual Hard Disk Wizard Before You Begin page.

Table 4.6 is an overview of what you can do with the wizard.

FIGURE 4.57   The Edit Virtual Hard Disk Wizard

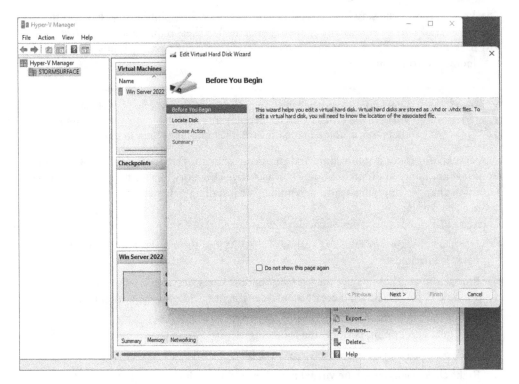

TABLE 4.6   Edit Disk overview

Action	Description
Compact	Reduces the size of a dynamically expanding or differencing disk by removing blank space from deleted files.
Convert	Converts a dynamically expanding disk to a fixed disk, or vice versa.
Expand	Increases the storage capacity of a dynamically expanding disk or a fixed virtual hard disk.
Merge	Merges the changes from a differencing disk into either the parent disk or another disk (applies to differencing disks only!).
Reconnect	If a differencing disk no longer finds its referring parent disk, this option can reconnect the parent to the disk.

Configure and Manage Checkpoints

Checkpoints record the state of a virtual machine at a certain point in time. It stores the existing data of a VM prior to any changes being made. Checkpoints allow you to restore a VM back to its original state if an error happens. Hyper-V checkpoints follow the same idea as Windows restore points.

Checkpoints were called snapshots in previous versions of Hyper-V. There are times when checkpoints may still be referred to as snapshots—as in some of the PowerShell commands later in this chapter.

A checkpoint is not a full backup and can cause data consistency issues with systems that replicate data between different nodes such as Active Directory. Before making software configuration changes, applying a software update, or installing new software, you may want to create a checkpoint.

Hyper-V includes two types of checkpoints (see Figure 4.58):

- Standard checkpoints take a snapshot of the VM and the state at the time the checkpoint is initiated.

- Production checkpoints use the Volume Shadow Copy Service or File System Freeze on a Linux virtual machine to create a data-consistent backup of the virtual machine. No snapshot of the virtual machine memory state is taken.

To create a checkpoint, perform the following steps:

1. In Hyper-V Manager, select the virtual machine.

2. Right-click the name of the virtual machine, and then click Checkpoint.

   When the process is complete, the checkpoint will appear under Checkpoints in the Hyper-V Manager.

You can also use PowerShell to create a checkpoint by using the `CheckPoint-VM` command.

If you want to revert your VM to a previous point in time, you can apply an existing checkpoint using either Hyper-V Manager or PowerShell:

1. In Hyper-V Manager, under Virtual Machines, select the virtual machine.

2. In the Checkpoints section, right-click the checkpoint that you want to use and click Apply.

3. A dialog box appears with the following options:

   - **Create Checkpoint and Apply:** Creates a new checkpoint of the VM before it applies the earlier checkpoint.

   - **Apply:** Applies only the checkpoint that you have chosen. You cannot undo this action.

   - **Cancel:** Closes the dialog box without doing anything.

FIGURE 4.58   Hyper-V Manager checkpoints

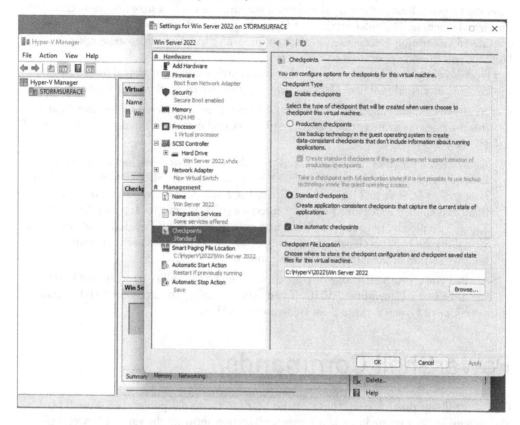

4.   Select either Create Checkpoint and Apply or the Apply option to create the checkpoint.

To see a list of checkpoints for a VM using PowerShell, use the `Get-VMCheckpoint` command, and to apply the checkpoint, use the `Restore-VMCheckpoint` command.

To change the checkpoint type, perform the following steps:

1.   Open the Hyper-V Manager.

2.   Right-click a virtual machine and select Settings.

3.   Under Management, select Checkpoints.

4.   Select the desired checkpoint type.

Generation 1 vs. Generation 2 VHDs

Previous versions of Hyper-V had some pretty major drawbacks. One big drawback was that Hyper-V could not boot a virtual machine from a virtual hard drive that was SCSI. Believe it or not, SCSI controllers were not even recognized by Hyper-V unless you installed the Integration Services component.

Another issue that the previous versions of Hyper-V had was the inability to copy files from the Hyper-V host to the virtual machines without the use of a network connection in the virtual machine. The older versions of Hyper-V, prior to Windows Server 2016, are now considered Generation 1 versions. Why is it so important to know which generations of Hyper-V you should use or need to use?

Hyper-V generations help determine what functionality and what virtual hardware you can use in your virtual machine. Hyper-V now supports two virtual machine generations:

- As already explained, previous versions of Hyper-V are considered *Generation 1*, and this provides the same virtual hardware to the virtual machine as in previous versions of Hyper-V.

- *Generation 2* provides better functionality of the virtual machines, including Secure Boot (which is enabled by default), the ability to boot from a SCSI virtual hard disk or boot from a SCSI virtual DVD, the ability to use a standard network adapter to PXE boot, and Unified Extensible Firmware Interface (UEFI) firmware support. Generation 2 gives you the ability to support UEFI firmware instead of BIOS-based firmware. On a virtual machine that is Generation 2, you can enable TPM and set security policies in the Security section of the virtual machine's properties.

So, when you create VHDs, one of your choices will be the ability to create the VHDs as a Generation 1 or a Generation 2 VHD. If you need the ability to have your VHDs run on older versions of Hyper-V, make them Generation 1 VHDs.

PowerShell Commands

One of the things that Microsoft has stated is that the exams are going to be more Power-Shell intensive. So, I wanted to add a PowerShell section showing the various PowerShell commands that you can use for Hyper-V. Table 4.7, taken directly from Microsoft's website, explains just some of the PowerShell commands that you can use with Hyper-V.

To see a more comprehensive list, please visit Microsoft's website at http://docs.microsoft.com/en-us/powershell/module/hyper-v/?view=windowsserver2019-ps.

TABLE 4.7 Hyper-V PowerShell commands

Command	Explanation
Add-VMDvdDrive	Adds a DVD drive to a virtual machine
Add-VMHardDiskDrive	Adds a hard disk drive to a virtual machine
Add-VMMigrationNetwork	Adds a network for virtual machine migration on one or more virtual machine hosts

Command	Explanation
Add-VMNetworkAdapter	Adds a virtual network adapter to a virtual machine
Add-VMSwitch	Adds a virtual switch to an Ethernet resource pool
Checkpoint-VM	Creates a checkpoint of a virtual machine
Convert-VHD	Converts the format, version type, and block size of a virtual hard disk file
Copy-VMFile	Copies a file to a virtual machine
Debug-VM	Debugs a virtual machine
Disable-VMConsoleSupport	Disables the keyboard, video, and mouse for virtual machines
Disable-VMMigration	Disables migration on one or more virtual machine hosts
Dismount-VHD	Dismounts a virtual hard disk
Enable-VMConsoleSupport	Enables the keyboard, video, and mouse for virtual machines
Enable-VMMigration	Enables migration on one or more virtual machine hosts
Enable-VMReplication	Enables replication of a virtual machine
Enable-VMResourceMetering	Collects resource utilization data for a virtual machine or resource pool
Export-VM	Exports a virtual machine to disk
Export-VMSnapshot	Exports a virtual machine checkpoint to disk
Get-VHD	Gets the virtual hard disk object associated with a virtual hard disk
Get-VHDSet	Gets information about a VHD set
Get-VHDSnapshot	Gets information about a checkpoint in a VHD set
Get-VM	Gets the virtual machines from one or more Hyper-V hosts
Get-VMDvdDrive	Gets the DVD drives attached to a virtual machine or snapshot
Get-VMHardDiskDrive	Gets the virtual hard disk drives attached to one or more virtual machines

TABLE 4.7 Hyper-V PowerShell commands *(continued)*

Command	Explanation
Get-VMMemory	Gets the memory of a virtual machine or snapshot
Get-VMNetworkAdapter	Gets the virtual network adapters of a virtual machine, snapshot, management operating system, or a virtual machine and management operating system
Get-VMProcessor	Gets the processor of a virtual machine or snapshot
Get-VMReplication	Gets the replication settings for a virtual machine
Get-VMSwitch	Gets virtual switches from one or more virtual Hyper-V hosts
Merge-VHD	Merges virtual hard disks
Mount-VHD	Mounts one or more virtual hard disks
Move-VM	Moves a virtual machine to a new Hyper-V host
New-VHD	Creates one or more new virtual hard disks
New-VM	Creates a new virtual machine
New-VMGroup	Creates a virtual machine group
New-VMSwitch	Creates a new virtual switch on one or more virtual machine hosts
Remove-VHDSnapshot	Removes a snapshot from a VHD set file
Remove-VM	Deletes a virtual machine
Remove-VMHardDiskDrive	Deletes one or more virtual hard disks from a virtual machine
Remove-VMNetworkAdapter	Removes one or more virtual network adapters from a virtual machine
Remove-VMReplication	Removes the replication relationship of a virtual machine
Remove-VMSan	Removes a virtual storage area network (SAN) from a Hyper-V host
Remove-VMSwitch	Deletes a virtual switch

Command	Explanation
Rename-VM	Renames a virtual machine
Rename-VMGroup	Renames virtual machine groups
Resize-VHD	Resizes a virtual hard disk
Restart-VM	Restarts a virtual machine
Save-VM	Saves a virtual machine
Set-VHD	Sets properties associated with a virtual hard disk
Set-VM	Configures a virtual machine
Set-VMBios	Configures the BIOS of a Generation 1 virtual machine
Set-VMMemory	Configures the memory of a virtual machine
Set-VMNetworkAdapter	Configures features of the virtual network adapter in a virtual machine or the management operating system
Set-VMProcessor	Configures one or more processors of a virtual machine
Set-VMReplicationServer	Configures a host as a Replica server
Set-VMSan	Configures a virtual storage area network on one or more Hyper-V hosts
Set-VMSwitch	Configures a virtual switch
Stop-VM	Shuts down, turns off, or saves a virtual machine
Suspend-VM	Suspends, or pauses, a virtual machine

Windows Sandbox

Windows Sandbox provides a desktop environment where you can test new apps or review files without affecting your computer. If you are testing a file and you notice that the file may be infected with malware, you can just shut the Sandbox down and the file will be erased and your computer will still be safe. With Windows Sandbox enabled, you can run software in a "sandboxed" environment and it will run separately from the host machine.

A sandbox is a short-term isolated environment. Once closed, all the software and files and the state will be deleted, and when you open a new instance, you will receive a brand-new instance of the sandbox.

Windows Sandbox has the following properties:

- Included in Windows 10/11 Pro and Enterprise. You do not need to download a VHD to use Windows Sandbox.

- Every time Windows Sandbox runs, it will be a clean new Windows environment.

- When you close the application, everything is deleted.

- Uses hardware-based virtualization for kernel isolation by relying on the Microsoft hypervisor to run a separate kernel. This isolates Windows Sandbox from the host.

- Uses the integrated kernel scheduler, smart memory management, and virtual GPU.

Prerequisites to Use Windows Sandbox

To use Windows Sandbox there are a few prerequisites that must be met:

- Windows 10/11 Pro, Enterprise, or Education (Windows Sandbox is currently not supported on Windows Home edition)

- AMD64 or (as of Windows 11 Build 22483) ARM64 architecture

- Virtualization capabilities enabled in BIOS

- At least 4 GB of RAM (8 GB recommended)

- At least 1 GB of free disk space (SSD recommended)

- At least two CPU cores (four cores with hyperthreading recommended)

Installing Windows Sandbox

To install Windows Sandbox, follow these steps:

1. Ensure that your machine is using Windows 10 Pro or Enterprise, Build 18305, or Windows 11.

2. Enable virtualization on the machine by doing one of the following:

   - If you're using a physical machine, make sure virtualization capabilities are enabled. We discussed enabling virtualization earlier in this chapter.

   - If you're using a virtual machine, run the following PowerShell command to enable nested virtualization:

     ```
     Set-VMProcessor -VMName \<VMName> -ExposeVirtualizationExtensions $true
     ```

3. If you're using Windows 10, in the search bar type **Turn Windows Features on or off** to access the Windows Optional Features tool. Select Windows Sandbox (see Figure 4.59) and then click OK. Restart the computer if you're prompted.

   If you're using Windows 11, open Settings ➤ Apps and click the Optional Features page on the right-hand side. If you do not see the Windows Sandbox option, it means that your computer does not meet the requirements to run Windows Sandbox. You can also enable Windows Sandbox by using PowerShell. Open PowerShell as an administrator and run **Enable-WindowsOptionalFeature -FeatureName "Containers-DisposableClientVM" -All -Online**.

4. Locate and select Windows Sandbox on the Start Menu to run it for the first time.

FIGURE 4.59   Selecting Windows Sandbox

Using the Windows Sandbox

Once Sandbox is enabled, it will create a copy of your Windows 10/11 installation in a virtual environment. You will not have access to personal folders when using Windows Sandbox, but you will still have Internet access. To use Sandbox:

1. To open the Windows Sandbox, type **Windows Sandbox** in the search box and then select it, or you can do a search using All Apps.

2. Windows Sandbox will open. It will be a secure version of your Windows client (see Figure 4.60). It looks very similar to a virtual machine.

3. Find the file (installer or executable) you want to run in the Sandbox and copy it from the host machine.

4. Switch to the Sandbox and paste the file into the Sandbox window. Or, you can download files directly from the Internet using the Edge browser that is included in the Sandbox.

FIGURE 4.60   The Windows Sandbox

5. Run the executable file or installer inside the Sandbox.

6. When you are done checking/testing the apps or files, close the Sandbox. You will see a dialog box that will verify that the Sandbox contents will be discarded and permanently deleted. Click OK.

Summary

Besides installing Windows client, configuring the operating system properly is one of the most important tasks that an IT team can perform.

Configuring the desktop environment allows you to create an environment that is comfortable for the end user, which in turn makes the user more productive.

Understanding the Start Menu and Control Panel options allows you to configure and operate the Windows 10/11 applications more efficiently. Knowing how to configure the System options properly in Control Panel allows you to fine-tune the Windows client operating system and get the best performance possible out of it.

In addition to using Control Panel to configure the Windows client, you can edit the Registry directly using the REGEDIT or REGEDT32 command. In Windows 10/11, REGEDT32 just opens REGEDIT.

Another important consideration when configuring Windows 10/11 is how the operating system will function when installed on a laptop or tablet (Windows Mobility). By configuring the mobility options on a laptop, you can allow that laptop to connect to your data in multiple ways.

We looked at services that run on Windows 10/11 and how to configure and troubleshoot them when they don't run properly. We also discussed how to configure virtual machines using the Hyper-V environment and how to create your own Hyper-V machines. I also showed you how to create and manage virtual machines. You also learned how to install and use Windows Sandbox to test applications and files without affecting your main system.

Exam Essentials

Be able to configure desktop settings.   Understand how to customize and configure the Windows 10/11 desktop settings. This includes setting up desktop personalization. It is also important to know how to configure the taskbar and Start Menu.

Be able to support mobile computers through power management features.   Understand the power features that are available in Windows 10/11, and be able to configure a laptop computer to use them.

Understand remote connections.   Know how to configure and connect to machines through remote connections. Know how to use Remote Assistance, Remote Desktop, and a VPN.

Know how to configure services.   Understand how to stop, start, monitor, pause, and configure services in Windows 10/11. Know how to configure the properties available through services.

Know Hyper-V's requirements and how to install it.   Know the hardware and software requirements as well as how to install Hyper-V and work with Windows Sandbox.

Video Resources

There are videos available for the following exercises:

   4.1

   4.2

   4.3

You can access the videos at www.wiley.com/go/sybextestprep.

Review Questions

1. You are the network administrator for StormWind Studios. You need to remove an old Registry key from a Windows 10/11 machine. Which of the following options could you use to remove the old Registry key?

   A. REGEDIT

   B. RGEDIT

   C. RGEDIT32

   D. REGEDITOR

2. You have a user, Rob, who uses a laptop computer running Windows 10/11. You have configured the laptop to enter Sleep mode after 30 minutes of inactivity. What will occur when the computer enters Sleep mode?

   A. The data will be saved to the hard disk and the computer will shut down.

   B. The data will be erased from RAM and the computer will shut down.

   C. The monitor will be turned off, but the hard disks will remain active.

   D. The data will be saved to memory and the computer will be put into a power-saving state.

3. You are the administrator for your company network. You have a Windows client laptop computer. A user reports that their battery seems to be having issues. You want to generate a report to review the battery life of the laptop that lists the expected battery life after a full charge. You'd also like to see the history of the battery life. What should you use to generate this report?

   A. From the command prompt, use the powercfg command.

   B. In Control Panel, use the Power Options settings.

   C. In the Settings app, use the Power & Sleep setting.

   D. Use Performance Monitor.

4. A new employee named Crystal has been supplied with a Windows client laptop computer. You have configured Crystal's computer with the Power Saver power plan, and you used the default options. Which of the following will occur after 20 minutes of inactivity on Crystal's computer?

   A. The display will be turned off, but the hard disk will remain active.

   B. The hard disk will be turned off, but the display will remain active.

   C. Both the hard disk and the display will be turned off.

   D. No components will be turned off.

5. You are the network administrator for a medium-sized company. You support all user desktop issues. Gary is using the default Windows client desktop on his laptop computer. Gary wants to change his desktop settings. Which of the following options should Gary use to configure the desktop in Windows 10/11?

    A. Right-click an empty space on the desktop and choose Personalize from the context menu.

    B. Select Control Panel ➢ System.

    C. Right-click My Computer and choose Manage from the context menu.

    D. Right-click My Computer and choose Properties from the context menu.

6. You work on the help desk for a large company. One of your users calls you and reports that they just accidentally deleted their `C:\Documents\Timesheet.xls` file. What is the easiest way to recover this file?

    A. In Folder Options, click the Show Deleted Files option.

    B. In Folder Options, click the Undo Deleted Files option.

    C. Click the Recycle Bin icon on the desktop and restore the deleted file.

    D. Restore the file from your most recent tape backup.

7. You are the system administrator for your company. You are configuring the services on a Windows client computer. You want to ensure that if a service fails to load, it will attempt to restart. Which tab of the service's Properties dialog box should you use?

    A. General

    B. Log On

    C. Recovery

    D. Dependencies

8. The system administrator of your network wants to edit the Registry, including setting security on the Registry keys. What primary utilities that support full editing of the Windows client Registry should the system administrator use? (Choose all that apply.)

    A. REGEDIT

    B. REDIT

    C. REGEDT32

    D. REGEDITOR

9. Kayla is dissatisfied with the configuration of her keyboard and mouse. She wants to reset the keyboard speed and the mouse pointer rate. What is one utility that she can use to configure the keyboard and mouse properties?

    A. Control Panel

    B. Computer Management

    C. Microsoft Management Console

    D. Registry Editor

10. Denise is using a laptop computer that uses ACPI. She wants to see what percentage of the battery power is still available. She also wants to know if hibernation has been configured. Which of the following utilities should she use?

    A. Device Manager

    B. Computer Manager

    C. Battery meter

    D. MMC

11. You are the administrator for your company network. You and a colleague are discussing a technology that allows you to run multiple operating systems concurrently on one computer. What is this technology called?

    A. Remote access

    B. A terminal server

    C. A virtual directory

    D. Virtualization

12. You and a colleague are discussing enabling device Sync settings. You'd like to sync the onscreen keyboard, sticky keys, filter keys, and toggle keys. What setting should you set in Sync?

    A. Ease of Access

    B. Language Preference

    C. Passwords

    D. Theme

13. You are the administrator for your company network. You have an application running that is causing issues. You open Task Manager and want to see what services are currently running on the computer. What tab do you use in Task Manager to stop a service from running?

    A. The Details tab

    B. The Services tab

    C. The Performance tab

    D. The Users tab

14. You are the administrator for your company network. You have several Windows client tablets. What should you do if you want to minimize power usage whenever a user presses the sleep button?

    A. Configure the sleep button setting to Hibernate using Power Options.

    B. Configure the sleep button setting to Sleep using Power Options.

    C. In the tablet's BIOS, disable the C-State control.

    D. Set the system cooling policy to passive by configuring the active power plan.

15. You are the administrator for your company network. You want to stop the computers in the IT department from sleeping. However, you still want the screens to shut off after a certain amount of time when the computer is not being used. What should you do if you want to configure and apply a standard power configuration scheme to the IT department's computers? (Choose all that apply.)

- **A.** On one of the computers in the IT department, use `powercfg /S` to modify the power scheme. Then, run `powercfg /export` to export the power scheme.
- **B.** On one of the computers in the IT department, use `powercfg /X` to modify the power scheme. Then, run `powercfg /export` to export the power scheme to the rest of the computers in the IT department.
- **C.** Use `powercfg /import` to import the power scheme to the rest of the IT department's computers. Then, run `powercfg /s` to set the power scheme to Active.
- **D.** Use `powercfg /import` to import the power scheme to the rest of the IT department's computers. Then run `powercfg /x` to set the power scheme to Active.

16. You are the administrator for your company network. Some employees want to change the wallpaper picture on their computers. What setting should you direct them to?

- **A.** Background
- **B.** Colors
- **C.** Theme
- **D.** Wallpaper

17. You are the administrator for your company network. Some employees want to change the screensaver on their computer. What setting should you direct them to?

- **A.** Background
- **B.** Lock Screen
- **C.** Screensaver
- **D.** Theme

18. You are the administrator for your company network. You want to use Windows PowerShell to create a service. What is the cmdlet that you will run?

- **A.** `Get-Service`
- **B.** `New-Service`
- **C.** `Restart-Service`
- **D.** `Start-Service`

19. You are the administrator for your company network. You support several Windows client laptops. You have been tasked to configure these laptops to support offline file access. What is the first step in configuring the laptops to meet your needs?

- **A.** Select Enable Offline Files.
- **B.** Select Manage Offline Files.
- **C.** Select Offline Files and then select Set Up.
- **D.** Select Set Up New Sync Partnerships.

20. You are the administrator for your company network. You and a colleague are discussing services. You want to change the service startup type, which can be set to automatic, manual, or disabled. What tab would you use to set this up?

A. The Dependencies tab

B. The General tab

C. The Log On tab

D. The Recovery tab

Chapter

5

Configuring Security and Devices

MICROSOFT EXAM OBJECTIVES COVERED IN THIS CHAPTER:

✓ **Configure and manage storage**

- Configure local storage.

✓ **Manage security settings on Windows client**

- Configure and manage Windows client firewall; manage virus and threat protection.

In this chapter, I am going to talk about configuring Windows 10/11. We'll look at how filesystems are configured and explore some of the security settings you can choose. Then we'll look at how to configure your hardware. Getting hardware up and running with today's operating systems is not usually a problem. With Plug and Play technology, the initial installation and configuration will typically go smoothly. However, you'll have to update the software controlling the hardware (drivers) over time and may need to roll back an update in case of an issue in a new package.

There will also be times when the drivers must be installed manually for legacy hardware. You may also have to verify the hardware configuration and make adjustments. The utility provided to perform these functions is Device Manager.

Device Manager displays all installed hardware. It also keeps information in storage, both removable and fixed, and displays communication devices like network interface cards and wireless and Bluetooth devices.

What you won't see for hardware in Device Manager are printers, unless of course they're USB. In that case, you will see the USB port and thus the printer will be identified, but you won't be able to configure the printer from Device Manager. You will use the Devices And Printers applet for configuring and troubleshooting printers in Control Panel or use Printers & Scanners in the Settings ➤ Devices section.

I will also discuss how to protect your Windows 10/11 devices by using the Windows Defender Firewall. The Windows Defender Firewall can help protect your client systems from being illegally breached, but when you're building a network, your Windows Defender Firewall should *not* be your only firewall. As you'll see, your network connection to the Internet should also be protected by another type of firewall. I will show you the different ways that you can protect your system using the Windows Security options.

Configuring Disk Storage

Windows 10/11 supports three types of disk storage: basic, dynamic, and GUID Partition Table (GPT). Basic storage is backward compatible with other operating systems and can be configured to support up to four partitions. Dynamic storage is supported by Windows 2000, Windows XP, Windows Vista, Windows 7, Windows 8, Windows 10 (and above), and Windows Server 2003 (and above) and allows storage to be configured as volumes. GPT support begins with the Windows 2003 SP1 release and allows you to configure volume sizes larger than 2 TB and up to 128 primary partitions. The following sections describe the basic storage, dynamic storage, and GPT storage configurations.

Basic Storage

Basic storage consists of primary and extended partitions and logical drives that exist within the extended partition. The first partition that is created on a hard drive is called a primary partition and is usually represented as the C: drive. Primary partitions use all of the space that is allocated to the partition, and a single drive letter is used to represent the partition. Only a single extended partition is allowed on any basic disk. Each physical drive can have up to four partitions. You can set up four primary partitions, or you can have three primary partitions and one extended partition. With an extended partition, you can allocate the space however you like, and each suballocation of space (called a logical drive) is represented by a different drive letter. For example, a 500 MB extended partition could have a 250 MB D: partition and a 250 MB E: partition.

At the highest level of disk organization, you have a physical hard drive. You cannot use space on the physical drive until you have logically partitioned the physical drive.

One of the advantages of using multiple partitions on a single physical hard drive is that each partition can have a different filesystem. For example, the C: drive might be FAT32 and the D: drive might be NTFS. Multiple partitions also make it easier to manage security requirements. I will discuss filesystem types later in this chapter.

Basic storage is the default, and this is the type that many users continue to use. But what if you want some additional functionality from your storage type? Let's look at some of the more advanced disk storage options.

Dynamic Storage

Dynamic storage is a Windows 10/11 feature that consists of a dynamic disk divided into dynamic volumes. Dynamic volumes cannot contain partitions or logical drives.

Dynamic storage supports three dynamic volume types: simple volumes, spanned volumes, and striped volumes. Dynamic storage also supports a Redundant Array of Independent Disks (RAID).

To set up dynamic storage, you convert or upgrade a basic disk to a dynamic disk. When converting a basic disk to dynamic, you do not lose any of your data. After the disk is converted, any partitions that existed on the basic disk are converted to dynamic simple volumes, and you can then create any additional dynamic volumes required within the dynamic disk.

You create dynamic storage with the Disk Management utility, which is discussed in the section "Using the Disk Management Utility" later in this chapter. Let's take a closer look at the different types of dynamic volumes.

Simple Volumes

A *simple volume* contains space from a single dynamic drive. The space from the single drive can be contiguous or noncontiguous. Simple volumes are used when you have enough disk space on a single drive to hold your entire volume. Figure 5.1 illustrates two simple volumes on a physical disk.

FIGURE 5.1   Two simple volumes

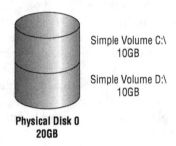

Simple Volume C:\
10GB

Simple Volume D:\
10GB

Physical Disk 0
20GB

Spanned Volumes

A *spanned volume* consists of disk space on two or more dynamic drives; up to 32 dynamic drives can be used in a spanned volume configuration. Spanned volume sets are used to dynamically increase the size of a dynamic volume. When you create spanned volumes, the data is written sequentially, filling space on one physical drive before writing to space on the next physical drive in the spanned volume set. Typically, administrators use spanned volumes when they are running out of disk space on a volume and want to dynamically extend the volume with space from another hard drive.

You do not need to allocate the same amount of space to the volume set on each physical drive. This means you could combine 500 MB on one physical drive with two 750 MB volumes on other dynamic drives, as shown in Figure 5.2.

FIGURE 5.2   A spanned volume set

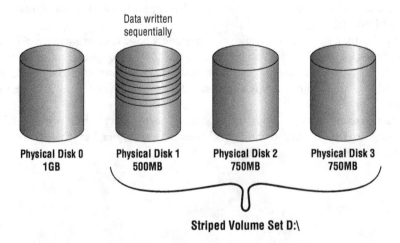

Data written
sequentially

Physical Disk 0   **Physical Disk 1**   **Physical Disk 2**   **Physical Disk 3**
1GB   **500MB**   **750MB**   **750MB**

Striped Volume Set D:

Because data is written sequentially, you do not see any performance enhancements with spanned volumes as you do with striped volumes (discussed next). The main disadvantage of spanned volumes is that if any drive in the spanned volume set fails, you lose access to all the data in the spanned set.

Striped Volumes

A *striped volume* stores data in equal stripes between two or more (up to 32) dynamic drives, as illustrated in Figure 5.3. Since the data is written sequentially across the stripe, you can take advantage of multiple I/O performance and increase the speed at which data reads and writes take place. Typically, administrators use striped volumes when they want to combine the space of several physical drives into a single logical volume and increase disk performance.

FIGURE 5.3   A striped volume set

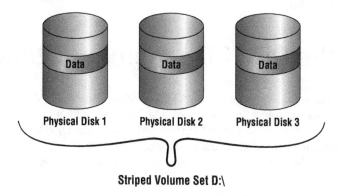

The main disadvantage of striped volumes is that if any drive in the striped volume set fails, you lose access to all the data in the striped set.

GUID Partition Table

The *GUID Partition Table (GPT)* is available for Windows 10/11 and was first introduced as part of the Extensible Firmware Interface (EFI) initiative from Intel. Basic and dynamic disks use the Master Boot Record (MBR) partitioning scheme that all operating systems have been using for years. Basic and dynamic disks use Cylinder-Head-Sector (CHS) addressing with the MBR scheme. CHS allows computers to assign addresses to data on the computer's hard disk drives. This has been an effective way to store data on a hard drive, but there is a newer, more effective way.

The GPT disk-partitioning system uses the GPT to configure the disk area. GPT uses an addressing scheme called Logical Block Addressing (LBA), which is a newer method of accessing hard disk drives. LBA uses a unique sector number only instead of using the cylinder, head, and sector number. Another advantage is that the GPT header and partition table are written to both the front and the back ends of the disk, which provides for better redundancy.

The GPT disk-partitioning system gives you many benefits over using the MBR system:

- Allows a volume size larger than 2 TB
- Allows up to 128 primary partitions
- Used for both 32-bit and 64-bit Windows 10 editions
- Includes cyclic redundancy check (CRC) for greater reliability

However, there is one disadvantage to using the GPT drives: you can convert a GPT drive only if the disk is empty and unpartitioned. I will show you the steps to creating a GPT disk later in this chapter.

To convert any disk or format any volume or partition, you can use the Disk Management utility. I will show you how to manage your disks using the Disk Management utility in the next section.

Using the Disk Management Utility

The Disk Management utility is a Microsoft Management Console (MMC) snap-in that gives administrators a graphical tool for managing disks and volumes within Windows 10/11. In the following sections, you will learn how to access the Disk Management utility and use it to perform basic tasks, including managing basic storage and dynamic storage. You will also learn about troubleshooting disks through disk status codes.

Understanding the Disk Management Utility

You can access the Disk Management utility in a few different ways. In Windows 10, you can right-click Computer in the Start Menu and select Manage, and then in Computer Management, select Disk Management. You could also use Control Panel ≻ Administrative Tools ≻ Computer Management. Or, in Windows 11, you can click the Start icon or press [Windows] key + X to launch the Quick Access menu and select Disk Management from the list of options.

First of all, to have full permissions to use the Disk Management utility, you must be logged on with local administrative privileges. The Disk Management utility's opening window, shown in Figure 5.4, displays the following information:

- The volumes that are recognized by the computer
- The type of disk, either basic or dynamic
- The type of filesystem used by each partition
- The status of the partition and whether the partition contains the system or the boot partition

- The capacity (amount of space) allocated to the partition
- The amount of free space remaining on the partition
- The amount of overhead associated with the partition

FIGURE 5.4 The Disk Management window

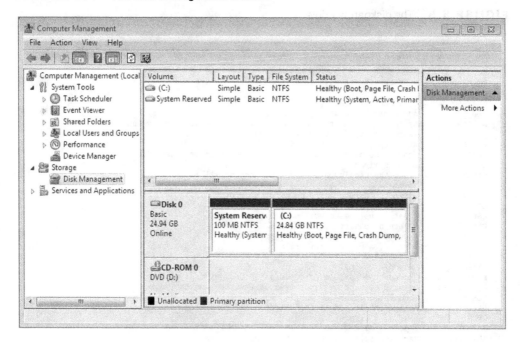

Windows 10/11 also includes a command-line utility called diskpart, which can be used as a command-line alternative to the Disk Management utility. You can view all the options associated with the diskpart utility by typing **diskpart** (as seen in Figure 5.5) at a command prompt and then typing **?** at the diskpart prompt.

The Disk Management utility allows you to configure and manage your disks. Let's take a look at some of the tasks that you can perform in disk administration.

Managing Administrative Hard Disk Tasks

The Disk Management utility allows you to perform a variety of hard drive administrative tasks:

- View disk properties.
- View volume and local disk properties.
- Add a new disk.
- Create volumes and partitions.

- Upgrade a basic disk to a dynamic or GPT disk.

- Change a drive letter and path.

- Delete partitions and volumes.

These tasks are discussed in the sections that follow.

FIGURE 5.5   The diskpart window

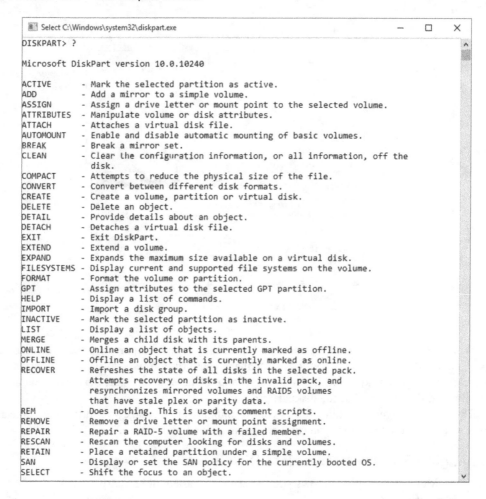

Viewing Disk Properties

To view the properties of a disk, right-click the disk number in the lower panel of the Disk Management main window and choose Properties from the context menu. This brings up the disk's Properties dialog box. Click the Volumes tab to see the volumes associated with the disk, as shown in Figure 5.6, which contains the following disk properties:

- The disk number
- The type of disk (basic, dynamic, CD-ROM, removable, DVD, or unknown)
- The status of the disk (online or offline)
- The partition style
- The capacity of the disk
- The amount of unallocated space on the disk
- The amount of space reserved on the disk
- The logical volumes that have been defined on the physical drive

 If you click the General tab of a disk's Properties dialog box, the hardware device type, the hardware vendor that produced the drive, the physical location of the drive, and the device status are displayed.

FIGURE 5.6 The Volumes tab of a disk's Properties dialog box

Viewing Volume and Local Disk Properties

On a dynamic disk, you manage volume properties. On a basic disk, you manage partition properties. Volumes and partitions perform the same function, and the options discussed in the following sections apply to both. (The examples here are based on a dynamic disk using a simple volume. If you are using basic storage, you will view the partition properties rather than the volume properties.)

To see the properties of a volume, right-click the volume in the upper panel of the Disk Management main window and choose Properties. This brings up the volume's Properties dialog box. Volume properties are organized on seven tabs: General, Tools, Hardware, Sharing, Security, Previous Versions, and Quota. The Security tab and Quota tab appear only for NTFS volumes. All these tabs are covered in detail in the following items.

General The information on the General tab of the volume's Properties dialog box, as shown in Figure 5.7, gives you a general idea of how the volume is configured. This dialog box shows the label, type, file system, used and free space, and capacity of the volume. The label is shown in an editable text box, and you can change it if desired. The space allocated to the volume is shown in a graphical representation as well as in text form.

FIGURE 5.7   General properties for a volume

The label on a volume or local disk is for informational purposes only. For example, depending on its use, you might give a volume a label such as APPS or ACCTDB.

The Disk Cleanup button starts the Disk Cleanup utility, which you can use to delete unnecessary files, thereby freeing disk space.

This tab also allows you to configure compression for the volume and to indicate whether the volume should be indexed.

Tools   The Tools tab of the volume's Properties dialog box, shown in Figure 5.8, provides access to two tools.

FIGURE 5.8   The Tools tab of the volume's Properties dialog box

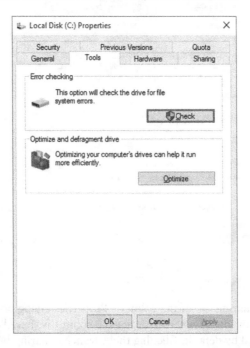

Click the Check button to run the Error-Checking utility to check the volume for errors. You may do this if you were experiencing problems accessing the volume or if the volume had been open during a system restart that did not go through a proper shutdown sequence.

Click the Optimize button to run the Disk Defragmenter utility. This utility defragments files on the volume by storing the files contiguously on the hard drive.

Hardware   The Hardware tab of the volume's Properties dialog box, shown in Figure 5.9, lists the hardware associated with the disk drives that are recognized by the Windows client operating system. The bottom half of the dialog box shows the properties of the device that is highlighted in the top half of the dialog box.

For more details about a hardware item, highlight it and click the Properties button in the lower-right corner of the dialog box. This brings up a Properties dialog box for the item. Your Device Status field should report, "This device is working properly." If that's not the case, you can click the Troubleshoot button (it will appear if the device is not working properly) to use a troubleshooting wizard that will help you discover the problem.

FIGURE 5.9   The Hardware tab of the volume's Properties dialog box

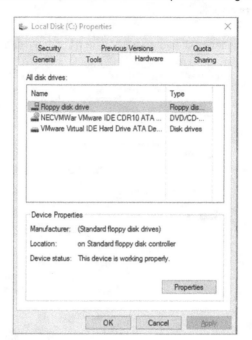

Sharing   On the Sharing tab of the volume's Properties dialog box, shown in Figure 5.10, you can specify whether or not the volume is shared on the network. Volumes are not shared by default. Clicking the Advanced Sharing button will allow you to specify whether the volume is shared and, if so, what the name of the share should be. You will also be able to specify who will have access to the shared volume.

Security   The Security tab of the volume's Properties dialog box, shown in Figure 5.11, appears only for NTFS volumes. The Security tab is used to set the NTFS permissions for the volume.

Previous Versions   The Previous Versions tab displays shadow copies of the files that are created by System Restore, as shown in Figure 5.12. Shadow copies of files are backup copies created by Windows in the background to allow you to restore the system to a previous state. On the Previous Versions tab, you can select a copy of the volume and either view the contents of the shadow copy or copy the shadow copy to another location. If System Restore is not enabled, then shadow copies of a volume will not be created.

FIGURE 5.10   The Sharing tab of the volume's Properties dialog box

FIGURE 5.11   The Security tab of the volume's Properties dialog box

FIGURE 5.12 The Previous Versions tab of the volume's Properties dialog box

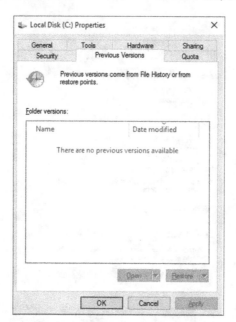

Quota   Quotas give you the ability to limit the amount of hard disk space that a user can have on a volume or partition (see Figure 5.13). By default, quotas are disabled. To enable quotas, select the Enable Quota Management check box. There are a few options that can be configured when enabling quotas.

FIGURE 5.13 The Quota tab of the volume's Properties dialog box

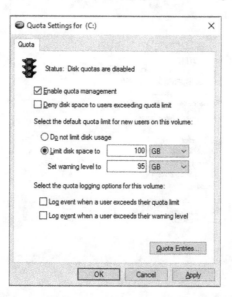

The Deny Disk Space To Users Exceeding Quota Limit check box is another option. When this box is selected, any user who exceeds their quota limit will be denied disk storage. You can choose not to enable this option, which allows you to just monitor the quotas. You also have the ability to set the quota limit and warning size and to log all quota events as they happen.

Adding a New Disk

New hard disks can be added to a system to increase the amount of disk storage you have. This is a fairly common task that you will need to perform as your application programs and files grow larger.

How you add a disk depends on whether your computer supports hot swapping of drives. Hot swapping is the process of adding a new hard drive while the computer is turned on. Most desktop computers do not support this capability. Remember, your user account must be a member of the Administrators group to install a new drive. The following list specifies configuration options:

Computer Doesn't Support Hot Swapping   If your computer does not support hot swapping, you must shut down the computer before you add a new disk. Then add the drive according to the manufacturer's directions. When you've finished, restart the computer. You should find the new drive listed in the Disk Management utility.

Computer Supports Hot Swapping   If your computer does support hot swapping, you don't need to turn off your computer first. Just add the drive according to the manufacturer's directions. Then open the Disk Management utility and select Action ➤ Rescan Disks. You should find the new drive listed in the Disk Management utility.

Creating Partitions and Volumes   Once you add a new disk, the next step is to create a partition (on a basic disk) or a volume (on a dynamic disk). Partitions and volumes fill similar roles in the storage of data on disks, and the processes for creating them are the same.

Creating a Volume or a Partition

Creating a volume or partition is a fairly easy process. To create the new volume or partition, right-click the unformatted free space and start the wizard.

Exercise 5.1 walks you through the New Volume Wizard for creating a new volume.

EXERCISE 5.1

Creating a New Volume

1. In the Disk Management utility, right-click an area of free storage space and choose the type of volume you want to create. If only one drive is installed, you will be able to create only a simple volume. You can click New Simple Volume to create a new simple volume.

2. The Welcome To The New Simple Volume Wizard appears. Click Next to continue.

3. The Select Volume Size screen appears. Select the size of volume to create, and then click Next to continue.

4. You should see the Assign Drive Letter Or Path screen. You can specify a drive letter, mount the volume as an empty folder, or choose not to assign a drive letter or drive path. If you choose to mount the volume into an empty folder, you can have a virtually unlimited number of volumes, negating the drive-letter limitation. If you choose not to assign a drive letter or path, users will not be able to access the volume. Make your selections, and click Next to continue (shown in Figure 5.14).

FIGURE 5.14   Assign Drive Letter Or Path screen

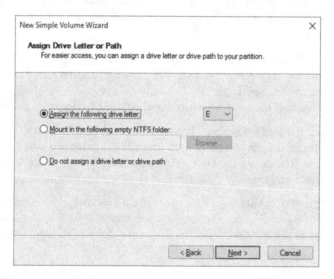

5. The Format Partition screen appears (see Figure 5.15). This screen allows you to choose whether you will format the volume. If you choose to format the volume, you can format it as FAT32 or NTFS. You can also select the allocation unit size, enter a volume label (for information only), specify whether or not you would like to perform a quick format, and choose whether or not to enable file and folder compression. After you've made your choices, click Next.

FIGURE 5.15   Format Partition screen

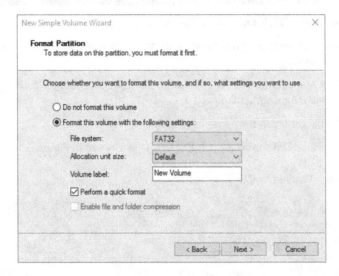

6. The Completing The New Volume Wizard screen appears. Verify your selections. If you need to change any of them, click the Back button to reach the appropriate screen. When everything is correctly set, click Finish.

Now that you know how to create a new volume or partition, let's see how to convert a basic disk to dynamic or GPT.

Upgrading a Basic Disk to a Dynamic or GPT Disk

When you perform a fresh installation of Windows 10/11, your drives are configured as basic disks. To take advantage of the features offered by Windows dynamic or GPT disks, you must upgrade your basic disks to either of those disk configurations.

Upgrading basic disks to dynamic disks is a one-way process as far as preserving data is concerned and is a potentially dangerous operation. Before you perform this upgrade (or make any major change to your drives or volumes), create a new backup of the drive or volume and verify that you can successfully restore the backup before proceeding with the change.

Any basic disk can be converted to a dynamic disk, but only a disk with all unformatted free space can be converted to a GPT disk. Exercise 5.2 walks you through converting an MBR-based disk to a GPT disk.

EXERCISE 5.2

Converting a Basic Disk to a GPT Disk

1. If the disk that you want to convert has partitions or volumes defined, first delete the partition or volume.

2. Open the Disk Management utility by clicking the Start button, right-clicking Computers, and choosing Manage.

3. Click Disk Management in the lower-left section.

4. Right-click the disk and choose Convert To GPT Disk (shown in Figure 5.16).

FIGURE 5.16 Convert To GPT Disk option

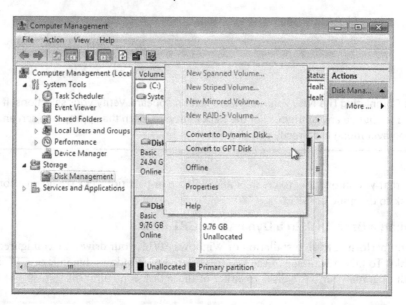

5. After the disk converts, you can right-click the disk and see that the Convert To MBR Disk option is now available.

There are a few other methods for converting an MBR-based disk to a GPT disk. You can use the diskpart utility and type the **Convert GPT** command. You can also create a GPT disk when you first install a new hard drive. After you install the new hard drive, during the initialization phase you can choose GPT Disk.

Another type of conversion that you may need to perform is that from a basic disk to a dynamic disk. Complete Exercise 5.3 to convert a basic disk to a dynamic disk.

EXERCISE 5.3

Converting a Basic Disk to a Dynamic Disk

1. In the Disk Management utility, right-click the disk you want to convert and select the Convert To Dynamic Disk option.

2. In the Convert To Dynamic Disk dialog box, check the disk that you want to convert and click OK.

3. In the Disks To Convert dialog box, click the Convert button.

4. A confirmation dialog box warns you that you will no longer be able to boot previous versions of Windows from this disk. Click Yes to continue to convert the disk.

As you are configuring the volumes or partitions on the hard drive, other things that you may need to configure are the drive letters and paths.

Changing the Drive Letters and Paths

There may be times when you need to change drive letters and paths when you add new equipment. Let's suppose you have a hard drive with two partitions: drive C: assigned as your first partition and drive D: assigned as your second partition. Your DVD drive is assigned the drive letter E:. You add a new hard drive and partition it as a new volume. By default, the new partition is assigned as drive F:. If you want your logical drives to be listed before the DVD drive, you can use the Disk Management utility's Change Drive Letter And Paths option to reassign your drive letters.

When you need to reassign drive letters, right-click the volume for which you want to change the drive letter and choose Change Drive Letter And Paths. This brings up the dialog box shown in Figure 5.17. Click the Change button to access the Change Drive Letter Or Path dialog box. Use the drop-down list next to the Assign The Following Drive Letter option to select the drive letter you want to assign to the volume.

FIGURE 5.17   The dialog box for changing a drive letter or path

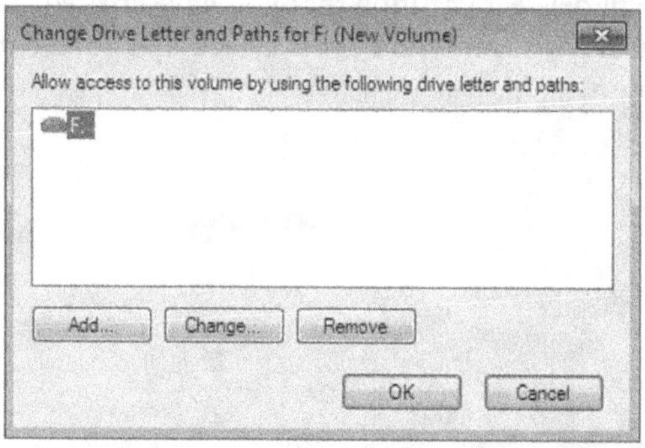

In Exercise 5.4, you will edit the drive letter of the partition you created.

EXERCISE 5.4

Editing a Drive Letter

1. Right-click Start ➤ Computer Management; then expand Storage ➤ Disk Management.

2. Right-click a drive that you have created and select Change Drive Letter And Paths.

3. In the Change Drive Letter And Paths dialog box, click the Change button.

4. In the Change Drive Letter Or Path dialog box, select a new drive letter and click OK.

5. In the dialog box that appears, click Yes to confirm that you want to change the drive letter.

Another activity that you may need to perform is deleting a partition or volume that you have created. The next section looks at these activities.

Deleting Partitions and Volumes

When configuring your hard disks, there may be a time that you want to reconfigure your drive by deleting the partitions or volumes on the hard drive. You may also want to delete a volume so that you can extend another volume. These are tasks that can be configured in Disk Management.

When deleting a volume or partition, you will see a warning that all the data on the partition or volume will be lost. You have to click Yes to confirm that you want to delete the volume or partition. This confirmation is important because once you delete a partition or volume, it's gone for good, along with any data content that was contained within it.

 The system volume, the boot volume, or any volume that contains the active paging (swap) file can't be deleted through the Disk Management utility. If you are trying to remove these partitions because you want to delete the Windows client, you can use a third-party disk-management utility.

In Exercise 5.5, you will delete a partition that you have created. Make sure that if you delete a partition or volume, it is empty; otherwise, back up all the data that you would like to retain before the deletion.

Deleting a Partition

1. In the Disk Management utility, right-click the volume or partition that you want to remove and choose Delete Volume.

2. A warning box appears, stating that once this volume is deleted, all data will be lost. Click Yes.

   The volume will be removed and the area will be returned as unformatted free space.

You may be worried that your users will remove devices from their Windows client machines. Microsoft has helped you in this situation. You can use removable-device policies to help restrict your users from removing their hardware. Removable-device policies can be created through the use of a Group Policy Object (GPO) on the server. GPOs are policies that are set on a computer or user and allow you to manipulate the Windows client environment.

Now that we have explored some of the basic administrative tasks of Disk Management, let's look at how to manage storage.

Managing Storage

The Disk Management utility offers support for managing storage. You can create, delete, and format partitions or volumes on your hard drives. You can also extend or shrink volumes on dynamic disks. Additionally, you can delete volume sets and striped sets.

Managing Dynamic Storage

As noted earlier in this chapter, a dynamic disk can contain simple, spanned, or striped volumes. Through the Disk Management utility, you can create volumes of each type. You can also create an extended volume, which is the process of adding disk space to a single simple volume. The following sections describe these disk-management tasks.

Creating Simple, Spanned, and Striped Volumes

As explained earlier, you use the New Volume Wizard to create a new volume. To start this wizard, in the Disk Management utility right-click an area of free space where you want to create the volume. Then, choose the type of volume you want to create: simple, spanned, or striped.

When you choose to create a spanned volume, you are creating a new volume from scratch that includes space from two or more physical drives, up to a maximum of 32 drives.

When you choose to create a striped volume, you are creating a new volume that combines free space from 2 to 32 drives into a single logical partition. The free space on all drives must be equal in size in a striped volume. Data in the striped volume is written across all drives in 64 KB stripes. (Data in spanned and extended volumes is written sequentially.) Striped volumes offer you better performance and are normally used for temporary files or folders. The problem with a striped volume is if you lose one of the drives in the volume, the entire striped volume is lost.

Another option that you have with volumes is to extend the volumes to create a larger storage area. In the next section, we will look at that process.

Creating Extended Volumes

When you create an extended volume, you are taking a single, simple volume (maybe one that is almost out of disk space) and adding more disk space to it, using free space that exists on the same physical hard drive. When the volume is extended, it is seen as a single drive letter. To extend a volume, the simple volume must be formatted as NTFS. You cannot extend a system or boot partition.

An extended volume is created when you are using only one physical drive. A spanned volume is created when you are using two or more physical drives. Exercise 5.6 shows you how to create an extended volume.

EXERCISE 5.6

Creating an Extended Volume

1. In the Disk Management utility, right-click the volume you want to extend and choose Extend Volume.

2. The Extend Volume Wizard starts. Click Next.

3. The Select Disks screen appears (see Figure 5.18). You can specify the maximum size of the extended volume. The maximum size you can specify is determined by the amount of free space that exists in all of the dynamic drives on your computer. Click Next to continue.

FIGURE 5.18 The Select Disks screen

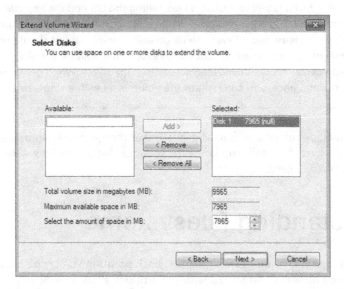

4. The Completing The Extend Volume Wizard screen appears. Click Finish. You will see the new volume.

Once a volume is extended, no portion of the volume can be deleted without losing data on the entire set. However, if there is unneeded space on a volume, you can shrink that volume without losing data by using the Shrink Volume option in Disk Management.

Real World Scenario

You're Running Out of Disk Space

Crystal, a user on your network, is running out of disk space. The situation needs to be corrected so she can be brought back up and running as quickly as possible. Crystal has a 250 GB drive (C:) that runs a very large customer database. She needs additional space added to the C: drive so the database will recognize the data because it must be stored on a single drive letter. Crystal's computer has a single IDE drive with nothing attached to the second IDE channel.

You have two basic options for managing space in this circumstance. One is to upgrade the disk to a larger disk, but this will necessitate reinstalling the OS and the applications and restoring the user's data. The other choice is to add a temporary second drive and extend the volume. This will at least allow Crystal to be up and running—but it should not be considered a permanent solution. If you do choose to extend the volume and then either drive within the volume set fails, Crystal will lose access to both drives. When her workload allows time for maintenance, you can replace the volume set with a single drive.

One issue you may run into with hard drives is that they go bad from time to time. If you have ever heard a hard drive fail, you know the sound: a distinct clicking. Once you have experienced it, you will never forget it.

Understanding Filesystems

A partition is a logical division of storage space. Each partition you create under Windows 10/11 must have a filesystem associated with it. Partitions allow a single physical device to be represented in the operating system as multiple drive letters and to be used as if there were multiple hard drives installed in the machine.

When selecting a filesystem, you can select FAT32 or NTFS. You typically select a filesystem based on the features you want to use and whether you will need to access the filesystem using other operating systems. If you have a FAT32 partition and want to update it to NTFS, you can use the Convert utility. The features of each filesystem and the procedure for converting filesystems are covered in the following sections.

Filesystem Selection

Your filesystem is used to track the storage of files on your hard drive in a way that is easily understood by end users while still allowing the operating system the ability to retrieve the files as requested. One of the fundamental choices associated with file management is the choice of your filesystem's configuration. It is recommended that you use the NTFS filesystem with Windows 10/11 because doing so will allow you to take advantage of features such as local security, file compression, and file encryption. You should choose the FAT32 filesystem only if you want to dual-boot your computer with a version of Windows that does not support NTFS because FAT32 is backward compatible with other operating systems.

Table 5.1 summarizes the capabilities of each filesystem, and they are described in more detail in the following sections. These volume size numbers were the values at the time this book was written. Make sure you continue to check with Microsoft to see if the volume sizes have increased since this book's publication.

TABLE 5.1   Filesystem capabilities

Feature	Fat32	NTFS
Supporting operating systems	All Windows operating systems above Windows 95	Windows NT, Windows 2000, Windows XP, Windows Server 2003, Windows Vista, Windows 7, Windows 8, Windows 10/11, and all Windows Server versions
Long filename support	Yes	Yes
Efficient use of disk space	Yes	Yes
Compression support	No	Yes
Encryption support	No (Before Windows 10) Yes (if formatted using Windows 10/11)	Yes
Support for local security	No	Yes
Support for network security	Yes	Yes
Maximum volume size	32 GB	16 TB with 4 KB clusters or 256 TB with 64 KB clusters

Windows 10/11 also supports Compact Disk File System (CDFS). However, CDFS cannot be managed. It is used only to mount and read CDs. Let's start looking at the supported disk filesystems.

FAT32

FAT32 is an updated version of File Allocation Table (FAT). The FAT32 version was first shipped with Windows 95 OSR2 (Operating System Release 2) and can be used by every Windows operating system since.

One of the main advantages of FAT32 is its support for smaller cluster sizes, which results in more efficient space allocation than was possible with FAT16. Files stored on a

FAT32 partition can use 20 to 30 percent less disk space than files stored on a FAT16 partition. FAT32 supports drive sizes from 512 MB up to 2 TB, although if you create and format a FAT32 partition through Windows 10/11, the FAT32 partition can only be up to 32 GB. Because of the smaller cluster sizes, FAT32 can also load programs up to 50 percent faster than FAT16 partitions can.

The main disadvantages of FAT32 compared to NTFS are that it does not provide as much support for larger hard drives and it does not provide very robust security options. It also doesn't offer native support for disk compression. Now that you understand FAT32, let's take a look at NTFS.

NTFS

NTFS, which was first used with the NT operating system, offers the highest level of service and features for Windows 10/11 computers. NTFS partitions can be up to 16 TB with 4 KB clusters, which is the default size, up to 8 PB (petabytes) on a 2048 KB cluster, which is the max size at the writing of this book. NTFS can support volumes as large as 8 PB on Windows Server 2019 and newer and Windows 10, version 1709 and newer (older versions support up to 256 TB). Volume sizes are affected by the number of clusters and the cluster size.

NTFS offers comprehensive folder-level and file-level security. This allows you to set an additional level of security for users who access the files and folders locally or through the network. For example, two users who share the same Windows client computer can be assigned different NTFS permissions so that one user has access to a folder but the other user is denied access to that folder. This is not possible on a FAT32 filesystem.

NTFS also offers disk-management features—such as compression and encryption capabilities—and data-recovery features. NTFS includes some of the following features:

- When files are read or written to a disk, they can be automatically encrypted and decrypted.

- Reparse points are used with mount points to redirect data as it is written or read from a folder to another volume or physical disk.

- There is support for sparse files, which are used by programs that create large files but allocate disk space only as needed.

- Remote storage allows you to extend your disk space by making removable media (for example, external tapes) more accessible.

- NTFS gives you the ability to resize volumes and partitions.

- You can use recovery logging on NTFS metadata, which is used for data recovery when a power failure or system problem occurs.

Now that you have seen the differences between FAT32 and NTFS, let's discuss how to convert a FAT32 drive to an NTFS drive.

Filesystem Conversion

In Windows 10/11, you can convert FAT32 partitions to NTFS. Filesystem conversion is the process of converting one filesystem to another without the loss of data. If you format a drive, as opposed to converting it, all the data on that drive will be lost.

To convert a partition, you use the Convert command-line utility. The syntax for the Convert command is as follows:

```
Convert [drive:]/fs:ntfs
```

For example, if you wanted to convert your D: drive to NTFS, you would type the following at a command prompt:

```
Convert D:/fs:ntfs
```

When the conversion process begins, it will attempt to lock the partition. If the partition cannot be locked—perhaps because it contains the Windows client operating system files or the system's page file—the conversion will not take place until the computer is restarted.

Using the Convert Command

You can use the /v switch with the Convert command. This switch specifies that you want to use verbose mode, and all messages will be displayed during the conversion process. You can also use the /NoSecurity switch, which specifies that all converted files and folders will have no security applied by default, so they can be accessed by anyone.

Configuring NTFS

As mentioned earlier, NTFS has many advantages over FAT32. The main advantages are NTFS Security, compression, encryption (EFS), and quotas. Let's take a look at some of these advantages in greater detail.

NTFS Security   One of the biggest advantages of NTFS is security. NTFS security is one of the most important aspects of an IT administrator's job. An advantage of NTFS security is that the security can be placed on individual files and folders. It does not matter whether you are local to the share (in front of the machine where the data is stored) or remote to the share (coming across the network to access the data); the security is always in place with NTFS. The default security permission is Users = Read on new folders or shares. Configuring NTFS security and managing how it works with shared permissions are covered in Chapter 3, "Managing Data."

Compression   *Compression* helps compact files or folders to allow for more efficient use of storage space. For example, a file that usually takes up 20 MB of space might use only 13 MB after compression. To enable compression on a file or folder, just open the Advanced Attributes dialog box in the properties and check the Compress Contents To Save Disk Space box.

If you have an entire drive that you'd like to compress, you don't have to compress all files and folders individually; you can compress the entire drive. To enable NTFS compression on a hard drive, perform the following:

1. Open File Explorer.
2. In the left pane, click This PC.
3. Under Devices And Drives, right-click the drive you'd like to compress and select Properties.
4. Select Compress This Drive To Save Disk Space.
5. Click Apply.
6. In the Confirm Attribute Changes dialog box, select Apply Changes To Drive (*drive letter*), Subfolders And Files option.
7. Click OK and then click OK again.

After you complete the steps, NTFS will enable compression on the entire drive.

If you want to undo the changes, you can use the same instructions, but in step 4, just clear the Compress This Drive To Save Disk Space box.

Encryption   The *Encrypting File System (EFS)* allows a user or administrator to secure files or folders by using encryption. Encryption employs the user's Security Identifier (SID) number to secure the file or folder. To implement encryption, open the Advanced Attributes dialog box for a file or folder, and select the Encrypt Contents To Secure Data check box.

If files are encrypted using EFS and an administrator has to unencrypt the files, there are two ways to do this. First, you can log in using the user's account (the account that encrypted the files) and unencrypt the files. Second, you can become a recovery agent and manually unencrypt the files. When configuring encryption in the command line or PowerShell utilities, administrators can use the Cipher command to manage and maintain encryption.

Until Windows 10 and Windows Server 2000, FAT32 did not support encryption. With the release of Windows 10 and Windows Server 2016, if you format FAT32 using one of these operating systems, encryption is available.

Quotas   Disk *quotas* give administrators the ability to limit how much storage space a user can have on a hard drive. You have a few options available to you when you set up disk quotas. You can set up disk quotas based on volume or on users.

Setting Quotas by Volume   One way to set up disk quotas is by setting the quota by volume, on a per-volume basis. This means that if you have a hard drive with C:, D:, and E: volumes, you would have to set up three individual quotas (one for each volume). This is your umbrella. This is where you set up an entire disk quota based on the volume for all users.

If you want to limit the available storage for all users by setting up a quota by volume, then perform the following steps:

1. Open File Explorer.
2. Click This PC in the left pane.
3. Under Devices And Drives, right-click the drive you'd like to limit and then choose Properties.
4. Select the Quota tab.
5. Click Show Quota Settings (as shown in Figure 5.19).

FIGURE 5.19   Show Quota Settings

6. Select Enable Quota Management.
7. Select the Deny Disk Space To Users Exceeding Quota Limit option.
8. Select Limit Disk Space To.
9. Set the amount of space you'd like and then specify the size unit (e.g., megabyte, gigabyte).

10. Set the amount of space before a warning is triggered to the user and specify the size unit (for example, megabyte or gigabyte).

11. Click Apply and then OK.

12. Restart the computer.

Once these steps are done, all accounts on the device will only be able to use a part of the total available storage on the hard drive. When a user is approaching their storage limit, they will receive a warning. If they reach their quota, then they will no longer be allowed to store any other files or documents.

By modifying the Limit Disk Space To and Set Warning Level To options, you can increase or decrease the amount of storage allowed.

Setting Quotas by User   You have the ability to set up quotas on volumes by user. Here is where you would individually let users have independent quotas that exceed your umbrella quota.

If you want to limit the available storage for a particular user, then perform the following steps:

1. Open File Explorer.

2. Click This PC in the left pane.

3. Under Devices And Drives, right-click the drive you'd like to limit and then choose Properties.

4. Select the Quota tab.

5. Click Show Quota Settings.

6. Select Enable Quota Management.

7. Select the Deny Disk Space To Users Exceeding Quota Limit option.

8. Click Quota Entries. If the user you want to restrict isn't listed, click Quota and select New Quota Entry.

9. On the Select Users tab, click Advanced.

10. Click Find Now and select the user you want to restrict.

11. Click OK and then click OK again.

12. Select the Limit Disk Space To option, set the amount of space you want, specify the size unit (for example, megabyte or gigabyte), set the amount of space before a warning is triggered to the user, and specify the size unit (for example, megabyte or gigabyte).

13. Click Apply and click OK.

Once these steps are done, the user will have limited disk space. If you wish, you can also disable or change the disk quota settings.

Specifying Quota Entries   You use quota entries to configure the volume and user quotas. You do this on the Quotas tab of the volume's Properties dialog box. There's a Quota Entries button in the Quota Settings window that shows you the current quotas that are already applied. You can use this tool to check the current disk space usage for all user accounts against the set quota. You can also create new quota entries, import/export, delete, and modify entries.

1. Open File Explorer.
2. Click This PC in the left pane.
3. Under Devices And Drives, right-click the drive you'd like to limit and then choose Properties.
4. Select the Quota tab.
5. Click Quota Entries.

Configuring Hardware

Configuring hardware properly is one of the most important tasks when setting up Windows 10/11. Windows 10/11 has included some tools to help users and administrators configure their hardware.

In Windows 10/11, there is a built-in functionality called Devices (under Settings). Devices offers an enhanced graphic output, giving better details about, and functionality to, installed devices such as cameras.

Hardware today follows the Plug and Play standard, so most of the time simply connecting hardware will allow Devices to automatically configure it. Devices that are not Plug and Play compatible can be installed manually from Devices as well.

Understanding Devices

Throughout the evolution of technologies and PCs, one of the greatest features is how we can use such a wide array of devices on PCs. Device Manager has allowed us to see all the hardware connected and make configuration changes, but utilizing the features of the devices themselves has been left up to programs outside the Windows interface. Windows 10/11 includes a specification for hardware vendors (knowing that most hardware comes with software for the user to interface with), allowing them to provide user access within Devices. Take, for example, a digital camera. Generally, when you connect a camera to a PC, the PC recognizes the device (this immediate recognition is called Plug and Play) and typically displays the camera as a mass storage device. Users wanting advanced features like downloading and editing the photos must use another program. When you plug in a device that is supported by Devices technology, on the other hand, Devices displays a single window that gives you easy access to common device tasks, such as, in the case of a camera, importing pictures, launching the vendor-supplied editing programs, and simply browsing pictures, all from one interface.

With Windows 10/11, you'll be able to access all your connected and wireless devices from the single Devices screen under Settings, and some devices may be displayed in the Windows client–enhanced taskbar. From here, you can work with your devices, browse files they might contain, and manage device settings.

Wireless and Bluetooth devices are also supported by Devices, making management of these resources much easier for the end user. As portable devices are disconnected and reconnected, the Devices screen will update in real time. Exercise 5.7 will guide you through opening and viewing devices recognized on your Windows client machine.

EXERCISE 5.7

Opening Devices

In Windows 10, perform the following:

1. Click Start ➤ Settings ➤ Devices.

2. Look through the various Devices sections to see what is attached to your current PC.

In Windows 11, perform the following:

1. Click Start ➤ Settings ➤ Bluetooth & Devices ➤ Devices.

2. Look through the various Devices sections to see what is attached to your current PC.

Next, we'll take a look at using Device Manager to configure devices.

Using Device Manager

Device Manager is the component in Windows 10/11 you'll use to see which devices are connected to your machine. You can use Device Manager to ensure that all devices are working properly and to troubleshoot misbehaving devices. For each device installed, you can view specific properties down to the resources being used, such as the assigned I/O (input/output) port and IRQs (interrupt requests). Through Device Manager, you can take the following specific actions:

- View a list of all hardware installed on your computer.
- Determine which device driver is installed for each device.
- Manage and update device drivers.
- Install new devices.
- Disable, enable, and uninstall devices.
- Use driver rollback to return to a previous version of a driver.
- Troubleshoot device problems.

More importantly, you can see which devices Windows 10/11 has recognized. That is, if you install or connect a new piece of hardware and Windows 10/11 doesn't recognize it at all, it won't be seen in Device Manager. This would be an unusual occurrence given the sophistication of today's hardware vendors and the Plug and Play standards that are implemented. However, using Device Manager is an important tool in seeing just which devices are known to Windows 10/11. Keep in mind that we've been using Device Manager for many versions of Windows, so what I'm discussing is applicable to legacy versions as well. In Exercise 5.8, you will view devices using Device Manager.

EXERCISE 5.8

Viewing Devices Using Device Manager

1. In Windows 10, click Start ≻ Windows System ≻ Control Panel ≻ Device Manager.

   In Windows 10/11, right-click the Start button and choose Device Manager.

2. Click the triangle next to Network Adapters (or double-click Network Adapters) to expand Network Adapters.

There are a number of ways to open Device Manager, as you saw in Exercise 5.8. These methods show you where the application resides, but administrators can launch Device Manager in other ways as well.

You can also just type **Device Manager** (or just **device**) into the Windows integrated search box and press Enter. All of these are means to the same end.

As shown in Figure 5.20, Device Manager has a fairly simple opening screen, but it has a lot of functionality behind it. From the opening screen, you get a good first feeling for the hardware that's installed and recognized and for any major issues, such as a device that's recognized but has no drivers installed or is not working correctly. You'll see a warning symbol displayed over the misbehaving device. For example, suppose you have just installed a new network adapter but the device does not seem to be working. You can open Device Manager and use the Network Adapter option to start the troubleshooting process. Figure 5.20 shows just such a network adapter.

To continue troubleshooting the network adapter within Device Manager, right-click the misbehaving adapter and choose Properties to open the Properties dialog box (Figure 5.21). This is just a small part of the functionality within Device Manager.

There are many reasons to view the devices installed and configured on a machine. One is to verify the type and status of hardware. For example, if someone in your organization has given you documentation for a user machine that includes the machine's hardware specifications and you are concerned that the stated network adapter for the machine may not be the one actually installed, you can use Device Manager on the machine in question to see the network adapters Windows 10/11 recognizes in the machine.

FIGURE 5.20   Device Manager screen

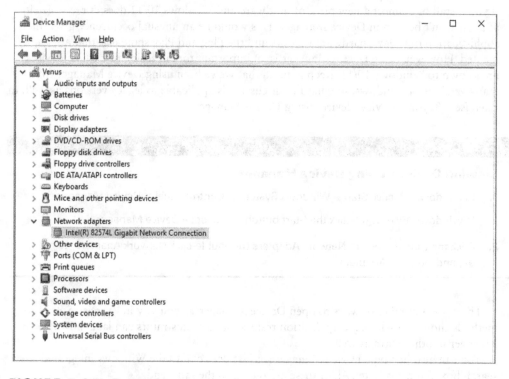

FIGURE 5.21   Device Manager network adapter properties

Device Properties Available Within Device Manager

Once you have opened Device Manager and have access to the installed devices on your machine, you can view their Properties dialog boxes. From there, you can view and change configuration parameters if necessary. You will find that the tabs available in the Properties dialog boxes will vary from device to device because the parameters that are available will vary with different hardware. Most devices will have at a minimum a General tab, a Driver tab, and a Details tab.

The Properties dialog box for most devices will include more specific tabs for the hardware configuration, such as for a network adapter, which also has an Advanced tab for more specific configuration parameters. Figure 5.22 shows a network adapter's Advanced tab selected with Adaptive Inter-Frame Spacing selected and the Value drop-down box active to show possible choices.

FIGURE 5.22   Advanced network interface properties

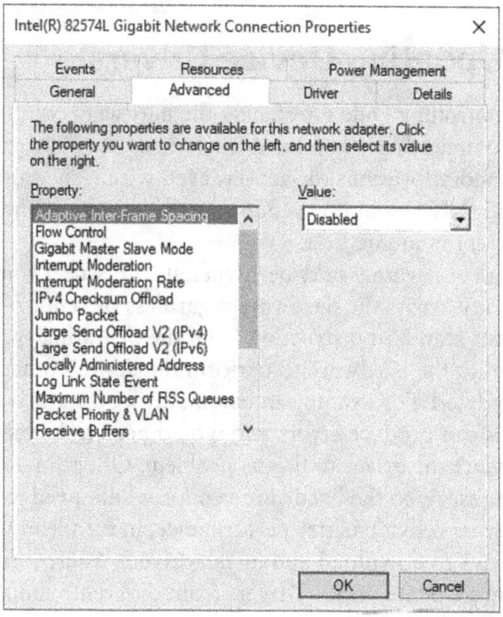

If you need to change the hardware configuration properties, Device Manager is the best way to access the parameters. Exercise 5.9 will show you how to view configurable properties for a network adapter through the Advanced tab.

EXERCISE 5.9

Configuring Network Adapter Advanced Properties

1.   Right-click the Start button and choose Device Manager.

2.   Click the triangle next to Network Adapters (or double-click Network Adapters) to expand it.

3.   Right-click your network adapter and select Properties.

4.   Choose the Advanced tab.

5.   Select various properties and view the parameters.

In addition to setting up devices, you will need to install and configure device drivers, which I will cover in the next section.

Installing and Updating Device Drivers

Device drivers are the controlling code interfacing the hardware components with the operating system. The commands are specific to each piece of hardware, and there may be different commands, memory locations, or actions even within the same type of hardware. A network interface card (NIC) from one vendor may have a different set of instructions than a NIC from a different manufacturer.

An operating system or software works best when it can issue a standard command and have the same functionality across the hardware regardless of vendor. This is where *drivers* come in; the driver takes a standard instruction from the operating system and interprets and then issues the command to the hardware to perform the desired function.

Drivers need to be updated. For example, a command set for a driver may perform a function incorrectly. This can produce errors and would need to be fixed. The hardware vendor will typically update the driver to fix the problem. Oftentimes, new or improved functionality may be necessary, so the hardware vendor would need to change the driver code to add functionality or provide better performance, in turn leading to an update.

There are different ways to download and install drivers. Microsoft drivers can be downloaded using the Windows Update utility. Drivers from different manufacturers can normally be downloaded from the manufacturer's website. Just access their website, search the product, and download the latest drivers. Then you can install those drivers using Device Manager.

Driver Code Causing an Arbitrary Nonreproducible Error

While working on a consulting job for a company where I was installing a new program and hardware to provide bar code scanning, I was plagued by the bar code readers connected to PCs randomly failing.

The bar code readers seemed to install correctly, and they showed as functioning properly within Device Manager. However, periodically the hardware readers would fail to input data into the application I was using. I could reboot the affected machine and the bar code reader would work fine again (for a while). It's easy to blame the operating system because the reboot seemed to fix the problem, but the operating system wasn't to blame.

After several days of troubleshooting and working with the manufacturer, it was determined that the driver interfacing the operating system with the hardware was not releasing memory resources correctly, causing the driver to fail. We received an updated driver and applied the update to the machines and the problem was resolved. Be careful not to blame the operating system prematurely, and be sure to investigate other areas for possible problems.

Typical first-time installation of drivers today happens automatically with the Plug and Play specification. After the hardware is installed, Windows 10/11 will recognize it and launch the driver installation program. Let's take, for example, the connection of a digital camera to the USB port of your computer.

Windows 10/11 will recognize that a device has been plugged in and will gather the information about the USB device. Windows 10/11 will then install the best driver it knows about (and if it doesn't know about the device, it will ask you how to proceed). Figure 5.23 shows the message indicating that the operating system found a driver and is installing it automatically in Windows 10.

The installation completes and the device is now available in Device Manager. If you need to review the driver details for your newly installed device, the network adapter in this case, you can right-click the device in Device Manager and choose Properties. Figure 5.24 shows the right-click menu (also known as the context menu); note that the top choice in this menu is a quick launch to update the driver software.

FIGURE 5.23   Automatic driver installation in Windows 10

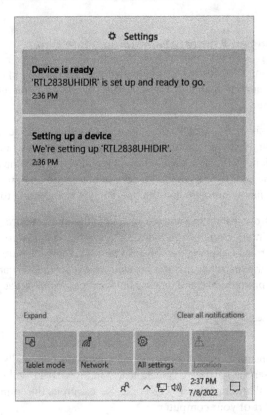

You may want to verify general information about the driver, like the provider or version. You can see that information in the Driver tab of the Properties dialog box. You can also choose to view the driver details, which are the supporting files and associated paths. Figure 5.25 shows the Properties dialog box of the network adapter that shows the Driver Details button on the Driver tab of the Properties dialog box for the network adapter.

Sometimes when you're having issues with a hardware device, you will go online and read forums or use search engine queries to attempt to find resolution ideas from other administrators. Someone might mention that they had a problem with a specific driver for the hardware you're researching. They might even mention the exact version of the driver and suggest a fix. Having the ability to view information on drivers and update them is helpful in a situation such as this. Exercise 5.10 walks you through looking at driver details.

FIGURE 5.24   Right-click menu for a device in Device Manager

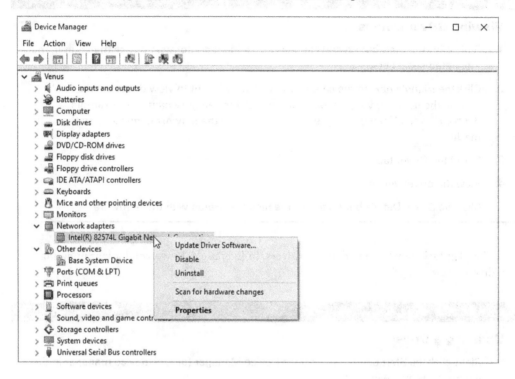

FIGURE 5.25   Driver details within Device Manager

EXERCISE 5.10

Viewing Driver Details

1. Right-click the Start button and choose Device Manager (or type **device manager** in the integrated search box).

2. Click the triangle next to the category in which you want to view driver details to expand the item list; you can also double-click the category name. For example, double-click the Network Adapters category to see the network connection to the machine.

3. Select the Driver tab.

4. View the driver version.

5. Click the Driver Details button to see the files associated with the hardware.

Another task may be to update the drivers. In Exercise 5.11 we will look at updating a driver.

EXERCISE 5.11

Updating a Driver

1. Right-click the Start button and choose Device Manager (or type **device manager** in the integrated search window).

2. Click the triangle next to category for which you want to update the driver to expand the item list; you can also double-click the category name.

3. Right-click the hardware item and select Properties.

4. Select the Driver tab.

5. Click the Update Driver button; a window launches asking how you want to search for the driver.

6. Choose Search Automatically For Updated Driver Software to have Windows search for you, or choose Browse My Computer For Driver Software if you have the new drivers already.

   Windows searches for and updates the drivers or reports back that you have the most current version.

Not only will you often need to update drivers because of a failure or hardware issue, but you will at times install new drivers for new or updated functionality. There will also be times when a hardware driver gets updated and the update breaks a piece of functioning hardware or doesn't solve a problem. In these cases, you will want to go back to the previous version, or "roll back" the driver. In Exercise 5.12, you will learn how to do a driver rollback.

EXERCISE 5.12

Rolling Back a Driver

1. Right-click the Start button and choose Device Manager (or type **device manager** in the integrated search window).

2. Click the triangle next to the category for which you want to roll back the driver to expand the item list; you can also double-click the category name.

3. Right-click the hardware item and select Properties.

4. Select the Driver tab.

5. Click the Roll Back Driver button. Note that if the Roll Back Driver button is grayed out, there isn't a previous version of the driver available.

   The previous driver will be installed and the hardware will return to its previous state of functionality.

The Driver tab for a piece of installed hardware in Device Manager also provides functionality for disabling and uninstalling a driver. Why would you want to disable a driver? There are several possibilities, but troubleshooting is one of the most common reasons.

Disabling the driver effectively disables the hardware; it will no longer function in the system. Uninstalling the device driver has a similar effect, but if the hardware is still installed, you can uninstall the driver and perform a scan to ensure that the hardware is still recognized and force a reinstallation.

I have often disabled a device from Device Manager to eliminate one part of an issue I am having with a system. If I'm confident that the problem is with the hardware, I will uninstall the driver and let the operating system reinstall it as part of the troubleshooting procedure. This works much of the time and is a good place to start. In Exercise 5.13, you will disable and enable a device driver.

EXERCISE 5.13

Disabling and Enabling a Device in Device Manager

1. Right-click the Start button and choose Device Manager (or type **device manager** in the integrated search window).

2. Click the triangle next to the appropriate category to expand the item list; you can also double-click the category name.

3. Right-click the hardware item and select Properties. Note that you can select Disable directly from the context menu if desired.

4. Select the Driver tab.

5. Click the Disable button. (This is a toggle button; it will be labeled Disable if the device is enabled and Enable if the device is disabled.)

6. The device driver and hence the device will be disabled and will no longer function. There will be a down arrow on the item in Device Manager, and the General tab will show that the device is disabled. Close the Properties dialog box for that device.

7. Right-click the hardware item and select Properties.

8. Select the Driver tab.

9. Click the Enable button. (Remember that this is a toggle button.)

10. The device driver will become enabled and the hardware will work as designed (barring any other issues).

11. Close Device Manager.

It may be beneficial at times to uninstall and reinstall a device driver. Many times when you do that, the default configuration parameters will be reset to their original specifications.

Any changes you have made will need to be reconfigured, but if the device driver worked previously and has stopped for some unknown reason (if you knew the reason, you'd simply fix it), uninstalling and reinstalling is worth a try. You may also consider using a different device driver than Windows 10/11 is set up to use via Plug and Play. Note that uninstalling a device driver does not delete the driver files from the machine; uninstalling the device driver removes the operating system configuration for the hardware.

You may want or need to find the driver files and delete them manually in some cases. Remember, you can find the files (and thus the filenames) from Driver Details on the Drivers tab of the Properties dialog box of the hardware within Device Manager.

If you have determined that the device driver for your misbehaving hardware is potentially causing the problem you are having, you can choose to uninstall and reinstall (automatically) the drivers. In Exercise 5.14, you will uninstall and then reinstall a device driver.

EXERCISE 5.14

Uninstalling and Reinstalling a Device Driver

1. Right-click the Start button and choose Device Manager (or type **device manager** in the integrated search window).

2. Click the triangle next to the category for the device you want to uninstall to expand the item list; you can also double-click the category name.

3. Right-click the hardware item and select Properties. Note that you can select Uninstall directly from the context menu.

4. Select the Driver tab.

5. Click the Uninstall button.

6. Click OK in the Confirm Device Uninstall dialog box. A progress box appears as the device driver is uninstalled. Once the driver is uninstalled, Device Manager will no longer show the device.

7. From Device Manager, choose the Action menu item and select Scan For Hardware Changes; alternatively, you can right-click the machine name in Device Manager and select Scan For Hardware Changes from the context menu.

   Windows 10 will initiate the process of discovering the Plug and Play device and will reinstall the device driver configuration into the operating system. The hardware will be available again within Device Manager.

A lot of hardware manufacturers would like you to install the driver files and some software for their device before the operating system has a chance to discover it. This is often so that the software program controlling some of the hardware functionality will be installed first so its configuration file can accurately reference the installed drivers, or it can also be to add the driver files to the driver configuration directories of the operating system before the operating system discovers the device.

The process of adding the drivers is usually done by inserting and running a setup program from a provided CD or DVD. I will say the hardware vendors know what's best. As an admin, it's sometimes hard not to just install the hardware and go from there, but following the vendor's recommendations will most often produce a better result.

 Real World Scenario

Follow the Hardware Vendor's Recommendation

Like many other admins, I sometimes think I know the right way to proceed in installing a piece of hardware. Seriously, how hard can it be? I once installed a new wireless USB adapter into a machine I was using by just plugging it in despite the great big red sticker that said, "Run the setup on the CD FIRST!"

Sure enough, Windows found the adapter and proceeded to install the drivers. The hardware showed up in Device Manager but would not work. Now, being the good trouble-shooter I am, I decided to run the Setup program on the CD. It turns out the driver files on the CD were a different version (actually older) than the installed files and Windows would not replace the installed drivers.

Even after I manually uninstalled them? Yes. I had to go back and find five different files in numerous locations and delete each one. Finding the files to delete was not a simple oper-ation; a lot of online research went into solving this problem, and several hours of my time were wasted.

Simply following the hardware-vendor instructions would have been much easier. I did the same installation on another machine following the vendor recommendations and every-thing worked perfectly. But then again, that's how we all learn these valuable lessons in life.

There are also situations we run into requiring a manual installation of hardware. There may be multiple reasons, including installation of legacy hardware, situations when drivers are not supplied in the operating system distribution files, or when drivers that may perform different functions from the default drivers are available. You can perform manual installa-tions from Device Manager through the Add Hardware Wizard.

In the manual installation process, you can have Windows 10/11 go out to the Internet to find a current driver, or you can specify a location of your choosing locally. From Device Manager, you launch the Add Hardware Wizard (Figure 5.26) by choosing Add Legacy Hardware from either the Action menu or the context menu of the machine.

FIGURE 5.26   Add Hardware Wizard initial window

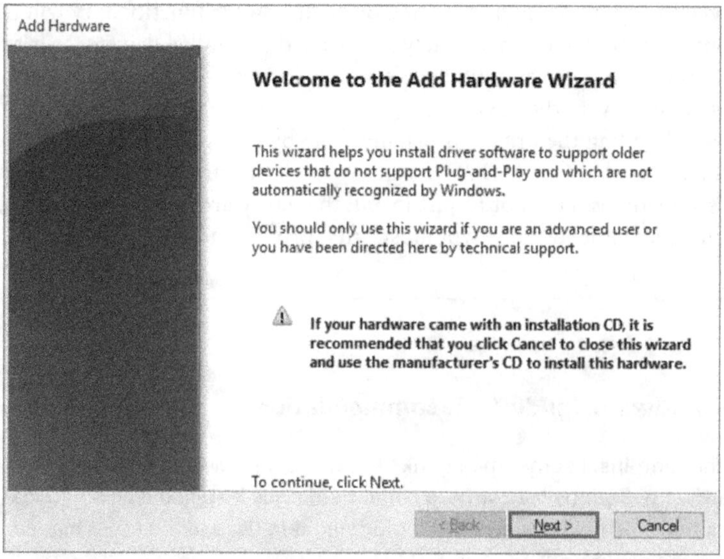

Add Hardware

Welcome to the Add Hardware Wizard

This wizard helps you install driver software to support older devices that do not support Plug-and-Play and which are not automatically recognized by Windows.

You should only use this wizard if you are an advanced user or you have been directed here by technical support.

⚠ If your hardware came with an installation CD, it is recommended that you click Cancel to close this wizard and use the manufacturer's CD to install this hardware.

To continue, click Next.

< Back   Next >   Cancel

The next step is to tell Windows where to look for the driver. This is the next page of the Add Hardware Wizard, as Figure 5.27 shows.

FIGURE 5.27   Driver file location choices

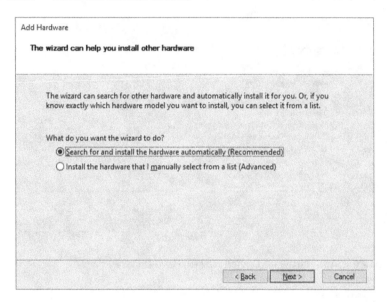

To choose a piece of hardware from a list of supplied drivers or, more important, to choose a specific path, select the option Install The Hardware That I Manually Select From A List (Advanced) and click Next. This allows you to select a device type or choose Show All Devices (Figure 5.28); selecting Show All Devices and clicking Next will give you the ability to choose a location.

If you have a disk or have the appropriate drivers stored in an accessible location, click the Have Disk button (as shown in Figure 5.29) and browse to the driver files you need to install. If all goes as planned, the hardware device drivers will be installed and Device Manager will display the newly installed hardware.

Driver Signing

In this world of hackers and viruses, one issue that needs to be addressed is the possibility that drivers that are downloaded come from an unrepeatable source and may have viruses or worms contained within the files. To help combat this problem, drivers that are created from reputable companies (like Dell or HP Compaq) assign a digital file certificate to the driver to show its validity.

FIGURE 5.28   Add Hardware Device Wizard hardware-selection window

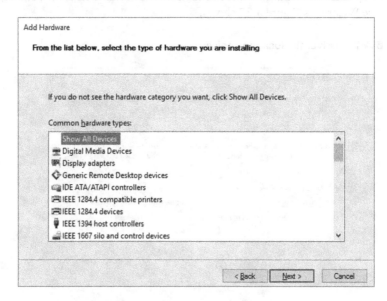

FIGURE 5.29   Add Hardware Device Wizard, Have Disk

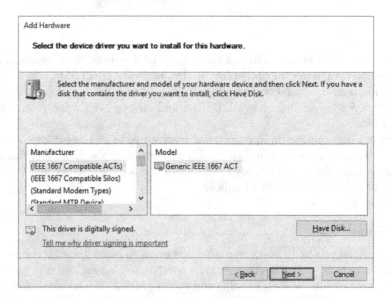

One way to ensure that all the drivers on your machine are verified is to run `sigverif`
`.exe`. The File Signature Verification Tool (`sigverif.exe`) helps identify unsigned drivers.
Exercise 5.15 walks you through the steps of verifying the drivers on your machine.

EXERCISE 5.15

Verifying Signed Drivers

1. Run the `sigverif.exe` program by typing **sigverif** in the Search The Web And Windows box, and then pressing Enter.

2. The File Signature Verification box appears. Click Start.

3. You will notice that the system scan begins. When the system has finished verifying the drivers, a message will appear stating that your files were all scanned. Click OK.

4. If there are any programs with unsigned drivers, they will be displayed at this time. Click Close to close the dialog box and then click Close to close the `sigverif.exe` program.

Knowing how to properly install and configure drivers is an important part of an IT professional's job. Another task that we must perform is managing input/output devices.

Managing I/O Devices

The devices you use to get information into and out of your Windows client machine are your I/O (input/output) devices. I/O devices include removable storage, keyboard, mouse, scanner, and printer. Your devices may be connected to your computer by standard cabling or by USB, or they may use a wireless technology such as IrDA (infrared) or RF (radio frequency).

Configuring Removable Storage Devices

Removable storage devices have been part of our computing world since the beginning. CDs, DVDs, and floppy disks are examples of removable storage. Today, we're using other types of removable storage as well, including flash-based electronics like USB sticks, memory cards, USB or FireWire external hard drives, cameras, phones, and so on. Windows 10/11 installs drivers for these devices (or media) dynamically as the devices are connected.

 We'll be concentrating in this section on dynamically connected devices utilizing the USB/FireWire connectivity and memory cards. These devices present challenges to the administrative team, because end users utilizing the technology may not follow guidelines for protecting their data from loss or for keeping it secure.

Windows 10/11 includes improvements to the Safely Remove Hardware (eject) menu. For example, it's now possible to eject just one memory card (from a single hub) and keep the ports available for future use.

To avoid losing data, it's important to remove external hardware like hard drives and USB drives safely.

Look for the Safely Remove Hardware icon on the taskbar (see Figure 5.30). If you don't see it, select Show Hidden Icons ^. Press and hold (or right-click) the icon and select the hardware you want to remove.

FIGURE 5.30 Safely Remove Hardware icon

In Widows 10, if you cannot find the Safely Remove Hardware icon, press and hold (or right-click) the taskbar and select Taskbar Settings. Under Notification Area, choose Select Which Icons Appear On The Taskbar. Scroll to Windows Explorer: Safely Remove Hardware And Eject Media and turn it on. If this doesn't work, then make sure the device has stopped all activity such as copying or syncing files, then select Start ➤ Settings ➤ Devices. Select the device and click Remove Device.

In Windows 11, if you cannot find the Safely Remove Hardware icon, press and hold (or right-click) the taskbar and select Taskbar Settings. In Windows 11, most app and system icons in the system tray are hidden. You can find hidden icons by clicking on the up arrow icon in the taskbar notification area. The flyout menu that displays hidden icons is the taskbar corner overflow menu. Scroll to Windows Explorer (when you hover over it, the tooltip will read Safely Remove Hardware And Eject Media) and turn it on. If this doesn't work, make sure the device has stopped all activity, then select Start ➤ Settings ➤ Bluetooth & Devices ➤ Devices. Select More (three vertical dots) next to the device, and click Remove Device.

Removable media are now listed under their label through Devices And Printers, as shown in Figure 5.31, rather than just their drive letter as they were in previous versions of Windows. This is also part of the Devices functionality of Windows 10/11; hardware vendors can include configuration information about portable devices and give users more resources from one location. There are a number of ways to access the Devices And Printers section:

- Using Control Panel (Windows 10/11): Open the Control Panel, make sure you are displaying the large icons, and then click Devices And Printers.

- Using Device Manager (Windows 10/11): Right-click the Start button and select Device Manager. On the Device Manager screen, click the Action tab and select Devices And Printers.

- Using Settings (Windows 10): Click Start ➢ Settings ➢ Devices and then click Devices And Printers under Related Settings on the right-hand side.

- Using Settings (Windows 11): Click Start ➢ Settings ➢ Bluetooth & Devices in the left pane. In the right pane, select the Devices tab. On the next screen, scroll down to the Related Settings section and select the Devices & Printers tab.

FIGURE 5.31   Devices and Printers with USB stick installed

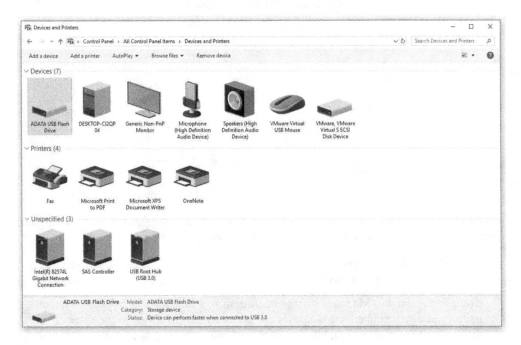

There are considerations in terms of data access performance with the portable devices as well. To make data access and saves faster, it's possible to have the operating system cache the data and write it to the portable device later when there's free processor time. However, this allows for the possibility of a user removing the portable device before the write is actually made, which would result in a loss of data.

Windows 10/11 defaults to writing the data immediately, minimizing the chance of data loss at the cost of performance. The configuration for optimizing the portable device for quick removal or better performance is found on the Policies tab of the Properties dialog box for the hardware device in Device Manager, as shown in Figure 5.32.

FIGURE 5.32   Policies tab

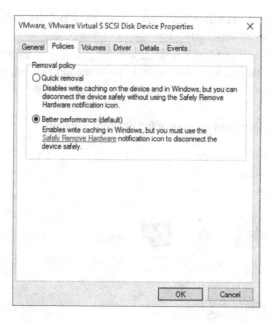

Windows defines two main policies—Quick Removal and Better Performance—that control how the system interacts with external storage devices:

Quick Removal   Manages storage operations in a manner that keeps the device ready to be removed at any time without using the Safely Remove Hardware process.

Better Performance   Manages storage operations in a manner that improves system performance. When in effect, Windows can cache write operations to the external device. But you have to use the Safely Remove Hardware process in order to remove the external drive safely.

Beginning in Windows 10 version 1809, the default policy is Quick Removal. In earlier versions the default policy was Better Performance. You can change the policy setting for each external device, and the policy that you set remains in effect if you disconnect the device and then connect it again to the same computer port.

In Exercise 5.16, we will walk through the steps to configure input/output devices through the use of Device Manager.

EXERCISE 5.16

Configuring an Input/Output Device

1. Open Device Manager using your preferred method.

2. Click the triangle next to Disk Drives (or double-click Disk Drives) to expand the item.

3. Right-click one of the storage device items and select Properties.

4. Select the Policies tab.

5. Click the Better Performance radio button and then click OK.

In Exercise 5.16, you changed the storage device to a write cache policy for better performance; this means writes to the portable device may be saved and written at a later time when the processor has clock cycles available. To ensure no loss of data, it is fairly important to properly eject the device using the Safely Remove Hardware tool before removing it.

Choosing the icon in the taskbar to eject the device initiates a stop for the hardware, forcing any cached writes in memory to be written to the device.

The device will close, meaning the writes have been made, and you will be presented with a window saying it's safe to remove the hardware.

Another important piece of hardware that needs to be configured is the printer. In the next section, we will discuss managing printers.

Managing Printers

Printers have been an issue for IT teams around the world and will likely continue to be. Every new update/release/version of an operating system has new software intelligence to make the installation and maintenance easier, but printer technology continues to grow and hardware vendors continue to make changes.

The driver base for all the different printers out there is huge, and even for the same printer there are numerous variations. Printers themselves have lots of options that can be made available, and this all has to be controlled by the operating system, through the drivers.

The Printer vs. the Print Device

I have referred in the preceding portion of this chapter to printers and devices; I have been talking about the physical piece of hardware and its functions.

In the IT world, we need to distinguish between the functionality of the hardware and of the software (both the driver software and the controlling software).

To this end, a lot of us know the physical device that has paper in it as the print device, not "the printer." The printer is the software application on the local machine controlling the print device. The printer driver is the software shim between the operating system and the locally installed software (the printer).

You will find in most organizations that there is not a print device attached to every computer. They are usually shared among users. This is cost effective on many levels, but it tends to cause issues. Most of us, end users and the IT team, need to print something once in a while, and so we send our documents or web pages to the print device to be printed.

The print device may be connected to someone's machine and shared for others to use, or it may be a stand-alone device. You may have a server on your network that has one or more print devices attached, and everyone sends their documents to a central location. Each user machine will have a printer installed and the appropriate drivers to allow Windows 10/11 to send the document to the print device through the printer with the appropriate instructions.

Of course, the print device can't physically print a document at the speed at which the printer can send the data to it. This is where a software component called the spool (spooler, print spool, and so on) comes in. There need to be software components that can buffer the print job until the print device can complete it. In fact, more than one user may be sending documents to be printed to the same print device at the same time, and the spool handles this as well.

What, No Spool?

I was working on a networking problem for a local veterinary clinic. The employees were complaining about issues they were having with their PCs being extremely slow sometimes but faster other times, and they were sure the network hardware was the cause. We discussed things that had changed recently—they had upgraded a piece of their software package to allow more functionality, which included having a couple of centralized printers for the docs and techs to use. It seemed as though every time someone printed, the network bogged down to the point of uselessness.

Casual discussions ensued. The network bog-down affected only the machine (or machines) actively sending a print job. Looking into the problem a little further showed that the vendor installation defaulted to printing directly to the print device, with no spooling. Each machine had to wait for the print job to complete before releasing any local resources (yes, that's right, not even background printing), and the other machines on the network ended up waiting as well. Allowing the machines to spool their print jobs solved the problem of slow networking (clearly not a networking issue in the end).

Installing Printers

Installing printers to a machine is done in two distinct ways: one where the print device is physically connected to the machine and one where it is not (it's connected over the network). There have to be software drivers in either case, and they can be on a CD/DVD, on a network share, downloaded on the Internet from the vendor, or even in the Windows distribution files. Printers in Windows 10/11 will be located in the Printers & Scanners window and will allow the device configuration to accommodate a full range of functionality from this one location.

To access the Printers & Scanners window:

- In Windows 10, click the Start button ➤ Settings ➤ Devices ➤ Printers & Scanners.
- In Windows 11, click the Start button ➤ Settings ➤ Bluetooth & Devices ➤ Printers & Scanners.

To add a printer to a machine locally, you will usually run the Setup program on the CD/DVD (following the manufacturer's instructions). The manufacturer's Setup program in a wizard format will ask the appropriate questions. You can set up the printer through Windows 10/11 as well as by using the Add A Printer Or Scanner function of Printers & Scanners. When USB printers are plugged in, they will be automatically detected and their drivers will be installed (or at least looked for automatically).

To add a printer using Windows 10, right-click the Start button ➤ Settings ➤ Devices and then click Add a printer or scanner, as shown in Figure 5.33.

To add a printer using Windows 11, click the Start button ➤ Settings ➤ Bluetooth & Services ➤ Printers & Scanners and then click the Add Device button in the Add A Printer Or Scanner section.

By choosing to add a printer/device option, you will notice that Windows 10/11 will automatically try to find the printer. If the printer that you want to install is not in the list, you can choose The Printer That I Want Isn't Listed in Windows 10 or click Add Manually in Windows 11. If the printer wasn't listed, then the next screen (shown in Figure 5.34) allows you to make the choice of installing the printer by the printer name, TCP/IP address, or Bluetooth discovery or by adding a local printer or network printer.

FIGURE 5.33 Adding a printer from Printers & Scanners in Windows 10

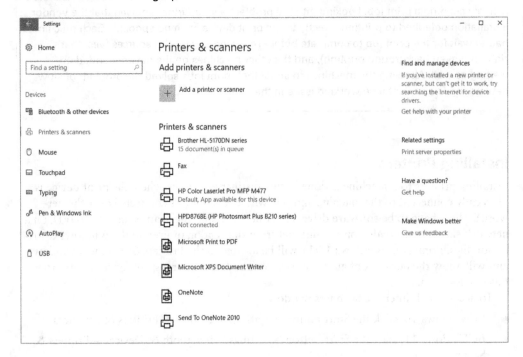

FIGURE 5.34 Add Printer Wizard local or remote choice

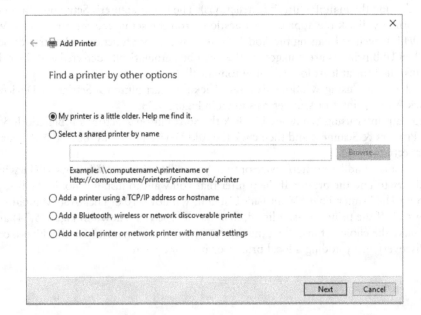

From the opening screen you can follow the steps in Exercise 5.17 to install the printer for a physically connected print device to a machine. We're going on the premise that the Setup program on the CD/DVD (if one existed) was not run and we're installing the printer from the wizard associated with Windows.

EXERCISE 5.17

Installing a Printer

1. In Windows 10, click the Start button ➤ Settings ➤ Devices.

   In Windows 11, click the Start button ➤ Settings ➤ Bluetooth & Devices ➤ Printers & Scanners.

2. In Windows 10, choose Add A Printer Or Scanner.

   In Windows 11, choose Add Device.

3. In Windows 10, select the option The Printer I Want Isn't Listed.

   In Windows 11, select the option Add Manually in The Printer I Want Isn't Listed section.

4. Choose the option "Add a local printer or network printer with manual settings" and click Next.

5. Select the option LPT1: (printer port) and click Next.

6. Under Manufacturer, choose Generic and then choose Generic / Text Only. Click Next.

7. For the printer name, leave the default Generic / Text. Click Next.

8. On the Printer Sharing screen, choose Do Not Share This Printer and click Next.

9. Make sure the check box Set As Default Printer is not selected and click Finish.

Do not remove the printer you just installed in this exercise.

Once you have completed the Add Printer Wizard to install your printer, you can open the Printers & Scanners window and see it. Using the context menu, you will have access to the Properties dialog box as well as some of the standard printing functions you've had in Windows in the past. As hardware vendors continue to implement functionality for Windows 10/11, you will have access to a full array of software components from the Printers & Scanners window, at least for the vendors who are going to participate in the Devices specifications for Windows 10/11.

What about installing a printer on a machine that needs to access a print device connected to another machine or on the network? In order to configure a printer to connect to a remote print device, you must launch the Add A Printer Or Scanner Wizard and go through the process of installing the printer, but point to a shared or stand-alone network printer by using the Add A Bluetooth, Wireless, Or Network Discoverable Printer option or by putting in its TCP/IP address.

Knowing that not all machines on any company's network are going to have print devices physically attached, there is functionality to allow sharing of networked devices and to install printers (software) on client machines. In Exercise 5.18, we will look at how to connect to a network printer. To complete this exercise, you need to have a network printer that you can connect to. If you do not have a network printer, skip this exercise.

EXERCISE 5.18

Installing a Shared Network Print Device

1. In Windows 10, click the Start button ➤ Settings ➤ Devices.

    In Windows 11, click the Start button ➤ Settings ➤ Bluetooth & Devices ➤ Printers & Scanners.

2. In Windows 10, choose Add A Printer Or Scanner.

    In Windows 11, choose Add Device.

3. In Windows 10, select the option The Printer I Want Isn't Listed.

    In Windows 11, select the option Add Manually in The Printer I Want Isn't Listed section.

4. Choose the option Add A Bluetooth, Wireless, Or Network Discoverable Printer and click Next.

    The Add Printer Wizard will search the local network for print devices that are available.

5. Select the networked print device in the Select A Printer section. If the device is not listed, you can choose The Printer That I Want Is Not Listed and enter the parameters for the networked print device.

    The print device will be detected, the driver will be discovered and installed, and you will be able to use the printer. It will be available at this time in Printers & Scanners.

Configuring Printers

Once the printer is installed for either a print device physically connected to the local machine or a network-connected print device, you can view the configuration parameters of the printer and modify them, if necessary, from the Properties dialog box. One way to access the properties is to select Control Panel ➤ Devices And Printers (Figure 5.35). Right-click the printer and select Properties for the hardware properties or Printer Properties for the software components.

FIGURE 5.35   Printer context menu from Devices And Printers

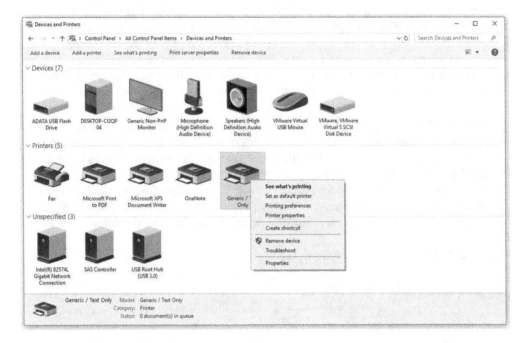

The Printer Properties dialog boxes for printers follow a standard that Microsoft has in place, but the content is really up to the manufacturer. Some vendors will supply more information than others. Most printers will provide a basic set of pages (tabs):

General Tab   The printer name, location, and comment are displayed here. The model is typically shown as well as the features of the specific print device and available paper. The printer preferences page is available by clicking the Preferences button, and you can print a test page by clicking the Print Test Page button.

Sharing Tab   The Sharing tab allows you to share a printer if it wasn't shared during its installation or to stop sharing it if it was previously shared. You can also add drivers for other flavors of operating systems so that the locally installed and shared printer can supply drivers for other machines attempting to connect and use it.

Ports Tab   Available ports and print devices connected to them can be viewed on the Ports tab. You can add a port, delete a port, and configure ports from the tab as well. Normally, operating systems just talk to the print device, but some print devices need to communicate with the operating system. This is known as bidirectional support (sending codes back from the print device to the printer for control).

Printer pooling is also available here. Printer pooling gives the IT staff the ability to configure multiple print devices (using identical drivers) to appear as one printer to connected users. The print jobs will be printed on one of the devices in the pool (the first available print device prints the job). If a print device fails, the others will keep working, making life better for the users (always a goal). It is important to keep all print devices near each other in a printing pool because the print job will print to the next available device. If you scatter the devices all over the company, users will have to search for their print jobs.

Advanced Tab   The Advanced tab provides various configuration parameters to control the printer and print device functions. One of the available settings is what time the printer is available. You can set specific hours or allow the printer to always be available (see Figure 5.36). Configuring the installed print driver is also an option, as is adding a new driver (by launching the Add Printer Driver Wizard). Spool options include whether or not to spool and whether to start printing immediately upon job submission or start printing after the last page is spooled. The Advanced tab includes the following buttons:

FIGURE 5.36   The Advanced tab

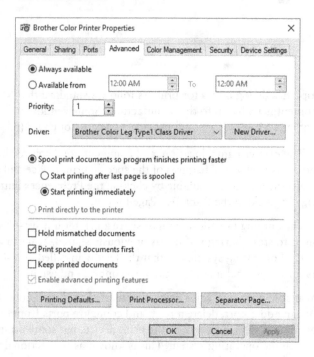

Printing Defaults Button   Launches the printer properties for the vendor as they apply to the documents.

Print Processor Button   Lets you choose whether to use the vendor-supplied print processor or the built-in Windows print processor. You can also choose the default data type to be sent to the print device.

Separator Page Button   Allows a specific page to be inserted between print jobs, making the separation of different documents easier.

Color Management Tab   If the print device has the capabilities of printing in color, there will be a Color Management tab. This tab gives you the ability to adjust the color management settings.

Security Tab   Group or user access permissions are controlled on the Security tab. Advanced permissions can be controlled here as well.

Device Settings Tab   Device settings–specific parameters for each print device are set up on the Device Settings tab (Figure 5.37). You can configure items like Form To Tray Assignment, Font Substitution, and other installable options for the print device here.

FIGURE 5.37   The Device Settings tab

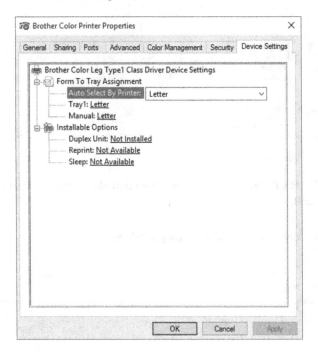

Managing Documents

Once the configuration is complete and the printer and print device are working in harmony, life is good. You can see the status of the document currently being printed as well as documents waiting to be printed. This is what we call the queue. The queue used to be viewed by choosing the queue option in the context menu for the printer. Windows 10/11 calls it See What's Printing (Figure 5.38).

FIGURE 5.38 See What's Printing

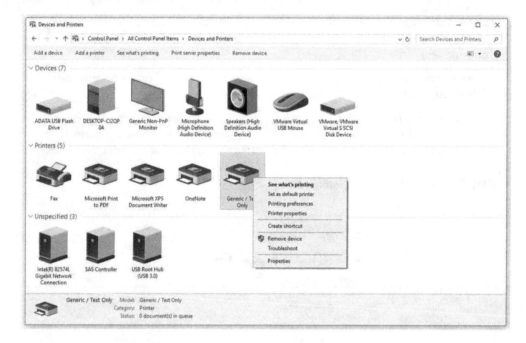

Selecting See What's Printing opens the window that shows your printer's document/job control (Figure 5.39).

FIGURE 5.39 See What's Printing display window

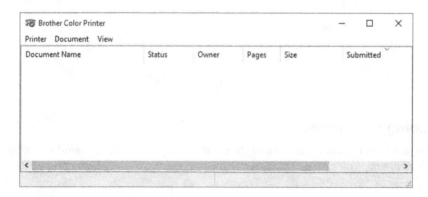

In Windows 10, you can get a graphical view of a device. To do this go to Control Panel, make sure you are displaying the large icons, and then click Devices And Printers. Double-click the printer to get a consolidated view and the popular (as decided by the vendor) menu choices. Figure 5.40 shows a printer and its options as seen when you double-click it in Windows 10. If you double-click a device in Windows 11, it will bring up the print queue.

FIGURE 5.40   Printer window from Devices And Printers in Windows 10

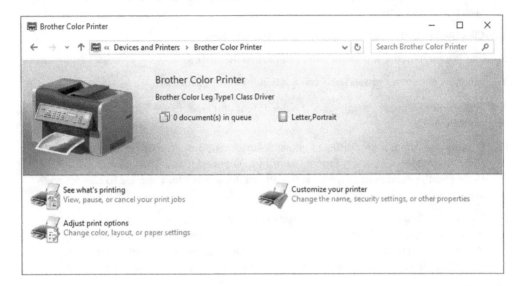

In Exercise 5.17 and Exercise 5.18, you installed printers for both a locally connected and a network-connected printer. In Exercise 5.19, let's take a look at sending a print job to the locally connected printer that you set up in Exercise 5.17 and view the document properties.

EXERCISE 5.19

Managing Documents in the Local Queue in Windows 10

1. Click the Start button ➤ Settings ➤ Devices ➤ Printers & Scanners.

2. Click the Generic printer that you installed during Exercise 5.17.

3. You will see three option buttons appear: Open Queue, Manage, and Remove Device. Click the Open Queue button.

4. Choose Printer ➤ Pause Printing from the menu.

5. View the status bar of the printer to verify that the printer is paused; there will also be a check mark next to Pause Printing in the menu.

EXERCISE 5.19 *(continued)*

Now let's send a test document to the paused locally connected printer:

1. In the Printer window, select Printer ➤ Properties.

2. On the General tab of the Properties window, click the Print Test Page button.

3. An information box will appear stating that a test page has been sent to the printer; click the Close button.

4. Click the OK button in the printer's Properties window.

5. The Printer window will display the print job in the queue.

You can view document properties from a job in the print queue:

1. In the Printer window, single-click the document you want to view (the print job you want to view).

2. Choose Document ➤ Properties to view the document properties; you can also right-click the print job and select Properties from the context menu. The General tab will show you the document properties; the other tabs are vendor supplied to control additional printer functionality for the document.

3. Click OK or Cancel to close the Properties window. Clicking OK will save any changes made and close the window; clicking Cancel will close the window without saving any changes. If you have made any configuration changes, the Apply button will become available; clicking Apply saves any changes made but does not close the window.

Now, let's delete a document from the queue:

1. In the Printer window, single-click the job you want to cancel (the document you want to delete).

2. Choose Document ➤ Cancel to delete the document. You can also right-click the document and select Cancel to delete the print job. Either method will prompt a confirmation message box asking Are You Sure You Want To Cancel The Document? Choose Yes.

3. The document will no longer be in the queue in the Printer window.

4. Choose Printer ➤ Close to close the Printer window.

Viewing the print queue in Windows 11 is done a bit differently than in Windows 10. To view the print queue on Windows 11, you want to perform the following steps:

1. Click the Start button ➤ Settings ➤ Bluetooth & Devices ➤ Printers & Scanners.

2. Click the printer you'd like to view the queue for (see Figure 5.41).

FIGURE 5.41 Printers & Scanners screen for a selected printer in Windows 11

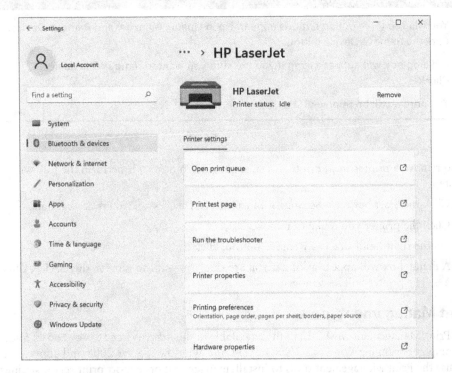

3. Select Open Print Queue. The Print Queue window will open and you can see what is printing. From here the queue screen is the same as in Windows 10. You can pause printing, cancel all documents, set up sharing, and so forth.

Deleting Printers

There may also be times you will want to delete a printer, either one that's locally connected or a network printer, from your Windows client machine. This may be due to a replacement of an older print device or may be necessary when moving a user to a new print device. The removal will be performed from the Printers & Scanners window. Removing a printer will remove the software configuration but not necessarily the driver files from the local machine. In Exercise 5.20, we will remove a printer.

EXERCISE 5.20

Removing a Printer from Printers & Scanners in Windows 10

1. Click the Start button ➤ Settings ➤ Devices ➤ Printers & Scanners.

2. Click the Generic printer that you installed during Exercise 5.17.

3. You will see three option buttons appear: Open Queue, Manage, and Remove Device. Click the Remove Device button.

4. A dialog box will appear asking if you are sure you want to remove this device. Click Yes.

5. The printer will be removed.

To remove a printer from Printers & Scanners in Windows 11, perform the following steps:

1. Click the Start button ➢ Settings ➢ Bluetooth & Devices ➢ Printers & Scanners.

2. Click the printer you'd like to remove.

3. On the right-hand side is a Remove button; click it.

4. A dialog box will appear asking if you are sure you want to remove this device. Click Yes. The printer will be removed.

Print Management Tools

The Print Management MMC Snap-in is available in the `Administrative Tools` folder on computers running Windows 7/8/8.1/10/11 and Windows Server 2008 and above. You can use the Print Management tools to install, manage, import/export print server settings, and view all the printers and print servers throughout your company.

You can use Print Management to install printers and to monitor print queues remotely. This feature allows you to use filters to find printers that are in an error condition and to receive email notifications or run scripts when a printer or print server needs attention. Depending on your printer, Print Management can also show you if a printer is low on ink or paper.

Print Management allows you to have a single application where you can monitor and manage your printers. For example, Print Management allows you to export print server information to a file and then take that file to another Windows system and import those print server settings into a new machine. This process is referred to as print server migration.

You can also use Print Management tools along with Group Policies. Group Policies are rules and policies that you can set on a server and those policies will be deployed to your users and computers automatically through the network.

Print Management also gives you the ability to automatically search for and install network printers on your local network. Besides the Print Management MMC, there is a command-line utility that you can use named `Printbrm.exe`. When using `Printbrm.exe`, you must be at a command prompt with administrative privileges.

Print Management allows you to complete the following tasks:

- Update and manage printer drivers.

- Control printer driver installation.

- Create new printer filters.

- View extended features of the printers.

- Pause or resume printing.

- Cancel all print jobs.

- List or remove printers from Active Directory.

- Delete printers.

- Import and export printer settings.

In Exercise 5.21, we will use the Print Migration tools to export our print server settings to a file. You can then take that file and import the settings into another print server. This is a way to export printers from one server and load them onto another.

EXERCISE 5.21

Using the Print Migration Tools

1. In the Windows client search box, type **Print Management**. Click the Print Management tool that appears.

2. Right-click Print Management and choose Migrate Printers (as shown in Figure 5.42).

EXERCISE 5.21 *(continued)*

FIGURE 5.42   Migrate Printers option

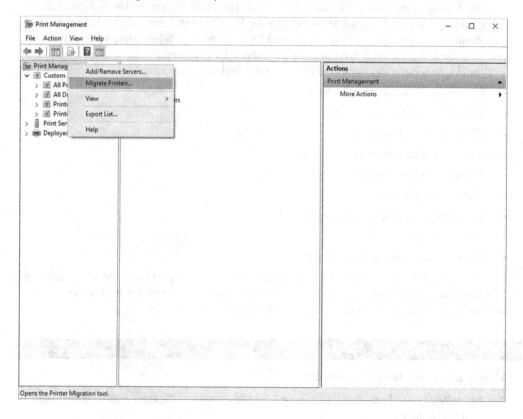

3.   At the Getting Started With Print Migration screen, choose to export printer queues and print drivers to a file. Click Next.

4.   Choose your print server and click Next.

5.   A screen will appear showing you which objects will be exported. Click Next.

6.   Type in a filename and location or click Browse to choose the filename and location. Click Next once completed.

7.   The settings will be exported. Once the export is complete, click the Finish button, as shown in Figure 5.43.

FIGURE 5.43 Export Complete screen

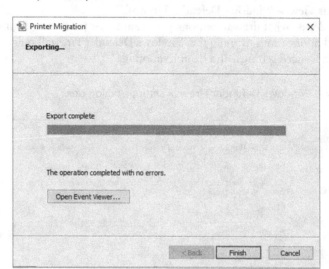

Now that the print server settings have been exported to a file, you can take that file to another machine and import those setting using the Print Migration tools. This is an easy way for administrators to move print servers without manually rebuilding the print server settings.

Configuring Windows Defender Firewall

Windows Defender Firewall, which is included with Windows 10/11, helps prevent unauthorized users or malicious software from accessing your computer. Windows Defender Firewall does not allow unsolicited traffic, which is traffic that was not sent in response to a request, to pass through the firewall. It also allows or blocks connections to and from other computers on a network. Windows Defender Firewall is sometimes referred to as Windows Defender for short, but it should not be confused with Microsoft Defender Antivirus software.

Understanding the Windows Defender Firewall Basics

The Windows Defender Firewall is the same app in Windows 10/11, but how you access them is a bit different. The only difference is the rounded corners that Windows 11 uses. Both Windows 10/11 use Control Panel to access the Windows Defender Firewall. In Windows 10, you configure Windows Defender Firewall by clicking Start ➤ Windows System ➤ Control Panel ➤ Large Icons View ➤ Windows Defender Firewall.

In Windows 11, the easiest way to access Control Panel is by searching for the app. Then select, Large Icons View ➢ Windows Defender Firewall.

You can then decide what firewall options you want to set (as seen in Figure 5.44) like changing firewall notifications, turning the Windows Defender Firewall on or off, restoring defaults, setting advanced settings, and troubleshooting.

FIGURE 5.44 Windows Defender Firewall settings dialog box

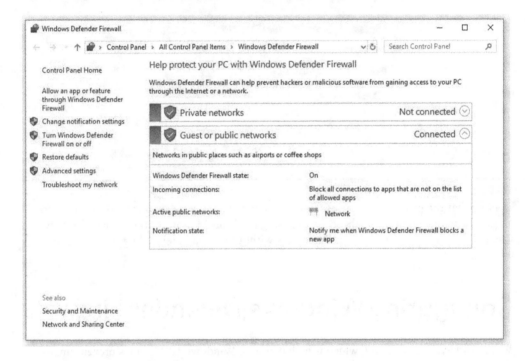

The Windows Firewall settings screen allows you to turn Windows Firewall on or off for both private and public networks. The On setting will block incoming sources, and the Turn Off Windows Firewall setting will allow incoming sources to connect.

There is also a check box for Block All Incoming Connections. This feature allows you to connect to networks that are not secure. When Block All Incoming Connections is selected, all incoming connections (even ones allowed in the Allowed Apps list) will be blocked by Windows Firewall.

I just wanted to point out, too, that sometimes a third- party security solution that you have installed on your device may take control of your firewall settings.

Windows Defender Firewall with Advanced Security

In Windows 10/11, you can configure more advanced settings by configuring Windows Firewall with Advanced Security (WFAS) by using the Advanced Settings link (on the left-hand side) in the Windows Defender Firewall app.

The Windows Defender Firewall With Advanced Security dialog box appears, as shown in Figure 5.45.

FIGURE 5.45   Windows Defender Firewall With Advanced Security

The left-hand pane shows that you can set up specific inbound and outbound rules, connection security rules, and monitoring rules. The central area shows an overview of the firewall's status when no rule is selected in the left pane. When a rule is selected, the central area shows the rule's settings. The right pane shows the same actions as the Action menu on the top. These are just shortcuts to the different actions that can be performed in Windows Firewall. Let's take a more detailed look at some of the elements in Windows Firewall.

Inbound and Outbound Rules

Inbound and outbound rules consist of many preconfigured rules that can be enabled or disabled. Obviously, inbound rules (see Figure 5.46) monitor inbound traffic, and outbound rules monitor outbound traffic. By default, many are disabled. Double-clicking a rule will bring up its Properties dialog box (Figure 5.47).

FIGURE 5.46 Inbound rules

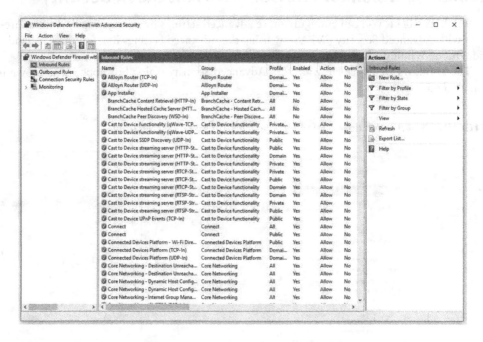

FIGURE 5.47 An inbound rule's Properties dialog box

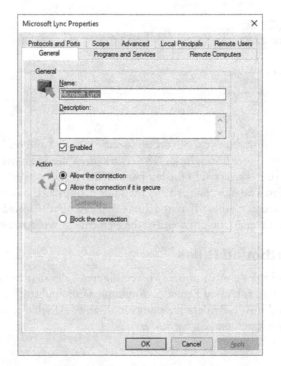

You can filter the rules to make them easier to view. Filtering can be based on the profile the rule affects, on whether the rule is enabled or disabled, or on the rule group. You can filter a rule by clicking which filter type you want to use in the right pane or by clicking the Action menu on the top of the screen.

If you can't find a rule that is appropriate for your needs, you can create a new rule by right-clicking Inbound Rules or Outbound Rules in the left-hand pane and then selecting New Rule. The New Inbound (or Outbound) Rule Wizard will launch, and you will be asked whether you want to create a rule based on a particular program, protocol or port, predefined category, or custom settings.

As you are setting up the firewall rules, you have the ability to configure authenticated exceptions. No matter how well your system security is set up, there are almost always times when computers on your network can't use IPsec. This is when you set up authenticated exceptions. Now it's important to understand that when you set up these authenticated exceptions, you are reducing the security of the network because it allows computers to send unprotected IPsec network traffic. So, make sure the computers that are added to the authenticated exceptions list are managed and trusted computers only.

Table 5.2 shows you some of the most common port numbers and what those port numbers are used for.

TABLE 5.2 Common port numbers

Port number	Associated application or service
20	FTP Data
21	FTP Control
22	Secure Shell (SSH)
23	Telnet
25	SMTP
53	DNS
67/68	DHCP/BOOTP
80	HTTP
102	Microsoft Exchange Server
110	POP3
443	HHTPS (HTTP with SSL)

Complete Exercise 5.22 to create a new inbound rule that will allow only encrypted TCP traffic.

Creating a New Inbound Rule

1. Open the Control Panel and select Large Icons View ➢ Windows Defender Firewall.

2. Click Advanced Settings on the left side.

3. Right-click Inbound Rules and select New Rule.

4. Select a rule type. For this exercise, select Custom so that you can see all the options available to you. Then click Next.

5. On the Program screen, choose All Programs. Then click Next.

6. Select the protocol type as well as the local and remote port numbers that are affected by this rule. For this exercise, choose TCP, and ensure that All Ports is selected for both Local Port and Remote Port. Click Next to continue.

7. On the Scope screen, choose Any IP Address for both Local and Remote. Then click Next.

8. On the Action screen, select Allow The Connection Only If It Is Secure. Click Next.

9. On the Users screen, you can experiment with these options if you want by entering users to both sections. Once you click one of the check boxes, the Add and Remove buttons become available. Click Next to continue.

10. On the Computers screen, you can choose what computers you will authorize or allow through this rule (exceptions). Again, you can experiment with these options if you want. Click Next to continue.

11. On the Profiles screen, select which profiles will be affected by this rule. Select one or more profiles and click Next.

12. Give your profile a name and description, and then click Finish. Your custom rule will appear in the list of inbound rules, and the rule will be enabled.

13. Double-click your newly created rule. Notice that you can change the options that you previously configured.

14. Delete the rule by right-clicking it and choosing Delete. A dialog box will appear asking if you are sure. Click Yes.

15. Close the Windows Firewall.

Connection Security Rules

Connection security rules are used to configure how and when authentication occurs. These rules do not specifically allow connections; that's the job of inbound and outbound rules. You can configure the following connection security rules:

Isolation   To restrict a connection based on authentication criteria.

Authentication Exemption   To specify computers that are exempt from authentication requirements.

Server-to-Server   To authenticate connections between computers.

Tunnel   To authenticate connections between gateway computers.

Custom   Use custom to create a customized connection security rule.

Monitoring

The Monitoring section shows detailed information about the firewall configurations for the Domain Profile, Private Profile, and Public Profile settings. These network location profiles determine what settings are enforced for private networks, public networks, and networks connected to a domain.

 **Real World Scenario**

Use More than Just Windows Defender Firewall

When doing consulting, it always concerns me when I see small to midsize companies using Microsoft Windows Defender Firewall and no other protection. Microsoft Windows Defender Firewall should be your *last* line of defense. You need to make sure that you have good hardware firewalls that separate your network from the world.

Also watch Windows Defender Firewall when it comes to printing. I have run into many situations where a printer that needs to communicate with the operating system has issues when Windows Defender Firewall is enabled. If this happens, make sure that the printer is allowed in the Allowed Programs section.

Now that you understand how to work with the Windows Defender Firewall, let's take a closer look at how to work with the Windows 10 Security Center.

Managing Windows Security

Windows 10/11 includes built-in Windows Security, which includes antivirus protection. Windows client devices are automatically protected from the very moment that your users start using Windows 10/11. Windows 10/11 Security is always scanning the system for viruses, malware (malicious software), and security dangers. Not only does Windows 10/11 provide real-time protection, Microsoft continually does updates to make sure that your corporate devices stay safe and that the devices are protected from any new threats.

Windows Security Center

Windows Security is built into Windows and includes an antivirus program called Microsoft Defender Antivirus. In early editions of Windows 10, Windows Security was known as Windows Defender Security Center. Windows Security starts automatically protecting your system. Figure 5.48 shows you the Windows Security dialog box and what's included.

FIGURE 5.48   Windows Security dialog box on Windows 11

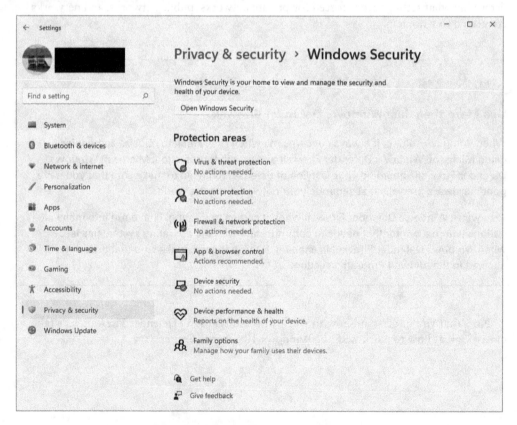

Windows Security has multiple options that you can set to help protect your system. So, let's take a look at some of these options:

Virus and Threat Protection   Windows 10/11 will automatically monitor for threats that can impact your device, run scans on your system, and get updates to help protect against any new threats. Windows 10/11 has an antivirus built in, and it will get automatic updates when your Windows client systems is updated.

Account Protection   Administrators can configure the user's sign-in options and account settings. These settings include using Windows Hello and Dynamic Lock.

Firewall & Network Protection   Windows 10/11 includes a Windows Firewall, and the Windows Firewall helps you prevent unauthorized users or malicious software from accessing your computer.

App & Browser Control   You can configure update settings for Windows Defender SmartScreen, and this helps protect your Windows 10/11 devices against potentially dangerous applications, downloads, files, and websites. This gives you the ability to control exploit protection and customize settings that will help protect your Windows client devices.

Device Security   Windows 10/11 Device Security allows you to use built-in security options to defend your organization's Windows client devices from malicious software attacks.

Device Performance & Health   Windows 10/11 allows you to view the status information about the device's performance health. This helps you keep your organization's devices clean and up-to-date with the latest version of Windows 10/11.

Family Options   The Family Options feature in Windows Security is not a feature that most administrators will configure in a corporate environment. These options provide tools to help manage children's computer access. Parents can use Family Options to help keep their children's devices clean and up-to-date with the latest version of Windows 10/11 and to protect their children when they are on the Internet.

You may notice status icons that indicate your level of safety. These include:

- Green means there are no recommended actions at this time.
- Yellow means that there is a recommended safety concern.
- Red means that there is a warning that something needs attention immediately.

In Exercise 5.23, I will show you how to run an advanced virus and threat scan on your Windows client device.

EXERCISE 5.23

Running an Advanced Scan

1. In Windows 10, click Start ➤ Settings ➤ Update & Security ➤ Windows Security and then choose Virus & Threat Protection.

   In Windows 11, click Start ➤ Settings ➤ Privacy & Security ➤ Windows Security and then choose Virus & Threat Protection.

2. Under Current Threats, select Scan Options (or in early versions of Windows 10, under Threat History, select Run A New Advanced Scan).

3. Make sure the Full Scan radio button is selected and click the Scan Now button.

   In the Scan Options menu (see Figure 5.49), you will see a list of four different types of scans you can perform:

   Quick Scan   Scans folders on your device where threats are usually found, such as the Downloads and Windows folders. This usually only takes a few minutes to finish.

   Full Scan   This scan will scan all files on your computer and all running programs. The scan may take longer to complete than other scans.

   Custom Scan   If you select this option, Windows Security will ask you for a specific file or folder location that you want to scan.

   Microsoft Defender Offline Scan   This option will restart your computer and will scan system files and programs while they are not running; this can be handy if there is malware running on the computer that may interfere with the scan.

4. The scan will take a while. After the scan finishes, close the Defender Security Center.

FIGURE 5.49 Scan options dialog box

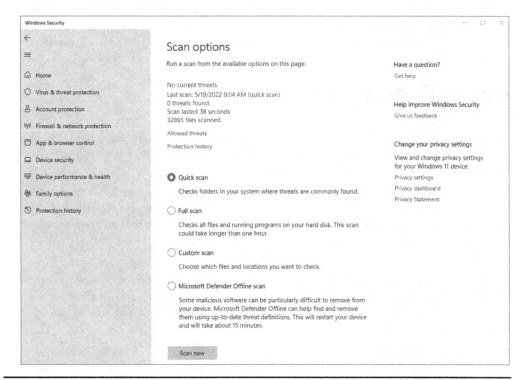

Summary

There are two ways that you can format your hard disk in a Windows 10/11 operating system: FAT32 and NTFS. NTFS has many advantages over FAT32, including security, encryption (before Windows 10 and Server 2016), disk quotas, and compression, just to name a few.

Devices and hardware are two important components that must be properly configured in Windows 10/11 to guarantee the best possible machine performance. Using Device Manager and Devices (under Settings) is an effective way to help manage these devices and drivers.

Another important task that we have to configure is setting up our print devices. The print devices are the physical machines that spit the print jobs out. The printer is the drivers that allow the print device to communicate with Windows 10/11.

Finally, we also discussed using Windows Firewall with Advanced Security. Windows Firewall helps prevent unauthorized users from connecting to the Windows 10/11 operating system. Windows Firewall is an extra line of defense, but it should not replace a perimeter firewall for your network. I also talked about protecting devices using Windows Security.

Exam Essentials

Understand the different file format options.   There are two ways to format a hard disk in Windows 10/11: FAT32 and NTFS. Understand that NTFS offers many benefits over FAT32, including security, compression, and disk quotas.

Know how to verify whether drivers are signed.   Microsoft includes with Windows 10/11 a utility called `sigverif.exe` for users to verify whether their drivers are digitally signed on their machines. `sigverif.exe` will scan your machine and verify that all drivers are properly signed. If they are not signed, `sigverif.exe` will show you which drivers are not signed.

Know how to configure devices and drivers.   Understand how to configure devices and drivers in Device Manager. Know how to roll back drivers and how to update drivers when newer versions are released. Know how to use Devices (under Settings) and how to add devices in Device Manager.

Know how to configure printers and print devices.   Understand how to configure printers and print devices in Printers & Scanners. Know how to connect to a print device and how to manage the jobs that are sent to the printer.

Know how to configure Windows Firewall.   Know how to set up and maintain Windows Firewall with Advanced Security. Know that you can set up inbound and outbound rules by using Windows Firewall. Know how to allow or deny applications by using Windows Firewall.

Know how to run scans with Windows Security.   Know how to set up and run virus scans using Windows Security.

Video Resources

There are videos available for the following exercises:

    5.1

    5.2

    5.4

You can access the videos at www.wiley.com/go/sybextestprep.

Review Questions

1. You are the network administrator for your organization. You have been asked by the owner of the company to verify that all drivers installed on the Windows 10/11 machines are signed drivers. How do you accomplish this task?

    A. Run `verify.exe` at the command prompt.

    B. Run a scan in Device Manager.

    C. Run `sigverif.exe` at the command prompt.

    D. Run `drivers.exe` at the command prompt.

2. You are the network administrator for your organization. You have a Windows client system called PS1 that is configured with multiple shared print queues. You need to migrate the print queues to a new machine called PS2. How do you do that?

    A. Use the Migrate Printers utility in the Print Management tool.

    B. Use the Migrate Printers utility in the Control Panel.

    C. Use the Migrate Printers utility in the Printers & Scanners utility.

    D. Use the Export Printers tool in the Print Management tool.

3. Your computer uses a SCSI adapter that supports a SCSI drive, which contains your Windows client system and boot partitions. After updating the SCSI driver, you restart your computer, but Windows will load but with errors. You need to get this computer up and running as quickly as possible. Which of the following strategies should you try first to correct your problem?

    A. Restore your computer's configuration with your last backup.

    B. Boot your computer with the System Image reload.

    C. Boot your computer and do a driver rollback.

    D. Boot your computer to the Recovery Console and manually copy the old driver back to the computer.

4. You are about to install a new driver for your CD-ROM drive, but you are not 100 percent sure that you are using the correct driver. Which of the following options will allow you to *most easily* return your computer to the previous state if the new driver is not correct?

    A. Safe Mode

    B. Roll Back Driver

    C. System Restore utility

    D. Startup Repair tool

5. You are the network administrator for your organization. Your organization has been using Windows 10/11 Enterprise. You need to run the Print Management tools from the command prompt. What command do you run?

   A. `Printmgmt.exe`

   B. `PrintMig.exe`

   C. `Prtmgmt.exe`

   D. `Printbrm.exe`

6. You are using Windows 10/11 Professional and you have a hardware component that is no longer needed. You do not want to delete the drivers but you do not want them active. What can you do to the drivers?

   A. Remove the drivers using Device Manager.

   B. Disable the drivers using Device Manager.

   C. Upgrade the drivers using Device Manager.

   D. Roll back the drivers using Device Manager.

7. You are the network administrator for a small organization. Your organization has implemented Windows 10/11 on all client machines. You want to implement another line of security on the Windows client machine so that unauthorized users can't access the machines. What can you implement?

   A. Windows Data Protection

   B. Windows Encryption Protection

   C. Windows Defender Firewall

   D. Windows Secure Data Protocol

8. You are the network administrator for a large organization. One of your users calls you and states that they think they are having issues with their network card. What tool can you use to see if the hardware is working properly?

   A. Device Hardware

   B. Manage Hardware

   C. Device Manager

   D. Device Configuration

9. You are the network administrator for a large organization. You have a Windows 10/11 machine that is working fine, but you downloaded and installed a newer version of the network adapter driver. After you load the driver, the network device stops working properly. Which tool should you use to help you fix the problem?

   A. Driver rollback

   B. Driver Repair utility

   C. Reverse Driver application

   D. Windows 10 Driver Compatibility tool

10. You are the administrator for your company network. You and a colleague are discussing Windows Security and Exploit Protection. Which section of Windows Security covers Exploit Protection mitigations?

   A. Account Protection

   B. App & Browser Control

   C. Device Security

   D. Virus & Threat Protection

11. You are the IT director for a large school system. You need to set up inbound and outbound rules on the Windows 10/11 machines. What do you need to do to accomplish this?

   A. Windows Defender Credential Guard

   B. Windows Defender Exploit Guard

   C. Windows Defender Application Control

   D. Windows Defender Firewall with Advanced Security

12. You are the administrator for StormWind Studios. You are trying to set up your Windows Defender Firewall to allow DNS inbound and outbound rules. Which port number would you set up?

   A. Port 20

   B. Port 25

   C. Port 53

   D. Port 80

13. You are the administrator for StormWind Studios. You are trying to set up your Windows Defender Firewall to allow SMTP inbound and outbound rules. Which port number would you set up?

   A. Port 20

   B. Port 25

   C. Port 53

   D. Port 80

14. You are the administrator for StormWind Studios. You are trying to set up your Windows Defender Firewall to allow FTP traffic. Which two port numbers would you set up?

   A. Ports 20 and 21

   B. Ports 25 and 53

   C. Ports 53 and 80

   D. Ports 80 and 443

15. You and a colleague are discussing how Windows Security monitors devices and provides a health report. You want to look at this report. Where does this report appear?

   A. Account Protection

   B. Device Performance & Health

   C. Device Security

   D. Virus & Threat Protection

16. You are the administrator for your company network. You and a colleague are discussing Microsoft Defender Antivirus. You know that there are a number of scan options available with Microsoft Defender Antivirus. You want to perform a scan that will scan the most likely areas on a hard disk that spyware, malware, and viruses are commonly known to infect. What scan option is being discussed?

   A. A custom scan

   B. A full scan

   C. A quick scan

   D. A Microsoft Defender offline scan

17. You and an assistant are discussing the `convert` command. What does the command `convert e: /fs:ntfs` do?

   A. It will convert the E: drive from FAT to NTFS.

   B. It will convert the E: drive from NTFS to FAT.

   C. It will format the E: drive to FAT.

   D. It will scan the E: drive for errors.

18. You are the administrator for your company network. You and a colleague are discussing troubleshooting a network adapter. What are some reasons why a network adapter may not be functioning properly? (Choose all that apply.)

   A. The network adapter is on the Hardware Compatibility List (HCL).

   B. The network adapter has outdated drivers.

   C. The network adapter is not recognized by Windows 10/11.

   D. The network adapter has been correctly configured.

19. You are the administrator for your company network. You have a Windows 10/11 Enterprise computer. You add a 1 TB hard drive and create a new volume that you've assigned as the D: drive letter. You format this new drive with NTFS. What should you do if you want to limit the amount of space that each user can use on this new drive? (Choose all that apply.)

   A. Select the default quota limit for new users on this volume by setting the Limit Disk Space To option.

   B. Run `convert d: /fs:ntfsNTFS`.

   C. Select Enable Quota Management.

   D. Select Deny Disk Space To Users Exceeding Quota Limit.

20. You are the administrator for your company network. You and a colleague are discussing the benefits of the NTFS filesystem. You are thinking about setting up disk quotas. By default, Windows 10/11 supports disk quota restrictions, but at what level?

A. The drive level is the default.

B. The folder level is the default.

C. The partition level is the default.

D. The volume level is the default.

Chapter

6

Configuring Network Connectivity

MICROSOFT EXAM OBJECTIVES COVERED IN THIS CHAPTER:

✓ **Configure networking and access**

- Configure client IP settings; configure mobile networking; configure VPN client by using built-in tools or Connection Manager Administration Kit (CMAK); configure and manage certificates on client devices; troubleshoot client connectivity.

When it comes to Windows 10/11, it's important to understand how to set up a network. In most IT departments, you install applications through the network. Also, when your users authenticate, they normally authenticate onto a network.

For most of us, our Windows client devices will be configured on some type of a network. It doesn't matter whether it's a home network or a corporate network; Windows 10/11 will normally belong to some type of network.

Because of this, knowing how to properly configure and design a Windows network is essential. In this chapter, we discuss Active Directory and how to configure Windows 10/11 to work within the Windows Server domain environment.

So, let's begin this chapter with the basics and what networking is all about.

Understanding the Basics

Microsoft uses two networking models: domain-based networks and workgroup networks. Corporations can use Azure as their network and not have an on-site network. This will be covered later in the book.

The way you design your network determines how you set up the rest of the computers and servers on that network. The choice you make here will be determined by many factors, including the number of users on your network and the amount of money you can spend.

Peer-to-Peer Networks

When setting up a Microsoft Windows *peer-to-peer network* (also referred to as a *workgroup*), it is important to understand that all computers on the network are equal. All of the peer-to-peer computers, also referred to as *nodes*, simultaneously act as both clients and servers.

Peer-to-peer networks are typically any combination of Microsoft Windows XP, Windows Vista, Windows 7, Windows 8 / 8.1, and Windows 10/11 machines connected by a centralized device such as a router, switch, or hub (see Figure 6.1).

FIGURE 6.1   Peer-to-peer model

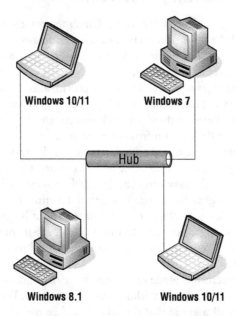

One of the biggest debates among IT professionals is when to use a peer-to-peer network. These types of networks have their place in the networking world. Most home networks use this type of configuration—where all of the computers are connected by a small Internet router. It's often the same for smaller companies, such as a dentist or an attorney's office. You would use this network configuration in a small environment with 10 or fewer users. This enables small organizations to still share resources without expensive equipment, server software, or an internal IT department.

But there is a downside to peer-to-peer networks; the biggest issues are manageability and security. Many new IT people like working on a small peer-to-peer network because of its size, but no matter what, a network with 10 users and 10 computers can be very difficult to manage, and security is extremely difficult to set up. Because there is no server to centralize user accounts on a peer-to-peer network, each Microsoft Windows 7, Windows 8/8.1, and Windows 10/11 computer must have a user account and password. So, if you have 10 users and 10 computers and all 10 users must be able to access all 10 computers, you end up creating 100 accounts: 10 accounts on each machine times 10 machines.

Another disadvantage of peer-to-peer networks is backups. Most IT departments do not back up individual user machines, and because there is no centralized server for data storage when using a peer-to-peer network, data recoverability can be an issue. However, today more solutions are available such as using cloud storage solutions like OneDrive, which takes away concern for performing backups regularly.

Now that you have seen the advantages and disadvantages of a peer-to-peer network, let's discuss the advantages and disadvantages of a domain-based network.

On-Site Active Directory Networks

A *domain-based* network uses Microsoft's *Active Directory*, which is a single distributed database that contains all the objects in your network. A domain is a logical grouping of objects into a distributed database. Some of these objects are user accounts, group accounts, and published objects (folders and printers).

The first of many advantages to Active Directory is centralized management. As just stated, the Active Directory database contains all the network information within a single, distributed data repository. Because these network objects are all located in the same database, you can easily manage the domain from one location.

Another major advantage to using Active Directory is domain security. You have the advantage of creating a unique username and password for each user within the domain. These usernames and passwords can be used to access all resources that an individual has the proper rights to access. You can determine, based on job function or position, which files or folders on the network a user should be granted access to and assign access to the user's single account. In our earlier peer-to-peer example, you needed to create 100 user accounts. With a domain, you would need to create only the 10 accounts, one per person.

An Active Directory structure is made up of one or more domains. As explained, a *domain* is a logical grouping of objects within your organization. For example, if we had the WillPanek.com domain, all users in that domain should be members of the WillPanek .com organization. The objects that are contained within a domain do not need to be in the same physical location. Domains can span the entire globe even though they are part of the same organization.

One of the advantages to using domains is the ability to have a *child domain*, which is a subdomain of another domain. You can build child domains based on physical locations, departments, and so forth. Figure 6.2 shows the hierarchy structure of WillPanek.com with its child domains (based on geographic location).

 Microsoft Active Directory domains are represented as triangles. You should remember that when taking any Microsoft exam.

Child domains give you greater scalability. Active Directory has the ability to store millions of objects within a single domain, but child domains give you the flexibility to design a structure that meets an organization's needs. For example, you may have a site located in a different state. Creating a child domain for that office allows that office to be an independent domain, and thus they can have their own security and domain settings. One or more domains that follow the same contiguous namespace are called a *tree*. For example, if my domain name is WillPanek.com and the child domains are NH.WillPanek.com, Arizona.WillPanek.com, and Florida.WillPanek.com, this would be a tree. All of these domains follow the WillPanek.com namespace.

FIGURE 6.2   Domain structure

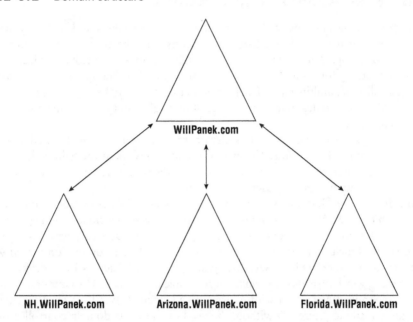

When you set up child domains, the parent and child domains automatically establish a trust relationship. *Trusts* allow users to be granted access to resources in a domain even when their accounts reside in a different domain. To make administration of trust relationships easier, Microsoft has made transitive two-way trusts the default relationship between domains within a forest. A forest is all the trees that are part of your Active Directory structure, and they share a schema and global catalog. This means that by default, all domains within the same forest automatically trust one another. As shown in Figure 6.2, WillPanek .com automatically trusts NH.WillPanek.com, Arizona.WillPanek.com, and Florida .WillPanek.com. This means that all the child domains implicitly trust one another.

The last Active Directory advantage that we will discuss is an extensible schema. The Active Directory schema contains all the objects and attributes of the database. For example, when you create a new user by using the Active Directory Users and Computers snap-in, the system asks you to fill in the user's first name, last name, username, password, and so forth. These fields are the attributes of the user object, and the way that the system knows to prompt for these fields is that the user object has these specific attributes assigned to it within the Active Directory schema. You have the ability to change or expand these fields based on organizational needs.

The major disadvantage to an Active Directory model is cost. When setting up an Active Directory domain, an organization needs a machine that's powerful enough to handle the Windows Server operating system, and as the size of an organization grows you would also need more powerful servers and then more than one domain server to ensure redundancy in case of failure. Also, most companies that decide to use a domain-based organization will require the IT personnel to manage and maintain the network infrastructure.

Cloud-Based Azure Active Directory

Now that you have been introduced to Active Directory, let's take a look at how you can have Microsoft manage your Active Directory with its cloud-based Active Directory called *Azure Active Directory*. Azure AD is Microsoft's subscription-based cloud service.

If you are working for a small to midsized company and you don't want to worry about employing a full-time, multiperson IT department, then this may be a great option for you. This allows Microsoft to deal with the worries of managing and maintaining a server room and all the hardware.

All your company would need to do is hire or train someone who would add and maintain the actual Azure AD accounts. This person could also work as the help desk or support individual. Now you have Microsoft worrying about the hardware and your IT people can focus on helping and maintaining users and accounts.

So how does Azure AD compare when it comes to adding Windows 10/11 to the domain? It really doesn't matter. As long as you have Internet access to the cloud-based system, your Windows 10/11 accounts will work the same way as if Active Directory was on-premises.

Windows 10/11 includes a feature for configuring and deploying corporation-owned Windows devices called Azure AD Join. Azure AD Join registers the Windows 10/11 devices in Azure Active Directory, which then allows them to be accessible and managed by your organization.

The one nice advantage is that with Azure Active Directory, Windows client devices authenticate directly to Azure AD without the need of an on-site domain controller. But, if you want, you can still have a domain controller on-site that works with the cloud-based Azure Active Directory.

When you are adding Windows 10/11 to Azure Active Directory, end users or domain admins can join their Windows client device (computer, tablet, or phone) to Azure AD during the out-of-box experience (OOBE). Because of this, organizations can assign devices to their users with no IT interaction or staging time.

Because of the Azure AD Join built into Windows 10/11, during the OOBE, the IT department would just add the device to the Azure Active Directory network.

Now that you understand the difference between a workgroup and a domain, let's explore some of the other networking terms that you will need to know.

Other Microsoft Networking Terms and Roles

Now that you have seen the different Microsoft networking models, let's talk about some of the server terminology that is used in the remainder of this chapter. You may be familiar with some of these terms, but it's always good to get a refresher.

Server A *server* is a machine that users connect to so they can access resources located on that machine. These resources can be files, printers, applications, and so forth. Usually, the type of server is dependent on the resource that the user needs. For example, a print server is a server that controls printers. A file server contains files. Application servers can run applications for the users. Sometimes you will hear a server referred to by the specific application that it may be running. For example, someone may say, "That's our SQL server" or "We have an Exchange server."

Domain Controller   This is a server that contains a replica of the Active Directory database. As mentioned earlier in this chapter, Active Directory is the database that contains all the security objects in your network along with any resources that you publish to Active Directory. A *domain controller* is a server that contains this database. All domain controllers are equal in a Windows Server network, and each can read from and write to the directory database unless it's a read-only domain controller (RODC). Some domain controllers may contain extra roles, but they are all part of the same Active Directory network.

Member Server   A *member server* is a server that is a member of a domain-based network but does not contain a copy of Active Directory. For example, Microsoft recommends that a Microsoft Exchange server be loaded on a member server instead of a domain controller. Both domain controllers and member servers can act as file, print, or application servers. Your choice of server type depends on whether you need that server to have a replica of Active Directory.

Network Discovery   *Network Discovery* is a setting that determines whether your Windows 10/11 system can locate other computers and devices on the network and if other computers on the network can see your computer. To enable or disable Network Discovery, you need to complete the following steps:

1. Open Control Panel using your preferred method; I suggest using the search feature.

2. Next, open Network And Sharing Center.

3. Click Change Advanced Sharing Settings on the left-hand side.

4. Click the arrow to expand your desired profile and then click Turn On/Turn Off Network Discovery.

5. Click the Save Changes button.

Stand-alone Server   A *stand-alone server* is not a member of a domain. Many organizations may use this type of server for virtualization. For example, say you load Windows Server with Hyper-V (Microsoft's virtualization server) on a stand-alone server. You can then create virtual machines that act as domain controllers to run the network.

Client Machine   A *client machine* is a computer that normally is used by a company's end users. The most common operating systems for a client machine are Windows 7, Windows 8/ 8.1, and Windows 10/11.

DNS Server   A *Domain Name Service (DNS)* server has the DNS service running on it. DNS is a name resolution service that resolves a hostname to a TCP/IP address (called forward lookup). DNS also has the ability to resolve a TCP/IP address to a name (called reverse lookup). When you install an operating system onto a computer, you assign that computer a hostname. The problem is that computers talk to each other by using TCP/IP addresses, such as 192.168.1.100. It would be difficult for most users to remember all the different TCP/IP addresses on a network. So normally you connect to a machine by using its hostname. DNS does the conversion of hostname to TCP/IP address for you.

The easiest way to understand how this works is to think of your phone number. If someone wants to call you but doesn't have your telephone number, they can call directory assistance. They give directory assistance your name, and they get your phone number. This is basically how a network works as well. DNS is directory assistance on your network. You give DNS a hostname, and it returns a network telephone number (TCP/IP address). DNS is a requirement if you want to install Active Directory. You can install DNS before or during the Active Directory installation, but DNS is required for an Active Directory installation to occur. DNS can help resolve either IPv4 or IPv6 TCP/IP addresses, both of which are explained later in this chapter, in the section "Understanding TCP/IP."

The reason that DNS can resolve both IPv4 and IPv6 is because of the Link-Local Multicast Name Resolution (LLMNR) protocol, which is based on DNS packet formats that allow both IPv4 and IPv6 hosts to perform name resolution for hosts on the same local network.

DHCP Server A *Dynamic Host Configuration Protocol (DHCP)* server runs the DHCP service, which assigns TCP/IP information to your computers dynamically. Every computer needs three settings to operate properly (with the Internet and an intranet): a TCP/IP address, a subnet mask, and a default gateway (router address). Your computers can get this minimum information two ways: manually, where someone manually types in the TCP/IP information on the machine, or dynamically, where the DHCP service automatically assigns the machine an address. DHCP can assign more than just these three settings. DHCP can assign any TCP/IP configuration information, including the address of a DNS server, WINS server, time servers, and so forth.

Continuing with our scenario from the DNS server description, DHCP would be the phone company. DHCP is the component that assigns the telephone number (TCP/IP number).

If you are using DHCP and your Windows 10/11 machine receives a 169.254.*x.x* TCP/IPv4 address, your client is not able to connect to the DHCP server. Windows 10/11 machines will automatically assign themselves a 169.254.*x.x* TCP/IPv4 number when DHCP is unavailable. This is called Automatic Private IP Addressing (APIPA). DHCP can issue both IPv4 or IPv6 TCP/IP addresses.

Global Catalog The *Global Catalog* is a database of all Active Directory objects in a forest with only a subset of the object attributes. Think of the Global Catalog as an index. If you needed to look something up in this Windows 10/11 book, you would go to the index and find what page you need to turn to. You would not just randomly look through the book for the information. This is the same purpose the Global Catalog serves in your Active Directory forest. When you need to find a resource in the domain (user, published printer, and so forth), you can search the Global Catalog to find its location.

Domain controllers need to use a Global Catalog to help with user authentication. Global Catalogs are a requirement on an Active Directory domain. All domain controllers can be Global Catalogs, but this is not always a good practice. Your network should have at least two Global Catalogs for redundancy, but too many can cause too much Global Catalog replication traffic unless you have a single-domain model.

Port Numbers   Port numbers are used by applications and services so that they can communicate with a network or a computer system. Think of port numbers as doorways that are used for the application or service. So, for example, if a user wants to connect to the Internet, they use port number 80.

Configuring NIC Devices

Before you can connect a Windows 10/11 machine to the domain, you must set up the *network interface card (NIC)*—a hardware component used to connect computers or other devices to the network to allow the machines to communicate with each other. NICs are responsible for providing the physical connection that recognizes the physical address of the device where they are installed.

 The Open Systems Interconnection (OSI) model defines the encapsulation technique that builds the basic data structure for data transport across an internetwork. The OSI model provides interoperability among hardware vendors, network protocols, and applications. The physical address is the OSI model Layer 2 address or, for Ethernet technologies, the MAC (Media Access Control) address. This is not an IP address, which is the OSI Layer 3, or Network layer, also generically defined as the logical address.

We generically call the interface between our network devices and the software components of the machines *network adapters* (also referred to as NICs). Most commonly, you see network adapters installed on computers, but you also see network adapters installed in network printers and specialized devices such as intrusion detection systems (IDSs) and firewalls. Network adapters do not need to be separate cards; they can be built in, as in the case of most PCs today or other network-ready devices, such as network cameras and network media players. These adapters (and all other hardware devices) need a driver to communicate with the Windows 10/11 operating system.

Before you physically install a network adapter, it's important to read the vendor's instructions that come with the hardware. Most network adapters you get today should be self-configuring, using Plug and Play capabilities. After you install a network adapter that supports Plug and Play, it should work following the installation procedure (which should be automated if the vendor says it is). You might have to restart, but our operating systems are getting much better with this, and you might just get lucky and be ready to use the device immediately.

If you happen to have a network adapter that is not Plug and Play, the operating system should detect the new piece of hardware and start a wizard that leads you through the process of loading the adapter's driver and setting initial configuration parameters. You can see your network connection and manage the network connection properties through the Network and Sharing Center.

Configuring a Network Adapter

After you have installed the network adapter, you configure it through its Properties dialog box. You can get to the network adapter properties pages via the Network and Sharing Center (detailed in the section "Configuring Wireless Network Settings" later in this chapter), through Computer Management or through Device Manager.

To use the Device Manager applet for the network adapter configuration, right-click Start and choose Device Manager. This launches the Device Manager MMC (Microsoft Management Console), shown in Figure 6.3.

FIGURE 6.3   Device Manager MMC

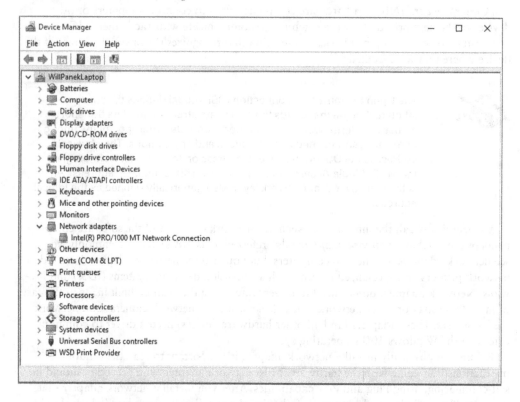

Figure 6.3 shows the Network Adapters device category expanded, and the adapter is installed in the machine. Accessing the network adapter properties allows us to view and change configuration parameters of the adapter. You do this by right-clicking the adapter in Device Manager and selecting Properties from the context menu. Each tab is detailed in the following list:

General Tab   The General tab of the network adapter's Properties dialog box (Figure 6.4) shows the name of the adapter, the device type, the manufacturer, and the location. The Device Status box reports whether the device is working properly. If not, the Device Status box gives you an error code and a brief description of what Windows 10/11 identifies as the issue. You can perform an Internet search for the error code(s) if the text is not sufficient.

FIGURE 6.4   General tab of the network adapter's Properties page

Advanced Tab   The contents of the Advanced tab of a Network Adapter's Properties dialog box vary depending on the network adapter and driver that you are using. Figure 6.5 shows an example of the Advanced tab for my Fast Ethernet adapter. To configure options in this dialog box, choose the property you want to modify in the Property list box and specify the desired value for the property in the Value box on the right.

Driver Tab   The Driver tab of the network adapter's Properties dialog box provides the following information about your driver:

- The driver provider
- The date the driver was released
- The driver version (useful in determining whether you have the latest driver installed)
- The digital signer (the company that provides the digital signature for driver signing)

FIGURE 6.5 Advanced tab of the network adapter's Properties page

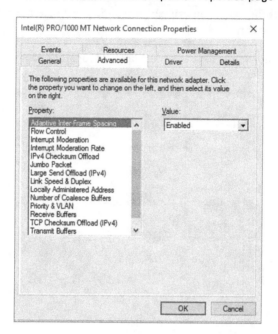

The Driver tab for my adapter is shown in Figure 6.6. The information here varies from driver to driver and even from vendor to vendor. The Driver Details button on the Driver tab brings up the Driver File Details dialog box, which provides the following details about the driver:

- The location of the driver file (useful for troubleshooting)
- The original provider of the driver
- The file version (useful for troubleshooting)
- Copyright information about the driver
- The digital signer for the driver

The Update Driver button starts a wizard to step you through upgrading the driver for an existing device. The Roll Back Driver button allows you to roll back to the previously installed driver if you update your network driver and encounter problems. In Figure 6.6, the Roll Back Driver button is grayed out (not available) because I have not updated the driver or a previous driver is not available. The Disable button is used to disable the device. After you disable the device, the Disable button changes into an Enable button, which you can use to enable the device. The Uninstall button removes the driver from your computer's configuration. You would uninstall the driver if you were going to remove the device from your system or if you want to completely remove the driver configuration from your system so that you can reinstall it from scratch either automatically or manually.

FIGURE 6.6   Driver tab of the network adapter's Properties page

Details Tab   The Details tab of the network adapter's Properties dialog box lists the resource settings for your network adapter. Information found on the Details tab varies by hardware device. I have included the Details tab information from my adapter in Figure 6.7, with the Property drop-down list box set to Device Description.

FIGURE 6.7   Details tab of the network adapter's Properties page

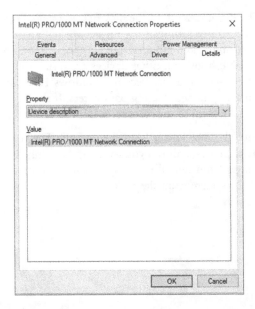

Events Tab   The Events tab (Figure 6.8) of the network adapter's Properties dialog box shows you some of the device events that have happened to this piece of hardware. There is also a View All Events button that opens the Event Viewer MMC, which shows you all events for this device. This is a good way to look to see if there have been any events or issues (like errors or warnings) for the device.

FIGURE 6.8   Events tab of the network adapter's Properties page

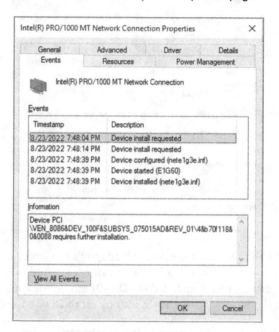

Resources Tab   The Resources tab of the network adapter's Properties dialog box (Figure 6.9) lists the resource settings for your network adapter. Resources include interrupt request (IRQ), memory, and input/output (I/O) resources. This information can be important for troubleshooting if other devices are trying to use the same resource settings. This is not normally the case because Windows 10/11 and the Plug and Play specification should set up nonconflicting parameters. If there are issues, the Conflicting Device List box at the bottom of the Resources tab will show the conflicts.

Power Management Tab   The Power Management tab (Figure 6.10) of the network adapter's Properties dialog box allows you to set up how this device can save power on the system. For example, you can allow the system to turn off this device and also allow this device to wake the system from sleep mode.

FIGURE 6.9   Resources tab of the network adapter's Properties page

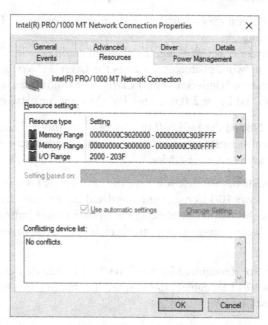

FIGURE 6.10   Power Management tab of the network adapter's Properties page

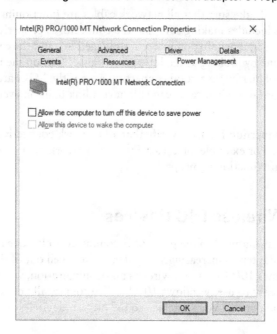

Troubleshooting a Network Adapter

When installing the NIC, you may encounter some problems or errors. Let's take a look at some NIC troubleshooting.

If your network adapter is not working, the problem might be with the hardware, the driver software, or the network protocols. I discuss the Layer 3 (Network layer) issues later in this chapter in the section "Understanding TCP/IP." The following are some common Layer 1 (Physical layer) and Layer 2 (Data Link layer) causes for network adapter problems:

Network Adapter Not on the HCL If the device is not on the Hardware Compatibility List (HCL), use your Internet resources to see if others have discovered a solution or contact the hardware vendor for advice.

Outdated Driver Make sure that you have the most current driver for your adapter. You can have Windows 10/11 check for an updated driver from the Driver tab of the Properties page for the adapter by clicking the Update Driver button and having Windows search for a better driver, or you can check for the latest driver on the hardware vendor's website.

Network Adapter Not Recognized by Windows 10/11 Check Device Manager to see whether Windows 10/11 recognizes the adapter. If you don't see your adapter, you can try to manually install it.

Improperly Configured Network Card Verify that the settings for the network card are correct for the parameters known within your network and for the hardware device the machine is connected to.

Cabling Problem Make sure that all network cables are functioning and are the correct type. This includes making sure that the connector is properly seated, the cable is straight or crossed (depending on where it's plugged in), and the cable is not broken. This is usually done by looking at the little green light (LGL) on the network adapter card. This does not guarantee a good connection even if the LGLs are illuminated. A single conductor failure in a cable can still have a link light on even if data is not passing.

Bad Network Connection Device Verify that all network connectivity hardware is properly working. For example, on a Fast Ethernet network, make sure the switch and port being used are functioning properly.

Configuring Wireless NIC Devices

Wireless technology has matured to the point of becoming cost effective and secure. The use of wireless network adapters is increasingly popular, scaling well out of the home and into the workplace. Windows 10/11 supports wireless autoconfiguration, which makes wireless network connections easy to use. Windows 10/11 will automatically discover the wireless networks available and connect your machine to the preferred wireless network.

One of the advantages to setting up Windows 10/11 and wireless connections is that once you have connected to a wireless access point (WAP), your Windows client will remember that and reconnect you to that preferred wireless network when your Windows 10/11 system is in range.

Configuring Wireless Network Settings

If you have a wireless network adapter compatible with Windows 10/11, it will be automatically recognized by the operating system. This can be a built-in adapter such as those most modern laptops come with, a wireless card you install in the machine, or even a wireless USB adapter. After it is installed, it is shown in Device Manager as well as in the Network and Sharing Center within the View Your Active Networks section.

We used Device Manager in the previous section for the network adapter configuration, so let's use the Network and Sharing Center for the wireless network configuration. Figure 6.11 shows the Network and Sharing Center with one active network, the wireless network connection called Trend.

FIGURE 6.11   Network and Sharing Center

At the time of writing this book, the Network and Sharing Center still exists in Control Panel within Windows 10/11. But, as I mentioned previously, Control Panel is slowly transitioning to the Settings app.

You can perform any of the following steps to access the Network and Sharing Center:

- The easiest way is to go directly to Control Panel in Windows 10/11 by opening the Start Menu search bar, typing **control panel**, and then select Network And Sharing Center (if the Control Panel view is Large Icons or Small Icons).

- Type **Network and Sharing Center** in the integrated search box of Windows 10/11.

- In Windows 10, click Start ➤ Windows System ➤ Control Panel ➤ Network And Internet ➤ Network And Sharing Center (if the Control Panel view is Category).

- In Windows 10, click Start ➤ Windows System ➤ Control Panel ➤ Network And Sharing Center (if the Control Panel view is Large Icons or Small Icons).

- In Windows 10, you can right-click the network icon in the lower-right taskbar and choose Open Network And Sharing Center.

- Click Start ➤ Settings ➤ Network And Internet and then choose either the Wi-Fi or the Ethernet Connection link.

Viewing the Wireless Network Connection Status

Windows 10/11 includes multiple ways to quickly check your computer's wireless network configuration. Some of the tools include using the Settings app, Task Manager, Control Panel, command prompt, and PowerShell.

Windows 10 allows you to quickly check your wireless network connection status by clicking Start ➤ Settings ➤ Network & Internet ➤ Status (as shown in Figure 6.12). If you're having issues with your wireless connection, you can run the Network troubleshooter to try to fix it. Or, on Windows 10 you can just click the Network icon in the lower right corner of the screen and it will inform you about your network connection and what state it's in.

FIGURE 6.12 Wireless network connection Status window in Windows 10

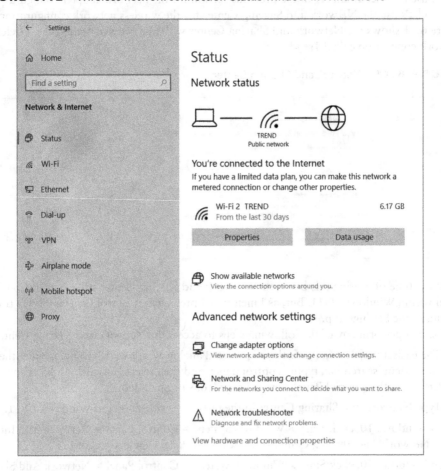

From the Status window you can view the properties, data usage, and available networks, and you also have the ability to look at advanced network settings. You can change adapter options, open the Network and Sharing Center, and run the Network troubleshooter.

In Windows 11, you can also check the status of the wireless network connection by clicking Start ➤ Settings ➤ Network & Internet. The status of your wireless network connection will appear at the top of the dialog box. In Windows 11, the Network icon is no longer displayed at the lower-right corner of the screen.

Viewing Wireless Network Connection Details

If you have a wireless adapter in your machine, perform Exercise 6.1 to view the network connection details for your wireless network connection.

EXERCISE 6.1

Viewing the Network Connection Details in Windows 10

1. Click Start ➤ Settings ➤ Network & Internet ➤ Status.

2. Click the Properties button to view the details.

Or, to view the network connection details in Windows 11:

1. Click Start ➤ Settings ➤ Network & Internet ➤ Status.

2. Along the top, click Properties to view the details.

Earlier we mentioned the Network and Sharing Center. There you can also modify adapter settings, change advanced sharing settings, set up a new connection or network, and troubleshoot problems. There are a number of ways to access the Network and Sharing Center: you can search for it, access it from Control Panel, or click the link under Advanced Network Settings in the Status dialog box. The Network and Sharing Center, as you saw in Figure 6.11, provides several options on the right-hand side. To view the network connections, click Change Adapter Settings on the right-hand side. This will open the Network Connections; from here, right-click the wireless device and select Properties. This will open the Wi-Fi Properties page. The Wi-Fi Properties page has a Networking tab (see Figure 6.13) that shows which network adapter is being used for this connection (which you can change if you have more than one available).

You can install or uninstall network clients, network services, and network protocols by clicking the appropriate button. You can also view the client, service, or protocol properties if they are available by first highlighting the item on the list and then clicking the Properties button for the selected item. If the Properties button is grayed out, a properties page is not available for the item.

FIGURE 6.13   Wi-Fi Properties page's Networking tab

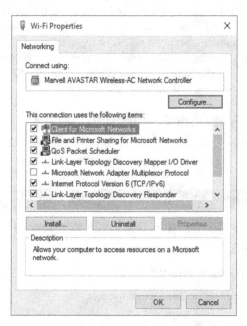

Perform Exercise 6.2 to access the network adapter properties from the network connection's Properties page.

EXERCISE 6.2

Viewing Wireless Network Connection Properties

1. Open Control Panel.

2. Select Network And Sharing Center (if the Control Panel view is Category).

3. Select Change Adapter Settings on the right-hand side.

4. Right-click the Wi-Fi connection and select Properties.

5. Click the Configure button.

6. View the various tabs regarding the network adapter properties.

7. Click Cancel to return to the Network Connection window.

Configuring Wireless Network Security

Wireless network security is a very large piece of setting up our wireless networks. The focal point for this is the wireless access point or wireless router to which we connect. Whether you are using a small wireless network or a large wireless infrastructure, you should have a plan for secure communication and should configure wireless network security. There are several basic parameters you can configure on your network access devices to increase the security of a wireless network:

- Disable broadcast of the SSID, which is the name of the wireless network. When SSID broadcast is disabled, the wireless network cannot be detected automatically until you manually configure your wireless network card to connect to that SSID.

- Create a MAC address filter list so that only specifically allowed wireless devices can connect to the wireless network, or you can require users attempting to connect to supply connection credentials.

- Enable encryption such as Wi-Fi Protected Access (WPA) or WPA2.

Wireless Connection Infrastructure or Ad Hoc?

You might not always be connecting to an access point or router; these connections are considered infrastructure mode connections. An infrastructure mode connection is similar to a wired connection of a PC to an outlet. Instead, you might connect in an ad hoc fashion, which could be a computer-to-computer connection to share information with other wireless network devices without another wireless device acting as an intermediary.

Ad hoc connections exist in a wired environment as well, when we connect two PCs' NICs together by using an Ethernet crossover cable. Securing data transfer in an ad hoc wireless setup is just as important as it is in infrastructure mode because the data is still traversing between devices using radio frequency (RF), and network sniffers today running the wireless adapter promiscuously (in monitor mode) have no problem viewing the data stream. If the data stream is not encrypted, sniffers will have access to it.

For large implementations, several vendors supply wireless access points under the control of a wireless director, which consists of software-based controllers that are responsible for allowing access points on the network, providing user access control, and enforcing encryption policies. For smaller implementations, this control functionality is done manually as the wireless routers or access points are set up.

The security policies put in place are configured on the wireless access device and the wireless client. Windows 10/11 client components must be set up to match the security settings of the wireless network access devices. During the setup of most wireless access devices provided by the hardware vendor, you will configure the security parameters. Configuring can be done during the setup process and/or through a web browser that can access the wireless access device configuration pages.

Most of our current devices have a built-in web server to allow the HTTP connection from a web browser. Windows 10/11 also has the ability to configure the wireless access device if the hardware vendor makes it available. If there is no specific component written, you can launch the web browser–based configuration from a convenient location—the Network and Sharing Center.

Whether you have Windows 10/11 configure the wireless network connection or you perform the setup through the manufacturer's process, you still need to configure your Windows 10/11 client access.

If you have performed the simplest configuration and there are no security parameters configured (bad idea, by the way), Windows 10/11 will connect automatically with a quick window showing the wireless network it's connecting to and providing access without much user intervention. Even canceling the screens will produce a successful (nonsecure) connection. This simple configuration process makes connecting a home or small network easy and straightforward for nontechnical users. However, this is not a good solution.

If you have configured wireless network security (a good idea!), then you need to configure the Windows client with the correct settings. Once again, the configuration screens are available from the convenient location known as the Network and Sharing Center.

In Exercise 6.3, you will access the Windows 10/11 client wireless network properties.

EXERCISE 6.3

Accessing the Windows Client Wireless Properties

1. Open Control Panel.

2. Select Network And Sharing Center (if the Control Panel view is Category).

3. Choose the Wireless Network Connection item within the View Your Active Networks section of the Network and Sharing Center.

4. Click the Wireless Properties button (shown in Figure 6.14) in the Connection area of the Wi-Fi Status window.

5. The Wireless Network Properties dialog box opens, displaying the current setup for the wireless network. Click Finish to close the dialog box.

FIGURE 6.14   Wireless Properties button

The Wireless Network Properties dialog box lets you set or change the Windows client configuration. The first tab is the Connection tab (Figure 6.15), which displays the following information:

FIGURE 6.15   Wireless Network Properties dialog box's Connection tab

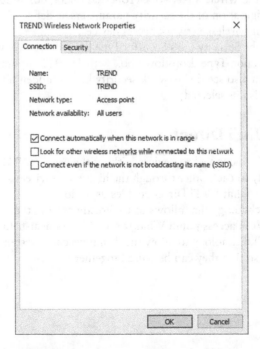

Name   The name assigned to the wireless network.

SSID   The SSID of the wireless connection. This defines a friendly name for the wireless network. This is normally an ASCII string and is usually broadcast by default, allowing a machine or users to select a wireless network with which to connect. Some wireless access devices will allow more than one SSID to be available (broadcast) at the same time, creating more than one wireless network within the same device.

Network Type   Displays the mode the wireless network is operating in. If the wireless network is in infrastructure mode, this parameter will be Access Point. If the wireless network is ad hoc, this will display Computer-To-Computer.

Network Availability   Displays the users to whom the wireless network is available— All Users or Me Only, for example.

Connect Automatically When This Network Is In Range   This option, when selected, allows automatic connection for this wireless network. Deselecting (clearing the check mark) requires the user to choose this wireless network for connection.

Look For Other Wireless Networks While Connected To This Network   Windows 10/11 will attempt to look for other wireless network connections even though you are connected to a network at the time. This allows a user to see if there is a better network connection available even after you have connected to your wireless access point.

Connect Even If The Network Is Not Broadcasting Its Name (SSID)   If the wireless network you are attempting to connect to is not broadcasting its SSID, you must select this option to allow Windows 10/11 to automatically connect.

The second tab on the Wireless Network Properties dialog box is Security (Figure 6.16), which allows the configuration of the security parameters as defined in your security policy and configured on your wireless network access devices.

Figure 6.16 shows the Security tab's Security Type drop-down box with WPA-Personal selected and the Encryption Type drop-down box with TKIP (Temporal Key Integrity Protocol) selected. You can also see the network security key as hidden text because the Show Characters check box is not selected.

Configuring Wi-Fi Direct

Think about being able to connect to devices without the use of a WAP. What if we could connect devices directly to each other through the high-speed wireless adapters in those devices? That is exactly what Wi-Fi Direct enables us to do.

Wi-Fi Direct is a technology that allows us to directly access other devices without requiring a separate Wi-Fi access point. Windows 10/11 uses near-field communication (better known as NFC) technology to allow the Windows client system to locate other NFC Wi-Fi enabled devices so that they can be paired together.

FIGURE 6.16   Wireless Network Properties Security tab

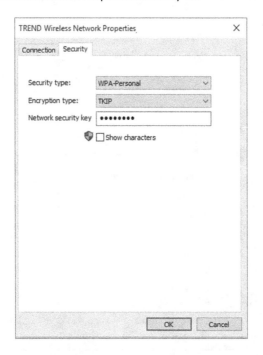

When devices are trying to pair together, the Near Field Proximity (NFP) receives pairing information from the device that is trying to connect. NFP then passes the pairing information to Windows 10/11. Windows 10/11 Wi-Fi Direct will then automatically follow the Wi-Fi Alliance Out-Of-Box pairing procedures for the connection.

If the pairing process connects, Windows will prompt the user for permission for the connection. If permission is given, Windows 10/11 will then attempt to finalize the connection. From that point on, no other user interaction is needed.

When Sync Settings is selected, Windows syncs the settings you choose across all your Windows 10/11 devices that you've signed into with your Microsoft account (see Figure 6.17).

To find Sync Settings, select Start ➤ Settings ➤ Accounts ➤ Sync Your Settings.

To sync in Windows 11, you will need to have Windows Backup turned on. Windows will back up the settings you selected across all your Windows 11 devices that you have signed into using your Microsoft account. To turn on Windows Backup in Windows 11, select Start ➤ Settings ➤ Accounts ➤ Windows Backup. You can back up OneDrive folder syncing and choose Remember My Apps and Remember My Preferences. Backup will be discussed later in this book.

FIGURE 6.17   Sync Settings on Windows 10

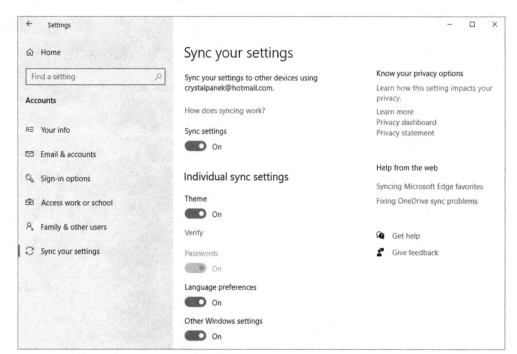

Troubleshooting Wireless Connectivity

There are a few common issues with wireless networking you can look at if you're having problems connecting to your wireless network. Following are a few problems and solutions:

Ensure that your wireless network card is enabled.   Here's one I see regularly: many newer laptops and tablets have either a switch or a hot-key setting that enables and disables the wireless device. Often, a laptop switch will be turned off, or a user will somehow press the key sequence to shut off the PC's wireless radio. The Physical layer is always a good place to start looking.

Ensure that your wireless card and the access devices are compatible.   Cards that are compatible with the 802.11b standard can connect to only 802.11b or 802.11b/g access devices configured to accept b. Cards using 802.11a can connect to only 802.11a or 802.11a/b/g access devices configured to accept a. An 802.11n card needs to connect to an 802.11n access device for efficiency, although most will auto-negotiate to the best specification available. The specification you're using on the card has to be available and turned on in the wireless access device.

Ensure that the access point signal is available.   I find radio frequency (RF) to be a funny thing. You can't see it, and you assume that it is everywhere. Not a good assumption. The output power of the signal might be fine, but the RF power is absorbed or attenuated as it goes through walls, insulation, or water. You need to make sure there is nothing that might be causing interference of the wireless signal.

Ensure that the security parameters are configured alike.   The SSID, encryption type, encryption algorithm, and passphrase/security key have to be set the same on both the wireless access device and the wireless client. Here's another one I see quite often: in the desire to make the initial setup and the secure setup easier for end users, some hardware vendors have a nice little button that allows the network access device to negotiate a secure set of parameters with the client. In one instance, after the wireless network had been working correctly for a while, a failure showed the parameters to be incompatible, thanks in large part to someone pressing the easy button just before the failure.

Ensure automatic connections if the SSID is not being broadcast.   If you are having trouble connecting to a network that does not broadcast its SSID, select the Connect Even If The Network Is Not Broadcasting check box in the Wireless Network Properties dialog box. I have solved several wireless network connection issues with this fix.

Consider how a wireless router interfaces with hardwired devices.   Many times when I troubleshoot a small or midsized network, I find that the company (or home user) is connected to a multifunction type of device. The wireless routers that are often deployed are technologically sophisticated. They have switch ports for connecting hardwired devices on the private network as well as an Internet port to connect to the outside world. The wireless portion of the device is like another switch port on the private side, allowing the wireless devices to interact with the hardwired devices.

When I troubleshoot and eliminate issues, I start with the hardwired devices and see whether they can communicate with each other and with the outside (the other side of your wireless router). Try to communicate between the hardwired and wireless as well to eliminate the router components. It's also not the best idea to use the wireless network to configure the wireless devices. Configuring through the wireless interface will ultimately cause you to lose connectivity in the middle of a configuration and may force you to connect with the cable, often leaving the access point unusable until you complete the task you started wirelessly.

Understanding TCP/IP

Another item that we need to configure before we can connect a Windows client machine to the domain is the protocol that will allow the Windows 10/11 machine to communicate with other machines. *Transmission Control Protocol/Internet Protocol (TCP/IP)* is the most commonly used network protocol. It is a suite of protocols that have evolved into the industry standard for network, internetwork, and Internet connectivity.

As I explained earlier in this chapter, when I teach my Microsoft Windows classes (both server and client classes), I like to use the following example for TCP/IP. Don't think of TCP/

IP as IP addresses—think of them as telephone numbers. When you need to contact a server or a website, you call its telephone number (TCP/IP).

We have a form of directory assistance on our networks as well: Domain Name Service (DNS) servers. That's all DNS does. It turns a name into a telephone number (name resolution). So, when you type **www.willpanek.com**, DNS turns willpanek.com into a TCP/IP number so that you can make your call to my website.

Now, just as with telephone numbers, there must be some device that acts like the telephone company that issues us our telephone numbers. Well, there is, and it's called a Dynamic Host Configuration Protocol (DHCP) server. DHCP gives your users a telephone (TCP/IP) number.

If you think of TCP/IP numbers as telephone numbers, I think it makes it much easier for anyone to understand why we use them and how they work.

The main protocols providing basic TCP/IP services include Internet Protocol (IP), Transmission Control Protocol (TCP), User Datagram Protocol (UDP), Address Resolution Protocol (ARP), Internet Control Message Protocol (ICMP), and Internet Group Management Protocol (IGMP).

Benefits and Features of TCP/IP

TCP/IP as a protocol suite was accepted as an industry standard in the 1980s and continues to be the primary internetworking protocol today. For a default installation of Windows 10/11, IPv4 and IPv6 are both installed by default. TCP/IP has the following benefits:

- TCP/IP is the most common protocol and is supported by almost all network operating systems. It is the required protocol for Internet access.

- TCP/IP is dependable and scalable for use in small and large networks.

- Support is provided for connectivity across interconnected networks, independent of the operating systems being used at the upper end of the OSI model or the physical components at the lower end of the OSI model.

- TCP/IP provides standard routing services for moving packets over interconnected network segments. Dividing networks into multiple subnetworks (or subnets) optimizes network traffic and facilitates network management.

- TCP/IP is designed to provide data reliability by providing a connection at the Transport layer and verifying that each data segment is received and passed to the application requiring the data by retransmitting lost information.

- TCP/IP allows for the classification of data in regard to its importance with quality of service. This allows important time-sensitive streams of data, such as Voice over IP, to get preferential treatment.

- TCP/IP is designed to be fault-tolerant. It is able to dynamically reroute packets if network links become unavailable, assuming alternate paths exist.

- Applications can provide services such as Dynamic Host Configuration Protocol (DHCP) for TCP/IP configuration and Domain Name Service (DNS) for hostname-to-IP-address resolution.

- Windows 10/11 continues to support Automatic Private IP Addressing (APIPA) used by small, local-connection-only networks without a DHCP server to allow Windows 10/11 to automatically assign an IP address to itself.

- Support for NetBIOS over TCP/IP (NetBT) is included in Windows 10/11. NetBIOS is a software specification used for identifying computer resources by name as opposed to IP address. We still use TCP/IP as the network protocol, so we map the NetBIOS name to an IP address.

- The inclusion of Alternate IP Configuration allows users to have a static and a DHCP-assigned IP address mapped to a single network adapter. This feature supports mobile users who roam between different network segments.

- IPv6 incorporates a much larger address space compared to IPv4 and, more important, incorporates many of the additional features of TCP/IP into a standardized protocol. This is important because a vendor that claims to support TCP/IP only has to support the 1980s version and may not support additional features such as Internet Protocol Security (IPsec). IPv6 as a standard includes these features, allowing a more robust network protocol.

Several of the features of TCP/IP included with Windows 10/11 are as follows:

- Allows a common structure for network communications across a wide variety of hardware and operating systems and a lot of applications that are specifically written to configure and control it.

- TCP/IP connectivity tools allowing access to a variety of hosts across a TCP/IP network. TCP/IP tools in Windows 10/11 include clients for HTTP, FTP, TFTP, Telnet, Finger, and so forth. Server components for the tools are available to install as well.

- Inclusion of a Simple Network Management Protocol (SNMP) agent that can be used to monitor performance and resource use of a TCP/IP host, server, or network hardware devices.

- TCP/IP management and diagnostic tools for maintenance and diagnostic support. TCP/IP management and diagnostic commands include `ipconfig`, `arp`, `ping`, `nbtstat`, `netsh`, `route`, `nslookup`, `tracert`, and `pathping`.

- Support for TCP/IP network printing, enabling you to print to networked print devices.

- Logical and physical multihoming, enabling multiple IP addresses on a single computer for single or multiple network adapters. Multiple network adapters installed on a single computer are normally associated with routing for internetwork connectivity.

- Support for internal IP routing, which enables a Windows client computer to route packets among multiple network adapters installed in one machine.

- Support for virtual private networks, which enable you to transmit data securely across a public network via encapsulated and encrypted packets.

Basics of IP Addressing and Configuration

Before you can configure TCP/IP, you should have a basic understanding of TCP/IP configuration and addressing. Let's review TCP/IP addressing. To configure a TCP/IP client, you must specify an IP address, subnet mask, and default gateway (if you're going to communicate outside your local network). Depending on your network, you might want to configure a DNS server and a domain name.

You can see the Windows client IPv4 Properties window in Figure 6.18. I have included it here because I am going to discuss the different configuration items in the following sections. Although normally set up for automatic configuration, these parameters have been manually assigned in this figure for clarity.

FIGURE 6.18   Windows client TCP/IP version 4 properties

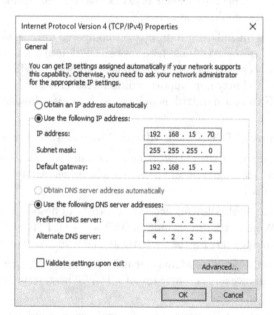

Understanding IPv4 Address Types

The IPv4 address scheme is one of two used by the Internet today, and TCP/IP is the only network protocol used by the Internet. There are three types of IPv4 addresses: broadcast, multicast, and unicast.

A *broadcast address* is read by all hosts that hear it (the broadcast will not go across a router, so only local devices hear the broadcast). The IPv4 broadcast address is 255.255.255.255; every single bit is a 1.

A *multicast address* is a special address that one or more devices will listen for by joining a multicast group. Only the local devices configured to listen for the address will respond and process the data in the multicast packet. A multicast address will have a value between 224 and 239 in the first octet (the leftmost number in the dotted decimal representation). A multicast example is 224.0.0.5.

A *unicast address* uniquely identifies a computer or device on the network. An IPv4 unicast address is a 32-bit address represented as a dotted decimal (an example is 131.107.1.200). Each number in the dotted decimal notation is a decimal representation of 8 bits, and the value of each is between 0 and 255 (255 is the numerically largest value that 8 bits can represent). A portion of the IPv4 unicast address is used to identify the network the device is on (or the network of a destination device), and a portion is used to identify the individual host on the local network or the unique host on a remote network.

IPv4 Address Classes

There are three classes of unicast IP addresses defined. Depending on the class you use, different parts of the address show the default network portion of the address and the host address. Table 6.1 shows the three classes of network addresses and the number of networks and hosts available for each network class.

TABLE 6.1   IPv4 class assignments

Network class	Address range of first octet	Number of unique networks available	Number of unique hosts per network
A	1–126	126	16,777,214
B	128–191	16,384	65,534
C	192–223	2,097,152	254

As you probably noticed, 127 is missing from the address ranges. 127.0.0.1 is the diagnostic loopback address, and because of that, no commercial TCP/IP range can start with 127.

The number of octets you can use for either the network ID or the host ID depends on which class you use for your network. For example, if I own a Class B address of 131.107.0.0, the first two octets (131.107) would be the network ID and the last two octets would be the host ID. Table 6.2 shows you the different classes and which octets are the network ID (represented by X) and which octets are the host ID (represented by Y). You are allowed to manipulate only the host IDs (Y) for your organization unless you are using a private IP address scheme.

TABLE 6.2 IPv4 network and host octets

Class	Example	Network ID	Host ID
A	17.1.10.10 (X.Y.Y.Y)	17 (X)	1.10.10 (Y.Y.Y)
B	131.107.14.240 (X.X.Y.Y)	131.107 (X.X)	14.240 (Y.Y)
C	192.168.1.10 (X.X.X.Y)	192.168.1 (X.X.X)	10 (Y)

IPv4 Subnet Mask

The *subnet mask* is used to specify which portion of the unicast IPv4 address defines the network value and which portion defines the unique host value. The subnet mask can be shown either as a dotted decimal, as with 255.255.255.0, or as a slash notation (called Classless Inter-Domain Routing, or CIDR), as in /24. The CIDR representation is the number of bits turned on in the subnet mask. For example, 255.255.224.0 is actually 11111111.1111111 1.11100000.00000000 (1s are on bits and 0s are off), which equals 19 bits turned on, or /19.

The standard for classful network addressing defines subnet masks for each class, as shown in Table 6.3.

TABLE 6.3 IPv4 default class subnet masks

Class	Default mask	Slash notation (CIDR)
A	255.0.0.0	/8
B	255.255.0.0	/16
C	255.255.255.0	/24

Another task of the subnet mask is to break down the ranges of your network. For example, 255.255.255.224 allows for six subnets. There should be six TCP/IP ranges that go with the six subnets. Table 6.4 shows the ranges for the different subnet masks.

What does this chart mean to you? Well, let's say that you have a subnet mask of 255.255.255.224. Because 224 allows for six subnets, the six ranges are in increments of 32. Table 6.5 shows a Class C subnet range for 224. Remember, in any range, you can't use the first number of the range (network ID) or the last number of any range (broadcast).

TABLE 6.4   Subnet mask ranges

Subnet mask number	Ranges
255	1
254	2
252	4
248	8
240	16
224	32
192	64
128	128

TABLE 6.5   Class C 224 subnet mask ranges

Subnets	Range	Usable
Range 1	0–31	1–30
Range 2	32–63	33–62
Range 3	64–95	65–94
Range 4	96–127	97–126
Range 5	128–159	129–158
Range 6	160–191	161–190
Range 7	192–223	193–222
Range 8	224-255	225-254

If this were a Class B subnet mask, the ranges would include a second octet that you would work with. Table 6.6 shows a Class B 224 subnet mask.

If this were a Class A subnet mask, the ranges would include three octets that you would work with. Table 6.7 shows a Class A 224 subnet mask.

TABLE 6.6   Class B 224 subnet mask range

Subnets	Range	Usable
Range 1	0.0–31.255	0.1–31.254
Range 2	32.0–63.255	32.1–63.254
Range 3	64.0–95.255	64.1–95.254
Range 4	96.0–127.255	96.1–127.254
Range 5	128.0–159.255	128.1–159.254
Range 6	160.0–191.255	160.1–191.254
Range 7	192.0–223.255	192.1–223.254
Range 8	224.0-255.255	224.1-255.254

TABLE 6.7   Class A 224 subnet mask range

Subnets	Range	Usable
Range 1	0.0.0–31.255.255	0.0.1-31.255.254
Range 2	32.0.0–63.255.255	32.0.1–63.255.254
Range 3	64.0.0–95.255.255	64.0.1–95.255.254
Range 4	96.0.0–127.255.255	96.0.1–127.255.254
Range 5	128.0.0–159.255.255	128.0.1–159.255.254
Range 6	160.0.0–191.255.255	160.0.1–191.255.254
Range 7	192.0.0–223.255.255	192.0.1–223.255.254

Using IPv6 Addresses

Through most of this discussion, we have been referencing TCP/IP as the network protocol. However, you should remember that it is really a suite of protocols running in Layer 3 and Layer 4 of the OSI model. Internet Protocol (IP) is the Layer 3 protocol responsible for assigning devices globally unique addresses (that is, unique in a whole company for private addresses and unique across the whole Internet for public addresses).

When the TCP/IP standard was adopted in the 1980s, it was unimaginable that we would ever need more than 4 billion addresses that are possible with IPv4, but with the dramatic growth of the use of computers in the home and workplace today, we do. In the 1990s, programmers realized that a new Layer 3 was going to be needed. This was not an easy task, and integration into the existing infrastructure was going to take a long time. An interim solution known as Network Address Translation (NAT) and Port Address Translation (PAT) emerged. NAT/PAT allowed more than one device to use the same IP address on a private network as long as there was one Internet address available. Cool enough, but this is not the real solution. IPv6 is the solution to the IPv4 address depletion.

As time has progressed from the IPv4 standard acceptance in the 1980s, we have needed new and better functionality. However, the way the standards process works around the world is that you can add functionality, but it may or may not be supported in any vendor's TCP/IPv4 network stack. What happened in IPv6 is that not only did the address space increase in size, but the additional functionality that may or may not have been included before has become part of the IPv6 standard.

For example, IPv4 is defined as having a variable-length header, which is cumbersome because we need to read an additional piece of data to see how big the header is. Most of the time, the header stays the same, so why not just fix its length and add an extension to the header if we need to carry more information? IPv6 uses a fixed-length IP header with the capability of carrying more information in an extension to the header, known as an *extension header*.

Microsoft has been including IPv6 in its operating systems since NT 4.0; it just has not been enabled by default. Windows 10/11 (as did Vista and Windows 7/8/8.1) natively supports both IPv4 and IPv6. The main differences you will notice between IPv4 and IPv6 are the format and size of the IP address. IPv6 addresses are 128 bits, typically written as eight groups of four hexadecimal characters. IPv4 addresses, as you saw earlier, are 32 bits—four decimal representations of 8 bits. Each of the eight groups of characters in an IPv6 address is separated by a colon; for example, 2001:4860:0000:0000:0012:10FF: FECD:00EF.

Leading zeros can be omitted, so we can write our example address as 2001:4860:0:0: 12:10FF:FECD:EF. Additionally, a double colon can be used to compress a set of consecutive zeros, so we could write our example address as 2001:4860::12:10FF:FECD:EF. The IPv6 address is 128 bits; when you see a double colon, it's a variable that says to fill enough zeros within the colons to make the address 128 bits. You can have only one set of double colons; two variables in one address won't work.

Will IPv6 take over the global address space soon? Even with IPv4's lack of address space, we are going to continue to use it for many years. The integration of IPv6 into the infrastructure is going to happen as a joint venture with IPv4 and IPv6 running at the same time in the devices and on some networks.

There are many mechanisms for enabling IPv6 communications over an IPv4 network, including the following:

Dual Stack   A computer or device running both the IPv4 and IPv6 protocol stacks at the same time

ISATAP   Intra-Site Automatic Tunnel Addressing Protocol

6to4   An encapsulation technique for putting IPv6 addresses inside IPv4 addresses

Teredo Tunneling   Another encapsulation technique for putting IPv6 traffic inside an IPv4 packet

Some IPv6-to-IPv4 dynamic translation techniques require that a computer's IPv4 address be used as the last 32 bits of the IPv6 address. When these translation techniques are used, it is common to write the last 32 bits as you would typically write an IPv4 address, such as 2001:4850::F8:192.168.122.26.

There are two ways to receive a TCP/IP address (for either IPv4 or IPv6): you can manually assign a TCP/IP address to the Windows 10/11 machine, or the Windows client machine can use DHCP.

There are several elements of the IPv4 protocol that could use some enhancements. Other elements have been added to IPv4 as extras to provide more functionality. IPv6 is designed to incorporate these enhancement/changes directly into the protocol specification.

The new concepts and new implementation of old concepts in IPv6 include the following:

- Larger address space (128-bit vs. 32-bit).

- Autoconfiguration of Internet-accessible addresses with or without DHCP (without DHCP it's called stateless autoconfiguration).

- More efficient IP header (fewer fields and no checksum).

- Fixed-length IP header (IPv4 header is variable length) with extension headers beyond the standard fixed length to provide enhancements.

- Built-in IP mobility and security (although available in IPv4, the IPv6 implementation is much better implementation).

- Built-in transition schemes to allow integration of the IPv4 and IPv6 spaces.

- ARP broadcast messages are replaced with a multicast request.

128-bit Address Space   The new 128-bit address space will provide unique addresses for the foreseeable future. I would like to say we will never use up all the addresses, but history may prove me wrong. The number of unique addresses in the IPv6 space is 2^{128}, or 3.4×10^{38} addresses. How big is that number? Enough for toasters and refrigerators (and maybe even cars) to all have their own addresses? Why yes, I believe it is.

For a point of reference, the nearest black hole to Earth is 1,600 light years away. If you were to stack 4 mm BB pellets from here to the nearest black hole and back, you would need 7.6×10^{21} BBs. This means you could uniquely address each BB from Earth to the black hole and back and still have quite a few addresses left over.

Or how about this: The IPv6 address space is big enough to provide well over 1 million addresses per square inch of the surface area of the earth (oceans included). No more running out of addresses for the Internet!

Stateful vs. Stateless Autoconfiguration   Autoconfiguration is another added/improved feature of IPv6. When you are choosing to use DHCP in IPv6, you can choose to set your systems up for stateful or stateless configuration. Stateful is what we currently do today with IPv4. Stateful means that DHCP is going to give our IPv6 clients all of their TCP/IP data (IP address, default gateway, and all DHCP options).

What if a Windows 10/11 client could ask the network itself what network it's on and, based on that information, create its own IP address and determine the default gateway? Well, that is what stateless configuration does. Stateless configuration means that the client's address is based on the router's advertisement messages. What this means is that the client creates their own IP address and default gateway based on the router's advertisement message and the machine's MAC address. They can still get all the other DHCP options, but they will not get an IP address and default gateway from DHCP.

Improved IPv6 Header   The IPv6 header is more efficient than the IPv4 header because it is fixed length (with extensions possible) and has only a few fields. The IPv6 header consists of a total of 40 bytes, broken down as follows: 32 bytes for source and destination IPv6 addresses and 8 bytes for the version field, traffic class field, flow label field, payload length field, next header field, and hop limit field.

We don't waste time with a checksum validation anymore, and we don't have to include the length of the IP header since it's fixed in IPv6; the IP header is variable length in IPv4, so the length must be included as a field.

IPv6 Mobility   IPv6 is only a replacement of the OSI Layer 3 component, and we are going to continue to use the TCP (and UDP) components as they currently exist; however, a TCP issue is addressed by IPv6. TCP is connection-oriented, meaning we establish an end-to-end communication path with sequencing and acknowledgments before we ever send any data, and then we have to acknowledge all pieces of data sent. This is done through a combination of an IP address, port number, and port type (socket).

If the source IP address changes, the TCP connection may be disrupted. But then, how often does this happen? More and more often, because more people are walking around with a wireless laptop or a wireless Voice over IP (VoIP) telephone. IPv6 mobility adds the capability by establishing a TCP connection with a home address, and when changing networks, it continues to communicate with the original endpoint from a care-of address as it changes LANs, which sends all traffic back through the home address. The handing off of network addresses does not disrupt the TCP connection state (the original TCP port number and address stay intact).

Improved Security   IPv6 has security built in. Internet Protocol security (IPsec) is a component we use today to authenticate and encrypt secure tunnels from a source to a destination. This can be from the client to the server or between gateways. IPv4 lets us do this by enhancing IP header functionality (basically adding a second IP header while encrypting everything behind it). In IPv6, we add this as standard functionality by using extension headers. Extension headers are inserted into the packet only if they are needed. Each header has a "next header" field, which identifies the next piece of information. The extension headers currently identified for IPv6 are Hop-By-Hop Options, Routing, Fragment, Destination Options, Authentication, and Encapsulating Security Payload. The Authentication header and Encapsulating Security Payload header are the IPsec-specific control headers.

IPv4-to-IPv6 Transmission   There are several mechanisms in place in IPv6 to make the IPv4 to IPv6 transition easy:

- A simple dual-stack implementation where both IPv4 and IPv6 are installed and used is certainly an option. In most situations (so far), this doesn't work so well because most of us aren't connected to an IPv6 network and our Internet connection is not IPv6 even if we're using IPv6 internally. So, Microsoft includes other mechanisms that can be used in several different circumstances.

- *Intra-Site Automatic Tunnel Addressing Protocol (ISATAP)* is an automatic tunneling mechanism used to connect an IPv6 network to an IPv4 address space that does not use NAT. ISATAP treats the IPv4 space as one big logical link connection space.

- *6to4* is a mechanism used to transition to IPv4. This method, like ISATAP, treats the IPv4 address space as a Logical Link Layer with each IPv6 space in transition using a 6to4 router to create endpoints using the IPv4 space as a point-to-point connection (kind of like a WAN, eh?). 6to4 implementations still do not work well through a NAT, although a 6to4 implementation using an application layer gateway (ALG) is certainly doable.

- *Teredo* is a mechanism that allows users behind a NAT to access the IPv6 space by tunneling IPv6 packets in UDP.

- Pseudointerfaces are used in these mechanisms to create a usable interface for the operating system. Another interesting feature of IPv6 is that addresses are assigned to interfaces (or pseudointerfaces), not simply to the end node.

New Broadcast Methods   IPv6 has moved away from using broadcasting. The three types of packets used in IPv6 are unicast, multicast, and anycast. IPv6 clients then must use one of these types to get the MAC address of the next Ethernet hop (default gateway). IPv6 makes use of multicasting for this along with new functionality of neighbor discovery. Not only does ARP utilize new functionality, but ICMP (also a Layer 3 protocol) is redone and known as ICMP6. ICMP6 is used for messaging (packet too large, time exceeded, and so on) as it was in IPv4, but it also is used for the messaging of IPv6 mobility. ICMP6 echo request and ICMP6 echo reply are still used for ping.

Additionally, there are several concepts to consider in IPv6 addressing. The format of the address has changed since IPv4, and we must get used to seeing and using it. There are three types of addresses we will use as well as predefined values used within the address space. You need to get accustomed to seeing these addresses and being able to identify their uses.

IPv6 Address Format

For the design of IPv4 addresses, remember that we present addresses as octets or the decimal (base 10) representation of 8 bits. Four octets add up to the 32 bits required. IPv6 expands the address space to 128 bits, and the representation is for the most part shown in *hexadecimal* (a notation used to represent 8 bits using the values 0–9 and A–F). The following is an example of a full IPv6 address: 2001:0DB8:0000:0000:1234:0000:A9FE:133E.

You can tell the implementation of DNS will make life a lot easier for even those of us who like to ping the address in lieu of the name. Fortunately, DNS already has the ability to handle IPv6 addresses with the use of an AAAA record. (*A* is short for *alias*.) An A record in IPv4's addressing space is 32 bits, so an AAAA record—4 *As*—is 128 bits. The Windows Server DNS server handles the AAAA and the reverse pointer (PTR) records for IPv6.

IPv6 Address Shortcuts

Here are some shortcuts you can use for writing an IPv6 address:

- :0: stands for:0000:
- You can leave out preceding 0s in any 16-bit word.

For example, :DB8: and :0DB8: are equivalent.

- :: is a variable standing for enough zeros to round out the address to 128 bits.
- :: can be used only once in an address.

You can use these shortcuts to represent the example address 2001:0DB8:0000:0000: 1234:0000:A9FE:133E as shown here:

- Compress :0000: into :0:
  2001:0DB8:0000:0000:1234:0:A9FE:133E
- Eliminate preceding zeros:
  2001:DB8:0000:0000:1234:0:A9FE:133E
- Use the special variable shortcut for multiple zeros:
  2001:DB8::1234:0:A9FE:133E

You can also use *prefix notation* or slash notation when discussing IPv6 networks. The network of the example address can be represented as 2001:DB8:0000:0000:0000:0000:000 0: 0000. This can also be expressed as 2001:DB8::/32. The /32 indicates 32 bits of network, and 2001:DB8: is 32 bits of network.

IPv6 Address Assignment

We can let Windows client dynamically or automatically assign its IPv6 address, or we can still assign it manually. With dynamic or automatic assignment, the IPv6 address is assigned either by a DHCPv6 server or by the Windows Server or client machine itself. If no DHCPv6 server is configured, Windows Server or the client can query the local LAN segment to find a router with a configured IPv6 interface. If so, the server will assign itself an address on the same IPv6 network as the router interface and set its default gateway to the router interface's IPv6 address.

To see your configured IP addresses (IPv4 and IPv6), you can still use the `ipconfig` command. I have configured a static IPv4 and IPv6 address on my server. The IPv6 address is the same as used in the previous example IPv6 address.

IPv6 Address Types

There are multiple types of addresses in IPv6:

 You will notice that there is an absence of the broadcast type that is included in IPv4. Ipv6 does not use broadcasts; they're replaced with multicasts.

Anycast Addresses   Anycast addresses are not really new. The concept of anycast existed in Ipv4 but was not widely used. An anycast address is an Ipv6 address assigned to multiple devices (usually different devices). When an anycast packet is sent, it is delivered to one of the devices, usually the closest one.

Unicast Addresses   A unicast packet uniquely identifies an interface of an Ipv6 device. The interface can be a virtual or *pseudointerface* or a real (physical) interface.

Unicast vs. Anycast

Unicast and anycast addresses look the same and may be indistinguishable from each other; it only depends on how many devices have the same address. If only one device has a globally unique Ipv6 address, it's a unicast address; if more than one device has the same address, it's an anycast address. Both unicast and anycast are considered one-to-one communication, although you could say anycast is one-to-"one of many."

There are several types of unicast addresses, as described here:

Global Unicast Address   As of this writing, the *global unicast address* space is defined as 2000:: /3. 2001::/32 are the IPv6 addresses being issued to business entities. I mentioned before that Microsoft has been allocated 2001:4898:: /32. You'll find most example addresses listed as 2001:DB8:: /32; this space has been reserved for documentation. A DHCPv6 server would be set up with scopes (ranges of addresses to be assigned) within this address space. There are some special addresses and address formats you will see in use as well. Do you remember the loopback address in IPv4—127.0.0.1? In IPv6, the loopback address is ::1 (or 0:0:0:0:0:0:0:0001). You may also see an address with dotted decimal used. A dual-stack Windows device may also show you 2001:DB8::4:2:165.55.4.2. This address form is used in an integration/migration model of IPv6 (or if you just can't leave the dotted decimal era).

Link-Local Address   *Link-local addresses* are defined as FE80:: /10. If you look at the ipconfig command, you will see the link-local IPv6 address as FE80::a425:ab9d:7da4:ccba. The last 8 bytes (64 bits) are random to ensure a high probability of randomness for the link-local address.

The link-local address is to be used on a single link (network segment) and will never be routed.

There is another form of the link-local IPv6 address called the Extended User Interface 64-bit (EUI-64) format. This is derived by using the MAC address of the physical interface and inserting an FFFE between the third and fourth bytes of the MAC. Again, looking at `ipconfig`, the EUI-64 address would take the physical (MAC) address 00–03–FF–11–02–CD and make the link-local IPv6 address FE80::0203:FFFF:FE11:02CD. I've left the preceding zeros in the link-local IPv6 address to make it easier for you to pick out the MAC address with the FFFE inserted.

AnonymousAddress   Microsoft Server uses the random address by default instead of EUI-64. The random value is called the AnonymousAddress in Microsoft Server. It can be modified to allow the use of EUI-64.

Unique Local Address   The unique local address can be FC00 or FD00 and is used like the private address space of IPv4. Unique local addresses are described in RFC 4193. They are not expected to be routable on the global Internet. They are routable inside a more limited area, such as a site. They may also be routed between a limited set of sites.

Multicast Address   Multicast addresses are one-to-many communication packets. Multicast packets are identifiable by their first byte (most significant byte, leftmost byte, leftmost 2 nibbles, leftmost 8 bits, etc.). A multicast address is defined as FF00::/8.

In the second byte shown (the 00 of FF00), the second 0 is what's called the scope. Interface local is 01; link-local is 02. FF01:: is an interface local multicast.

There are several well-known (already defined) multicast addresses. For example, if you want to send a packet to all nodes in the local-link scope, you send the packet to FF02::1 (also shown as FF02:0:0:0:0:0:0:1). The all-routers multicast address is FF02::2.

We also use multicasting to get the logical link layer address (MAC address) of a device we are trying to communicate with. Instead of using the ARP mechanism of IPv4, IPv6 uses the ICMPv6 neighbor solicitation (NS) and neighbor advertisement (NA) messages. The NS and NA ICMPv6 messages are all part of the new Neighbor Discovery Protocol (NDP). This new ICMPv6 functionality also includes router solicitation and router advertisements as well as redirect messages (similar to the IPv4 redirect functionality).

Table 6.8 outlines the IPv6 address space known prefixes and some well-known addresses.

TABLE 6.8   IPv6 address space known prefixes and addresses

Address prefix	Scope of use
2000:: /3	Global unicast space prefix
FE80:: /10	Local-link address prefix
FC00:: /7	Unique local unicast prefix
FF00:: /8	Multicast prefix
2001:DB8:: /32	Global unicast prefix used for documentation
::1	Reserved local loopback address
2001:0000: /32	Teredo prefix
2002:: /16	6to4 prefix

IPv6 Integration/Migration

It's time to get into the mindset of integrating IPv6 into your existing infrastructure with the longer goal of migrating over to IPv6. This is not going to be an "OK, Friday the Internet is changing over" rollout. We are going to bring about the change as a controlled implementation. It could easily be three to five years before a solid migration occurs and probably longer. The migration is just below getting the world migrated to the metric system on the overall timeline. The process of integration/migration is made up of several mechanisms:

Dual Stack   Simply running both IPv4 and IPv6 on the same network, utilizing the IPv4 address space for devices only using IPv4 addresses and utilizing the IPv6 address space for devices using IPv6 addresses

Tunneling   Using an encapsulation scheme for transporting one address space inside another

Address Translation   Using a higher-level application to transparently change one address type (IPv4 or IPv6) to the other so that end devices are unaware that one address space is talking to another

IPv6 Dual Stack

The default implementation in Windows 10/11 is an enabled Ipv6 configured along with Ipv4; this is dual stack. The implementation can be dual IP Layer or dual TCP/IP stack. Windows 10/11 uses the dual IP Layer implementation. When an application queries a DNS server to resolve a hostname to an IP address, the DNS server may respond with an Ipv4 address or an Ipv6 address. If the DNS server responds with both, Windows 10/11 will prefer the Ipv6 addresses. Windows 10/11 can use both Ipv4 and Ipv6 addresses as necessary for network communication. When looking at the output of the `ipconfig` command, you will see both address spaces displayed.

Ipv6 Tunneling

Windows 10/11 includes several tunneling mechanisms for tunneling Ipv6 through the Ipv4 address space. They include the following:

ISATAP: Intra-Site Automatic Tunnel Addressing Protocol used for unicast Ipv6 communication across an Ipv4 infrastructure. ISATAP is enabled by default in Windows Server 2008 and above.

6to4: Used for unicast Ipv6 communication across an Ipv4 infrastructure.

Teredo: Used for unicast Ipv6 communication with an Ipv4 NAT implementation across an Ipv4 infrastructure.

With multiple tunneling protocols available and enabled by default, you might ask what the difference is and why one is used over the others. They all allow us to tunnel Ipv6 packets through the Ipv4 address space (a really cool thing if you're trying to integrate/migrate).

ISATAP ISATAP is the automatic tunnel addressing protocol providing Ipv6 addresses based on the Ipv4 address of the end interface (node). The Ipv6 address is automatically configured on the local device, and the dual-stack machine can use either its Ipv4 or Ipv6 address to communicate on the local network (within the local network infrastructure). ISATAP can use the neighbor discovery mechanism to determine the router ID and network prefix where the device is located, thus making intrasite communication possible even in a routed infrastructure.

The format of an ISATAP address is [64 bits of prefix] [32 bits indicating ISATAP] [32 bits Ipv4 address].

The center 32 bits indicating ISATAP are actually 0000:5EFE (when using private Ipv4 addresses). The ISATAP address of my Windows client machine using the link-local Ipv6 address is FE80::5EFE. Each node participating in the ISATAP infrastructure must support ISATAP. If you're routing through an IPv4 cloud, a border router (a router transitioning from an Ipv6 to Ipv4 space) must support ISATAP. Windows 10/11 can be configured as a border router and will forward ISATAP packets. ISATAP is experimental and is defined in RFC 4214.

6to4 6to4 specifies a procedure for Ipv6 networks to communicate with each other through an Ipv4 space without having the Ipv6 nodes having to know what's going on.

The Ipv6 nodes do not need to be dual stacked to make this happen. The border router is the device responsible for knowing about the Ipv6-to-Ipv4 transition. The Ipv6 packets are encapsulated at the border router and decapsulated at the other end or on the way back. There is an assigned prefix for the 6to4 implementation; 2002:: /16. 6to4 is defined in RFC 3056.

Teredo   Teredo (named after a genus of shipworm that drills holes in the wood of ships) is a protocol designed to allow IPv6 addresses to be available to hosts through one or more layers of NAT. Teredo uses a process of tunneling packets through the IPv4 space using UDP. The Teredo service encapsulates the IPv6 data within a UDP segment (packet) and uses an IPv4 address to get through the IPv4 cloud. Having a Layer 4 (Transport layer) available to use as a translation functionality is what gives us the ability to be behind a NAT. Teredo provides host-to-host communication and dynamic addressing for IPv6 nodes (dual stack), allowing the nodes to have access to resources in an IPv6 network and the IPv6 devices to have access to the IPv6 devices that have connectivity only to the IPv4 space (just as home users who have an IPv6-enabled operating system connecting to IPv6 resources and their home ISP have only IPv4 capabilities). Teredo is defined in RFC 4380.

In Windows 10/11, an IPv4 Teredo server is identified and configured (using the `netsh` command interface). The Teredo server provides connectivity resources (address) to the Teredo client (the node that has access to the IPv4 Internet and needs access to an IPv6 network/Internet). A Teredo relay is a component used by the IPv6 router to receive traffic destined for Teredo clients and forward the traffic appropriately. The defined prefix for Teredo addresses is 2001:: /32 (does it look better like this? – 2001:0000:: /32). Teredo does add overhead like all the implementations discussed. It is generally accepted that we should use the simplest model available. However, in the process of integration/migration for most of us behind a NAT, Teredo will be the process to choose.

In Windows 10/11, use the `ipconfig /all` command to view the default configurations including IPv4 and IPv6. You may notice a notation we didn't discuss: the percent sign at the end of the IPv6 address. The number after the percent sign is the virtual interface identifier used by Windows 10/11.

Information Commands Useful with IPv6

There are numerous commands you can use to view, verify, and configure the network parameters of Windows 10/11. You can use the `netsh` command set and the `route` command set as well as the standard `ping` and `tracert` functions.

Use the `netsh` command interface to examine and configure IPv6 functionality (as well as the provided dialog boxes if you like). The `netsh` command issued from the command interpreter changes into a network shell (`netsh`) where you can configure and view both IPv4 and IPv6 components.

Don't forget to use the ever-popular `route print` command to see the Windows 10/11 routing tables (IPv4 and IPv6). The other diagnostic commands are still available for IPv4 as well as IPv6. In previous versions of Microsoft operating systems, `ping` was the IPv4 command and `ping6` was the IPv6 command.

This has changed for Windows 10/11; `ping` works for both IPv4 and IPv6 to test Layer 3 connectivity to remote devices. The command is now `tracert` for both IPv4 and IPv6 and will show you every Layer 3 (IP) hop from source to destination (assuming all the administrators from here to there want you to see the hops and are not blocking ICMP and also assuming your packets are not traversing IP tunnels; you won't see the router hops in the tunnel either).

Overall, the consortium of people making up development of the Internet and Internet protocols have tried to make all changes to communication infrastructures easy to implement (this is a daunting task with so many vendors and various infrastructures currently in place).

The goal is not to daze and confuse administrators; it's to provide the most flexibility with the greatest functionality. IPv6 is going to provide the needed Layer 3 (Network layer, Global Addressing layer, Logical Addressing layer . . . call it what you like) functionality for the foreseeable future.

Configuring TCP/IP on Windows 10

Windows 10/11 can use either IPv4 or IPv6 to communicate with other machines on a network, but the Windows client machine must receive the TCP/IP address. There are two ways that a Windows client machine can get a TCP/IP address: statically or dynamically.

Assigning Static TCP/IP Numbers

As an administrator, you may find it necessary to configure a Windows client machine manually (static configuration). To do so, you must know the following:

- Which TCP/IP address the machine will receive
- What the subnet mask is for the segment
- What the default gateway (router's TCP/IP address) is
- What the DNS server TCP/IP addresses are

Complete Exercise 6.4 to configure a Windows 10 machine to use a static TCP/IP address. How to configure a static TCP/IP address on a Windows 11 machine will be right after this exercise. This example uses TCP/IP addresses for a local network, but you can use your own TCP/IP addresses if you know what they should be.

EXERCISE 6.4

Configure a Static TCP/IP Address in Windows 10

1. Select Start ➤ Settings ➤ Network & Internet.

2. Do one of the following:

   For a Wi-Fi network, select Wi-Fi ➤ Manage Known Networks. Choose the network you want to change the settings for, then select Properties.

   For an Ethernet network, select Ethernet, then select the Ethernet network you're connected to.

3. Under IP Assignment, select Edit.

EXERCISE 6.4 *(continued)*

4. Under Edit IP Settings, select Manual. You can choose between either IPv4 or IPv6 (both steps are included here).

a. To specify IPv4 settings manually:

i. Under Edit IP settings, choose Manual, then turn on IPv4.

ii. Enter the following IP address settings:

IP Address: **192.168.1.50**

Subnet Mask: **255.255.255.0**

Default Gateway: **192.168.1.1**

iii. To specify a DNS server address, in the Preferred DNS and Alternate DNS boxes, type the addresses of the primary and secondary DNS servers. Enter **8.8.8.8** (unless you want to use your own settings).

b. Or, to specify IPv6 settings manually:

i. Under Edit IP settings, choose Manual, then turn on IPv6.

ii. Enter the following IP address settings:

IP Address: **192.168.1.50**

Subnet Mask: **255.255.255.0**

Default Gateway: **192.168.1.1**

iii. To specify a DNS server address, in the Preferred DNS and Alternate DNS boxes, type the addresses of the primary and secondary DNS servers. Enter **8.8.8.8** (unless you want to use your own settings).

5. When you're done, click Save.

In Exercise 6.4, you configured a static TCP/IP address on a Windows 10 machine. The steps for configuring a static TCP/IP address on a Windows 11 machine are basically the same; a few of the names are a bit different and you have another option. Here is how you would do it:

1. Select Start ➢ Settings ➢ Network & internet.

2. Do one of the following:

   ▪ For a Wi-Fi network, select Wi-Fi ➢ Manage known networks. Choose the network for which you want to change the settings.

   ▪ For an Ethernet network, select Ethernet, then select the Ethernet network you're connected to.

3. Next to IP assignment, select Edit.

4. Under Edit network IP settings or Edit IP settings, select Manual. You can choose between either IPv4 or IPv6 (both steps are included below).

- To specify IPv4 settings manually:
  - Under Edit network IP settings or Edit IP settings, choose Manual, then turn on IPv4.
  - To specify an IP address, in the IP address, Subnet mask, and Gateway boxes, type the IP address settings.
  - To specify a DNS server address, in the Preferred DNS and Alternate DNS boxes, type the addresses of the primary and secondary DNS servers.
  - To specify if you want to use an encrypted (DNS over HTTPS) or unencrypted connection to the DNS server you specify, for Preferred DNS encryption and Alternate DNS encryption, choose the setting you want.
- To specify IPv6 settings manually:
  - Under Edit Network IP Settings or Edit IP Settings, choose Manual, then turn on IPv6.
  - To specify an IP address, in the IP address, Subnet prefix length, and Gateway boxes, type the IP address settings.
  - To specify a DNS server address, in the Preferred DNS and Alternate DNS boxes, type the addresses of the primary and secondary DNS servers.
  - To specify if you want to use an encrypted (DNS over HTTPS) or unencrypted connection to the DNS server you specify, for Preferred DNS encryption and Alternate DNS encryption, choose the setting you want.

5. When you're done, select Save.

Configuring a Windows 10/11 Machine to Use DHCP

Dynamic IP configuration assumes that you have a DHCP server on your network that is reachable by the DHCP clients. DHCP servers are configured to automatically provide DHCP clients with all their IP configuration information, including IP address, subnet mask, and DNS server.

For large networks, DHCP is the easiest and most reliable way of managing IP configurations. By default, a Windows 10/11 machine is configured as a DHCP client for dynamic IP configuration.

Complete Exercise 6.5 to configure a Windows 10/11 machine to use a dynamic IP configuration.

EXERCISE 6.5

Using DHCP in Windows 10/11

1. Select Start ➢ Settings ➢ Network & Internet.

2. Do one of the following:

For a Wi-Fi network, select Wi-Fi ➢ Manage Known Networks. Choose the network you want to change the settings for, then select Properties.

EXERCISE 6.5 *(continued)*

For an Ethernet network, select Ethernet, then select the Ethernet network you're connected to.

3. Under IP Assignment, select Edit.

4. Under Edit IP Settings/Edit Network IP Settings, select Automatic (DHCP). When you select Automatic (DHCP), the IP address settings and the DNS server address setting are set automatically by your router or other access point (recommended).

5. When you're done, click Save.

If you are using DHCP and you are not connecting to other machines properly, you can type **ipconfig /all** at a command prompt to see what your TCP/IP address is. If your TCP/IP address starts with 169.254.*x.x*, you are not connecting to the DHCP server. Instead, your Windows 10/11 machine is using APIPA.

Understanding APIPA

Automatic Private IP Addressing (APIPA) is used to automatically assign private IP addresses for home or small business networks that contain a single subnet, have no DHCP server, and are not using static IP addressing. If APIPA is being used, clients will be able to communicate only with other clients on the same subnet that are also using APIPA. The benefit of using APIPA in small networks is that it is less tedious and has less chance of configuration errors than statically assigning IP addresses and configuration.

APIPA is used with Windows 10/11 under the following conditions:

- When the client is configured as a DHCP client but no DHCP server is available to service the DHCP request

- When the client originally obtained a DHCP lease from a DHCP server but when the client tried to renew the DHCP lease, the DHCP server was unavailable and the lease period expired

APIPA uses a Class B network address space that has been reserved for its use. The address space is the 169.254.0.0 network, where the range of 169.254.0.1–169.254.255.254 is available for the host to assign to itself. APIPA uses the following process:

1. The Windows client attempts to use a DHCP server for its configuration, but no DHCP servers respond.

2. The Windows client selects a random address from the 169.254.0.1–169.254.255.254 range of addresses and will use a subnet mask of 255.255.0.0.

3. The client uses a duplicate address-detection method to verify that the address it selected is not already in use on the network.

4. If the address is already in use, the client repeats steps 1 and 2. If the address is not already in use, the client configures its network interface with the address it randomly selected. Given the number of the addresses the APIPA client can select from (65,534 addresses), the odds of selecting a duplicate are very slim.

5. The Windows 10/11 network client continues to search for a DHCP server every five minutes. If a DHCP server replies to the request, the APIPA configuration is dropped, and the client receives new IP configuration settings from the DHCP server.

You can determine whether your network interface has been configured using APIPA by looking at your IP address from the command prompt by using the `ipconfig /all` command.

Testing Your IP Configuration

After you have installed and configured the TCP/IP settings, you can test the IP configuration by using the `ipconfig`, `ping`, and `nbtstat` commands. These commands are also useful in troubleshooting IP configuration errors. You can also graphically view connection details through the Ethernet Status section of the Network and Sharing Center.

Using the *ipconfig* Command

The `ipconfig` command displays your IP configuration. Table 6.9 lists the command switches that you can use with the `ipconfig` command.

TABLE 6.9   `ipconfig` switches

Switch	Description
/?	Shows all of the help options for `ipconfig`
/all	Shows verbose information about your IP configuration, including your computer's physical address, the DNS server you are using, and whether you are using DHCP
/allcompartments	Shows IP information for all compartments
/release	Releases an IPv4 address that has been assigned through DHCP
/release6	Releases an IPv6 address that has been assigned through DHCP
/renew	Renews an IPv4 address through DHCP
/renew6	Renews an IPv6 address through DHCP
/flushdns	Purges the DNS resolver cache
/registerdns	Refreshes DHCP leases and re-registers DNS names
/displaydns	Displays the contents of the DNS resolver cache
/showclassid	Lists the DHCP class IDs allowed by the computer
/setclassID	Allows you to modify the DHCP class ID

Using Other TCP/IP Commands

You can use numerous commands to view, verify, and configure the network parameters of Windows 10/11. Specifically, you can use the `netsh` command set and the `route` command set as well as the standard `ping` and `tracert` functions.

Use the `netsh` command interface to examine and configure IPv6 functionality (as well as the provided dialog boxes if you want). The `netsh` command issued from the command interpreter changes into a network shell (`netsh`) where you can configure and view both IPv4 and IPv6 components. Don't forget to use the ever-popular `route print` command to see the Windows 10/11 routing tables (IPv4 and IPv6). `ping` works for both IPv4 and IPv6 to test Layer 3 connectivity to remote devices. As already mentioned, the command is `tracert` for both IPv4 and IPv6 and will show you every Layer 3 (IP) hop from source to destination (assuming all the administrators from here to there want you to see the hops and are not blocking ICMP and also assuming your packets are not traversing IP tunnels, or you won't see the router hops in the tunnel either).

TCP/IP Troubleshooting

If you are having trouble connecting to network resources, consider the following:

- If you can access resources on your local subnet but not on a remote subnet, check the default gateway settings on your computer. Pinging a remote host and receiving a Destination Unreachable message is also related to default gateway misconfiguration.

- If you can access some but not all resources on your local subnet or remote subnet, you should check your subnet mask settings, the wiring to those resources, or the devices between your computer and those resources.

- Use the `ipconfig` command to ensure that you are not configured with an APIPA address. If you are, determine why you are not receiving IP settings from your DHCP server.

- If you can access a resource (for example, by pinging a computer) by IP address but not by name, check the DNS settings on your computer.

After we have TCP/IP set up on our Windows 10/11 machine, we can connect the Windows client machine to the network. In the next section, we will look at how to do that.

Configuring Windows Client on a Network

In a corporate environment, the client machines (Windows 7/8/8.1, and Windows 10/11) will be connected to the domain environment either from the Windows 10/11 operating system domain or from Active Directory. Having the Windows 10/11 machine on the network offers many benefits to administration:

- You can deploy GPOs from one location instead of LGPOs on each machine.

- Users can store their data on a server. This way, the nightly backups capture user information. Most Windows 10/11 machines will *not* be backed up separately.

- You can manage users and groups from one central location (Active Directory) instead of on each Windows 10/11 machine.

- You can manage resource security on servers instead of on each Windows client machine.

Adding Windows 10/11 to the Domain

It does not matter which way you choose to connect the machine to the domain. I usually connect the Windows client machine through the Windows operating system. Many IT administrators add the Windows 10/11 system by using the Active Directory Users and Computers MMC, but either way does the same task.

Complete Exercise 6.6 to connect a Windows 10/11 machine to a Windows Server domain via the Windows 10/11 OS. To complete this exercise, you will need to have a Windows Server domain that the Window client machine can connect to.

EXERCISE 6.6

Connecting a Windows Client Machine to the Domain

1. This can be done in different ways; you can use either Settings or Control Panel. Click Start ≻ Settings ≻ System ≻ About. Or open Control Panel using your preferred method, and select System ≻ About.

2. The next step depends on whether you are on a Windows 10 or a Windows 11 machine:

   - In Windows 10, under Related Links on the right-hand side, click Advanced System Settings.

   - In Windows 11, look for Related Links below the Device specifications and select Domain or Workgroup.

3. The System Properties dialog box opens; ensure that you are on the Computer Name tab.

4. Click the Change button next to the To Rename This Computer Or Change Its Domain Or Workgroup section.

5. In the Member Of section, click the Domain radio button (shown in Figure 6.19) and type the name of your Windows Server domain.

FIGURE 6.19   Computer Name/Domain Changes screen

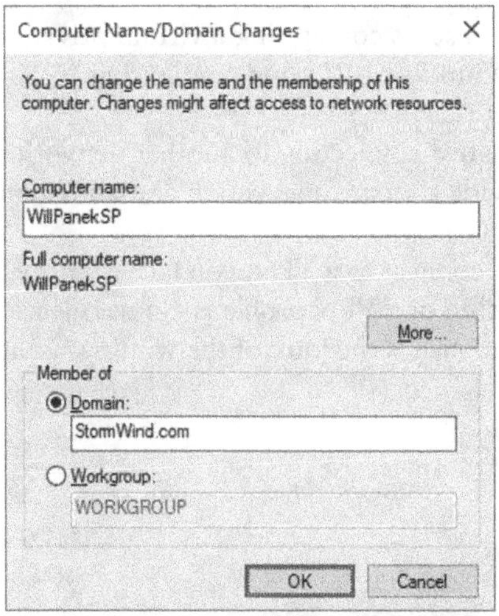

6. A Credentials box appears, asking for a username and password. Enter an account with administrative credentials to join the machine to the domain. Click OK.

7. A dialog box stating that you are part of the domain appears. Click OK and reboot the machine.

8. From the Windows client machine, log onto the domain with your username and password.

You can also add a Windows client computer to a domain by using PowerShell by following these steps:

1. Launch the PowerShell as an administrator.

2. Run the following command:
    Add-Computer -DomainName "Domain Name" -Credential "Domain Username".

3. Press Enter, and you will be prompted to enter your domain user password.

4. Restart the computer to finish.

You can also use the command prompt to join a Windows client to an Active directory domain. Here's how:

1. On the Windows client computer, open the command prompt using your preferred method.

2. Run the following command: **netdom join <computername> /domain:<yourADdomain> /UserD:<username> /PasswordD:<password>**.

3. Restart the Windows client computer to finish.

Configure VPN Clients

In this section I am going to discuss configuring a virtual private network (VPN) client by using the built-in tools on Windows 10/11 and configuring VPNs by using the Connection Manager Administration Kit (CMAK).

A VPN allows you to create a connection to another network securely over the Internet. A VPN connection can provide a secure connection and allow you to access your corporate network over the Internet.

However, before you can connect to a VPN, you have to have a VPN profile set up on your computer. The creation of a VPN profile is almost identical on Windows 10 and Windows 11. The main difference is the look of the windows, but the steps are basically the same.

Create a VPN Profile

To create a VPN profile in Windows 10/11, perform the following steps:

1. Select Start ➤ Settings ➤ Network & Internet ➤ VPN ➤ Add A VPN Connection in Windows 10 (as shown in Figure 6.20) or click Add VPN in Windows 11 (as shown in Figure 6.21).

FIGURE 6.20   Add A VPN Connection option in Windows 10

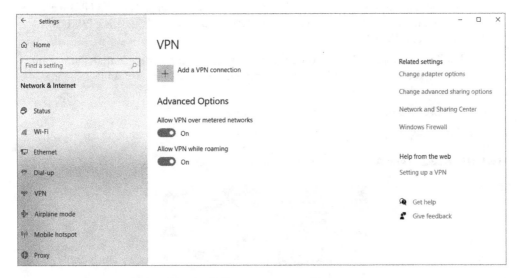

FIGURE 6.21   Add VPN in Windows 11

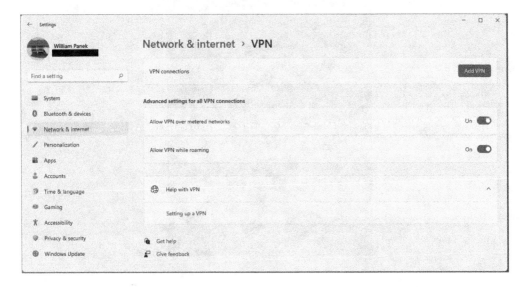

2. In Add A VPN Connection (as shown in Figure 6.22) for Windows 10 (or the Add VPN in Windows 11—the information requested is the same), enter the following:

    ▪   For VPN Provider, choose Windows (built-in).

    ▪   In the Connection Name box, enter a recognizable name.

    ▪   For Server Name Or Address, enter the address for the VPN server.

    ▪   For VPN Type, choose the type of VPN connection you want to create. You'll need to know which kind of VPN connection your company or VPN service uses. Your options are: Automatic, Point to Point Tunneling Protocol (PPTP), L2TP/IPsec With Certificate, L2TP/IPsec With Pre-shared Key, Secure Socket Tunneling Protocol (SSTP), and IKEv2.

    ▪   For Type Of Sign-in Info, choose the type of sign-in info (or credentials) you want to use. Your options are: User Name And Password, Smart Card, One-Time Password, and Certificate.

    ▪   For User Name (Optional), enter a username.

    ▪   For Password (Optional), enter a password.

FIGURE 6.22   Add A VPN Connection window on Windows 10

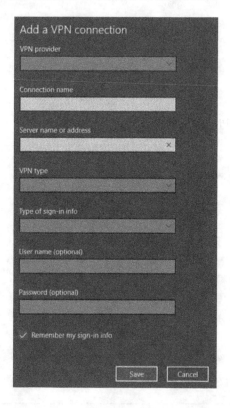

3. When done, click Save.

If you need to edit the VPN connection information or set additional settings, such as proxy settings, choose the VPN connection and then select Advanced Options.

Connect to a VPN

Now, that you have the VPN profile established, you need to connect to the VPN. The steps to connect to a VPN will be different depending on the Windows version you are using.

To connect to a VPN from a Windows 10 machine:

1. On the far right of the taskbar, click the Network icon.

2. Select the VPN connection you want to connect to and then do either of the following depending on what happens when you select the VPN connection:

- If the Connect button displays under the VPN connection, click it.

- If the VPN section in Settings opens, select the VPN connection there, then select Connect.

3. If prompted, enter your username and password or other logon information.

When you are connected to the VPN, the VPN connection name will show that you are connected underneath it, as shown in Figure 6.23.

FIGURE 6.23   VPN connection on Windows 10 showing a Connected status

To connect to a VPN from a Windows 11 machine:

1. Select Start ➤ Settings ➤ Network & Internet ➤ VPN.

2. Next to the VPN connection you want, click Connect.

3. If prompted, enter your username and password or other logon information.

When you are connected to the VPN, the VPN connection name will show that you are connected underneath it.

Connection Manager Administration Kit (CMAK)

Connection Manager Administration Kit (CMAK) is a client network connection tool that lets a user connect to a remote network, such as a corporate network that is protected by a VPN server. You will create a profile that is made up of connection settings that will allow users to connect to a VPN from a local machine to a remote network. The profile that is created will be an executable file (EXE) that, once distributed to the users, they can run and connect to the remote network.

CMAK is an optional component that is not installed by default. Installing and creating CMAK profiles is done on a server machine. You must first enable it on the server:

1. Open Control Panel using your preferred method.

2. Click Programs And Features.

3. On the left-hand side, click the Turn Windows Features On Or Off link.

4. Depending on which version you are using this has been called Connection Manager Administration Kit or RAS Connection Manager Administration Kit. Select the feature you want by clicking the check box.

5. Click OK, when prompted, and restart your computer.

Once the feature is installed, you can then run the Connection Manager Administration Kit Wizard to create the profile that the clients will use to access the VPN (see Figure 6.24).

FIGURE 6.24 Connection Manager Administration Kit Welcome screen

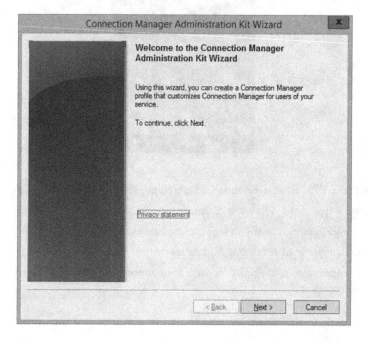

Once you have gone through all the necessary steps using the CMAK Wizard, the Connection Manager profile is created. The profile, by default, is stored in the `C:\Program Files\CMAK\Profiles` directory, which is automatically created by CMAK.

The new profile package can then be distributed to the end users by either copying the files in the CMAK directory or by sharing the CMAK directory and providing users with the path information. Users can then run the executable file and connect to the desired VPN.

Configure and Manage Certificates on Client Devices

The main function of a certificate is to authenticate the identity of the owner of the certificate. A certificate or digital certificate is a digitally signed document that is unique and that recognizes an individual or organization. A public key can be used to encrypt the messages that are sent from the owner of the certificate. Certificates must be issued by a certification authority, which is often a third-party issuer of certificates.

In Windows, there are three primary ways to manage certificates: the Certificates Manager Console (`certmgr.msc`) which is a Microsoft Management Console (MMC) snap-in; PowerShell; or the `certutil` command-line tool. The `certutil` command-line tool is used on Windows Server machines and is installed as part of Certificate Services. You can use `certutil` to display certification authority (CA) configuration information, to configure Certificate Services, to back up and restore CA components, and to verify certificates, key pairs, and certificate chains. Using `certutil` is beyond the scope of this book, but it is another way that you can manage certificates on a Windows machine.

When working with certificates, you may need to view and examine their properties. There are three different types of certificate stores that you can examine with the MMC on a Windows device. They are:

Service Account   This store is local to a particular service on the device.

Current User   This store is local to the current user account on the device.

Local Device   This store is local to the device and global to all users on the device.

The Certificates Manager Console (`certmgr.msc`) is a part of the MMC. The Certificate Manager allows you to:

- Delete or request new certificates
- Export certificates
- Import certificates
- Modify certificates
- View details about certificates

To view certificates in the MMC snap-in, follow these steps:

1. Right-click the Start button and select Run, then type **mmc** and click OK. The MMC will open.

2. Select File ➤ Add/Remove Snap-in. The Add Or Remove Snap-ins window will open.

3. From the Available Snap-ins list, choose Certificates, then click Add, as shown in Figure 6.25.

FIGURE 6.25 Add Or Remove Snap-ins window

4. In the Certificates Snap-in window, you can select My User Account, Service Account, or Computer Account. Select your desired option. If you select Service Account or Computer Account, you will need to click Next. If you select My User Account, just click Finish and move to step 6.

5. If you selected Service Account or Computer Account, select your desired options and continue through the dialog windows and then click Finish.

6. In the Add Or Remove Snap-in window, click OK.

7. This step is optional: you can save the MMC console for later use. To do that, choose File ➤ Save or Save As.

8. To view your certificates in the MMC snap-in, select Console Root in the left pane, then expand your desired certificate type. A list of directories for each type of certificate will appear. Then, from each certificate directory, you can view, export, import, and delete certificates.

If you want to just view certificates for the current user, follow these steps:

1. Right-click the Start button and select Run, then type **certmgr.msc** and click OK. The Certificate Manager tool for the current user appears, as shown in Figure 6.26.

FIGURE 6.26 Certificate Manager tool for the current user

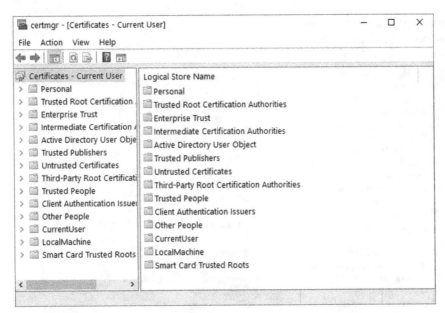

2. To view certificates, under Certificates – Current User in the left pane, expand the directory for the type of certificate you want to view.

If you want to view certificates for the local device, perform these steps:

1. Right-click the Start button and select Run, then type **certlm.msc** and click OK. The Certificate Manager tool for the local device appears, as shown in Figure 6.27.

2. To view certificates, under Certificates – Local Computer in the left pane, expand the directory for the type of certificate you want to view.

You can also use PowerShell to view and manage certificates on a local machine. The default PowerShell Get-ChildItem cmdlet allows for accessing the local certificate store. To see all the certificates in the root directory, use Get-ChildItem Cert: \LocalMachine\Root.

FIGURE 6.27 Certificate Manager tool for the local device

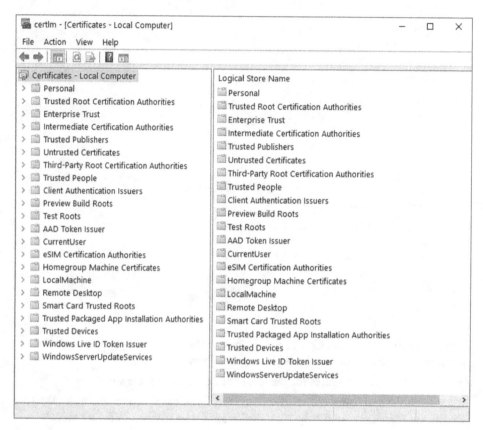

Summary

In this chapter, we discussed the different types of Windows networks: domain-based and peer-to-peer (workgroup) based. Computers need to use a communication device called a NIC device in order to communicate with each other across the network. You can set up Windows 10/11 to use both wired and wireless NIC devices. Windows 10/11 also has new features to help with setting up your wireless networks.

To allow computers to communicate on a network, you must use a *protocol*—a set of communication standards that all computers will use. The main protocol that Windows 10/11 uses is TCP/IP. There are two versions of TCP/IP that Windows 10/11 can use: IPv4 and IPv6. IPv4 is the most commonly used protocol, but IPv6 is the newest version of TCP/IP and gives organizations flexibility and growth potential.

We also discussed how to configure a VPN client by using built-in tools as well as working with the Connection Manager Administration Kit (CMAK). And we discussed how to configure and manage certificates on client devices.

Exam Essentials

Understand Microsoft networking. Know the difference between the Microsoft networks that you can set up. Know the difference between workgroups and domains. Know about working with Azure Active Directory versus on-site Active Directory.

Understand how to configure network settings. Know how to install and configure both wired and wireless networks. Understand how Windows 10/11 has built-in wireless network support. Know how to set up your preferred wireless network.

Understand IPv4 and IPv6. Know and understand IPv4 and IPv6. Understand how to configure and maintain both IPv4 and IPv6 networks. Know how to subnet an IPv4 network. Understand that APIPA will automatically assign an IP address to a Windows client machine if DHCP is not available.

Understand how to configure a VPN client. Know how to configure a VPN client using built-in tools and working with the Connection Manager Administration Kit tool (CMAK).

Understand how to view certificates on client devices. Know how to configure and manage certificates on client devices using the Microsoft Management Console (MMC).

Video Resources

There are videos available for the following exercises:

6.1

6.2

6.4

You can access the videos at www.wiley.com/go/sybextestprep.

Review Questions

1. You have two DHCP servers on your network. Your computer accidentally received the wrong IP and DNS server configuration from a DHCP server that was misconfigured. The DHCP server with the incorrect configuration has been disabled. What commands could you use to release and renew your computer's DHCP configuration? (Choose two.)

   A. `ipconfig /release`

   B. `ipconfig /registerdhcp`

   C. `ipconfig /renew`

   D. `ipconfig /flushdhcp`

2. You are the network administrator for your company. Your service provider has assigned you the network address 192.168.154.0. You have been granted the entire range to use. What class of address have you been assigned?

   A. Class A

   B. Class B

   C. Class C

   D. Class D

3. You are the network administrator for your company. After configuring a new computer and connecting it to the network, you discover that you cannot access any of the computers on the remote subnet by IP address. You can access some of the computers on the local subnet by IP address. What is the most likely problem?

   A. Incorrectly defined IP address

   B. Incorrectly defined subnet mask

   C. Incorrectly defined default gateway

   D. Incorrectly defined DNS server

4. A user cannot access a server in the domain. After troubleshooting, you determine that the user cannot access the server by name but can access the server by IP address. What is the most likely problem?

   A. Incorrectly defined IP address

   B. Incorrectly defined subnet mask

   C. Incorrectly defined DHCP server

   D. Incorrectly defined DNS server

5. You have a Windows client machine that needs to have a static TCP/IP address. You assign the IP address to the machine and you now want to register the computer with DNS. How can you do this from the Windows client machine?

   A. `ipconfig /renewdns`

   B. `ipconfig /flushdns`

   C. `ipconfig /dns`

   D. `ipconfig /registerdns`

6. You have been hired as a TCP/IP contractor for an organization who wants to redo their network. The company currently uses a 192.168.*x.x* class but they are projecting a hiring of over 500 new employees this year. They currently have 175 employees. They do not want to buy a new TCP/IP class. What can you do to help them? (Choose all that apply.)

    A. Change the network to 10.0.0.0/8.

    B. Change the network to 172.16.0.0/16.

    C. Change the network to 224.10.0.0/24.

    D. Change the network to 192.10.0.0/24.

7. You are hired by a small company to set up a network. The company sells pocket watches and they have only five employees. They can't afford a server and client access licenses. What type of network can you set up for them?

    A. Set up all Windows 10/11 clients on a workgroup.

    B. Create a HomeGroup.

    C. Set them up on Azure Active Directory.

    D. Load Windows Server onto a Windows 10 system.

8. Which of the following IP addresses are Class A addresses? (Choose all that apply.)

    A. 131.107.10.15

    B. 128.10.14.1

    C. 10.14.100.240

    D. 65.102.17.9

9. Which of the following IP addresses are Class B addresses? (Choose all that apply.)

    A. 131.107.10.150

    B. 189.10.14.1

    C. 10.14.100.240

    D. 198.102.17.9

10. You are the network administrator for a large organization with many laptop users who go on the road. Your organization would like to start moving away from users connecting in by VPN to get data. They have decided that they want to start moving the entire IT department to the cloud. What version of Active Directory can they start using?

    A. Azure Active Directory

    B. OneDrive

    C. Windows Server Active Directory

    D. DirectAccess

11. You are the administrator for your company network. You have a Windows client machine that needs to be able to communicate with all computers on the internal network. The company decides to add 15 new segments to its IPv6 network. How should you configure the IPv6 address so that the server can communicate with all of the segments?

    A. Configure the address as fd00::2b0:e0ff:dee9:4143/8.

    B. Configure the address as fe80::2b0:e0ff:dee9:4143/32.

    C. Configure the address as ff80::2b0:e0ff:dee9:4143/64.

    D. Configure the address as fe80::2b0:e0ff:dee9:4143/64.

12. You are the administrator for your company network. You and a colleague are discussing configuring a VPN client. Which tab of the Connection Properties dialog box is where you would want to enter the VPN server address or hostname?

    A. The General tab

    B. The Networking tab

    C. The Options tab

    D. The Security tab

13. You are the administrator for your company network. You and a colleague are discussing subnet masks and how to determine the Classless Inter-Domain Routing (CIDR) number. Given the subnet mask 255.255.224.0, what would the CIDR equivalent be?

    A. /17

    B. /18

    C. /19

    D. /20

14. You are the administrator for your company network. Your network contains an Active Directory domain that has more than 1,000 Windows client computers. What should you do if you want to prevent the computers from one department from appearing in the Network in File Explorer?

    A. You should configure DNS to use an external provider.

    B. You should disable the Network List Service.

    C. You should modify the file in the %systemroot%\system32\drivers\etc\ networks directory.

    D. You should turn off Network Discovery.

15. You are the administrator for your company network. The network is using the address 137.25.0.0; it is composed of 20 subnets, with a maximum of 300 hosts on each subnet. The company is on a merger-and-acquisitions spree, and your manager has told you to prepare for an increase to 50 subnets with some containing more than 600 hosts. Using the existing network address, which of the following subnet masks would work for this requirement?

    A. 255.255.240.0

    B. 255.255.248.0

    C. 255.255.252.0

    D. 255.255.254.0

16. You are the administrator for your company network. Your network has a DNS server that contained corrupted data. You fix the issues on the server. One of the users in the network is complaining that they are still unable to access Internet resources. You check to see whether things are working on another computer on the same subnet. What command should you run to fix the issue?

   A. You should run the `DNS /flushdns` command.

   B. You should run the `ipconfig /flush` command.

   C. You should run the `ipconfig /flushdns` command.

   D. You should run the `ping /flush` command.

17. You are the administrator for your company network. You and a colleague are discussing Classless Inter-Domain Routing (CIDR). Which of the following subnet masks represents the CIDR of /27?

   A. 255.255.255.224

   B. 255.255.255.240

   C. 255.255.255.248

   D. 255.255.255.254

18. You are the administrator for your company network. You and a colleague are discussing troubleshooting methods for checking network connectivity. One method that you are discussing is by pinging the loopback address at the command prompt. What is the IPv4 diagnostic loopback address?

   A. You should ping `127.0.0.0`.

   B. You should ping `127.0.0.1`.

   C. You should ping `127.0.1.0`.

   D. You should ping `127.1.0.0`.

19. You are the administrator for your company network. You and a colleague are discussing troubleshooting methods for checking network connectivity. One method that you are discussing is pinging the loopback address at the command prompt. What is the IPv6 diagnostic loopback address?

   A. You should ping `::1`.

   B. You should ping `::01`.

   C. You should ping `0:0:0:0:0:0:0:1111`.

   D. You should ping `1:0:0:0:0:0:0:0011`.

20. You are the administrator for your company network. A user is using a computer running a Windows client. When this user connects to the corporate network, they are unable to access the internal company servers but can access the servers on the Internet. You run the `ipconfig /all` command and receive the following:

```
Connection-specific DNS Suffix . :
Description . . . . . . . . . . . : Ethernet 1
Physical Address . . . . . . . . : 00-50-B6-7B-E4-81
DHCP Enabled . . . . . . . . . . : Yes
Autoconfiguration Enabled . . . : Yes
Link-local IPv6 Address . . . . : fe80::5d56:3419:eB3b:3c46%17 (Preferred)
IPv4 Address . . . . . . . . . . : 192.168.0.121(Preferred)
Subnet Mask . . . . . . . . . . : 255.255.255.0
Lease Obtained . . . . . . . . . : Friday, August 5, 2022 11:38:12 AM
Lease Expires . . . . . . . . . : Friday, August 5, 2022 11:38:12 PM
Default Gateway . . . . . . . . : 192.168.0.1
DHCP Server . . . . . . . . . . : 192.168.0.2
DHCPv6 IAID . . . . . . . . . . : 536891574
DHCPv6 Client DUID . . . . . . . : 00-01-00-01-22-AC-5F-64-00-50-B6-7B-
E4-81
DNS Servers . . . . . . . . . . : 131.107.10.60
       192.168.0.3
NetBIOS over Tcpip . . . . . . . : Enabled
```

You send a ping request and can ping the default gateway, the DNS servers, and the DHCP server successfully. What configuration could be causing the issue?

A. The issue is with the default gateway address.

B. The issue is with the DNS servers.

C. The issue is with the IPv4 address.

D. The issue is with the subnet mask.

Chapter

7

Configuring Recovery

MICROSOFT EXAM OBJECTIVES COVERED IN THIS CHAPTER:

✓ **Configure Windows settings**

- Configure startup options.

✓ **Configure and manage storage**

- Optimize local drives by using Disk cleanup or Storage Sense.

✓ **Perform system and data recovery**

- Troubleshoot boot and startup processes; recover Windows client; recover files; create and manage restore points; restore from restore points.

✓ **Monitor and manage Windows**

- Configure and analyze event logs; monitor and manage performance and reliability, configure scheduled tasks, manage Registry.

One of the tasks that administrators will need to do on a daily basis is fixing Windows client systems that are having issues. There are many ways to determine what issues a Windows client system may be having, and there are many tools to help you solve the issues.

The best way to protect any Windows client system is to make sure the users' files are stored on a network server and backed up daily or use cloud storage such as OneDrive. But you may encounter situations where you need to back up your Windows 10/11 system.

Windows 10/11 includes a full backup and restore application (Backup and Restore [Windows 7]) that allows a user or an administrator to maintain a backup copy of any of the Windows client component files and data files that are considered critical to the operation of your day-to-day business.

There may also be times when a Windows client doesn't start properly and you will need to identify and resolve the Windows error to get the system booting up properly again. Many different utilities are available that allow you to troubleshoot and fix startup issues; these tools include Safe Mode, the Startup Repair tool, the Backup and Restore Center, Driver Rollback, and System Restore.

Finally, there will be times when you need to monitor the Windows client system. Sometimes, performance optimization can feel like a luxury, but it can be very important, especially if you can't get your Windows client system to run applications the way they are intended to run. The Windows 10/11 operating system has been specifically designed to keep your mission-critical applications and data accessible even in times of failures.

The most common cause of such problems is a hardware configuration issue. Poorly written device drivers and unsupported hardware can cause problems with system stability. Failed hardware components (such as system memory) may do so as well. Memory chips can be faulty, electrostatic discharge can ruin them, and other hardware issues can occur. No matter what, a problem with your memory chip spells disaster for your Windows client system.

Usually, third-party hardware vendors provide utility programs with their computers that can be used for performing hardware diagnostics on machines to help you find problems. These utilities are a good first step to resolving intermittent problems, but Windows 10/11 comes with many utilities that can help you diagnose and fix your issues.

In this chapter, I'll cover the tools and methods used for measuring performance and troubleshooting failures in Windows 10/11. Before you dive into the technical details, however, you should thoroughly understand what you're trying to accomplish and how you'll meet this goal.

Understanding Recovery

One of the worst events you may experience is a computer that won't boot. An even worse experience is discovering that there is no recent backup for that computer. The first step in preparing for disaster recovery is to expect that a disaster will happen at some point and to ensure that you take proactive measures to plan your recovery before the failure occurs. Here are some of the preparations you can make:

- Keep your computer up-to-date with Windows Update (covered in Chapter 1, "Windows Client Installation").

- Perform regular system backups.

- Use current software to scan for malware (such as viruses, spyware, and adware), and make sure you have the most recent updates.

- Perform regular administrative functions, such as monitoring the logs in the Event Viewer utility.

No matter how many safeguards you enact, eventually you'll likely need to recover a system. Table 7.1 summarizes some of the Windows 10/11 utilities and options you can use to assist in performing system recovery. All these Windows 10/11 recovery techniques are covered in detail in this chapter.

TABLE 7.1   Windows 10/11 recovery techniques

Recovery technique	When to use
Event Viewer	If the Windows client operating system can be loaded through normal mode or Safe Mode, one of the first places to look for hints about the problem is Event Viewer. Event Viewer displays system, security, and application logs.
Safe Mode	This is generally your starting point for system recovery. Safe Mode loads the absolute minimum of services and drivers that are needed to boot Windows 10/11. If you can boot your computer to Safe Mode and you suspect that you have a system conflict, you can temporarily disable an application or processes, troubleshoot services, or uninstall software.
Startup Repair tool	If your computer will not boot to Safe Mode, you can use the Startup Repair tool to replace corrupted system files. This option will not help if you have hardware errors, however.
Backup and Restore	You should use this utility to safeguard your computer. If necessary, you can use the Backup and Restore (Windows 7) utility to restore personal files from backup media and to restore a complete image of your computer.

TABLE 7.1   Windows 10/11 recovery techniques *(continued)*

Recovery technique	When to use
Driver Rollback	If you install a driver that causes issues on your system, you can use the Driver Rollback utility to return the driver to its previous version. Use Device Manager to access the Driver Rollback utility. Right-click the hardware component and choose Properties. Then click the Driver tab, and the Roll Back Driver button (Driver Rollback) will be there.
System Restore	System Restore is used to create known checkpoints of your system's configuration. In the event that your system becomes misconfigured, you can restore the system configuration to an earlier version of the checkpoint.

Knowing the Startup/Boot Options

The Windows 10/11 advanced boot options can be used to troubleshoot errors that keep Windows 10/11 from successfully booting. Figure 7.1 shows the Advanced Boot Options screen. These advanced boot options are covered in the following sections.

FIGURE 7.1   Advanced Options screen

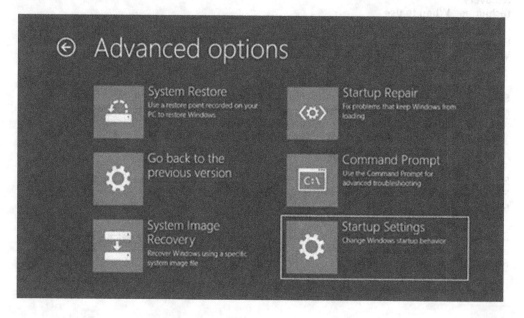

In Windows 7 and earlier versions, to access the advanced boot options, you pressed the F8 key during startup. Starting with Windows 8, Microsoft changed this. To access the Windows 10/11 advanced boot options, hold the Shift key down and choose the Restart option (from either the login screen or the Start Menu). This will bring up the Advanced Boot Options menu, which offers numerous options for booting Windows 10/11.

Starting in Safe Mode

When your computer will not start, one of the fundamental troubleshooting techniques is to simplify the configuration as much as possible. This is especially important when you do not know the cause of your problem and you have a complex configuration. After you have simplified the configuration, you can determine whether the problem is in the basic configuration or is a result of your complex configuration.

If the problem is in the basic configuration, you have a starting point for troubleshooting. If the problem is not in the basic configuration, you should proceed to restore each configuration option you removed, one at a time. This helps you to identify what is causing the error.

If Windows 10/11 will not load, you can attempt to load the operating system in Safe Mode. When you run Windows 10/11 in Safe Mode, you are simplifying your Windows configuration as much as possible. There are two versions: Safe Mode and Safe Mode with Networking. Safe Mode with Networking adds the network drivers and services that you will need in order to access the Internet and other computers on the network.

The Windows Recovery Environment (WinRE) will automatically boot after two failed attempts to boot the operating system. You can then perform a Safe Mode boot from the advanced boot options.

The drivers that are loaded with Safe Mode include basic ones for the mouse, monitor, keyboard, hard drive, standard video driver, and default system services.

Safe Mode is considered a diagnostic mode, so you do not have access to all of the features and devices in Windows 10/11 that you have access to when you boot normally.

Windows 10/11 offers a few startup settings when you're trying to repair your Windows client system. Figure 7.2 shows the settings that are offered when you boot into Startup Settings.

When the Startup Settings screen appears, you then have the ability to choose to enter a Safe Mode (three versions). Once a computer is booted into Safe Mode, you will see the text Safe Mode in the four corners of your desktop, as shown in Figure 7.3.

FIGURE 7.2   Startup Settings screen

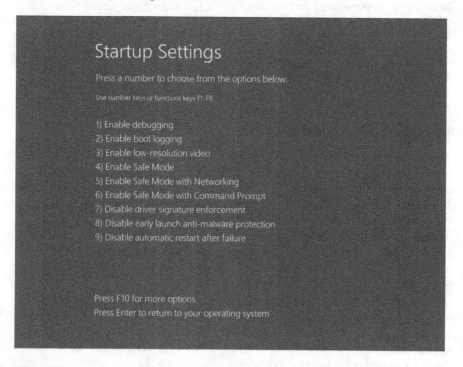

FIGURE 7.3   A computer running in Safe Mode

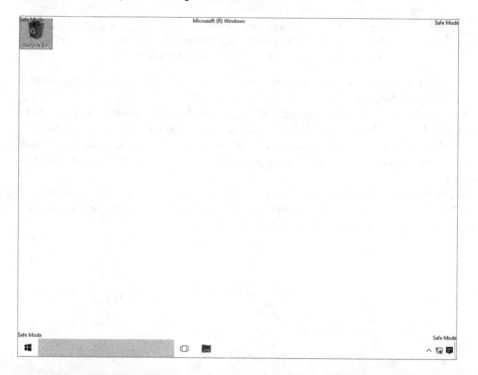

If you boot to Safe Mode, check all of your computer's hardware and software settings in Device Manager and try to determine why Windows 10/11 will not boot properly. After you take steps to fix the problem, try to boot to Windows client as you normally would.

In Exercise 7.1, you will boot your computer to Safe Mode.

EXERCISE 7.1

Booting Your Windows 10/11 Computer to Safe Mode from the Sign-In Screen

1. On the Windows sign-in screen, press and hold the Shift key while you select Power ≫ Restart.

2. After the computer restarts to the Choose An Option screen, select Troubleshoot, as shown in Figure 7.4.

FIGURE 7.4   Choose An Option screen

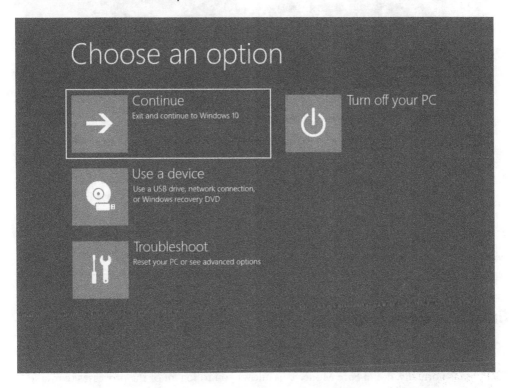

EXERCISE 7.1 *(continued)*

3. On the Troubleshoot screen, select Advanced Options (shown in Figure 7.5).

FIGURE 7.5   Troubleshoot screen

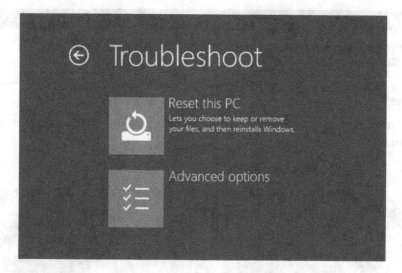

4. On the Advanced options screen, select Startup Settings.

5. On the Startup Settings screen, click the Restart button. The system will reboot into the Startup Settings screen.

6. After the computer restarts, you'll see a list of options. Select 4 or press F4 to start your PC in Safe Mode. Or if you'll need to use the Internet, select 5 or press F5 for Safe Mode with Networking.

7. When Windows 10 starts, log in.

Don't restart your computer yet; you will do this as a part of the next exercise.

Enabling Boot Logging

Boot logging creates a log file that tracks the loading of drivers and services. When you choose the Enable Boot Logging option from the Advanced Boot Options menu, Windows 10/11 loads normally, not in Safe Mode. This allows you to log all of the processes that take place during a normal boot sequence. If you select the option Enabling Boot Logging from the Advanced Boot Options menu, you can perform the steps in Exercise 7.2 to view the results.

There are several other ways to enable boot logging in Windows 10/11. One way is by using MSConfig, a GUI tool that allows you to configure various startup operating system options.

To enable boot logging in Windows 10/11 using MSConfig, perform the following:

1. Press [Windows] key + R and type **msconfig** in the Run box. Press Enter.

2. If it appears, confirm the UAC prompt and then go to the Boot tab.

3. Under the Boot options, select the check box next to Boot Log.

4. You may be prompted to restart the computer. If you click Restart, the operating system will be rebooted.

This log file can be used to troubleshoot the boot process. When logging is enabled, the log file is written to `C:\WINDOWS\Ntbtlog.txt`. A sample of the `Ntbtlog.txt` file is shown in Figure 7.6.

FIGURE 7.6   A Windows 10/11 boot log file

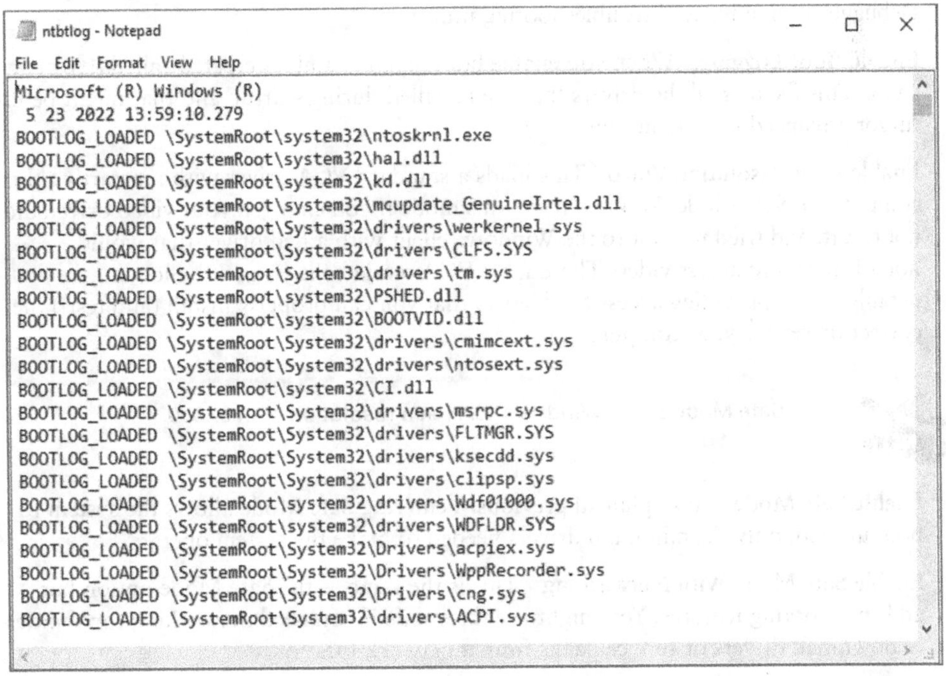

```
ntbtlog - Notepad                                           —   □   ✕
File   Edit   Format   View   Help
Microsoft (R) Windows (R)
 5 23 2022 13:59:10.279
BOOTLOG_LOADED \SystemRoot\system32\ntoskrnl.exe
BOOTLOG_LOADED \SystemRoot\system32\hal.dll
BOOTLOG_LOADED \SystemRoot\system32\kd.dll
BOOTLOG_LOADED \SystemRoot\system32\mcupdate_GenuineIntel.dll
BOOTLOG_LOADED \SystemRoot\System32\drivers\werkernel.sys
BOOTLOG_LOADED \SystemRoot\System32\drivers\CLFS.SYS
BOOTLOG_LOADED \SystemRoot\System32\drivers\tm.sys
BOOTLOG_LOADED \SystemRoot\system32\PSHED.dll
BOOTLOG_LOADED \SystemRoot\system32\BOOTVID.dll
BOOTLOG_LOADED \SystemRoot\System32\drivers\cmimcext.sys
BOOTLOG_LOADED \SystemRoot\System32\drivers\ntosext.sys
BOOTLOG_LOADED \SystemRoot\system32\CI.dll
BOOTLOG_LOADED \SystemRoot\System32\drivers\msrpc.sys
BOOTLOG_LOADED \SystemRoot\System32\drivers\FLTMGR.SYS
BOOTLOG_LOADED \SystemRoot\System32\drivers\ksecdd.sys
BOOTLOG_LOADED \SystemRoot\System32\drivers\clipsp.sys
BOOTLOG_LOADED \SystemRoot\system32\drivers\Wdf01000.sys
BOOTLOG_LOADED \SystemRoot\system32\drivers\WDFLDR.SYS
BOOTLOG_LOADED \SystemRoot\System32\Drivers\acpiex.sys
BOOTLOG_LOADED \SystemRoot\System32\Drivers\WppRecorder.sys
BOOTLOG_LOADED \SystemRoot\System32\Drivers\cng.sys
BOOTLOG_LOADED \SystemRoot\System32\drivers\ACPI.sys
```

In Exercise 7.2, you will view the boot log file.

EXERCISE 7.2

Viewing the Boot Log File

1. Click File Explorer (the folder icon on the taskbar) and browse to `C:\WINDOWS\Ntbtlog.txt`. Double-click this file.

2. Examine the contents of your boot log file.

3. Shut down your computer and restart it without using Advanced Boot Options.

The boot log file is cumulative. Each time you boot to Safe Mode, you are writing to this file. This enables you to make changes, reboot, and see whether you have fixed any problems. If you want to start from scratch, you should manually delete this file and reboot to an Advanced Boot Options menu selection that supports logging (Enable Boot Logging).

Using Other Startup Setting Options

In this section, you will learn about additional Startup Settings menu modes. These include the following options:

Enable Debugging   This runs the Kernel Debugger, if it is installed. The Kernel Debugger is an advanced troubleshooting utility.

Enable Boot Logging   When you enable boot logging, a file is created called Ntbtlog .txt. This file lists all the drivers that are installed during startup and that might be useful for advanced troubleshooting.

Enable Low-Resolution Video   This loads a standard VGA driver without starting the computer in Safe Mode. You might use this mode if you changed your video driver, did not test it, and tried to boot to the Windows client with a bad driver that would not allow you to access video. The Enable VGA mode bails you out by loading a default driver, providing access to video so that you can properly install (and test!) the correct driver for your computer.

Safe Mode starts Windows 10/11 at a resolution of 800×600.

Enable Safe Mode   As explained previously, entering Safe Mode allows the system to boot up with only the minimum drivers needed to make the system operate.

Enable Safe Mode With Networking   This is the same as the Safe Mode option but adds networking features. You might use this mode if you need networking capabilities to download drivers or service packs from a network location.

Enable Safe Mode With Command Prompt   This starts the computer in Safe Mode, but after you log into Windows 10/11, only a command prompt is displayed. This mode does not provide access to the desktop. Experienced troubleshooters use this mode.

Disable Driver Signature Enforcement   This allows drivers to be installed even if they do not contain valid signatures.

Disable Early Launch Anti-Malware Protection   Windows 10/11 has a feature called Secure Boot. Secure Boot helps protect the Windows boot configuration and its components. Secure Boot also loads an Early Launch Anti-malware (ELAM) driver. Choosing this option disables the Early Launch Anti-malware driver.

Disable Automatic Restart After Failure   This prevents Windows from restarting when a critical error causes Windows to fail. This option should be used only when Windows fails every time you restart, preventing you from accessing the desktop or any configuration options.

Press F10 for more options   If you select F10, you will see another menu with a single item that allows you to launch the Windows Recovery Environment. This is what you access when you boot from a Recovery Drive. Press F10 again to return to the first menu or press Enter to start Windows normally. The Windows Recovery Environment (WinRE) is used to repair common causes of bootable operating systems problems. By default, WinRE is preloaded into the Windows 10/11 for Desktop editions (Home, Pro, Enterprise, and Education).

Press Enter to Return to Your Operating System   This boots the Windows client system in the default manner.

Understanding System Restore

System restores are actually a two-part process. First, in the Windows client operating system you create system restore points. These are snapshots of the Windows 10/11 system so that in the event you need to revert to one of these snapshots, you can.

So, after you create some system restore points, the System Restore option in the Advanced Options allows you to revert your PC to an earlier point in time. Restore points are generated when you or a user installs a new application, driver, or Windows update or when you manually create a restore point.

When you restore to a previous point, the user's personal files won't be affected, but restores do remove applications, drivers, and updates installed after the restore point was made.

To enable System Protection (needed to create restore points), in Control Panel click the System icon. System Protection and restore points will be covered in greater detail later in this chapter. This will open the About page; on Windows 10, on the right-hand side under Related Settings, select System Protection. If using Windows 11, the System Protection link will be under the Device Specifications section. When you click the link, it will open the System Properties dialog box. Click the Configure button (see Figure 7.7) to turn on System Protection.

Once you have enabled System Protection in Control Panel, you then need to open the System Restore application. To do that, follow these steps:

1. Open Control panel using your preferred method.

2. Click Recovery in Control panel.

3. In the Recovery window, click Configure System Restore (as shown in Figure 7.8).

4. On the next screen, click Create. This will allow you to create a system restore point.

FIGURE 7.7 Configure button for System Protection

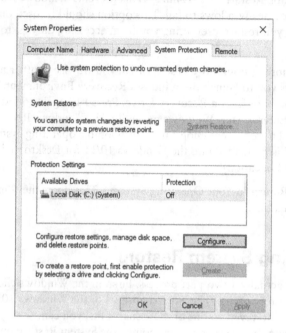

FIGURE 7.8 Open System Restore

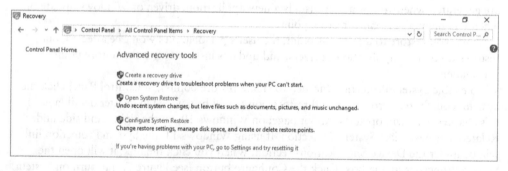

 The steps to create restore points as well as restore and clean up old restore points will be explained in the section "Maintaining Windows 10/11 with Backup and Restore" later in this chapter.

Before you can use System Restore to fix a crashed computer, you need to create a recovery drive. Recovery drives allow you to create a backup drive in the event that a PC can't start. After the recovery drive is created, you can then use that drive to recover from a system crash.

To use the recovery drive to fix a crashed computer, boot the system into the Advanced Options and then choose System Restore. You will be asked for a username and then a password, and the system will continue using one of the restore points that was selected.

Using the System Image Recovery

Another way to protect your Windows client computer system is to create and use system images. System images are exact copies of the Windows client drive. System images, by default, include the drives that are needed for Windows to function properly. System images include Windows and all of the system settings, programs, and files.

System images work well in the event of a major hard disk or computer crash. System images allow you to restore all of the contents of the crashed system and get the system back up and running. When you restore a crashed system from an image, the entire system is restored. It's a complete restore of the computer system. This means that you can't pick and choose what programs you want to install. It's an all-or-nothing restore.

This is the reason you should also make sure that you do regular backups. By making sure all of your backups are up-to-date and by making sure you have a system image, you are completely covered in the event of a major crash.

To create a system image, open Control panel using your preferred method. In Control panel, open File History. Once you're in the File History application, click the System Image Backup link in the lower-left corner (see Figure 7.9).

FIGURE 7.9   System Image Backup link

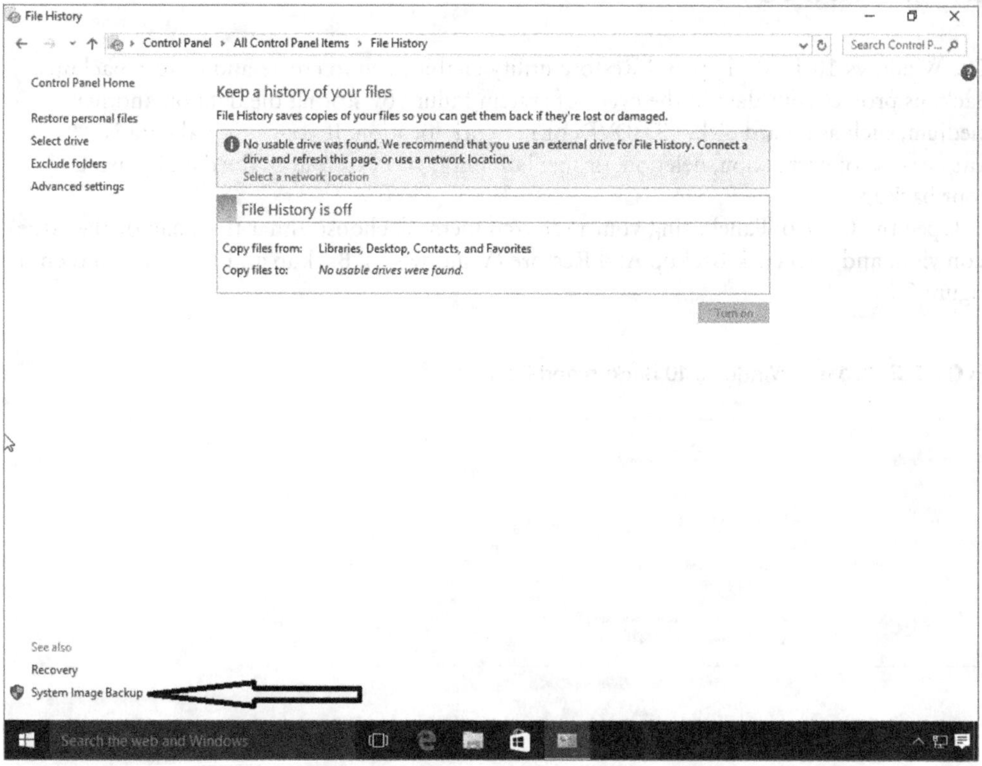

The steps to create a System Image Backup will be explained later in this chapter in the section "Maintaining Windows 10/11 with Backup and Restore."

Using the Startup Repair Tool

Another option that is available in the Advanced Options menu is the Startup Repair tool. If your Windows client computer will not boot because of missing or corrupted system files, you can use the Startup Repair tool to correct these problems. Startup Repair cannot repair hardware failures. Additionally, Startup Repair cannot recover personal files that have been corrupted, damaged by viruses, or deleted. To ensure that you can recover your personal files, you should use the Backup and Restore utility discussed in the next section.

If Startup Repair is unable to correct the problem, you might have to reinstall Windows 10/11, but this should be done as a last resort. This is one reason you should always back up your Windows client machine.

Maintaining Windows 10/11 with Backup and Restore

The Windows 10/11 Backup and Restore utility enables you to create and restore backups. Backups protect your data in the event of system failure by storing the data on another medium, such as a hard disk, CD, DVD, or network location. If your original data is lost because of corruption, deletion, or media failure, you can restore the data by using your backup.

Open the Control Panel using your preferred method, choose either the small or the large icon view, and then click Backup And Restore (Windows 7). Backup and Restore is shown in Figure 7.10.

FIGURE 7.10   Windows 10 Backup and Restore

Creating a Backup

You can see in Figure 7.10 that no backups of this Windows client machine have been made. To set up a backup, click the Set Up Backup link on the right side of the Backup And Restore window. Choosing Set Up Backup launches a wizard that takes you through the process of creating a backup. The Backup Wizard first asks you for a location to save your backup. This location can be a hard disk (removable or fixed), a CD, a DVD, or even a network location.

Next, you are asked to either let Windows 10/11 choose the files and folders to back up or let you manually select the resources you want to back up. In your manual selection, you can choose just the data libraries of Windows 10/11 for you as a user or other users. You can also choose to create a backup of the Windows client system files. If you want to choose other files and folders, you have the option of selecting any resources individually on your hard disk(s).

The final page of the wizard enables you to view the items you have selected as well as set up a schedule for your backups to occur. If you're happy with the setup, click the Save Settings And Run Backup button. The backup commences, and you are able to restore the resources, if necessary, in the future. Figure 7.11 shows my Windows client machine right after I chose to save the settings and run a backup. You can see the backup in progress and the date and time of my last backup.

FIGURE 7.11   Windows client backup status

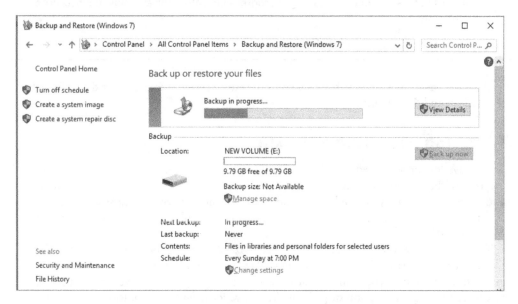

Windows 10/11 *cannot* back up encrypted files. To back up encrypted files, you need to manually copy all encrypted files to an external hard drive or decrypt the files before the backup.

In Exercise 7.3, you will make a backup of your files. This exercise assumes that you haven't yet configured an automatic backup.

EXERCISE 7.3

Backing Up Files

1. Open Control Panel using your preferred method, ensure that you are using either small or large icons, and then select Backup And Restore (Windows 7).

2. Click the Back Up Now button.

3. Select the location where you want to save your backup, and then click Next. In this example, I will use my D: drive.

4. The What Do You Want To Back Up? screen appears. Click the Let Me Choose radio button and then click Next.

5. Select the files that you would like to back up. Click Next.

6. On the Review Your Backup Settings screen, you can select how often you want a backup to be automatically performed. To start the backup, click the Save Settings And Run Backup button.

    Windows begins backing up files, and a progress indicator indicates how the backup is progressing.

7. When the backup is complete, click Close.

After you have created your backup, you can restore system files and user data files with the Backup and Restore utility.

Restoring Files from a Backup

If you have lost or destroyed files that you still want on your Windows client system, you can restore them from your backup. To restore files to your computer, launch the Backup and Restore program by typing **backup and restore** in the Windows client search box. Assuming the media where your backup was saved is available, you can click the Restore My Files button.

Clicking Restore My Files launches a restore wizard that prompts you to search for the files you want to restore. You can select multiple files and folders. When you have selected all the files and folders you want to restore, click Next, and you will have one final option: restore to the original location or pick an alternative location for restoration. After you make the restore-location decision, click Restore. The restore operation commences, and your original files and folders are available for you from the backup media.

You also have options in the Backup And Restore window to restore all users' files or to select another backup to restore files from. You would use this second option if you saved your backup to multiple locations and the last one (the one listed in the backup section) is not the set of backup files you want to use in your current session. Other than just restoring files and folders, you have the choice to use other advanced backup options.

In Exercise 7.4, you will restore some files. This exercise assumes that you created a backup in Exercise 7.3.

EXERCISE 7.4

Restoring Files

1. Open Control Panel, ensure that you are using either small or large icons, and then select Backup And Restore (Windows 7).

2. Click the Restore My Files button.

3. At the Restore Files screen, click the Browse For Folders button.

4. Click the Microsoft Windows Backup link in the left window. Then double-click the backup that you created in the previous exercise. Choose the folder that you want to restore (I chose the `Program Files` folder, but you need to choose a folder with enough free space) and click Add. Click Next to continue.

5. Select whether you want files saved in the original location or a different location. To begin the restore, click Restore.

6. When the restore is complete, click Finish.

Recovering Files from OneDrive

As explained in Chapter 3, "Managing Data," Microsoft has a subscription-based storage system called OneDrive. Microsoft's OneDrive is built into Windows 10/11 by default. One-Drive is a cloud-based storage subscription service so home users can store their documents and then access those documents from anywhere in the world (provided that you have Internet access).

OneDrive was designed for the average home user who is looking to store data in a safe, secure, cloud-based environment. OneDrive, when first released, was also a consideration for corporate environments, but with the release of Windows Azure, OneDrive is really intended for the home user or corporate user who wants to store some of their own personal documents in the cloud. Corporations would be more inclined to use Microsoft Azure with all of its corporate benefits.

Exercise 7.5 will show you how to set up a OneDrive account for your user account. To do this, you must have a Microsoft account. You get 5 GB for free from Microsoft on the OneDrive cloud-based storage.

If you did Exercise 3.2 in Chapter 3, please skip the following exercise.

EXERCISE 7.5

Configuring OneDrive

1. Open OneDrive using your preferred method.

2. Log into OneDrive using your Microsoft account.

3. You will get a screen that shows where your files will be located on your system. Click the Next button.

4. On the Sync Files screen, choose what folders you want to sync with Microsoft and then click Next.

   A screen will appear telling you that your OneDrive is set up and ready to go.

5. Click the Open My OneDrive Folder button to open your folders and Microsoft OneDrive.

6. Close OneDrive.

Now that the OneDrive subscription has been set up, you can recover files and folders by clicking Windows Explorer and then choosing OneDrive from the left side. You can recover any of the files and folders that were stored on OneDrive.

Using the WBAdmin Command Utility

Administrators have the ability to configure and manage backups and restores through the command prompt using a utility called WBAdmin. WBAdmin replaces the NTBackup utility that was released with previous versions of Windows. WBAdmin allows you to back up and restore your operating system, volumes, files, folders, and applications, all from a command prompt.

You must be a member of the Administrators group to configure a regularly scheduled backup. To perform any other tasks using WBAdmin, you must be a member of either the Backup Operators group or the Administrators group, or you must have been delegated the appropriate permissions.

To run Wbadmin.exe, you must start it from an elevated command prompt. As mentioned earlier in this book, you can access the command prompt on Windows 10 by clicking Start, right-clicking Command Prompt, and then selecting Run As Administrator. However, on Windows 11, the command prompt is not located directly on the Start Menu; it is now located in the Windows Tools folder. To open the command prompt in Windows 11, click the Start button and then select All Apps. Scroll down and select the Windows Tools folder. Right-click Command Prompt and select Run As Administrator.

Table 7.2 shows the Windows 10/11 Wbadmin command switches and their descriptions.

TABLE 7.2 Wbadmin switches

Command	Description
Wbadmin Start Backup	Runs a one-time backup
Wbadmin Stop job	Stops the currently running backup or recovery job
Wbadmin get versions	Shows the details of a backup
Wbadmin get items	Lists items contained in a backup
Wbadmin get status	Shows the status of the currently running operation

Using Advanced Backup Options

In the main Backup And Restore window, you have options in the left pane to turn off the schedule, create a system image, and create a system repair disk.

Choosing the Turn Off Schedule option lets you take your backup out of the current backup scheduling in Task Scheduler. Creating a system image lets you back up critical operating system files for restoration later if your operating system becomes corrupted. Creating a system repair disc allows you to create a bootable disc with which you will have a limited set of repair utilities and the ability to restore your backup files if necessary.

Creating a System Image

A *system image* enables you to take a snapshot of the entire hard disk and capture that image to a specific location so that you can restore that image at a later date.

To create a system image of your entire computer, select the Create A System Image link on the left side of the Backup and Restore utility. When creating a system image, you can save that image to a hard disk, a DVD, or a network location.

In Exercise 7.6, you will create a system image and save it to a local hard disk.

EXERCISE 7.6

Creating a System Image

1. Open Control Panel, ensure that you are using either small or large icons, and then select Backup And Restore (Windows 7).

2. Click the Create A System Image link on the left side.

3. Choose the location where you want to save the image. I am choosing the local D: drive. Click Next.

4. On the Confirm screen, click Start Backup.

5. A dialog box may appear, asking whether you want to create a system repair disc. Click the No button. If you want to create a system repair disc, you will need a DVD burner and a DVD.

6. When the image is complete, click the Close button.

After you create a system image, you may need to restore it. Let's take a look at the steps needed to complete a restore.

Restoring an Image

When you need to restore an image, you will use the System Image Recovery tool. To restore an image using this tool, you must perform the following steps:

1. Boot your computer by using the Windows 10/11 media, or use the recovery partition instructions provided by your computer manufacturer.

2. When the Install Windows dialog box appears, select the language, the time and currency format, and the keyboard or input method. Click Next to continue.

3. The Install Now button appears in the center of the screen. Click Repair Your Computer in the lower-left corner.

4. This opens the Windows Recovery Environment (WinRE), where you will choose the Troubleshoot option, then choose Advanced Options.

5. The Advanced Options dialog box appears. You can choose one of the following options:

- System Restore
- Startup Repair
- Uninstall Updates
- Command Prompt
- System Image Recovery
- UEFI Firmware Settings (if applicable)

Choose System Image Recovery to continue.

6. Select the user account that has administrative privileges and then enter the password for that user account.

7. The Re-image Your Computer Wizard will appear and the Use The Latest Available System Image (Recommended) option will be selected by default. If the image is okay, you can click Next to continue.

8. If you want to select a different image, you can choose Select A System Image, then click Next and follow the prompts to select the location of the image and the image you want to restore.

9. You will then be presented with a dialog box where you can select additional restore options, such as installing drivers, and formatting and repartitioning disks as well as choosing if the system will automatically install updates and reboot. Click Next.

10. You will be asked to review your selections. Click Finish to continue.

11. You will be warned one final time that all the data on the drive is to be replaced; you can then click Yes to continue.

 If you were not provided with the Windows 10/11 media when you purchased your computer, the computer manufacturer might have placed the files on a recovery partition. Check with the manufacturer for more information.

Another way of restoring an image using the System Image Recovery is by performing the following. In Windows 10, go to Start ➤ Settings ➤ Update & Security ➤ Recovery. In the Advanced Startup section on the right, click the Restart Now button under Advanced Startup. In Windows 11, go to Start ➤ Settings ➤ System ➤ Recovery and then click the Restart Now button next to Advanced Startup.

Now, in either Windows 10 or Windows 11, in the Choose An Option window, choose Troubleshoot ➤ Advanced Options ➤ System Image Recovery ➤ See More Recovery Options. Select System Image Recovery. Then, follow the prompts to restore the image file.

Using System Protection

System Protection, as mentioned earlier, is a feature of Windows 10/11 that creates a backup and saves the configuration information of your computer's system files and settings on a regular basis. System Protection saves multiple previous versions of saved configurations rather than just overwriting them. This makes it possible to return to multiple configurations in your Windows 10/11 history, known as *restore points.* These restore points are created before most significant events, such as installing a new driver. Restore points are also created automatically every seven days. System Protection is turned on by default in Windows 10/11 for any drive formatted with NTFS.

You manage System Protection and the restore points from the System Protection tab of the System Properties dialog box, which was mentioned previously and shown in Figure 7.7. You can also access this tab directly by typing **restore point** into the Windows client search box or by clicking the Recovery icon in Control Panel.

Clicking the System Restore button launches the System Restore Wizard, which walks you through the process of returning your Windows client to a previous point in time.

Also on the System Protection tab of the System Properties dialog box is the Protection Settings section, where you can configure any of your available drives. Select the drive for which you would like to modify the configuration and click the Configure button. The System Protection configuration dialog box for the drive appears.

The System Protection dialog box allows you to enable or disable system protection for the drive. When you enable protection, you can opt for previous versions of files or previous versions of files and system settings. You also have the ability to set the maximum disk space that the restore points will use for storage. Another function of the System Protection dialog box for the selected disk is to delete all restore points (including system settings and previous versions of files) by clicking the Delete button.

One tool included with restore points is shadow copies. Shadow copies are copies of files and folders that Windows automatically saves as part of a restore point. Normally, restore points are made only once a day if you have enabled System Protection. If System Protection is enabled, Windows will then automatically create shadow copies of files that have been modified since the last restore point was made.

One advantage of using restore points and shadow copies is the ability to restore files and folders using the Previous Versions tab. When you click any folder and choose Properties, the last tab on the right is Previous Versions. You can easily restore any folder by choosing one of these previous versions.

Creating Restore Points

Restore points contain Registry and system information as it was at a certain point in time. These restore points are created at the following times:

- Weekly
  - Before installing applications or drivers
  - Before significant system events
  - Before System Restore is used to restore files (so you can undo the changes if necessary)
  - Manually upon request

In Exercise 7.7, you will manually create a restore point.

EXERCISE 7.7

Creating a Restore Point

1. Open Control Panel.

2. Select Recovery.

3. In the Recovery window, select Configure System Restore.

4. Click the Create button at the bottom of the screen.

5. In the System Protection dialog box, enter a description for the restore point. Click Create.

6. A dialog box states that the restore point was created. Click Close.

Restoring Restore Points

You can restore previously created restore points with System Restore. The restore operation will restore system files and settings but will not affect your personal files.

WARNING

System Restore will also remove any programs that have been installed since the restore point was created.

In Exercise 7.8, you will revert your system configuration to a previously captured restore point.

EXERCISE 7.8

Restoring a Restore Point

1.   Open Control Panel.

2.   Select System ➤ System Protection.

3.   Click the System Restore button. Click Next on the Restore System Files And Settings screen to continue.

4.   Choose the restore point created in the previous exercise and click Next to continue.

5.   Review your restore point selection, and click Finish to continue.

6.   Click Yes to confirm that you want System Restore to continue.

7.   System Restore will restore your system and reboot your computer to apply the changes. You should see a message stating that System Restore has restored your computer. Click OK to close the dialog box.

Cleaning Up Old Restore Points

One problem with creating multiple restore points is that they start to take up a large amount of your hard disk. You will need to clean up old restore points from time to time, and you can accomplish this task by using the Disk Cleanup utility.

The Disk Cleanup utility removes temporary files, empties the Recycle Bin, and removes a variety of system files and other items that you no longer need. When using the Disk Cleanup utility, you can also click the More Options tab and choose Programs And Features and System Restore And Shadow Copies to clean them up as well.

NOTE

The More Options tab is available when you choose to clean up files from all users on the computer.

In Windows 10, to use the Disk Cleanup utility click Start ≻ Windows System ≻ Control Panel ≻ Administrative Tools ≻ Disk Cleanup.

Or, in both Windows 10 and Windows 11, to delete temporary files, follow these steps:

1. In the search box on the taskbar, type **disk cleanup**, and select Disk Cleanup from the list of results.

2. Select the drive you want to clean up, and then click OK.

3. Under Files To Delete, select the file types you want to get rid of.

4. Click OK.

In Windows 11, Microsoft introduced a version of the Storage Sense tool that takes care of your drive and makes sure that it doesn't run out of free space. Storage Sense will be discussed in greater detail in the next section. However, if you are more comfortable with using the Disk Cleanup utility, you can still use it in Windows 11, but it has been moved and is a bit harder to locate. There are several methods to open the Disk Cleanup utility on a Windows 11 machine; you can:

- Press [Windows] key + R and type **cleanmgr.exe** to run the Disk Cleanup tool.

- Search for Disk Cleanup and select the Disk Cleanup app.

- Depending on the build of Windows 11 you are using, you can open File Explorer, navigate to the This PC folder, right-click the drive, and select Properties. In the Properties dialog box, select Disk Cleanup or Storage Usage.

Storage Sense

Storage Sense is used to manage your computer's storage. It works with OneDrive, as a silent assistant, to automatically free up space. When configured, it can empty the Recycle Bin, delete temporary files, and do other things automatically.

Storage Sense is available for Windows 10 version 1809 and later. Storage Sense runs only on the C: drive, so your OneDrive location must reside on the system partition (C:\). Storage Sense ignores other locations, including physical drives, such as CD and DVD drives, and logical partitions, such as D: drives.

To use Storage Sense, you must first enable it. To do so, follow these steps:

1. Click Start ≻ Settings ≻ System ≻ Storage.

2. Use the toggle switch to turn on Storage Sense.

Once Storage Sense has been enabled, you can then customize how it runs. You will see the following options:

Cleanup Of Temporary Files   Enable this toggle if you want to delete temporary files.

Automatic User Content Cleanup   Enable this toggle to run Storage Sense automatically.

Configure Cleanup Schedules ➤ Run Storage Sense   From here you can select when you want Storage Sense to run. The options are:

- Every Day
- Every Week
- Every Month
- During Low Free Disk Space (default)

Configure Cleanup Schedules ➤ Delete Files In My Recycle Bin If They Have Been There For Over   Select the lifespan of your bin files. Storage Sense will delete the files at the selected option. The options are:

- Never
- 1 Day
- 14 Days
- 30 Days
- 60 Days

Configure Cleanup Schedules ➤ Delete Files In My Download Folders If They Haven't Been Opened For More Than Use this section to delete redundant downloads. The options are:

- Never
- 1 Day
- 14 Days
- 30 Days
- 60 Days

Locally available cloud content   Use this section to clean up unused items from your cloud storage. The options are:

- Never
- 1 Day
- 14 Days
- 30 Days
- 60 Days

To tell Storage Sense how often to run and what to clean up, perform these steps:

1. Click Start ➤ Settings ➤ System ➤ Storage.
2. Select Configure Storage Sense or run it now.
3. Select your desired settings, including when to run and how often files are cleaned up.

With Storage Sense you can select your preferences for deleting temporary files. Under the section Temporary Files, you can choose when files from your Recycle Bin or Downloads folder are deleted. Options include:

- Items in the Recycle Bin will be deleted based on how long they have been in the Recycle Bin.

- Items in the Downloads folder will be deleted based on how long they have been unopened. The default is to never delete these files unless you specify.

- Keep Delete temporary files that my apps aren't using selected to clean up unneeded files associated with apps on your PC.

Cloud files can exist locally on the disk or be available online-only when you are signed into your cloud account. To manage that content, you can choose the conditions for when inactive files are made online-only; under Content Will Become Online-Only If Not Opened For More Than, select your preferred amount of time (see Figure 7.12).

FIGURE 7.12 Storage Sense Locally Available Cloud Content

Locally available cloud content

Storage sense can free up space by removing unused cloud-backed content from your device. Content flagged as "Always keep on this device" will not be affected.

Click here for more information

OneDrive - Personal
Content will become online-only if not opened for more than:

| Never | ∨ |

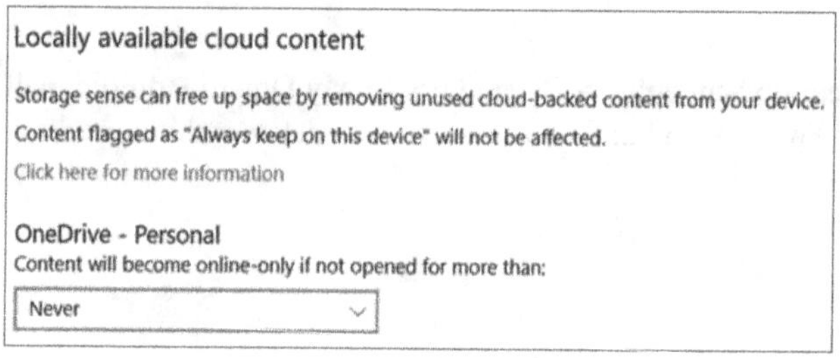

Using the Recycle Bin

Now we are going to talk about an icon that we have seen on our desktop for many years called the Recycle Bin. The Recycle Bin is a temporary storage container that holds deleted files. The advantage of having a temporary storage container is that you can restore or recycle the files to their original location. So basically, it allows you to undelete a deleted file.

When a file or folder is deleted on a computer, it isn't actually deleted. When files or folders get deleted, they get placed into the Recycle Bin. This works well because if you change your mind or realize that you actually need the file or folder, you can undelete it and it gets restored. The Recycle Bin allows you to perform a refresh or recycle of files that were deleted but shouldn't have been.

The Recycle Bin allows you to restore files or folders multiple ways. You can right-click the item and choose Restore or you can use the Manage tab (as shown in Figure 7.13).

FIGURE 7.13   Manage tab in Recycle Bin

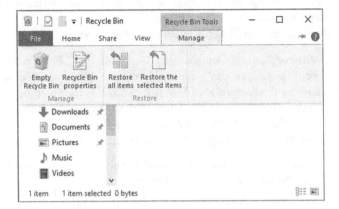

In Exercise 7.9, you will create a document and then delete the document. Then you will use the Recycle Bin to restore the document to its original location.

EXERCISE 7.9

Using the Recycle Bin

1. On the Windows client desktop, right-click and choose New Text Document.

2. Create a new test document called **Test.txt**.

3. After the document is created, right-click the document and choose Delete.

4. Double-click to open the Recycle Bin.

5. You can either right-click the Test.txt document and choose Restore or click the document, and then on the Manage tab, choose Restore The Selected Item.

6. Close the Recycle Bin, and the document should be back on the desktop.

Monitoring Windows

Because performance monitoring and optimization are vital functions in network environments of any size, Windows 10/11 includes several monitoring and performance tools.

Introducing Performance Monitor

The first and most useful tool is the Windows 10/11 *Performance Monitor*, which was designed to allow users and system administrators to monitor performance statistics for various operating system parameters. Specifically, you can collect, store, and analyze information about CPU, memory, disk, and network resources using this tool, and these are only a handful of the things you can monitor. By collecting and analyzing performance values, you can identify many potential problems.

You can use the Performance Monitor in the following ways:

Performance Monitor ActiveX Control   The Windows 10/11 Performance Monitor is an ActiveX control that you can place within other applications. Examples of applications that can host the Performance Monitor control include web browsers and client programs such as Microsoft Word and Microsoft Excel. This functionality can make it easy for application developers and system administrators to incorporate the Performance Monitor into their own tools and applications.

Performance Monitor MMC   For more common performance monitoring functions, you'll want to use the built-in Microsoft Management Console (MMC) version of the Performance Monitor.

Data Collector Sets   Windows 10/11 Performance Monitor includes the Data Collector Set. This tool works with performance logs, telling Performance Monitor where the logs are stored and when the log needs to run. The Data Collector Sets also define the credentials used to run the set.

There are numerous ways to access the Performance Monitor MMC:

- In both Windows 10 and 11, you can just search for **performance monitor** or **permon** in the search bar and click it from the best match section.
- In Windows 10, you can open Control Panel, click Administrative Tools, and select Performance Monitor.
- In Windows 11, you can click the Start Menu and select All Apps. Then, scroll down and click Windows Tools. Then click Performance Monitor. The Performance Monitor will open with a handful of default counters.

You can choose from many different methods of monitoring performance when you are using Performance Monitor. A couple of examples are listed here:

- You can look at a snapshot of current activity for a few of the most important counters. This allows you to find areas of potential bottlenecks and monitor the load on your servers at a certain point in time.
- You can save information to a log file for historical reporting and later analysis. This type of information is useful, for example, if you want to compare the load on your servers from three months ago to the current load.

You'll get to take a closer look at this method and many others as you examine Performance Monitor in more detail.

In the following sections, you'll learn about the basics of working with the Windows 10/11 Performance Monitor and other performance tools. Then you'll apply these tools and techniques when you monitor the performance of your network.

NOTE Your Performance Monitor grows as your system grows, and whenever you add services to Windows 10/11, you also add to what you can monitor. You should make sure that, as you install services, you take a look at what it is you can monitor.

Deciding What to Monitor

The first step in monitoring performance is to decide what you want to monitor. In Windows 10/11, the operating system and related services include hundreds of performance statistics that you can track easily. For example, you may want to monitor the processor. This is just one of many items that can be monitored. All performance statistics fall into three main categories that you can choose to measure:

Performance Objects   A *performance object* within Performance Monitor is a collection of various performance statistics that you can monitor. Performance objects are based on various areas of system resources. For example, there are performance objects for the processor and memory as well as for specific services.

Counters   *Counters* are the actual parameters measured by Performance Monitor. They are specific items that are grouped within performance objects. For example, within the Processor performance object, there is a counter for % Processor Time. This counter displays one type of detailed information about the Processor performance object (specifically, the amount of total CPU time all of the processes on the system are using). Another set of counters you can use will allow you to monitor print servers.

Instances   Some counters will have *instances*. An instance further identifies which performance parameter the counter is measuring. A simple example is a server with two CPUs. If you decide you want to monitor processor usage (using the Processor performance object)—specifically, utilization (the % Total Utilization counter)—you must still specify *which* CPU(s) you want to measure. In this example, you would have the choice of monitoring either of the two CPUs or a total value for both (using the Total instance).

To specify which performance objects, counters, and instances you want to monitor, you add them to Performance Monitor using the Add Counters dialog box. Figure 7.14 shows the various options that are available when you add new counters to monitor using Performance Monitor.

The items that you will be able to monitor will be based on your hardware and software configuration. For example, if you have not installed and configured Hyper-V, the options available within the Hyper-V Server performance object will not be available. Or, if you have multiple network adapters or CPUs on the Windows client system, you will have the option of viewing each instance separately or as part of the total value.

FIGURE 7.14   Adding a new Performance Monitor counter

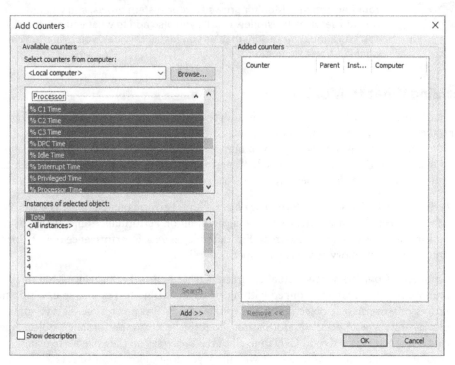

Viewing Performance Information

The Windows 10/11 Performance Monitor was designed to show information in a clear and easy-to-understand format. Performance objects, counters, and instances may be displayed in each of three views. This flexibility allows you to quickly and easily define the information you want to see once and then choose how it will be displayed based on specific needs. Most likely, you will use only one view, but it's helpful to know what other views are available depending on what it is you are trying to assess.

You can use the following main views to review statistics and information on performance:

Line View   The *Line view* is the default display that is presented when you first access the Windows 10/11 Performance Monitor. The chart displays values using the vertical axis and time using the horizontal axis. This view is useful if you want to display values over a period of time or see the changes in these values over that time period. Each point that is plotted on the graph is based on an average value calculated during the sample interval for the measurement being made. For example, you may notice overall CPU utilization starting at a low value at the beginning of the chart and then becoming much higher during later measurements. This indicates that the server has become busier (specifically, with CPU-intensive processes). Figure 7.15 provides an example of the Line view.

FIGURE 7.15   Viewing information in Performance Monitor Line view

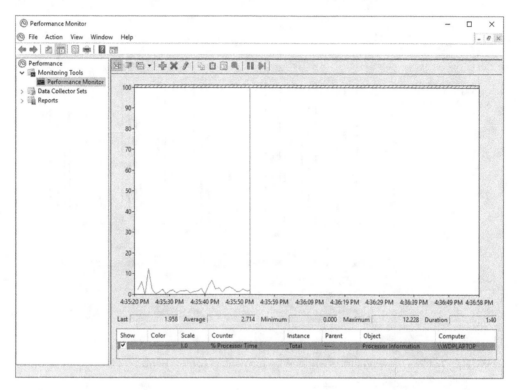

Histogram View   The *Histogram view* shows performance statistics and information using a set of relative bar charts. This view is useful if you want to see a snapshot of the latest value for a given counter. For example, if you were interested in viewing a snapshot of current system performance statistics during each refresh interval, the length of each of the bars in the display would give you a visual representation of each value. It would also allow you to compare measurements visually relative to each other. You can set the histogram to display an average measurement as well as minimum and maximum thresholds. Figure 7.16 shows a typical Histogram view.

Report View   Like the Histogram view, the *Report view* shows performance statistics based on the latest measurement. You can see an average measurement as well as minimum and maximum thresholds. This view is most useful for determining exact values because it provides information in numeric terms, whereas the Chart and Histogram views provide information graphically. Figure 7.17 provides an example of the type of information you'll see in the Report view.

FIGURE 7.16 Viewing information in Performance Monitor Histogram view

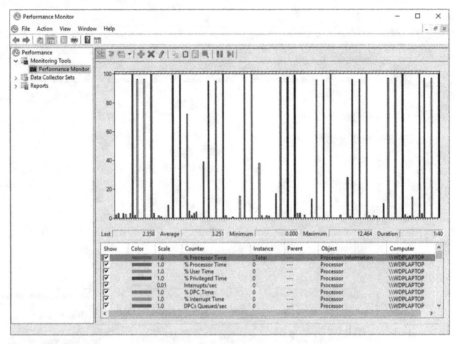

FIGURE 7.17 Viewing information in Performance Monitor Report view

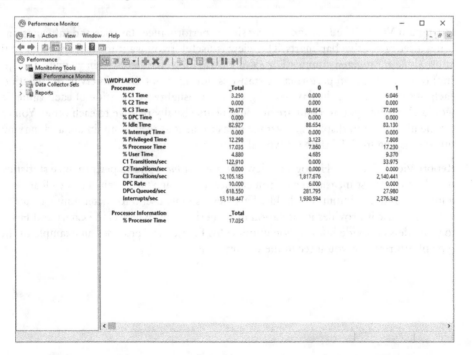

Managing Performance Monitor Properties

You can specify additional settings for viewing performance information within the properties of Performance Monitor. You can access these options by clicking the Properties button in the taskbar or by right-clicking the Performance Monitor display and selecting Properties. You can change these additional settings by using the following tabs:

General Tab   On the General tab (shown in Figure 7.18), you can specify several options that relate to Performance Monitor views:

- You can enable or disable legends (which display information about the various counters), the value bar, and the toolbar.

- For the Report and Histogram views, you can choose which type of information is displayed. The options are Default, Current, Minimum, Maximum, and Average. What you see with each of these options depends on the type of data being collected. These options are not available for the Graph view because the Graph view displays an average value over a period of time (the sample interval).

- You can also choose the graph elements. By default, the display will be set to update every second. If you want to update less often, you should increase the number of seconds between updates.

FIGURE 7.18   General tab of the Performance Monitor Properties dialog box

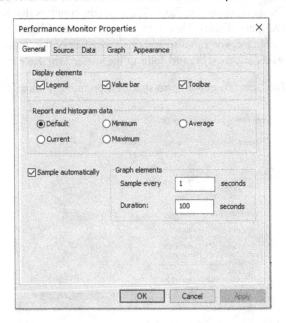

Source Tab   On the Source tab (shown in Figure 7.19), you can specify the source for the performance information you want to view. Options include Current Activity (the default setting) or data from a log file. If you choose to analyze information from a log file, you can also specify the time range for which you want to view statistics. I'll cover these selections in the next section.

FIGURE 7.19　　Source tab of the Performance Monitor Properties dialog box

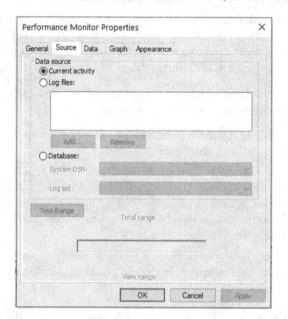

Data Tab　The Data tab (shown in Figure 7.20) lists the counters that have been added to the Performance Monitor display. These counters apply to the Chart, Histogram, and Report views. Using this interface, you can also add or remove any of the counters and change the properties, such as the width, style, and color of the line and the scale used for display.

FIGURE 7.20　　The Data tab of the Performance Monitor Properties dialog box

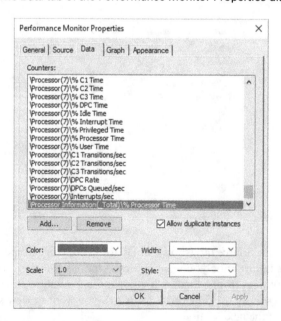

Graph Tab   On the Graph tab (shown in Figure 7.21), you can specify certain options that will allow you to customize the display of Performance Monitor views. First, you can specify what type of view you want to see (Line, Histogram, or Report). Then you can add a title for the graph, specify a label for the vertical axis, choose to display grids, and specify the vertical scale range.

FIGURE 7.21   The Graph tab of the Performance Monitor Properties dialog box

Appearance Tab   Using the Appearance tab (see Figure 7.22), you can specify the colors for the areas of the display, such as the background and foreground. You can also specify the fonts that are used to display counter values in Performance Monitor views. You can change settings to find a suitable balance between readability and the amount of information shown on one screen. Finally, you can set up the properties for a border.

Now that you have an idea of the types of information Performance Monitor tracks and how this data is displayed, we'll take a look at another feature—saving and analyzing performance data.

Saving and Analyzing Data with Performance Logs and Alerts

One of the most important aspects of monitoring performance is that it should be done over a given period of time (referred to as a *baseline*). So far, I have shown you how you can use Performance Monitor to view statistics in real time. I have, however, also alluded to using Performance Monitor to save data for later analysis. Now let's take a look at how you can do this.

FIGURE 7.22   The Appearance tab of the Performance Monitor Properties dialog box

When viewing information in Performance Monitor, you have two main options with respect to the data on display:

View Current Activity   When you first click the Performance Monitor icon in the `Administrative Tools` folder or from `Windows Tools`, the default option is to view data obtained from current system information. This method of viewing measures and displays various real-time statistics on the system's performance.

View Log File Data   This option allows you to view information that was previously saved to a log file. Although the performance objects, counters, and instances may appear to be the same as those viewed using the View Current Activity option, the information itself was actually captured at a previous point in time and stored into a log file.

Log files for the View Log File Data option are created in the Performance Logs And Alerts section of the Windows 10/11 Performance tool.

Three items allow you to customize how the data is collected in the log files:

Counter Logs   *Counter logs* record performance statistics based on the various performance objects, counters, and instances available in Performance Monitor. The values are updated based on a time interval setting and are saved to a file for later analysis.

Circular Logging   In *circular logging*, the data that is stored within a file is overwritten as new data is entered into the log. This is a useful method of logging if you want to record information only for a certain time frame (for example, the past four hours). Circular logging also conserves disk space by ensuring that the performance log file will not continue to grow over certain limits.

Linear Logging   In *linear logging*, data is never deleted from the log files, and new information is added to the end of the log file. The result is a log file that continually grows. The benefit is that all historical information is retained.

Now that you have an idea of the types of functions that are supported by the Windows 10/11 Performance tools, let's see how you can apply this information to the task at hand— monitoring and troubleshooting your Windows network.

 Real World Scenario

Real-World Performance Monitoring

In our daily jobs as system engineers and administrators, we come across systems that are in need of our help and may even ask for it. You, of course, check your Event Viewer and Performance Monitor and perform other tasks that help you troubleshoot. But what is really the most common problem that occurs? From my experience, I'd say that you suffer performance problems many times if your Windows 10/11 operating system is installed on a subpar system. Either the system's hardware minimum requirements weren't addressed or the operating system is not configured properly.

Using Other Performance-Monitoring Tools

Performance Monitor allows you to monitor different parameters of the Windows client operating system and associated services and applications. However, you can also use three other tools to monitor performance in Windows 10/11. They are Reliability Monitor, Task Manager, and Event Viewer. All three of these tools are useful for monitoring different areas of overall system performance and for examining details related to specific system events. In the following sections, you'll take a quick look at these tools and how you can best use them.

Reliability Monitor

Windows 10/11 Reliability Monitor is part of the Windows Reliability and Performance Monitor Snap-in for Microsoft Management Console (MMC). The easiest way to access Reliability Monitor is to type **perfmon /rel** in the Run command box ([Windows] key + R) and press Enter.

Reliability Monitor provides a system stability overview and allows you to get details about events that may be impacting the Windows client reliability. Reliability Monitor calculates a stability index based on a certain period of time, and it then shows that stability index in the System Stability Chart.

Reliability Monitor shows information, all on their own separate lines, about application failures, Windows failures, miscellaneous failures, warnings, and information. It shows you a period of time on the Windows client system, and you can click any of the events during that specific period of time and see what information, warnings, or errors occurred during that time period.

You can then use the information gathered by Reliability Monitor to help diagnose the issues that the Windows 10/11 system may be having.

Task Manager

Performance Monitor is designed to allow you to keep track of specific aspects of system performance over time. But what do you do if you want to get a quick snapshot of what the local system is doing? Creating a System Monitor chart, adding counters, and choosing a view is overkill. Fortunately, the Windows 10/11 Task Manager has been designed to provide a quick overview of important system performance statistics without requiring any configuration. Better yet, it's always readily available.

You can easily access Task Manager in several ways:

- On Windows 10, right-click the Windows taskbar, and then select Task Manager.
- Press Ctrl+Alt+Del, and then select Task Manager.
- Press Ctrl+Shift+Esc.
- Type **Taskman** in the Windows search box.

Each of these methods allows you to access a snapshot of the current system performance quickly.

Once you access Task Manager, you will see the following seven tabs:

These tabs can be different on Windows client machines. For example, Windows 10/11 Home can vary from Windows 10/11 Enterprise.

Also, I just wanted to point out at the time this book was written this is what the current Task Manager looked like. Microsoft has been looking at redesigning Task Manager for future releases of Windows 11 and may be moving options such as processes to a new menu. Also, the new Task Manager may have a left-hand side menu.

Processes Tab   The Processes tab shows you all the processes that are currently running on the local computer. By default, you'll be able to view how much CPU time and memory a particular process is using. By clicking any of the columns, you can quickly sort by the data values in that particular column. This is useful, for example, if you want to find out which processes are using the most memory on your server.

By accessing the performance objects in the View menu, you can add columns to the Processes tab. Figure 7.23 shows a list of the current processes running on a Windows client computer.

FIGURE 7.23   Viewing process statistics and information using Task Manager

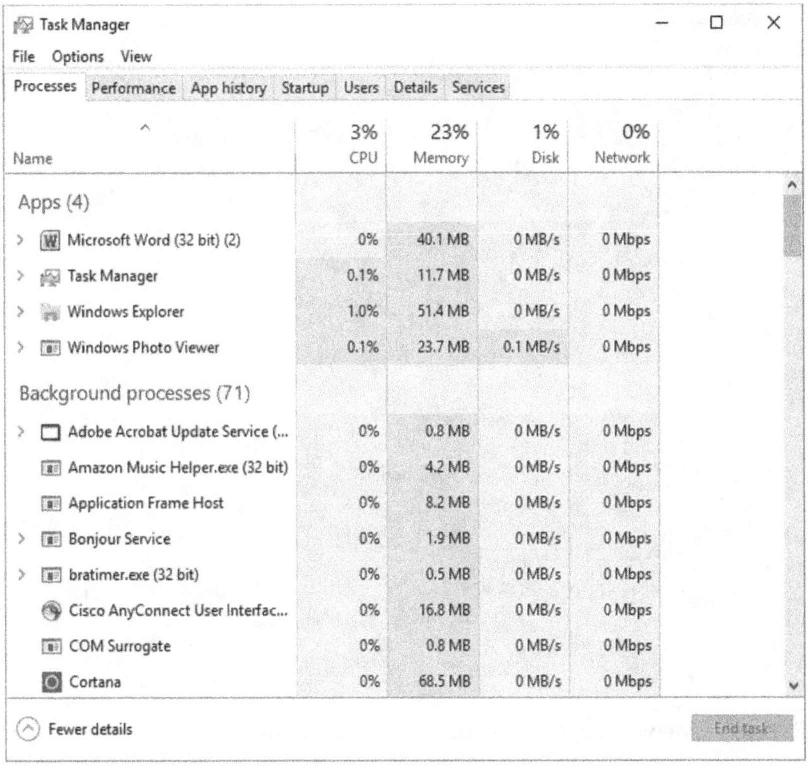

Performance Tab   One of the problems with using Performance Monitor to get a quick snapshot of system performance is that you have to add counters to a chart. Most system administrators are too busy to take the time to do this when all they need is basic CPU and memory information. That's where the Performance tab of Task Manager comes in. Using the Performance tab, you can view details about how memory is allocated on the computer and how much of the CPU is utilized (see Figure 7.24).

App History   This tab shows you all of the recent applications that have been running on the Windows client system. Users have the option Delete Usage History on this tab.

Startup   The Startup tab shows you which applications get started when the machine first starts up. Some applications require that services start at system startup for the applications to run properly.

Users Tab   The Users tab (see Figure 7.25) lists the currently active user accounts. This is particularly helpful if you want to see who is online and quickly log off or disconnect users.

FIGURE 7.24 Viewing CPU performance information using Task Manager

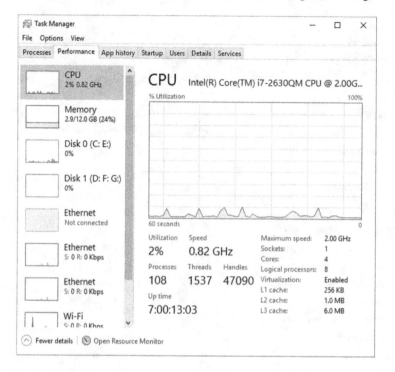

FIGURE 7.25 Viewing user information using Task Manager

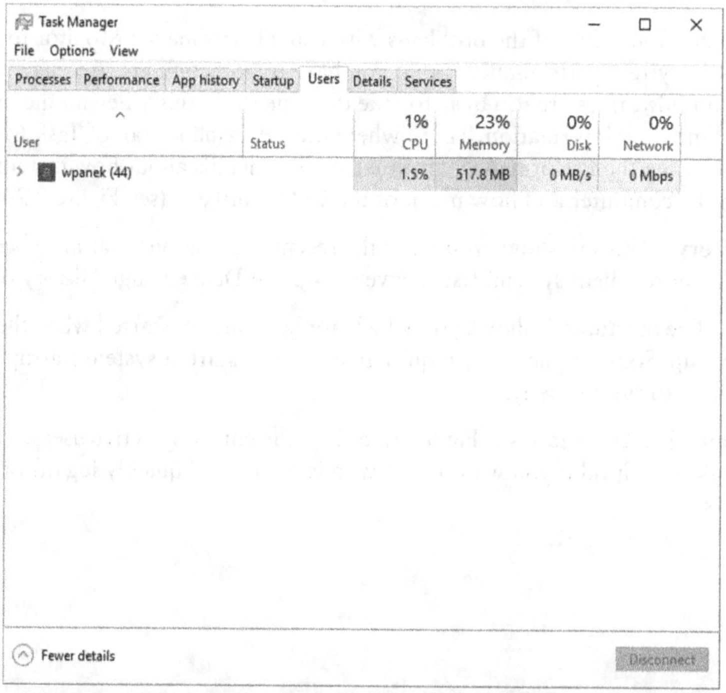

Details Tab   The Details tab (see Figure 7.26) shows you what applications are currently running on the system. From this location, you can stop an application from running by right-clicking the application and choosing Stop. You also have the ability to set your affinity level here. By setting the affinity, you can choose which applications will use which processors on your system.

FIGURE 7.26   Viewing currently running applications using Task Manager

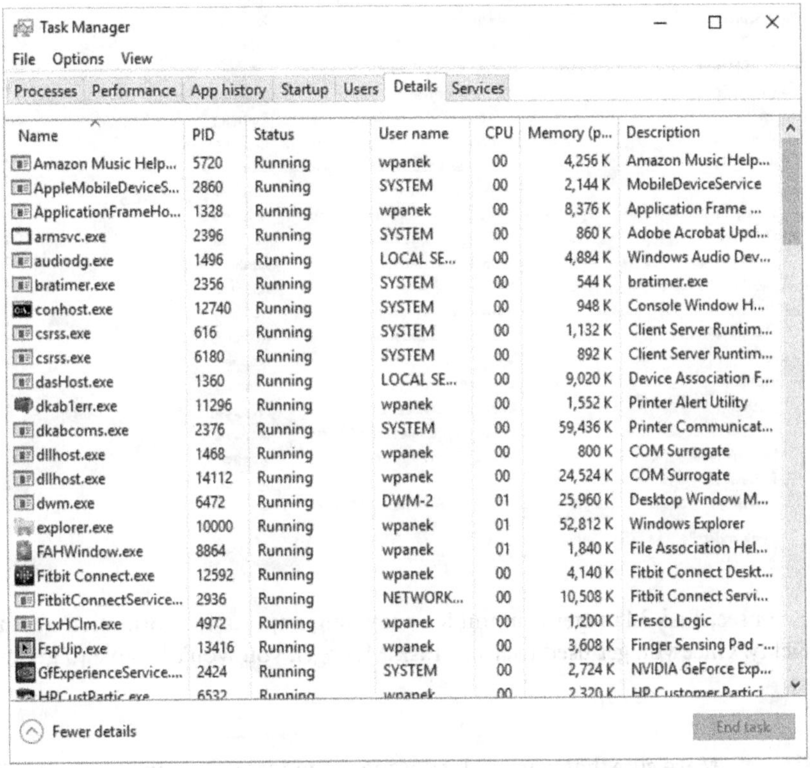

Services Tab   The Services tab (see Figure 7.27) shows you what services are currently running on the system. From this location, you can stop a service from running by right-clicking the service and choosing Stop. The Open Services link launches the Services MMC.

FIGURE 7.27   Viewing services information using Task Manager

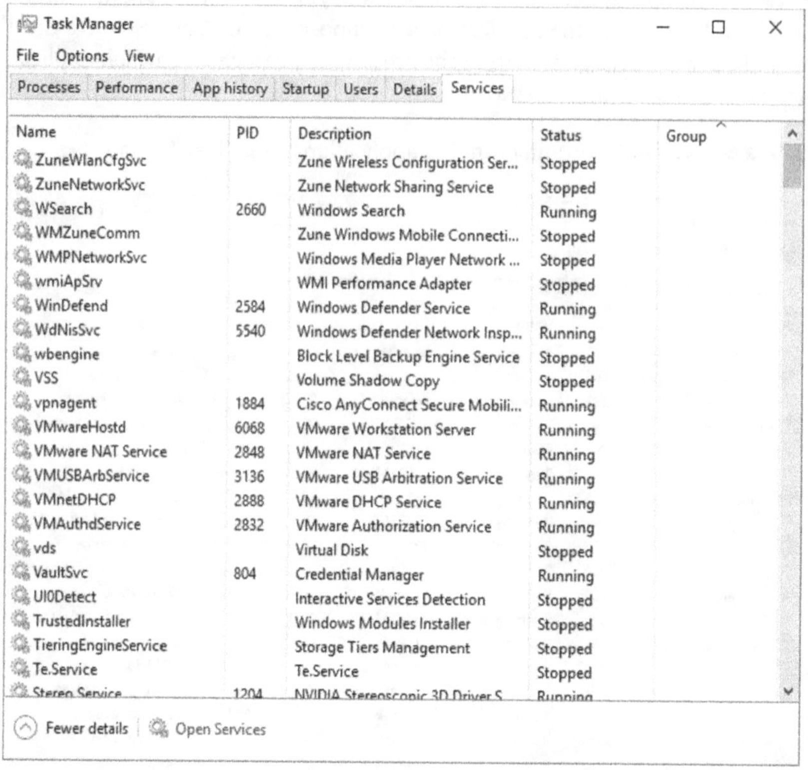

Name	PID	Description	Status	Group
ZuneWlanCfgSvc		Zune Wireless Configuration Ser...	Stopped	
ZuneNetworkSvc		Zune Network Sharing Service	Stopped	
WSearch	2660	Windows Search	Running	
WMZuneComm		Zune Windows Mobile Connecti...	Stopped	
WMPNetworkSvc		Windows Media Player Network ...	Stopped	
wmiApSrv		WMI Performance Adapter	Stopped	
WinDefend	2584	Windows Defender Service	Running	
WdNisSvc	5540	Windows Defender Network Insp...	Running	
wbengine		Block Level Backup Engine Service	Stopped	
VSS		Volume Shadow Copy	Stopped	
vpnagent	1884	Cisco AnyConnect Secure Mobili...	Running	
VMwareHostd	6068	VMware Workstation Server	Running	
VMware NAT Service	2848	VMware NAT Service	Running	
VMUSBArbService	3136	VMware USB Arbitration Service	Running	
VMnetDHCP	2888	VMware DHCP Service	Running	
VMAuthdService	2832	VMware Authorization Service	Running	
vds		Virtual Disk	Stopped	
VaultSvc	804	Credential Manager	Running	
UI0Detect		Interactive Services Detection	Stopped	
TrustedInstaller		Windows Modules Installer	Stopped	
TieringEngineService		Storage Tiers Management	Stopped	
Te.Service		Te.Service	Stopped	
Stereo Service	1204	NVIDIA Stereoscopic 3D Driver S...	Running	

As you can see, Task Manager is useful for providing important information about the system quickly. Once you get used to using Task Manager, you won't be able to get by without it!

 Make sure that you use Task Manager and familiarize yourself with all that it can do; you can end processes that have become intermittent, kill applications that may hang the system, view NIC performance, and so on. In addition, you can access this tool quickly to get an idea of what could be causing you problems. Event Viewer and Performance Monitor are both great tools for getting granular information on potential problems.

Event Viewer

Event Viewer is also useful for monitoring network information. Specifically, you can use the logs to view any information, warnings, or alerts related to the proper functioning of the network (see Figure 7.28). There are a number of ways to access the Event Viewer; you can:

- Search for Event Viewer in the search bar by typing **event** or **event viewer**.

- Right-click the Start button and choose Event Viewer.

- In Windows 10, select Start ➤ Windows Administrative Tools ➤ Event Viewer.

- In Windows 11, select Start ➤ All Apps ➤ Windows Tools ➤ Event Viewer.

Clicking any of the items in the left pane displays the various events that have been logged for each item.

Each event that is preceded by a blue "i" icon designates that these events are informational and do not indicate problems with the network. Rather, they record benign events such as Microsoft Office startup or a service starting.

Problematic or potentially problematic events are indicated by a yellow warning icon or a red error icon (see Figure 7.29). Warnings usually indicate a problem that wouldn't prevent a service from running but that might cause undesired effects with the service in question.

FIGURE 7.28   Event Viewer

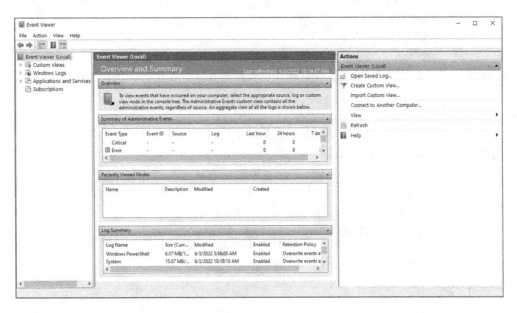

Error events almost always indicate a failed service, application, or function. For instance, if the dynamic registration of a DNS client fails, Event Viewer will generate an error. As you can see, errors are more severe than warnings because, in the case of DNS, the DNS client cannot participate in DNS at all because of the error.

FIGURE 7.29   Information, errors, and warnings in Event Viewer

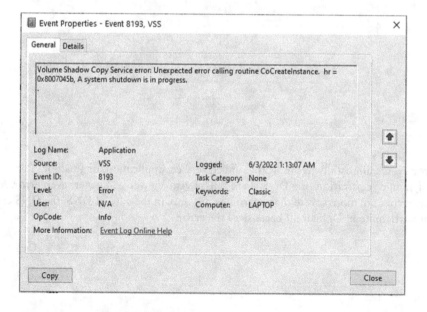

Double-clicking any event opens its Event Properties dialog box, as shown in Figure 7.30, which displays a detailed description of the event.

FIGURE 7.30   An Event Properties dialog box

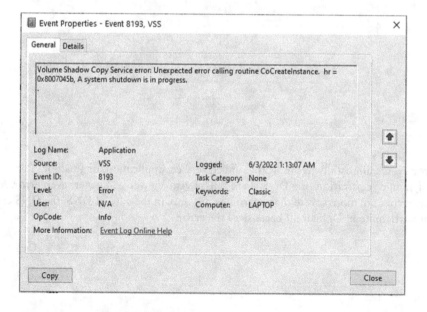

Event Viewer can display thousands of different events, so it would be impossible to list them all here. The important points of which you should be aware are the following:

- Information events are always benign.
- Warnings indicate noncritical problems.
- Errors indicate showstopping events.

Let's discuss some of the logs and the ways that you can view data:

Applications and Services   The *applications and services logs* are part of Event Viewer where applications (for example, Hardware events) and services log their events. Internet Explorer events would be logged in this part of Event Viewer. An important log in this section is the Key Management Service log (see Figure 7.31). This is where all of your Key Management Service events get stored.

FIGURE 7.31   The applications and services logs

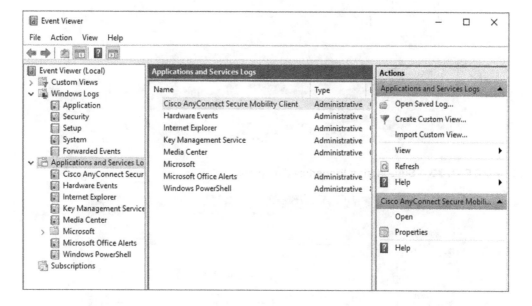

Custom Views   *Custom views* allow you to filter events (see Figure 7.32) to create your own customized look. You can filter events by event level (critical, error, warning, and so on), by logs, and by source. You also have the ability to view events occurring within a specific time frame. This allows you to look only at the events that are important to you.

Subscriptions   *Subscriptions* allow a user to receive alerts about events that you predefine. In the Subscription Properties dialog box (see Figure 7.33), you can define what type of events you want notifications about and the notification method. The Subscriptions section is an advanced alerting service to help you watch for events.

FIGURE 7.32   Create Custom View dialog box

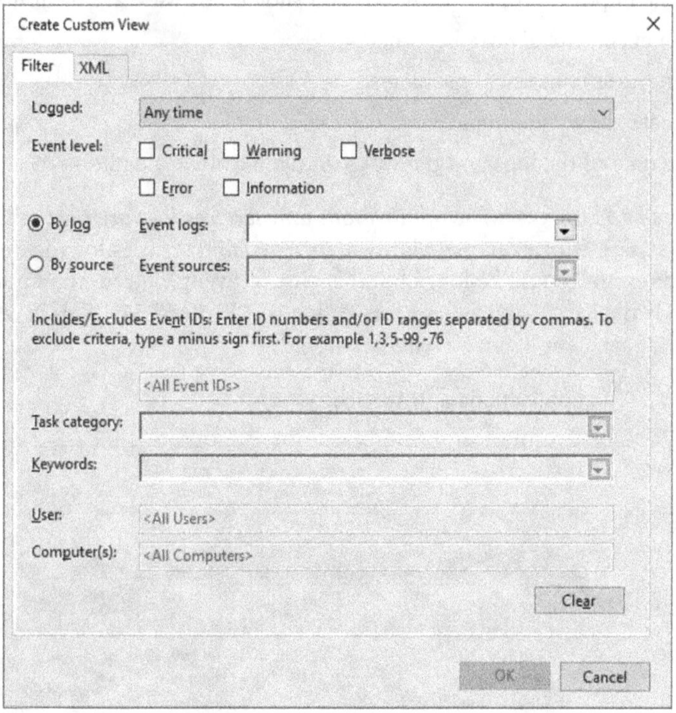

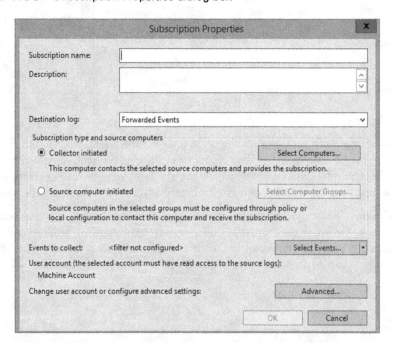

FIGURE 7.33   Subscription Properties dialog box

Manage the Registry

Microsoft uses the Windows Registry, which is a collection of databases that contains all the configuration settings for the operating system. It stores the information and settings for software programs, hardware devices, user preferences, and operating system configurations. The Registry can be accessed and configured directly by using the Registry Editor program.

It's important to note that you should only directly modify the Registry if you know what you are doing—incorrect modifications to the Registry will affect the entire system and could prevent it from working properly.

If you don't feel comfortable modifying the Registry directly, you can utilize the GUI utilities, Control Panel, and/or Settings. Both Control Panel and Settings will allow you to configure the Registry without using the Registry Editor.

However, if you do want to configure a system directly by using the Registry you can use the Registry Editor by using either Regedit or Regedt32.

As I mentioned previously, Windows 10/11 actually only uses the regedit command. If you type **regedt32**, it will just open the Regedit command utility.

So, to open the Registry Editor, right-click the Start button and select Run. Then type **regedit** and press Enter. The Registry Editor will open, as shown in Figure 7.34.

FIGURE 7.34   The Registry Editor

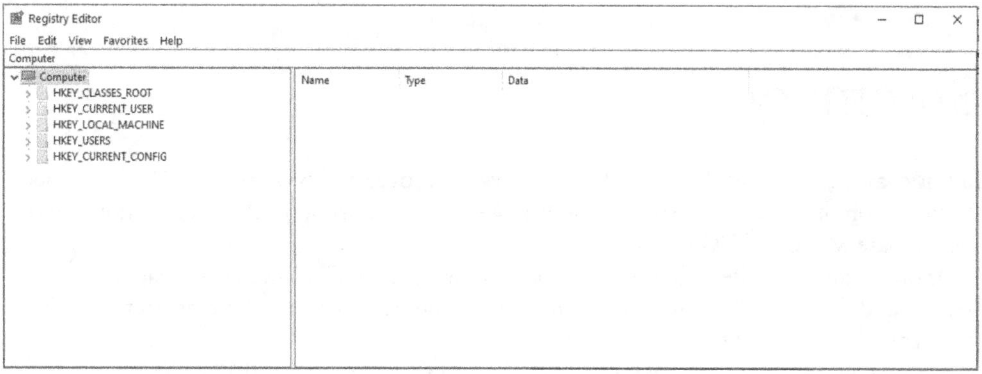

You can minimize or expand the Registry keys by selecting the small > icon next to each key. On the left-hand side of the screen, the Registry hives appear as folders. All keys that are considered hives begin with HKEY and are at the top of the Registry hierarchy as shown in Figure 7.34.

A hive is a logical group of keys, subkeys, and values. Within each hive you can modify subkeys. The Registry is constantly looked at by Windows and other programs.

Here is a list of the most common Registry hives:

HKEY_CLASSES_ROOT   This hive contains the information needed for Windows to know what to do when you ask it to do something, such as viewing the contents of a drive.

This area is where the file types of software are registered and associated so Windows will know how to open and process them.

HKEY_CURRENT_USER   This hive contains the configuration information for Windows and software-specific information to a user that is currently logged in.

HKEY_LOCAL_MACHINE   This hive contains most of the configuration information for the software that is installed on the system as well as the Windows operating system. It also contains information regarding hardware and device drivers.

HKEY_USERS   This hive contains user-specific configuration information for all active users on the computer. So, if you have multiple users on the same system, this hive will show you that configuration information for each user.

HKEY_CURRENT_CONFIG   This hive doesn't store any information. It is basically a shortcut to the Registry key that keeps the information about the hardware profile currently being used, the \SYSTEM\CurrentControlSet\Hardware Profiles\ Current\ Registry key.

Again, I always like to stress that discretion should be taken when editing the Registry directly because the settings that are critical to Windows functionality are stored here. If you edit the wrong Registry value, this may cause services to fail and could potentially prevent Windows from working.

Summary

In this chapter, you looked at the different ways to recover and protect your Windows client machine from hardware and software issues. We discussed using the Advanced Boot Options such as Safe Mode and VGA Mode.

Another important item that needs to be completed on a Windows client machine is Backup and Restore (Windows 7). Backing up a Windows 10/11 machine protects data in the event of a hardware or software failure.

We also discussed how to back up a complete copy of Windows 10/11 by using images. An image allows you to copy the entire Windows client machine and then reimage the machine in the event of a major failure. Another way to protect data is by the use of shadow copies. Shadow copies, which are a part of System Protection, allow you to keep previous versions of data and revert to a previous version in the event of a problem.

The chapter also covered monitoring the Windows 10/11 system. Monitoring performance on Windows 10/11 is imperative to rooting out any issues that may affect your network. If your systems are not running at their best, your end users may experience issues such as latency, or worse, you may experience corruption in your network data. Either way, it's important to know how to monitor the performance of your systems.

We also examined how to use the various performance-related tools that are included with Windows 10/11. Tools such as Performance Monitor, Task Manager, and Event Viewer can help you diagnose and troubleshoot system performance issues. These tools will help you find typical problems related to memory, disk space, and any other hardware-related issues you may experience. Knowing how to use tools to troubleshoot and test your systems is imperative, not only to passing the exam, but also to performing your duties at work. To have a smoothly running network environment, it is vital that you understand the issues related to the reliability and performance of your Windows client systems.

We discussed the Registry and the Registry Editor and the importance of knowing what you are doing before working with the Registry Editor.

Exam Essentials

Understand the different options for managing system recovery. Know how to use the Startup Repair tool, System Restore, and the Backup and Restore (Windows 7) and when it is appropriate to use each option.

Be able to perform file recovery with the Backup and Restore (Windows 7) and shadow copies. Understand the options that are supported through Backup and Restore (Windows 7) and the files that are backed up using this tool. Know how to manually create a shadow copy and how to keep only the last shadow copy version.

Know how to troubleshoot using Advanced Boot Options. Be able to list the options that can be accessed through Advanced Boot Options, and know when it is appropriate to use each option. Know the difference between Safe Mode and Enable Low-Resolution Video.

Know the importance of common performance counters. Several important performance-related counters deal with general system performance. Know the importance of monitoring memory, print server, CPU, and network usage on a busy server.

Understand the role of other troubleshooting tools. Windows Task Manager and Event Viewer can both be used to diagnose and troubleshoot configuration- and performance-related issues.

Understand how to troubleshoot common sources of server reliability problems. Windows 10/11 has been designed to be a stable, robust, and reliable operating system. Should you experience intermittent failures, you should know how to troubleshoot device drivers and buggy system-level software.

Video Resources

There are no videos for this chapter.

Review Questions

1. You need to stop an application from running in Task Manager. Which tab would you use to stop an application from running?

    A. Performance

    B. Users

    C. Options

    D. Details

2. You and a colleague are discussing a Microsoft utility that allows you to collect information in a log and analyze the data in real time. What is this utility called?

    A. Disk Cleanup

    B. Event Viewer

    C. Performance Monitor

    D. Resource Monitor

3. You need to back up the existing data on a computer before you install a new application. You also need to ensure that you are able to recover individual user files that are replaced or deleted during the installation. What should you do?

    A. Create a system restore point.

    B. Perform an Automated System Recovery (ASR) backup and restore.

    C. In the Backup And Restore (Windows 7) window, click the Back Up Now button.

    D. In the Backup And Restore (Windows 7) window, click the Back Up Computer button.

4. Your data recovery strategy must meet the following requirements:

    - Back up all data files and folders in C:\Data.

    - Restore individual files and folders in C:\Data.

    - Ensure that data is backed up to and restored from external media.

    What should you do?

    A. Use the Previous Versions tab to restore the files and folders.

    B. Use the System Restore feature to perform backup and restore operations.

    C. Use the NTBackup utility to back up and restore individual files and folders.

    D. Use the Backup and Restore utility to back up and restore files.

5. You need to ensure that you can recover system configuration and data if your computer hard disk fails. What should you do?

    A. Create a system restore point.

    B. Create a backup of all file categories.

    C. Create a Backup and Restore image.

    D. Perform an Automated System Recovery (ASR) backup.

6. You have a computer that runs Windows 10/11. Your computer has two volumes, C: and D:. Both volumes are formatted by using the NTFS filesystem. You need to disable previous versions on the D: volume. What should you do?

   A. From System Properties, modify the System Protection settings.

   B. From the properties of the D: volume, modify the Quota settings.

   C. From the properties of the D: volume, modify the Sharing settings.

   D. From the Disk Management Snap-in, convert the hard disk drive that contains the D: volume to Dynamic.

7. You have a computer that runs Windows client. You configure a backup job to back up all files and folders on an external NTFS filesystem hard disk drive. The backup job fails to back up all files that have the encryption attribute set. You need to back up all encrypted files. The backed-up files must remain encrypted. What should you do?

   A. Manually copy the encrypted files to the external hard disk drive.

   B. Schedule a backup job to occur when you are not logged on to the computer.

   C. Enable Volume Shadow Copy on the external drive and schedule a backup job.

   D. Add the certificate of the local administrator account to the list of users who can transparently access the files, and schedule a backup job.

8. You have a computer that runs Windows 10/11. You use Windows Backup and Restore to create a backup image. You need to perform a complete restore of the computer. What are two possible ways to begin the restore? (Each correct answer presents a complete solution. Choose two.)

   A. Open the Windows Backup and Restore Center and click Advanced Restore.

   B. Open the Windows Backup and Restore Center and click Restore Computer.

   C. Start your computer. From the Advanced Boot Options menu, select Repair Your Computer.

   D. Start the computer by using the Windows 10/11 installation media. Select Repair Your Computer.

9. You are the network administrator for your organization. You are asked by a junior administrator when he should create restore points. Which of the following are times when restore points should be created? (Choose all that apply.)

   A. Manually upon request

   B. Before installing applications or drivers

   C. Before significant system events

   D. Before System Restore is used to restore files (so you can undo the changes if necessary)

10. You install Windows 10/11 on a new computer. You update the video card driver and restart the computer. When you start the computer, the screen flickers and then goes blank. You restart the computer and receive the same result. You need to configure the video card driver. What should you do first?

    A. Restart the computer in Safe Mode.

    B. Restart the computer in Debugging Mode.

    C. Restart the computer in low-resolution video mode.

    D. Insert the Windows 10/11 installation media into the computer, restart, and use System Recovery to perform a startup repair.

11. You and a colleague are discussing user profiles. You know that a user profile contains an `ntuser.dat` file. When a user signs on to a Windows machine, the system loads the file into the Registry and maps it to a specific Registry subtree. To what Registry subtree is the `ntuser.dat` file mapped?

A. `HKEY_USERS\.DEFAULT`

B. `HKEY_CURRENT_USER`

C. `HKEY_CURRENT_CONFIG`

D. `HKEY_LOCAL_MACHINE\Security`

12. You are the administrator for your company network. During the boot process, you want to see what is being loaded. Using the Advanced Boot Options menu, you have enabled boot logging. Where will the log file be stored?

A. The log file will be stored as `\Windows\Bootlog.txt`.

B. The log file will be stored as `\Windows\Logging.txt`.

C. The log file will be stored as `\Windows\Ntbtlog.txt`.

D. The log file will be stored as `\Windows\Startup.txt`.

13. You are the administrator for your company network. A user has informed you that their Windows client computer will not boot because of missing or corrupted system files. The machine is not able to boot into Safe Mode. What tool can you use to replace the corrupted system file?

A. System Restore

B. Startup Repair

C. System Image Recovery

D. Uninstall Updates

14. You are the administrator for your company network. Some of your duties require that you perform the following tasks:

- Collect data from local or remote Windows client computers on the network. Collect data either from a single computer or from multiple computers concurrently.

- View data as it is being collected in real time or historically from collected data.

What Windows 10/11 application should you use?

A. Computer Monitor

B. Event Viewer

C. Performance Monitor

D. Reliability Monitor

15. You are the administrator for your company network. You want to edit the Registry without using Control Panel. What are the two utilities that are supported by Windows 10/11 to edit the Registry manually? (Choose two.)

A. Regedit

B. Regedt32

C. Regeditor

D. Registryeditor

16. You are the administrator for your company network. You have a Windows 10/11 Professional computer. You receive a SMART alert that the hard disk on this computer will soon be failing. You connect an external hard disk to the computer. What should you use if you need to create a backup that you can use to restore the operating system and the user documents from the external drive?

   A. `Start-OB Backup`

   B. `Start-WB Backup`

   C. `vssadmin.exe`

   D. `wbadmin.exe`

17. You are the administrator for your company network. You have a Windows 10/11 Enterprise computer that has File History and System Protection turned on for the C: drive. You accidentally press the Delete key on the keyboard, deleting a folder on the C: drive. What is the easiest way to recover this folder?

   A. Use a manually selected restore point.

   B. Use File History.

   C. Use the latest restore point.

   D. Use the Recycle Bin.

18. You are the administrator for your company network. You and a colleague are discussing the output modes for Performance Monitor. You view the output mode, as shown in the following graphic:

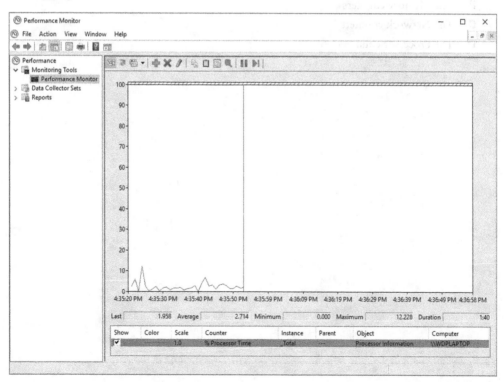

What output mode are you observing?

A. Grid view

B. Histogram view

C. Line view

D. Report view

19. You are the administrator for your company network. You have a Windows client computer that is taking a long time to start. What tool should you use if you want to identify what applications might be causing the greatest delays when starting this computer?

    A. Performance Monitor

    B. Resource Monitor

    C. System Configuration

    D. Task Manager

20. You are the administrator for your company network. A few users have indicated that a particular application is taking too long to load. You use Performance Monitor to create a baseline report for one of the computers. You monitor the processor, the disk subsystem, and the network subsystem. You notice that the disk subsystem has a high load of activity. What other counters should you also monitor to know for sure whether there is a disk subsystem bottleneck?

    A. The Application counters

    B. The Memory counters

    C. The Network counters

    D. The Processor counters

Exam MD-101

Chapter

8

Deploy Windows Client

MICROSOFT EXAM OBJECTIVES COVERED IN THIS CHAPTER:

✓ **Plan a Windows client deployment**

- Assess infrastructure readiness by using Endpoint Analytics; select a deployment tool based on requirements; choose between migrate and rebuild; choose an imaging and/or provisioning strategy; plan and implement changes to Windows edition by using subscription activation or MAK license management.

✓ **Plan and implement Windows client provisioning by using Windows Autopilot**

- Choose an Autopilot deployment method based on requirements, including user-driven mode, self-deploying mode, autopilot reset, and pre-provisioning; configure device registration for Autopilot; create, validate, and assign deployment profiles; provision Windows devices by using Autopilot; troubleshoot an Autopilot deployment.

✓ **Plan and implement Windows client deployment by using Microsoft Deployment Toolkit (MDT)**

- Plan and implement an MDT deployment infrastructure; choose configuration options based on requirements, such as boot images, OS images, upgrade packages, task sequences, and drivers; create, manage, and deploy images; plan and implement PXE boot by using Windows Deployment Services (WDS); create and use task sequences; manage application and driver deployment; customize an MDT deployment by using customsettings.ini and bootstrap.ini; monitor and troubleshoot deployment; plan and configure user state migration.

The next few chapters of this book are for exam MD-101, Managing Modern Desktops. This is the second of two Windows client exams (MD-100 and MD-101) for the Microsoft 365 Certified: Modern Desktop Administrator Associate.

The upcoming chapters will focus on how to deploy and update Windows clients using the least amount of administrative effort by using modern technologies and tools. You will learn how to plan and deploy Windows clients and how to choose a deployment method that works best for your environment. Then I will discuss some different ways to manage Windows clients by using Azure Active Directory and Microsoft Intune. I will go over how to keep your client devices secure and up-to-date and how to manage device and user authentication by utilizing the cloud.

Plan a Windows Client Deployment

In this chapter I will be discussing Windows client deployments and a variety of deployment tools. I will discuss client provisioning using Windows Autopilot and planning and implementing deployments by using the Microsoft Deployment Toolkit (MDT).

If you need to install Windows 10/11 on multiple computers, you could manually install the operating system on each computer, as described in Chapter 1, "Windows Client Installation." However, automating the deployment process will make your job easier, more efficient, and more cost effective if you have a large number of client computers on which to install Windows 10/11.

Windows 10/11 comes with several utilities that can be used for deploying and automating the Windows client installation. With access to multiple utilities with different functionality, you have increased flexibility in determining how to best deploy Windows 10/11 within a large corporate environment.

In this chapter I will delve more into using the modern technologies that can be used to aid in the deployment of Windows clients. I will start off this chapter by discussing Microsoft Endpoint Manager (MEM).

Microsoft Endpoint Manager (MEM) Overview

Before I delve into Endpoint Analytics, it's important to know more about Microsoft Endpoint Manager (MEM). MEM is used for maintaining, monitoring, and protecting your endpoints. Whether you are using the cloud or on-premise networks, MEM will help keep your data safe and secure. It consists of the tools and services that you can use to monitor and maintain your endpoints whether they are corporate-owned or personally owned devices. Endpoints include:

- Apps
- Desktop computers
- Embedded devices
- Mobile devices
- Servers
- Shared devices
- Virtual machines

Microsoft Endpoint Manager includes a variety of services such as:

- Azure Active Directory (Azure AD)
- Desktop Analytics/Endpoint Analytics
- Microsoft Defender for Endpoint
- Microsoft Endpoint Configuration Manager
- Microsoft Intune
- Windows Autopilot

MEM uses Azure Active Directory (Azure AD) to identify devices, groups, multifactor authentication (MFA), and users.

Co-management is used to join an already existent on-premises Configuration Manager asset to the cloud by using either Intune or another Microsoft 365 cloud service. You will determine which service will be the management authority.

Endpoint Analytics is a cloud-based service that works in conjunction with Configuration Manager and Intune. It helps you make important decisions regarding the update readiness of a Windows client. Endpoint Analytics looks at the data from your company along with data collected from millions of other devices that are connected to the Microsoft cloud to help provide information on apps, security updates, and more. Endpoint Analytics is used to keep Windows 10/11 devices current.

 Endpoint Analytics is the newer version of Desktop Analytics. Microsoft will be phasing out the Desktop Analytics solution on November 30, 2022, when it will be included into the Microsoft Endpoint Manager Admin Center portal. Desktop Analytics is used to assess the compatibility of Windows endpoints. Some of its capabilities associated with Windows 11 readiness assessments have already been incorporated into the Endpoint Analytics solution, which is used by the Endpoint Manager.

The Endpoint Manager Admin Center is a website that manages devices and creates policies. Here you can access the Microsoft Intune service, as well as other device management-related settings. Microsoft has changed the URL for the Microsoft Endpoint Manager Admin

Center (formerly known as Microsoft 365 Device Management) to `https://endpoint.microsoft.com`.

Endpoint Manager can be thought of in three separate parts; the cloud, on-premises, and cloud + on-premises. Each one is described here:

Cloud   All your data is stored in Azure. This method provides you with the benefits of mobility on the cloud as well as the security advantages that are provided by Azure.

On-premises   If you aren't ready to use the cloud, you can keep your existing systems in-house. All hardware and software applications are hosted on-site.

Cloud + On-premises   This is also referred to as a hybrid. These environments use a combination of both cloud and on-premise solutions.

There are a number of benefits of using Microsoft Endpoint Manager. These benefits are used to manage and protect your endpoints; you can do the following:

- Confirm that user devices are configured and protected according to corporate policies.
- Confirm that your corporate security rules are in place.
- Ensure that corporate services are available to your end users and on all their devices.
- Ensure that your company is using correct credentials in order to access and share corporate information.
- Protect the apps and devices that access your resources.
- Protect the data that your users are accessing.

If you have Microsoft Endpoint Configuration Manager or Microsoft Intune, then you already have Microsoft Endpoint Manager. These are all now one management system.

Microsoft Intune is a cloud-based mobile device management (MDM) and mobile application management (MAM) provider that you use for apps and devices. With the cloud, Intune can be used to create and check for compliance, deploy apps, and change device features and settings on a variety of devices.

Windows Autopilot is used to streamline the way devices get deployed, reset, and repurposed by using a deployment method that requires no interaction from the IT department. Autopilot is used to preconfigure devices and to automatically enroll devices into Intune. Your users simply unbox the device and turn it on, and Windows Autopilot will configure it from the cloud using just a few steps. I will be discussing Autopilot in greater detail later in this chapter.

Endpoint Analytics

Now, let's discuss Microsoft Endpoint Analytics. Endpoint Analytics is part of the Microsoft Productivity Score. The Microsoft Productivity Score provides the following:

Metrics   Metrics help you to see where they are on their digital transformation, which is the process of using digital technologies to modify or create new business processes and customer experiences in order to meet the needs of the ever-changing business and market requirements.

Insights   Insights about the data are provided to help you identify opportunities to improve productivity and satisfaction.

Recommended Actions   You can use these recommended actions to use Microsoft 365 products more efficiently.

These analytics give you a score based on how your company is working and the quality of the experience that you are giving your end users. It identifies policy or hardware issues that could potentially slow down devices and helps you make improvements.

Endpoint Analytics Requirements

You can enroll devices via Configuration Manager or Microsoft Intune. Let's take a look at the requirements of enrolling devices using Intune and Configuration Manager, as shown in Table 8.1.

> The information in Table 8.1 was taken directly from Microsoft's website and documentation and was current as of this writing.

TABLE 8.1   Endpoint Analytics requirements

To enroll devices via Intune	To enroll devices via Configuration Manager
<ul><li>Intune enrolled or co-managed devices running the following:<ul><li>Windows 10 version 1903 or later.</li><li>July 2021 cumulative update or later.</li><li>Pro, Pro Education, Enterprise, or Education. Home and long-term servicing channel (LTSC) aren't supported.</li></ul></li><li>Windows devices must be Azure AD joined or hybrid Azure AD joined. Workplace joined or Azure AD registered devices aren't supported.</li><li>Network connectivity from devices to the Microsoft public cloud.</li><li>The Intune Service Administrator role is required to start gathering data.<ul><li>After clicking Start for gathering data, other read-only roles can view the data.</li></ul></li></ul>	<ul><li>A minimum of Configuration Manager version 2002 with KB4560496 - Update rollup for Microsoft Endpoint Configuration Manager version 2002 or later.</li><li>The Configuration Manager clients upgraded to version 2002 (including KB4560496) or later.</li><li>Microsoft Endpoint Manager tenant attach enabled.</li><li>Enable Endpoint analytics for devices uploaded to Microsoft Endpoint Manager.</li></ul>

Endpoint Analytics Licensing Requirements

Devices that are enrolled in Endpoint Analytics must have a valid license. In order to use Endpoint Analytics, you will need to have a license for the Microsoft Endpoint Manager product, plus E3 or E5 Windows 10/11 Enterprise or Education licensing. Also, the Intune Service Administrator is required to enable data collection, since Endpoint Analytics is a cloud-based service.

Endpoint Analytics Built-in Role Permissions

The roles shown in Table 8.2 already have access to Endpoint Analytics.

 The information in Table 8.2 was taken directly from Microsoft's website and documentation and was current as of this writing.

TABLE 8.2   Built-in roles that already have access to Endpoint Analytics

Role name	Azure Active Directory role	Intune role	Endpoint Analytics permissions
Global Administrator	Yes		Read/Write
Intune Service Administrator	Yes		Read/Write
School Administrator		Yes	Read/Write
Endpoint Security Manager		Yes	Read Only
Help Desk Operator		Yes	Read Only
Read Only Operator		Yes	Read Only
Reports Reader	Yes		Read Only

Using Endpoint Analytics

To get started using Endpoint Analytics, follow these steps:

1. Navigate to https://endpoint.microsoft.com and sign in.
2. Click Reports.
3. Select Endpoint Analytics.

4. Click the Start button, as shown in Figure 8.1. By default, most settings are automatically enabled for all of your devices when you select Start to enable user-experience analytics. If you wish to further modify the settings, you may do so by selecting the Settings option in Microsoft Endpoint Manager Admin Center ➢ Endpoint Analytics ➢ Settings.

FIGURE 8.1   Starting Endpoint Analytics

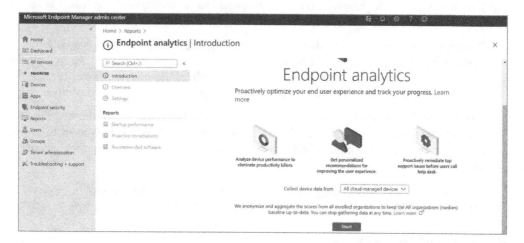

When you sign into the Microsoft Endpoint Manager Admin Center it will open to the Overview page, where you will be presented with several score charts, as shown in Figure 8.2 (this graphic has come directly from Microsoft's website).

FIGURE 8.2   Endpoint Analytics Overview screen

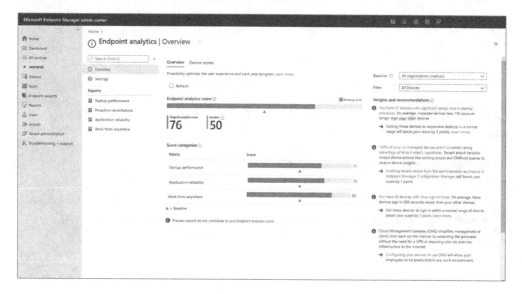

Some key features you will want to look at are the scores and if there are insights and recommendations for you. Here is a brief overview on each of the components you will want to watch for (these can also be seen in Figure 8.2):

Scores   Endpoint Analytics scores range from 0 to 100. The lower the score, the more improvement is needed. If you see a status that indicates insufficient data, that means you do not have enough devices reporting to provide a score. Currently, at least five devices are required to provide scoring.

Baselines   Baseline scores are shown on charts as triangle markers. There is a built-in baseline for All organizations (median), which will let you compare your score to a typical enterprise. You have the ability to create new baselines depending on your current metrics. This allows you to track progress or view regressions over a period of time.

Insights and Recommendations   The Overview page provides a prioritized list of things you can do to improve your score. The recommendations will tell you how to increase the score and how many points the score will gain once you have completed the recommended action.

Later in Chapter 13, "Monitoring Devices," I will touch more on how to monitor devices using the Endpoint Manager Admin Center and Endpoint Analytics.

Deployment Options

So, what deployment method should you use? This is a question that is often asked. There really is no right or wrong answer—you use what works best for you or your organization, and you need to consider what you want to achieve. You can start with Windows Autopilot if you are continually provisioning new devices, or you can use Intune if you add rules and control settings for your apps, devices, and users.

Windows client deployments fall into one of three categories:

- Modern
- Dynamic
- Traditional

Microsoft recommends using the modern deployment methods unless you must use a different procedure. These methods utilize existing tools such as Microsoft Deployment Toolkit (MDT) and Microsoft Endpoint Configuration Manager. Modern deployment methods support both traditional on-premises and cloud services to deliver the deployment. Dynamic deployment methods allow you to configure specific use case applications and settings. Traditional deployment methods deploy operating system images by using existing tools.

Table 8.3 summarizes the various Windows client deployment scenarios.

 The information in Table 8.3 was taken directly from Microsoft's website and documentation and was current as of this writing.

TABLE 8.3 Windows deployment categories and scenarios

Deployment category	Scenario	Description
Modern	Windows Autopilot	Customize the out-of-box-experience (OOBE) and deploy a new system with apps and settings already configured.
Modern	In-Place Upgrade	Use Windows Setup to update the OS and migrate apps and settings. Rollback data is saved in the `Windows.old` folder.
Dynamic	Subscription Activation	Switch from Windows 10/11 Pro to Enterprise when a subscribed user signs in.
Dynamic	Azure AD/MDM	The device is automatically joined to Azure Active Directory and is configured by Mobile Device Management.
Dynamic	Provisioning Packages	Using the Windows Imaging and Configuration Designer tool, create provisioning packages that can be applied to devices.
Traditional	Bare Metal	Deploy a new device, or wipe an existing device and deploy with a fresh image.
Traditional	Refresh	Also called wipe and load. Redeploy a device by saving the user state, wiping the disk, then restoring the user state.
Traditional	Replace	Replace an existing device with a new one by saving the user state on the old device and then restoring it to the new device.

I discussed deployment methods in Chapter 1.

Choose an Imaging and/or Provisioning Strategy

Disk imaging is the process of taking a checkpoint of a computer and then using that checkpoint to create new computers, thus allowing for automated deployments. The reference, or source, computer has Windows 10/11 installed and is configured with the settings and applications that should be installed on the target computers. The image (checkpoints) is then created and can be transferred to other computers, thus installing the operating system, settings, and applications that were defined on the reference computer.

A provisioning package (with the extension .ppkg) is a container for a collection of configuration settings. With Windows client, you can create provisioning packages that let you quickly configure a device without having to install a new image.

You can use the Windows Configuration Designer (WCD) to work with images and provisioning packages. The WCD allows you to:

- View and configure all the settings and policies for a Windows 10/11 image or provisioning package.
- Create Windows provisioning answer files.
- Allow an answer file to add third-party drivers, apps, or other assets.
- Create variants and specify the settings that apply to each variant.
- Build and flash a Windows image.
- Build a provisioning package.

The Windows Configuration Designer gives you many options on how to deploy and set up Windows 10/11 clients. WCD includes the following tools:

- Configure and edit images by using the Deployment Image Servicing and Management (DISM) utility.
- Create Windows Preinstallation Environment (Windows PE) images.
- Migrate user data and profiles using the User State Migration Tool (USMT).
- Windows Configuration Designer (WCD).

I discussed using the WCD and other different deployment methods in Chapter 1, "Windows Client Installation."

Subscription Activation/MAK License Management

Subscription Activation is a Windows feature that is available for qualifying devices running Windows 10 or Windows 11. Subscription Activation enables users to switch from Windows Professional to Enterprise. Microsoft refers to this as "step-up." This feature is available in both Windows 10 and Windows 11 if you subscribed to Windows 10/11 Enterprise E3 or E5. This also works for Education editions of Windows 10/11. You cannot upgrade from Windows 10 to Windows 11 by using Subscription Activation.

When an Azure AD user signs in with an assigned Windows 10/11 Enterprise E3 or E5 license, Subscription Activation can provide automatic activation with no activation keys or reboots. Azure AD will assign the licenses to users or groups.

Multiple Activation Key (MAK) License Management

A Multiple Activation Key (MAK) is typically used in by small- or mid-sized companies that have a volume licensing agreement. A MAK will activate systems on a one-time basis by using Microsoft's hosted activation services, either through the Internet or by phone. This requires a connection with a Microsoft activation server. Once a system has been activated, there will be no additional communication with Microsoft.

To use a MAK, the devices to be activated have to have a MAK installed. Each MAK can be used a certain number of times. You can download MAK keys using the Microsoft Volume Licensing Service Center (VLSC) website. The VLSC is an online tool used for managing volume licensing agreements, to download products, and to access license keys. Each MAK comes with a certain number of activations. This number is based on the number of licenses that have been purchased. You can increase the number of activations available by contacting Microsoft.

Deploying with Windows Autopilot

Let's now take a look at how to deploy Windows 10/11 machines from the cloud. Microsoft has introduced a way to deploy Windows 10/11 by using Intune and Windows Autopilot.

Windows Autopilot is a group of multiple technologies that allow you to set up and configure brand-new devices directly from the manufacturer. These devices can go directly into the production environment, and when the user logs into Intune, the device will be automatically configured for your environment.

You can also use Windows Autopilot to reconfigure, recover, and repurpose devices that are already in your corporate environment. This allows you to quickly and easily repurpose machines so that they can be assigned to different users. Since Windows Autopilot is a benefit of using Microsoft Intune, your IT department does not need to set up an on-site infrastructure to support this service. This helps reduce the cost of building machines for your IT department.

So, what does this actually mean to your IT department? Let's take a look at just a couple scenarios where Windows Autopilot can help your IT department quickly set up or repurpose Windows client devices.

When you purchase Windows 10/11 machines from different vendors, currently you need to make sure that you have custom images for each vendor. The reason for this is that each vendor puts in its own hardware and that hardware needs custom drivers to work properly. With Windows Autopilot, you can have the vendor send the machines directly to your remote users or IT department for immediate deployment.

When the user logs into Windows Azure with their email address and password, Windows Autopilot will automatically apply settings, policies, and applications and, if need be, even change the version of Windows 10/11 (for example, from Pro to Enterprise) on the machine. The machine will automatically be ready for use in your corporate environment without any need for the IT department to manually make any changes to the new machine.

Another scenario of using Windows Autopilot is when you need to repurpose machines within your organization. Currently, when many of us get a new machine for a user, you need to load an image onto that machine and set it up for that specific user. After the machine is given to the user, you normally take their machine, reimage it, and pass it on to someone with an older machine. This can result in a large chain of repurposed machines.

With Windows Autopilot, when a user gets a machine from another user, once they log into their Azure account, the machine can reload a clean operating system with all of the policies and applications they need to do their job. The IT department doesn't need to reimage machines before they are redeployed.

After the IT department deploys or repurposes the Windows client machines, those machines can then be managed by using Microsoft Intune, System Center Configuration Manager (SCCM), Windows Update for Business, and other compatible tools. Windows Autopilot allows your organization to complete the following tasks:

- Join Windows client devices automatically to Azure Active Directory (Azure AD) or to your on-site Active Directory (via Hybrid Azure AD Join).

- Automatically enroll Windows client devices into MDM services, such as Microsoft Intune (this requires an Azure AD Premium subscription).

- Restrict the creation of the Administrator account.

- Build and automatically assign Windows client devices to configuration groups based on the Windows 10/11 device profile.

- Customizable OOBE content that is specific to your organization.

Windows Autopilot Requirements

So now that you understand the benefits of using Windows Autopilot, let's take a look at what's required so that you can use Windows Autopilot in your organization.

First, and most importantly, Windows Autopilot depends on the version and specific capabilities of Windows 10/11. Second, you will need to have an Azure subscription set up with Azure AD. Finally, you will need to add the Mobile Device Management (MDM) services along with Intune to your Azure subscription so that you can set up and manage Windows Autopilot.

Hardware Requirements

If you want to deploy a new machine directly from a vendor using Windows Autopilot, a unique hardware ID for the device needs to be captured and uploaded. This step can be done directly by the hardware vendor, but if you need to get this information manually, you can do so through a data gathering process that collects the device data. For this to be done, your version of Windows 10 must be version 1703 or later.

The hardware ID (commonly called a hardware hash) contains data details about the Windows client device. This data includes the manufacturer information (including the model), the device's serial number, the hard drive's serial number, and many other factors that are used to uniquely identify the device.

To manually gather this information, you can use Microsoft System Center Configuration Manager (version 1802 or higher). After all of the hash information is collected, the data can be exported from System Center Configuration Manager into a comma-separated values (CSV) file.

Once you have met the hardware requirements, you need to look at the software requirements of Windows 10/11.

Software Requirements

As stated earlier, one of the main requirements for Windows Autopilot is Windows 10/11. Windows 10 must meet the following minimum requirements:

- Windows 11 must be one of the following editions in order to use Windows Autopilot:
  - Windows 11 Pro
  - Windows 11 Pro Education
  - Windows 11 Pro for Workstations
  - Windows 11 Enterprise
  - Windows 10 Education
- Windows 10 version 1703 (Semi-Annual Channel) or higher.
- Windows 10 must be one of the following editions in order to use Windows Autopilot:
  - Windows 10 Pro
  - Windows 10 Pro Education
  - Windows 10 Pro for Workstations
  - Windows 10 Enterprise
  - Windows 10 Education

Besides meeting the minimum software requirements, your organization must also meet minimum networking requirements

Networking Requirements

Windows Autopilot depends on a variety of Internet-based services. Access to these services must be provided for Autopilot to function properly. These include an Azure subscription setup with Azure AD. Your organization must also subscribe to MDM services along with using Microsoft Intune.

After your organization sets up the Microsoft cloud–based subscriptions, you will need to ensure that the proper access to these services has been configured. This access may change based on how your Azure subscription is set up. For example, if you are using a hybrid setup (where you have an on-site network and an Azure network working together), you need to make sure that your firewall and DNS settings are set up properly. If you are using just an Azure network, you need to make sure that access to that Azure network is set up properly.

Since Windows Autopilot requires access to Internet-based services, you need to ensure that, at a minimum, the following settings are set up:

- You must properly configure DNS name resolution for your Internet DNS names.
- Firewalls must allow all hosts to have access to port 80 (HTTP), 443 (HTTPS), and 123 (UDP/NTP).
- If your organization requires that users authenticate before gaining Internet access, white-list access may be needed so that your users can access the required services.

After you have met the required software and hardware configuration, the next step is to set up Windows Autopilot profiles.

Windows Autopilot Deployment Scenarios

Windows Autopilot has an ever-expanding list of deployment scenarios. These will differ depending on the type of organization you have, how your organization is progressing on moving to Windows 10/11, and how far your organization has transitioned to modern management.

Some Windows Autopilot scenarios include:

User-Driven Mode   An end user can deploy and configure devices for themselves.

Self-Deploying Mode   Deployed devices will be automatically configured for shared use, such as a kiosk, or as a digital signage device.

Windows Autopilot Reset   A device will be redeployed in a business-ready state.

Pre-provisioning   A device will be pre-provisioned with up-to-date applications, policies, and settings.

Support for Existing Devices   An existing Windows 7 or 8.1 device will be deployed with Windows 10/11.

Now let's take a look at each of these in detail.

User-Driven Mode

User-driven mode allows you to configure new devices to automatically change from a factory state to a ready-to-use state. You do not need to touch the devices. The devices are shipped directly to the end user with the following instructions:

1. Unbox the device, plug it in, and turn it on.
2. If it uses multiple languages, select a language, locale, and keyboard.
3. Connect the device to a wireless or wired network with Internet access. If using wireless, connect to the Wi-Fi network first.
4. Specify an email address and password for your corporate account.

The rest of the process is automated. The device performs the following:

1. Joins the organization.
2. Enrolls in Microsoft Intune or another MDM service.
3. Gets configured as defined by your organization.

Self-Deploying Mode

Self-deploying mode allows you to deploy a device with no interaction from the user. No user interaction is needed for devices that are using an Ethernet connection. If the devices will be connected by Wi-Fi, then the user must select the language, locale, and keyboard and then establish a network connection. Self-deploying mode allows you to deploy a Windows device as a kiosk, a digital signage device, or a shared device. Self-deploying mode provides the following:

- Devices are joined to Azure AD. Self-deploying mode does not support Active Directory Join or Hybrid Azure AD Join. All devices will be joined to Azure AD.
- Devices are enrolled in Intune (or another MDM service) using Azure AD for automatic MDM enrollment.

- Ensures that all policies, applications, certificates, and networking profiles are provisioned on the device.

- Uses the Enrollment Status Page to prevent access until the device is fully provisioned.

To deploy in self-deploying mode, the following steps need to be performed:

1. An Autopilot profile for self-deploying mode with your required settings needs to be created. This step must be done using Microsoft Intune. You cannot create a profile using Microsoft Store for Business or Partner Center.

2. Create a device group in Azure AD and assign the Autopilot profile to that group. Make sure that the profile has been assigned to the device.

3. Then, boot the device; if using Wi-Fi, connect the device; and then wait for the provisioning process to finish.

Windows Autopilot Reset

Windows Autopilot Reset will transform a device back to a business-ready state by:

- Removing the previous users' personal files, apps, and settings. The device's primary user will be removed and the new user who signs in after reset will be set as the primary user.

- Reapplying the original settings of the device.

- Changing the region, language, and keyboard back to their original values.

- Keeping the device's Azure AD device membership and MDM enrollment information.

- Maintaining the device's management connection to Intune.

- Maintaining the Wi-Fi connection information.

- Maintaining any provisioning packages that were previously applied to the device.

- A provisioning package present on a USB drive when the reset process is started.

Autopilot Reset will prevent the new user from accessing the desktop until all information has been restored. This includes the reapplying of provisioning packages, and if a device is enrolled in an MDM service, the MDM sync must be finished.

A full device wipe will be required if the device is a Hybrid Azure AD joined device. It may take up to 24 hours for the device to be ready to be deployed again. I will go into further details on wiping a device in Chapter 11, "Managing Devices."

Autopilot Reset supports two different scenarios: local reset and remote reset. A local reset is started in-house by an administrator and a remote reset is started remotely by using an MDM service such as Microsoft Intune.

If performing a local Autopilot Reset, it involves a two-step process. The reset must first be triggered and then authenticated. To trigger a local Autopilot Reset:

1. From the Windows device lock screen, press Ctrl+[Windows] key + R. This will open a custom login screen for the local Autopilot Reset. This screen will:

   a. Confirm and verify that the end user has the right to trigger a local Autopilot Reset.

   b. Inform the user that if a provisioning package was created using Windows Configuration Designer, it will be used as part of the reset process.

2. Sign in using the admin account credentials. If a provisioning package was created, plug in the USB drive and trigger the local Autopilot Reset. Once triggered, the reset process will start. When complete, the device will be ready to be used.

If using Intune to trigger a remote restart, perform the following steps:

1. In the Intune console, navigate to the Devices tab.

2. In the All Devices view, select the device to be reset and click More to view device actions.

3. Select Autopilot Reset. If the device is not running Windows 10 build 17672 or higher, the Autopilot Reset option will not be enabled in Intune.

4. Once the reset is complete, the device is ready for use.

Pre-provisioning

Windows Autopilot helps provision new devices by using the preinstalled OEM image and drivers. Pre-provisioning can install apps, policies, profiles, and so forth. With a pre-provisioned deployment, the provisioning process is split. The more time-consuming sections are performed by the IT staff, partners, or original equipment manufacturers (OEMs), and the end user just needs to perform tasks such as settings and policies and then they can begin to use the device.

 Windows Autopilot for pre-provisioned deployment used to be called the Windows Autopilot white glove feature.

Pre-provisioning deployments require:

- Windows 10, version 1903 or later.
- Windows Pro, Enterprise, or Education editions.
- An Intune subscription.
- Physical devices that support TPM 2.0 and device attestation. Virtual machines aren't supported.
- Physical devices with Ethernet connectivity. Wi-Fi connectivity isn't supported because of the requirement to choose a language, locale, and keyboard to make a Wi-Fi connection.

Windows Autopilot for pre-provisioned deployment supports two separate scenarios that each consist of two parts: a technician flow and a user flow.

- User-driven deployments with Azure AD Join: The device will be joined to an Azure AD tenant.
- User-driven deployments with Hybrid Azure AD Join: The device will be joined to an on-premises AD domain and separately registered with Azure AD.

Support for Existing Devices

Windows Autopilot lets you deploy the latest version of Windows to existing devices. The apps that an end user needs can be installed automatically.

Windows Autopilot for existing devices only supports user-driven Azure AD and hybrid Azure AD profiles. Self-deploying and pre-provisioning profiles aren't supported.

Support for existing devices has a few prerequisites:

- A currently supported version of Microsoft Endpoint Configuration Manager current branch

- Assigned Microsoft Intune licenses

- Azure AD Premium

- A supported version of Windows 10 or Windows 11 imported into Configuration Manager as an OS image

Configure Device Registration for Autopilot

Before a device can be deployed using Windows Autopilot, it must be registered. For a device to be successfully registered, two processes must be completed. The device's hardware hash (unique hardware identity) must be captured and uploaded to the Autopilot service, and the device must be associated to an Azure tenant ID. Typically, these processes are completed by the distributor, reseller, or OEM from where the devices were bought.

You can also register from within your organization by collecting the hardware identity from new or existing devices and uploading it manually. If devices meet certain requirements, they can also be configured for automatic registration with Windows Autopilot.

You can perform Windows Autopilot device registration by manually collecting the hardware identity of devices (hardware hashes) and upload the information in a CSV file.

Before you can manually configure device registration for Autopilot, you must meet a few prerequisites and requirements:

- Intune subscription

- Windows automatic enrollment enabled

- Azure Active Directory Premium subscription

- Intune Administrator or Policy and Profile Manager permissions

To get a hardware hash from existing devices, you can use the following methods:

- Use Microsoft Endpoint Configuration Manager to automatically collect the hardware hashes for existing Windows devices.

- Use Windows PowerShell script `Get-WindowsAutopilotInfo.ps1` to get a device's hardware hash and serial number.

- From the desktop select Settings ➢ Accounts.

- Use the Diagnostics page during OOBE (Windows 11 only).

To Add Devices

Now that the hardware hashes have been captured into a CSV file, you can add the devices by importing the file. To import the file using Intune, perform the following:

1. In the Microsoft Endpoint Manager Admin Center, select Devices ➤ Windows ➤ Windows Enrollment ➤ Devices (under Windows Autopilot Deployment Program), as shown in Figure 8.3.

FIGURE 8.3   Microsoft Endpoint Manager Admin Center

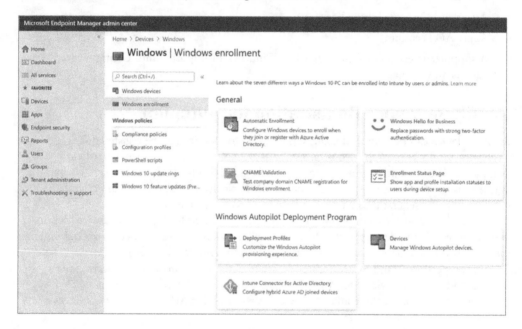

2. Select Import, the Add Windows Autopilot Devices window opens.

3. Then, under the "Specify the path to the list you want to import," browse to the CSV file that lists the devices you want to add.

4. Click the Import button. Note that this may take several minutes to complete.

5. Once the import is finished, select Devices ➤ Windows ➤ Windows Enrollment ➤ Devices (under Windows Autopilot Deployment Program) ➤Sync. Again, this process may take several minutes to complete.

6. Once the process completes, refresh to see the new added devices.

Windows Autopilot Profiles

Windows Autopilot profiles allow you to choose how the Windows client system will be set up and configured on Azure AD and Intune. This allows your organization to set up different options depending on the requirements needed for configuring the Windows devices. The following Windows Autopilot profiles are available:

Skip Cortana, OneDrive And OEM Registration Setup Pages   Any device that registers with Windows Autopilot will automatically skip the Cortana, OneDrive, and OEM registration setup pages during the OOBE process.

Automatically Set Up For Work Or School   Any device that registers with Windows Autopilot will automatically be configured as a work or school device. Because of this, these questions will not be asked during the OOBE process.

Sign In Experience With Company Branding   Instead of presenting your user with a generic Azure Active Directory sign-in page, any device that registers with Windows Autopilot will automatically be presented with a customized sign-in page. This page can be configured with the organization's name, logon, and additional help text, as configured in Azure AD.

Skip Privacy Settings   Any device that registers with Windows Autopilot will not be asked about privacy settings during the Windows 10/11 OOBE process. This setting is used if the organization is going to configure these privacy settings using Intune.

Disable Local Admin Account Creation On The Device   Organizations can decide whether the user who is registering with Windows Autopilot will have administrator access once the process is finished.

Skip End User License Agreement   If your organization is using Windows 10 version 1709 or later, organizations can allow users to skip the End-User License Agreement (EULA) page during the OOBE process. When an organization chooses this profile setting, the organization accepts the EULA terms on their users' behalf.

If you decide that you want to use PowerShell when configuring Windows Autopilot, after the software and hardware requirements are met, you can use the `Install-Module WindowsAutopilotIntune` cmdlet to configure Windows Autopilot.

Autopilot deployment profiles are used to configure the Autopilot devices. You can create up to 350 profiles per tenant. To create an Autopilot deployment profile, perform the following:

1. In the Microsoft Endpoint Manager Admin Center, choose Devices ➤ Windows ➤ Windows Enrollment ➤ Deployment Profiles ➤ Create Profile ➤ Windows PC.

2. On the Basics page, type a required Name and an optional Description (as shown in Figure 8.4).

FIGURE 8.4 Create Profile window on the Basics page

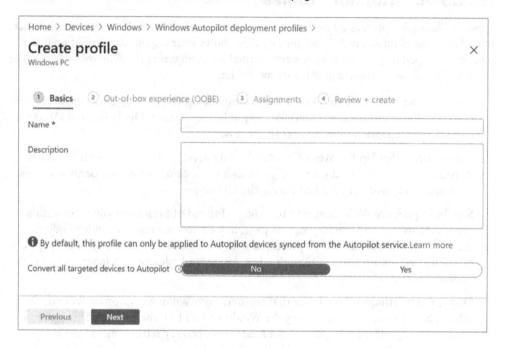

3. If you want all devices in the assigned groups to automatically convert to Autopilot, set Convert All Targeted Devices To Autopilot to Yes. You need to allow up to 48 hours for the registration to be processed. Then, click Next.

4. On the Out-Of-Box Experience (OOBE) page, as shown in Figure 8.5, under Deployment mode you can select one of two options:

   - **User-Driven:** If you select this option, devices with this profile are associated with the user who is enrolling the device by using their user credentials.

   - **Self-Deploying (Preview):** If you select this option, which requires Windows 10, version 1809 or later, devices aren't associated with the user who is enrolling the device. User credentials aren't required to enroll the device.

5. From the Join To Azure AD As drop-down list, select Azure AD Joined.

6. Configure the following options:

   - **End-User License Agreement (EULA) - (Windows 10, version 1709 or later):** Select this option if you want to show the EULA to users.

   - **Privacy Settings:** Select this if you want to show privacy settings to users.

   - **Hide Change Account Options (requires Windows 10, version 1809 or later):** Select Hide to prevent change account options from displaying on the company sign-in and domain error pages. If you select this option, it requires company branding to be configured in Azure AD.

FIGURE 8.5   Create Profile window on the Out-of-Box-Experience (OOBE) page

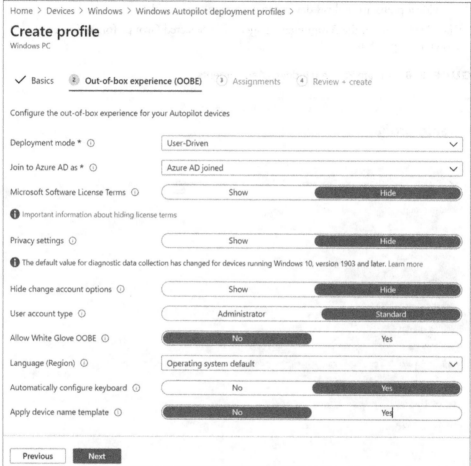

- **User account type:** Select the user's account type (Administrator or Standard user).
- **Allow White Glove OOBE (requires Windows 10, version 1903 or later; additional physical requirements):** Select Yes to allow pre-provisioning support.
- **Language (Region):** Select the language you want to use for the device.
- **Automatically Configure Keyboard:** If you specified a Language (Region), click Yes to skip the Keyboard Selection page.
- **Apply Device Name Template (requires Windows 10, version 1809 or later, and Azure AD join type):** Select Yes to create a template to use when naming a device during enrollment. Names must be 15 characters or less, and can have letters, numbers, and hyphens. Names can't be all numbers. Use the %SERIAL% macro to add

a hardware-specific serial number, or use the %RAND:*x*% macro to add a random string of numbers, where *x* equals the number of digits to add. You can only provide a prefix for hybrid devices in a domain join profile.

7. Click Next, and on the Assignments page, select Selected Groups for Assign To, as shown in Figure 8.6.

FIGURE 8.6 Create Profile window – Assignments

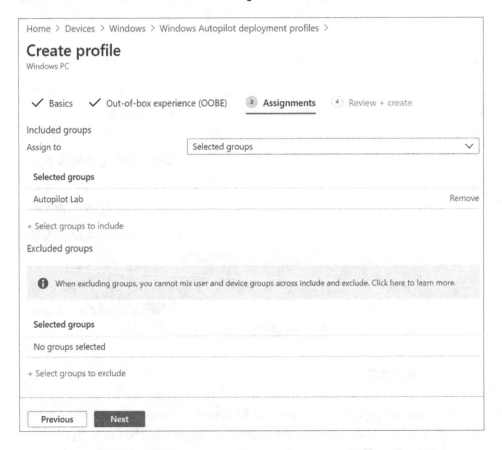

8. Choose Select Groups To Include, and select the groups you want to include in this profile. If you want to exclude any groups, choose Select Groups To Exclude, and select the groups you want to exclude. Then, click Next.

9. On the Review + Create page, review and validate your selected options and then click Create to create the profile.

Provision Windows Devices by Using Autopilot

As I mentioned previously, Windows Autopilot for pre-provisioned deployment supports two distinct scenarios that each consist of two parts: the technician flow and the user flow.

Technician Flow

After a customer or Admin has selected all the apps and settings they want for their devices through Intune, the pre-provisioning technician can begin the pre-provisioning process that I discussed previously in this chapter. The technician can be a member of the IT staff, a services partner, or an OEM. Regardless of the scenario, the process performed by the technician is the same. The technician will:

1. Boot the device.
2. On the first OOBE screen (which could be a language selection or locale selection screen), don't click Next. Instead, press the [Windows] key five times to view an additional options dialog box. From that screen, select the Windows Autopilot Provisioning option and then click Continue, as shown in Figure 8.7.

FIGURE 8.7   What Would You Like To Do? screen

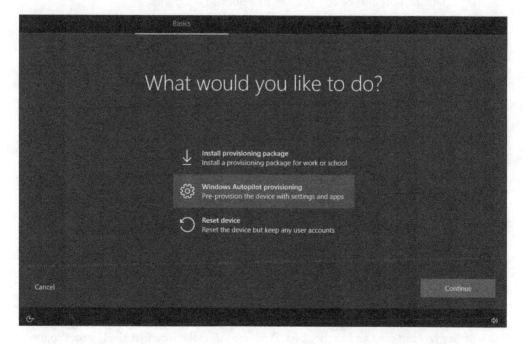

3. On the Windows Autopilot Configuration screen, information about the device will displayed, including the Autopilot profile assigned, the organization name, the user assigned (if there is one), and a QR code that contains a unique identifier. You can use

the QR code to look up the device in Intune. Validate the information that is shown. If you need to make any changes, make the changes and then select Refresh.

4. Click Provision to begin the provisioning process.

5. If the pre-provisioning process is successful then a green status screen will appear showing details about the device. Select Reseal to shut down the device. The device can now be sent to the end user. If the pre-provisioning process fails, then a red status screen will appear showing details about the device. You can then view diagnostic logs from the device and make changes, and then you can set the device to restart the pre-provisioning process.

User Flow

When the end user receives the device, they will complete a normal Windows Autopilot user-driven process by following these steps:

1. Turn on the device.

2. Choose the appropriate language, locale, and keyboard settings.

3. Connect to a network (if using Wi-Fi). Internet access is required. If using Hybrid Azure AD Join, there must also be connectivity to a domain controller.

4. On the sign-on screen, enter the user's Azure AD credentials.

5. If using Hybrid Azure AD Join, the device will reboot; after the reboot, the user enters their Active Directory credentials. Additional policies and apps may be delivered, as tracked by the Enrollment Status Page (ESP). Once complete, the user can utilize the desktop.

So, with the provisioning of Windows client devices using Autopilot (User-Driven Azure AD Joined), the configured devices are sent to the users directly and all the end user has to do is power on the device, connect to Wi-Fi, and enter their Azure AD credentials to start the Autopilot deployment. The rest of the configuration tasks will be automatic.

Troubleshoot an Autopilot Deployment

Windows Autopilot is designed to make all parts of the Windows device life cycle simple, but issues may arise, so it's important to know how to troubleshoot any problems.

Troubleshooting an Autopilot deployment can be broken down into different areas of interest. When troubleshooting, these areas include possible network connectivity issues, deployment profile or OOBE issues, Azure AD issues, and/or MDM enrollment issues.

The first thing that should be checked is the network connection. Can the device access the services needed for networking? Be sure to check if the device has obtained an IP address and whether you can ping an Internet URL. You need to make sure that the Internet connection is working for a successful Autopilot deployment.

Another key issue to check for is reviewing the configuration information. Has Azure AD, Microsoft Intune, or another MDM service been configured as needed to run Windows

Autopilot? Is the Autopilot OOBE behavior working as expected, and are the correct screens being seen? Is the device able to join Azure AD? Possibly there could be MDM enrollment issues. Is the device able to enroll in Microsoft Intune or another MDM service?

You can also check the Windows event logs in Event Viewer. You can get to these logs by going to Application And Service Logs ➤ Microsoft ➤ Windows ➤ Provisioning-Diagnostics-Provider ➤ Autopilot.

Whenever an error happens, an error code gets created. An error code is a number that indicates what the error is. This code is useful when you're trying to find a resolution to the issue. Autopilot also has some error codes associated with it. Some of the common Autopilot error codes are:

0x80070032 You will get this error if Windows Autopilot Reset is used to prepare an existing device and the Windows Recovery Environment (WinRE) is incorrectly configured and isn't enabled.

0x800705B4 This error is caused by the device being either a virtual machine or not having TPM 2.0.

0x801c03ea This error means that the device is TPM 2.0-capable but that the TPM still needs to be upgraded from 1.2 to 2.0. This error indicates that TPM attestation failed, causing a failure to join Azure AD with a device token.

0x801c0003 This error will generate a message that states, "Something went wrong," which indicates that the Azure AD join failed.

0x801C03F3 This issue can happen if Azure AD can't find an Azure AD device object for the device that you're trying to deploy.

0x80180014 After the first Autopilot deployment, devices with a targeted Autopilot self-deployment mode or pre-provisioning mode profile can't automatically reenroll using Autopilot.

0x80180018 This error will generate a message that states, "Something went wrong," which indicates the MDM enrollment failed.

0x81039023 This is a code generated on Windows 11 indicating that TPM attestation has failed during the pre-provisioning technician flow or self-deployment mode.

0xc1036501 This error indicates that the device can't do an automatic MDM enrollment because there are multiple MDM configurations in Azure AD.

In the following sections, I will delve into greater detail regarding a few of the errors that Autopilot may encounter.

Device Import and Enrollment Troubleshooting

Some issues may happen when importing and enrolling devices into Intune. Devices using Autopilot self-deployment mode or pre-provisioning mode profile may not be automatically enrolled using Autopilot and receive an error code 0x80180014. In order to reuse a device, you must first delete the device record created by Intune. The resolution to this error code is to redeploy the device through Autopilot by deleting the device record in Intune and then redeploying the Autopilot deployment profile.

Another issue that may arise with device import and enrollment is that the Windows MDM enrollment is disabled in the Intune tenant. To fix this, follow these steps:

1. In the Microsoft Endpoint Manager Admin Center, choose Devices ➤ Enrollment Restrictions, and then select a device type restriction.

2. Choose Properties ➤ Edit next to Platform Settings and then select Allow For Windows (MDM).

3. Click Review and then Save.

Autopilot OOBE Troubleshooting

If you're having issues with an OOBE, it is helpful to first check whether the device received an Autopilot profile.

If you get an error stating that "Something went wrong" or "Can't connect to the URL of your organization's MDM terms of use. Try again, or contact your system administrator with the problem information from this page," this is usually due to a licensing issue. You need to ensure that the user who is signing into the device has a valid license.

If you need to reboot a computer during OOBE, you can use the shutdown command. shutdown is a command prompt command that powers off, restarts, logs off, or hibernates a computer. If you have access over the network, the shutdown command can also remotely shut down or restart a computer. To force an Autopilot profile to be downloaded, you should reboot the device during OOBE to allow the device to retrieve the profile. Press Shift+F10 to open a command prompt at the start of the OOBE and then enter **shutdown /r /t 0** to restart the device immediately or enter **shutdown /s /t 0** to shut down immediately. The /s switch will shut down the local machine. The /t switch is the time, in seconds, between the execution of the shutdown command and the actual shutdown or restart.

Azure Active Directory Join Troubleshooting

The most common problem when joining a device to Azure AD is permissions. You need to ensure that the correct configuration is in place to allow users to join devices to Azure AD.

Another issue that can occur is that the user has exceeded the number of devices that they are allowed to join. This limit is configured in Azure AD.

Windows Autopilot Diagnostics Page

If you are using Window 11, Autopilot has a diagnostics page that allows you to view additional troubleshooting information regarding the provisioning process. This page is enabled through the Autopilot Enrollment Status Page (ESP). To deploy the ESP to devices, you have to create an ESP profile in Microsoft Intune. The diagnostics page is enabled by going to the ESP profile and selecting Yes to turn on log collection and diagnostics page for end users. Then you click the View Diagnostics button or press the keyboard shortcut Ctrl+Shift+D to access the information. The diagnostics page is currently supported for commercial OOBE and Autopilot user-driven mode.

Using Microsoft Deployment Toolkit (MDT)

The Microsoft Deployment Toolkit (MDT) is a free tool that is offered by Microsoft for automating Windows and Windows Server operating system deployments and to help take advantage of the Windows Assessment and Deployment Kit (ADK).

MDT can be used to create images or used as a complete deployment solution. It is used to help automate the deployment of Windows operating systems and applications to desktop, portable, and server computers. MDT supports the deployment of Windows 10 as well as Windows 7, Windows 8.1, and Windows Server. However, at the time of writing this book, MDT is not supported for Windows 11.

You can download Microsoft Deployment Toolkit (MDT) for free from Microsoft's website: www.microsoft.com/en-us/download/details.aspx?id=54259.

I discussed installing and working with the MDT in Chapter 1, "Windows Client Installation."

Planning MDT Deployments

When planning an MDT deployment, there are a number of questions you must first ask yourself and factors to consider. These questions and factor considerations will help you determine the best deployment path to meet your needs. MDT supports three types of deployment methods:

Lite Touch Installation (LTI)   Requires limited user interaction.

User-Driven Installation (UDI)   Requires complete intervention, manually, to respond to all installation prompts, such as machine name, password, or language settings.

Zero Touch Installation (ZTI)   Is a completely automated deployment plan that does not require any interaction with any user for installation.

Table 8.4 provides a checklist that you can use to help in the planning process. This is not a complete list of questions to ask yourself. To see an entire list of possible questions, please visit Microsoft's website at https://docs.microsoft.com/en-us/mem/configmgr/mdt/use-the-mdt#PlanningMdtDeployments.

 The information in Table 8.4 was taken directly from Microsoft's website and documentation and was current as of this writing.

TABLE 8.4   MDT planning deployment questions/planning checklist

Question	Overview
Where will you store your distribution files?	Files for the operating system and applications are stored in deployment shares for LTI and distribution points for ZTI and UDI.
Will you deploy across the network, with removable media, or both?	If you are deploying across the network, verify that there is sufficient bandwidth between the deployment shares, distribution points, and the target computers, and provide regional distribution points.
What is your imaging and source file strategy?	The MDT deployment process allows for the creation of customized images that are first deployed to a reference computer, then captured from the reference computer, and finally deployed to target computers.
Will you deploy a full set of operating system files or a custom image?	As part of the planning process, determine the types of images that you will create.
How will you handle product keys and licensing?	Small organizations might assign each user an individual product key. Larger organizations should use Key Management Service (KMS) or Multiple Activation Key (MAK) activation.

MDT Configuration Options

There are a number of configuration options you can set depending on your needs when using MDT. Some of these options include:

Boot Images   Boot images are the Windows PE images that are used to initiate deployments. Boot images can be started from a CD or DVD, an ISO file, a USB device, or over the network using a Preboot Execution Environment (PXE) server. The boot images connect to the deployment share on the server and start the deployment.

Operating Systems   You can import the operating systems you wish to deploy by using the Deployment Workbench. You can import either the full source or a custom image. The full source operating systems are typically used to create reference images.

Packages   You can add any Microsoft package using the Deployment Workbench. The most commonly added packages are language packs. You also can add security and other updates this way. However, Microsoft recommends using the Windows Server Update Services (WSUS) for operating system updates.

Task Sequences   Task sequences are the heart of a deployment solution. When creating a task sequence, you need to select a template. The templates are located in the `Templates` folder in the MDT installation directory, and determine which actions are present in the sequence.

Driver Repository   You can use the Deployment Workbench to import drivers into a driver repository. The driver repository will reside on the server.

Plan and Implement PXE Boot by Using Windows Deployment Services (WDS)

Windows Deployment Services (WDS) is a suite of components that allows you to remotely install Windows on client computers.

A WDS server installs Windows 10 on the client computers. The WDS server must be configured with the Preboot Execution Environment (PXE) boot files, the images to be deployed to the client computers, and the answer file. WDS client computers must be PXE-capable. PXE is a technology that is used to boot to the network when no operating system or network configuration has been installed and configured on a client computer.

I discussed installing WDS in Chapter 1, "Windows Client Installation."

Create and Use Task Sequences

A task sequence is a list of actions and conditions that will be run in a certain order. Some examples include:

Apply Operating System   The sequence will use ImageX to apply an image.

Format and Partition   The sequence will create the partition(s) and format them.

Gather   The sequence will read configuration settings from the deployment server.

Inject Drivers   The sequence will figure out what drivers a machine needs and will download the appropriate drivers from a central driver repository.

Windows Update   The sequence will connect to a WSUS server and update the machine.

When the task sequence is run, the actions of each step are performed at the command-line level without requiring user intervention.

To create a task sequence, open the MDT Workbench, right-click the Task Sequences node, and then click New Task Sequence. This will open the New Task Sequence Wizard, which consists of a combined series of steps that are designed to complete an action, as shown in Figure 8.8.

FIGURE 8.8   New Task Sequence Wizard

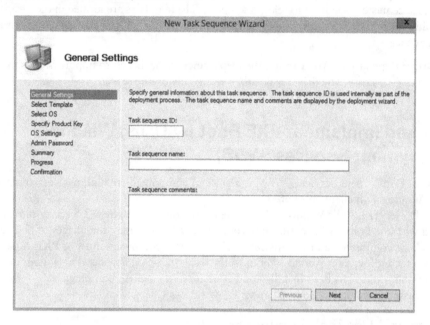

MDT comes with several default task sequence templates that you can utilize. You can also create your own templates as long as they are stored in the Templates folder. The task sequence templates that are included with MDT are shown in Table 8.5.

TABLE 8.5   Task sequence templates

Task sequence template	Description
Sysprep and Capture Task Sequence	Used to run the System Preparation (Sysprep) tool and capture an image of a reference computer.
Standard Client Task Sequence	Most frequently used. This template will create reference images and is used for deploying clients.
Standard Client Replace Task Sequence	Used to run User State Migration Tool (USMT) backup and the optional full Windows Imaging (WIM) backup action. This template can also be used to perform a secure wipe of a machine that is going to be decommissioned.
Custom Task Sequence	Used to create a custom task sequence with only one default action.

Task sequence template	Description
Standard Server Task Sequence	Used as the default task sequence for deploying operating system images to servers. The main difference between this template and the Standard Client template is that it does not contain any USMT actions because USMT is not supported on servers.
Lite Touch OEM Task Sequence	Used to preload operating systems images on the computer hard drive. Typically used by computer OEMs, but some enterprise organizations also use this feature.
Post OS Installation Task Sequence	Used to run actions after the operating system has been deployed. Very useful for server deployments but not often used for client deployments.
Deploy to VHD Client Task Sequence	Similar to the Standard Client task sequence template but also creates a virtual hard disk (VHD) file on the target computer and deploys the image to the VHD file.
Deploy to VHD Server Task Sequence	Same as the Deploy to VHD Client task sequence but for servers.
Standard Client Upgrade Task Sequence	Used to perform an in-place upgrade from Windows 7, Windows 8, or Windows 8.1 directly to Windows 10, automatically preserving existing data, settings, applications, and drivers.

Manage Application and Driver Deployment

Use the Deployment Workbench to create a folder in the Applications directory:

1. In the Deployment Workbench, expand the Deployment Share.
2. Right-click Applications, then select New Folder.
3. On the General tab, add a folder name. This is a required step.
4. If you wish, add comments to describe the folder.

To import applications using the Deployment Workbench, perform the following steps:

1. Open the Deployment Workbench and expand the Deployment Share.
2. Right-click the Applications directory, and select New Application. This will open the New Application Wizard.
3. On the Application Type page, select Application With Source Files and click Next.
4. Enter the name of the application, the publisher, version, and language and then click Next.

5. Enter the location of the installer and source files in the Source Directory, then click Next.

    Select the Move The File check box if you want to only keep the files in the deployment share and not in the original location.

6. On the Destination page, enter a name for the folder that will be created in the Application directory of the deployment share. Then click Next.

7. On the Command Details page, add the name of the executable that will install the software. Then click Next.

8. On the summary page, review the options and click Next.

    After completion, the confirmation page displays the output.

A key to successful management of drivers for MDT is to have a driver repository. Make sure to visit the vendor's website to download the appropriate drivers. For boot images, you need to have storage and network drivers; for the operating system, you need to have the full suite of drivers. From this repository, you can import drivers into MDT for deployment. When you import drivers to the MDT driver repository, MDT will create a single instance folder structure based on the driver class names.

Customsettings.ini and *Bootstrap.ini*

Customsettings.ini and Bootstrap.ini are the main files of your configuration. They are the rules that control the Windows Deployment Wizard on the client side.

The Bootstrap.ini file can be edited to include information that is site-specific and can include information such as the Default Gateway IP address or MAC address. The Bootstrap.ini file is processed first when you boot into WinPE. The CustomSettings .ini is processed after the Welcome screen and at various times during the task sequence. Bootstrap.ini can be accessed in one of two ways:

-   On the Rules tab of the Deployment Share properties, click the Edit Bootstrap.ini button.

-   Access the Bootstrap.ini file in the Control subdirectory the Deployment Share.

CustomSettings.ini specifies the instructions to perform actions and set parameters in MDT. You can access CustomSettings.ini in one of two ways:

-   On the Rules tab of the Deployment Share properties

-   The CustomSettings.ini file in the Control subdirectory of the Deployment Share

Monitor and Troubleshoot Deployment

There is a chance, at some point, that you may encounter an issue during the deployment process. It could be one of a number of different things, such as a missing driver, incorrect settings, or an improper script syntax. That is where log file can help.

When running, each MDT script creates a log file automatically. These log files are a useful tool if you need to troubleshoot an issue. The MDT log files end with a .log extension. You can use either CMTrace or Configuration Manager to view the MDT log files. The names of the log files match the name of the script.

For troubleshooting, you can locate MDT log files in three locations:

- `X:\MININT\SMSOSD\OSDLOGS` before the image is applied to a device
- `C:\MININT\SMSOSD\OSDLOGS` during the deployment process
- `%WINDIR%\SMSOSD` or `%WINDIR%\TEMP\SMSOSD` after a successful deployment

MDT creates the following log files:

BDD.log   This file is the combined MDT log file that is copied to a network location at the end of the deployment if you specify the `SLShare` property in the `Customsettings.ini` file.

LiteTouch.log   This file is created during LTI deployments. It resides in `%WINDIR%\TEMP\DeploymentLogs` unless you specify the `/debug:true` option.

***Scriptname**.log**   This file is created by each MDT script. *Scriptname* represents the name of the script.

SMSTS.log   This file is created by the Task Sequencer and describes all Task Sequencer transactions. Depending on the deployment scenario, it may reside in `%TEMP%`, `%WINDIR%\System32\ccm\logs`, `C:\_SMSTaskSequence`, or `C:\SMSTSLog`.

Wizard.log   The deployment wizard creates and updates this file.

WPEinit.log   This file is created during the Windows PE initialization process and is useful for troubleshooting errors encountered while starting Windows PE.

DeploymentWorkbench_id.log   This log file is created in the `%temp%` folder when you specify `/debug` when starting the Deployment Workbench.

Plan and Configure User State Migration

The User State Migration Tool (USMT) is included with the Windows Assessment and Deployment Kit (Windows ADK) for Windows 10/11. The USMT is used by administrators to migrate users from one computer to another via a command-line utility.

You can use the USMT to simplify user state migration during deployments of the Windows operating system. The USMT captures user accounts, user files, operating system settings, application settings, and then migrates those settings to a new Windows installation.

You can automate the user profile migration process by using deployment automation tools, such as System Center Configuration Manager or the MDT for large-scale deployments.

USMT uses configurable migration rule (.xml) files to control exactly which user accounts, files, operating system settings, and application settings are migrated and how they are migrated. You can use USMT for both side-by-side migrations, where one piece of hardware is being replaced, or wipe-and-load (or refresh) migrations, when only the operating system is being upgraded.

USMT includes command-line tools that must be run under an account with local administrator permissions, they are:

- ScanState.exe
- LoadState.exe
- UsmtUtils.exe

USMT also includes a set of four .xml files that can be modified, they are:

- MigApp.xml contains rules for transferring the user's data.
- MigDocs.xml contains document transfer rules.
- MigUser.xml contains rules for transferring users' profiles.
- Config.xml contains information on the components that are excluded from the transfer.

USMT allows you to write data to a local disk, removable USB drive, or a shared network folder. It cannot directly transfer data across the network from the source to the target device.

The scanstate command syntax is as follows:

```
scanstate [StorePath] [/apps] [/ppkg:FileName] [/i:[Path\]FileName]
[/o] [/v:VerbosityLevel] [/nocompress] [/localonly] [/encrypt
/key:KeyString|/keyfile:[Path\]FileName] [/l:[Path\]FileName]
[/progress:[Path\]FileName] [/r:TimesToRetry] [/w:SecondsBeforeRetry]
[/c] [/p] [/all] [/ui:[DomainName|ComputerName\]UserName]
[/ue:[DomainName|ComputerName\]UserName]
[/uel:NumberOfDays|YYYY/MM/DD|0] [/efs:abort|skip|decryptcopy|copyraw]
[/genconfig:[Path\]FileName[/config:[Path\]FileName] [/?|help]
```

For a complete list and description of the options for the scanstate command, check out Microsoft's website at https://docs.microsoft.com/en-us/windows/deployment/usmt/usmt-scanstate-syntax.

The LoadState command syntax is as follows:

```
loadstate StorePath [/i:[Path\]FileName] [/v:VerbosityLevel]
[/nocompress] [/decrypt /key:KeyString|/keyfile:[Path\]FileName]
[/l:[Path\]FileName] [/progress:[Path\]FileName] [/r:TimesToRetry]
[/w:SecondsToWait] [/c] [/all]
[/ui:[DomainName|ComputerName\]UserName]
[/ue:[[DomainName|ComputerName\]UserName]
[/uel:NumberOfDays|YYYY/MM/DD|0] [/md:OldDomain:NewDomain]
[/mu:OldDomain\OldUserName:[NewDomain\]NewUserName] [/lac:[Password]]
[/lae] [/config:[Path\]FileName] [/?|help]
```

For a complete list and description of the options for the `LoadState` command, visit Microsoft's website at `https://docs.microsoft.com/en-us/windows/deployment/usmt/usmt-loadstate-syntax`.

`UsmtUtils.exe` is used for deleting a hard-link store, validating a compressed file store, and extracting data from a compressed file store. The syntax for `UsmtUtils.exe` is as follows:

```
usmtutils [/ec | /rd <storeDir> | /verify <filepath> [options] |
/extract <filepath> <destinationPath> [options]]
```

For a complete list and description of the options for the `UsmtUtils.exe` command, visit Microsoft's website at `https://docs.microsoft.com/en-us/windows/deployment/usmt/usmt-utilities`.

USMT Phases

There are three phases that occur when migrating files and settings using USMT:

- **Phase 1:** Plan the migration.
- **Phase 2:** Collect the files and settings from the source computer.
- **Phase 3:** Prepare the destination computer and restore files and settings.

In Phase 1, there are several steps when planning your migration using USMT:

1. Determine if the migration will be refreshing or replacing computers; you can choose an online migration or an offline migration using Windows Preinstallation Environment (WinPE) or the files in the `Windows.old` directory.

2. Specify what you'd like to migrate.

3. Specify where you'd like to store the data.

4. Use the `/GenMigXML` command-line option to determine which files will be included in the migration and to determine whether any modifications are necessary.

5. Modify copies of the `Migration.xml` and `MigDocs.xml` files and create custom .xml files, if needed.

6. Create a `Config.xml` file if you want to exclude any components from the migration. For example, the following command creates a `Config.xml` file by using the `MigDocs.xml` and `MigApp.xml` files:
   ```
   scanstate /genconfig:config.xml /i:migdocs.xml /i:migapp.xml
   /v:13 /l:scanstate.log
   ```

7. Review the migration state of the components listed in the `Config.xml` file, and specify `migrate=no` for any components that you do not want to migrate.

In Phase 2, you collect the files and settings from the source computer:

1. Back up the source computer.

2. Close all applications.

3. Run the `scanstate` command on the source computer to collect files and settings. Make sure to specify all of the .xml files that you want the `scanstate` command to use—for example,

```
scanstate \\server\migration\mystore /config:config.xml
/i:migdocs.xml /i:migapp.xml /v:13 /l:scan.log
```

4. Run the USMTUtils command with the /Verify command to ensure that the store you created is not corrupted.

In Phase 3, you prepare the destination computer and restore files and settings:

1. Install the operating system on the destination computer.

2. Install all applications that were on the source computer.

3. Close all applications.

4. Run the LoadState command on the destination computer. Specify the same .xml files that you specified when you used the scanstate command. For example, the following command migrates the files and settings:

```
loadstate \\server\migration\mystore /config:config.xml
/i:migdocs.xml /i:migapp.xml /v:13 /l:load.log
```

5. Log off after you run the LoadState command. Some settings may not take effect until the next time the user logs on.

Summary

This chapter discussed Windows client deployments and a variety of deployment tools offered by Microsoft. I discussed assessing your infrastructure readiness by using Endpoint Analytics, which is part of the Microsoft Endpoint Manager (MEM). I covered imaging and provisioning strategies and how to implement changes to Windows editions by using subscription activation or using Multiple Activation Key (MAK) license management.

I also talked about installing Windows client devices using Windows Autopilot. I explained how Windows Autopilot is used and configured and the requirements needed to use it. I also explained the different profiles that you can use with Windows Autopilot. I covered client provisioning using Windows Autopilot and planning and implementing deployments by using the Microsoft Deployment Toolkit (MDT).

Microsoft Deployment Toolkit (MDT) is a way of automating desktop and server deployment. With MDT, you can deploy desktops and servers through the use of a common console, which allows for quicker deployments, having standardized desktop and server images and security and zero-touch deployments of Windows clients.

Exam Essentials

Know how to use Endpoint Analytics.   Assess infrastructure readiness by using Endpoint Analytics. Endpoint Analytics is a cloud-based service that works in conjunction with

Configuration Manager and Intune that helps you to make important decisions regarding the update readiness of a Windows client.

Understand Subscription Activation or MAK license management.   Subscription Activation enables users to switch from Windows Professional to Enterprise. Microsoft refers to this as "step-up." A Multiple Activation Key (MAK) is used by companies that have a volume licensing agreement. A MAK will activate systems on a one-time basis by using Microsoft's hosted activation services.

Know how to select a deployment tool based on requirements.   Which deployment method should you use? There really is no right or wrong answer—you use what works best for you or your organization, and you need to consider what you want to achieve. Windows client deployments fall into one of three categories: modern, dynamic, and traditional.

Be able to choose an imaging or provisioning strategy.   Again, there is no right or wrong— you select what will work best for you. The reference computer is installed and configured with the settings and applications that should be installed on the target computers. The image is then created and can be transferred to other computers. A provisioning package (.ppkg) is a collection of configuration settings. You can create provisioning packages that let you quickly configure a device without having to install a new image.

Be familiar with using Windows Autopilot.   Windows Autopilot is a group of multiple technologies that allow you to set up and configure brand-new devices, repurpose current machines, and even recover corporate machines.

Understand the Microsoft Deployment Toolkit (MDT).   Know that the MDT is a way of automating desktop and client deployment. Understand that the MDT allows you to deploy desktops and servers through the use of a common console.

Video Resources

There are no videos for this chapter.

Review Questions

1. You are the administrator for your company network. You and a colleague are discussing Windows Autopilot error codes. Which of the following codes shows error code ERROR_ NOT_SUPPORTED when you have used Windows Autopilot Reset?

   A. 0x800705B4

   B. 0x801c0003

   C. 0x80180018

   D. 0x80070032

2. You are the network administrator for StormWind Studios. Your network contains an Active Directory domain. The domain contains 300 computers that run Windows 10/11. You have both an on-site Active Directory network and a Microsoft Azure Active Directory (Azure AD) with Microsoft Intune. You need to automatically register all the existing computers to the Azure AD network and also enroll all of the computers in Intune. What should you use?

   A. Use a DNS Autodiscover address record.

   B. Use a Windows Autopilot deployment profile.

   C. Use an Autodiscover service connection point (SCP).

   D. Set up a Group Policy Object (GPO).

3. You are the administrator for your company network. You and a colleague are discussing a way to create an inventory of applications that are currently running within your company. There is a service that works in conjunction with Configuration Manager that allows you to create an inventory of applications. What is this service called?

   A. Delivery Optimization

   B. Endpoint Analytics

   C. Upgrade Readiness

   D. Windows Analytics

4. You are the administrator for your company network. You use Windows Autopilot to configure the computer settings of computers that are issued to employees. An employee has been using an issued Windows client computer and then leaves the company. You'd like to transfer that computer to a new user. You need to make sure that when the new user first starts the computer, they will be prompted to select the language settings and to agree to the license agreement. What should you do?

   A. You should create a new Windows Autopilot self-deploying deployment profile.

   B. You should create a new Windows Autopilot user-driven deployment profile.

   C. You should perform a local Windows Autopilot Reset.

   D. You should perform a remote Windows Autopilot Reset.

5. You are the administrator for your company network. You are using Windows Deployment Service (WDS) to install a number of Windows 10 computers. When users attempt to use WDS, they are not able to complete the unattended installation. You suspect that the WDS server has not been configured to respond to user requests. To respond to user requests, which one of the following utilities should you use to configure the WDS server?

A. You should use Active Directory Users and Computers.

B. You should use Active Directory Users and Groups.

C. You should use the Windows Deployment Service (WDS) MMC snap-in.

D. You should use the WDSMAN utility.

6. You have computers that run Windows 10 Pro. The computers are joined to Microsoft Azure Active Directory (Azure AD) and enrolled in Microsoft Intune for Mobile Device Management (MDM). You need to upgrade the computers to Windows 10 Enterprise. What should you configure in Intune?

A. A device enrollment policy

B. A device cleanup rule

C. A device compliance policy

D. A Windows Autopilot device profile

7. You are the administrator for your company network. You and a colleague are discussing the different deployment scenarios and the categories into which certain scenarios fall. You are discussing Subscription Activation. Which category does this fall into in regard to deployment scenarios?

A. Contemporary deployment category

B. Dynamic deployment category

C. Modern deployment category

D. Traditional deployment category

8. You are the administrator for your company network. The network has an Active Directory domain. The domain contains several thousand Windows client computers. You implement hybrid Microsoft Azure Active Directory (Azure AD) and Microsoft Intune. You have to register all of the existing computers automatically to Azure AD and enroll the computers in Intune. What should you do while using the least amount of administrative effort?

A. You should configure an Autodiscover address record.

B. You should configure an Autodiscover service connection point (SCP).

C. You should configure a Group Policy object (GPO).

D. You should configure a Windows Autopilot deployment profile.

9. You are the administrator for your company network. You have several computers that are running Windows client and have been configured by using Windows Autopilot. A user performs the following tasks on one of the computers:

- Creates a VPN connection to the corporate network

- Installs a Microsoft Store app named App1

- Connects to a Wi-Fi network

You perform a Windows Autopilot Reset on the computer. What will be the state of the Wi-Fi connection on the computer when the user signs in?

A. The Wi-Fi connection will be removed.

B. The Wi-Fi connection will be retained, and the passphrase will be retained.

C. The Wi-Fi connection will be retained, but the passphrase will be reset.

D. The Wi-Fi connection will be removed, but the passphrase will be retained.

10. You are the administrator for your company network. Your company infrastructure is comprised of the following:

- A Microsoft 365 tenant
- An Active Directory forest
- A Microsoft Store for Business
- A Key Management Service (KMS) server
- A Windows Deployment Services (WDS) server
- A Microsoft Azure Active Directory (Azure AD) Premium tenant

You purchase 100 new Windows 10/11 computers, and you want to make sure that the new computers are automatically joined to the Azure AD by using Windows Autopilot. What information will be required from each computer?

A. You will need the device serial number and hardware hash.

B. You will need the MAC address and computer name.

C. You will need the volume license key and computer name.

D. No additional information will be needed.

11. You are the administrator for your company network. You have several computers that are running Windows 10/11 and have been configured using Windows Autopilot. A user performs the following tasks on one of the computers:

- Creates a VPN connection to the corporate network
- Installs a Microsoft Store app named App1
- Connects to a Wi-Fi network

You perform a Windows Autopilot Reset on the computer. What will be the state of App1 on the computer when the user signs in?

A. The app will be reinstalled at sign-in.

B. The app will be removed.

C. The app will be retained.

D. Nothing will happen; it can't be done.

12. You are the administrator for your company network. Your company has a Microsoft Azure Active Directory (Azure AD) tenant. You have a volume licensing agreement and use product keys to activate Windows 10. You are planning on deploying Window 10 Pro to several hundred new computers by using the Microsoft Deployment Toolkit (MDT) and Windows Deployment Services (WDS). What should you configure if you need to make sure the new computers will be configured with the correct product keys during the installation?

   A. The Device settings in Azure AD

   B. An MDT task sequence

   C. A WDS boot image

   D. A Windows Autopilot deployment profile

13. You are the administrator for your company network. You and a colleague are discussing Autopilot and what needs to be done if a device has not downloaded the Autopilot profile. You first reboot the device during an OOBE to allow the device to try to retrieve the profile, but that doesn't work. What should you do next?

   A. At the start of the OOBE, you should press Shift+F10 to open a command prompt and then enter **shutdown /r /t 0**.

   B. At the start of the OOBE, you should press Shift+F10 to open a command prompt and then enter **shutdown /s /t 0**.

   C. At the start of the OOBE, you should press Shift+F8 to open a command prompt and then enter **shutdown /h /t 60**.

   D. At the start of the OOBE, you should press Shift+F8 to open a command prompt and then enter **shutdown /o /t 60**.

14. You are the administrator for your company network. A remote user buys a new laptop that has Windows 10 Professional installed. They will be using this laptop for corporate business. You need to configure the laptop as follows:

   ▪ You must modify the layout of the Start Menu.

   ▪ You must upgrade Windows 10 Professional to Windows 10 Enterprise.

   ▪ You must join the laptop to the Microsoft Azure Active Directory (Azure AD) corporate domain.

   What should you do?

   A. You should create a custom Windows image (.wim) file that contains an image of Windows 10 Enterprise and upload the file to a Microsoft user.

   B. You should create a provisioning package (.ppkg) file and email the file to the user.

   C. You should create a Sysprep Unattend (.xml) file and email the file to the user.

   D. You should create a Windows To Go workspace and ship the workspace to the user.

15. You are the administrator for your company network. You have a hybrid Microsoft Azure Active Directory (Azure AD) tenant. You configure a Windows Autopilot deployment profile. The deployment profile is configured as follows:

Name: Autopilot1

Convert all targeted devices to Autopilot: No

Deployment Mode: User-Driven

Join to Azure AD as: Azure AD joined

You want to apply the profile to a new computer. What should you do first?

A. Assign a user to a specific Autopilot device.

B. Enroll the device in Microsoft Intune.

C. Import a CSV file into Windows Autopilot.

D. Join the device to Azure AD.

16. You are the administrator for your company network. You have a hybrid Microsoft Azure Active Directory (Azure AD) tenant. You configure a Windows Autopilot deployment profile. The deployment profile is configured as follows:

Name: Autopilot1

Convert all targeted devices to Autopilot: No

Deployment Mode: User-Driven

Join to Azure AD as: Azure AD joined

When the Windows Autopilot profile is applied to the computer, the computer will be which of the following?

A. Joined to Active Directory only

B. Joined to Azure AD only

C. Registered in Azure AD only

D. Joined to Active Directory and registered in Azure AD

17. You are the administrator for your company network. There is a Microsoft tool that allows a Windows client computer to be set up with all applications and operating systems automatically without any administrator intervention. What is this called?

A. Deployment Image Servicing and Management (DISM)

B. Windows 10 Admin setup

C. Windows Autopilot

D. Windows Internal Database (WID) Server

18. You are the administrator for your company network. Your network contains several hundred Windows 7 computers. Some of these computers are used by multiple users. You are planning to refresh the operating system of the computers to Windows 10, but you need to retain the personalization settings to applications before you refresh the computers. Your solution must minimize network bandwidth and network storage space. What command should you run on the computers?

A. `dism.exe /i myapp.xml /genconfig:myfile1.xml /nocompress /ui :mysite\*`

B. `scandisk /i myapp.xml /genconfig:myfile1.xml /nocompress /ui :mysite\*`

C. `scanstate /i myapp.xml /genconfig:myfile1.xml /nocompress /ui :mysite\*`

D. `usmtutils.exe /i myapp.xml /genconfig:myfile1.xml /nocompress /ui :mysite\*`

19. You are the administrator for your company network. You have a Microsoft Intune subscription. You configure a Windows Autopilot deployment profile. The deployment profile is configured as follows:

Name: Profile1

Convert all targeted devices to Autopilot: No

Deployment Mode: User-Driven

Out-of-box experience (OOBE): Defaults configured

End user license agreement (EULA): Hide

Privacy settings: Hide

Hide change account settings: Hide

User account type: Standard

Apply computer name template (Windows Insider only): No

During the deployment, users can configure which of the following?

A. Users can configure the computer name.

B. Users can configure the Cortana settings.

C. Users can configure the keyboard layout.

D. Users can configure the wallpaper settings.

20. You are the administrator for your company network. You and a colleague are discussing files that can be used with the User State Migration Tool (USMT). What file extension is used with the migration files?

A. `.csv`

B. `.docx`

C. `.txt`

D. `.xml`

Chapter

9

Managing Identity and Access

MICROSOFT EXAM OBJECTIVES COVERED IN THIS CHAPTER:

✓ **Manage identity**

- Enable users and groups from Azure Active Directory (Azure AD) to access Windows client; register devices in and join devices to Azure AD; manage AD DS and Azure AD groups; manage AD DS and Azure AD users; configure Enterprise State Roaming in Azure AD.

✓ **Plan and implement conditional access policies**

- Plan conditional access; set up conditional access policies; determine which users are affected by a conditional access policy; troubleshoot conditional access.

Now that you understand how to create a Windows client device, it's time to work with Active Directory. There are different ways to set up Active Directory. As an administrator, you can set up Active Directory on your local networks or in an Azure virtual machine. But you can also set up Active Directory within the Azure desktop.

For all of you administrators who currently work on an Active Directory network, Azure Active Directory is not really the Active Directory that we all know. It is a database that controls access, and yes, you can join computers to an Azure Active Directory network, but that's almost where the similarities stop.

So, I think the best way to talk about Active Directory in this chapter is to talk about what it does and how Azure Active Directory differs from that. Then the features and limitations of Azure Active Directory will be a lot clearer to you.

Active Directory vs. Azure Active Directory

One of the most confusing things that Microsoft can do at times is assign to a new feature or service a name that's similar to the name of an existing feature or service. This is what happened here with Active Directory and Azure Active Directory.

A perfect example of this is Universal Group Membership Caching (UGMC). UGMC has *nothing* to do with Universal Groups. Universal Groups are a type of group and UGMC helps a site, with no Global Catalog, with logins. But because they both have the words Universal Groups, people think that they are connected.

Azure Active Directory is not the Active Directory that most of us use on a daily basis. This might be overstating it a bit. Think of Azure Active Directory as Active Directory lite. So, let's look at Active Directory and then look at Azure Active Directory so that you can see the differences between the two.

Understanding Active Directory

There are different ways that you can set up a network. If all of the machines can work both as clients and servers, this type of network is referred to as a workgroup or peer-to-peer network. The downside of this type of network is that it is too small and that each computer has its own authentication database. This means that every user has to have an account on every computer. This can lead to all types of issues, and it is also a very difficult network to manage.

This is where Active Directory comes in. Active Directory at its core is just a database. It's a single database that all of your users can belong to. This makes it much easier to manage a network, and it also allows you to have better control over the users and their permissions.

Active Directory is built on the database standard called Directory Services. Directory Services got its "claim to fame" with Novell. Novell used Directory Services to control access to their networks. When Microsoft decided to move their network over to Directory Services, they decided to name their version Active Directory.

Active Directory networks are grouped together in units known as domains (shown as triangles). A domain is a logical grouping of objects into a distributed database. Some of these objects are user accounts, group accounts, and published objects (folders and printers).

It is very important to understand that domains are a logical grouping of objects. *Logical* is the key word in this description. Domains are logical, not physical. For example, Microsoft.com is a worldwide entity. Not all of the domain users are located in Redmond, Washington. They are scattered all over the world.

Active Directory can be a local version by loading Active Directory onto an on-site server or setting up Active Directory in a virtual machine on Azure. But Active Directory is Active Directory no matter how you set it up. It's a database that you set up to help control access to your network. It doesn't matter if that network is on-site or in a VM in the cloud.

One of the advantages to using domains is the ability to have a *child domain*, which is a subdomain of another domain. You can build child domains based on physical locations, departments, and so forth.

Child domains give you greater scalability. Active Directory child domains give an administrator the flexibility to design a structure that meets an organization's needs. For example, you may have a site located in other states or countries. Creating a child domain for that office allows that office to be an independent domain, and thus they can have their own security and domain settings. One or more domains that follow the same contiguous namespace are called a *tree*. So, if my domain name is Stormwind.com and the child domains are NH.Stormwind.com, Arizona.Stormwind.com, and Florida.Stormwind.com, this would be a tree. All domains here follow the Stormwind.com namespace.

Another Active Directory advantage is the ability to extend the Active Directory schema. The Active Directory schema contains all the objects and attributes of the database. For example, when you create a new user in Active Directory, the system asks you to fill in the user's first name, last name, username, password, and so forth. These fields are the attributes of the user object, and the way that the system knows to prompt for these fields is that the user object has these specific attributes assigned to it within the Active Directory schema. You have the ability to change or expand these fields based on organizational needs.

Let's take a look at some of the advantages of Active Directory:

Active Directory Certificate Services Active Directory Certificate Services (AD CS) provides a customizable set of services that allows you to issue and manage public key infrastructure (PKI) certificates. These certificates can be used in software security systems that employ public key technologies.

Active Directory Domain Services   Active Directory Domain Services (AD DS) includes features that make deploying domain controllers simpler and lets you implement them faster. AD DS also makes the domain controllers more flexible, both to audit and to authorize access to files. Moreover, AD DS has been designed to make performing administrative tasks easier through consistent graphical and scripted management experiences.

Active Directory Rights Management Services   Active Directory Rights Management Services (AD RMS) provides management and development tools that let you work with industry security technologies, including encryption, certificates, and authentication. Using these technologies allows organizations to create reliable information protection solutions.

Kerberos Authentication   Windows Server uses the Kerberos authentication protocol and extensions for password-based and public-key authentication. The Kerberos client is installed as a security support provider (SSP), and it can be accessed through the Security Support Provider Interface (SSPI).

Kerberos Constrained Delegation   Kerberos constrained delegation (KCD) is an authentication protocol that administrators can set up for delegating client credentials for specific service accounts. For example, KCD may be a requirement for services in SharePoint 2019. If you are planning on using SharePoint 2019 Analysis Services and Power Pivot data, you will need to configure KCD. KCD allows a service account to impersonate another service account, and this allows access to specific resources.

Managed Service Accounts   *Managed Service Accounts* are Windows Server accounts that are managed by Active Directory. Regular service accounts are accounts that are created to run specific services such as Exchange and SQL Server. Normally when an administrator creates a service account, it's up to that administrator to maintain the account (including changing the password). Managed Service Accounts are accounts that an administrator creates but the accounts are managed by Active Directory (including password changes). To create Managed Service Accounts, you must use the New-ADServiceAccount PowerShell command. You must use PowerShell in order to create a Managed Service Account.

Group Managed Service Accounts   The group Managed Service Account (gMSA) provides the same functionality within the domain as Managed Service Accounts, but gMSAs extend their functionality over multiple servers. These accounts are very useful when a service account needs to work with multiple servers as with a server farm (for Network Load Balancing).

There are times when the authentication process requires that all instances of a service use the same service account. This is where gMSAs are used. Once group Managed Service Accounts are used, Windows Server will automatically manage the password for the service account. The network administrator will no longer be responsible for managing the service account password.

Security Auditing Security auditing gives an organization the ability to help maintain the security of an enterprise. By using security audits, you can verify authorized or unauthorized access to machines, resources, applications, and services. One of the best advantages of security audits is the ability to verify regulatory compliance.

TLS/SSL (Schannel SSP) Schannel is a security support provider (SSP) that uses the Secure Sockets Layer (SSL) and Transport Layer Security (TLS) Internet standard authentication protocols together. The Security Support Provider Interface (SSPI) is an API used by Windows systems to allow security-related functionality, including authentication.

Windows Deployment Services Windows Deployment Services allows an administrator to install Windows operating systems remotely. Administrators can use Windows Deployment Services to set up new computers by using a network-based installation.

Now when it comes to setting up Active Directory on-site or on a virtual machine, that server becomes a Domain Controller. Microsoft only has three server types: Domain Controller, Member Server, or Stand-Alone Server. So, it's important that you understand how each server works. Let's take a look at servers and what types of Microsoft servers you can have.

Server A *server* is a dedicated computer, device, or program that provides a service to another computer or user (known as clients). Servers manage network resources that users can connect to. These resources can be files, printers, applications, and so forth. Usually, the type of server is dependent on the resource that the user needs. For example, a print server is a server that controls printers. A file server contains files. Application servers can run applications for the users. Sometimes you will hear a server referred to by the specific application that it may be running. For example, someone may say, "That's our SQL server" or "We have an Exchange server."

Domain Controller This is a server that contains a replica of the Active Directory database. As mentioned earlier in this chapter, Active Directory is the database that contains all the objects in your network. A *domain controller* is a server that contains this database. All domain controllers are equal in a Windows Server network, and each can read from and write to the directory database. Some domain controllers may contain extra roles, but they all have the same copy of Active Directory.

Member Server A *member server* is a server that is a member of a domain-based network but does not contain a copy of Active Directory. For example, Microsoft recommends that a Microsoft Exchange server be loaded on a member server instead of a domain controller. Both domain controllers and member servers can act as file, print, or application servers. Your choice of server type depends on whether you need that server to have a replica of Active Directory.

Stand-Alone Server A *stand-alone server* is not a member of a domain. Many organizations may use this type of server for virtualization. For example, say you load Windows Server with Hyper-V (Microsoft's virtualization server) on a stand-alone server. You can then create virtual machines that act as domain controllers to run the network.

Another component of a Microsoft network is a Global Catalog. The *Global Catalog* is a database of all Active Directory objects in a forest with only a subset of the object attributes. In other words, the Global Catalog is a partial representation of the Active Directory objects. Think of the Global Catalog as an index. If you needed to look something up in this Windows client book, you would go to the index and find what page you need to turn to. You would not just randomly look through the book for the information. This is the same purpose the Global Catalog serves in your Active Directory forest. When you need to find a resource in the forest (user, published printer, and so forth), you can search the Global Catalog to find its location.

Domain controllers need to use a Global Catalog to help with user authentication. Global Catalogs are a requirement on an Active Directory domain. All domain controllers can be Global Catalogs, but this is not always a good practice. Your network should have at least two Global Catalogs for redundancy, but too many can cause too much Global Catalog replication traffic unless you have a single-domain model.

Read-Only Domain Controllers

Windows Server supports another type of domain controller called the *read-only domain controller (RODC)*. This is a full copy of the Active Directory database without the ability to write to Active Directory. The RODC gives an organization the ability to install a domain controller in a location (on-site or off-site) where security is a concern.

RODCs need to get their Active Directory database from another domain controller. So, if you have a network with no domain controllers set up yet for the domain, the RODC option will not be available (the option will be grayed out). Implementing an RODC is the same as adding another domain controller to a domain. The installation is exactly the same except that when you get to the screen to choose domain controller options, you check the box for RODC. Again, this is *only* available if there are other domain controllers already in the domain.

Installing Active Directory On-Site or in Azure

Before you install Active Directory into your network, you must first make sure that your network and the server meet some minimum requirements. Table 9.1 will show you the requirements needed for Active Directory.

TABLE 9.1 Active Directory requirements

Requirement	Description
Adprep	When adding the first Windows Server domain controller to an existing Active Directory domain, Adprep commands run automatically as needed.
Credentials	When installing a new AD DS forest, the administrator must be set to local Administrator on the first server. To install an additional domain controller in an existing domain, you need to be a member of the Domain Admins group.
DNS	Domain Name System needs to be installed for Active Directory to function properly. You can install DNS during the Active Directory installation.

Requirement	Description
NTFS	The Windows Server drives that store the database, log files, and SYSVOL folder must be placed on a volume that is formatted with the NTFS file system.
RODCs	Read-only domain controllers can be installed as long as another domain controller (Windows Server 2008 or newer) already exists on the domain. Also, the forest functional level must be at least Windows Server 2003.
TCP/IP	You must configure the appropriate TCP/IP settings on your domain, and you must configure the DNS server addresses.

The Installation Process

Windows Server computers are configured as either member servers (if they are joined to a domain) or stand-alone servers (if they are part of a workgroup). The process of converting a server to a domain controller is known as *promotion*. Through the use of a simple and intuitive wizard in Server Manager, system administrators can quickly configure servers to be domain controllers after installation. Administrators also have the ability to promote domain controllers using Windows PowerShell.

The first step in installing Active Directory is promoting a Windows Server computer to a domain controller. The first domain controller in an environment serves as the starting point for the forest, trees, domains, and the operations master roles.

Exercise 9.1 shows the steps you need to follow to promote an existing Windows Server computer to a domain controller. To complete the steps in this exercise, you must have already installed and configured a Windows Server computer. I am using a Windows Server 2022 computer for this exercise. You also need a DNS server that supports SRV records. If you do not have a DNS server available, the Active Directory Installation Wizard automatically configures one for you. I would recommend that you do this lab on a test box. This lab is needed later so that I can show you how to connect your on-site setup with Azure.

EXERCISE 9.1

Setting Up an On-Site Domain Controller

1. Install the Active Directory Domain Services by clicking the Add Roles And Features link in Server Manager's Dashboard view.

2. On the Before You Begin screen, click Next.

3. The Select Installation Type screen will appear. Make sure that the Role-Based radio button is selected and click Next.

4. On the Select Destination Server screen, choose the local machine. Click Next.

5. On the Select Server Roles screen, click the Active Directory Domain Services check box.

6. A pop-up menu will appear asking you to install additional features. Click the Add Features button.

7. Click Next.

8. On the Select Features screen, accept the defaults and click Next.

9. Click Next on the information screen.

10. Click the Install button on the Confirmation Installation screen.

11. The Installation Progress screen will show you how the installation is progressing. After the installation is complete, click the Close button.

12. On the left-side window, click the AD DS link.

13. Click the More link next to Configuration Required For Active Directory Domain Services.

14. Under the Post-Deployment Configuration section, click the Promote This Server To A Domain Controller link.

15. At this point, you will configure this domain controller. You are going to install a new domain controller in a new domain in a new forest. On the Deployment Configuration screen, click the Add A New Forest radio button. You then need to add a root domain name. In this exercise, I will use StormWindAD.com (see Figure 9.1). Click Next.

FIGURE 9.1   New Forest screen

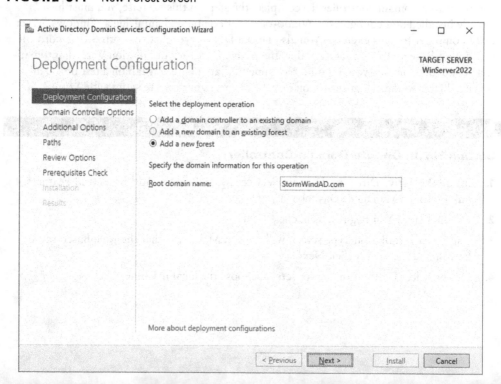

16. On the Domain Controller Options screen, set the following options (see Figure 9.2):

- Function levels: Windows Server 2022 (for both)

- Verify that the DNS and Global Catalog check boxes are checked. Notice that the RODC check box is grayed out. This is because RODCs need to get their Active Directory database from another domain controller. Since this is the first domain controller in the forest, RODCs are not possible. If you need an RODC, complete the previous steps on a member server in a domain where domain controllers already exist.

- Password: **P@ssw0rd**

Then click Next.

FIGURE 9.2   Domain Controller Options screen

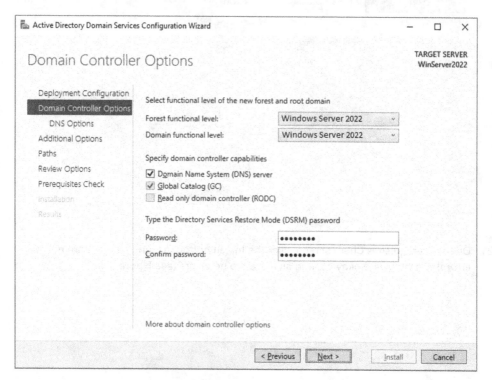

17. On the DNS screen, click Next.

18. On the Additional Options screen, accept the default NetBIOS domain name and click Next.

19. On the Paths screen, accept the default file locations and click Next.

20. On the Review Options screen (see Figure 9.3), verify your settings and click Next. At this screen, there is a View Script button. This button allows you to grab a PowerShell script based on the features you have just set up.

FIGURE 9.3   Review Options screen

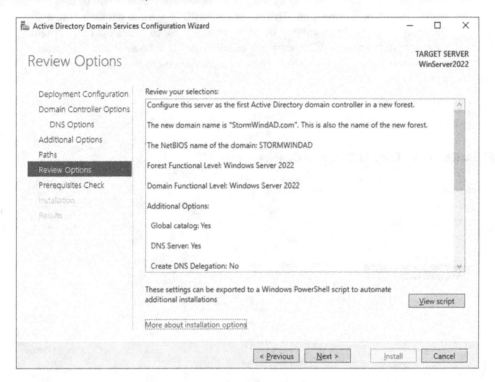

21. On the Prerequisites Check screen, click the Install button (as long as there are no errors). Warnings are okay as long as there are no errors (see Figure 9.4).

FIGURE 9.4   Prerequisites Check screen

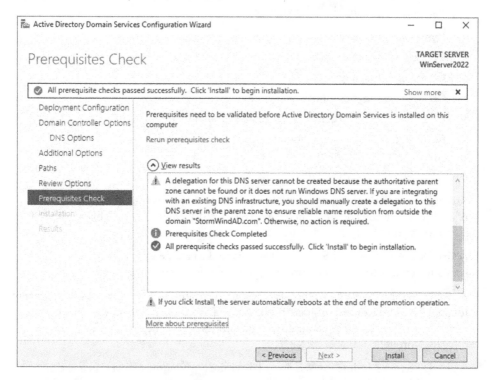

22. After the installation completes, the machine will automatically reboot. Log in as the administrator.

23. Close Server Manager.

24. Press the Start button on the keyboard and choose Administrative Tools. You should see new MMC snap-ins for Active Directory.

25. Close the Administrative Tools window.

Using Active Directory Administrative Tools

After a server has been promoted to a domain controller, you will see that various tools are added to the Administrative Tools program group, including the following:

Active Directory Administrative Center   This is a *Microsoft Management Console (MMC)* snap-in that allows you to accomplish many Active Directory tasks from one central location. This MMC snap-in allows you to manage your directory services objects, including doing the following tasks:

- Reset user passwords
- Create or manage user accounts
- Create or manage groups
- Create or manage computer accounts
- Create or manage organizational units (OUs) and containers
- Connect to one or several domains or domain controllers in the same instance of Active Directory Administrative Center
- Filter Active Directory data

Active Directory Domains and Trusts   Use this tool to view and change information related to the various domains in an Active Directory environment. This MMC snap-in also allows you to set up shortcut trusts.

Active Directory Sites and Services   Use this tool to create and manage Active Directory sites and services to map to an organization's physical network infrastructure.

Active Directory Users and Computers   User and computer management is fundamental for an Active Directory environment. The Active Directory Users and Computers tool allows you to set machine- and user-specific settings across the domain. This tool is discussed throughout this book.

Active Directory Module for Windows PowerShell   *Windows PowerShell* is a command-line shell and scripting language. The Active Directory Module for Windows PowerShell is a group of cmdlets used to manage your Active Directory domains, Active Directory Lightweight Directory Services (AD LDS) configuration sets, and Active Directory Database Mounting Tool instances in a single, self-contained package. The Active Directory Module for Windows PowerShell is a normal PowerShell window. The only difference is that the Active Directory PowerShell module is preloaded when you choose the Active Directory Module for Windows PowerShell.

A good way to make sure that Active Directory is accessible and functioning properly is to run the Active Directory Users and Computers tool. When you open the tool, you should see a configuration similar to that shown in Figure 9.5. Specifically, you should make sure the name of the domain you created appears in the list. You should also click the `Domain Controllers` folder and make sure that the name of your local server appears in the right pane. If your configuration passes these two checks, Active Directory is present and configured.

FIGURE 9.5   Viewing Active Directory information using the Active Directory Users and Computers tool

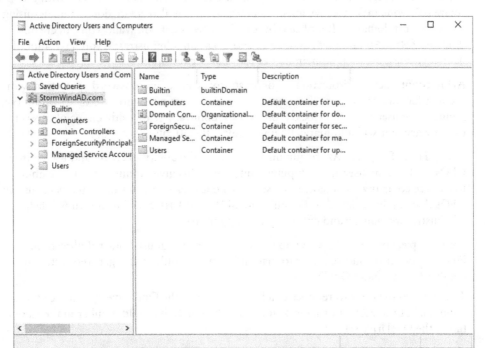

Understanding Azure Active Directory

So now that you understand how to install Active Directory on your on-site network, it's time to see how to configure your Azure Active Directory. One big misconception is that Azure Active Directory is set up and configured the same way that your on-site Active Directory is set up. The advantage of Azure Active Directory is that there is no installation. As soon as you set up your Azure subscription, Azure Active Directory is ready to go.

So, before we begin setting up your Azure Active Directory, let's take a look at some of the features that Azure Active Directory delivers. The following features are just some of the features available in Azure AD managed domains.

Simple Deployment   Administrators can easily enable Azure AD Domain Services for their Azure AD directory. Managed domains include cloud-only user accounts and user accounts synchronized from an on-premises directory.

Domain-Join   Administrators have the ability to easily join computers to the Azure domain. Administrators can even combine the Azure domain with Windows 10/11 so that the clients can automatically join the domain with automated domain joining tools.

Setting Domain Names   Azure administrators have the ability to create custom domain names (for example, WillPanek.com) that are either verified or unverified with the Azure AD Domain Service wizards. Administrators can also create domain names using the Microsoft domain suffix of onmicrosoft.com. So, if you want, you can create a domain of WillPanek.onmicrosoft.com. So as an administrator, you have a lot of flexibility when creating domain names for your organization.

AD Account Lockout Protection   Administrators can set up password protection with account lockout protection. If a user enters an improper password five times within two minutes, the user account is locked out for 30 minutes. The nice advantage of this is that the user account will automatically unlock after the 30 minutes are up.

Group Policy Support   Azure administrators have the ability to create and use built-in GPOs for both the user and computer containers. This gives administrators the ability to enforce company compliances for security policies. Administrators can create custom GPOs that can be assigned to Organizational Units (OUs), and this in turn will help administrators manage and enforce company policies.

For example, you can set a GPO up so that your users will use Folder Redirection. Folder Redirection allows a user to place a file in one folder but it gets redirected to another (this includes OneDrive).

To use a Group Policy to redirect OneDrive, you need the OneDrive sync to be at least build 18.111.0603.0004 or later. You can see the OneDrive build number in the About tab of the OneDrive settings.

> The Group Policy Object for "OneDrive Known Folder Move" won't work if an administrator has already set up a Windows Folder Redirection policy to redirect a user's Documents, Pictures, or Desktop folders to a storage location other than OneDrive. If this has been done, the administrator must first remove the Redirection Group Policy Object that has already been created. The redirection for OneDrive doesn't affect the Music and Videos folders. So, an administrator can keep them redirected with the Windows Group Policy object that is already created.

Azure AD Integration   One of the nice advantages of Azure is that administrators do not need to manage or configure Azure AD replication. Azure user accounts, group membership, or even user passwords are automatically replicated between Azure AD and Azure AD Domain Services. Azure AD tenant information is automatically replicated and synchronized to your on-site or Azure AD domains.

NTLM and Kerberos Authentication Support   Some applications, like Exchange, require Windows integrated authentication. Since Azure AD supports NTLM and Kerberos support, any service or application that needs to work with NTLM and Kerberos will work within the Azure AD domain.

LDAP Integration   Administrators have the ability to use any application, service, or LDAP security measure with Azure AD. LDAP is an industry standard, and any LDAP-compatible application or feature can be integrated with your Azure AD network.

DNS Support   Administrators have the ability to set up, configure, and integrate DNS with their Azure network. DNS is a hostname resolution service and Azure allows administrators to easily configure DNS with many of the same DNS administration tools that they are currently familiar with.

Working with Organizational Units   Organizational Units (OUs) are Active Directory storage containers that administrators can use to manage users, computers, and groups accounts. One of the nice advantages of using OUs is the ability to set policies on each individual OU. So, administrators have the ability to set different policies for different OUs and this gives an organization better control on how policies are administered.

High Availability   One of the most important requirements for any IT department is the ability to keep their network up and running. Some organizations require minimum downtime requirements. This means that your organization can only be down for a certain amount of time per year. Azure AD Domain Services offers an organization the ability to set up high availability for your Azure domains.

This feature guarantees higher service resiliency and uptime. With built-in health monitoring, Azure offers automatic failure recovery by spinning up a new instance to take over for any failed instances. This feature provides automatic and continued services for your organization's Azure network.

Management Tools Support   Administrators have the ability to use the same tools that they are familiar with for managing their current domains. The Active Directory Administrative Center and Active Directory PowerShell utilities can be used when managing their Azure AD domains.

Azure AD Questions and Answers

This section consists of questions and answers about features and functionality of Azure Active Directory. The text was taken directly from Microsoft's website (http://docs .microsoft.com/en-us/azure/active-directory-domain-services/ active-directory-ds-faqs). I recommend that you visit this page often for updates about features and Services.

Q. Can I create multiple managed domains for a single Azure AD directory?

Answer: No. You can only create a single managed domain serviced by Azure AD Domain Services for a single Azure AD directory.

Q. Can I enable Azure AD Domain Services in an Azure Resource Manager virtual network?

Answer: Yes. Azure AD Domain Services can be enabled in an Azure Resource Manager virtual network. Classic Azure virtual networks are no longer supported for creating new managed domains.

Q. Can I migrate my existing managed domain from a classic virtual network to a Resource Manager virtual network?

Answer: Yes, Azure Active Directory Domain Services (Azure AD DS) supports a one-time move for customers currently using the Classic virtual network model to the Resource Manager virtual network model.

Q. Can I enable Azure AD Domain Services in an Azure CSP (Cloud Solution Provider) subscription?

Answer: Yes. You can enable Azure AD Domain Services in Azure CSP subscriptions.

Q. Can I enable Azure AD Domain Services in a federated Azure AD directory? I do not synchronize password hashes to Azure AD. Can I enable Azure AD Domain Services for this directory?

Answer: No. Azure AD Domain Services needs access to the password hashes of user accounts, to authenticate users via NTLM or Kerberos. In a federated directory, password hashes are not stored in the Azure AD directory. Therefore, Azure AD Domain Services does not work with such Azure AD directories.

Q. Can I make Azure AD Domain Services available in multiple virtual networks within my subscription?

Answer: The service itself does not directly support this scenario. Your managed domain is available in only one virtual network at a time. However, you may configure connectivity between multiple virtual networks to expose Azure AD Domain Services to other virtual networks. See how you can connect virtual networks in Azure.

Q. Can I enable Azure AD Domain Services using PowerShell?

Answer: Yes. You can enable Azure AD Domain Services using PowerShell.

Q. Can I enable Azure AD Domain Services using a Resource Manager Template?

Answer: Yes, you can create an Azure AD Domain Services managed domain using a Resource Manager template. A service principal and Azure AD group for administration must be created using the Azure portal or Azure PowerShell before the template is deployed.

Q. Can I add domain controllers to an Azure AD Domain Services managed domain?

Answer: No. The domain provided by Azure AD Domain Services is a managed domain. You do not need to provision, configure, or otherwise manage domain controllers for this domain—these management activities are provided as a service by Microsoft. Therefore, you cannot add additional domain controllers (read-write or read-only) for the managed domain.

Q. Can guest users invited to my directory use Azure AD Domain Services?

Answer: No. Guest users invited to your Azure AD directory using the Azure AD B2B invite process are synchronized into your Azure AD Domain Services managed domain. However, passwords for these users are not stored in your Azure AD directory. Therefore, Azure AD Domain Services has no way to sync NTLM and Kerberos hashes for these users into your managed domain. As a result, such users cannot log into the managed domain or join computers to the managed domain.

Q. Can I connect to the domain controller for my managed domain using Remote Desktop?

Answer: No. You do not have permissions to connect to domain controllers for the managed domain via Remote Desktop. Members of the AAD DC Administrators group can administer the managed domain using AD administration tools such as the Active Directory Administration Center (ADAC) or AD PowerShell. These tools are installed using the Remote Server Administration Tools feature on a Windows server joined to the managed domain.

Q. I've enabled Azure AD Domain Services. What user account do I use to domain-join machines to this domain?

Answer: Members of the administrative group AAD DC Administrators can domain-join machines. Additionally, members of this group are granted remote desktop access to machines that have been joined to the domain.

Q. Do I have domain administrator privileges for the managed domain provided by Azure AD Domain Services?

Answer: No. You are not granted administrative privileges on the managed domain. Both Domain Administrator and Enterprise Administrator privileges are not available for you to use within the domain. Members of the domain administrator or enterprise administrator groups in your on-premises Active Directory are also not granted domain/enterprise administrator privileges on the managed domain.

Q. Can I modify group memberships using LDAP or other AD administrative tools on managed domains?

Answer: No. Group memberships cannot be modified on domains serviced by Azure AD Domain Services. The same applies for user attributes. You may however change group memberships or user attributes either in Azure AD or on your on-premises domain. Such changes are automatically synchronized to Azure AD Domain Services.

Q. How long does it take for changes I make to my Azure AD directory to be visible in my managed domain?

Answer: Changes made in your Azure AD directory using either the Azure AD UI or PowerShell are synchronized to your managed domain. This synchronization process runs in the background. Once initial synchronization is complete, it typically takes about 20 minutes for changes made in Azure AD to be reflected in your managed domain.

Q. Can I extend the schema of the managed domain provided by Azure AD Domain Services?

Answer: No. The schema is administered by Microsoft for the managed domain. Schema extensions are not supported by Azure AD Domain Services.

Q. Can I modify or add DNS records in my managed domain?

Answer: Yes. Members of the AAD DC Administrators group are granted DNS Administrator privileges, to modify DNS records in the managed domain. They can use the DNS Manager console on a machine running Windows Server joined to the managed domain, to manage DNS. To use the DNS Manager console, install DNS Server Tools, which is part of the Remote Server Administration Tools optional feature on the server. More information on utilities for administering, monitoring, and troubleshooting DNS is available on TechNet.

Q. What is the password lifetime policy on a managed domain?

Answer: The default password lifetime on an Azure AD Domain Services managed domain is 90 days. This password lifetime is not synchronized with the password lifetime configured in Azure AD. Therefore, you may have a situation where users' passwords expire in your managed domain, but are still valid in Azure AD. In such scenarios, users need to change their password in Azure AD and the new password will synchronize to your managed domain. Additionally, the Azure AD password policy for `DisablePasswordExpiration` is synchronized to a managed domain. When `DisablePasswordExpiration` is applied to a user in Azure AD, the `UserAccountControl` value for the synchronized user in the managed domain has `DONT_EXPIRE_PASSWORD` applied.

Q. Does Azure AD Domain Services provide AD account lockout protection?

Answer: Yes. Five invalid password attempts within 2 minutes on the managed domain cause a user account to be locked out for 30 minutes. After 30 minutes, the user account is automatically unlocked. Invalid password attempts on the managed domain do not lock out the user account in Azure AD. The user account is locked out only within your Azure AD Domain Services managed domain.

Q. Can I fail over Azure AD Domain Services to another region for a DR (disaster recovery) event?

Answer: Yes, to provide geographical resiliency for a managed domain, you can create an additional replica set to a peered virtual network in any Azure region that supports Azure AD DS. Replica sets share the same namespace and configuration with the managed domain.

Q. Can I get Azure AD Domain Services as part of Enterprise Mobility Suite (EMS)? Do I need Azure AD Premium to use Azure AD Domain Services?

Answer: No. Azure AD Domain Services is a pay-as-you-go Azure service and is not part of EMS. Azure AD Domain Services can be used with all editions of Azure AD (Free, Basic, and, Premium). You are billed on an hourly basis, depending on usage.

Managing Azure AD

So now that we have looked at some of the features of Azure AD along with the common questions and answers about Azure AD, it's time to go through the Azure AD Dashboard. Figure 9.6 shows you dashboard (you get to the Azure AD dashboard by clicking Azure Active Directory on the left side menu of the main dashboard). You can choose the default mode for the portal menu. It can be docked or it can act as a flyout panel. When the portal menu is in flyout mode, it will be hidden until you need it. Select the menu icon to open or close the menu. Let's take a look at some of the options on the left side, starting with Overview.

Overview

The Overview section of the Azure AD Dashboard is the figure you are looking at in Figure 9.6. The first thing you will notice in the center of the screen is the default Azure AD directory and the number of sign-ins on Azure.

FIGURE 9.6   Viewing the Azure AD Dashboard

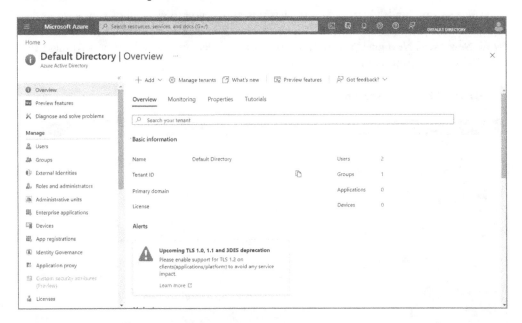

Below the Sign-ins section are all the different services that you have with Azure AD. You can click the All Services check box to see every service, or you can click an individual service and see the details of just those services on Azure AD.

On the right-hand side, you can see the role that your user is currently logged in as, and you can also search for individual objects in the Find section.

Also, on the right-hand side you can add Users, Guest Users, Groups, Enterprise Applications, and App Registrations. Below that you will see that you can access Other capabilities like Identity Protection, Privilege Identity Management, Tenant Restrictions, Azure AD Domain Services, and Access Reviews.

Below that section, you can view Getting Started With Azure AD, and you have the ability to create a directory.

Preview Features

The Preview Features section (on the left side under Overview) is an area that allows you to evaluate features. When you click a feature, a window will open telling you more about the selected feature, such as an overview, what you will see in the preview, as well as documentation and learning links.

Diagnose and Solve Problems

The Diagnose and Solve Problems section allows you to explore the most common problems for your resources. You can search for common problems, or you can select Troubleshoot to run an automated troubleshooter.

Users

The Users section (under Manage) on the left side allows you to view all of your current Azure AD user accounts (see Figure 9.7). Under the Users section, an administrator can also create New users, New guest users, Reset passwords, Delete users, Multi-Factor Authentication, Refresh your screen, or set up your columns.

FIGURE 9.7   Users section

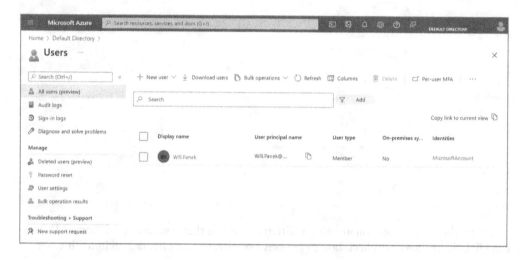

Another task that you can do in the Users section is manipulate user settings. The User Settings link allows you to set up how the user can launch and view applications, how the user can register applications, and if the user can access the Azure AD administration portal. Administrators can also manage external users and access panel control from the Settings section.

The Users section also allows administrators to see how often the user is logging into Azure (this allows you to perform an access review), and administrators can also get audit information about the user account. Finally, in the Users section, you can troubleshoot user issues and open a support ticket with Microsoft for additional help.

Groups

The Groups section allows an administrator to create and manage groups (see Figure 9.8). In the Groups section, you can create new groups, manage group settings for all groups, manage group membership, and delete groups. Administrators can also perform auditing on groups along with troubleshooting group issues or opening a support ticket with Microsoft for additional help.

FIGURE 9.8   Group section

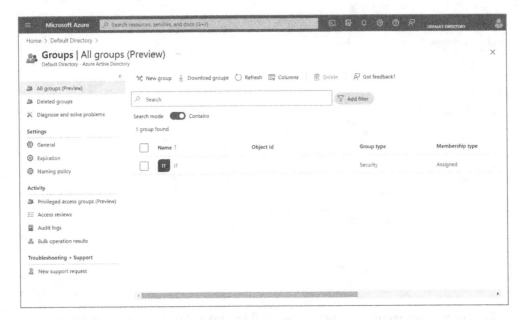

External Identities

The External Identities section allows you to work with user accounts from other organizations.

Azure AD External Identities is part of Microsoft Entra. Microsoft Entra is the product name for Microsoft's existing identity and access management services. The Microsoft Entra product has three segments:

- Microsoft Azure Active Directory

- Permissions Management, which is a service for detecting human and machine identities and activities

- Verified ID, which at the time this book was written is a product still in development

External Identities combine all your external identities and user directories into one portal to help you manage them. It provides more ways for you to share resources or apps with users who are not in your organization.

The External Identities section also allows you to invite users who already own an Azure AD account or a Microsoft Account. If they have one of these account types already set up, they can automatically sign in without any further configuration from an administrator.

In the External Collaboration Settings section of External Identities (see Figure 9.9), Administrators can set up what guest accounts can do regarding Azure. For example, an Administrator can decide if guest user access is limited or if users can invite other users to use your organization's Azure network. Finally, you can set up collaboration restrictions (such as which domains you can invite users from) for your guest user accounts.

FIGURE 9.9   External Collaboration Settings

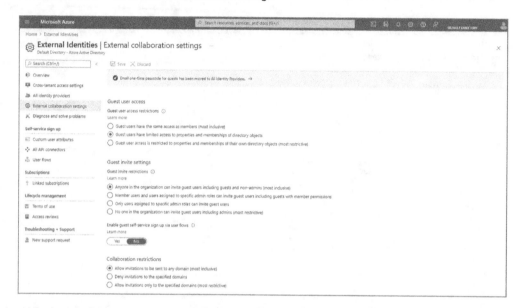

The Lifecycle Management section of External Identities also allows an Administrator to set up terms of use agreements while also allowing Administrators to perform auditing of their guest users. Terms of use provide a method that you can use to present information to end users in a PDF format. The PDF file can be any content, such as existing contract documents, that allows you to collect end-user agreements during the user sign-in process. Finally, Administrators can troubleshoot issues or open a support ticket with Microsoft for additional help.

Roles and Administrators

The Roles and Administrators section allows you to see all of the available Azure AD roles and what each role does. In Table 9.2, I will show you some of the roles that are available and what each role does in Azure AD. This is not a complete list of all available roles.

Azure AD Roles

When you are in the Azure AD Roles and Administrators section, you can click any of these roles to see who currently has this role in your organization. There are a number of roles available.

TABLE 9.2 Azure roles

Role	Description of role permission
Application administrator	Allows you to create and manage all aspects of app registrations and enterprise apps
Application developer	Allows you to create application registrations independent of the Users Can Register Applications setting
Azure Information Protection administrator	Allows you to manage all aspects of the Azure Information Protection product
Billing administrator	Allows you to perform common billing-related tasks like updating payment information
Cloud application administrator	Allows you to create and manage all aspects of app registrations and enterprise apps except App Proxy
Cloud device administrator	Allows you to have full access to manage devices in Azure AD
Compliance administrator	Allows you to read and manage compliance configuration and reports in Azure AD and Office 365
Conditional Access administrator	Allows you to manage conditional access capabilities
Customer LockBox access approver	Allows you to approve Microsoft support requests to access customer organizational data
Desktop Analytics administrator	Allows you to access and manage desktop management tools and services
Dynamics 365 administrator	Allows you to manage all aspects of the Dynamics 365 product
Exchange administrator	Allows you to manage all aspects of the Exchange product
Global administrator	Allows you to manage all aspects of Azure AD and Microsoft services that use Azure AD identities
Guest inviter	Allows you to invite guest users independent of the Members Can Invite Guests setting
Intune administrator	Allows you to manage all aspects of the Intune product
License administrator	Allows you to have the ability to assign, remove, and update license assignments

TABLE 9.2 Azure roles *(continued)*

Role	Description of role permission
Message center reader	Allows you to read messages and updates for your organization in Office 365 Message Center only
Password administrator	Allows you to reset passwords for non-administrators and help desk administrators
Power BI administrator	Allows you to manage all aspects of the Power BI product
Privileged role administrator	Allows you to manage role assignments in Azure AD and all aspects of Privileged Identity Management
Reports reader	Allows you to read sign-in and audit reports
Security administrator	Allows you to read security information and reports and manage configuration in Azure AD and Office 365
Security reader	Allows you to read security information and reports in Azure AD and Office 365
Service support administrator	Allows you to read service health information and manage support tickets
SharePoint administrator	Allows you to manage all aspects of the SharePoint service
Skype for Business administrator	Allows you to manage all aspects of the Skype for Business product
Teams communications administrator	Allows you to manage calling and meetings features within the Microsoft Teams service
Teams Communications Support Engineer	Allows you to troubleshoot communications issues within Teams using advanced tools
Teams Communications Support Specialist	Allows you to troubleshoot communications issues within Teams using basic tools
Teams devices administrator	Allows you to manage Teams certified devices from the Teams admin center
User administrator	Allows you to manage all aspects of users and groups, including resetting passwords for limited admins

Administrative Units

An administrative unit is an Azure AD resource that can be a container for other Azure AD resources. It can contain only users, groups, or devices, and it can restrict permissions in a role to any portion of your organization that you define.

Enterprise Applications

The Enterprise applications section allows an Administrator to view, set up, and configure your organization's Enterprise applications (see Figure 9.10). Administrators can also set up an Application proxy within this section. An Application proxy allows an Administrator to provide single sign-on (SSO) and secure remote access for web applications hosted on your on-premises network.

FIGURE 9.10   The Enterprise Applications section

The Enterprise applications section also allows an Administrator to set up user settings for your Enterprise applications. These settings include users giving consent to applications accessing data on their company networks, users adding applications to their Access panel, and if users can only see Office 365 in the O365 portal.

The Enterprise applications section allows an Administrator to also set up Conditional access (setting up application policies), seeing who has logged into the applications, and perform auditing. Administrators can also troubleshoot application issues or open a support ticket with Microsoft for additional help.

> In the main Azure AD dashboard, there are a few other menu options on the left-hand side that have to do with Enterprise applications. These options (App Registrations and Application Proxy) can be accessed in the Enterprise Applications section or directly using the Azure AD dashboard menu. Either link gets you to the same settings. Because of this, I will not add them while explaining the Azure AD menu options.

Devices

The Devices section allows an Azure AD Administrator to specify which devices can access Azure AD. Administrators can also manage device settings and device roaming settings (Enterprise State Roaming). Finally, Administrators can do auditing and troubleshooting from the Device section.

Identity Governance

The Identity Governance section allows you to manage digital identities. You can review the most common use cases and sets of capabilities for your governance needs.

Licenses

The Licenses section lets you view purchased licensing for additional Azure AD components. If you purchase additional Azure AD components (for example: Azure Active Directory Premium P2 or Enterprise Mobility + Security E5), those additional components will show up in the Licenses section. You can also see if there are any licensing issues in this section.

The Licenses section also allows you to view additional components that are available and what those components do. Administrators can also view auditing and perform troubleshooting from this section.

Azure AD Connect

Azure AD Connect (see Figure 9.11) allows an Administrator to integrate Azure AD with your Windows Server AD or another directory on your network. One of the nice advantages of the Azure AD Connect section is that it allows an Administrator to download and install Azure AD Connect by using the Download link.

Azure AD Connect helps you integrate your on-premises Active Directory with Azure AD. This allows your users to be more productive, by giving those users access to both cloud and on-premises resources by using a common user account for accessing both networks. By using Azure AD Connect, users and organizations can take advantage of the following features:

- Users can have a common hybrid identity that lets them access on-site or cloud-based services that use both Windows Server Active Directory and Azure Active Directory.

- Administrators have the ability to provide conditional access based on their device and user identity, network location, application resource, and multifactor authentication.

- Users can use this common identity in Azure AD, Office 365, Intune, SaaS apps, and third-party applications.

FIGURE 9.11   The Azure AD Connect section

Developers can create applications that use the common identity model, thus integrating applications into on-site Active Directory or cloud-based Azure applications.

To use Azure AD Connect, your on-site network must be using Windows Server 2008, Windows Server 2008 R2, Windows Server 2012, Windows Server 2012 R2, Windows Server 2016, Windows Server 2019, and/or Windows Server 2022.

The Azure AD Connect section allows you to specify how your users will seamlessly pass through between both networks. Administrators can establish seamless connections by using a Federation server (including Active Directory Federation Services (AD FS)), Seamless single sign-on, or Pass-through authentication.

Custom Domain Names

The Custom Domain Names section allows you to add and verify new domain names (see Figure 9.12). When you first build your Azure subscription, your new Azure AD tenant comes with an initial domain name (for example, wpanek.onmicrosoft.com).

Administrators can't change or delete the initial domain name that is created, but they do have the ability to add their organization's domain names to the list of supported names. Adding custom domain names allows an administrator to create user names that are familiar to their users.

FIGURE 9.12   The Custom Domain Names section

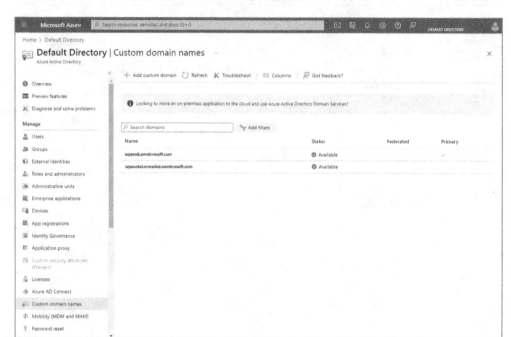

Mobility (MDM and MAM)

One feature that many organizations have started to implement is the ability for their employees to bring their own devices to work (Bring Your Own Device, or BYOD). Because of this, Microsoft has tools like Mobile Device Management (MDM) and Mobile Application Management (MAM) to help IT administrators manage corporate data on personal devices.

Also, many organizations have started issuing devices like tablets to their employees, and many companies do not mind personal use of those devices. These are reasons Microsoft has implemented mobility tools into its Azure AD networks.

Windows client devices (either personal or corporate) have the ability to be connected to a corporate Azure AD network either by using the Windows 10/11 Settings app or through any of the Universal Windows Platform (UWP) apps.

Windows 10/11 Mobile Devices

When a user connects their personal device to a corporate network, they should understand that corporate policies may affect their devices and settings.

Password Reset

The Password Reset section allows an administrator to determine if they want to enable self-service password reset (SSPR). If an organization decides to enable this feature, users will be able to reset their own passwords or unlock their accounts. The use of security questions is available only in Azure AD SSPR. If security questions are used, Microsoft recommends that they be used in conjunction with another security method. Security questions are stored privately and securely on a user object in the directory, and they can only be answered by users during registration. There is no way for an administrator to read or modify a user's questions or answers.

An administrator can allow all accounts to use SSPR (see Figure 9.13) or they can choose certain groups that will have the ability to use SSPR.

FIGURE 9.13   Self-service password reset

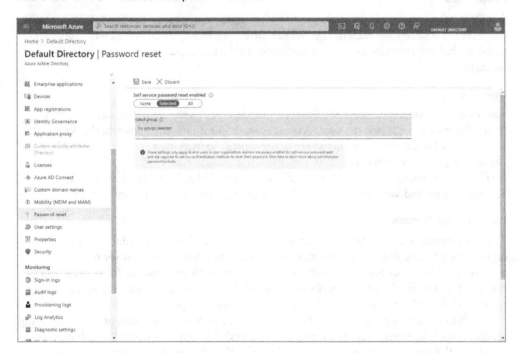

In the Password Reset section, administrators can also choose to use authentication methods. Authentication methods allow an organization to verify that the user is who they say they are. Methods for this include verification by mobile app notification, mobile app code, email, mobile phone, office phone, or security question. Administrators can choose between a single verification or multiple verifications.

Administrators can require registrations when a user logs into Azure AD and can also set up password resets so that the user is notified if their password changes. Administrators can also choose to be notified when administrator passwords are reset.

Also, admins can choose to enable a custom help desk link for users and configure password changes to be replicated back to an Active Directory network. Administrators can perform auditing and troubleshooting from the Password Reset section as well.

User Settings

The User Settings section allows an administrator to manage how end users will launch and view their applications. You can set the App Registrations settings, set Administrator Portal Access (to restrict access to the Azure AD administration portal), set LinkedIn account connections, as well as manage external users' collaboration settings and manage user features.

Properties

The Properties section allows an Azure AD administrator to change the Default Directory properties. These settings include the Default Directory name, language, technical contact email, global privacy contact, privacy statement URL, and access management person for Azure.

Security

The Security section, allows an administrator to view your security policies and security issues. Security is a big part of Azure AD because, unlike an on-site network, the Azure AD network can be accessed from anywhere in the world. So, making sure your Azure AD security is strong is a very important task for any Azure administrator.

This section contains settings for Conditional Access, Identity Protection, view the Security Center and Verifiable Credentials (Preview), as you can see in Figure 9.14.

Conditional Access

The Conditional Access section (see Figure 9.15) allows an Azure AD Administrator to set security policies. When it comes to Azure, one of the biggest concerns for organizations is cloud-based security. Azure allows users to access their networks from anywhere in the world and from almost any device. Because of this, just securing resource access is not enough. This is where Conditional Access policies come into play.

Conditional Access policies allow an organization to set how resources are accessed using access control decisions (who has access to resources) through Azure AD. We will discuss Conditional Access policies in greater detail later in this chapter. Setting up Conditional Access policies allows an organization to have automated access control decisions based on the policies that your organization sets. Some of the situations that Conditional Access policies can help with are sign-in risk, network location risk, device management, and client applications.

FIGURE 9.14   Security section's Getting Started page

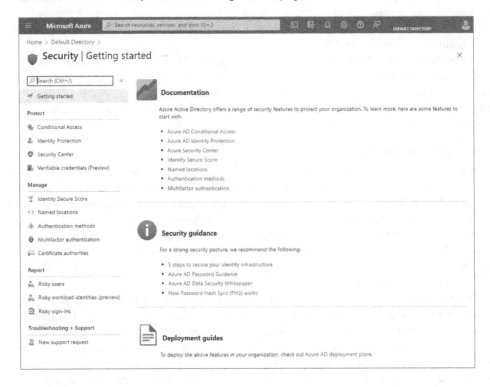

FIGURE 9.15   Conditional Access Policies section

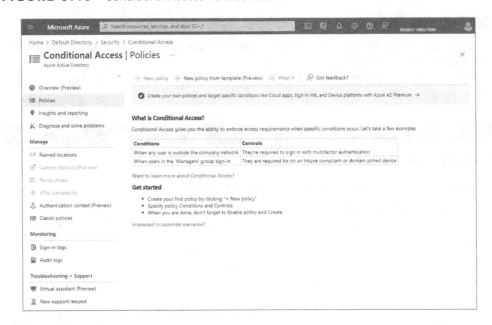

If a device complies with the policy rules that you have configured, that device can access data, email, and other company resources. If the device does not meet the minimum policies that you have set up, then that device will not have access to any of the company's resources. This is how conditional access works.

If you decide that you do not want to use Conditional Access, you can still use compliance policies. If you decide to use compliance policies without Conditional Access, you can access reports showing the device compliance status. Administrators can evaluate this information and decide whether Conditional Access is needed or if you can continue to use Azure without any Conditional Access policies.

Identity Secure Score

Under the Manage section of the Security page, the Identity Secure Score allows an Administrator to view their Azure AD Identity Secure Score. The Identity Secure Score is an indicator for how aligned Azure AD is with Microsoft's best practices recommendations for your organization's security setup. The Identity Secure Score is an integer number between 1 and 248. The higher the number, the better your security settings align with Microsoft's recommendations. The score helps an organization objectively measure their identity security position, plan for identity security improvements, and review the successful implementation of your organization's improvements.

On the Identity Secure Score dashboard, an organization will be able to view your organization's score, comparison graph, trend graph, and a list of identity security best practices.

So, the way this works is that Azure views your security configuration every 48 hours. Its then takes what it sees and compares your organization's settings against Microsoft's best practices. Based on that evaluation, your organization's security score is calculated. Based on that security score, an administrator can adjust their security settings and policies to make improvements.

Configuring Objects

Now that we have looked at some of the sections within Azure AD, let's explore how to create objects like users and groups.

User accounts allow employees to log into the Azure network. In Exercise 9.2, you learn how to create a user account in Azure AD.

EXERCISE 9.2

Creating an Azure AD User Account

1. Log into the Azure portal at https://portal.azure.com.
2. Click the Azure Active Directory link.
3. Under Manage, click the Users link.
4. Click the link +New User.

5. Type the name of your user and a username. For this lab, I used George Washington as my user's name and GWashington@wpanek.onmicrosoft.com as the username (see Figure 9.16). You can enter a First name and Last name as well.

FIGURE 9.16 New user information

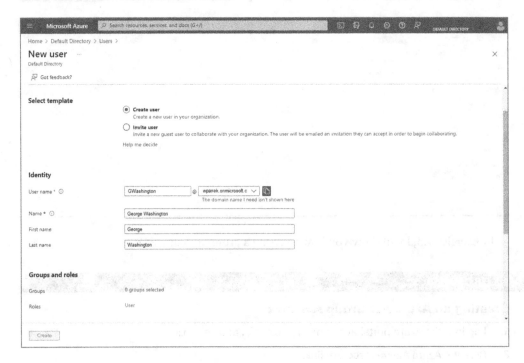

6. We are not going to add this user to a group yet. Be sure Roles is set to User.

7. You can also specify Settings if you wish, such as whether you want to block sign-in; just leave this set to No.

8. If you wish, you can fill out the Job Info section, including such information as Job Title, Department, Company Name, and Manager.

9. Click the Create button.

10. You should now see your user account (see Figure 9.17). If you would like to change any user information, double-click the user account and make changes. Be sure to save any changes that are made.

EXERCISE 9.2 *(continued)*

FIGURE 9.17   New user created

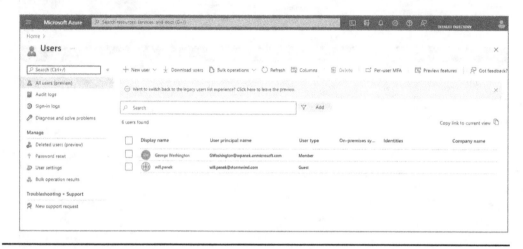

In Exercise 9.3, I will show you how to create a group in Azure AD.

EXERCISE 9.3

Creating an Azure AD Group Account

1. Log into the Azure portal at https://portal.azure.com.

2. Click the Azure Active Directory link.

3. Under Manage, click the Groups link.

4. Click the link New Group.

5. From the Group Type pull-down, choose Security. Security groups are the group type you use when you want the group to be assigned to resources. Office 365 groups allow users to collaborate with other users by giving them access to a shared mailbox, calendar, files, SharePoint site, and more.

6. In the Group Name box, type the name of your group. I used Marketing for my group name.

7.   In the Group Description field, type a description for your group.

8.   From the Membership Type pull-down, choose Assigned. Assigned groups allow an administrator to add specific users as members of the group and to give them unique permissions. Dynamic user groups allow an administrator to use dynamic group rules to automatically add and remove members. Dynamic device groups allow an administrator to use dynamic group rules to automatically add and remove devices.

9.   Click Create.

Self-Service Password Reset

As stated earlier, the Password Reset section allows an Administrator to determine if they want to enable self-service password resets (SSPR). If an organization decides to enable this feature, users will be able to reset their own passwords or unlock their accounts.

An Administrator can allow all accounts to use the SSPR, or they can just choose certain groups that will have the ability to use SSPR. Before setting up SSPR, you must meet the following prerequisites:

■   An Azure AD tenant subscription with the minimum of at least one trial license enabled

■   A Global Administrator account that can be used to enable SSPR

■   A non-administrator test account with a password that you know

■   A pilot group account to test with the non-administrator test account (the user account needs to be a member of this group)

In Exercise 9.4, I will show you how to set up the Self-Service Password Reset option in Azure Active Directory. To complete this exercise, you must have created a user and group in Exercise 9.2 and Exercise 9.3.

EXERCISE 9.4

Setting Up Self-Service Password Reset

1.   From your existing Azure AD tenant, click the Azure Active Directory.

2.   Select Password Reset.

3.   On the Properties page, under the option Self Service Password Reset Enabled, click the Selected option (see Figure 9.18).

EXERCISE 9.4 *(continued)*

FIGURE 9.18   Choosing the Selected option

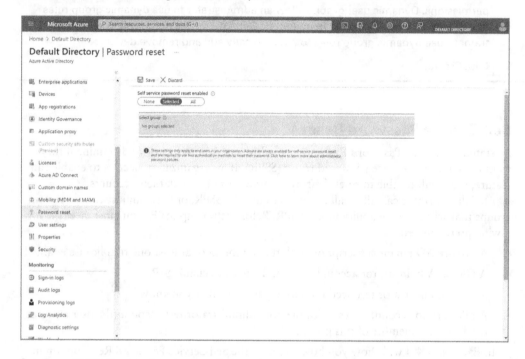

4.   From Select Group, choose your pilot group.

5.   Click Save.

6.   On the Authentication Methods page, make the following choices and then click Save:

Number of methods required to reset: 1

Methods available to users

Mobile phone

Office phone

7.   On the Registration page, make the following choices:

Require users to register when they sign in: Yes

Set the number of days before users are asked to reconfirm their authentication information: 365

In Exercise 9.5, I will show you how to test the Self-Service Password Reset option. To complete this exercise, you must have completed Exercise 9.4. This test must be done with a normal user account. You can't run this test using an administrator account.

EXERCISE 9.5

Testing the Self-Service Password Reset

1. Open a new browser window in InPrivate or incognito mode, and browse to `https://aka.ms/ssprsetup`.

2. Sign in with a non-administrator test user, and register your authentication phone.

3. Once complete, click the Looks Good button and close the browser window.

4. Open a new browser window in InPrivate or incognito mode, and browse to `https://aka.ms/sspr`.

5. Enter your non-administrator test user's user ID and the characters from the CAPTCHA, and then click Next.

6. Follow the verification steps to reset your password.

Configuring Azure AD Identity Protection

Azure AD Identity Protection is a feature that can help any organization protect themselves. Azure Active Directory Identity Protection is a feature of the Azure AD Premium P2 edition. It allows an organization to:

- Identify possible vulnerabilities that can affect your organization's identities.

- Set up automated reactions to detect suspicious actions.

- Identify suspicious events and take proper action to resolve those events.

Azure AD Identity Protection allows an Azure Administrator to use the same type of protection that Microsoft uses to protect and secure users' identities.

One of the most common security breaches that hackers use to gain access to an organization is by stealing and using a current user's identity. In recent years, hackers have developed more effective ways of stealing user data by using common attacks like phishing for data and hacking into third-party organizations.

Detecting a compromised user account is no easy task. Azure AD helps by using an adaptive learning algorithm and heuristics to determine irregularities and suspicious events. Once these events are recognized, Identity Protection produces a report and generates an alert that allows an Azure Administrator to view the issues and take appropriate actions to stop the attack.

There are advantages to using Identity Protection because Identity Protection is more than just a monitoring and reporting utility. It lets you create policies that automatically detect and respond to events that meet a specific risk level. These policies can automatically stop the hack by blocking the user account and requiring that the user's password be reset. During the password reset, multifactor user authentication is then enforced.

To use Azure AD Identity Protection, you must add the service to your Azure subscription. In Exercise 9.6, I will show you how.

EXERCISE 9.6

Adding Azure AD Identity Protection

1. Log into the Azure portal at `https://portal.azure.com`.

2. Click Marketplace; if the option is not visible, select More Services and then locate Marketplace.

3. Click Identity.

4. Enter **identity protection** in the Search The Marketplace box to narrow down your options, and then click Azure AD Identity Protection (see Figure 9.19).

FIGURE 9.19 Choosing Azure AD Identity Protection

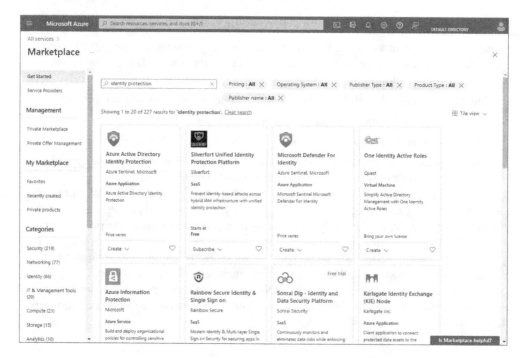

5. When the Azure AD Identity Protection information page appears, click Create.

6. If a page appears showing that Directory is set to Default Directory, you can choose a different directory and then click Create. If the default directory is fine, don't click Create.

7. You should see a message (see Figure 9.20) that states that the Default Directory is protected. Click that message to open the Azure AD Identity Protection dashboard. If this message does not appear, click Create and then click Azure Active Directory on the left side. On the right side under Your Role, you should see a section called Other Capabilities. Click Identity Protection to see this message. This is also how you can access the Identity Protection dashboard later.

FIGURE 9.20 Clicking the message to open the Identity Protection Dashboard

8. At this point, you should see the Azure AD Identity Protection dashboard (Figure 9.21). Take a few minutes and look at the different sections within the dashboard. Under the Investigation section, click Users Flagged For Risk, Risk Events, and Vulnerabilities.

FIGURE 9.21   Identity Protection Dashboard

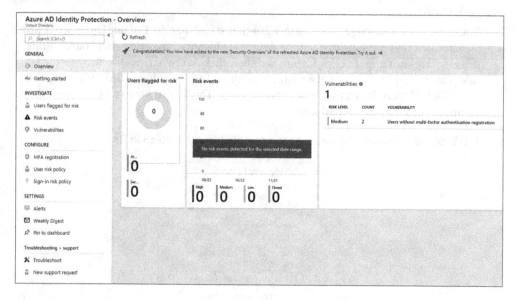

9. In the Configure section, click User Risk Policy.

10. Under Users, make sure all users are selected.

11. Click Set Condition. Under User Risk, click Select A Risk Level, and select Medium And Above. Click the Select button and then the Done button.

12. Under Controls, select a control. Under Select The Controls To Be Enforced, select Allow Access and make sure Require Password Change is selected. Click the Select button.

13. Under Enforce Policy, click On if you want to enforce this policy. If you do not want this policy to go live, do not click On.

14. Click Save.

15. You can also set a sign-in risk policy by clicking Sign-in Risk Policy. Under Users, choose All Users. Under Conditions, choose Medium And Above. Under Controls, Access, make sure you select Allow Access and select the Require Multi-factor Authentication check box. Choose either On or Off for Enforce Policy (choose Off if you just want to see how the policy is created), and then click Save.

16. Under Settings, click Alerts. Choose the level of risk you want to set. For this lab, I am choosing Medium. Click the link under Emails Are Sent To The Following Users and choose who the alerts should be sent to. Click Add and choose an email address. Click Done and then Save.

Managing Hybrid Networks

One nice feature of using both an on-site and Azure network is that Microsoft has many different tools to help you connect both networks. Connecting both networks is important so that users can seamlessly move between the two networks.

Microsoft's identity solutions extend your organization's on-site network with the Azure network features. These solutions create a common user identity for authentication and authorization to all resources. The advantage is that the users can access these resources no matter where they reside. This is what Microsoft refers to as *hybrid identity*.

To properly set up your hybrid identity, use one of the following authentication methods. Which one you decide on all depends on your environment scenario. The three available methods are:

- Password hash synchronization (PHS)

- Pass-through authentication (PTA)

- Federation

So, what is the real advantage of setting up both networks using one of these methods? When you choose one of the authentication methods, you are providing your users with *Single Sign-On (SSO)* capabilities. Single sign-on allows your users to sign in once but have access to resources on both networks. This is what gives your users seamless access to all resources. So, let's take a look at some of the available identity solutions.

Password Hash Synchronization with Azure AD

One of the hybrid identity sign-in methods that you can use is called *password hash synchronization*. Azure AD and your on-site Active Directory synchronize with each other by using a hash value. The hash value is created based on the user's password. This way, the two systems can stay in sync with each other. Azure AD Connect is also required for this setup to function properly.

Password hash synchronization is a feature that is part of the Azure AD Connect Sync, and it allows you to log into Azure AD applications like Office 365. The advantage is that your users log into their account using their on-site username and password. This helps users because it reduces the number of username and passwords that they need to know.

Another advantage to your organization is that they can use password hash synchronization as a backup sign-on method if your organization decides to use Federation services with Active Directory Federation Services (AD FS). To set up password hash synchronization, your environment needs to implement the following:

- Azure AD Connect

- Directory synchronization between your on-site Active Directory and your Azure AD instance

- Have password hash synchronization enabled

Azure Active Directory Pass-Through Authentication

Another option for allowing your users to sign in to both on-site and cloud-based applications using the same passwords is *Azure AD Pass-through Authentication*. Organizations can use Azure AD Pass-through Authentication instead of using Azure AD Password Hash Synchronization. The organizational benefits for using Azure AD Pass-through Authentication is the ability to enforce on-site Active Directory security and password policies.

Azure AD Pass-through Authentication utilizes an agent installed onto an on-premise server. This allows Azure AD to validate the username and password directly on one of the on-premises AD domain controllers.

This will help your organization with costs because your IT support desk will not be inundated by users who can't remember their different passwords. This will help lower your IT department budget for total cost of ownership (TCO). Fewer calls to support means less support people needed. Some of the key benefits to using Azure AD Pass-through Authentication are as follows:

- Better user experience
  - Users can use the same account password to sign into both your Azure AD and on-site AD networks.
  - Users don't need to talk to IT as often to reset passwords for multiple accounts.
  - Azure AD allows your users to do their own password management using the Self-Service Password Management tools.
- Easy deployment
  - There is no need to deploy a large infrastructure on-site. Azure AD network can handle most of your networking services.
  - A lower budget is needed for on-site IT departments. Since your Azure AD and your on-site AD can easily integrate with each other, there is no need for large IT departments on-site.
- Security
  - On-site passwords will never be stored in the Azure cloud.
  - Users' accounts are protected using Azure AD Conditional Access policies. These policies include using Multi-Factor Authentication (MFA), filtering for brute-force password attacks, and stopping legacy authentication.
  - The Azure agent will only allow outbound connections from within your network. The advantage of this is that you are not required to load an agent on your perimeter network.
  - With the use of certificate-based authentication, organizations get secure connections between the Azure agent and Azure AD.
- Highly available
  - By installing additional Azure agents onto on-site servers, you can get high availability for Azure sign-in requests.

Federation with Azure AD

To understand what Federation can do for your organization, you must first understand trusts. Federation is just trusts on steroids. Understanding what a trust can do for your organization will help you understand why we use Federation services.

Understanding Trusts

Trust relationships make it easier to share security information and network resources between domains. Standard transitive two-way trusts are automatically created between the domains in a tree and between each of the trees in a forest. Figure 9.22 shows an example of the default trust relationships in an Active Directory forest.

FIGURE 9.22   Default trusts in an Active Directory forest

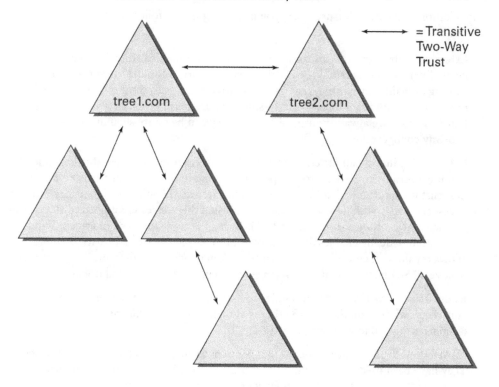

When configuring trusts, consider two main characteristics:

Transitive Trusts   By default, Active Directory trusts are *transitive trusts*. The simplest way to understand transitive relationships is through this example: if Domain A trusts Domain B and Domain B trusts Domain C, then Domain A implicitly trusts Domain C. If you need to apply a tighter level of security, trusts can be configured as intransitive.

One-Way vs. Two-Way   Trusts can be configured as one-way or two-way relationships. The default operation is to create *two-way trusts*, or *bidirectional trusts*. This makes it easier to manage trust relationships by reducing the trusts you must create. In some cases, however, you might decide against two-way trusts. In one-way relationships, the trusting domain allows resources to be shared with the trusted domain but not the other way around.

When domains are added together to form trees and forests, an automatic transitive two-way trust is created between them. Although the default trust relationships work well for most organizations, there are some reasons you might want to manage trusts manually:

- You may want to remove trusts between domains if you are absolutely sure you do not want resources to be shared between domains.

- Because of security concerns, you may need to keep resources isolated.

In addition to the default trust types, you can configure the following types of special trusts:

External Trusts   An *external trust* is a one-way nontransitive trust that is created manually. This trust is established with an external domain outside the forest of the trusting domain. You use external trusts to provide access to resources on a domain or forest that cannot use a forest trust. In some cases, external trusts are your only option. External trusts are always nontransitive, but they can be established in a one-way or two-way configuration.

Default SID Filtering on External Trusts   When you set up an external trust, remember that it is possible for hackers to compromise a domain controller in a trusted domain. If this trust is compromised, a hacker can use the Security Identifier (SID) history attribute to associate SIDs with new user accounts, granting themselves unauthorized rights (this is called an *elevation-of-privileges attack*). To help prevent this type of attack, Windows Server automatically enables SID filter quarantining on all external trusts. SID filtering allows the domain controllers in the trusting domain (the domain with the resources) to remove all SID history attributes that are not members of the trusted domain.

Realm Trusts   *Realm trusts* are similar to external trusts. You use them to connect to a non-Windows domain that uses Kerberos authentication. Realm trusts can be transitive or nontransitive, one-way or two-way.

Cross-Forest Trusts   *Cross-forest trusts* are used to share resources between forests. They have been used since Windows Server 2000 domains and cannot be nontransitive, but you can establish them in a one-way or a two-way configuration. Authentication requests in either forest can reach the other forest in a two-way cross-forest trust. If you want one forest to trust another forest, you must set it (at a minimum) to at least the forest function level of Windows Server 2003.

Selective Authentication vs. Forest-Wide Authentication   Forest-wide authentication on a forest trust means that users of the trusted forest can access all the resources of the trusting forest. Selective authentication means that users cannot authenticate to a domain controller or resource server in the trusting forest unless they are explicitly allowed to do so.

Shortcut Trusts   In some cases, you may want to create direct trusts between two domains that implicitly trust each other. Such a trust is sometimes referred to as a *shortcut trust*, and it can improve the speed at which resources are accessed across many different domains. Let's say you have a forest, as shown in Figure 9.23.

FIGURE 9.23   Example of a forest

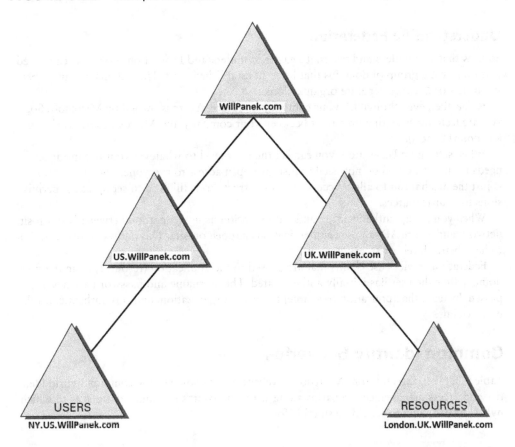

Users in the NY.US.WillPanek.com domain can access resources in the London .UK.WillPanek.com domain, but the users have to authenticate using the parent domains to gain access (NY.US.WillPanek.com to US.WillPanek.com to WillPanek.com to UK.WillPanek.com to finally reach London.UK.WillPanek.com).

This process can be slow. An administrator can set up a one-way trust from London .UK.WillPanek.com (trusting domain) to NY.US.WillPanek.com (trusted domain) so that the users can access the resources directly.

Perhaps the most important aspect to remember regarding trusts is that creating them only *allows* you to share resources between domains. The trust does not grant any permissions between domains by itself. Once a trust has been established, however, system administrators can easily assign the necessary permissions.

Understanding Federation

So now that you understand trusts, it's easier to understand Federation services because Federation is just a group of domains that have an established trust. These domains can be between sites or between separate organizations.

Remember, even though it's your company on Azure, Azure is owned by Microsoft. So, you are technically setting up a trust between your company and Microsoft's network (on Microsoft.com).

When setting up Federation, you can set the trust level to whatever your organization needs for its users. You do not need to just give open access to everyone. Also, Federation is just the mechanism to allow access across the trust. You still need to set up users' permissions to your resources.

When you set up authentication and authorization using Federation between your on-site network and Azure AD, all user authentications happen on-site. This allows an organization to have better levels of access control.

Federation services use claims that are passed to the application (resource) from the user domain after the user has initially authenticated. The username and password are never passed. Instead, the application (resource) trusts the organization, and this authenticates the user's claims.

Common Identity Scenarios

Table 9.3, taken directly from Microsoft's website, shows some of the common hybrid identity and access management scenarios along with Microsoft's recommendations as to which hybrid identity option would be suitable for each.

In Table 9.3, the three headers are abbreviated. Column 2, PHS and SSO, stands for Password hash synchronization with single sign-on. Column 3, PTA and SSO, stands for Pass-through authentication and single sign-on. Finally, Column 4 stands for Federated single sign-on using Active Directory Federation Services.

TABLE 9.3   Common identity scenarios and recommendations

Scenario	PHS and SSO	PTA and SSO	AD FS
Sync new user, contact, and group accounts created in my on-premises Active Directory to the cloud automatically.	X	X	X
Set up my tenant for Microsoft 365 hybrid scenarios.	X	X	X
Enable my users to sign in and access cloud services using their on-premises password.	X	X	X
Implement single sign-on using corporate credentials.	X	X	X
Ensure no password hashes are stored in the cloud.		X	X
Enable cloud multifactor authentication solutions.	X	X	X
Enable on-premises multifactor authentication solutions.			X
Support smart card authentication for my users.			X
Display password expiry notifications in the Office portal and on the Windows 10 desktop.			X

Azure AD Connect

Once you decide that you want your on-site network to be integrated with Azure AD, you need to install a component that allows both versions of Active Directory to work together. That component is called Azure AD Connect.

Azure AD Connect is a Microsoft utility that allows you to set up a hybrid design between Azure AD and your on-site AD. It provides some of the following features:

- Password hash synchronization
- Pass-through authentication
- Federation integration
- Synchronization
- Health monitoring

Azure AD Connect Health Monitoring

Azure AD Connect Health Monitoring is a way that an administrator can monitor their on-site identity infrastructure and maintain a constant connection to all of your Azure services.

To access the Azure AD Connect Health information, connect to the Azure AD Connect Health portal. The portal can be used to view alerts, usage information, performance monitoring, and other key information. The Azure AD Connect Health portal gives you a one-stop shop for all of your Azure AD Connect monitoring.

Installing Azure AD Connect

Before you can install Azure AD Connect, make sure that your infrastructure and your Azure network meet the prerequisites. The following is a list of requirements for installing Azure AD Connect:

- Azure AD
- On-site Active Directory
- Azure AD Connect server
- SQL Server database used by Azure AD Connect
- Azure AD Global Administrator account
- Enterprise Administrator account
- Connectivity between networks
- PowerShell and .NET Framework setup
- Enabled TLS 1.2 for Azure AD Connect

In Exercise 9.7, I will show you how to download and install Azure AD Connect. To complete this exercise, you must have an on-site version of AD that can be connected to Azure.

EXERCISE 9.7

Installing Azure AD Connect

1. Log into the Azure portal at https://portal.azure.com.
2. Click Azure Active Directory.
3. Click Azure AD Connect.
4. Click the Download Azure AD Connect link.
5. Click the Download button.
6. When the download box appears, choose to download the AzureADConnect.msi file to a network location. Once the download is complete, close the download box.
7. Log into the server (where you wish to install Azure AD Connect) as the local administrator.
8. Navigate to the AzureADConnect.msi file and double-click the file to start the installation.

9. On the Welcome screen, select the box to agree to the license terms and then click Continue.

10. On the Express Settings page, click Use Express Settings.

11. On the Connect To Azure AD page, enter the Azure Global administrator's username and password and then click Next.

12. The Connect To AD DS page will appear. Enter the username and password for an on-site enterprise admin and then click Next.

13. The Azure AD sign-in configuration page will appear. Review every domain marked Not Added and Not Verified. Make sure domains are verified in Azure AD. Once the domains are verified in Azure, click the Refresh symbol. If you need to verify your domains, go into Azure Active Directory, and then select Custom Domain Names. Enter the domain names for your on-site domain.

14. On the Ready To Configure page, click Install.

15. When the installation completes, click Exit.

16. You must sign off and sign in again before you can use or set up any other services.

Azure VPN Gateway

As I have stated throughout this book, most companies will have both an on-site network and an Azure network. Because of this, you will need to know how to connect both networks together. This is where you would use a site-to-site VPN (virtual private network) gateway connection.

Site-to-site VPN gateway connections allow you to connect both networks together over a secure IPsec/IKE (Internet Key Exchange) VPN tunnel. To make this type of connection between networks, you need to have a VPN device located on-site. This VPN device will require a public IP address on the external side (the side facing the Internet) of the device.

To use a site-to-site VPN connection, you must meet the following requirements:

- Compatible VPN device with an administrator who can configure the device.

- An external public IP address for that VPN device.

- Knowledge of your on-site IP configuration and subnetting. None of your on-site IP subnets can overlap your Azure virtual network subnets.

Example Values for Site-to-Site VPN Connection

To help IT people better understand and configure site-to-site VPN connections, Microsoft released example values on their website. These example values can be used to set up a test environment, or they can be used to help you better understand what values are needed to set up a site-to-site VPN connection.

The following examples were taken directly from Microsoft's website: http://docs.microsoft.com/en-us/azure/vpn-gateway/tutorial-site-to-site-portal.

- VNet Name: TestVNet1.

- Address Space: 10.1.0.0/16.

- Subscription: The subscription you want to use.

- Resource Group: TestRG1.

- Location: East US.

- Subnet: FrontEnd: 10.1.0.0/24, BackEnd: 10.1.1.0/24 (optional for this exercise).

- Gateway Subnet name: GatewaySubnet (this will auto-fill in the portal).

- Gateway Subnet address range: 10.1.255.0/27.

- DNS Server: 8.8.8.8—Optional. The IP address of your DNS server.

- Virtual Network Gateway Name: VNet1GW.

- Public IP: VNet1GWIP.

- VPN Type: Route-based.

- Connection Type: Site-to-site (IPsec).

- Gateway Type: VPN.

- Local Network Gateway Name: Site1.

- Connection Name: VNet1toSite1.

- Shared Key: For this example, we use abc123. But you can use whatever is compatible with your VPN hardware. The important thing is that the values match on both sides of the connection.

Creating the VPN Gateway

Now that you have an understanding of why you would need a VPN gateway, let's look at what it takes to create a VPN gateway. Since every VPN device is different, I will show you how to create the actual site-to-site VPN connection in Exercise 9.8. You need to have someone create the connection on the VPN device.

EXERCISE 9.8

Creating the Site-to-Site VPN Connection

1. Log into the Azure portal at https://portal.azure.com.

2. On the left side of the portal page, click + Create A Resource (if the portal menu is not visible, click Show Portal Menu in the upper left-hand corner and then click + Create A Resource) and then type **Virtual Network Gateway** in the search box. In the Results section, click Virtual Network Gateway (as shown in Figure 9.24).

FIGURE 9.24   Choosing Virtual Network Gateway

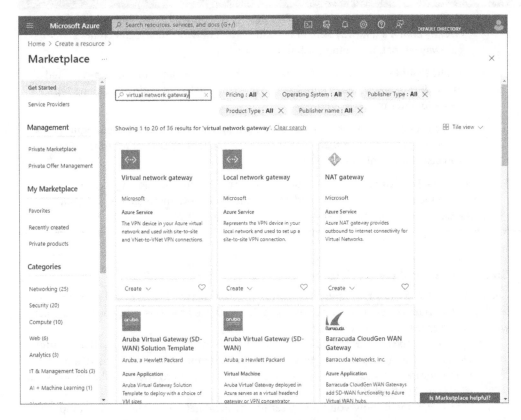

3.   On the Virtual Network Gateway page, click the Create button.

4.   On the Create Virtual Network Gateway page, enter the values for your virtual network gateway settings.

- **Name:** This is the name of your gateway object.

- **Gateway Type:** Select VPN. VPN gateways use the VPN type.

- **VPN Type:** Choose the VPN type that fits your configuration. Route-based VPNs are the most common type.

- **SKU:** Select your gateway SKU. This will depend on the VPN type you select.

- **Enable Active-Active Mode:** If you are creating an active-active gateway configuration, choose this check box. If you are not creating an active-active gateway configuration, leave this check box unselected.

- **Location:** Choose your appropriate geographical location.

- **Virtual Network:** Choose the virtual network you want for this gateway.

EXERCISE 9.8 *(continued)*

- **Gateway Subnet Address Range:** This setting will only be seen if you did not already create a gateway subnet for your virtual network. If you did create a valid gateway subnet, this setting will not appear.

- **Public IP Address:** This setting specifies the public IP address that gets associated to the VPN gateway. Make sure Create New is the selected radio button and type a name for your public IP address.

- Unless your configuration specifically requires BGP ASN, leave this configuration's check box unchecked. If BGP ASN is required, the default setting for ASN is 65515. You can change this if needed.

5. Click Create. The settings will be validated and you'll see the "Deploying Virtual network gateway" message on the dashboard. This can take up to 45 minutes. Refresh your portal page to see the current status.

Creating the Local Network Gateway

The next step that we must complete is creating the local network gateway. The local network gateway refers to your on-site network. What you need to do is give your on-site network a name that Azure can use to access that network.

After you name the on-site network on Azure, you then need to tell Azure what IP address that it needs to use to access the on-site VPN device. You must also specify the IP address prefix (that is located on your on-site location) that will be used to route traffic through the VPN gateway and to the VPN device.

In Exercise 9.9, I will show you how to set up the local network gateway. To complete this exercise, you need to know the IP address information for your on-site test or live network.

EXERCISE 9.9

Creating the Local Network Gateway

1. Log into the Azure portal at https://portal.azure.com.

2. On the left side of the portal page, click + Create A Resource and then type Local network gateway in the search box. In the Results section, click Local Network Gateway (as shown in Figure 9.25).

FIGURE 9.25   Choosing a local network gateway

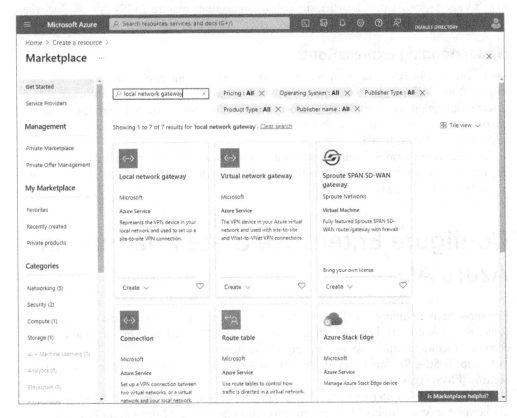

3. On the Local Network Gateway page, click Create.

4. On the Create Local Network Gateway page, enter the values for your local network gateway settings:

    - **Name:** Specify the name of your local network gateway.

    - **IP address:** This is the public IP address of the VPN device.

    - **Address Space:** This is the IP address ranges for the local network.

    - **Configure BGP settings:** Use this setting when configuring BGP. Otherwise, don't select this option.

    - **Subscription:** Verify your current Azure subscription is showing.

    - **Resource Group:** You can create a new resource group or choose one that you have already created.

    - **Location:** Choose your appropriate geographical location.

5. Click the Create button.

Once you have finished creating the VPN connection, you will need to configure the company's VPN device. As stated earlier, site-to-site connections require a VPN device. Once the VPN device is configured properly, your site-to-site communications are completed.

Understanding ExpressRoute

ExpressRoute allows you to set up another way to connect your two networks. ExpressRoute lets you connect your internal network to your external network using a private connection supplied by your connection provider. Using ExpressRoute allows you to connect your internal network with any or all of the different Microsoft cloud services such as Azure and Microsoft 365.

Since the connection is through your connection provider and not the Internet, ExpressRoute is much faster, more reliable, and offers better security and lower latency connections over the Internet.

Configure Enterprise State Roaming in Azure AD

Enterprise State Roaming is a Windows 10/11 feature that allows users that are using a device that is Azure AD device registered (either Azure AD joined or hybrid joined) to synchronize their application and user settings to the cloud.

Enterprise State Roaming is available with an Azure AD Premium or Enterprise Mobility + Security (EMS) license.

When you enable Enterprise State Roaming, you are automatically given a free, limited-use license for Azure Rights Management protection from Azure Information Protection. This free subscription is limited to encrypting and decrypting enterprise settings and application data synced by Enterprise State Roaming. To have full capabilities of the Azure Rights Management service, you must have a paid subscription.

Requirements of Enterprise State Roaming

You must meet these requirements:

- Windows 10 or newer, with the latest updates, and a minimum Version 1511 (OS Build 10586 or later) is installed on the device.

- The device is Azure AD joined or hybrid Azure AD joined.

- Enterprise State Roaming needs to be enabled for the tenant in Azure AD. You can enable roaming for all users or for only a selected group of users.

- The user is assigned an Azure Active Directory Premium license.

- The device must be restarted, and the user must sign in again to access Enterprise State Roaming features.

Enable Enterprise State Roaming

Follow these steps:

1. Log into the Azure portal.
2. Browse to Azure Active Directory ➤ Devices ➤ Enterprise State Roaming.
3. Select Users May Sync Settings And App Data Across Devices.

NOTE   For a Windows 10 or newer device to use the Enterprise State Roaming service, the device must authenticate using an Azure AD identity. For devices that are joined to Azure AD, the user's primary sign-in identity is their Azure AD identity, so no other configuration is required. For devices that use on-premises Active Directory, the administrator must configure hybrid Azure Active Directory joined devices.

Enterprise State Roaming data is partitioned on three major geographic regions: North America, EMEA (Europe, the Middle East, and Africa), and APAC (Asia-Pacific Countries). Enterprise State Roaming data is hosted in one or more Azure regions that align with the country/region value that is set in the Azure Active Directory instance. The data for the tenant is located locally within the geographical region and isn't replicated across regions. The country/region value is set as part of the Azure AD directory creation process and it cannot be changed.

View Per-User Device Sync Status

To view a per-user device sync status report, perform the following:

1. Sign into the Azure AD Admin Center at `https://aad.portal.azure.com`.
2. Select Azure Active Directory ➤ Users ➤ All Users.
3. Select the user and then select Devices.
4. Select View Devices Syncing Settings And App Data to show sync status.

Devices syncing for the user are shown and can be downloaded.

Data that is synced to the cloud using Enterprise State Roaming is retained until it is deleted manually or until the data is deemed to be "stale." Data that hasn't been accessed for one year (the retention period) will be treated as stale and may be deleted from the cloud. This data retention policy isn't configurable, and once the data is permanently deleted, it is not recoverable.

Plan and Implement Conditional Access Policies

We discussed Conditional Access policies earlier in this chapter, but in this section, we will delve into the topic a bit deeper.

Conditional Access policies are basically if-then statements; if a user wants access to a specific resource, then they must meet certain actions or criteria. The Azure AD Conditional Access feature will analyze users, devices, and locations in order to automate decisions and enforce your access policies. Conditional Access policies allow an administrator to create certain conditions that can block access, require multifactor authentication, or can even restrict the user's session.

There are some prerequisites when working with Conditional Access policies:

- An Azure AD tenant with Azure AD Premium or trial license enabled

- An account with Conditional Access administrator privileges

- A test user (non-administrator) who will verify that policies work as needed prior to affecting actual users

- A group that the non-administrator user is a member of

Sometimes the hardest part when setting up Conditional Access policies is to determine which users should be affected. There are some common questions you can ask. The policies will answer questions about who should have access to corporate resources, what resources they can access, and what conditions need to be met. These policies can grant access, limit access, or block access. You will create Conditional Access policies by defining the if-then statements, meaning that IF an assignment is met, then certain conditions and controls can be applied.

According to Microsoft, there are some common questions that you should ask when determining policies. Make sure to document the answers to the questions for each prior to creating the policy. These questions were taken directly from Microsoft's website at `http://docs.microsoft.com/en-us/azure/active-directory/conditional-access/plan-conditional-access`.

- Users or workload identities
  - Which users, groups, directory roles, and workload identities will be included in or excluded from the policy?
  - What emergency access accounts or groups should be excluded from the policy?

- Cloud apps or actions: Will this policy apply to any application, user action, or authentication context? If yes. . .
  - What application(s) will the policy apply to?
  - What user actions will be subject to this policy?
  - What authentication contexts will this policy be applied to?

- Conditions
  - Which device platforms will be included in or excluded from the policy?
  - What are the organization's trusted locations?

- What locations will be included in or excluded from the policy?
- What client app types will be included in or excluded from the policy?
- Do you have policies that would drive excluding Azure AD joined devices or Hybrid Azure AD joined devices from policies?
- If using Identity Protection, do you want to incorporate sign-in risk protection?

- Grant or Block: Do you want to grant access to resources by requiring one or more of the following?
  - Require MFA
  - Require device to be marked as compliant
  - Require hybrid Azure AD joined device
  - Require approved client app
  - Require app protection policy
  - Require password change
  - Use Terms of Use
- Session control: Do you want to enforce any of the following access controls on cloud apps?
  - Use app enforced restrictions
  - Use Conditional Access App control
  - Enforce sign-in frequency
  - Use persistent browser sessions
  - Customize continuous access evaluation

A Conditional Access policy must, at a minimum, contain the following in order to be enforced (as shown in Figure 9.26):

- Name of the policy
- Assignments
  - Users and/or groups to apply the policy to
  - Cloud apps or actions to apply the policy to
- Access controls
  - Grant or block controls

FIGURE 9.26   Creating a conditional access policy

Create a Conditional Access Policy

To create a Conditional Access policy:

1. Sign in to the Azure portal, `https://portal.azure.com`, using an account with Global Administrator permissions.
2. Select Azure Active Directory.
3. Once Azure AD is open, select Security from the menu on the left-hand side.
4. Select Conditional Access, select + New Policy, and then click Create New Policy.
5. Enter a name for the policy.
6. Under Assignments, select the current value under Users Or Workload Identities.
7. Under What Does This Policy Apply To?, select your desired option.
8. Next you can choose to either choose to Include or Exclude - select your desired option.
9. Click the link that allows you to specify users and groups. Select your desired user or groups.

10. Continue to modify the policy to suit your needs. Once you are satisfied with your options, you can activate the policy by selecting On in the Enable Policy section. Then click Create.

 When choosing which users and groups to include, keep in mind that there is a limit to the number of individual users that can be added directly to a Conditional Access policy. If you have a large number of individual users, Microsoft recommends placing them into a group and then assigning the group to the Conditional Access policy.

Troubleshooting Conditional Access

If a user is having an issue with a Conditional Access policy, collect the following information from them in order to help troubleshoot:

- User principal name
- User display name
- Operating system name
- Time stamp (approximate is okay)
- Target application
- Client application type (browser vs. client)
- Correlation ID (this is unique to the sign-in)

If the user received a message with a More Details link, have them click the link to provide more details.

Azure AD Audit Log

The Azure AD audit log can be a helpful tool when troubleshooting Conditional Access policy changes. By default, audit log data is kept for only 30 days. If you want to edit the diagnostic settings, you can go to the Azure portal ➤ Azure Active Directory ➤ Diagnostic settings ➤ Edit.

To use the audit log:

1. Sign into the Azure portal as a global administrator, security administrator, or Conditional Access administrator.

2. Select Azure Active Directory ➤ Audit Logs.

3. Select your required Date Range.

4. Select Activity and choose one of the following:

- **Add Conditional Access Policy:** This option lists newly created policies.
- **Update Conditional Access Policy:** This option lists changed policies.
- **Delete Conditional Access Policy:** This option lists deleted policies.

Troubleshoot Sign-in Problems

If a user experiences a sign-in problem, they will receive an error message, or if signing in using a web browser, the error page itself will have detailed information. Just click the More Details link to display useful troubleshooting information.

Here are some additional Conditional Access error codes that a user may receive when signing in:

- 53000 – Device Not Compliant
- 53001 – Device Not Domain Joined
- 53002 – Application Used Is Not An Approved App
- 53003 – Blocked By Conditional Access
- 53004 – Proof Up Blocked Due To Risk

So, what should you do if you get locked out of the Azure portal due to an incorrect setting in a Conditional Access policy? First, you want to check if there are other administrators in your company who aren't blocked. Another administrator with access to the Azure portal can disable the policy that is affecting your sign-in. But if no other administrators can update the policy, you will have to submit a support request. Microsoft Support will review and help you fix the policy that is preventing access.

To find out which Conditional Access policy or policies are applied, view them by following these steps:

1. Sign in to the Azure portal as a global or security administrator, or as a global reader.
2. Select Azure Active Directory ➤ Browse to Azure Active Directory ➤ Sign-ins.
3. Locate the event you wish to review. You can add or remove different filters and columns to meet your needs.
4. Once you locate the event you want to review, select the Conditional Access tab. This tab will show the specific policy or policies that resulted in the sign-in interruption.

   - Information on the Troubleshooting And Support tab may provide a reason why a sign-in failed.

   - To investigate further, click the policy name. This will show the policy configuration user interface for the selected policy for review and editing.

5. To view the policy details, click the ellipsis on the right side of the policy in a sign-in event. This will show you more information about why a policy was or wasn't applied. If the information still isn't clear, you can use the sign-in diagnostic tool located under Basic Info ➤ Troubleshoot Event.

Troubleshoot Using the What If Tool

The What If tool is also useful when you're trying to determine why a policy was or wasn't applied. Access the tool by going to the Azure portal and selecting Azure Active Directory ➤ Security ➤ Conditional Access ➤ What If (as shown in Figure 9.27).

FIGURE 9.27   What If tool

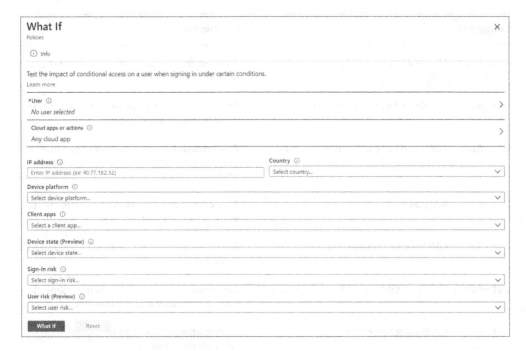

The What If tool only requires a User or Workload identity to get started. At any point, you can click Reset to clear any criteria input and return to the default state.

Using PowerShell Commands

Table 9.4 shows some of the PowerShell commands available for Azure Active Directory. You must be using a newer version of PowerShell on your on-site servers or client machines. If you run into any issues trying to run these commands, please check out a newer version of Microsoft PowerShell on Microsoft's website.

TABLE 9.4   PowerShell commands for Azure Active Directory

Command	Description
`Add-AzureADAdministrativeUnitMember`	This command allows an Azure admin to add an administrative unit member.
`Add-AzureADApplicationPolicy`	Administrators can use this command to add an application policy.
`Add-AzureADScopedRoleMembership`	This command allows an Azure admin to add a scoped role membership to an administrative unit.

TABLE 9.4   PowerShell commands for Azure Active Directory *(continued)*

Command	Description
Add-AzureADServicePrincipalPolicy	Administrators can use this command to add a service principal policy.
Get-AzureADAdministrativeUnit	This command allows an Azure admin to view an administrative unit.
Get-AzureADAdministrativeUnitMember	Administrators can use this command to view a member of an administrative unit.
Get-AzureADApplicationPolicy	This command allows an Azure admin to view an application policy.
Get-AzureADDirectorySetting	Administrators can use this command to view a directory setting.
Get-AzureADDirectorySettingTemplate	This command allows an Azure admin to view a directory setting template.
Get-AzureADObjectSetting	Administrators can use this command to view an object setting.
Get-AzureADPolicy	This command allows an Azure admin to view a policy.
Get-AzureADPolicyAppliedObject	Administrators can use this command to view the objects to which a policy is applied.
Get-AzureADScopedRoleMembership	This command allows an Azure admin to view a scoped role membership from an administrative unit.
Get-AzureADServicePrincipalPolicy	Administrators can use this command to view the service principal policy.
New-AzureADAdministrativeUnit	This command allows an Azure admin to create an administrative unit.
New-AzureADDirectorySetting	Administrators can use this command to create a directory settings object.
New-AzureADObjectSetting	This command allows an Azure admin to create a settings object.

Command	Description
`New-AzureADPolicy`	Administrators can use this command to create a policy.
`Remove-AzureADAdministrativeUnit`	This command allows an Azure admin to remove an administrative unit.
`Remove-AzureADAdministrativeUnitMember`	Administrators can use this command to remove an administrative unit member.
`Remove-AzureADDirectorySetting`	This command allows an Azure admin to delete a directory setting in Azure Active Directory.
`Remove-AzureADObjectSetting`	Administrators can use this command to delete settings in Azure Active Directory.
`Remove-AzureADPolicy`	This command allows an Azure admin to delete a policy.
`Remove-AzureADScopedRoleMembership`	Administrators can use this command to remove a scoped role membership.
`Set-AzureADDirectorySetting`	This command updates a directory setting in Azure Active Directory.
`Set-AzureADObjectSetting`	This command allows an Azure admin to update object settings.
`Set-AzureADPolicy`	Administrators can use this command to update a policy.
`Get-AzureADApplicationProxyConnector GroupMembers`	This command retrieves the members of an Application Proxy connector group.

Summary

This chapter covered the basics of implementing an Active Directory within your organization. We looked at the various pieces of an Active Directory on-site (or Azure VM) setup.

We then examined the components of Azure AD. We discussed the benefits and features of Azure AD in addition to the common questions and answers about Azure AD directly from Microsoft's website.

You were introduced to the Azure AD dashboard and many of its sections. I showed you how to create an Azure AD users account and an Azure AD group. You then learned about the Azure AD Password Reset option and how to configure that feature.

This chapter also covered the benefits of using the Azure AD Identity Protection feature, and how to add that feature to your subscription. You learned how to configure Identity Protection and set up an email address so that you can receive alerts.

You also learned how to set up a hybrid network and the importance of setting up an on-site network along with your Azure AD network. This chapter then covered various authentication methods and explained what each method can do for you. We also discussed Azure AD Connect and how it can link your on-site AD with Azure AD.

You learned the benefits of using site-to-site VPN gateway connections. We discussed the requirements and how to set up and configure the components needed for site-to-site VPN gateway connections. You saw how to configure Enterprise State Roaming in Azure AD, and we discussed planning and implementing Conditional Access policies in greater detail and how to troubleshoot them.

Exam Essentials

Understand the difference between Active Directory and Azure Active Directory (Azure AD).   Make sure you understand the features and benefits of using Azure AD. Not only is this important for taking the Microsoft exams, but it is also important to determine if Azure AD is the correct choice for your organization.

Understand the Q&As of Azure AD.   This is very important for a couple of reasons. First, and most obvious, for the Microsoft exam you need to understand what Azure AD can do and not do. Second, you need to make sure that Azure AD can handle all the services your organization is trying to provide.

Know the Azure AD Dashboard.   You need to understand the Azure AD dashboard and where you configure the various components for Azure AD. You also need to know how to access other dashboards (like the Azure AD Identity Protection dashboard) so that you can properly navigate Azure AD and its features.

Know how to set up and configure password resets.   You should understand what the process is for password resets and how to configure different authentication methods. Understand how to verify the users by using text messages or emails for verification.

Understand Azure AD Identity Protection.   Know how to add Azure AD Identity Protection to your Azure subscription. Make sure you know how to configure the different policies and how to set alerts for an Azure administrator.

Know about hybrid networks.   It is important to understand why we use hybrid networks and the different authentication methods that can be used for setting up a hybrid network.

Understand Azure AD Connect.   Understand why we use Azure AD Connect. Azure AD Connect allows you to connect your on-site AD with Azure AD. This allows your user accounts and passwords to be replicated.

Be familiar with site-to-site VPN gateway connections.   Know and understand what site-to-site VPN gateways can do for your company. Site-to-site VPN gateway connections allow you to connect both of your networks together over a secure IPsec/IKE VPN tunnel.

Understand and configure Enterprise State Roaming in Azure AD.   Understand and configure Enterprise State Roaming in Azure AD. Enterprise State Roaming gives users who are using an Azure AD registered device the ability to synchronize their application and user settings to the cloud.

Plan and implement Conditional Access policies and troubleshoot them in Azure AD.   Be able to configure Conditional Access policies and know how to troubleshoot them. Conditional Access policies are basically if-then statements; if a user wants access to a specific resource, then they must meet certain actions or criteria.

Know the Azure AD PowerShell commands.   Microsoft announced that all of their Microsoft exams would start asking questions about using PowerShell. This is going to be true for all chapters in this book, but make sure you understand the basic Azure AD PowerShell commands.

Video Resources

There are no videos for this chapter.

Review Questions

1. You are the system administrator of a large organization that has recently decided to add an Azure AD subscription. Your boss has asked you about Azure security and making sure that user logins are secure. What feature can you explain to your boss to ease their concerns?

   A. Azure AD User Security

   B. Azure AD Identity Protection

   C. Azure AD Security add-on

   D. Azure Identity Protection

2. You want to create a new Azure Active Directory policy for your users. What PowerShell command would you use to accomplish this task?

   A. `New-AzurePolicy`

   B. `New-AzureActiveDirectoryPolicy`

   C. `Set-AzurePolicy`

   D. `New-AzureADPolicy`

3. You want to look at an Azure Active Directory policy for your users. What PowerShell command would you use to accomplish this task?

   A. `Get-AzureADPolicy`

   B. `Get-AzurePolicy`

   C. `View-AzurePolicy`

   D. `View-AzureADPolicy`

4. You are the administrator for a large organization that has subscribed to a new Azure AD subscription. You want your users to be able to reset passwords themselves. What Azure AD feature allows this to happen?

   A. User-enabled password resets

   B. Azure password reset feature

   C. Self-service password reset

   D. Password reset service

5. You are the new Azure AD Global Administrator for your organization. Your company wants to set up a way to integrate their on-site AD with Azure AD. What tool can you use to do this?

   A. Site-to-site VPN gateway connectors

   B. Azure AD Connect

   C. Azure AD Replication

   D. Active Directory Replicator

6. You want to look at an Azure Active Directory application policy for your users' applications. What PowerShell command would you use to accomplish this task?

    A. `Add-AzureADPolicy`

    B. `Add-AzureADApplicationPolicy`

    C. `Create-AzurePolicy`

    D. `Install-AzureADPolicy`

7. You want to change an Azure Active Directory policy for your users. What PowerShell command would you use to accomplish this task?

    A. `New-AzureADPolicy`

    B. `Edit-AzureADPolicy`

    C. `New-AzurePolicy`

    D. `Set-AzureADPolicy`

8. You are the new Azure AD Global Administrator for your organization. Your company has an Azure AD domain name of `ContosoAzure.onmicrosoft.com`. Your bosses want you to change the default domain name to `Contoso.onmicrosoft.com`. How can you change the initial domain name?

    A. Use the Custom Domain Names section of Azure AD and change the name.

    B. In Azure AD, go to default directories and change the domain name.

    C. Use PowerShell to change the default domain name.

    D. This can't be done.

9. You are the new Azure AD Global Administrator for your organization. Your company has an Azure AD domain name of `ContosoAzure.onmicrosoft.com`. Your bosses want you to add a new domain name for `Contoso.onmicrosoft.com`. How can you add the new domain name to your existing domain?

    A. Use the Custom Domain Names section of Azure AD and change the name.

    B. In Azure AD, go to default directories and add the domain name.

    C. Use the Azure Administrative Center to add the new domain name.

    D. This can't be done.

10. You want to view your Azure AD directory settings for your Azure AD subscription. What PowerShell command would you use to accomplish this task?

    A. `View-AzureADDirectorySetting`

    B. `Get-AzureADDirectorySetting`

    C. `Add-AzureADDirectorySetting`

    D. `Set-AzureADDirectorySetting`

11. You are the administrator for your company network. You want to look at an Azure Active Directory application policy for your user's applications. What PowerShell command should you use?

    A. `Add-AzureADPolicy`

    B. `Get-AzureADApplicationPolicy`

    C. `Create-AzurePolicy`

    D. `Install-AzureADPolicy`

12. You are the administrator for your company network. You have 20 Windows client computers that are joined to Azure AD. You have a Microsoft 365 subscription. You are planning to replace these computers with new computers that also run Windows 10/11. The new computers will be joined to Azure AD. What should you configure if you need to ensure that the desktop background, the Favorites, and the browsing history are available on the new computers?

    A. You should configure Enterprise State Roaming.

    B. You should configure Folder Redirection.

    C. You should configure system settings.

    D. You should configure roaming user profiles.

13. You are the administrator for your company network. You and a colleague are discussing different authentication methods. Which one of the following tools allows for the use of security questions?

    A. Azure AD Self-Service Password Reset (SSPR).

    B. Azure Multifactor Authentication (Azure MFA).

    C. Password Manager (PassMgr).

    D. This can't be done.

14. You are the administrator for your company network. You have an Azure AD tenant. All corporate devices are enrolled. You have a web-based application that uses Azure AD to authenticate. What should you configure if you need to prompt all users of the application to agree to the protection of corporate data when they access the app from both corporate and non-corporate devices?

    A. You should configure notifications in Device Compliance.

    B. You should configure Terms and Conditions in Device Enrollment.

    C. You should configure Terms of Use in Conditional Access.

    D. You should configure an Endpoint Protection Profile in Device Configuration.

15. You are the administrator for your company network. You need to ensure that when managers join Azure AD that their computers are enrolled automatically into Mobile Device Management (MDM). What tool should you use to do this?

    A. The Configuration Manager console

    B. The Group Policy Management Editor

    C. The Azure portal

    D. The Microsoft Intune portal

16. You are the administrator for your company network. You and a colleague are discussing conditional access policies and how to set one up. One section of the conditional access policy controls the who, what, and where of the conditional access policy. What section is being discussed?

    A. Access Controls

    B. Admission Control

    C. Assignments

    D. Tasks

17. You are the administrator for your company network. You and a colleague are discussing a feature used by Azure AD to bring together signals, to make decisions, and to enforce organizational policies. What is this tool called?

    A. Conditional access

    B. Device access

    C. Microsoft Cloud App Security (MCAS)

    D. Microsoft Empowerment

18. You are the administrator for your company network. You and a colleague are discussing the ability of Windows 10/11 Azure AD users to roam their profile data between multiple devices, allowing the user and app settings to sync between the devices regardless of where the user is located. What is this called?

    A. Azure Readiness Roaming

    B. Enterprise State Roaming

    C. Mandatory User Profile

    D. Roaming User Profile

19. You are the administrator for your company network. You and a colleague are discussing a tool that allows an organization to automate the detection and remediation of identity-based risks. What is this tool called?

    A. Azure AD User Security

    B. Azure AD Identity Protection

    C. Azure AD Security add-on

    D. Azure Identity Protection

20. You are the administrator for your company network. You and a colleague are discussing roles and permissions. You are using Azure AD and you want to assign permissions to users for maintaining conditional access. What role should you assign to the users if you'd like them to be able to view, create, modify, and delete conditional access policies?

    A. The Application Administrator role

    B. The Compliance Administrator role

    C. The Conditional Access Administrator role

    D. The Conditional Admission Administrator role

Chapter

10

Planning and Managing Microsoft Intune

MICROSOFT EXAM OBJECTIVES COVERED IN THIS CHAPTER:

✓ **Manage device lifecycle**

  ▪ Configure enrollment settings in Intune; configure automatic and bulk enrollment in Intune; configure policy sets; restart, retire, or wipe devices.

✓ **Manage device updates**

  ▪ Plan for device updates; create and manage quality update policies by using Intune; create and manage feature update policies by using Intune; create and manage iOS/iPadOS update policies by using Intune; manage Android updates by using device configuration profiles; monitor updates; troubleshoot updates in Intune; configure Windows client delivery optimization by using Intune; create and manage update rings by using Intune.

✓ **Deploy and update applications**

  ▪ Deploy apps by using Intune; configure Microsoft 365 Apps deployment by using Microsoft 365 Apps Admin Center; deploy Microsoft 365 Apps by using Intune; manage Office app settings by using group policy or Intune; deploy apps by using Microsoft Store for Business, Apple store, and Google store.

✓ **Implement app protection and app configuration policies**

  ▪ Plan app protection policies; plan app configuration policies for iOS and Android; implement app protection policies; implement app configuration policies for iOS and Android; manage app protection policies, manage app configuration policies.

In this chapter, we'll talk about Microsoft Intune and how you can use it to manage devices and software. You'll learn how to manage device updates using Intune, including creating update rings. We'll also discuss how to deploy apps using the Microsoft 365 Apps Admin Center and different app stores. Then, we'll discuss app protection and app configuration policies.

The chapter begins by talking about managing devices using Intune. You'll learn how to provision user accounts and enroll devices. We'll also discuss how to manage and configure devices using the Microsoft Intune subscription.

Next, you'll learn how to deploy and configure updates using Intune. We'll discuss how to use the in-console monitoring tools and how to approve and decline updates.

Then, the chapter focuses on working with mobile devices, including Windows tablets, broadband metering and tethering, and how to wipe mobile devices for employees who leave the company.

Finally, this chapter shows you how to use Intune to help deploy and maintain your company's software packages. We'll discuss sideloading applications into your users' devices, and explore the various types of reports that you can run to check on the hardware and software in your environment.

So, let's get started with using Microsoft Intune to help manage and maintain your corporate devices.

Managing Devices with Microsoft Intune

The first thing we need to discuss in this chapter is exactly what Microsoft Intune is. Microsoft Intune is a device management system (see Figure 10.1) that allows administrators to manage mobile devices, mobile applications, and PC management capabilities all from the cloud.

Administrators using Intune can provide their users with access to corporate applications, data, and resources from almost anywhere and on almost any device while also keeping your corporate information secure. It also helps you save money because Intune allows you to license users instead of licensing devices. So, if you have a user who works from multiple devices (laptop, tablet, and Windows phone) you only pay once for the user license instead of multiple times for all of the user's devices.

FIGURE 10.1   Microsoft Intune dashboard

Administrators can use Intune to support and manage Windows clients. Administrators can use Intune on a Windows 10/11 device to accomplish the following tasks:

- Enrollment
- Organization resource access
- Application management
- Policies
- Inventory
- Reporting
- Remote wipe

Intune is built on Microsoft Azure Active Directory and System Center. Active Directory is a Directory Services database created by Microsoft. Directory Services was originally designed by Novell, and starting in Windows Server 2000, Microsoft's version, Active Directory, was introduced to the world. To put this in an easy way to think about, Active Directory is just a database that allows administrators to control access to the network. Microsoft has taken Active Directory to a new level with cloud-based Active Directory, or Azure AD. Now instead of having to buy Windows Server and the required hardware, you can just use a cloud-based version of Active Directory.

Microsoft System Center Configuration Manager (SCCM) allows administrators to have a wide-ranging solution for change and configuration management. Configuration Manager allows an administrator to perform some of the following tasks:

- Deploy corporate operating systems, applications, and updates.
- Monitor and fix computers for compliance requirements.
- Monitor hardware and software inventory.
- Remotely administer devices.

Understanding Microsoft Intune Benefits

Microsoft Intune provides many different benefits to help an IT department be more productive and keep systems running all on the same software. Intune allows an IT department the ability to keep corporate data secure while allowing users to access the same company software from any device that they want to work from. Let's take a look at some other Intune benefits:

- Multiple device enrollments for users. Licenses are per user and not per device. So, users can work from multiple devices.
- Corporate data security for users and applications like Microsoft Exchange, Outlook, and Office.
- The ability to use Office 365 from any approved device.
- Since Intune is a cloud-based system, the IT department is not required to build an infrastructure. This saves the additional cost of buying and maintaining hardware and software.
- Intune extends your SCCM through both the cloud and on-premises versions by connecting the two systems together through the use of an application connector.
- Microsoft 24/7 support is available through worldwide phone or online support. Also, administrators have access to Microsoft.com for Intune FAQs and a knowledge base.
- Corporations have multiple licensing options available. Intune is also part of Microsoft's Enterprise Mobility + Security (EMS) suite by default.

Configuring Intune Subscriptions

When you are considering using Microsoft Intune, you must think about the subscription type you want. You can start with a free 30-day trial or move directly into a full paid subscription. Either choice allows you to start managing mobile devices and corporate computers immediately.

One of the nice advantages of Intune subscriptions is available if you decide to add at least 150 user licenses. If you reach 150 licenses, you get to use Microsoft's FastTrack Benefits Center. This benefit also allows a Microsoft specialist to work with your organization as part of the FastTrack benefits. The Microsoft specialist helps you get the most out of using Intune and all of its benefits.

The process to start using Microsoft Intune is easy and free. You go to Microsoft's website and sign up for a free 30-day trial of Intune. Then you start adding your users, groups, and devices. If you decide that Microsoft Intune is right for your organization, you can then sign up for one of the monthly rates.

Once you have decided to take that next step, you need to start redesigning your company's infrastructure to include the cloud-based subscription. This can be as easy as setting up your DNS servers to include the cloud-based services or as complex as adding all your devices to the cloud and phasing out many of the infrastructure servers that you currently have running in-house.

Whatever you decide, one of the most important phases of moving to a cloud-based system is planning. Once you have made the decision to move to the cloud, that's when the real work and planning comes into play. Planning includes asking these questions:

- Will you be moving all users to Azure AD?

- Will you be using the cloud just for device and software deployment?

- Will you be phasing out in-house equipment?

- Will you allow users to use their own devices(Bring Your Own Device [BYOD])?

- If users want to use their personal devices, will you supply them with corporate software applications?

- Will you be using Office 2019/2021 or Office 365?

When you sign up for an Intune account, you will specify a domain for your Intune subscription. After you sign up, Microsoft will send you an email like the one in Figure 10.2 containing your Intune information.

In Exercise 10.1, you will learn how to set up a free Intune 30-day trial account. You will need to complete this exercise to do some of the other exercises in this chapter.

FIGURE 10.2 Intune Welcome email

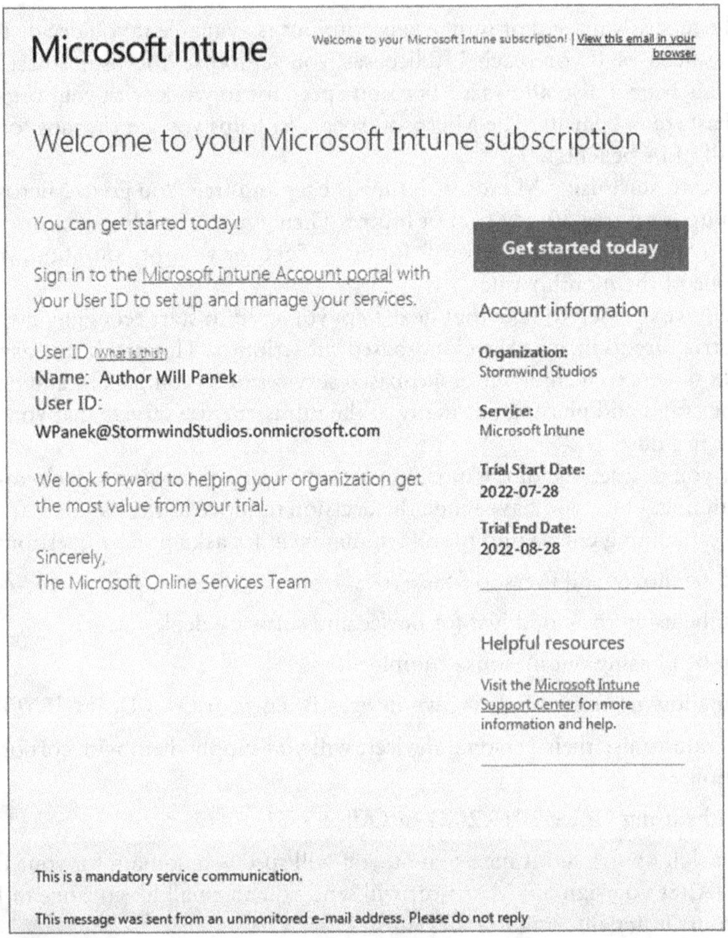

Microsoft Intune

Welcome to your Microsoft Intune subscription! | View this email in your browser

Welcome to your Microsoft Intune subscription

You can get started today!

Sign in to the Microsoft Intune Account portal with your User ID to set up and manage your services.

User ID (what is this?)
Name: Author Will Panek
User ID:
WPanek@StormwindStudios.onmicrosoft.com

We look forward to helping your organization get the most value from your trial.

Sincerely,
The Microsoft Online Services Team

Get started today

Account information

Organization:
Stormwind Studios

Service:
Microsoft Intune

Trial Start Date:
2022-07-28

Trial End Date:
2022-08-28

Helpful resources

Visit the Microsoft Intune Support Center for more information and help.

This is a mandatory service communication.

This message was sent from an unmonitored e-mail address. Please do not reply

---

EXERCISE 10.1

Setting Up an Intune Account

1. Go to the Microsoft Intune free trial sign-up website (`https://docs.microsoft.com/en-us/mem/intune/fundamentals/free-trial-sign-up`).

2. Navigate to the Intune set up account page by clicking the link provided.

3. Enter your email address and click Next, as shown in Figure 10.3. If you already have an account set up with another Microsoft service using your email address, you can choose to sign in using that account for the Intune trial, or you can create a new account. These steps assume you are creating a new account.

FIGURE 10.3   Microsoft Intune sign-up

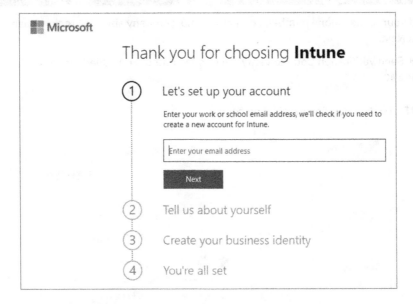

4. Click Set Up Account to create a new account, as shown in Figure 10.4.

FIGURE 10.4   Creating a new account

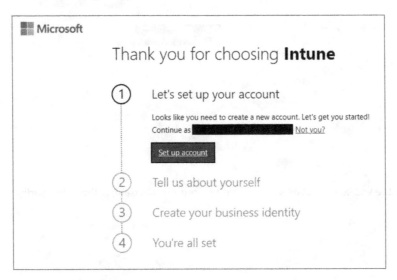

5. Add your name, phone number, company name, company size, and region. Then, click Next.

6. Click Send Verification Code to verify the phone number you added, as shown in Figure 10.5.

FIGURE 10.5 Sending verification code

7. Enter the verification code you receive on your mobile device, then click Verify.

8. Add a domain name for your trial that represents your business or organization. Your name will be added before the `.onmicrosoft.com`. Click Check Availability and then click Next, as shown in Figure 10.6. If you like, you can later change this domain name to your custom domain name.

FIGURE 10.6   Checking availability

9. Add a username and password that you will use to log into Microsoft Intune. Review the trial agreement and privacy statement. Click Sign Up to create your account, as shown in Figure 10.7.

FIGURE 10.7   Adding your username

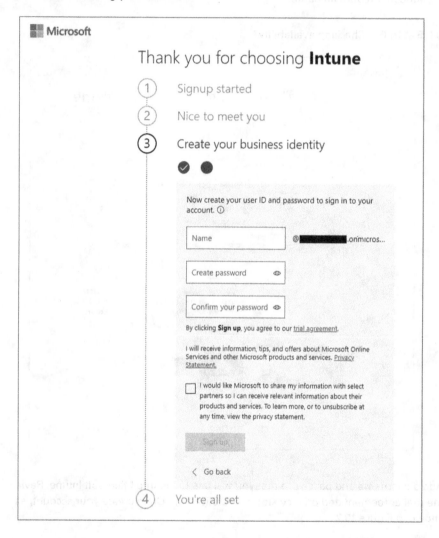

After the account has been created, you will see your username. You will also receive an email message that contains your account information that was shown previously in Figure 10.2. This email will confirm that the subscription is now active.

Provisioning User Accounts

Once you have signed up for Intune, you can start assigning your corporate users and groups to Intune. This step involves choosing which individuals will have access to the cloud-based services of Intune. At this point, the IT department can start using all of the Intune benefits.

As stated previously, once you sign up, you will receive an email with your user information along with a link to the Microsoft Endpoint Manager admin center portal. Click that link and then sign in. Once you do, you will automatically be redirected to the Microsoft Endpoint Manager admin center dashboard. This is where you can start creating your users and groups.

During the Intune subscription process, you create a domain name and that domain is added to a Microsoft extension by default. So, for example, if I choose a domain named Stormwind, then the default Microsoft subscription will look like this: Stormwind .onmicrosoft.com. If your company already owns its own domain name, then you can use that domain instead of the default Microsoft option.

Setting Administrator Accounts

Be sure to decide which way you want to set up your cloud-based domain. If you decide to just use Microsoft's default, all of your users will end up with an onmicrosoft.com extension for their User Principal Name (UPN). Using a preowned domain name can make your life in IT much easier because your users will log in using the same domain name that they are accustomed to using on a daily basis.

During setup, you can have the cloud-based version of Active Directory (Azure AD) work with the on-premises server-based version of Active Directory by using the Azure AD Connect tool (formerly known as the Directory Synchronization tool, Directory Sync tool, or the DirSync.exe tool).

 You can download the Azure AD Connect tool on Microsoft's Azure website. After logging into your Azure dashboard, choose Azure AD and then choose the Azure AD Connect link.

The Azure AD Connect tool is a server-based application that can be installed onto a server that is currently joined to your local domain. The Connect tool allows your corporate on-site users to synchronize to your cloud-based services.

When you decide to connect your cloud-based Azure Active Directory to your on-site server–based Active Directory, user administration becomes much easier for your IT department members. It allows your users to use a single sign-on to access both the local resources and the cloud-based resources. When users have to log in using different accounts, it puts more stress on the IT department and/or help desk.

The first users that you should add to Intune are your administrators. That way, they can start helping build other user accounts. When assigning administrative privileges, you have three choices: Tenant Administrator, Service Administrator, or Device Enrollment Manager. Let's take a look at each of them.

Tenant Administrator

Tenant Administrators are used for very specific tasks. Normally, they are assigned only one administrator role. This one role determines the administrative scope for the user and the tasks they can manage. Tenant Administrators can be assigned any of the following roles:

Billing Administrator   The Billing Administrator is allowed to make purchases, handle company subscriptions, manage support items, and handle service health issues.

Global Administrator   The Global Administrator has the ability to access all administrative features. By default, the administrator who signs up for the Intune subscription is the Global Administrator for your organization.

- Global Administrators are the only administrators that can assign other administrators their rights.
- You can have more than one Global Administrator in your organization.

Intune Administrator   The Intune Administrator has all Intune Global Administrator permissions except permission to create administrators with Directory Role options.

Password Administrator   Password Administrators have the ability to deal with user password issues like resetting passwords, managing requests, and monitoring service health. Password Administrators are allowed to reset passwords for users and other Password Administrators.

Service Support Administrator   The Service Support Administrators can manage service requests and handle service health requests.

User Administrator   User Administrators deal with user issues like resetting passwords, handling service health requests, and managing user accounts and groups.

Service Administrator

This is a tough role to truly understand because Intune really doesn't assign an Intune Service Administrator role. Actually, the Intune Service Administrator role is just a Tenant Administrator role with the Global Administrator permission assigned to the individual who signed up for the Intune subscription, which we discussed in the previous section. This role is also known as the Intune Administrator. Intune Service Administrators use the administrative console to handle the daily tasks for Intune.

Device Enrollment Manager

One of the great benefits of using Intune is the ability of users to enroll multiple devices. If you want a user to help other users enroll devices, then you can also make a user a Device Enrollment Manager (DEM). This role allows an administrator or user to enroll devices for other users. This is also useful for companies that have kiosk-type machines. Your DEM can enroll these types of systems. Individuals signed into a DEM account can enroll and manage up to 1,000 devices, whereas a standard non-admin account can enroll 15 devices. However, there are limitations on the number of devices that the DEM can enroll. Here are some of the limitations a DEM can encounter (as of this writing):

Android Enterprise   Can enroll up to 10 personally owned devices with work profiles. These devices cannot be corporate-owned with a work profile or fully managed.

Apple Automated Device Enrollment (ADE)   DEM is not compatible with ADE.

Apple Volume Purchase Apps   DEM-enrolled devices can install Volume Purchase Program (VPP) apps if they have Apple VPP device licenses.

Azure AD   Applying an Azure AD device restriction to a DEM account will prevent you from reaching the 1,000-device limit that the DEM account can enroll.

Conditional Access   This is only supported with DEM on devices running Windows 10, version 1803, and later.

Device Limit Restrictions   DEM enrolls Windows 10/11 devices in Shared Device mode, so device limit restrictions won't work on them.

Intune Company Portal   Only the local device appears in the Company Portal app or Company Portal website. Device users can't wipe DEM-enrolled devices from the Company Portal.

Number of Accounts   There's a limit of 150 DEM accounts in Intune.

A DEM can use the following to enroll devices in Intune:

- Windows Autopilot
- Windows devices bulk enrollment
- DEM-initiated via Company Portal enrollment
- DEM-initiated via Azure AD-join

Creating a User in Intune

Once you have decided to use Intune, you must start setting up user accounts within Intune so that your users can start accessing the benefits of using Intune.

For users to access Intune, they must have a valid license. When a user has a valid user license, they can then enroll up to 15 of their devices. This way, they can use different devices to do different tasks from both work and home.

When adding users to the Intune portal, you can do it either one user at a time or by bulk import from a CSV file. When adding users, you must assign licenses to each of these users. No matter how you add a user, adding a license to that user is not needed at the time the user is created. But a license must be associated to that user before that user can access Intune.

If you decide to import your users from your on-site Active Directory to the cloud, the users will not have a license. You will be required to assign licenses to your users after the Active Directory merger to Intune.

You can manually add users to your Intune subscription using either the Microsoft 365 Admin Center or the Microsoft Endpoint Manager admin center. An administrator can also edit user accounts to assign Intune licenses. So, let's take a look at how easy it is to create a new user. Exercise 10.2 walks you through the process of creating a new user in the Microsoft Endpoint Manager admin center.

EXERCISE 10.2

Adding Users to Intune

1. Open the Microsoft Endpoint admin center by clicking the link in the email that you received after creating your subscription in Exercise 10.1.

2. Click Users ➤ All Users.

3. Click the +New User link.

4. Specify the following, as shown in Figure 10.8:

   - User Name: The new name that the user will use to sign in to Azure Active Directory

   - Name: The user's given name

   - First name (optional)

   - Last name (optional)

FIGURE 10.8 Creating an Intune new user

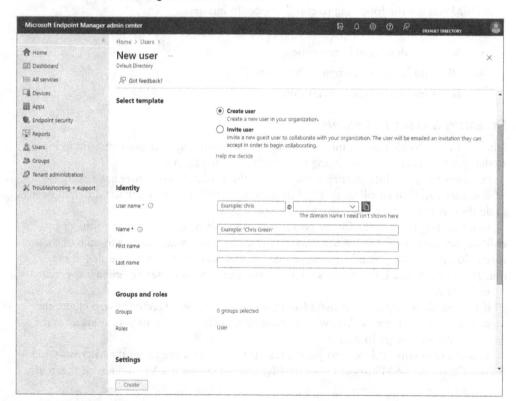

5. To assign the new user to groups (optional), click 0 Groups Selected to open the Groups pane. Here you can select the groups you want to assign to the user. When finished selecting groups, click Select.

6. By default, the new user is assigned the role of User. If you want to add roles to the user, click User under Groups And Roles. In the Directory Roles pane, select the roles you want to assign to the user and then click Select.

7. If you want to block the user from signing in, you can select Yes for Block Sign In under Settings. Be sure to switch this back to No when you're ready to let the user sign in.

8. Choose a Usage Location for the new user. Usage Location is required before you can assign the new user an Intune license.

9. Optionally, you can provide Job Title, Department, Company Name, and Manager.

10. Click Create to add the new user to Intune.

Now that we have looked at creating a user in the Microsoft Endpoint Manager admin center, let's take a look at how to create groups.

To manage devices and users, Intune uses Azure AD groups. An administrator can use groups to fit your organization's needs. Creating groups in Intune helps administrators have more flexibility when it comes to Intune management. Administrators can set up groups based on devices, users, geographic locations, departments, or even hardware types. Creating the groups are done in about the same way, but deciding which groups to create is where the planning and decision-making takes place.

Administrators can add these group types:

- **Assigned groups:** Manually add users or devices into a static group.

- **Dynamic groups:** Automatically add users or devices to user groups or device groups based on a created expression. Dynamic groups require Azure AD Premium.

Any users and groups that are created can also be seen in the Microsoft 365 admin center, the Azure AD admin center, and in the Microsoft Endpoint Manager admin center portal. Microsoft recommends that if an administrator's primary role is device management, that they utilize the Microsoft Endpoint Manager admin center. In Exercise 10.3, I will show you how to create a new group.

EXERCISE 10.3

Creating a New Group

1. Open the Microsoft Endpoint Manager admin center and sign in.

2. Select Groups ➢ New Group, as shown in Figure 10.9.

FIGURE 10.9 Clicking New Group

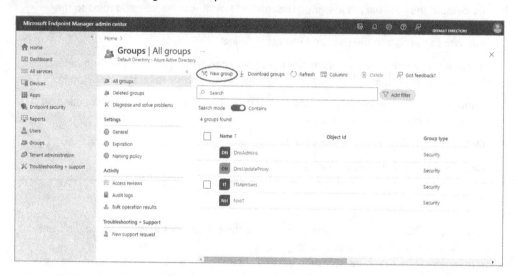

3. For Group Type, choose one of the following options:

   - **Security:** Security groups are used to define who has access to resources. Security groups are recommended for groups in Intune.

   - **Microsoft 365:** These groups provide access to a shared mailbox, calendar, files, SharePoint site, and more. This option gives people outside of your organization access to the group.

4. Enter a name and description for the new group so that others will know what the group is used for.

5. Enter the membership type (see Figure 10.10). You have several options:

   - **Assigned:** an administrator manually assigns users or devices to this group and can remove users or devices.

   - **Dynamic User:** an administrator creates membership rules to add and remove members automatically.

   - **Dynamic Device:** an administrator creates dynamic group rules to add and remove devices automatically.

FIGURE 10.10   Choosing the membership type

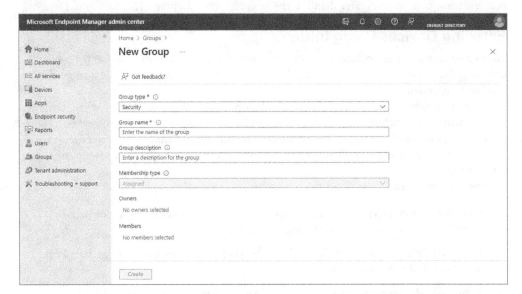

6.   To add the new group, click Create. The new group now appears in the list.

After you create the new group, you can manage that group from the administrative console. Administrators have the ability to change the group membership at any time. Managing and maintaining groups is easily accomplished from the administrative console.

Now that you have seen how to create users and groups, let's take a look at how to set up Intune policies.

Creating Intune Policies

Administrators have the ability to place rules on security settings, firewall settings, and Endpoint Protection settings on your Intune mobile devices and applications. Think of Intune policies as network group policies—they are rules that you can put on devices or users.

Once you decide to move to Intune for your devices, it's important to use Intune policies to help manage the devices on your network and set up Endpoint Protection. Intune helps your IT staff deploy devices and applications, and Intune policies allow the IT team to manage the settings on these deployments. When you build a policy, you can deploy that policy to the user groups that you set up in the previous section. Then when the users log into Intune, the policy becomes their baseline policy.

You can create policies for the different types of devices available for Intune. You can create policies for Androids, iOS, macOS, Windows, software, Computer Manager, and common mobile device settings. We will discuss Intune device compliance policies and device configuration policies in greater detail in the next chapter, Chapter 11, "Managing Devices."

Enrolling Devices Using Intune

To take advantage of using Intune, you must enroll devices in the Intune system. To enroll clients in this system, you must download the Intune client software onto the devices that need to be enrolled.

To manage devices in Intune, devices must first be enrolled in the Intune service. Both personally owned and corporate-owned devices can be enrolled for Intune management. There are two ways to enroll devices in Intune: Users can either self-enroll their devices, or an administrator can configure policies that will force automatic enrollment without any user involvement.

Users can self-enroll their Windows device by using any of these methods:

Bring Your Own Device (BYOD)   Users enroll their personally owned devices by downloading and installing the Company Portal App.

Azure AD Join   Joins the device with Azure AD and enables users to sign into Windows with their Azure AD credentials.

Autopilot   Automates Azure AD Join and enrolls new corporate-owned devices into Intune.

MDM-Only Enrollment   Lets users enroll an existing Workgroup, Active Directory, or Azure AD joined PC into Intune. Users enroll from Settings on the existing Windows PC.

Administrators can set up the following methods of enrollment that require no user interaction:

Hybrid Azure AD Join   Administrators can configure Active Directory Group Policy to automatically enroll devices that are hybrid Azure AD joined.

Configuration Manager Co-management   Administrators can enroll their existing Configuration Manager managed devices into Intune to obtain dual benefits of Intune and Configuration Manager.

Device Enrollment Manager (DEM)   DEM is a special service account. DEM accounts have permissions that allow authorized users to enroll and manage multiple corporate-owned devices.

Bulk Enroll   Allows an authorized user to join large numbers of new corporate-owned devices to Azure AD and Intune.

Windows IoT Core Dashboard   Enrolling Windows IoT Core devices is accomplished by using the Windows IoT Core Dashboard to prepare the device, and then using Windows Configuration Designer to create a provisioning package.

Now for some of the different devices on the market today, you may need to take additional steps in order for them to work with your Intune network. For example, to use Apple iOS, an Apple MDM Push Certificate must be imported from Apple so that you can manage iOS devices. This certificate allows Intune administrators to manage iOS.

When an administrator goes to enroll the many different devices on the Intune network, as stated, some of the different devices require different installation options:

Apple iOS/iPadOS   Before you can begin to enroll iOS/iPadOS devices with Apple Automated Device Enrollment (ADE), you will need to obtain an ADE token file (with the extension .p7m) from Apple. This token allows Intune to sync information about ADE devices and allows Intune to upload enrollment profiles to Apple and to assign devices to those profiles. You use the Apple Business Manager (ABM) or Apple School Manager (ASM) portal to create this token.

Intune enables MDM of iPads and iPhones to give users secure access to company email, data, and apps. Administrators need to import an Apple MDM Push Certificate from Apple so that you can manage iOS/iPad devices. Administrators need to sign into the Microsoft Endpoint Manager admin center and then select Devices ➤ Enroll Devices ➤ Apple Enrollment ➤ Apple MDM Push Certificate. Then perform the following steps:

Step 1. Grant Microsoft permission to send user and device information to Apple by selecting I Agree (as shown in Figure 10.11).

Step 2. Download the Intune certificate signing request required to create an Apple MDM push certificate by selecting Download Your CSR. Intune will download and save the request file on the local machine. The file is used to request a trust relationship certificate from the Apple Push Certificates portal.

Step 3. Create an Apple MDM push certificate by following these steps:

1. Select Create Your MDM push Certificate to go to the Apple Push Certificates portal.

2. Sign in with your organization's Apple ID.

3. Click Create A Certificate.

4. Read and agree to the terms and conditions and then click Accept.

5. Click Choose File and then select the CSR file you downloaded in Intune.

6. Click Upload.

7. On the confirmation page, click Download. Intune downloads the certificate file (with the extension .pem) to your device. Save this file for later.

Step 4. Enter the Apple ID used to create your Apple MDM push certificate by returning to the admin center and entering your Apple ID.

Step 5. Browse to your Apple MDM push certificate to upload by clicking the Folder icon and then selecting the certificate file you downloaded in the Apple portal. Then click Upload to finish configuring the MDM push certificate.

FIGURE 10.11 Configure MDM Push Certificate screen

Configure MDM Push Certificate ✕

🗑 Delete

∧ Essentials

Status	Days until expiration
✅ Active	365
Last updated	Expiration
7/12/2022	7/12/2023
Apple ID	Subject ID
Serial number	

You need an Apple MDM push certificate to manage Apple devices with Intune.
Steps:

1.   I grant Microsoft permission to send both user and device information to Apple. More information on Microsoft permission.

☑ I agree.

2.   Download the Intune certificate signing request required to create an Apple MDM push certificate.

Download your CSR

3.   Create an Apple MDM push certificate. More information on Apple MDM push certificate.

Create your MDM push Certificate ☐↗

4.   Enter the Apple ID used to create your Apple MDM push certificate.

Apple ID *

[   ]

5.   Browse to your Apple MDM push certificate to upload

Apple MDM push certificate *

[   ] 📁

Upload

You can then create a user enrollment profile in Intune by going to the Microsoft End-point Manager admin center, selecting Devices ➤ iOS/iPadOS ➤ iOS Enrollment ➤ Enrollment Types (Preview) ➤ Create Profile ➤ iOS/iPadOS. This profile is where you will set up the enrollment experience your iOS/iPadOS end users will encounter.

Android Devices   To select the appropriate enrollment method for Android devices, you need to consider the enrollment type that you will be using and whether the device is a personal device or a corporate-owned device. As an Intune administrator, you can enroll Android devices in the following ways:

> **Android Enterprise**   Use the Android Enterprise Personally Owned With A Work Profile option when you want personal devices to have permission to access corporate data. Administrators manage the work accounts, apps, and data. Any personal data that is on the device is kept separate from the work data, and the administrators do not control the personal settings or data.
>
> Android Enterprise Dedicated is for corporate-owned, single-use devices, such as digital signage or inventory management. Administrators will lock down the usage of the device for a limited set of apps and web links and prevent users from adding other apps or performing other actions on the device.
>
> Android Enterprise Fully Managed is for corporate-owned, single-user devices that are used solely for work and not personal use. Administrators can manage the entire device and enforce policy controls.
>
> Android Enterprise Corporate-Owned With A Work Profile is for corporate-owned, single-user devices that are intended for corporate and personal use.
>
> **Android Device Administrator**   This should be used in areas where Android Enterprise or Google Mobile Services (GMS) is unavailable.
>
> **Android Open Source Project (AOSP)**   This option offers a set of enrollment options for devices that aren't integrated with Google Mobile services.
>
> Corporate-Owned, User Associated Devices is for corporate-owned, single-user devices that are solely for corporate use and not for personal use. The administrator can manage the entire device.
>
> Corporate-Owned, Userless Devices is for corporate-owned, shared devices where the administrator can manage the entire device.

To enroll an Android device, perform the following steps:

1. On the Android device, open the Google Store.

2. Search for the Intune Company portal app and install it. When prompted about permissions, click Accept.

3. Launch the Intune Company portal app. If prompted to accept the organization's terms and conditions, click Accept All.

4. Sign in using your user account from your Microsoft 365 subscription.

5. Follow any instructions provided. These will vary depending on the settings that you have configured in Intune. You may be asked to accept new settings on the device. Click Continue on each screen to proceed through the setup and enrollment.

6. Then you will need to activate the Device Administrator. Click Activate and your device is now registered.

7. You may be asked to define a device category. When finished, click Done.

8. Click Done again. Once the deployment is finished, you can use the Microsoft 365 Device Management portal to view the enrolled device, which will appear in the Devices node.

Windows Phone   Administrators must set up some management requirements before Windows Phones will work with your Intune network. DNS Administrators need to create CNAME records in order for users to connect to the Intune network resources. Windows Phones also require a certificate to establish encrypted communications between the client device and the Intune cloud-based system.

Windows Devices   Windows devices are connected in basically the same way as Windows Phones. The DNS Administrators have to create a CNAME record, and then applications can be sideloaded into the Windows computer. Users can also connect to Intune by using the Intune Company portal.

Sideloading applications using Intune will be explained in greater detail later in this chapter. Sideloading basically means loading pre-bought or company applications using the Microsoft Store for Business, Intune, or images.

Administrators can use the Mobile Device Management (MDM) tools to help your company users enroll different devices and manage their Intune accounts. MDM has some of the following benefits:

- MDM allows users to enroll their own devices through the use of the self-service company portal. After users enroll their devices, the users can install corporate applications.

- Once a device is enrolled, MDM helps deploy certificates, Wi-Fi, VPN, and email profiles automatically. This gives users access to corporate resources with the necessary security configuration options.

- MDM allows administrators to use broad management tools for managing mobile devices, passcode resets, device lockouts, data encryption, and allows you to fully wipe a stolen device to help protect against corporate data loss.

- MDM helps simplify the enrollment of corporate devices with bulk enrollment tools like the Apple Configurator.

- MDM allows administrators to easily enroll Apple iOS devices with the Device Enrollment Program (DEP).

- MDM allows administrators to enforce a much stricter lockdown policy for iOS, Android, and Windows Phone devices.

To enroll clients into the Intune network, you can install the software in a variety of ways. The company administrator can provide an installation package to allow users to enroll their systems. Administrators can set up a Group Policy that can be used to enroll computers into Intune, or users can self-enroll using the Intune portal.

If you decide to use MDM, you must first set up the mobile device management authority. This enables management of device platforms and allows your devices to be enrolled with the company portal app.

Before enrolling your Windows client, you must confirm which version of Windows that you have installed. Microsoft provides several ways to confirm which version of Windows you are running. You can search for winver in the search box or use the ver command from the command prompt. Exercise 10.4 walks you through another way of verifying which version you are using.

EXERCISE 10.4

Confirming the Windows Version

1. To display Windows Settings options, right-click the Windows Start icon and select Settings (see Figure 10.12).

FIGURE 10.12   Windows Settings screen

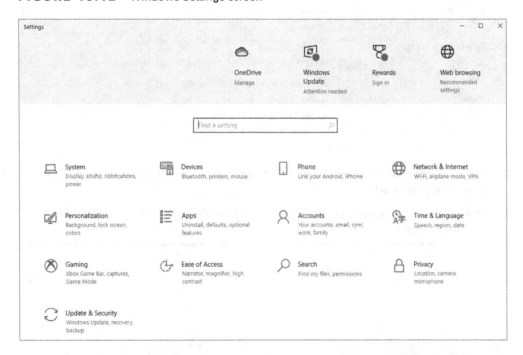

EXERCISE 10.4 *(continued)*

2. Select System ➤ About (see Figure 10.13).

FIGURE 10.13 Windows About screen

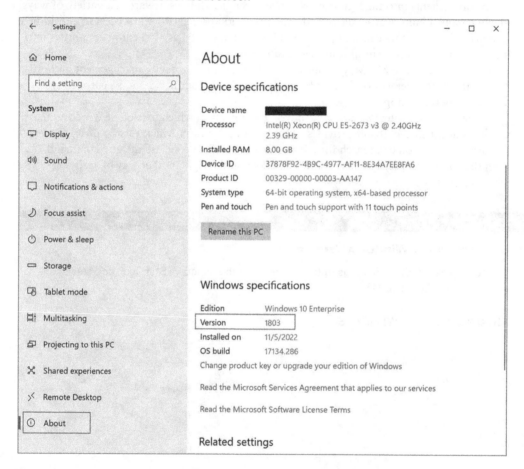

3. In the Settings window you will see a list of Windows specifications for your computer. Locate the version in this list.

4. Confirm that the Windows version is Windows 10 (version 1607 or later) or Windows 11 (version 21H2 or later).

The steps presented in this book are for Windows 10 (version 1607 or later) or Windows 11 (version 21H2 or later); if the version you are using is 1511 or lower, follow the steps on Microsoft's website: `http://docs.microsoft.com/en-us/intune-user-help/ enroll-windows-10-device#enroll-windows-10-version-1511-and-earlier- device`. Exercise 10.5 shows you how to enroll a Windows 10 desktop version 1607 or higher device.

EXERCISE 10.5

Enrolling Windows 10 Desktop Version 1607 or Higher

1. Return to Windows Settings and click Accounts (see Figure 10.14).

FIGURE 10.14 Windows Settings screen

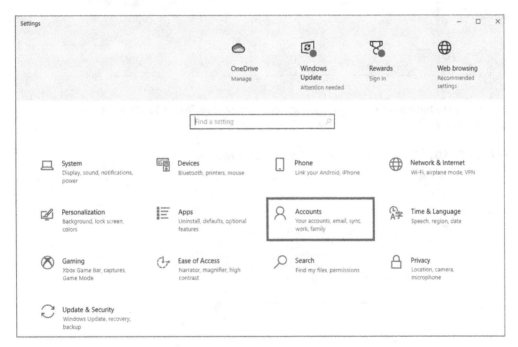

2. Select Access Work Or School ➢ Connect (see Figure 10.15).

EXERCISE 10.5 *(continued)*

FIGURE 10.15   Access Work or School Screen

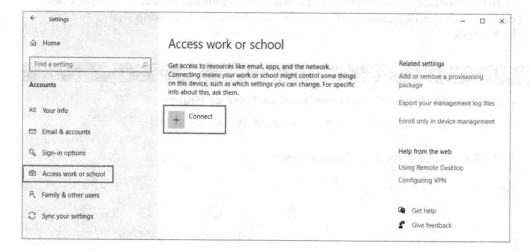

3.   Sign in to Intune with your work or school account (see Figure 10.16) and then click Next.

FIGURE 10.16   Set Up A Work Or School Account screen

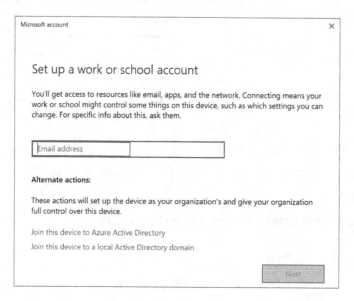

You will see a message showing that the device is registering with your company or school.

4.   When you see the "You're all set!" screen, click Done.

5. You will now see the added account as part of the Access Work Or School settings on your Windows desktop (see Figure 10.17).

FIGURE 10.17   Added Account screen

6. Confirm that the device is enrolled in Intune by signing into the Microsoft Endpoint Manager admin center as a Global Administrator or an Intune Service Administrator.

7. To view the enrolled devices in Intune, click Devices.

8. Verify that the device is enrolled within Intune, as shown in Figure 10.18.

FIGURE 10.18   Intune Enrolled Devices screen

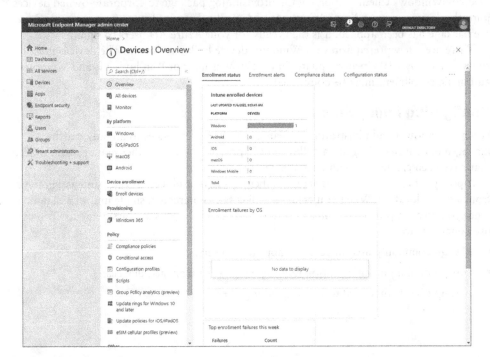

Configuring Automatic MDM Enrollment

Automatic enrollment allows users to enroll their Windows devices in Intune. To enroll, users add their work account to their personally owned devices or join corporate-owned devices to Azure AD. Prerequisites for enabling Windows automatic enrollment includes an Azure AD Premium subscription, a Microsoft Intune subscription, and Global Administrator permissions. To configure automatic MDM enrollment, perform the following steps:

1. Sign into the Azure portal at https://portal.azure.com and select Azure Active Directory ➤ Mobility (MDM And MAM) ➤ Microsoft Intune.

2. Configure the MDM User Scope. Choose which devices should be managed by Intune. These Windows devices can automatically enroll for management with Microsoft Intune:

   - **None:** MDM automatic enrollment disabled.

   - **Some:** Select the groups that can automatically enroll their Windows client devices.

   - **All:** All users can automatically enroll their Windows client devices.

3. Use the default values for the MDM Terms Of Use URL, the MDM Discovery URL, and the MDM Compliance URL. Then click Save.

Configuring Bulk Enrollment in Intune

An administrator can join a large number of devices to Azure AD and Intune. To bulk-enroll devices for your Azure AD tenant, you will first create a provisioning package with the Windows Configuration Designer (WCD) app. I discussed provisioning packages in Chapter 8, "Deploy Windows Client." Applying the provisioning package to corporate-owned devices joins the devices to your Azure AD tenant and enrolls them for Intune management. Once the package has been applied, it is then ready for your Azure AD users to sign in.

There are a few prerequisites for Windows device bulk enrollment. The devices must be running Windows 10 Creator update (build 1709) or later or Windows 11, and Windows automatic enrollment must be configured.

Configuring Policy Sets

Policy sets allow an administrator to create a bundle of references to already existing management entities. They are a collection of apps, policies, and other management objects that have been created and can be assigned.

A policy set enables you to select a number of different objects at once and assign them from a single location. When you create a policy set, you create a single unit of assignment. Once you create a policy set, you can review and edit its objects and assignments. You can use policy sets to:

- Assign commonly used or relevant apps to all users.

- Assign minimum configuration requirements on all managed devices.

- Group objects that need to be assigned together.

You can include the following objects in a policy set:

- Apps
- App configuration policies
- App protection policies
- Device configuration profiles
- Device compliance policies
- Windows autopilot deployment profiles
- Enrollment status page
- Settings catalog policies

Creating a Policy Set

To create a policy set:

1. Sign into the Microsoft Endpoint Manager admin center.
2. Select Devices ➤ Policy Sets ➤ Policy Sets ➤ + Create.
3. On the Basics page, add the following values, as shown in Figure 10.19:
   - **Policy set name:** Give a name for the policy set.
   - **Description (optional):** Provide a description for the policy set.

FIGURE 10.19   Intune policy set

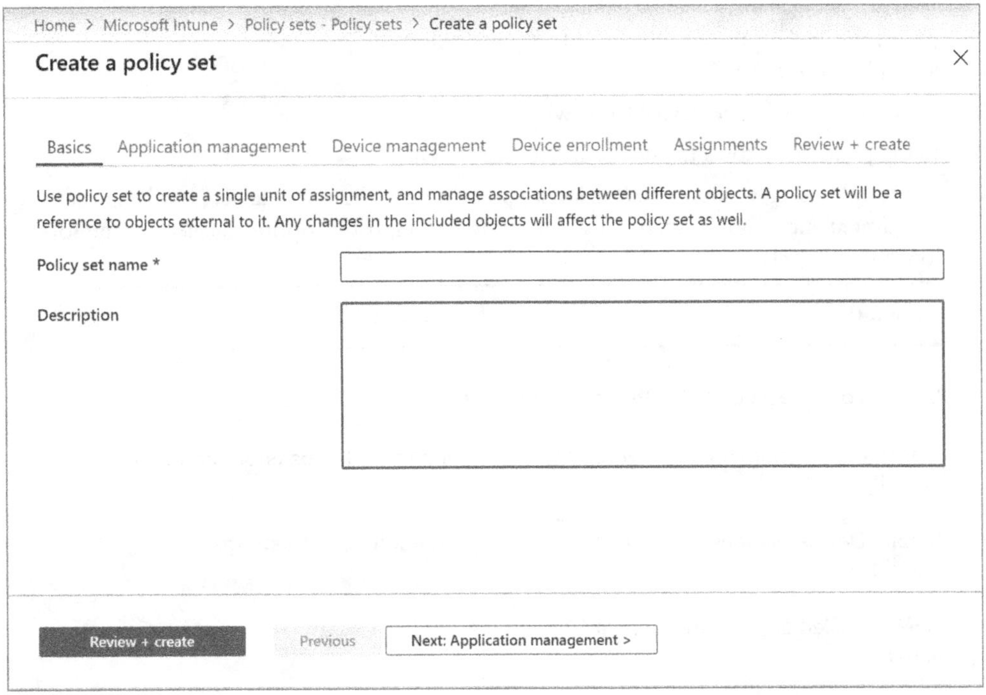

Home > Microsoft Intune > Policy sets - Policy sets > Create a policy set

Create a policy set   ×

| Basics | Application management | Device management | Device enrollment | Assignments | Review + create |

Use policy set to create a single unit of assignment, and manage associations between different objects. A policy set will be a reference to objects external to it. Any changes in the included objects will affect the policy set as well.

Policy set name *

Description

Review + create   Previous   Next: Application management >

4. Click Next: Application Management. If you want, on this page you can add apps, app configuration policies, and app protection policies to your policy set.

5. Click Next: Device Management. This page allows you to add device management objects to the policy set, such as device configuration profiles and device compliance policies.

6. Click Next: Device Enrollment. This page allows you to add device enrollment objects to the policy set, such as device type restrictions, Windows Autopilot deployment profiles, and enrollment status page profiles.

7. Click Next: Assignments. This page lets you assign the policy set to users and devices. You can assign a policy set to a device whether or not it's managed by Intune.

8. Click Next: Review + Create to review the values you entered for the policy set.

9. Click Create.

Using Intune to Restart, Retire, or Wipe Devices

If a device is no longer needed, is being repurposed, or is missing, you can use the Retire or Wipe actions to remove devices from Intune. You can also issue a remote command from the Intune Company portal to devices that are enrolled in Intune.

The Wipe action will restore a device to its factory default settings. The user data will be kept if the Retain Enrollment State And User Account option has been selected. Otherwise, all data, apps, and settings will be removed. The Wipe action is not available for iOS/iPadOS devices enrolled with User Enrollment.

To wipe a device, perform the following steps:

1. Sign into the Microsoft Endpoint Manager admin center.

2. Select Devices ➤ All Devices.

3. Select the name of the device to be wiped.

4. In the pane that shows the device name, select Wipe.

5. For Windows 10 version 1709 or later, you also have the Wipe device, but keep the enrollment state and associated user account option. If this option is selected, the following will apply:

Retained	Not retained
User accounts associated with the device	User files
Machine state (domain join, Azure AD joined)	User-installed apps (store and Win32 apps)
Mobile Device Management (MDM) enrollment	Nondefault device settings
OEM-installed apps (store and Win32 apps)	

Retained	Not retained
User profile	
User data outside of the user profile	
User autologon	

6. The Wipe device, and continue to wipe even if device loses power option ensures that the Wipe action cannot be stopped by turning off the device. This option will keep trying to reset the device until successful.

7. For iOS/iPadOS eSIM devices, the cellular data plan is preserved by default when you wipe a device. If you want to remove the data plan from the device when you wipe the device, select the Also Remove The Devices Data Plan option.

8. To confirm the wipe, click Yes.

The Retire action will remove managed app data, settings, and email profiles that were assigned using Intune, and the device will be removed from Intune. The device will be removed the next time the device checks in and receives the remote Retire action. The device will still show up in Intune until the device checks in. If you want to remove a device immediately, then you will want to use the Delete action instead. If you use Retire, it will still leave all the user's personal data on the device.

There may be times when you need to restart a device. The Restart Device action causes the selected device to be restarted, usually within 5 minutes. However, it's important to note that the device's owner will not be notified of the restart and they may lose work if not notified. The platforms that are supported for a restart include:

- Android Enterprise dedicated devices, Android 8.0 and later
- Android Enterprise fully managed devices, Android 8.0 and later
- iOS/iPadOS
- macOS
- Windows 8.1 and later

At the time this book was written, devices that are not supported for using Restart include Android and Android Enterprise personally owned work profile devices and Android Enterprise corporate-owned with work profile devices.

To restart a device, perform the following steps:

1. Sign into the Microsoft Endpoint Manager admin center.

2. Select Devices ➤ All Devices.

3. In the list of devices, select the desired device, click Restart, then click Yes.

4. To check the status of the restart, select Devices ➤ Device Actions.

Configuring the Intune Connector Site

To understand how connectors work, you must first understand what a connector does and why we use them in the computer industry. Connectors allow different types of devices to communicate with each other. So, for example, let's say we had a Microsoft Exchange server and a Unix-based mail server. You would add a connector to the Exchange server so that it could communicate and understand the Unix mail server. That's how Intune connectors work also.

Intune connectors allow Microsoft Intune to communicate and understand other types of devices and software. So, if we decide to use Azure AD and Azure Exchange, we can install a connector so that the Azure Exchange can work with the corporate Exchange mail server.

Exchange devices have the ability to be managed through both the on-premises Exchange servers and the hosted Exchange Servers in the cloud. The Exchange connector connects your users with your Exchange deployments, and the connector lets you manage your mobile devices through the Intune console.

Administrators who have been using System Center Configuration Manager to manage their computers, Macs, and Unix-based devices can add the Intune connector so that they can manage all of these devices from one console.

To configure connectors, in the Microsoft Endpoint Manager admin center, select Devices ➤ Windows ➤ Windows Enrollment ➤ Intune Connector For Active Directory ➤ Add. Then follow the instructions to download the connector.

Configuring Intune Alerts

One of the nice advantages of using Intune is the ability to monitor and see alerts within Intune. When looking at these Intune alerts, there are different levels of severity within the alerts. Table 11.1 shows you the various alert types and what each type means.

TABLE 11.1   Intune alert types

Alert	Description
🛑 Critical	This alert shows you that you have a serious issue that needs to be investigated and fixed.
⚠️ Warning	This alert shows you that there may be an issue but that issue is not very serious at this time. These alerts need to be investigated to make sure that they do not become a problem in the future.
ℹ️ Informational	This alert shows you that there is some information about a product but that it's not a problem. For example, an informational alert may tell you that there is an upgrade to a connector that you have installed.

When dealing with Intune monitoring and alerts, there are a few settings that you can set up to help configure how alerts work. For example, under the Alerts section in the Azure portal, you can set up recipients who will receive emails when alerts happen.

So, if you get a critical error, an email can be sent to an administrator so that you or your Intune administrators can work on resolving the issue as fast as possible. If you don't set up email alerts, someone will need to monitor the Intune system daily to watch for issues. Intune Administrators have the ability to set different email recipients for different alert types so that critical alerts go to one IT person and warnings go to another.

Administrators also have the ability to enable or disable certain alert types. So, if you are getting a warning that you know is not going to affect your Intune system, you can disable the warning to remove it completely. This way, it's not a message your Intune administrators need to see on a daily basis.

Supporting Applications

Intune lets you deploy and maintain software from the cloud. The advantage to this is that the software issued through Intune is licensed to the user and not the hardware. So, what this means is that you can deploy a copy of Office to a user using multiple devices and when that user works on corporate data, that data is secure. That's the real advantage to Intune. It allows your users to work securely from their iPhone, Windows laptops, or tablet.

Intune also allows an organization to use their current business apps by using the Intune App Wrapping tool. The Intune App Wrapping tool is a command-line application that builds a package around the in-house application. Then the business application can be managed by the Intune mobile application management policies.

The Intune App Wrapping tool also gives you secure data viewing through the Intune Managed Browser, AV Player, Image viewer, and the PDF viewer. Administrators also have the ability to prevent specific applications or web addresses from being accessed by specific types of mobile devices. Finally, when dealing with corporate data and security, Administrators have the ability to wipe out a device in the event that the device is stolen or lost, or the employee leaves the company.

Deploying Applications Using Intune

The way that we do business in the corporate world continues to change on a daily basis. Today, many of our users bring in their own devices (Bring Your Own Device [BYOD]). Because of BYOD, it is getting harder for IT departments to deploy software.

As stated earlier in this chapter, Intune is a cloud-based desktop and MDM tool that helps IT departments provide their users with access to company applications, data, and resources. The users have the ability to access these resources from any type of device (i.e., Apple, Android, or Windows devices).

One of the issues that we face as IT administrators is that we have multiple copies of software throughout a company and multiple version types (Apple versions of Office compared to Windows versions). Let's take a look at Office as our example. Many times, we have older versions of Office (Office 2010/2016) and newer versions of Office (Office 2019/Office 365).

This is where Intune can help out an IT department. You can upload software packages to Intune and your users can get current copies of the software from the web. Also, Intune helps your organization protect its software by giving you extra security and features. Intune also allows you to set up application management policies that allow you to manage applications on different devices.

As long as a device is compatible with Intune, you can deploy the applications to that device. Depending on the device and the application, deployment options may vary. You have the ability to upload your applications to Intune or link a Microsoft Store for Business application to Intune storage.

To deploy applications using Intune, you must use the proper software installation type based on the different devices that your users may be using. Microsoft gives you a trial subscription of 2 GB of cloud storage. You can purchase more storage depending on how much money you want to spend.

Using Intune to Sideload Apps

Sideloading an application means that you are loading an application that you already own or one that your company created into a delivery system (i.e., Intune, Microsoft Store for Business, or images).

You may be familiar with sideloading apps into the Microsoft Store for Business. This is the process of building or buying your own application and then adding it to the Microsoft Store for Business so that all of your users can download and use that app. Sideloading an application into Intune means the same thing. You are taking an application that you built or bought and adding it to Intune for user downloads.

Think about how you deploy software today. You buy a package and either manually install the software to your users or use some type of deployment package like System Center Configuration Manager. The only difference now is that the application gets loaded into the cloud and can be deployed to any device that is compatible with the application.

On Windows 10/11 devices, Intune supports many different app types and deployment scenarios. After you have added an app to Intune, you can then assign that app to users and devices.

The app types supported on Windows 10/11 devices are line-of-business (LOB) apps and Microsoft Store for Business apps.

An LOB app is one that is added from an app installation file. The following steps will help you add a Windows LOB app to Intune.

Adding a Windows LOB App to Intune

Step 1: Specify the software setup file:

    a.   Sign in to the Microsoft Endpoint Manager admin center.

    b.   Select Apps ➢ All Apps ➢ Add.

    c.   In the Select App Type pane, under Other App Types, select Line-Of-Business App.

    d.   Click Select. The Add App steps are displayed.

Step 2: Select the app package file:

    a.   Click Select App Package File in the Add App pane.

    b.   Click the Browse button in the App Package File pane. Then select a Windows installation file with the extension `.msi`, `.appx`, or `.appxbundle`.

    c.   Click OK when done.

Step 3: Configure app information:

    a.   Select App Information in the Add App pane.

    b.   In the App Information pane, configure the information such as name, description, publisher, and so forth.

    c.   Click Next to display the Scope Tags page. If you wish to use scope tags, complete the Scopes section.

    d.   Click Next to display the Assignments page.

    e.   Set up the assignments, then click Next to display the Review + Create page.

Step 4: Finish up:

    a.   Review the values and settings you entered for the app.

    b.   When you are done, click Create to add the app to Intune.

Step 5: Update a line-of-business app:

    1.   Sign into the Microsoft Endpoint Manager admin center.

    2.   Select Apps ➢ All Apps.

    3.   Find and select your app from the list of apps.

    4.   Click Properties under Manage in the App pane.

    5.   Click Edit next to App Information.

    6.   Click the listed file next to Select File To Update. The App Package File pane is displayed.

    7.   Click the folder icon and browse to the location of your updated app file. Click Open. The app information is updated with the package information.

    8.   Verify that App version reflects the updated app package.

An administrator can install apps on a Windows client device in one of two ways depending on the app type. The app types are:

- **User Context:** The app is installed for that user on the device when the user signs into the device.

- **Device Context:** The app is installed directly to the device by Intune.

After you add an app to Intune, you can then assign the app to users and devices. An administrator can assign an app to a device whether or not that device is managed by Intune.

Once an application has been uploaded to Intune, you'll want to deploy the app to your users. To do this, you'll need to assign the app to an Intune group. The following steps show you how:

1. Sign into the Microsoft Endpoint Manager admin center.

2. Select Apps ➢ All Apps.

3. Select the app you want to assign in the Apps pane.

4. Select Assignments in the Manage section of the menu.

5. Click Add Group to open the Add Group pane.

6. Next, you will want to select the assignment type. Several options are available:

    - **Available For Enrolled Devices:** Assigns the app to groups of users who can install the app from the Company portal app or website.

    - **Available With Or Without Enrollment:** Assigns the app to groups of users whose devices are not enrolled with Intune.

    - **Required:** The app is installed on devices in the selected groups.

    - **Uninstall:** The app is uninstalled from devices in the selected groups.

7. Click Included Groups to select the groups of users.

8. After you have selected one or more groups, click Select.

9. Click OK in the Assign pane.

10. Click Exclude Groups if you want to exclude any groups.

11. Click Select if you have chosen to exclude any groups.

12. Click OK in the Add Group pane.

13. Click Save in the App Assignments pane.

To monitor the properties of apps:

1. Sign into the Microsoft Endpoint Manager admin center.

2. Select Apps ➢ All Apps.

3. Select an app to monitor in the list of the apps. This will open the App pane, which shows an overview of the device status and the user status.

Microsoft 365 App Deployment

For administrators who deploy and manage Microsoft 365 apps, they can use the Microsoft 365 Apps admin center. To access the Microsoft 356 Apps admin center, use your administrator account to sign in at `https://admin.microsoft.com`. To sign in you must have the Global or Security administrator, or Office Apps administrator role assigned.

On the left-hand side, you will see the following options:

Home   This is the dashboard for the admin center.

Users   This is where you can create and manage users as well as set permission levels or reset passwords.

Groups   This is where you create and manage groups.

Resources   This is where you create and manage resources.

Billing   This is where you view, purchase, or cancel subscriptions.

Support   This is where you view existing service requests or create new ones.

Settings   This is where you will manage global settings for apps such as email, sites, and the Office suite. You can also change your password policy and its expiration date. In addition, you can add and update domain names, change your organization profile, and release preferences.

Setup   This is where you can manage existing domains, turn on and manage multi-factor authentication, manage admin access, migrate user mailboxes to Office 365, manage feature updates, and help users install their Office apps.

Reports   This is where you will see how your organization is using Microsoft 365, with detailed reports on email use, Office activations, and more.

Health   This is where you can see your service health and the health history.

Admin Centers   This will open separate Admin Centers for Exchange, Skype for Business, SharePoint, Yammer, and Azure AD. Each Admin Center includes all available settings for that service.

Microsoft 365 Apps is offered as a subscription. You can deploy Microsoft 365 Apps either from the cloud or from a local source, or by using Configuration Manager. Users can install Microsoft 365 Apps on up to five different computers using a single Office 365 license. Users can also install Microsoft 365 Apps on up to 5 tablets and 5 phones. To use Microsoft 365 Apps, a user must have an Office 365 (or Microsoft 365) account and must have been assigned a license. Even though users do not have to be connected to the Internet all the time to use Microsoft 365 Apps, they will need to connect to the Internet at least once every 30 days.

Configuring Microsoft 365 Apps using the Office Deployment Toolkit or Office Customization Tool

Another way that you can configure Microsoft 365 Apps is by using either the Office Deployment Toolkit (ODT) or the Office Customization Tool.

The ODT is a command-line utility that an administrator can download and use to deploy Microsoft 365 Apps to client computers. To download the ODT, go to: www .microsoft.com/en-us/download/details.aspx?id=49117. After downloading the file, run the executable file. This contains the setup.exe and a sample configuration file (configuration.xml). The ODT allows an administrator to control an Office installation by defining which products and languages are installed and how they should be updated.

To work with the ODT, edit the configuration file to meet your needs, and then run setup.exe from the command line. When creating the configuration file, Microsoft recommends starting with the sample configuration file and editing it to meet your needs. The sample configuration file looks like this:

```
<Configuration>
  <Add SourcePath="\\Server\Share"
      OfficeClientEdition="64"
      Channel="MonthlyEnterprise" >
    <Product ID="O365ProPlusRetail">
      <Language ID="en-us" />
    </Product>
    <Product ID="VisioProRetail">
      <Language ID="en-us" />
    </Product>
  </Add>
  <Updates Enabled="TRUE"
          UpdatePath="\\Server\Share" />
  <Display Level="None" AcceptEULA="TRUE" />
</Configuration>
```

The sample configuration file includes elements and attributes that are most commonly used when downloading and installing Office on a client computer. Each section is described below:

- Add SourcePath="\\Server\Share": Office will be downloaded to "\\server\ share" on the network and deployed using the installation files found at this location.

- Add OfficeClientEdition="64": Downloads and installs the 64-bit edition of Office.

- Add Channel="MonthlyEnterprise": Office will be installed using the Monthly Enterprise Channel.

- Product ID="O365ProPlusRetail": Downloads and installs Microsoft 365 Apps for Enterprise.

- `Language ID="en-us"`: Downloads and installs the English version of Office.
- `Updates Enabled="TRUE"`: Office will check for updates.
- `Updates UpdatePath="\\Server\Share"`: Office will check for updates at "\server\share" on your network.
- `Display Level="None" AcceptEULA="TRUE"`: When installing Office, there will be no user interface displayed. EULA is an End-User License Agreement.

For a complete list of all available attributes that can be configured, please check out Microsoft's website at: `https://learn.microsoft.com/en-us/deployoffice/ office-deployment-tool-configuration-options`.

Once you have created your configuration file, from a command prompt, run the ODT executable in download mode. Example: `setup.exe / download <yourconfigurationfile.xml>`. Then, after running the command, go to the download location you defined in the configuration file and look for an Office folder with the appropriate files in it.

Another option is by using the Office Customization Tool. This tool will walk you through the steps of creating a configuration file. Just as the sample configuration file used in the ODT, these configuration files provide control over an Office installation. After creating the configuration files, you can use them with the ODT to deploy the customized version of Office. To use the Office Customization Tool, go to: `https://config.office.com`.

You will have the option to either create a new configuration file by selecting the Create button or import/edit a configuration file by clicking Import.

To create a new configuration file, perform the following:

1. Go to Office Customization Tool at `https://config.office.com` and select the Create button.

2. In the Product and Releases section, select the architecture you want to deploy. Each configuration file can only deploy one architecture.

3. Select the products and applications that you want to be deployed.

4. Select the update channel you want to deploy. The update channel determines how often your client devices are updated.

5. Select which version to deploy. Microsoft recommends selecting the most current version.

6. In the Language section, select the language. You can use multiple languages and you can select Match Operating System to automatically install the same languages that are being used on the client device.

7. In the Installation section, select whether to install the Office files directly from the cloud or from your local network.

8. Select whether to display the installation to your end users and whether you'd like to pin the Office icons to the taskbar.

9. In the Update and Upgrade section, select whether to install updates directly from the cloud, from your local network, or with Configuration Manager.

10. Select whether to automatically remove all MSI-versions of Office, and whether to automatically install the same language as the removed MSI-version of Office.

11. In the Licensing and Activation settings, if you are deploying a volume-licensed version of Office, Visio, or Project, specify the appropriate license key.

12. In the General section, type your organization name and a description.

13. Select if you want to automatically accept the EULA.

14. Select if you want to enable shared computer activation. Shared computer activation allows you deploy Microsoft 365 Apps to a computer in your organization that is accessed by multiple users.

15. In the Application Preferences section, select what preferences to apply when deploying Office. You can search for a particular setting, filter preferences by Office app, and get more information about each setting by selecting it and reviewing the detailed description.

16. Select Finish, review the settings in the right-hand pane, and then select Export.

17. Then, accept the terms in the license agreement, name the configuration file, and then select Export or, if you're saving the configuration file to the cloud, select Done.

18. You can now use the configuration file in your Office deployment by using the ODT.

Using Intune to Deep-Link Applications

One of the nice advantages of using Windows 10/11 is that you can purchase Microsoft Store applications. After you purchase the applications, you can deploy the Microsoft Store for Business application (deep-link) to all of your users.

Supporting Broadband Connectivity

Administrators have a few weapons in their broadband arsenal. Two different options that we can set up as Administrators is the ability to see how much network or software bandwidth is being used (metering) and setting up Windows 10/11 devices to use your cellular Internet connections (tethering).

Understanding Metering

Administrators have the ability to limit and monitor network usage by configuring the network as a metered network. Network metering allows you to watch or meter network downloading, and then administrators can charge users or departments for their network usage.

This is becoming something that many IT departments have started doing due to budgeting. Many IT departments are non-revenue-generating departments, and because of this, it can be difficult for them to get a budget passed. But with network metering, you can charge other departments for the amount of bandwidth and network that is being used.

When you're setting up your company's Internet connection, your ISP can charge by the amount of data used. That's called a metered Internet connection. If you have a metered Internet connection, setting your network connection to metered in Windows can help you reduce the amount of data you send and receive. To set this up in Windows, take the following steps:

1. Click Start ➤ Settings, and then tap Network & Internet.

2. Tap or click the Wi-Fi link and then select Manage Known Networks.

3. Select Wi-Fi Network ➤ Properties and then turn on/off Set As Metered Connection.

Administrators also have the ability to limit how much bandwidth a user or department gets to use when downloading applications. This is referred to as software metering. To set up software metering, an Administrator must use a combination of Intune and System Center Configuration Monitor.

Understanding Broadband Tethering

Tethering allows a user to use their Windows 10/11 mobile device through their cellular phone. If you have a Windows client mobile device and want it to access the Internet, you can go through your cell coverage to get online.

Tethering can also involve connecting one mobile device to another mobile device for Internet access. So, let's say I have an iPad with a cellular Internet connection. I can connect another Windows 10/11 tablet to that iPad to gain Internet access. So tethering is the ability to connect one device to another for Internet access. Before you set up tethering, there are a few things that you should know:

- There may be extra charges when connecting your data connection with another device.

- Applications and updates may not be downloaded over a metered connection, and by default, tethered and mobile broadband connections are metered.

- Many cellular carriers require that you pay an extra fee for allowing your phone to be a hotspot for tethering. To enable tethering on most devices, set up your mobile device as an Internet hotspot.

Understanding Data Synchronization

Data synchronization allows you to synchronize your devices with your servers. These servers can be network-based or cloud-based. Administrators have the ability to synchronize work folders, and use the Sync Center to use one application for all of their synchronization needs.

To enable synchronization on a Windows 10/11 device, click the Start button and choose Settings. When you are in the Settings window, click the Accounts link to set up your user accounts and synchronization (see Figure 10.20).

Once you enter into the Account link, you can choose the bottom option (Sync Your Settings) to set up all of your synchronization settings (see Figure 10.21).

FIGURE 10.20 Accounts link in the Settings window

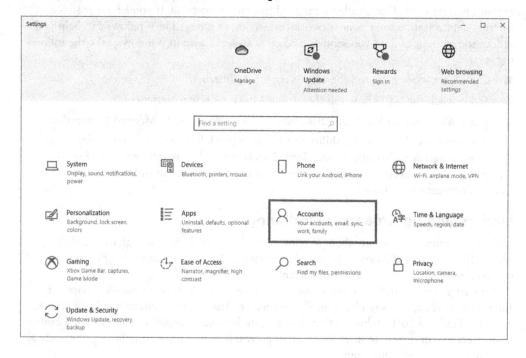

FIGURE 10.21 Syncing your settings

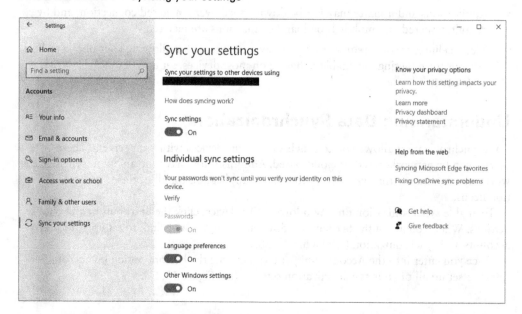

One of the final things that you want to look at in the Accounts window is the Access Work Or School link. This link allows you to connect your device to your work or school, sign into Azure, and enroll in device management using the links provided under Related Settings, as shown in Figure 10.22.

FIGURE 10.22   Related Settings in the Access Work Or School window

Using Mobile Application Management

One of the advantages to using Intune is the ability to download applications to many different platforms. One concern that IT departments may have is that their users will download corporate applications on personal devices. Since many companies now allow BYOD, there needs to be tools that allow a company to control company data on personal devices. This is where *Mobile Application Management (MAM)* can help your organization.

MAM is part of Intune and it is a suite of administrator management tools that allow you to manage, configure, publish, update, and monitor applications for your mobile devices.

The advantage to using MAM is that an administrator has the ability to manage and protect the company's data from within the application that the user is using. For example, an administrator can manage a work-related application that has confidential information on it and that application can be on almost any type of device (including personal devices).

MAM will work with many of the Microsoft productivity applications, including:

- Bookings
- Edge
- Excel
- Kaizala
- Launcher

- Lens
- Lists
- Office
- OneDrive
- OneNote
- Outlook
- Planner
- PowerApps
- PowerPoint
- SharePoint
- Skype for Business
- Teams
- To-Do
- Visio Viewer
- Whiteboard
- Word
- Yammer

 NOTE For a complete list of applications that Intune and MAM will support, please visit Microsoft's website at http://docs.microsoft.com/en-us/intune/apps-supported-intune-apps.

There are two configurations that are supported by Intune MAM:

- Intune MDM + MAM
- Unenrolled devices with MAM managed applications

With Intune MDM + MAM, administrators can manage apps by using MAM and app protection policies only on devices that are enrolled with Intune MDM. To manage apps using MDM + MAM, you should use Intune in the Microsoft Endpoint Manager admin center.

With Unenrolled devices with MAM managed applications, you can manage apps using MAM and app protection policies on devices that are not enrolled with Intune MDM. Apps can be managed by using Intune on devices that are registered with third-party Enterprise Mobility Management (EMM) providers. To manage apps using MAM, customers should use Intune in the Microsoft Endpoint Manager admin center.

Understanding Updates

Deploying updates can be a very difficult process for many organizations. Depending on the number of users that you have and the number of applications that each uses, updates can be a time-consuming process.

Many organizations install a Microsoft server called a Windows Server Update Services (WSUS). WSUS servers allow administrators to deploy Microsoft product updates to computers that are running Windows. Administrators can manage all of their organization's Microsoft updates from one application.

The downside to WSUS is that it is used for Microsoft updates. So, you can deploy updates to all of your applications, Microsoft and non-Microsoft, by using the Intune management portal.

Deploying Software Updates Using Intune

When you decide to use Intune to deploy your updates, you get a lot of options that you get to consider and set up. For example, do you want to approve all your updates, or do you want the updates to automatically deploy? Many administrators like to approve all their updates so that they have a chance to test them first before deploying.

Intune stores only the update policy assignments, not the actual updates. The devices still need to access Windows Update to obtain the updates.

Intune provides the following policy types to manage updates:

Update Rings for Windows 10 and Later   A collection of settings that configures devices that run Windows 10 and Windows 11 updates. Update ring policies are supported on devices that run Windows 10 version 1607 or later and Windows 11.

Feature Updates for Windows 10 and Later (Public Preview)   Updates devices to the Windows version that you specify and freezes the feature set on those devices until you choose to update them. Figure 10.28 shows the Windows 10 update ring.

To create and assign update rings, follow these steps:

1. Sign into the Microsoft Endpoint Manager admin center.
2. Select Devices ➤ Windows ➤ Update Rings For Windows 10 And Later ➤ + Create Profile.
3. Under Basics, specify a name and a description (optional), and then click Next (as shown in Figure 10.23).

FIGURE 10.23   Create Update Ring for Windows 10 and Later

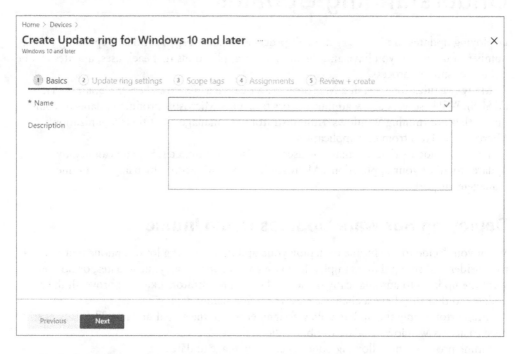

4.   Under Update Ring Settings, configure your required settings. After configuring update
     and user experience settings, click Next.

5.   If you want to apply scope tags, you can do that under Scope Tags. Click + Select Scope
     Tags to open the Select Tags pane. Choose one or more tags, and then click Select and
     return to the Scope Tags page. Click Next to continue to Assignments.

6.   Under Assignments, click + Select Groups To Include and then assign the update ring to
     one or more groups. Click Next to continue.

7.   Under Review + Create, review the settings and then click Create.

To manage your Windows update rings, go to the portal, navigate to Devices ➤ Windows
➤ Update Rings For Windows 10 And Later, and select the policy you want to manage. This
will open the policy's Overview page. Here you can view the rings' assignment status. You
can also delete, pause, resume, extend, and uninstall the update ring by selecting the actions
from the top of the Overview pane (see Figure 10.24):

Delete   Click Delete to stop enforcing the settings of the selected Windows update ring.
Deleting a ring will remove its configuration from Intune and will no longer apply or
enforce those settings.

Pause   Click Pause to prevent assigned devices from receiving feature or quality updates
for up to 35 days from the time that you paused it. After the maximum days have

passed, the pause functionality will expire and the device will scan Windows Updates for applicable updates. Once the scan is complete, you can then pause the updates again. If you resume a paused update ring and then pause it again, the pause period will reset to 35 days.

Resume   If an update ring is paused, you can click Resume to restore feature or quality updates for that ring to activate operation. After you resume an update ring, you can pause it again.

Extend   If an update ring is paused, you can click Extend to reset the pause period for both feature and quality updates for that update ring to 35 days.

Uninstall   Uninstall will uninstall or roll back the latest feature update or quality update for an active or paused update ring. After uninstalling one type, you can then uninstall the other type. Intune doesn't support or manage the ability of users to uninstall updates. For an uninstall to be successful, the device must be running Windows 10 April 2018 update (version 1803) or later or Windows 11.

FIGURE 10.24   Overview pane actions

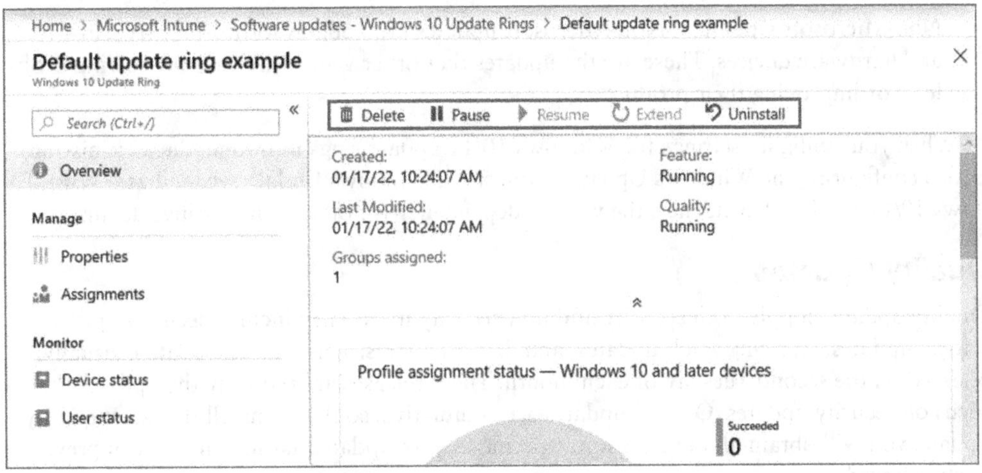

Identifying Required Updates

When you decide to use Intune for updates, you need to decide which type of updates that you want to install. Administrators have the ability to choose what type of updates they want to install:

All Updates   All updates section means just that—all updates. Every possible update that can be deployed will be shown under the All Updates section.

Critical Updates   Critical updates are those that are released to fix a specific issue that is for a critical bug that is not security-related.

Security Updates Security updates are those that need to be applied to fix a security issue. These security issues are used by hackers to hack into a device or software.

Definition Updates Definition updates are normally software updates that contain additions to a product's definition database. Definition databases are used to identify objects that have very specific attributes. These attributes look for malicious code, phishing websites, or junk mail.

Service Packs Service packs are a collective set of all current hotfixes, security updates, critical updates, and updates. Normally service packs also contain additional fixes for known issues that are found since the release of the product. Service packs may also contain customer-requested design changes or features.

Update Rollups Update rollups are current hotfixes, security updates, critical updates, and updates that are bundled together for easy deployment. Update rollups are normally used to target a specific component or software package.

Mandatory Updates Mandatory updates are those that are released to either fix or replace a software or hardware issue. You must run mandatory updates or the device or Windows system may stop functioning properly.

Non-Microsoft Updates Non-Microsoft updates are updates for third-party software and hardware devices. These are the updates that other vendors release for solving problems or improving their product.

When you configure settings for Windows 10/11 update rings in Intune, the administrator is also configuring the Windows Update settings. If a Windows Update setting has a Windows 10/11 version dependency, the version dependency is noted in the settings details.

Quality Updates

Quality updates supply both security and non-security fixes. They include security updates, critical updates, servicing stack updates, and driver updates. This type of update is usually released on the second Tuesday of each month. These releases are typically the updates that focus on security updates. Quality updates are cumulative, so if you install the latest quality update, you will obtain all the fixes for a specific feature update that may have been previously released.

Creating and managing quality updates was discussed earlier in this chapter in the section "Deploying Software Updates Using Intune."

Feature Updates for Windows 10 and Later

With feature updates for Windows 10 and later, the administrator selects the Windows feature version that they want devices to stay at. When a device receives a feature updates policy, the device will update to the version of Windows specified. If a device already runs a later version of Windows, then it will remain at its current version.

Feature updates are typically released annually. They add new features and functionality to Windows 10/11. Until you modify or remove the feature updates policy, devices won't install a new Windows version. If the policy is edited to specify a newer version, devices can then install the features from that Windows version.

To create and assign feature updates for Windows 10 and later, follow these steps:

1. Sign into the Microsoft Endpoint Manager admin center.

2. Select Devices ➤ Windows ➤ Feature Updates For Windows 10 And Later ➤ + Create Profile.

3. Under Deployment Settings, specify a name and a description (optional), and for Feature Update To Deploy, select the version of Windows with the feature set you want, and then click Next. You can also configure Rollout options that are used to manage when Windows Updates makes the update available to devices that receive this policy.

4. Under Assignments, click + Select Groups To Include and then assign the update ring to one or more groups. Click Next.

5. Under Review + Create, review the settings and click Create to save.

To manage feature updates for Windows 10 and later, follow these steps:

1. In the admin center, go to Devices ➤ Windows ➤ Feature Updates For Windows 10 And Later and select the policy you want to manage. The policy opens to its Overview pane. For each profile, you can view:

    - **Feature Update Version:** The feature update version in the profile

    - **Assigned:** Whether the profile is assigned to one or more groups

    - **Support:** The status of the feature update:

        - **Supported:** The feature update version is supported and can be deployed to devices.

        - **Support Ending:** The feature update version is within two months of its support end date.

        - **Not supported:** Support for the feature update has expired and it no longer deploys to devices.

    - **Support End Date:** The end of support date for the feature update version.

2. From the Overview pane, the administrator can configure the following options:

    - Click Delete to delete the policy from Intune and remove it from devices.

    - Click Properties to modify the deployment. On the Properties pane, click Edit to open the deployment settings or assignments to modify the deployment.

    - Click End User Update Status to view information about the policy.

Using Device Configuration Profiles to Manage Android Updates

In a world where more and more people are using their mobile devices to connect to the network, you need to know how to manage those mobile devices. So, you will want to set up the MDM authority to Intune. Chapter 11 discusses device configuration profiles in greater detail.

To set up an Android device administrator in Intune, perform the following steps:

1. Sign into the Microsoft Endpoint Manager admin center.

2. Select Devices ➤ Android ➤ Android Enrollment ➤ Personal And Corporate-Owned Devices With Device Administration Privileges ➤ Use Device Administrator To Manage Devices. This will set up the Android device administrator.

3. Inform your users how you want them to enroll their devices.

4. Once a user has enrolled their device, you can begin to manage that device using Intune, including assigning compliance policies, managing apps, and more.

Once a device is enrolled, Intune will sync with the device every eight hours. During the sync process, the apps will:

■ Download any policies or updates.

■ Send hardware inventory updates.

■ Send company app inventory updates.

If a device is out of sync or no longer meets the requirements, it will show a status of Not Compliant. If that is the case, then the device's access to resources may be revoked until it meets the requirements again. The Company Portal app will notify you about any issues and will give you the steps for resolving the out-of-sync issue.

Troubleshooting Updates

One of the first things you can do is check the policy deployment status in the Intune portal. You can see whether or not the status was successful.

You can also verify that update policies are managed by MDM by going to the targeted device and selecting Settings ➤ Updates And Security ➤ Windows Update ➤ Advanced Options. Click View Configured Update Policies, then verify that the policy type is Mobile Device Management.

Configuring a Windows Client Delivery Optimization

With Intune, use Delivery Optimization settings for your Windows devices to reduce bandwidth consumption when those devices download applications and updates. Configure Delivery Optimization as part of your device configuration profiles. After you create a profile, you can then assign or deploy that profile to your Windows devices.

For a complete list of delivery optimization options, check out Microsoft's website at `http://docs.microsoft.com/en-us/mem/intune/configuration/delivery-optimization-settings`.

To create a delivery optimization profile, perform the following steps:

1. Sign into the Microsoft Endpoint Manager admin center.

2. Select Devices ➤ Configuration Profiles and then click + Create Profile.

3. Enter the following properties:
   - **Platform:** Select Windows 10 and later.
   - **Profile:** Select Templates ➤ Delivery Optimization.
4. Click Create.
5. On the Basics page, enter the following properties:
   - **Name:** Enter a descriptive name for your profile.
   - **Description (optional):** Enter a description for the profile.
6. Click Next.
7. On the Configuration Settings page, define how you want updates and apps to download. When you're done, click Next.
8. On the Scope (Tags) page, click Select Scope Tags to open the Select Tags pane, where you can assign scope tags to the profile. Click Next to continue.
9. On the Assignments page, select the groups that will receive this profile. Then, click Next.
10. On the Applicability Rules page, use the Rule, Property, and Value options to define how this profile applies within assigned groups.
11. On the Review + Create page, when you're done, click Create. The profile is created and appears in the list. The policy will be applied the next time the device checks in.

Using Intune Compliance Reports

An administrator can use Intune to deploy Windows updates to Windows 10/11 devices. The administrator will want to review a policy report on the deployment status for the configured policies for Update rings for Windows 10 and later and Feature updates for Windows 10 and later. To do so, follow these steps:

1. Sign into the Microsoft Endpoint Manager admin center.
2. Select Devices ➤ Monitor.
3. Under Software Updates, select Per Update Ring Deployment State and choose the deployment ring you want to review.

Using Intune Reports

One of the best tools that Intune offers is the ability to obtain all of the different types of reports. Intune reports help an Administrator monitor the status of your enrolled devices and see if there are any issues that need to be addressed. The reports also allow an Administrator to examine both the hardware and software inventory.

With Intune reports, you can monitor the health and activity of endpoints and view other reporting data across Intune. Examples include device compliance, device health, and device trends. You can also build custom reports.

Intune reports are categorized into the following areas of focus:

- **Operational:** Provides targeted data that helps an administrator focus and take action.
- **Organizational:** Provides a wider summary of an overall view, such as device management state.
- **Historical:** Provides patterns and trends over a period of time.
- **Specialist:** Allows an administrator to use raw data to create their own custom reports.

Using Intune reports allows an administrator to search and sort, perform data paging, review performance, and export data.

- **Search and sort:** Search and sort across every column.
- **Data paging:** Scan data based on paging, either page by page or by jumping to a specific page.
- **Performance:** Quickly generate and view reports created from large tenants.
- **Export:** Export reporting data generated from large tenants.

Implement App Protection and App Configuration Policies

App protection policies (APPs) can be applied to apps that are running on devices that may or may not be managed using Intune. APPs are rules that will ensure that your corporate data stays safe and contained within the managed app, which is an app that has an APP applied to it and that can be managed by Intune.

App configuration policies help to get rid of app setup issues by allowing you to assign configuration settings to a policy before the end user runs the app. The settings you configure will be applied automatically on the end user's device without them taking any actions other than running the app. Configuration settings are unique for each app.

In this section, I will delve into more detail regarding App Protection and App Configuration policies.

App Protection Policies

App protection policies (APPs) can be configured for apps that run on devices that are:

- **Enrolled in Intune:** These devices are usually corporate owned.
- **Enrolled in a third-party MDM solution:** These devices are usually corporate owned.
- **Not enrolled in any mobile device management solution:** These devices are usually employee-owned devices that aren't managed or enrolled in Intune or other MDM solutions.

Using APPs offers a number of benefits:

- APPs protect corporate data at the app level; management is based on the user's identity. This will eliminate the need for device management.

- End-user productivity is not affected and the policies do not apply when using the app in a personal context—APPs only apply to corporate data.

- APPs ensure that app-layer protection is in place, such as requiring a PIN to open a work app, controlling the sharing of data between apps, and making it so that the end user cannot save corporate app data to a personal storage location.

- MDM and MAM ensure that the device is protected. You can require a PIN to access the device or deploy a managed app. Or, you can deploy apps to devices using your MDM solution to provide more control over app management.

Creating an iOS/iPadOS or Android App Protection Policy (APP)

To create an APP for iOS/iPadOS and Android apps, perform the following steps:

1. Sign into the Microsoft Endpoint Manager admin center.

2. Select Apps ➤ App Protection Policies. This selection opens the App protection policies details, where you create new policies and edit existing policies.

3. Click + Create Policy and select iOS/iPadOS or Android to open the Create Policy pane.

4. On the Basics page, complete the following:

   - **Name:** The name of the profile that appears in the Microsoft Endpoint Manager admin center

   - **Description:** A description of the profile

   - **Platform:** A value you wish to assign

5. Click Next. On the Apps page, you can choose how you want to apply the policy to apps on different devices. You must add at least one app.

Value/option	Description
Target To Apps On All Device Types	Use this option to target your policy to apps on devices of any management state. Click No to target apps on specific devices types.
Device Types	Use this option to specify whether this policy applies to MDM managed devices or unmanaged devices. For iOS/iPadOS APP policies, select from Unmanaged and Managed devices. For Android APP policies, select from Unmanaged, Android Device Administrator, and Android Enterprise.
Target Policy To	Use this drop-down box to target your app protection policy to All Apps, Microsoft Apps, or Core Microsoft Apps.

6. Click Next to display the Data protection page, which provides the settings for data loss prevention (DLP) controls, such as cut, copy, paste, and save-as restrictions. These settings determine how users interact with data in the apps that this app protection policy applies. Data protection settings include iOS/iPadOS Data Protection and Android Data Protection. Click Next.

7. On the Access Requirements page, configure the PIN and credential requirements for iOS/iPadOS access or Android access. Click Next.

8. On the Conditional Launch page, set the sign-in security requirements for the app protection policy. Select a Setting and enter the Value that users must meet to sign into your company app.

9. Select the Action you want to take if users do not meet your requirements. In some cases, multiple actions can be configured for a single setting. Conditional launch settings include iOS/iPadOS conditional launch and Android conditional launch settings. Click Next.

10. On the Assignments page, you assign the app protection policy to groups of users. You must apply the policy to a group of users to have the policy take effect.

11. Click Next: Review + Create to review the values and settings you entered for this APP.

12. When you are done, click Create to create the app protection policy in Intune.

App Configuration Policies

An app configuration policy helps reduce app setup issues by allowing you to assign configuration settings to a policy before the end user runs the app. You use app configuration policies in Intune to provide custom configuration settings for an app. These settings are unique for each app. App configuration policies, under Device Enrollment Type, can either be Managed Devices or Managed Apps. Managed Devices refer to apps that are deployed and managed by Intune. Managed Apps refer to apps that are configured with an Intune APP on devices regardless of the enrollment state.

Creating an App Configuration Policy for iOS/iPadOS

1. Sign into the Microsoft Endpoint Manager admin center.

2. Select Apps ➢ App Configuration Policies ➢ Add ➢ Managed Devices. Note that you can choose between Managed Devices and Managed Apps.

3. On the Basics page, set the following details:
   - **Name:** The name of the profile that will appear in the Microsoft Endpoint Manager admin center
   - **Description:** A description of the profile
   - **Device Enrollment Type:** Managed Devices

4. Select iOS/iPadOS as the platform.

5. Click Select App next to Targeted App. The Associated App pane is displayed.

6. In the Targeted App pane, choose the managed app to associate with the configuration policy and click OK.

7. Click Next to display the Settings page.

8. In the drop-down box, select the Configuration settings format. Select one of the following methods to add configuration information:

   ▪ Use Configuration Designer.

   ▪ Enter XML Data.

9. Click Next to display the Assignments page.

10. In the drop-down box next to Assign to, select either Selected Groups, All Users, All Devices, or All Users And All Devices to assign the app configuration policy to, as shown in Figure 10.25. For this example, select All Users.

FIGURE 10.25   App configuration policy: assigning groups

11. Click Select Groups To Exclude to display the related pane.

12. Choose the groups you want to exclude and then click Select.

13. Click Next to display the Review + Create page.

14. Click Create to add the app configuration policy to Intune.

PowerShell Commands

Table 11.2 is a list of just some of the PowerShell commands that administrators can use to manage, configure, and view applications in Azure.

TABLE 11.2   PowerShell commands

Command	Description
Add-AzureADApplicationOwner	Adds an owner to an application
Add-AzureADApplicationPolicy	Adds a policy to an application
Get-AzureADApplication	Allows you to view an application
Get-AzureADApplicationExtensionProperty	Allows you to view the extension properties of an application
Get-AzureADApplicationOwner	Allows you to see who the owner of an application is
Get-AzureADApplicationPasswordCredential	Allows you to view an application password
Get-AzureADApplicationPolicy	Allows you to view an application policy.
New-AzureADApplication	Creates a new application in Azure
New-AzureADApplicationExtensionProperty	Creates extension properties of an application
New-AzureADApplicationPasswordCredential	Creates password credentials for an application.
Remove-AzureADApplication	Deletes an application

Command	Description
Remove-AzureADApplicationExtensionProperty	Removes an extension property of an application
Remove-AzureADApplicationOwner	Removes an owner from an application
Remove-AzureADApplicationPasswordCredential	Removes the password credentials from an application
Set-AzureADApplication	Updates an application

Summary

This chapter discussed the cloud and Intune. You learned how Intune can help you manage devices and software. You learned how to set up and configure an Intune subscription and how you can use that subscription to help your network users get the most out of their network resources and software.

We also talked about managing devices using Intune. You learned how to provision user accounts and enroll devices. We also discussed how to manage and configure devices using the Intune subscription. Then we discussed deploying and configuring software and updates using Intune.

Next you learned how to work with mobile devices, including Windows tablets, broadband metering, and tethering. We discussed how to wipe mobile devices for employees who leave the company and how you can set policies to control how applications are deployed to your users. You then learned how to use Intune to deploy and maintain your company's software packages and updates.

This chapter showed you the different types of reports that you can run using Intune. These reports can help you see what devices still need updates and also what hardware may need to be installed or replaced.

Exam Essentials

Understand Microsoft Intune. Understand what Intune can do to improve your network. Make sure you know how to connect users and devices to Intune.

Know how to configure an Intune subscription. Understand how to set up and manage an Intune subscription. Be able to configure a device to use Intune.

Understand the benefits of Intune.   Understand how these benefits, such as remote wipe, can help you protect your corporate data.

Know how to use Intune connectors.   Be able to use Intune connectors to work with software within a network. The connector allows the cloud-based software to communicate properly with the infrastructure-based software.

Know how to set up Intune alerts.   Understand each type of Intune alert and which alerts are important to fix immediately or which alerts just are giving you information. Know how to set up notifications for each alert type.

Know how to work with Intune reports.   Understand how to use the various reports to monitor the status of Intune managed devices. These reports give you information on the status of software updates, software installed, and certificate compliance. Reports also let you examine the inventory of your network's hardware and software.

Know how to manage device updates.   Understand how to plan for device updates, as well as how to create and manage quality and feature update policies. Create and manage iOS/iPadOS update policies, and know how to manage Android updates and how to monitor updates, as well as create and manage update rings.

Know how to implement app protection and app configuration policies.   Understand how to plan and manage app protection policies and app configuration policies, including policies for iOS and Android.

Video Resources

There are no videos for this chapter.

Review Questions

1. You are the network administrator for your organization. Your users use both desktops and tablets to access the network. Your tablet users use a 4G mobile broadband Wi-Fi connection. You need to watch how much data your users are using on this connection. How do you do that?

   A. Configure the broadband connection as a metered network.

   B. Turn on network resource monitoring.

   C. Enable performance monitoring.

   D. Enable tablet metering in the tablets settings.

2. You manage 1,000 Windows client computers. All of the computers are enrolled in Intune. You manage the servicing channel settings by using Intune. What should you do if you want to review the servicing status of a computer?

   A. From Device Configuration Profiles, view the device status.

   B. From Device Compliance, view the device compliance.

   C. From Software Updates, view the audit logs.

   D. From Software Updates, view the Per Update Ring Deployment State.

3. You are the IT manager of a large manufacturing company. Sales personnel are allowed to bring their own personal Windows client devices to the office. The company allows the salespeople to install company software and use their devices to retrieve company mail by using the management infrastructure agent. One of your salespeople reports that their Windows client laptop was stolen. You need to make sure that no one can steal any of the corporate data or access any corporate emails. Which two actions should you perform? Each correct answer presents part of the solution. (Choose two.)

   A. Prevent the computer from connecting to the corporate wireless network.

   B. Remove the computer from the management infrastructure.

   C. Reset the user's password.

   D. Do a remote wipe on the user's laptop.

4. You are the IT director for a large school system. The school has decided that students can bring in their own devices to do school work with. Your organization uses Azure Active Directory and Intune for all the students' applications and network authentication. You need to be sure that students who are using iPads as well as Windows client devices have full access. What do you need to do to ensure that all iOS devices have access?

   A. Add a Student Portal app from the Apple App Store.

   B. Create a Device Enrollment Manager account.

   C. Configure an Intune Service connector for Exchange.

   D. Import an Apple Push Notification service (APNs) certificate.

5. You have 200 Windows client computers that are joined to Azure AD and enrolled in Intune. You want to enable Self-Service Password Reset on the sign-in screen. Which settings should you configure from the Intune blade?

   A. Device configuration

   B. Device compliance

   C. Device enrollment

   D. Conditional access

6. You are the IT manager for WillPanek.com. The company has an Active Directory domain and a cloud-based Azure Active Directory. The two are synchronized by using the Azure Active Directory Synchronization tool. The company also uses System Center Configuration Manager. You need to use Configuration Manager to manage devices registered with Intune. What do you need to do to accomplish this? (Choose two.)

   A. Create a new Device Enrollment Manager account in Intune.

   B. In Intune, configure an Active Directory connector.

   C. Configure the Intune Connector role in Configuration Manager.

   D. Create the Microsoft Intune subscription in Configuration Manager.

7. Your company has an Azure subscription. All the users in the Marketing department use their own personal devices that run either iOS or Android systems. All the devices are enrolled in Intune. The company has developed a new mobile application named App1 for the Marketing department. You need to ensure that only the Marketing department users can download App1. What should you do first?

   A. Add App1 to Intune.

   B. Add App1 to a local server for users to use.

   C. Add App1 to Microsoft Store for Business.

   D. Configure the iOS and Android systems to use the new application.

8. You are the IT director for a large company that has decided to move to the cloud. The company wants to use Azure AD and Intune. The company has been looking into this because users have been using multiple devices to get their job done. When your users get added to Intune and get licensed, how many devices can each user add by default?

   A. 4.

   B. 10.

   C. 15.

   D. None. Device administrators are the only people who can add devices to Intune.

9. You are the administrator of a company that builds its own applications. You have decided that you want to install a company application for all employees by using the Microsoft Store for Business. Which term is used to refer to installing corporate apps through the Microsoft Store for Business?

   A. WS installations

   B. BranchCache

   C. Image installation

   D. Sideloading

10. You are the IT director for Stormwind Training Studios. Your company has decided to start using Intune for all of their software deployments. You want to set up a notification system so that you see all alerts and your IT manager only gets notified for critical alerts. How do you accomplish this? (Choose all that apply.)

A. Set up all event notifications for the IT manager in Intune.

B. Set up all event notifications for the IT director in Intune.

C. Set up critical event notifications for the IT manager in Intune.

D. Set up critical event notifications for the IT director in Intune.

11. You are the administrator for your company network. You have a Microsoft 365 subscription. Users have iOS devices that are not enrolled in Microsoft 365 Device Management. You create an app protection policy for the Microsoft Outlook app. The policy is configured as follows:

Name: Policy1

Platform: iOS

Target To All App Types: No

App Types: Apps On Unmanaged Devices

Apps: 1 app selected

Settings ➤ Data Protection: Default settings are configured

Settings ➤ Access Requirements: Default settings are configured

Settings ➤ Conditional Branch: Default settings are configured

Settings ➤ Scope (Tags): 0 scope(s) selected

You want to configure the policy to meet the following requirements:

- Prevent users from using the Outlook app if the operating system version is less than 12.0.0.

- Require users to use an alphanumeric passcode to access the Outlook app.

What should you configure in an app protection policy to prevent the users from using Outlook if the operating system version is less than 12.0.0?

A. Access requirements

B. Conditional launch

C. Data protection

D. A scope

12. You are the administrator for your company network. Your network has an Active Directory domain that runs Windows client computers that are enrolled in Intune. Updates are deployed by using Windows Update for Business. Users in a group must meet the following requirements:

- Update installations can happen any day, but only between 00:00 and 05:00.

- Updates must be downloaded from Microsoft and from other company computers that have already downloaded the updates.

What two settings should you modify if you need to configure the Windows 10 and later update rings in Intune to meet the requirements? (Choose two.)

A. Update Settings ➤ Quality Update Deferral Period (Days)

B. Update Settings ➤ Servicing Channel

C. User Experience Settings ➤ Automatic Update Behavior

D. User Experience Settings ➤ Delivery Optimization Download Mode

13. You are the administrator for your company network. You and a colleague are discussing Apple Mobile Device Management (MDM) push certificates. How long is an Apple push certificate valid?

A. One year.

B. Two years.

C. Three years.

D. It does not expire.

14. You are the administrator for your company network. You and a colleague are discussing device enrollment. When a device is enrolled in Intune, it is supplied with a Mobile Device Management (MDM) certificate that is used to communicate with the Intune service. You know that there are several ways to enroll a device depending on the device's ownership, device type, and management requirements. One of these methods includes personally owned phones, tablets, and computers. The users install and run the Company Portal app to enroll the devices. What is this method known as?

A. Apple Automated Device Enrollment (ADE)

B. Bring your own device (BYOD)

C. Corporate-owned device (COD)

D. Device Enrollment Manager (DEM)

15. You are the administrator for your company network. Your company implements Azure AD, Microsoft 365, Intune, and Azure Information Protection. The company's security policy states the following:

- Personal devices do not need to be enrolled in Intune.

- Users must authenticate by using a PIN before they can access corporate email data.

- Users can use their personal iOS and Android devices to access corporate cloud services.

- Users must be prevented from copying corporate email data to a cloud storage service other than Microsoft OneDrive for Business.

What should you create if you want to configure a solution to meet the corporate security policies?

A. You should add an app protection policy from the Intune admin center.

B. You should add a data loss prevention (DLP) policy from the Security & Compliance admin center.

C. You should add a device configuration profile from the Intune admin center.

D. You should add a supervision policy from the Security & Compliance admin center.

16. You are the administrator for your company network. You install a feature update on a Windows client computer. You are worried about how the update will affect a specific application. How many days do you have to roll back the update?

    A. 5 days

    B. 10 days

    C. 14 days

    D. 30 days

17. You are the administrator for your company network. You have two Windows client computers that are enrolled in Intune:

    - Computer1 is a member of Group1.

    - Computer2 is a member of Group1 and Group2.

    In Intune, Windows 10 and later update rings are defined as shown:

Name	Quality deferral (days)	Assigned
Ring1	3	Yes
Ring2	10	Yes

    You assign the update rings as shown:

Name	Include	Exclude
Ring1	Group1	Group2
Ring2	Group2	Group1

    What will the quality deferral (days) be on Computer1?

    A. 3 days

    B. 7 days

    C. 10 days

    D. 13 days

18. You are the administrator for your company network. Your network contains an Active Directory domain that is synced to Azure AD. All of the network computers are enrolled in Intune. The domain contains the following computers:

Name	Operating System
Computer1	Windows 8.1 Enterprise
Computer2	Windows 10 Enterprise without the latest feature update
Computer3	Windows 10 Enterprise without the latest feature update

You are evaluating which Intune actions you can use to reset the computers to run Windows 10 Enterprise with the latest update. On which computers do you perform a Clean Wipe action?

A. Computer1 only

B. Computer2 only

C. Computer3 only

D. Computer2 and Computer3 only

E. Computer1, Computer2, and Computer3

19. You are the administrator for your company network. You and a colleague are discussing Windows Update for Business and the different types of updates that it provides. One of the update types is typically released on the second Tuesday of each month and includes security, critical, and driver updates. What type of update is being discussed?

A. Feature updates

B. Non-deferrable updates

C. Pilot updates

D. Quality updates

20. You are the administrator for your company network. Your company has an Azure AD tenant. You use Intune to manage your iOS, Android, and Windows client devices. You want to purchase 1,000 new iOS devices, and each will be assigned to a specific user. You need to ensure that the iOS devices are automatically enrolled in Intune the first time that the assigned user signs on. What actions should you perform? (Choose three.)

A. Add an Apple Automated Device Enrollment (ADE) token.

B. Create a device compliance policy.

C. Create an Apple enrollment profile.

D. Create a Device Enrollment Manager (DEM) account.

E. Assign an enrollment profile.

Chapter

11

Managing Devices

MICROSOFT EXAM OBJECTIVES COVERED IN THIS CHAPTER:

✓ **Implement device compliance policies**

- Plan device compliance policies; implement device compliance policies; manage notifications for device compliance policies, monitor device compliance; troubleshoot device compliance policies.

✓ **Plan and implement device configuration profiles**

- Plan device configuration profiles; implement device configuration profiles; monitor and troubleshoot device configuration profiles; configure and implement assigned access on public devices, including kiosks and dedicated devices.

This chapter shows you how to set up and manage your Windows 10/11 devices both on-site and using Intune, which is part of Microsoft Endpoint Manager and Azure AD.

When you install Windows 10/11, you designate the initial configuration for your disks. Through Windows 10/11's utilities and features, you can change that configuration and perform disk management tasks.

One of the advantages of using Azure is the ability to connect to your Azure network using many different device styles (Microsoft, Apple, etc.). But that means you have to set up Azure to accept these different device types.

Also, you have the ability to set up policies and rules for the devices that connect to your Azure network. This chapter is going to show you how to set up those policies.

So, after you purchase your licenses and you are ready to go, you can then configure Azure AD with compliance policies. These policies allow you to configure how Windows client devices will work.

Before we dive into policies and profiles for your devices, let's take another look at Microsoft Intune. Intune was discussed in greater detail in Chapter 10, "Planning and Managing Microsoft Intune," but this chapter covers a bit of what Intune can do for you. It's important to understand Intune because even though these policies and profiles are added to devices and users, you create them in Intune.

Intune allows you to manage mobile devices, mobile applications, and PC management capabilities, all from the cloud. Using Intune, you can provide your users with access to corporate applications, data, and resources from almost anywhere and on almost any device while also keeping your corporate information secure. Using Intune also helps you save money because it allows you to license *users* instead of *devices*. So, if you have a user who works from multiple devices (laptop, tablet, and Windows phone), you only pay once for the user license instead of multiple times for all of the user's devices.

Administrators can use Microsoft Intune to support and manage Windows 10/11. Administrators can use Intune on a Windows client device for the following:

- Enrollment
- Organization resource access
- Application management
- Policies
- Inventory
- Reporting
- Remote wipe

Intune is an add-on to your Azure subscription, but if you want to deploy software using the cloud or set up rules for how your devices and users will function, Intune is a subscription that you should add to your cloud-based utilities. Let's now take a look at how you can set up policies and profiles for your devices and users.

Compliance Policies

One of the advantages of using Azure is the ability to protect the corporate data by ensuring that users and devices meet certain requirements. When using Intune, this is referred to as compliance policies. Compliance policies are rules and settings that your users and their devices must follow in order to connect and access Intune.

Compliance policies, along with conditional access, ensures that administrators can stop users and devices that don't follow the rules that your organization has determined as necessary for access. For example, the Intune administrator can ensure that:

- Corporate users enter a password on their mobile devices to access data.

- Their devices haven't been cracked, rooted, or jail broken. Administrators can ensure that devices are under a minimum threat level.

- Devices have a minimum operating system along with updates.

Azure Active Directory, along with conditional access, allows Intune to enforce the compliances that your organization demands. When you enroll a device in Intune, the registration begins with Azure AD and the device information is placed into Azure AD. A part of this registration process is the device's compliance status, which is used by the conditional access policies, and based on that, corporate resources are either blocked or allowed.

One advantage that you get by using compliance policies is that you can assign the policy to either a user (using a user group) or a device (using a device group). If a policy is assigned to a user, all the user's devices are also checked for policy compliance.

 Microsoft recommends that if you are using Windows 10 version 1803 or higher, the policy should be deployed to the device group if the user doesn't enroll the device. By using device groups, Azure administrators can use compliancy reporting to ensure that the devices meet complexity.

Conditional Access

The Conditional Access options in Azure (see Figure 11.1) allow an Azure AD administrator to set security policies. When it comes to Azure, one of the biggest concerns for organizations is cloud-based security. Azure allows users to access their networks from anywhere in the world and from almost any device. Because of this, just securing resource access is not enough. This is the purpose of conditional access policies. As you'll recall, we discussed conditional access in detail in Chapter 9, "Managing Identity and Access."

FIGURE 11.1   Conditional Access: Policies section of Azure AD

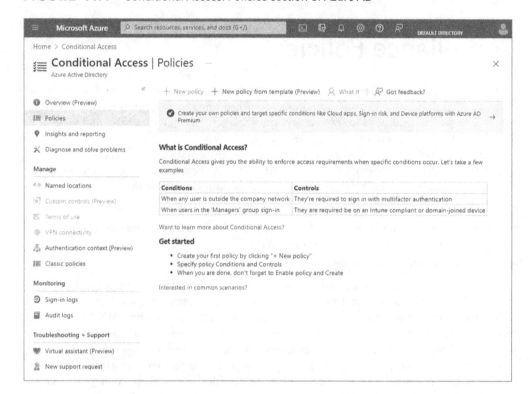

Conditional access policies allow an organization to set how resources are accessed using access control decisions through Azure AD. Some of the situations that conditional access policies can help with are sign-in risk, network location risk, device management, and client applications.

With Conditional Access

If a device complies with the policy rules that you have configured, that device can get access to data, email, and other company resources. If the device does not meet the minimum policies that you have set up, that device will not have access to any of the company's resources. This is how conditional access works.

Without Conditional Access

If you decide that you do not want to use conditional access, you can still use compliance policies. With compliance policies without conditional access, you can still access reports showing the device compliance status. Administrators can then evaluate this information and decide if conditional access is needed or if you can continue to use Azure without any conditional access policies.

Plan Device Compliance Policies

Mobile Device Management (MDM) solutions can help you protect your data by making sure users and devices meet certain requirements.

Compliance policies are the settings and rules that need to be met in order for your users and devices to be compliant. They include the actions that will result if a device is not compliant. Compliance policies can also be combined with conditional access, which blocks the users and devices that don't meet your requirements.

Compliance policies have two parts: compliance policy settings and device compliance policy. Compliance policy settings are the tenant-wide settings that every device will receive. Device compliance policies are the platform-specific rules that you deploy to groups of users or devices. To be compliant, the devices must meet these rules.

Many companies have laws and regulations that must be met in order to be compliant. To remain compliant, be sure to configure and manage your devices in accordance with those requirements. Examples of these regulations include:

- General Data Protection Regulation (GDPR) consists of the ground rules for collecting personal data from any individual residing in the European Union. It enforces the accountability for processing personal data and sets up countermeasures in the event of a data breach.

- Gramm–Leach–Bliley Act is a U.S. federal law that requires financial institutions to explain how they share and protect their customers' private information.

- The Health Insurance Portability and Accountability Act of 1996 (HIPPA) is a U.S. federal law that protects patient health information from being disclosed without the patient's consent. HIPPA requires data privacy and security provisions for safeguarding medical information. The law has emerged into greater importance recently with the explosion of health data breaches caused by cyberattacks and ransomware attacks on health insurers and providers.

- Sarbanes–Oxley Act is a U.S. federal law that was created to protect investors by making corporate disclosure more reliable and accurate. CEOs and CFOs must review all financial reports and ensure that the reports do not contain misrepresentations. Your goal is to keep financial data secure and free from any tampering, theft, and deletion.

Examples of device compliance policies include rules that specify whether devices must be running a minimum OS version and that a jailbroken or rooted device not be used.

Creating a Device Compliance Policy

To create a compliance policy, the Azure administrator needs to ensure that a few steps are completed before creating the policies. The following requirements are needed to set up compliance policies:

- Subscriptions
  - Microsoft Intune.
  - To use conditional access, your organization needs Azure AD Premium edition. If using Intune compliance only, your organization doesn't require an Azure AD subscription.
- Supported platforms
  - Android Device Administrator
  - Android AOSP (preview)
  - Android Enterprise
  - iOS/iPadOS
  - macOS
  - Windows 8.1 and later
  - Windows 10/11

The administrator must also enroll devices in Intune (which is required to see the compliance status). It is also necessary to enroll the devices for one user or enroll the device without a primary user assigned. Enrolling devices to multiple users is not supported.

Once you have ensured that your organization has met the minimum requirements to set up compliance policies, then the next step is to create the policy. The following steps will walk you through the process:

1. Sign into the Microsoft Endpoint Manager admin center at `https://endpoint .microsoft.com`.
2. Select Devices ➤ Compliance Policies ➤ Policies ➤ Create Policy.
3. Select a platform for the policy, you can use one of the options listed above under supported platforms. For Android Enterprise, you can also select a policy type: Fully Managed, Dedicated, Corporate-Owned Work Profile, or Personally-Owned Work Profile.
4. Click Create to open the Create Policy Configuration window.
5. On the Basics tab, specify a Name and a Description.
6. On the Compliance Settings tab, expand the available categories and configure all the settings you want for your policy.
7. On the Actions For Noncompliance tab, specify a sequence of actions to apply automatically to devices that don't meet this compliance policy. You can add multiple actions and configure schedules and additional details for some actions.

8. On the Scope tags tab, select tags to help filter policies to specific groups, if desired.

9. On the Assignments tab, assign the policy to your groups by clicking + Select Groups, then include and assign the policy to one or more groups.

10. On the Review + Create tab, review the settings and click Create when you're ready to save the compliance policy.

Now, when your users or devices that are targeted by the policy check in with Intune, they will be evaluated for compliance. The policy is now created and it will now show up in the policy list.

Monitoring Device Compliance

Within Intune there is a dashboard that will show you the compliance status of devices. This will help you learn why a device failed to meet the compliance configurations and see if there are any compliance-related problems. You can view the overall compliance states of devices, check the status of individual settings and policies, and dig deeper into specific settings and policies to see how they will affect devices.

To open the Intune Device Compliance dashboard:

1. Sign into the Microsoft Endpoint Manager admin center at `https://endpoint .microsoft.com`.

2. Select Devices ➤ Overview.

3. Select the Compliance Status tab (shown in Figure 11.2).

FIGURE 11.2 Compliance Status tab in the Devices section

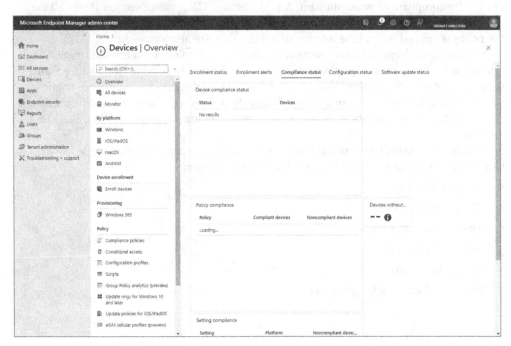

When the dashboard opens, you will see an overview of all the compliance reports. You can use these reports to view the overall device compliance, view the policy compliance, and the setting compliance.

The Compliance Status section shows the compliance states for all your Intune-enrolled devices. The device compliance states are kept in the Intune and Azure AD databases. The states include:

- Compliant means that one or more device compliance policy settings has been successfully applied.

- In-Grace Period means that a device has been targeted with a device compliance policy but the policy hasn't been applied yet by the user. It is basically not compliant, but the device is still within the grace period that you established.

- Not Evaluated is the initial state for newly enrolled devices, but there are some other reasons that a device may fall under this status. These include: devices that haven't been assigned a compliance policy, devices that haven't checked in since an updated compliance policy, devices not associated to a specific user, and devices enrolled with a device enrollment manager (DEM) account.

- Not-Compliant means that the device failed to apply one or more of the device compliance policy settings or the user hasn't complied with the policies.

- Device Not Synced means that a device failed to report its device compliance policy status because the device is offline or failed to communicate with Intune or Azure AD, or the device received an error message.

The Policy Compliance section shows the policies that have been set up and how many devices are compliant or noncompliant. And the Setting Compliance section shows all the device compliance policy settings for all the different compliance policies, the platforms that the policy is applied to, and the number of devices that are noncompliant.

You can delve deeper into each section by clicking on it to obtain more information. For example, if you are showing devices as not compliant in the device Compliance Status section, you can click the Not Compliant section to open the Device Compliance window, which will display the devices in a Device Status chart. This will show you additional details regarding the devices, including their operating system platform, when they last checked in, and more.

In addition to using the charts in Compliance Status, you can go to Reports ➤ Device Compliance. Some of the available compliance reports you can view are:

- Device compliance
- Noncompliant devices
- Devices without compliance policy
- Setting compliance
- Policy compliance
- Noncompliant policies (preview)

- Windows health attestation report
- Threat agent status

Migrating Policies to MDM

Once your organization decides to move to Azure, one of the tasks that an administrator will need to consider is moving on-site Group Policy object settings (GPOs) to MDM. You must analyze your current GPOs and figure out what needs to be moved to the MDM management tool in Azure.

Microsoft understands that GPO analysis needs to be done and that's why they developed the MDM Migration Analysis Tool (MMAT) to help administrators complete this task. MMAT looks at your organization's GPOs to see which ones have been created for a user or computer. MMAT then generates a report that shows you which equivalent MDM policies will need to be set. The report that MMAT generates can be in both XML and HTML formats.

Microsoft is starting to phase out MMAT. If you are currently using MMAT, then it's another utility that can help you out. If you are not currently using MMAT, I would recommend using newer Azure/Microsoft tools.

If your Azure administrator decides that they want to use the MMAT, they will need to complete the following steps:

1. Install the Remote Server Administration Tools.
2. Install the zipped folder for MMAT to your computer and unzip the folder.
3. Open Windows PowerShell as an administrator.
4. In PowerShell, change the directory location to where you installed the MMAT files (these files include PowerShell scripts).
5. Run the following PowerShell script:

```
Set-ExecutionPolicy -ExecutionPolicy Unrestricted -Scope
Process $VerbosePreference="Continue" ./Invoke-
MdmMigrationAnalysisTool.ps1 -collectGPOReports -
runAnalysisTool
```

After the `Invoke-MdmMigrationAnalysisTool.ps1` script has run, the Azure administrator will have three reports that they can look at:

MDMMigrationAnalysis.xml   This file is the XML version of the MMAT report, and it contains information about the policies that are set for the targeted user and computer. It will also show you how these policies map to MDM.

MDMMigrationAnalysis.html   This file is the HTML version of the same XML report.

MDMMigrationAnalysisTool.log   This file is a log file that will give Azure administrators more information about how the MMAT tool ran.

Device Configuration Profiles

Another way to set up Intune rules as an administrator is a *device configuration profile*. Profiles work like policies since they are another way to use rules for your Intune devices.

Intune, along with device configuration profiles, allows an administrator to configure settings and features that can be enabled or disabled on the various devices that your users will connect with.

Device Configuration Profile Options

Device configuration profile settings and features are added to your configuration profiles. Administrators can build these profiles for devices and platforms, including iOS, Android, and Windows. After these profiles are built, then an Intune administrator can apply or assign these profiles to their devices. These device configuration settings and features can include some of the following:

Administrative Templates   Administrative templates have hundreds of Windows 10 (and above) settings that an administrator can set for programs and features such as Microsoft Edge, OneDrive, Office, and other programs. These settings are very similar to setting up GPOs but they are all cloud-based settings.

Certificates   Certificate settings allow an Intune administrator to configure certificates for applications like Wi-Fi, VPN, and email profiles. These settings can be configured for many different devices, including Android and Android Enterprise, iOS and macOS, Windows 8.1, and Windows 10 and later.

Custom Profile   Custom profile settings allow an Intune Administrator to configure options that are not automatically included with Intune. For example, an administrator can set a custom profile that allows you to create an ADMX-backed policy or enable self-service password resets. Custom profiles let you set options for Android and Android Enterprise, iOS and macOS, and Windows 10/11 devices.

Delivery Optimization   Delivery optimization allows Intune administrators to set up and configure updates to Windows 10 (and above) devices that connect to the cloud.

Device Features   Device features make it easy for administrators to configure iOS/iPadOS and macOS devices. These settings allow administrators to configure things like AirPrint, notifications, and lock screen messages.

Device Restrictions   Device restrictions allow an Intune administrator to configure settings for things like hardware, data, and security settings on your devices. Device restrictions can be created to prevent iOS/iPadOS device users from using their device's camera. Device restrictions can be used on Android and Android Enterprise, iOS/iPadOS, macOS, Windows 10 Team, and Windows 10 and later devices.

Edition Upgrade   Edition Upgrade allows you to upgrade Windows 10 (and later) devices to a newer version of Windows.

Email   Email options allow you to create, monitor, and assign Exchange ActiveSync email settings for your devices. For example, email profiles allow your users to access your organization's email while using their personal devices. Email options can be set for Android Device Administrator, Android Enterprise, iOS/iPadOS, Windows, and Windows 10 and later devices.

Endpoint Protection   Endpoint Protection allows you to set Windows 10 (and above) options for BitLocker and Windows Defender settings. For example, you can set Windows Defender for a threat score setting. If a user with a high threat score rating attempts to access cloud-based resources, you can stop this device from accessing your resources.

Identity Protection   Identity Protection allows an Intune administrator to control the Windows Hello for Business experience on Windows client devices. Identity protection settings allow you to configure options for devices such as PINs and gestures for Windows Hello for Business.

Kiosk   Kiosk settings allow an administrator to configure a Windows 10 (and later) device to run a single application or run many applications. Kiosk systems are normally designed for use in a location where many people can use the same device and that device will run only limited applications. Administrators have the ability to customize other features, including a Start Menu and a web browser. Kiosk settings are also available for Android, Android Enterprise, and iOS/iPadOS devices, but you need to configure these devices as device restrictions so they can still function as Kiosk devices, although they're configured differently.

Shared Multiuser Device   Shared multiuser devices are devices used by multiple users to perform day-to-day activities. This is different than a kiosk-based machine in that kiosk-based machines are used by many users but they run limited programs, whereas shared multiuser devices are devices that users use to do their job while at work but other users will use the same device. These devices normally run all of the organization's software so that people can do their jobs. For example, if you are in an environment where you have shift workers, you may have multiple shifts, and different people will use a machine when they are working during their shift.

Shared multiuser device settings allow an administrator to control many of the devices' features and manage these shared devices through Intune.

 To see a complete or updated list of device configuration profile settings, please visit Microsoft's website at http://docs.microsoft.com/en-us/intune/device-profiles.

Building Device Configuration Profiles

Intune includes settings and features you can either enable or disable on a variety of devices. These settings and features are added to configuration profiles. You can create profiles for different devices on several platforms, including iOS/iPadOS, Android Device Administrator, Android Enterprise, and Windows. Then, you use Intune to assign the profile to the devices.

As part of your MDM solution, you can use these configuration profiles to perform various tasks. Intune has a wide selection of templates that include groups of settings that are specific to a feature, such as certificates, VPN, email, and more.

One nice advantage is that building device configuration profiles work a lot like building device compliances. Many of the same settings are available as you build the device configuration profile.

To build a device configuration profile, complete the following steps:

1. Sign into the Microsoft Endpoint Manager admin center at `https://endpoint .microsoft.com`.

2. Select Devices ➢ Overview (shown in Figure 11.3). Administrators can choose from the following options:

FIGURE 11.3   Devices: Overview screen

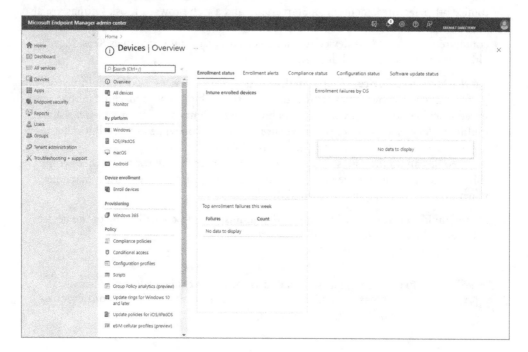

- **Overview:** This will show you the status of your profiles and provides additional details on the different profiles that you have assigned to your users and devices.
- **Monitor:** This screen allows an administrator to check the status of profiles for success or failure, as well as view logs on the profiles.
- **By platform:** This section allows an administrator to create and view policies and profiles by platform. This view may also show specific platform features.
- **Policy:** This option allows an administrator to create device profiles, upload custom PowerShell scripts, and add data plans to devices using eSIM.

3. Click Configuration Profiles, as shown in Figure 11.4.

FIGURE 11.4   Devices: Configuration Profiles page

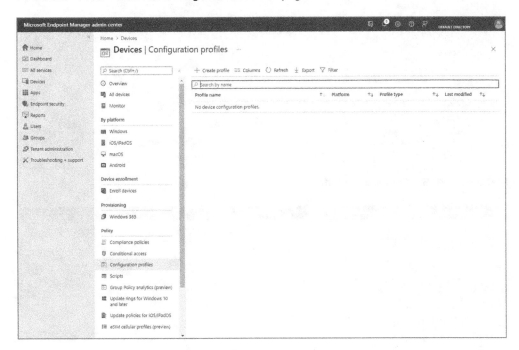

4. Click + Create Profile to create a profile, as shown in Figure 11.5.
5. When you create a profile, you can choose your platform, as shown in Figure 11.6, and then choose the profile type.

FIGURE 11.5   The Create Profile page

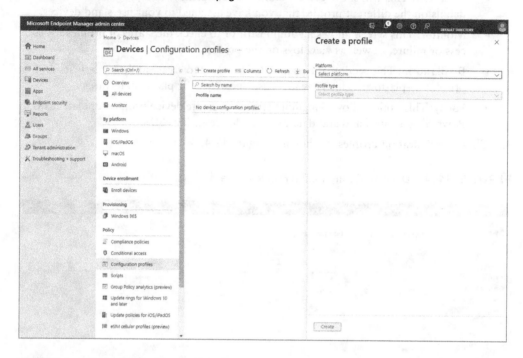

FIGURE 11.6   Choosing a platform

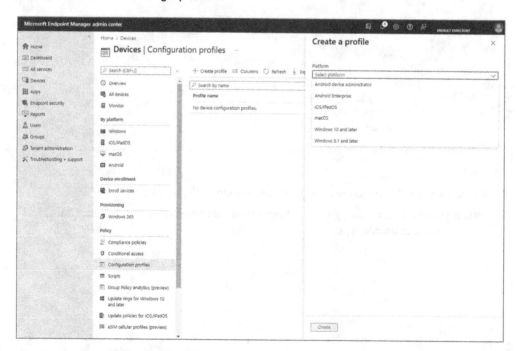

Depending on the platform you select, the settings that you can configure will be different. There are a wide variety of profile types to choose from:

- Administrative Templates (Windows)
- Custom
- Delivery Optimization (Windows)
- Derived Credential (Android Enterprise, iOS, iPadOS)
- Device Features (macOS, iOS, iPadOS)
- Device Firmware (Windows)
- Device Restrictions
- Domain Join (Windows)
- Edition Upgrade and Mode Switch (Windows)
- Education (iOS, iPadOS)
- Email
- Endpoint Protection (macOS, Windows)
- Extensions (macOS)
- Identity Protection (Windows)
- Kiosk
- Microsoft Defender for Endpoint (Windows)
- Mobility Extensions (MX) Profile (Android Device Administrator)
- Network Boundary (Windows)
- OEMConfig (Android Enterprise)
- PKCS Certificate
- PKCS Imported Certificate
- Preference File (macOS)
- SCEP Certificate
- Secure Assessment (Education) (Windows)
- Shared Multi-User Device (Windows)
- Telecom Expenses (Android Device Administrator, iOS, iPadOS)
- Trusted Certificate
- VPN
- Wi-Fi
- Windows Health Monitoring
- Wired Networks (macOS)

6.   Once you select your platform and profile type, click Create. You will now see tabs along the top that include Basics, Configuration Settings, Scope tags, Assignments, and Review + Create.

7.   In Basics, enter the following properties and then click Next:

   ▪   **Name:** Enter a descriptive name for the profile.

   ▪   **Description:** Enter a description for the profile. This setting is optional but recommended.

8.   In the Configuration settings, select All Settings to see an alphabetical list of all the settings. Or, you can configure settings that apply to devices (Computer Configuration) and settings that apply to users (User Configuration). Select the options you wish and then click OK to save your changes and click Next.

9.   On the Scope Tags (Optional) page, assign a tag to filter the profile to specific groups, and then click Next.

10.   On the Assignments page, select the user or groups that will receive the profile, and then click Next.

11.   Finally, on Review + Create page, review the settings you set. When you click Create, your changes will be saved and the profile will be assigned. The policy will also appear in the profiles list.

Monitoring and Troubleshooting Device Configuration Profiles

Intune has several features that help you monitor and manage device configuration profiles. When you create your device profile, Intune shows graphical charts that display the profile status, such as whether the profile is being assigned to devices successfully or there is a conflict.

To view existing profiles, sign into the Microsoft Endpoint Manager admin center, then select Devices ➢ Configuration Profiles. You will see a list of all your profiles, including the platform, the type of profile, and whether the profile is assigned.

To see additional information about a particular profile, click the profile. Then, select the Overview tab, which shows the profile assignment status:

Succeeded   The policy was successfully applied.

Error   Intune failed to apply the policy and displays an error code with a link to an explanation.

Conflict   This status indicates that two settings are applied to the same device and Intune can't sort out the conflict. When this happens, be sure to review the policy.

Pending   The device hasn't yet checked in with Intune to receive the policy.

Not Applicable   The device can't receive the policy.

In the Profiles list, you can also modify and edit the profile. When you click a profile, it will open the profile overview page, as shown in Figure 11.7. You can use the options under

Properties to change the name of the policy or modify the configuration settings that are currently in effect. To edit the scope tags used in a policy, under Scope Tags, click Edit to add or remove a scope tag. To edit the users and groups that receive a policy, under Assignments, click Edit. This will allow you to update the policy assignment and to add or remove a filter. To edit the Applicability Rules, in this section click Edit to add or remove applicability rules.

On the Properties Overview page, you will also see the device and user check-in status. This indicates the number of users or devices that have checked in using your selected profile. If you click the View Report button shown in Figure 11.7, you can see which devices received the profile, the usernames with devices that received the profile, and the check-in status, including the last time the user or device checked in with the profile.

FIGURE 11.7   Device: Configuration Profile properties

The Device Assignment Status section allows you to generate a report to see the latest profile assignment states for devices that have received the selected profile. You also have the ability to filter the assignment status to search for particular statuses.

The Per Setting Status section displays the individual settings within the profile and their status.

Viewing Conflicts

By selecting Devices ➢ All Devices, you can see if any settings are causing a conflict. If there is a conflict, you can see all the profiles that may contain the conflicting setting. This allows you to troubleshoot and fix any discrepancies.

If a device displays a Conflict state, then select that row. In the new window, you see all the profiles and the profile names that have the setting that is causing the conflict.

Troubleshooting Device Configuration Profiles

If there happen to be two or more policies assigned to the same user or device, then the setting that gets applied happens at the individual setting level:

- Compliance policy settings always take precedence over configuration profile settings.

- If a compliance policy evaluates against the same setting in another compliance policy, then the most restrictive compliance policy setting gets applied.

- If a configuration policy setting conflicts with a setting in another configuration policy, this conflict is shown in Intune. You will manually need to resolve these conflicts.

Another way to troubleshoot device configuration policies and profiles is by using the built-in Troubleshooting + Support option, shown in Figure 11.8. This feature allows you to review different compliance and configuration statuses.

FIGURE 11.8   Troubleshooting + Support option

To use the built-in Troubleshoot pane, perform the following steps:

1. In the Microsoft Endpoint Manager admin center, select Troubleshooting + Support ➢ Troubleshoot, as shown in Figure 11.9.

2. Click Select User and then select the user having an issue. Then click Select.

3. Confirm that both the Intune License and Account Status each show green check marks.

FIGURE 11.9   Troubleshoot options

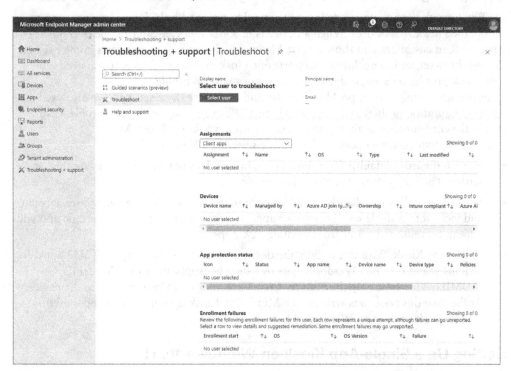

4. Under Devices, locate the device that is having an issue. There are different columns here:

- **Managed:** For a device to receive a compliance or configuration policy, this property must show MDM or EAS/MDM. If you do not see MDM or EAS/MDM, that means the device is not enrolled. It will not receive a compliance policy until it has been enrolled.

- **Azure AD Join Type:** This should be set to Workplace or AzureAD. If this column is showing a status of Not Registered, then there may be an issue with enrollment. You can unenroll and re-enroll the device to help resolve this issue.

- **Intune Compliant:** This column should show Yes. If you see No, there may be an issue with a compliance policy or the device isn't connected to the Intune service.

- **Azure AD Compliant:** This column should show Yes. If you see No, then there may be an issue with a compliance policy or the device isn't connected to the Intune service.

- **Last Check In:** This column shows a time and date of last check-in. By default, Intune devices check in every 8 hours.

Configuring and Implementing Assigned Access on Public Devices

On Windows devices, you can use Intune to run devices as a kiosk. These devices are sometimes called *dedicated* devices. When a device is in Kiosk mode, it can run one or more apps. Also, you can customize and show a Start Menu, add different apps, specify a home page on the web browser, and more. Intune supports one kiosk profile per device. If you need multiple kiosk profiles on a single device, you can use a custom profile.

Intune uses configuration profiles to create and customize these settings. We discussed creating configuration profiles earlier in this chapter. When creating the kiosk's profile, ensure that in the configuration settings you choose the option Select A Kiosk Mode.

Intune includes several options when you're selecting a Kiosk mode:

- **Not Configured (default):** With this option, Intune does not change or update this setting. The policy doesn't enable Kiosk mode.

- **Single App, Full-Screen Kiosk:** With this option, the device runs as a single-user account and locks it to a single web browser or app. So, when the user logs in, a specific app will appear, preventing the user from opening new apps.

- **Multi-App Kiosk:** With this option, the device runs multiple Store apps, Win32 apps, web browsers, or inbox Windows apps by using the Application User Model ID (AUMID). However, only the apps that you have added will be available on the device. At the time this book was written, the Multi-App Kiosk option is only supported on Windows 10 and not on Windows 11.

Setting Up a Single-App Kiosk on Windows 10/11

A single-app kiosk uses the Assigned Access feature to run a single app above the lock screen. When the kiosk account signs in, the app will be automatically started. The person who is using the kiosk will not be able to do anything else on the device other than use what you set up in the profile. Using Kiosk mode over a remote desktop connection is not supported.

The kiosk users must sign in on a physical device that has been set up as the kiosk device. Users will not be able to copy and paste when apps are run in Kiosk mode.

You have several options for configuring your single-app kiosk:

- On the device, locally in Settings, select the Set Up A Kiosk (which was previously called Set Up Assigned Access) option. This option is supported in Windows 10 Pro, Enterprise, and Education, and Windows 11.

- PowerShell: You can use Windows PowerShell cmdlets to set up a single-app kiosk. First, you need to create the user account on the device and install the kiosk app for that account. This option is supported in Windows 10 Pro, Enterprise, and Education, and Windows 11.

- Windows Configuration Designer (WCD): You can use the kiosk wizard in WCD. WCD is a tool that produces a provisioning package. A provisioning package includes configuration settings that can be applied to one or more devices during the first-run experience (OOBE), or after OOBE is done (runtime). We discussed provisioning packages in Chapter 4, "Managing the Windows Client Environment." By using the kiosk wizard, you can create the kiosk user account, install the kiosk app, and configure your required settings. This option is supported in Windows 10 Pro version 1709+, Enterprise, and Education, and Windows 11.

- Microsoft Endpoint Manager or another Mobile Device Management (MDM) provider: You can use MDM to set up a kiosk configuration for your devices. When creating the profile, the Configuration Profiles window is where you select the option to create a profile; then select Kiosk, as shown in Figure 11.10, and set your required options, as shown in Figure 11.11.

FIGURE 11.10 Creating a kiosk profile in Endpoint Manager

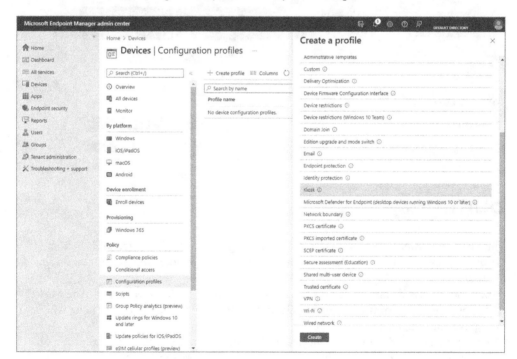

FIGURE 11.11   Kiosk Configuration Settings window

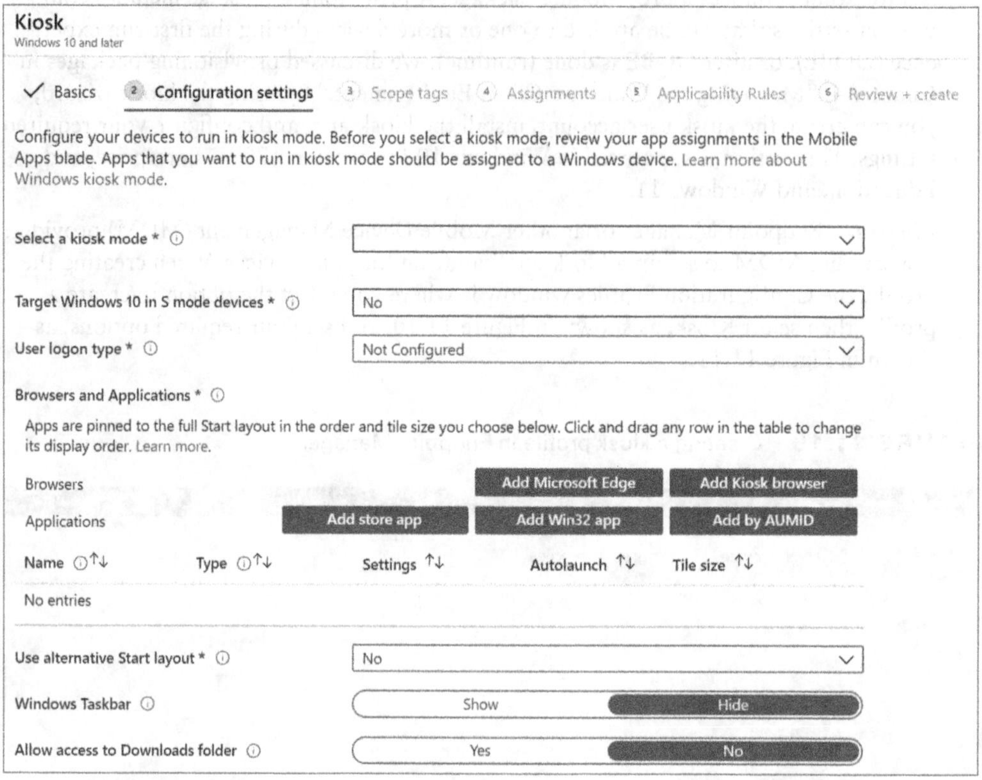

Summary

This chapter showed how compliance policies, along with conditional access, help administrators stop users and devices that don't follow the rules that your organization has deemed necessary for access.

We also discussed converting on-site GPOs to MDM using the MMAT tool. The MMAT tool allows an administrator to analyze GPOs and determine which MDM policies will be the equivalent setting.

Finally, you learned about using device configuration profiles. Device configuration profiles work like GPO policies but they are designed strictly for cloud-based rules.

Exam Essentials

Know how compliance policies work. Understand how compliance policies, along with conditional access, ensures that administrators can stop users and devices that don't follow the rules that your organization has determined as necessary for access.

Understand how to use MMAT. Understand that GPO analysis needs to be done and how the MDM Migration Analysis Tool (MMAT) helps administrators complete this task.

Know how to create device configuration profiles. Know how to add settings and features to your configuration profiles. Administrators can build these profiles for devices and platforms, including iOS, Android, and Windows, and these settings are for cloud-based Intune devices.

Video Resources

There are no videos for this chapter.

Review Questions

1. You are the administrator for an organization that has 100 devices that run Windows 10 Pro. The devices are joined to Azure AD and enrolled in Intune. You need to upgrade the computers to Windows 10 Enterprise. What should you configure in Intune?

    A. A device enrollment policy

    B. A device cleanup rule

    C. A device compliance policy

    D. A device configuration profile

2. You are creating a device configuration profile in Intune. You need to implement an ADMX-backed policy. Which profile type should you use?

    A. Identity protection

    B. Custom

    C. Device restrictions

    D. Device restrictions (Windows 10 Team)

3. You are the network administrator for a large training organization. Your organization plans to deploy Windows client tablets to 50 meeting rooms. These tablets will be managed by using Intune. The tablets have an application named Storm1 that many users will use. You need to configure the tablets so that any user can use Storm1 without having to sign in. Users must not be able to use other applications on the tablets. Which device configuration profile type should you use?

    A. Kiosk

    B. Endpoint protection

    C. Identity protection

    D. Device restrictions

4. You have 175 computers that run Windows 10/11. The computers are joined to Azure AD and enrolled in Intune. You have been asked to enable self-service password reset on the sign-in screen. Which settings should you configure in Microsoft Intune?

    A. Device configuration

    B. Device compliance

    C. Device enrollment

    D. Conditional access

5. You and a colleague are discussing a law that regulates how financial institutions handle their customers' personal information. What is this law called?

    A. Federal Information Processing Standard (FIPS) Publication 140-2 (FIPS PUB 140-2)

    B. Gramm–Leach–Bliley Act of 1999 (GLBA)

    C. Health Insurance Portability and Accountability Act of 1996 (HIPPA)

    D. Sarbanes–Oxley Act of 2002

6. You are the administrator for your company network. Your company has several hundred Windows client computers that are managed by using Intune. Windows updates are currently being downloaded without using Delivery Optimization. What should you do in Intune if you'd like to configure the computers to use Delivery Optimization?

    A. Configure an app protection policy.

    B. Create a device configuration profile.

    C. Configure a device compliance policy.

    D. Configure a Windows 10 update ring.

7. You are the administrator for your company network. Your company has a Microsoft 365 subscription. You manage all devices using Intune. The company uses conditional access to restrict access to Microsoft 365 services for devices that do not comply with the company's security policies. What should you use if you need to identify which devices will be prevented from accessing Microsoft 365 services?

    A. The Conditional Access blade in the Azure Active Directory admin center

    B. The Device Compliance blade in the Intune admin center

    C. The Device Health solution in Desktop Analytics

    D. The Windows Defender Security Center

8. You are the administrator for your company network. You and a colleague are discussing which law requires that healthcare-related organizations must be in compliance with certain security standards. What is this law called?

    A. Federal Information Processing Standard (FIPS) Publication 140-2 (FIPS PUB 140-2)

    B. Gramm-Leach-Bliley Act of 1999 (GLBA)

    C. Health Insurance Portability and Accountability Act of 1996 (HIPPA)

    D. Sarbanes-Oxley Act of 2002

9. You have been asked by your boss to set up a device configuration profile in Intune to allow your users to be able to reset their own passwords. Which device configuration profile option should you configure in Intune?

    A. Kiosk

    B. Endpoint Protection

    C. Identity Protection

    D. Custom

10. Your company uses Intune to manage all devices. The company uses conditional access to restrict access to Microsoft 365 services for devices that do not comply with the company's security policies. You want to view which devices will be prevented from accessing Microsoft 365 services. What should you use?

    A. The Device Health solution in Windows Analytics

    B. The Windows Defender Security Center

    C. Device compliance in the Intune admin center

    D. The Conditional access blade in the Azure Active Directory admin center

11. You are the administrator for your company network. Your company plans to deploy tablets to all of your conference rooms. The tablets are managed using Intune and have a corporate application installed. You want to configure the tablets so that any user can use the app without having to sign in. The users must be prevented from using other applications on the tablets. What device configuration profile type should you use?

- **A.** The Device restrictions profile type
- **B.** The Endpoint Protection profile type
- **C.** The Identity Protection profile type
- **D.** The Kiosk profile type

12. You are the administrator for your company network. You and a colleague are discussing setting up a device in the lobby that will run a corporate line-of-business (LOB) app. What is this device known as if it will only serve the function of running this corporate app?

- **A.** Computer stall
- **B.** Kiosk
- **C.** Rotunda
- **D.** Stand-alone computer

13. You are the administrator for your company network. You and a colleague are discussing a set of rules put onto devices that allow them access to resources within your organization by using Intune. What are these sets of rules known as?

- **A.** Accordance policies
- **B.** Compliance policies
- **C.** Device rules
- **D.** System compliance policies

14. You are the administrator for your company network. You and a colleague are discussing creating Intune policies. There is a setting that you can assign and filter policies to specific groups. What is the name of this item that you can add to a profile?

- **A.** Device groups
- **B.** Intune licenses
- **C.** Roles
- **D.** Scope tags

15. You are the administrator for your company network. You and a colleague are discussing reports and how to customize the view to meet your needs. You want to generate a custom device inventory report to show the Device Name, Managed By, and OS Version information. What should you modify to see the needed information?

- **A.** Columns
- **B.** Export
- **C.** Filter
- **D.** Refresh

16. You are the administrator for your company network. You and a colleague are discussing common issues and troubleshooting when using Intune policies and profiles. Which statement is true when two profile settings are applied to the same device?

A. When two profile settings are applied to the same device, the most restrictive value will be applied.

B. When two profile settings are applied to the same device, the least restrictive value will be applied.

C. When two profile settings are applied to the same device, both values will be applied.

D. When two profile settings are applied to the same device, neither value will be applied.

17. You are the administrator for your company network. You and a colleague are discussing the time it takes for a Windows 10/11–enrolled device to check in with Intune. What is the default time that it takes for the device to check in?

A. Every hour

B. Every 4 hours

C. Every 8 hours

D. Once a day

18. You are the administrator for your company network. You and a colleague are discussing device profiles. You are discussing a profile type that will allow you to run devices as a dedicated device. What is this profile type called?

A. Administrative Templates

B. Device Restrictions

C. Kiosk

D. Windows Information Protection

19. You are the administrator for your company network. You and a colleague are discussing compliance policy and configuration policy interactions. Which of the following statements is *not* true regarding how the policies will interact?

A. Compliance policy settings will take priority over configuration profile settings.

B. Configuration profile settings will take priority over compliance policy settings.

C. If you have a compliance policy and it includes the same settings that are found in another compliance policy, then the most restrictive setting will be applied.

D. If you have a configuration policy setting that clashes with the setting in another configuration policy, then the issue will be displayed in Intune, and the administrator will need to resolve the issue manually.

20. You are the administrator for your company network. You and a colleague are discussing systems that are normally designed to be in one location where many people can use them. This is usually the same device, and that device will run only a limited number of applications. What is this called?

A. Computer stalls

B. Kiosks

C. Rotundas

D. Stand-alone computers

Chapter

12

Managing Security

MICROSOFT EXAM OBJECTIVES COVERED IN THIS CHAPTER:

✓ **Plan and implement endpoint protection**

  ▪ Plan endpoint security; implement and manage security base-
    lines in Intune; create and manage configuration policies for
    Endpoint Security including antivirus, encryption, firewall,
    endpoint detection and response, and attack surface reduction;
    onboard devices into Microsoft Defender for Endpoint; mon-
    itor Microsoft Defender for Endpoint; investigate and respond
    to threats.

This chapter dives into ways of protecting Windows clients by using tools such as Windows Security and the Microsoft Defender Admin Center. You'll learn what endpoints are and how to protect them.

We'll discuss how to implement and manage security baselines in Intune as well as how to create and manage configuration policies for Endpoint Security. Then you'll learn how to onboard devices into Defender for Endpoint and how to investigate and respond to threats.

Finally, we'll discuss other ways to protect your devices and data by using tools such as Microsoft Defender Application Guard, Microsoft Defender Credential Guard, Microsoft Defender Exploit Guard, and Windows Defender Application Control.

Windows Security

Windows Security is built into Windows and includes an antivirus program called Microsoft Defender Antivirus. In early versions of Windows 10, Windows Security was called Microsoft Defender Security Center. Windows Security is where the tools that protect a device and data can be found. This is one of many ways that you can protect your system.

Windows Security can be accessed in a number of ways in both Windows 10/11. One way, in Windows 10, is by going to Start ➤ Settings ➤ Update & Security ➤ Windows Security, as shown in Figure 12.1.

In Windows 11, you can access Windows Security by going to Start ➤ Settings ➤ Privacy & Security.

The protection areas include:

- **Virus & Threat Protection:** Here you can monitor threats to a device, run scans, and get updates to help detect the latest threats.

- **Account Protection:** Here you can access sign-in options and account settings, including Windows Hello and Dynamic Lock.

- **Firewall & Network Protection:** Here you can manage firewall settings and monitor your network and Internet connections.

- **App & Browser Control:** Here you can update settings for Microsoft Defender SmartScreen to help protect a device against potentially dangerous apps, files, sites, and downloads. You can also customize protection settings for the device.

- **Device Security:** Here you can review built-in security options to help protect a device from attacks by malicious software.

- **Device Performance & Health:** Here you can view the status information about a device's performance health, and keep the device clean and up-to-date with the latest version of Windows.

- **Family Options:** Here you can keep track of a child's online activity and the devices within your household.

You may notice status icons on the protection areas; these indicate the level of safety:

- Green indicates that there aren't any recommended actions that need to be taken right now.

- Yellow indicates that there is a safety recommendation.

- Red indicates that there is a warning that something needs immediate attention.

FIGURE 12.1   Windows Security in Windows 10

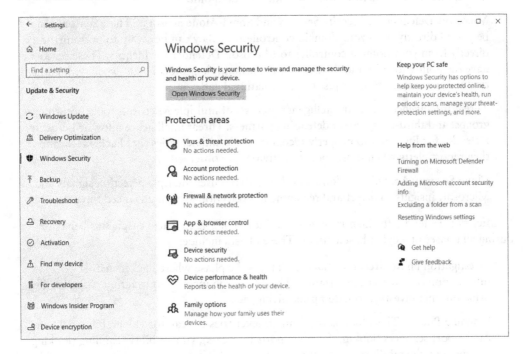

Planning and Implementing Endpoint Protection

When talking about Microsoft Defender, it can be a little confusing to people. The reason for this is that Windows 10/11 comes with Microsoft Defender, and Azure also now comes with Microsoft Defender. So, when IT people are discussing Defender, it's important that they specify which version they are talking about. We'll discuss Azure's version of Microsoft Defender and the benefits that it provides to organizations.

Microsoft Defender for Identity (previously called Azure Advanced Threat Protection) allows organizations to monitor domain controller traffic while Microsoft Defender for Endpoint (previously called Microsoft Defender Advanced Threat Protection) allows organizations to monitor endpoints (for example, users' devices). Organizations can use both of these defenses together for the best possible protection, and both can be managed by using a single Azure interface.

When deciding to integrate Microsoft Defender for Identity and Microsoft Defender for Endpoint together, you get the benefits of both systems working together. Some of these benefits are as follows:

Endpoint Behavioral Sensors   Endpoint behavioral sensors are sensors that are built into the Windows 10/11 operating system, and these sensors gather and process behavioral data for things like the Registry, files, processors, and communications. This data is then sent to the Microsoft Defender for Endpoint.

Microsoft Defender for Identity Sensors and Stand-Alone Sensors   These sensors can be placed directly onto your domain controllers, or they can be set up to port mirror directly from your domain controller to Microsoft Defender for Identity. These sensors have the ability to collect and parse traffic for multiple protocols that work with authentication or authorization, or just for informational gathering.

Threat Intelligence   Threat intelligence consists of multiple Microsoft tools, security groups, and third-party threat defending partners. Threat intelligence allows Microsoft Defender for Endpoint to properly recognize tools and activities that hackers use and then report alerts when those tools or activities are observed.

Cloud Security Analytics   Cloud security analytics uses multiple detection signals and Microsoft insights to detect and recommend protection against advanced threats.

Microsoft Defender for Identity uses several technologies to detect suspicious behavior during all phases of a cyber-based attack. These phases include:

Investigation Phase (Reconnaissance)   This is the phase where hackers gather information on a target organization. This phase can include information gathering by using Internet investigation, dumpster diving, etc.

Scanning Phase   This phase is when an attacker tries to scan for vulnerabilities. These can be port scanners (looking for open ports to access), vulnerability scanning (looking for known vulnerabilities), and network scanning (looking at network components like routers and firewalls).

Access Phase   This is the phase when hackers try to gain access to your network based on the investigation and scanning phases.

Maintaining Access Phase   This is the phase when hackers try to put back doors or software in place so that they can continue to gain access to your network.

Clearing Their Tracks Phase   Hackers who are any good will try to clear their tracks so that no one knows they were there. In this phase, hackers will try to delete logs and any evidence that the hack even took place.

Microsoft Defender for Endpoint uses Microsoft technologies and expertise to help detect and stop the different phases of a hacker. Microsoft has put in advanced methods to detect hacking before the hacks take place.

Endpoint Security

Endpoints are the devices that connect to a computer network. Endpoints include desktops, laptops, tablets, mobile devices, servers, IoT devices, virtual machines, and more. Endpoint security helps to protect these endpoints from cyberattacks by using a wide variety of services and solutions. The first endpoint security tools were the traditional antivirus and anti-malware software. Now, endpoint security has expanded to include more advanced cloud solutions. Some of the more common endpoint security risks are as follows:

Device Loss   This is when a device is physically lost, allowing an attacker to access important corporate information.

Drive-by Downloads   This type of attack uses the automated download of software to a device without the user's knowledge or consent.

Malware Ads   These attacks use online ads to spread malware and hack into systems.

Outdated Patches   If devices are not updated regularly, then this may expose vulnerabilities that will allow an attacker to break into a device and steal information.

Phishing   This attack is a form of social engineering attack that tricks the target into sharing sensitive information.

Ransomware   This is a malware attack that will hold the target's information or system hostage until the attacker is paid to release it.

Endpoint Security Best Practices

To help protect against cyberattacks, there are some best practices that you can follow. One of the more important things you can do is educate your users. When it comes to endpoint security, you are the first line of defense. Keep your users up-to-date on security and compliance training. Keep track of devices that are connected to your network, and make sure that your endpoints have the most current updates and patches. You can add another layer of protection to devices and information by encrypting your endpoints. You can implement strong passwords by using complex passwords, enforcing regular password updates, and prohibiting users from using old passwords.

Microsoft Defender for Endpoint was designed to help enterprise networks prevent, detect, investigate, and respond to advanced threats. It is a cloud-powered endpoint security solution that will help protect against ransomware, file-less malware, and other attacks on Windows, macOS, Linux, Android, and iOS.

Managing Endpoint Security in Microsoft Intune

You can use Intune to configure device security to manage security tasks for devices by using the Endpoint security node. Endpoint security policies are created to help you reduce risks and focus on device security. The Endpoint Security node (as shown in Figure 12.2) is where you will find the tools that you can use to keep your devices secure. You will be able to perform the following:

Create Compliance Policies   You can set up device and user requirements using compliance policies. These are the rules that devices and users must meet to be considered compliant. We discussed compliance policies in Chapter 11, "Managing Devices."

Deploy Security Baselines   Intune includes security baselines for Windows devices and a list of applications, such as Microsoft Defender for Endpoint and Microsoft Edge. The security baselines are preconfigured groups of Windows settings that help you apply a recommended configuration. We will discuss security baselines more in the next section.

Integrate Intune with Your Microsoft Defender for Endpoint Team   By integrating the two, you can access security tasks. Security tasks help your security team identify devices that may be at risk and include steps on how to correct any issues.

Manage Security Configurations   Endpoint security policies focus on device security such as antivirus, disk encryption, firewalls, and more through the use of Microsoft Defender for Endpoint.

Review Managed Device Statuses   You can use the All Devices section to see whether devices are in compliance, and if they're not, you can use this section to see how to resolve issues for the devices that are not in compliance.

Managing Security Baselines

In Intune, security baselines are preconfigured groups of settings that are best practice recommendations from the Microsoft security teams for that product. These recommendations protect your users and devices. Intune supports security baselines for Windows 10/11 device settings, Microsoft Edge, Microsoft Defender for Endpoint Protection, and more. Security baselines are supported for devices that run Windows 10 version 1809 and later, and Windows 11.

Prior to deploying security baselines, you can customize them in order to enforce only the settings and values you want. Because in most situations, the default settings of a security baseline are the most restrictive, you want to ensure that the default settings do not interfere with other policy settings you have established already. When you create a security baseline profile in Intune, you are creating a template that consists of multiple device configuration profiles. In Intune, security baselines are deployed to groups of users or devices.

FIGURE 12.2   Endpoint Security node

To access security baselines, go to the Microsoft Endpoint Manager admin center ➤ Endpoint Security ➤ Security Baselines (as shown in Figure 12.3). You will then see a list of all the available baselines. The list will show you the name of the baseline template, how many profiles you have that use that type of baseline, how many versions of the baseline type are available, and the last published date that shows when the latest version of the baseline template became available.

FIGURE 12.3   Security Baselines

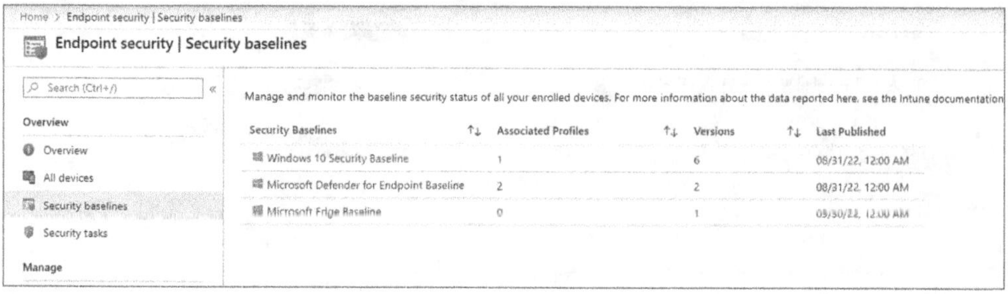

Security Baselines	Associated Profiles	Versions	Last Published
Windows 10 Security Baseline	1	6	08/31/22, 12:00 AM
Microsoft Defender for Endpoint Baseline	2	2	08/31/22, 12:00 AM
Microsoft Edge Baseline	0	1	08/30/22, 12:00 AM

In order to manage security baselines in Intune, you must have an account with the Policy and Profile Manager built-in role, and you may have to have an active subscription to additional services, such as Microsoft Defender for Endpoint.

Some common tasks when working with security baselines include creating a profile, changing the version, and removing a baseline assignment. To create a profile, follow these steps:

1. Sign into the Microsoft Endpoint Manager admin center, at `https://endpoint` `.microsoft.com`.

2. Select Endpoint Security ➤ Security Baselines to view the list of available baselines (as shown in Figure 12.3 earlier).

3. Select the baseline you want to use and then click Create Profile.

4. On the Basics tab, specify the Name and Description. The description is optional but we recommend that you include it. Then click Next to go to the next tab.

5. On the Configuration Settings tab, view the available baseline settings you can select. You can expand a group to view the settings in that group, and the default values for those settings in the baseline (as shown in Figure 12.4).

FIGURE 12.4   Security Baselines: Configuration Settings

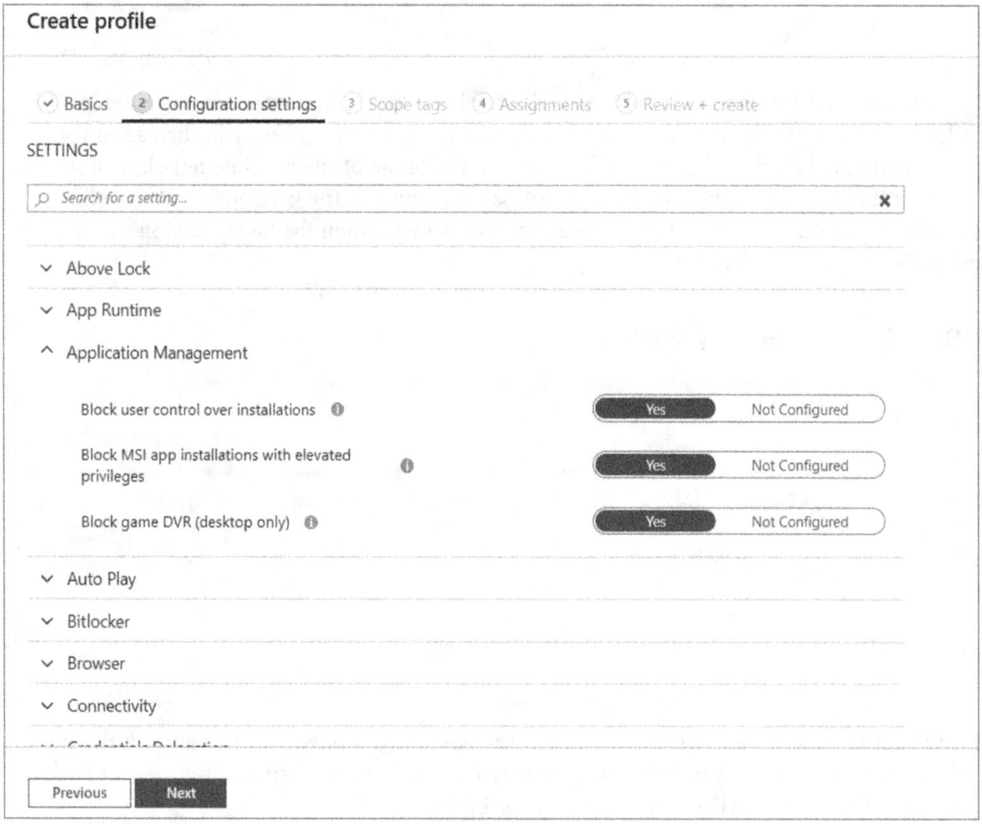

6. On the Scope Tags tab, click Select Scope Tags to open the Select Tags pane, where you can assign scope tags to the profile.

7. On the Assignments tab, click Select Groups To Include and then assign the baseline to one or more groups.

8. When you are ready to deploy the baseline, select the Review + Create tab and review the details for the baseline. Click Create to save and deploy the profile. As soon as the profile is created, it will be pushed to the assigned group and immediately applied.

Once a profile has been created, you can edit it by going to Endpoint Security ➤ Security Baselines, selecting the baseline type that you configured, and then selecting Profiles. Then, select the profile from the list of available profiles, and click Properties. You can edit settings from all the available configuration tabs, and click Review + Save to commit your changes.

Changing the Baseline Version for a Profile

There may be times where you need to change the baseline version for a profile. Perform the following steps to change the baseline version:

1. Sign into the Microsoft Endpoint Manager admin center at `https://endpoint.microsoft.com`.

2. Select Endpoint Security ➤ Security Baselines and then select the tile for the baseline type that has the profile you want to change.

3. Next, click Profiles, select the check box for the profile you want to edit, and then select Change Version, as shown in Figure 12.5.

FIGURE 12.5   Endpoint Security – Change Version

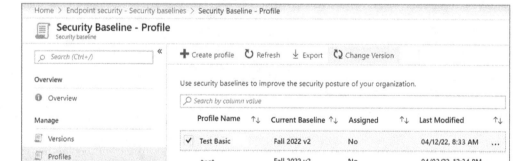

4. In the Change Version pane, open the Select A Security Baseline To Update To drop-down list, and select the version you want to use.

5. Click Review Update to download a CSV file that will display the differences between the profiles. Review the file so that you know which settings are new or removed, and what the default values for these settings are in the updated profile. When ready, continue to the next step.

6. Select one of the two options for Select A Method To Update The Profile:

   - **Accept Baseline Changes But Keep My Existing Setting Customizations:** This option keeps the customizations you made to the baseline profile and applies them to the new version you've chosen to use.

   - **Accept Baseline Changes And Discard Existing Setting Customizations:** This option overwrites your original profile completely. The updated profile will use the default values for all settings.

7. Finally, click Submit. The profile updates to the selected baseline version, and after the conversion is complete, the baseline immediately redeploys to assigned groups.

Managing Device Security Using Policies

You can use the security policies that are located under the Manage section in the Endpoint Security node to configure device security, as shown in Figure 12.6.

FIGURE 12.6   Endpoint Security – Manage section

Endpoint security policies are one of several ways in which Intune is used to configure device settings. Each endpoint security profile focuses on a specific subset of device settings and is used to configure one particular aspect. It's important to note that in Intune, security baselines, device configuration policies, and endpoint security policies are all treated equally as sources of device configuration settings, and a settings conflict can happen when a device receives multiple configuration settings from different sources. Here are some of the items you can manage, along with a brief description of each:

- **Antivirus:** These policies help you focus on managing antivirus settings for managed devices.

- **Disk encryption:** This focuses on only the settings that are relevant for a device's built-in encryption method, such as FileVault or BitLocker.

- **Firewall:** Use this section to configure the built-in firewall for devices that run macOS and Windows 10/11.

- **Endpoint detection and response (EDR):** These policies are used when you integrate Microsoft Defender for Endpoint with Intune. The policies are used to manage EDR settings and to onboard devices to Microsoft Defender for Endpoint.

- **Attack surface reduction:** When Defender antivirus is in use on your Windows 10/11 devices, use this to manage those settings.

- **Account protection:** This is used to help you protect the identity and accounts of your users. The account protection policy focuses on the settings for Windows Hello and Credential Guard.

Also found under Manage are device compliance and conditional access policies. These policy types aren't focused security policies for configuring endpoints but are important tools for managing devices and access to your company resources.

To create an endpoint security policy, perform the following steps:

1. Sign into the Microsoft Endpoint Manager admin center at `https://endpoint.microsoft.com`.

2. Select Endpoint Security and then select the type of policy you want to configure; then click Create Policy. Choose from the following policy types:

    - Antivirus
    - Disk encryption
    - Firewall
    - Endpoint detection and response
    - Attack surface reduction
    - Account protection

3. Enter the following properties:

    - **Platform:** Choose the platform that you are creating the policy for. The available options will vary depend on the policy type you select.
    - **Profile:** Choose from the available profiles for the selected platform.

4. Click Create.

5. On the Basics page, enter a name and description for the profile, then click Next.

6. On the Configuration Settings page, expand each group of settings, and configure the settings you want to manage. When done, click Next.

7. On the Scope Tags page, choose Select Scope Tags to open the Select Tags pane, where you can assign scope tags to the profile. Click Next to continue.

8. On the Assignments page, select the groups you want to receive the profile and then click Next.

9. On the Review + Create page, when you're done, click Create.

Duplicating a Policy

There may be times when you need to create another endpoint security policy that is nearly identical to another except for one small difference. Suppose you want to assign similar policies but to different groups. Instead of creating a new policy from scratch, you can simply duplicate the policy and then edit it to fit your requirements. When you create a duplicate of a policy, it will come with all the original configuration settings and scope tags, but it will not have any assignments and you will have to assign it a new name. You can duplicate the following types of endpoint security policies:

- Account protection
- Antivirus
- Attack surface reduction
- Disk encryption
- Endpoint detection and response
- Firewall

To duplicate an endpoint security policy, perform the following steps:

1. Sign into the Microsoft Endpoint Manager admin center at `https://endpoint.microsoft.com`.

2. Select the policy that you want to copy. Next, click Duplicate or click the ellipsis (. . .) to the right of the policy and select Duplicate.

3. Give the policy a new name and then click Save.

Then you can edit the policy to suit your needs. To edit an endpoint security policy, perform the following steps:

1. Select the new policy and then select Properties.

2. Select Settings to expand a list of the configuration settings in the policy to review the current configuration, then click Edit for each category to modify the policy. Select each tab and make your changes. The tabs are:

  - Basics
  - Assignments

- Scope Tags
- Configuration Settings

3. Edits to one category must be saved before you can edit other categories. You do this by clicking Save.

Troubleshooting an Endpoint Security Baseline

There may be times when you have deployed an endpoint security baseline but the deployment status is showing an error. What should you do? Microsoft has provided you with the tools you need to troubleshoot the error. To figure out what the error might be, perform the following steps:

1. In Intune, select Security Baselines ➤ select a baseline ➤ Profiles.

2. Select a profile ➤ Under Monitor ➤ Per-setting status.

3. A table will show you all the settings along with a status of each. Select the Error or the Conflict column to see the setting causing the error.

Implementing Microsoft Defender for Endpoint

Microsoft Defender for Endpoint is an enterprise endpoint security platform that helps you prevent, detect, investigate, and respond to advanced threats. Microsoft Defender for Endpoint was previously called Microsoft Defender Advanced Threat Protection.

Microsoft Defender for Endpoint provides the following, as shown in Figure 12.7.

FIGURE 12.7   Microsoft Defender for Endpoint

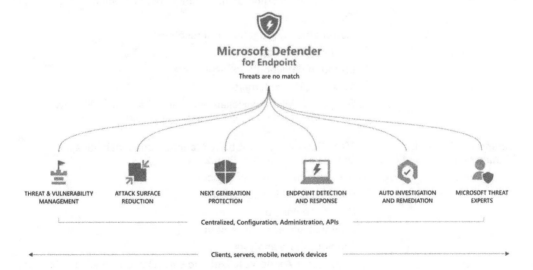

As of this writing, Microsoft Defender for Endpoint is available in two plans, Defender for Endpoint Plan 1 and Plan 2. A new add-on called Microsoft Defender Vulnerability Management is available for Plan 2. These plans provide you with advanced threat protection, with antivirus and antimalware protection, ransomware mitigation, and more. They also provide centralized management and reporting.

This information in Table 12.1 was taken directly from Microsoft's website.

TABLE 12.1 Comparison of Microsoft's endpoint security plans

Plan	What's included
Defender for Endpoint Plan 1	Next-generation protection (includes antimalware and antivirus)
	Attack surface reduction
	Manual response actions
	Centralized management
	Security reports
	APIs
	Support for Windows 1011, iOS, Android OS, and macOS devices
Defender for Endpoint Plan 2	All of the Defender for Endpoint Plan 1 capabilities, plus:
	Device discovery
	Device inventory
	Core Defender Vulnerability Management capabilities
	Threat Analytics
	Automated investigation and response
	Advanced hunting
	Endpoint detection and response
	Microsoft Threat Experts
	Support for Windows (client and server) and non-Windows platforms (macOS, iOS, Android, and Linux)
Defender Vulnerability Management add-on	More Defender Vulnerability Management capabilities for Defender for Endpoint Plan 2:
	Security baselines assessment
	Block vulnerable applications
	Browser extensions
	Digital certificate assessment
	Network share analysis
	Support for Windows (client and server) and non-Windows platforms (macOS, iOS, Android, and Linux)

Microsoft Defender for Endpoint Plan 1 is available as a stand-alone subscription for commercial and education customers and is also included as part of Microsoft 365 E3/A3. Microsoft Defender for Endpoint Plan 2, which was previously called Microsoft Defender for Endpoint, is available as a stand-alone subscription. It's also included as part of the following plans:

- Windows 11 Enterprise E5/A5
- Windows 10 Enterprise E5/A5
- Microsoft 365 E5/A5/G5 (which includes Windows 10 or Windows 11 Enterprise E5)
- Microsoft 365 E5/A5/G5/F5 Security
- Microsoft 365 F5 Security & Compliance

Planning Your Microsoft Defender for EndpointDeployment

When planning your Microsoft Defender for Endpoint deployment you want to plan it so that you can get the most out of its security capabilities to protect your environment from cyberattacks. Microsoft provides the following graphic to help you when planning a Microsoft Defender for Endpoint deployment. Figure 12.8 provides guidance on how to identify your environment architecture, select the best type of deployment tool, and guides you on how to configure your required capabilities. For more information regarding planning your Microsoft Defender for Endpoint deployment, check out Microsoft's website at, `https://learn.microsoft.com/en-us/microsoft-365/security/defender-endpoint/deployment-strategy?view=o365-worldwide`.

FIGURE 12.8   Planning your Microsoft Defender for Endpoint deployment

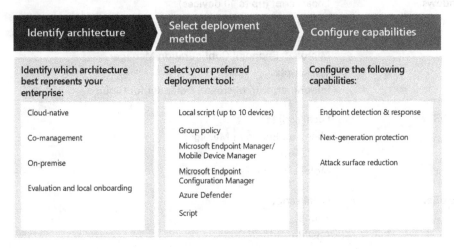

Because every environment is different, some tools may be better suited to meet your deployment needs. Because there are so many different ways to plan your deployment, we

want to share an extremely helpful web page that can assist with the planning phase. This web page allows you to download a variety of PDFs that cover the multitude of ways to plan your deployment. The information included with the guides provide information on prerequisites, design, and configuration options. So, check out Microsoft's website at `https://docs.microsoft.com/en-us/microsoft-365/security/defender-endpoint/deployment-strategy`.

Microsoft Defender for Endpoint Deployment

Once you plan your Microsoft Defender for Endpoint deployment, the next phase will be the actual deployment phase. The deployment phase has its own phases that include:

- **Phase 1** – Prepare: Determine what should be considered, such as stakeholder approvals, environment considerations, access permissions, and adoption order of capabilities.

- **Phase 2** – Setup: The initial steps needed so you can access the portal, such as licensing validation, tenant configuration using the setup wizard, and network configuration.

- **Phase 3** – Onboard: Depending on the operating system and deployment method, you can use one of the tools in Table 12.2 to onboard devices to Defender for Endpoint.

The following table lists the available tools based on the endpoint that you need to onboard. The information in Table 12.2 was taken directly from Microsoft's website.

TABLE 12.2   Onboarding tool options

Endpoint	Tool options
Windows	Local script (up to 10 devices)
	Group Policy
	Microsoft Endpoint Manager/Mobile Device Manager
	Microsoft Endpoint Configuration Manager
	VDI scripts
	Integration with Microsoft Defender for Cloud
macOS	Local scripts
	Microsoft Endpoint Manager
	JAMF Pro
	Mobile Device Management
Linux Server	Local script
	Puppet
	Ansible
iOS	Microsoft Endpoint Manager
Android	Microsoft Endpoint Manager

As you can see in Table 12.2, there are a number of ways to onboard devices to Defender for Endpoint depending on the operating system and deployment method. You can use the onboarding wizard to help guide you through the process. You will go through the onboarding section of the Defender for Endpoint portal to onboard any of the supported devices. Depending on the device, you will be provided with instructions and package files to meet your needs for the device chosen.

Monitoring Microsoft Defender for Endpoint

You can view information on device compliance and onboarding by using the Microsoft Endpoint Manager admin center. To monitor the state of devices that have a Microsoft Defender for Endpoint compliance policy, perform the following steps:

1. Sign into the Microsoft Endpoint Manager admin center at `https://endpoint.microsoft.com`.

2. Select Devices ➢ Monitor ➢ Policy Compliance.

3. Locate the Microsoft Defender for Endpoint policy that you want from the list and check to see which devices are compliant or noncompliant.

You can also take a look at the operational report for noncompliant devices by going to Devices ➢ Monitor ➢ Noncompliant Devices to see a list of all devices that are in noncompliance.

If you want to learn the onboarding status of your Intune-managed devices, you can select Endpoint Security ➢ Microsoft Defender For Endpoint. Here you can also onboard more devices to Microsoft Defender for Endpoint by creating a device configuration profile.

Endpoint Detection and Response

Microsoft Defender for Endpoint provides you with near-real-time detection and response capabilities. This allows you to take actions quickly if a threat is encountered. If a threat is detected, then an alert will be created. Microsoft Defender for Endpoint collects process information, network activity, user login activity, Registry and file system changes, and more, which is kept for six months.

To view threats, you can use the Security Operations dashboard. Here you will see an overview of threats that have been detected and when response actions are required. The dashboard shows you an overview of the following, as you can see in Figure 12.9:

- Active alerts
- Devices at risk
- Sensor health
- Service health
- Daily devices reporting
- Active automated investigations
- Automated investigations statistics
- Users at risk
- Suspicious activities

FIGURE 12.9   Security Operations dashboard

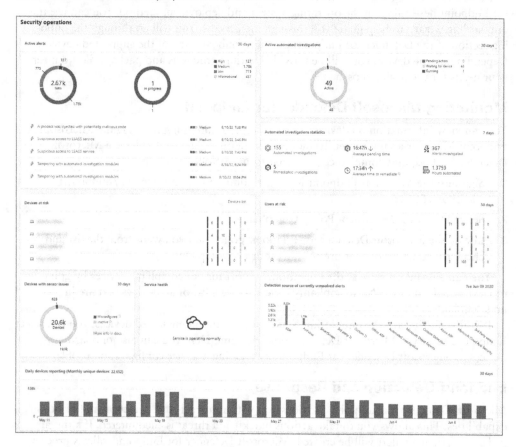

From the dashboard, you can quickly explore and investigate alerts and devices to see if there are any threats or suspicious activity. The dashboard also has tiles that you can click that will provide more information on your overall health state.

If you click Active Alerts, you can view the overall number of active alerts for the past 30 days. Alerts are grouped into New and In Progress, as shown in Figure 12.10.

You can click the number inside each alert ring to see that category's queue (New or In Progress). Each will be sorted by their alert severity levels. The Alerts queue will show you a list of alerts that have been flagged from devices on your network. By default, the queue displays any alerts that were seen in the last 30 days, with the most recent alert being at the top of the list. Each row will include an alert severity category and a brief description. If you click an alert, you will see a detailed view. From the Alerts Queue page, you can customize the alerts view to suit your needs. On the top navigation, you can:

- Add or remove columns.

- Apply filters.

- Display the alerts for a particular duration (1 Day, 3 Days, 1 Week, 30 Days, and 6 Months).
- Export the alerts list to Microsoft Excel.
- Manage alerts.

FIGURE 12.10 Active Alerts

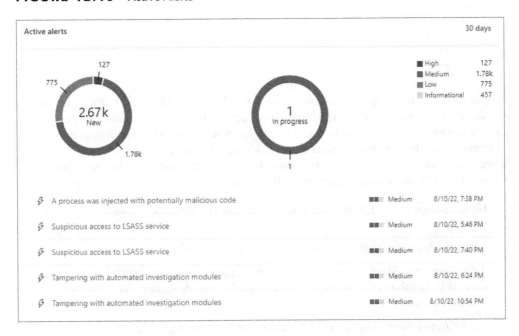

You will also notice that the Alerts Queue page displays the severity levels by color, as shown in Figure 12.11:

- High (Red): These alerts indicate a high risk because of the severity of damage they can inflict on devices.
- Medium (Orange): These alerts indicate endpoint detection and response behaviors that might be a part of an advanced persistent threat (APT) such as Registry changes or the execution of a suspicious file.
- Low (Yellow): These alerts may be associated with malware attacks, such as logs being cleared. These threats do not indicate that there was an attack, but it's best to investigate.
- Informational (Gray): These alerts may not be considered harmful but could be a security issue.

FIGURE 12.11   Alerts Queue page

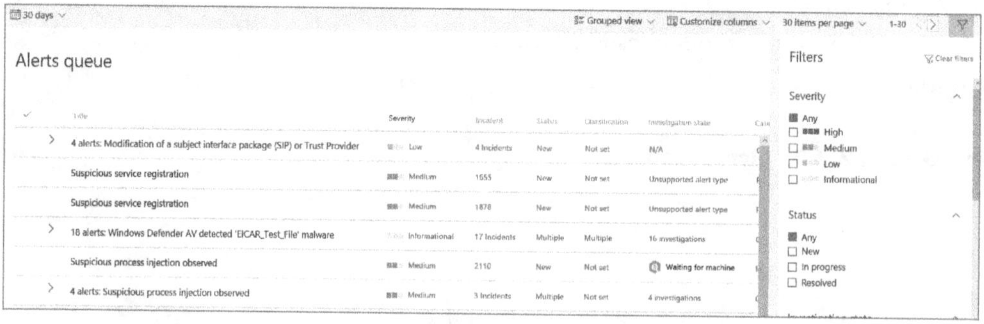

Also on the Security Operations dashboard, if you look at the Devices At Risk tile, this will show you a list of devices that have the most active alerts. For each device, the total number of alerts is shown in a circle next to the device name and then further categorized by severity level. To view more details about a device, just click the name of the device. When you select a device to investigate, you will see a device summary page, as shown in Figure 12.12. On the summary page you will see the following:

Device Details   This provides information such as the domain, OS, and health state of the device.

Response Actions   These are tasks you can perform for the given device.

Tabs (Overview, Alerts, Timeline, Security Recommendations, Software Inventory, Discovered Vulnerabilities, Missing KBs)   These tabs provide security and threat prevention information.

Cards (Active Alerts, Logged On Users, Security Assessment, Device Health Status)   Cards display an overview of alerts related to the device and their risk level.

On the Device Summary page, there are also a number of response actions that you can take, as shown in Figure 12.13. These actions include:

- Manage Tags
- Initiate Automated Investigation
- Initiate Live Response Session
- Collect Investigation Package
- Run Antivirus Scan
- Remove App Restrictions
- Isolate Device
- Consult A Threat Expert
- Action Center

FIGURE 12.12   Device Summary

FIGURE 12.13   Response actions

On the Security Operations dashboard, if you look at the Devices with sensor issues tile, this will give you information on a device's ability to provide sensor data to the Microsoft Defender for Endpoint service. It shows how many devices require attention and helps you identify devices that may have problems, as shown in Figure 12.14.

Here you will see two different status indicators:

- **Misconfigured:** This is the number of devices that may have configuration errors that need to be corrected.

- **Inactive:** This is the number of devices that have stopped reporting to the Microsoft Defender for Endpoint service for more than seven days within the past month.

The Service Health tile shows whether the service is active or if there are issues, as shown in Figure 12.15.

If you click this tile, it will open the Service Health page, which shows the health state of each cloud service in a table format, as shown in Figure 12.16.

FIGURE 12.14   Devices With Sensor Issues tile

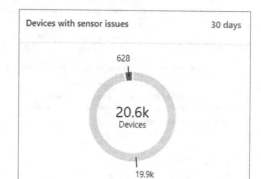

FIGURE 12.15   Service Health tile

The default view is the All Services tab, which shows all services, their current health state, and any active incidents or advisories. An icon and status in the Health column indicate the state of each service.

On the security operations dashboard, if you look at the Daily Devices Reporting tile (as shown in Figure 12.17), this will show you a bar graph that shows the number of devices that are reporting within the last 30 days. You can hover over an individual bar on the graph to see the exact number of devices reporting that day.

On the security operations dashboard, if you look at the Active Automated Investigations tile (shown in Figure 12.18), this will show you the number of automated investigations from the last 30 days. The number of investigations are categorized into Pending Action, Waiting For Device, and Running.

FIGURE 12.16 Service Health page

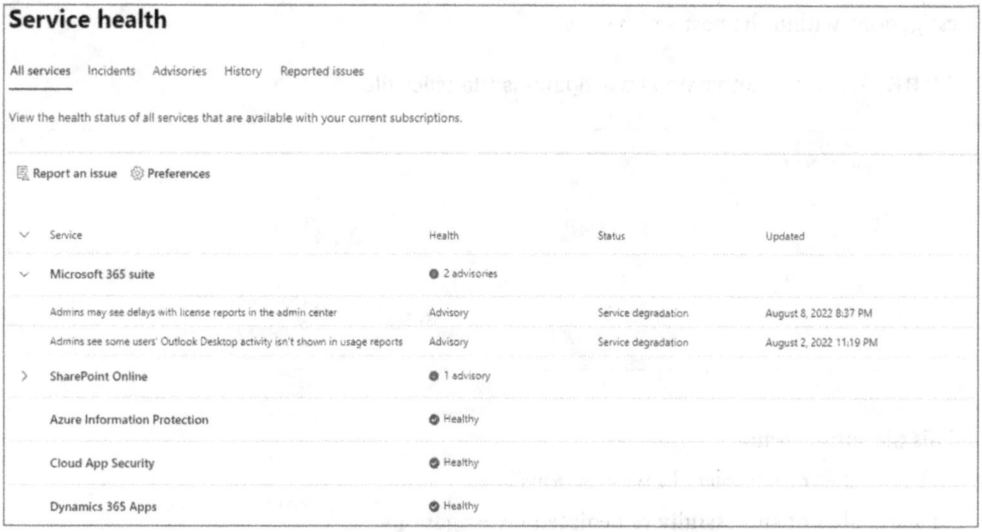

Service health
All services
Incidents
Advisories
History
Reported issues
View the health status of all services that are available with your current subscriptions.
Report an issue
Preferences
Service
Health
Status
Updated
Microsoft 365 suite
2 advisories
Admins may see delays with license reports in the admin center
Advisory
Service degradation
August 8, 2022 8:37 PM
Admins see some users' Outlook Desktop activity isn't shown in usage reports
Advisory
Service degradation
August 2, 2022 11:19 PM
SharePoint Online
1 advisory
Azure Information Protection
Healthy
Cloud App Security
Healthy
Dynamics 365 Apps
Healthy

FIGURE 12.17 Daily Devices Reporting tile

Daily devices reporting (Monthly unique devices: 22,652)
30 days

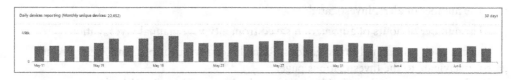

FIGURE 12.18 Active Automated Investigations tile

Active automated investigations
30 days
Pending action 0
Waiting for device 48
Running 0
48
Active
48

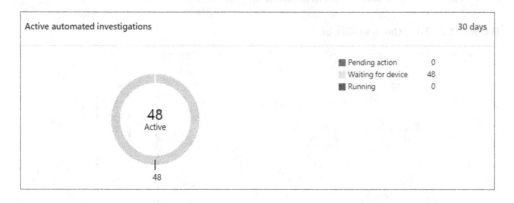

On the security operations dashboard, if you look at the Automated Investigations Statistics tile (shown in Figure 12.19), this will show you statistics pertaining to automated investigations within the past seven days.

FIGURE 12.19   Automated Investigations Statistics tile

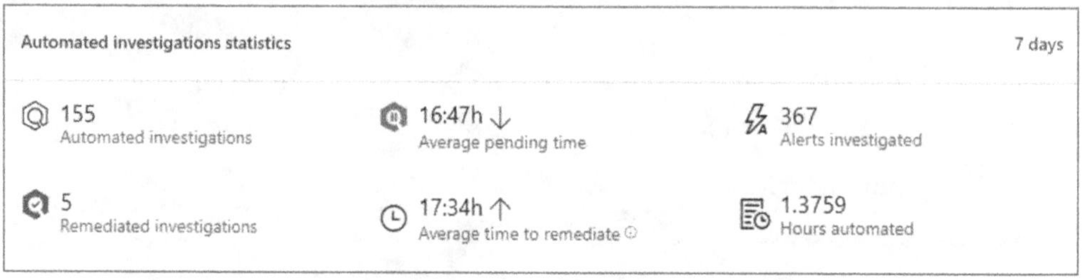

This tile shows you:

- The number of completed investigations
- The number of successfully remediated investigations
- The average pending time it takes for an investigation to be initiated
- The average time it takes to remediate an alert
- The number of alerts investigated
- The number of hours of automation saved from a typical manual investigation

You can click Automated Investigations, Remediated Investigations, and Alerts Investigated to navigate to the Investigations page.

On the security operations dashboard, if you look at the Users At Risk tile (shown in Figure 12.20), this tile will show you a list of user accounts that have the most active alerts and the number of alerts seen on high, medium, or low alerts.

FIGURE 12.20   Users at Risk tile

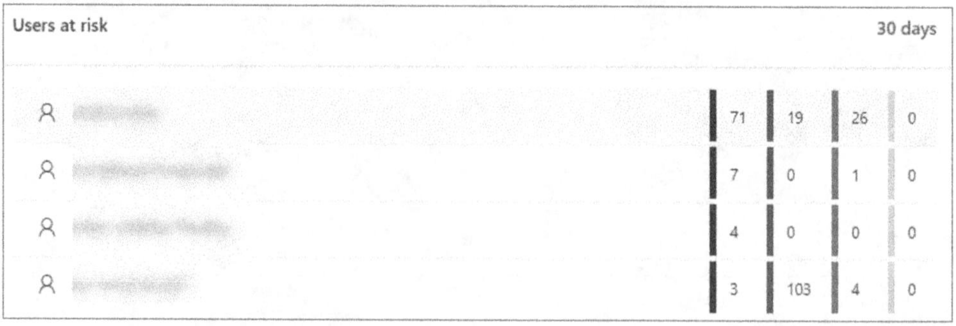

By selecting a user account, you can see more details about that user, as shown in Figure 12.21:

- User account details, Microsoft Defender for Identity alerts, and logged-on devices, role, logon type, and other details
- Overview of the incidents and the user's devices
- Alerts related to this user
- Observed in organization (devices logged on to)

FIGURE 12.21 Users account details

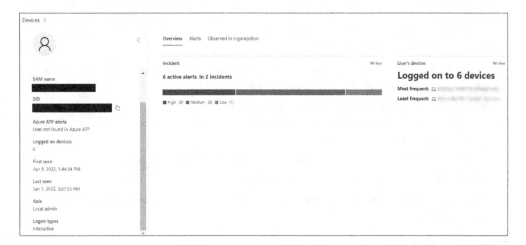

Understanding Microsoft Defender Application Guard

One of the biggest issues that we have in IT is the Internet. It's a world gamechanger and a company gamechanger. But that also means it's an IT gamechanger. We in IT have to rethink how we protect our networks, and that's because of the Internet.

Years ago, hackers had to use phone lines, and that helped prevent a lot of hacker wannabes. Phone lines were easy to track, and it could be expensive for a young hacker to spend a lot of money on phone calls—especially if they were unsuccessful with their hacks.

Today, anyone can hack from anywhere because of the World Wide Web, and they pay only a monthly fee for Internet access. So, we must rethink how we protect our data and our companies. This is where Application Guard can help us.

Application Guard was specifically designed for Windows 10/11 and Microsoft Edge. Application Guard works with Microsoft Edge to isolate untrusted websites, thus protecting your organization's network and data while your users are working on the Internet.

As an Enterprise Administrator, you can pick which websites are defined as trusted sites. These sites can be internal websites, external websites, company websites, and cloud-based organizations. If a site is not on the trusted list, it is then considered untrusted and automatically isolated when a user visits the site.

When a user accesses a website that is not on the trusted list, Microsoft Edge will be automatically opened in an isolated Hyper-V-enabled container. This container will be a separate environment from the host operating system, and this will help protect untrusted websites from causing damage to the Windows client system. Also, since the website will be isolated, any type of attack will not affect the corporate network or its data.

Microsoft Defender Application Guard is disabled by default. It works in two modes: Standalone or Enterprise. Standalone mode allows a noncorporate user to use Microsoft Defender Application Guard without any administrator-configured policies. Enterprise mode is used in an enterprise environment and can be configured automatically by the Enterprise Administrator.

For you to use Microsoft Defender Application Guard, your environment must meet a few hardware requirements. These include the following:

- **64-bit CPU:** A 64-bit computer with a minimum of four cores (logical processors) is required for hypervisor and virtualization-based security (VBS).

- **CPU virtualization extensions:** Extended page tables, also called Second-Level Address Translation (SLAT), and either one of these virtualization extensions for VBS: VT-x (Intel) or AMD-V.

- **Hardware memory:** Microsoft requires a minimum of 8 GB of RAM.

- **Hard disk:** 5 GB of free space, solid-state disk (SSD) recommended.

- **Input/Output Memory Management Unit (IOMMU) support:** Not required but recommended.

Microsoft Defender Application Guard Standalone Mode

If a user wants to use Standalone mode, they need to be using either Windows 10 Enterprise edition (version 1709 or higher), Windows 10 Pro edition (version 1803), or Windows 11. The user must install Application Guard manually on their Windows 10/11 device, and then they need to manually start Microsoft Edge in Application Guard while they are browsing untrusted sites.

Exercise 12.1 will show you how to install Microsoft Defender Application Guard using the Control Panel.

EXERCISE 12.1

Installing Microsoft Defender Application Guard

1. Right-click Start and choose Windows System ≻ Control Panel ≻ Large Icon View ≻ Programs And Features.

2. Click the link Turn Windows Features On Or Off.

3. Scroll down and check the box for Microsoft Defender Application Guard (shown in Figure 12.22), and then click OK.

FIGURE 12.22   Installing Microsoft Defender Application Guard

4. After Microsoft Defender Application Guard installs, close Control Panel.

You can also install Microsoft Defender Application Guard by using PowerShell. To do this, you need to right-click on PowerShell and choose the top option, Run As Administrator (see Figure 12.23).

FIGURE 12.23   Opening PowerShell as an administrator

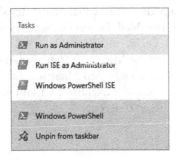

Once you are in the PowerShell window, run the following PowerShell command and then restart the Windows client device:

```
Enable-WindowsOptionalFeature -online -FeatureName
Windows-Defender-ApplicationGuard
```

You can also install Microsoft Defender Application Guard using Intune. To do so, perform the following steps:

1. Go to the Microsoft Endpoint admin center at `https://endpoint.microsoft.com` and sign in.

2. Choose Devices ➢ Configuration Profiles ➢ + Create Profile, and do the following:

   a. In the Platform list, select Windows 10 and later.

   b. In the Profile list, select Endpoint Protection.

   c. Click Create.

3. Specify the following settings for the profile:

   ▪ Name and description.

   ▪ In the Select A Category To Configure Settings section, choose Microsoft Defender Application Guard.

   ▪ In the Application Guard list, click Enabled for Edge.

   ▪ Choose your preferences for Clipboard Behavior, External Content, and the remaining settings.

4. Click OK, and then click OK again.

5. Review your settings, and then click Create.

6. Click Assignments, and then do the following:

   a. On the Include tab, in the Assign To list, choose an option.

   b. If you have any devices or users you want to exclude from this endpoint protection profile, specify them on the Exclude tab.

   c. Click Save.

After the profile is created, any devices to which the policy should apply will have Microsoft Defender Application Guard enabled. However, the users may have to restart their devices in order for protection to begin.

Exercise 12.2 shows you how to use Microsoft Defender Application Guard in Standalone mode. You will be using Windows 10 and Microsoft Edge for this exercise. To complete this exercise, you must complete Exercise 12.1 and install Microsoft Defender Application Guard on your Windows 10 device.

Using Microsoft Defender Application Guard

1. Open Microsoft Edge.

2. From the options menu, choose New Application Guard Window (see Figure 12.24).

FIGURE 12.24   New Application Guard Window option

3. You will need to wait for Application Guard to set up the isolated environment (see Figure 12.25). This may take a few moments.

FIGURE 12.25 Application Guard starting screen

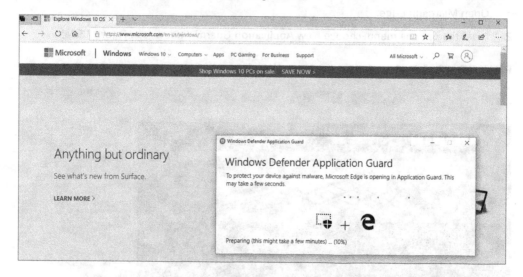

4. As you can see in Figure 12.26, we opened Microsoft's website in Application Guard mode, and you can see that in the upper-left-hand corner of the window. Close Edge.

FIGURE 12.26 Microsoft's website in Application Guard mode

Microsoft Defender Application Guard Enterprise Mode

Microsoft Defender Application Guard in the enterprise environment is not much different for the user as in Standalone mode. The main difference is that the Enterprise Administrator configures the Microsoft Defender Application Guard application. The Enterprise Administrator sets up and configures the application. When a user accesses an untrusted website, Microsoft Defender Application Guard automatically starts.

So, let's take a look at some of the enterprise-based systems that will benefit from Microsoft Defender Application Guard:

Enterprise Desktops and Laptops   Enterprise desktops are machines that are joined to your domain and managed by your company's administrators. Enterprise Administrators can configure Microsoft Defender Application Guard through Configuration Manager or Microsoft Intune.

Bring Your Own Device (BYOD) Laptops   Normally organizations that allow users to use their own devices for company business need to follow company rules. So, these devices are normally managed by the Enterprise Administrators through Intune. If a user wants to use a personal device but they don't want to follow corporate rules, most companies won't allow the use of the personal device.

Exercise 12.3 shows you how to use Microsoft Defender Application Guard in Enterprise mode. Before your organization can use Application Guard in Enterprise mode, administrators must install Windows 10 Enterprise edition (version 1709 or higher) on their corporate network or the needed functionality will not work.

EXERCISE 12.3

Microsoft Defender Application Guard Enterprise

1.   Install Application Guard using one of the methods listed earlier.

2.   Restart the device, and then start Microsoft Edge.

3.   Set up the Network Isolation settings in Group Policy as shown in Figure 12.27:

   a.   Click the Windows icon, type **Group Policy**, and then click Edit Group Policy.

   b.   Go to the Administrative Templates\Network\Network Isolation\Enterprise Resource Domains Hosted In The Cloud setting.

   c.   For the purposes of this scenario, type **.microsoft.com** into the Enterprise Cloud Resources box.

FIGURE 12.27   Network Isolation GPO

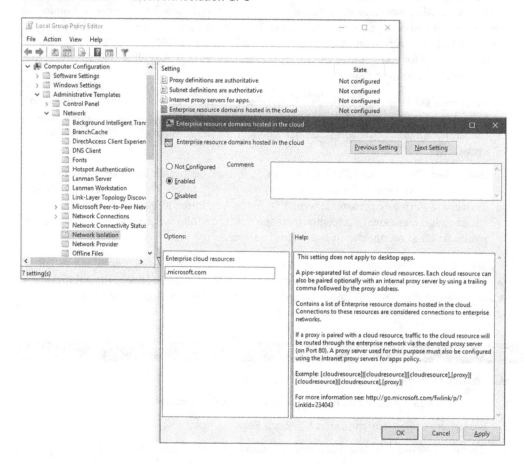

4. Next, go to the Administrative Templates\Network\Network Isolation\Domains Categorized As Both Work And Personal setting. Enter in the websites that you trust in the Neutral Resources box, as shown in Figure 12.28.

FIGURE 12.28   Domains Categorized As Both Work And Personal setting

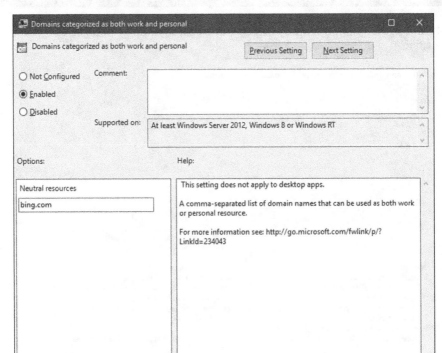

5. Next, go to the Computer Configuration\Administrative Templates\Windows Compo-
    nents\Microsoft Defender Application Guard\Turn On Microsoft Defender Application
    Guard In Enterprise Mode setting.

6. Click the Enabled radio button, choose Option 1 (see Figure 12.29), and click OK.

FIGURE 12.29   Turn On Microsoft Defender Application Guard In Enterprise Mode setting

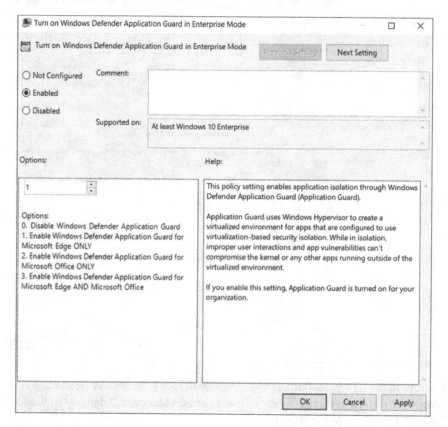

7.   Close the GPO editor.

Understanding Microsoft Defender Credential Guard

Microsoft Defender Credential Guard is a virtualization-based security service to help isolate critical files so that only system software that is privileged can access those critical files.

Once the feature is enabled, a Windows client machine that is part of Active Directory or Azure Active Directory will have the system's credentials protected by Microsoft Defender Credential Guard.

After an administrator enables Microsoft Defender Credential Guard, the Local Security Authority (LSA) process in the operating system works with a new component called the isolated LSA. The isolated process stores and protects the system's critical data.

Once data is stored by the isolated LSA process, the system then uses the virtualization-based security to protect the data and that data is no longer accessible to the rest of the operating system.

To enable Microsoft Defender Credential Guard, you must meet the following requirements:

- Machine must support virtualization-based security (required).

- Secure boot (required).

- TPM 1.2 or 2.0, either discrete or firmware (preferred; provides binding to hardware).

- UEFI lock (preferred; prevents attacker from disabling with a simple Registry key change).

The virtualization-based security requires the following:

- 64-bit CPU

- CPU virtualization extensions plus extended page tables

- Windows hypervisor (does not require Hyper-V Windows Feature to be installed)

If an administrator wants to use Microsoft Defender Credential Guard in a Hyper-V virtual machine, the following requirements need to be met:

- Windows 10 (version 1607 or higher) or Windows Server 2016 or higher and the system must have Hyper-V with Input Output Memory Management Unit (IOMMU).

- The Hyper-V virtual machine must be set as Generation 2 and virtual TPM needs to be enabled.

Once administrators have met the minimum requirements for setting up Microsoft Defender Credential Guard, they can enable it with any of the following methods:

- Using Group Policy

- Modifying the Registry

- Using the Hypervisor-Protected Code Integrity (HVCI)

- Using the Windows Defender Credential Guard hardware readiness tool

Exercise 12.4 shows how to enable Microsoft Defender Credential Guard using a Group Policy object (GPO).

EXERCISE 12.4

Enabling Microsoft Defender Credential Guard Using a GPO

1. Open the Group Policy Management editor on a Windows Server machine.

2. Create a new GPO, click the GPO, and choose Edit.

EXERCISE 12.4 *(continued)*

3. Go to Computer Configuration ➤ Administrative Templates ➤ System ➤ Device Guard.

4. Select Turn On Virtualization Based Security and then choose the Enabled option (see Figure 12.30).

FIGURE 12.30   Turn On Virtualization Based Security setting

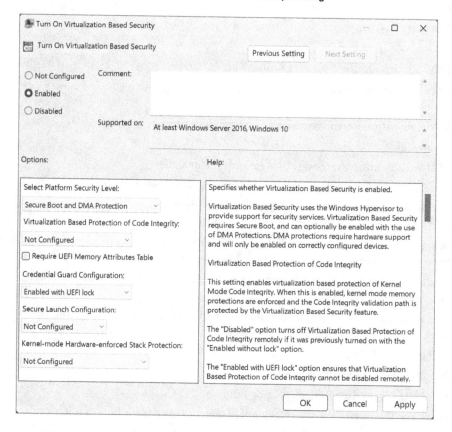

5. In the Select Platform Security Level box, choose Secure Boot or Secure Boot And DMA Protection.

6. In the Credential Guard Configuration box, select Enabled With UEFI Lock, and then click OK. (If you want to be able to turn off Windows Defender Credential Guard remotely, choose Enabled Without Lock.)

7. In the Secure Launch Configuration box, choose Not Configured, Enabled, or Disabled.

8. Click OK and then close the Group Policy Management Console.

9. To enforce processing of the Group Policy, run **gpupdate /force**.

You can also enable Windows Defender Credential Guard by using Microsoft Endpoint Manager. To do so, perform the following steps:

1. From the Microsoft Endpoint Manager admin center, select Devices.

2. Select Configuration Profiles.

3. Select Create Profile ➤ Windows 10 And Later ➤ Settings Catalog ➤ + Create.

4. Configuration Settings: Select Device Guard as the category and add your required settings.

Implementing and Managing Microsoft Defender Exploit Guard

Another way that Microsoft has started protecting systems is by using Microsoft Defender Exploit Guard. Microsoft Defender Exploit Guard helps protect your Windows client systems against malware, ransomware, and other types of attacks. It does this by reducing the attack surface of a device.

So, what does it mean when someone says that they are reducing the attack surface of a system? The way I always explain it is in this way. I am a huge hockey fan. When I lived in New Jersey, I used to go to dozens of hockey games.

Now think of a hockey net (or soccer net) as the Windows system. During one of the hockey intermissions (when the players get a break), they would bring out a piece of plexiglass and on the bottom of the plexiglass, there was an opening just a bit bigger than a hockey puck. Then they would give someone a stick and a puck and allow them to shoot at the net from the center of the ice. If the puck went in, they would win a car or money or whatever the prize was that night.

Now think of the open net as Windows 10/11. You can have a great goaltender (your firewall), but if someone is good enough, they can still get the puck by the goaltender. Now think of the plexiglass. The only way that someone can score is by getting the puck in that tiny little opening. This is an example of a reduced attack surface. The goaltender doesn't need to protect the entire net. They just need to protect that tiny opening.

Microsoft Defender Exploit Guard is your plexiglass on the Windows client operating system. By protecting common ways that hackers exploit the system, the hackers now have to get into the system by using that tiny little opening.

Microsoft Defender Exploit Guard helps protect your system from common malware hacks that use executable files and scripts that attack applications like Microsoft Office (for example, Outlook). Microsoft Defender Exploit Guard also looks for suspicious scripts or behavior that is not normal on the Windows 10/11 system.

One of the common hacks today is ransomware. This is when a hacker takes over your system and requests a ransom to release your files. During this time, the hackers hold your documents hostage until you pay. Once Microsoft Defender Exploit Guard is enabled, folders and files are assessed to determine if the files are safe from ransomware threats.

There are numerous ways to turn on Microsoft Defender Exploit Guard—you can use any of the following tools:

- Windows Security app
- Intune
- MDM
- Microsoft Endpoint Manager
- Microsoft Endpoint Configuration Manager
- Group Policy
- PowerShell

You can configure and deploy Configuration Manager policies that manage all four components of Microsoft Defender Exploit Guard. These components include:

- Attack surface reduction
- Controlled folder access
- Exploit protection
- Network protection

Exercise 12.5 shows how to enable Microsoft Defender Exploit Guard using Intune.

EXERCISE 12.5

Enabling Microsoft Defender Exploit Guard Using Intune

1. Open Settings by clicking the Start button and then clicking the Settings (spoke) icon.

2. Select Update And Security.

3. Select Windows Security and click Virus And Threat Protection.

4. Click Ransomware Protection and make sure the setting is turned on (see Figure 12.31).

FIGURE 12.31   Turning on the Ransomware setting

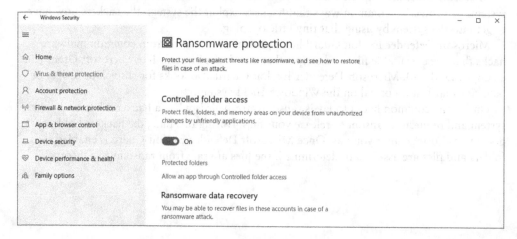

5. Click Protected Folders to see what folders are currently protected (Figure 12.32). You can click + Add A Protected Folder to add additional folders.

FIGURE 12.32 Protected Folders screen

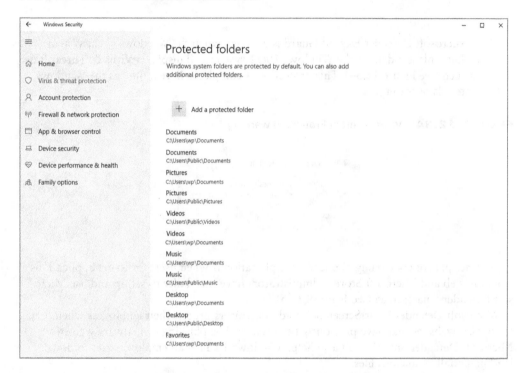

6. If you would like an application to have access, you can click the link Allow An App Through Controlled Folder Access. Once you click the link, you can add an application that will be allowed access (see Figure 12.33).

FIGURE 12.33 Allow An App Through Controlled Folder Access screen

7. Close the Security Center (reboot if you made any changes).

Once Microsoft Defender Exploit Guard is enabled, when the Windows client system suspects that a file is a danger, the Windows 10/11 system will display a Virus & Threat Protection screen (see Figure 12.34). This protection is completed in real time as the Windows 10/11 system is operating.

FIGURE 12.34   Virus & Threat Protection warning

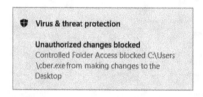

Another part of controlling application exploitation is when users try to get applications from the web and Microsoft Store. Administrators have the ability to set up and use Microsoft Defender SmartScreen (see Figure 12.35).

Microsoft Defender SmartScreen helps administrators protect their employees when they try to visit websites that have previously been reported as phishing or malware websites. Microsoft Defender SmartScreen also helps Windows 10/11 if an employee tries to download potentially malicious files.

SmartScreen allows Windows to determine if a downloaded application or an application installer may be potentially malicious:

- SmartScreen checks if downloaded files are on a list of known malicious software sites or if programs that are being downloaded are known to be unsafe. If any file or program is on these lists, SmartScreen will prompt the user with a warning to let that user know that the data or site might be malicious.

- When a user downloads a file or program that isn't on the list, SmartScreen will show the user a warning prompt, to advise caution.

Another way that your organization can help protect users against downloading applications that are possibly harmful is by using Microsoft Defender Application Control.

FIGURE 12.35   Microsoft Defender SmartScreen

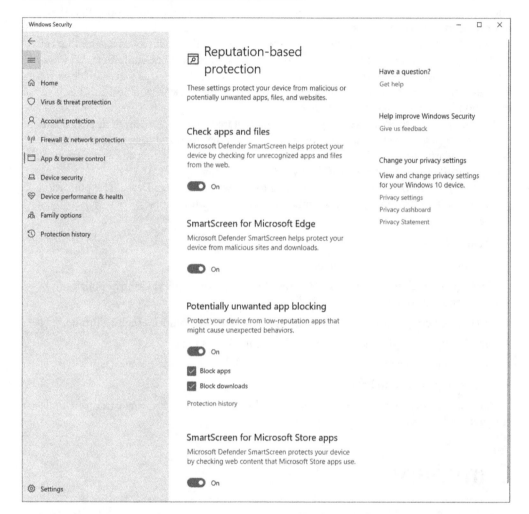

Using Windows Defender Application Control

So now that we have discussed how to protect your system and system files, let's talk about protecting applications. When an application runs, it has the ability to access data with the same access to data that a user has. Because of this, Microsoft has created Windows Defender Application Control (WDAC) to help stop data attacks through the use of applications.

For many years, if a user had local admin rights and they wanted to install an application onto a corporate machine, they just did it. Users just assumed that applications that they buy or download were trustworthy.

Administrators can now use Windows Defender Application Control to ensure that only applications that you explicitly allow can run on the Windows client computers. Windows Defender Application Control has a big advantage over using antivirus software alone by stopping an application from running unless you explicitly allow it, you add another layer of protection in your war against data theft.

For many years, top-level security analysts have stated that some form of application control would be a good way to address the many threats that executable-based malware pose. Now, administrators can add that additional layer of security by listing the applications that can specifically run on your own Windows 10/11 corporate system.

If an administrator wants to create policies to use with Windows Defender Application Control, first make sure you meet the following system requirements:

- Windows 10
- Windows 11
- Windows Server 2016 and higher

There are several ways to deploy Windows Defender Application Control policies to managed endpoints, including:

- Deploying using a Mobile Device Management (MDM) solution, such as Intune
- Deploying using Microsoft Endpoint Configuration Manager
- Deploying via script
- Deploying via Group Policy

After Windows Defender Application Control is set up, administrators can create and configure policies by using GPOs or Intune.

Summary

This chapter discussed Windows Security, the tools that help protect a device and its data. This is one of many ways that you can protect your system.

We discussed Endpoint Protection and what endpoints are. Endpoint security helps you protect your endpoints from cyberattacks by using a wide variety of services and solutions.

Then we covered endpoint security using Intune and creating and monitoring security baselines. In Intune, security baselines are preconfigured groups of settings that are recommended best practices from the Microsoft security teams for that product.

We then explored working with Microsoft Defender for Endpoint. We described the plans available and the deployment steps. We also discussed the numerous ways that you can onboard devices to Defender for Endpoint, which vary depending on the operating system and deployment method you are using.

You learned how to monitor your devices using Microsoft Defender for Endpoint and how you can view information about device compliance and onboarding by using the Microsoft Endpoint Manager admin center.

We also discussed Endpoint Detection and Response by using the Security Operations dashboard to view a wide variety of tiles such as Active Alerts, Devices At Risk, Devices With Sensor Issues, Service Health, and Daily Devices Reporting. We explored the response actions you can take.

You then learned about Microsoft Defender Application Guard, specifically designed for Windows 10/11 and Microsoft Edge. Application Guard works with Edge to isolate untrusted websites, thus protecting your organization's network and data while users are working on the Internet.

Then we focused on Microsoft Defender Credential Guard, a virtualization-based security service to help isolate critical files so that only system software that is privileged can access those critical files.

You learned how to use Microsoft Defender Exploit Guard to protect your Windows 10/11 system against malware, ransomware, and other types of attacks. Microsoft Defender Exploit Guard does this by reducing the attack surface of a device.

Finally, we explained how Windows Defender Application Control allows an administrator to control applications and stop them from running unless you explicitly allow it.

Exam Essentials

Know how to plan and implement Endpoint Protection.   Know and understand what endpoints are and how to plan endpoint security.

Know how to use Security Baselines in Intune.   Know what Security Baselines are and how to implement and manage them in Intune.

Understand Endpoint Security.   Know how to create and manage configuration policies for Endpoint Security, including antivirus, encryption, firewall, endpoint detection and response, and attack surface reduction.

Know how to use Microsoft Defender for Endpoint.   Know what Microsoft Defender for Endpoint can do for you as well as how to onboard devices into Microsoft Defender for Endpoint. Also, know how to monitor Microsoft Defender for Endpoint as well as how to investigate and respond to threats using the Security Operations dashboard and response actions.

Understand how to use Microsoft Defender Application Guard.   Understand how Application Guard works with Edge to isolate untrusted websites and how to set up Standalone and Enterprise modes.

Understand how to use Microsoft Defender Credential Guard. Know how Microsoft Defender Credential Guard uses virtualization-based security to help isolate critical files so that only system software with privileges can access those critical files.

Understand how to use Microsoft Defender Exploit Guard. Know how Microsoft Defender Exploit Guard helps protect your Windows client system against malware, ransomware, and other types of attacks.

Know how to use Windows Defender Application Control. Understand how Windows Defender Application Control allows an administrator to control which applications are allowed on a Windows 10/11 system.

Video Resources

There are no videos for this chapter.

Review Questions

1. You are the administrator for an organization with 275 computers that all run Windows 10/11. These computers are all joined to Microsoft Azure Active Directory and all computers are enrolled in Intune. You need to make sure that only approved applications are allowed to run on all of these computers. What should you implement to ensure this?

    A. Microsoft Defender Credential Guard

    B. Microsoft Defender Exploit Guard

    C. Microsoft Defender Application Guard

    D. Microsoft Defender Antivirus

2. You are the administrator of a large training company. All of your machines run Windows 10/11. You have a Windows client machine that has a virus that was caused by a malicious font. You need to stop this type of threat from affecting your corporate computers in the future. What should you use?

    A. Microsoft Defender Exploit Guard

    B. Microsoft Defender Application Guard

    C. Microsoft Defender Credential Guard

    D. Microsoft Defender System Guard

3. You are the administrator for an organization where all computers run Windows 10/11. You need to make sure that critical files are isolated so that only system software with privileges can access those critical files. What should you implement to ensure this?

    A. Microsoft Defender Credential Guard

    B. Microsoft Defender Exploit Guard

    C. Microsoft Defender Application Control

    D. Microsoft Defender Antivirus

4. You are the administrator for your company network. You and a colleague are discussing enabling Microsoft Defender Credential Guard by using Intune. When enabling Microsoft Defender Credential Guard using Intune, what profile type should you use?

    A. The Endpoint Protection profile type

    B. The Administrative Templates profile type

    C. The Identity Protection (Windows) profile type

    D. The Device Restrictions profile type

5. You are the administrator for your company network. You want to enable Microsoft Defender Credential Guard on computers that are running Windows 10/11. What should you install on these computers?

    A. Containers

    B. A guarded host

    C. Hyper-V

    D. Microsoft Defender Application Guard

6. You are the IT manager for WillPanek.com. The company has an Active Directory domain and a cloud-based Azure Active Directory. You need to protect your systems from common malware hacks that use executable files and scripts that attack applications like Microsoft Office (for example, Outlook). What do you need to do to accomplish this?

A. Microsoft Defender Credential Guard

B. Microsoft Defender Exploit Guard

C. Microsoft Defender Application Guard

D. Microsoft Defender Firewall with Advanced Security

7. You are the administrator for your company network. You and a colleague are discussing Microsoft Defender Application Guard. You know that there are a few hardware requirements that must be met to be able to use this feature. What is the minimum amount of RAM that Microsoft recommends to use Microsoft Defender Application Guard?

A. 2 GB

B. 4 GB

C. 8 GB

D. 12 GB

8. You are the administrator for a large organization and all your computers run Windows 10/11. These computers are all joined to Microsoft Azure Active Directory and all computers are enrolled in Intune. You need to ensure that all applications installed on the Windows client systems are only applications that are approved by the IT department. What should you implement to ensure this?

A. Microsoft Defender Application Guard

B. Microsoft Defender Credential Guard

C. Microsoft Defender Exploit Guard

D. Microsoft Defender Antivirus

9. You are the administrator of a large publishing company. All of your corporate machines run Windows 10/11. You need to ensure that no software will affect the Windows client machines from common malware hacks that use executable files and scripts to attack applications. What should you use?

A. Microsoft Defender Application Guard

B. Microsoft Defender Credential Guard

C. Microsoft Defender System Guard

D. Microsoft Defender Exploit Guard

10. You and a colleague are discussing how to implement Microsoft Defender for Endpoint. You have the following devices:

- Device 1: Window 10 Pro machine that is not a domain member
- Device 2: Windows 10 Enterprise machine that is a domain member
- Device 3: Windows 11 Pro machine that is a domain member
- Device 4: Mac OS X machine that is not a domain member

Which devices can be onboarded to Microsoft Defender for Endpoint using Microsoft Endpoint Configuration Manager?

A. Device 3 only

B. Device 1, Device 2, and Device 3 only.

C. Device 1, Device 2, Device 3, and Device 4

D. Device 2 and Device 3 only

11. You are the administrator for your company network. You and a colleague are discussing Microsoft Defender for Endpoint and its built-in features and capabilities. Once this capability is put in place, it will detect, investigate, and respond to advanced threats. What is the name of this Microsoft Defender for Endpoint capability?

A. Attack Surface Reduction

B. Endpoint Detection and Response

C. Next Generation Protection

D. Threat & Vulnerability Management

12. You are the administrator for your company network. You and a colleague are discussing Windows Security. One section of Windows Security covers the Microsoft Defender SmartScreen settings and Exploit Protection mitigations. What section is being discussed?

A. Account Protection

B. App & Browser Control

C. Device Security

D. Virus & Threat Protection

13. You are the administrator for your company network. You and a colleague are discussing Microsoft Defender Application Guard. You know that you can configure the mode used by Microsoft Defender Application Guard. What mode allows users to manage their own device settings?

A. Enterprise mode

B. Readiness mode

C. Standalone mode

D. User mode

14. You are the administrator for your company network. You and a colleague are discussing Microsoft Defender Application Guard. You know that it is turned off by default, and you want to install it using Control Panel. Where in Control Panel do you install it?

A. Ease of Access

B. Network and Internet

C. Programs and Features

D. System and Security

15. You are the administrator for your company network. You and a colleague are discussing setting up security baselines by using Intune. Which Intune built-in role account can create the security baselines?

A. Application Manager

B. Help Desk Operator

C. Policy and Profile Manager

D. Read Only Operator

16. You are the administrator for your company network. You and a colleague are discussing endpoint security risks. One of these risks is when an attack uses an automated download of software to a device without the user's consent. What risk type are you discussing?

A. Drive-by downloads

B. Malware ads

C. Phishing

D. Ransomware

17. You are the administrator for your company network. You and a colleague are discussing Microsoft Defender for Endpoint and the Security Operations dashboard. One of the tiles shows you a list of devices that have the most active alerts. What is the name of this tile?

A. Active Alerts

B. Devices At Risk

C. Sensor Health

D. Service Health

18. You are the administrator for your company network. You and a colleague are discussing Microsoft Defender Exploit Guard components. One of the components consists of rules that help prevent attack vectors that are applied by scripts, email, and Office-based malware. What is being discussed?

A. Attack surface reduction rules

B. Controlled folder access

C. Exploit protection

D. Network protection

19. You are the administrator for your company network. You and a colleague are discussing Microsoft Defender Application Guard. You know that there are a few hardware requirements that must be met to utilize this feature. What is the minimum amount of hard disk space that Microsoft recommends to utilize Microsoft Defender Application Guard?

A. 5 GB of free space

B. 10 GB of free space

C. 15 GB of free space

D. 20 GB of free space

20. You are the administrator for your company network. You and a colleague are discussing the ways to enable Microsoft Defender Credential Guard. Microsoft Defender Credential Guard can be enabled by using Group Policy, the Registry, or the Hypervisor-Protected Code Integrity (HVCI) and the Microsoft Defender Credential Guard hardware readiness tool. You decide that you'd like to enable it using Group Policy. What setting in Group Policy should you enable?

A. Deploy Microsoft Defender Application Control

B. Install Microsoft Defender Application Control

C. Turn On Virtualization Based Security

D. Turn Off Virtualization Based Security

Chapter

13

Monitoring Devices

MICROSOFT EXAM OBJECTIVES COVERED IN THIS CHAPTER:

✓ **Monitor devices**

- Monitor devices by using Azure Monitor; monitor device hardware and software inventory by using Endpoint Manager Admin Center; monitor devices by using Endpoint Analytics.

One of the daily tasks that you as an administrator will need to do is fix Windows client systems that are having issues. There are many ways to determine what issues a Windows client system may be having, and several tools are available to help you solve those issues.

The best way to protect any Windows client system is to make sure the users' files are stored on a network server and backed up daily. But there may be times when you need to back up the Windows 10/11 system.

Windows 10/11 includes a full backup and restore application called Backup and Restore (Windows 7) that allows a user or an administrator to maintain a backup copy of any of the Windows 10/11 component files and data files that are considered critical to the operation of their day-to-day business. In this chapter we will discuss using different tools for monitoring devices such as Azure Monitor, Endpoint Manager Admin Center, Endpoint Analytics, and the Microsoft Azure Backup utility. You'll see how easy it is for your users and IT administrators to quickly and easily back up their documents to the cloud.

There will be times when you need to monitor the Windows 10/11 system. Sometimes, performance optimization can feel like a luxury, but it can be very important, especially if you can't get your Windows client system to run applications the way they are intended to run. The Windows 10/11 operating system has been specifically designed to keep your mission-critical applications and data accessible even in times of failures.

The most common cause of such problems is a hardware configuration issue. Poorly written device drivers and unsupported hardware can cause problems with system stability. Failed hardware components (such as system memory) may do so as well. Memory chips can be faulty, electrostatic discharge can ruin them, and other hardware issues can occur. No matter what, a problem with your memory chip spells disaster for your Windows 10/11 system.

Usually, third-party hardware vendors provide utility programs with their computers that can be used for performing hardware diagnostics on machines to help you locate the source of problems. These utilities are a good first step to resolving intermittent problems, but Windows 10/11 comes with several utilities that can help you diagnose and fix your issues.

In this chapter, we'll cover the tools and methods used for measuring performance and troubleshooting failures in Windows 10/11. Before you dive into the technical details, however, you should thoroughly understand what you're trying to accomplish and how you'll meet this goal.

Monitoring Windows

Because performance monitoring and optimization are vital functions in network environments of any size, Windows 10/11 includes several monitoring and performance tools, including Performance Monitor, Reliability Monitor, Task Manager, and Event Viewer.

Performance Monitor allows you to monitor different parameters of the Windows 10/11 operating system and associated services and applications. You can also use one of the other tools to monitor performance in Windows 10/11. Reliability Monitor, Task Manager, and Event Viewer are all useful for monitoring different areas of overall system performance and for examining details related to specific system events. I discussed these tools in greater detail in Chapter 7, "Configuring Recovery."

Monitor Cloud-Based Tools

Microsoft offers a couple of different cloud-based tools for monitoring services:

- Azure Monitor, which is designed for the cloud but can also be used to monitor on-premises systems
- System Center Operations Manager (SCOM), which is designed for on-premises and for the cloud

These tools provide core monitoring services, which include alerts, service uptime tracking, health monitoring for application and infrastructure, diagnostics, and analytics.

Azure Monitor

Azure Monitor is software that runs as a service (SaaS). All of the supporting infrastructure runs in Azure and is handled by Microsoft. Azure Monitor was created to perform analytics, diagnostics, and monitoring. The core components of the infrastructure, such as collectors, metrics and logs store, and analytics, are run by Microsoft (see Figure 13.1).

Many of the following figures were taken directly from Microsoft's website. Since many of the figures point out specific issues, most of the figures were taken from Microsoft's website to demonstrate those points. For more information on Azure Monitor, please check out Microsoft's website at: https://learn.microsoft.com/en-us/azure/azure-monitor.

Here are a few things that you can do with Azure Monitor:

- With Application Insights, you can detect and diagnose issues across applications and dependencies.
- With VMs and Azure Monitor for Containers, you can compare infrastructure issues.

- By using Log Analytics for troubleshooting and deep diagnostics, you can monitor data.
- By using smart alerts and automated actions, you can support operations at scale.
- By using Azure dashboards and workbooks, you can create visualizations.

FIGURE 13.1   Azure Monitor dashboard

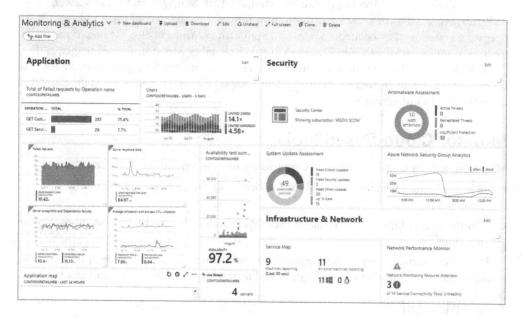

Figure 13.2 provides a view of how Azure Monitor works. In the middle are the two fundamental types of data used by Azure Monitor; these are the data stores for metrics and logs. On the left side are the sources that populate the data stores. On the right side are the various functions that Azure Monitor can perform with this collected data.

As mentioned earlier, all the data that is collected by Azure Monitor fits into one of two fundamental types:

- *Metrics* are numerical values that express a piece of the system at a specific point in time. They are capable of supporting real-time scenarios.

- *Logs* contain other kinds of data, which is arranged into records with different sets of properties for each type.

Data collected by Azure Monitor will appear on the right-hand side on the Overview page in the Azure portal. You may notice several charts that display the performance metrics. Click any of the graphs to open the data in Metrics Explorer, shown in Figure 13.3, so that you can chart the values of various metrics over a given period of time. You can also view the charts or pin them to a dashboard to view them with other visualizations.

FIGURE 13.2   How Azure Monitor works

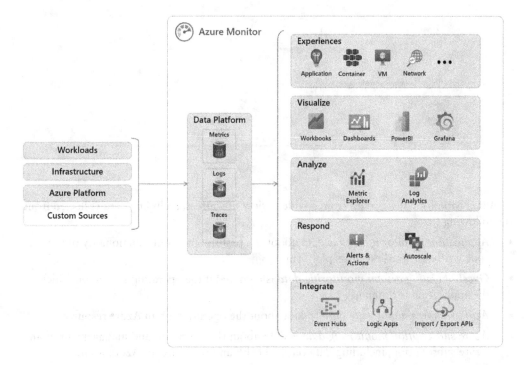

FIGURE 13.3   Metrics Explorer

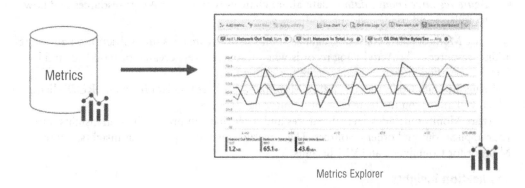

Metrics Explorer

Log data that is accumulated with Azure Monitor can be analyzed by using queries. You can create and test queries by using Log Analytics in the Azure portal (see Figure 13.4).

FIGURE 13.4   Log Analytics

Log Analytics

Azure Monitor collects data from a wide variety of sources, including data collected from the following tiers:

- *Application monitoring data* is data about the performance and functionality of the code written, regardless of its platform.

- *Guest operating system monitoring data* is data about the operating system on which the application is running.

- *Azure resource monitoring data* is data about the operation of an Azure resource.

- *Azure subscription monitoring data* is data about the operation and management of an Azure subscription, including data on the health and operation of Azure itself.

- *Azure tenant monitoring data* is data about the operation of tenant-level Azure services, such as Azure Active Directory.

- *Azure resource change data* is data about changes within your Azure resources and how to address and triage incidents and issues.

Azure Monitor starts collecting data as soon as you create an Azure subscription and start adding resources. The Activity log records when resources were created or modified, and the Metrics will show how the resources are performing.

Using the Data Collector API, Azure Monitor can collect log data from any REST client, which will allow you to create custom monitoring scenarios.

Azure Monitor includes several features and tools that can provide helpful insights into your applications and other resources. These features include Application Insights, Azure Monitor for Containers, and VM Insights.

Application Insights

Application Insights monitors the availability, performance, and usage of web applications that are hosted either in the cloud or on-premises. It uses Azure Monitor to provide insight into an application's operations and to diagnose problems without waiting for a user to report it. Application Insights includes connection points to several different development tools and can integrate with Visual Studio to support DevOps processes (see Figure 13.5).

FIGURE 13.5   Application Insights

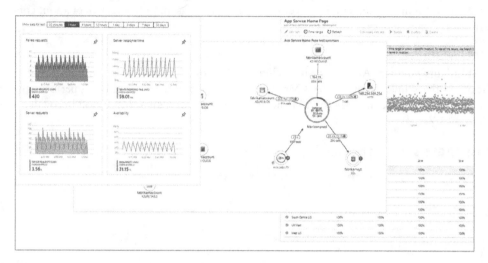

Container Insights

Container Insights is a feature intended to monitor the performance of container workloads. It shows performance visibility by collecting memory and processor metrics from controllers, nodes, and containers. Container logs are also collected (see Figure 13.6).

FIGURE 13.6   Container Insights

Container Insights monitors the performance and health of Azure Kubernetes Services or Azure Container Instances. It also collects container logs and inventory data about containers and their images.

VM Insights

VM Insights monitors Azure virtual machines (VMs) by analyzing the performance and health of the Windows and Linux VMs. This includes support for monitoring performance and application dependencies for VMs hosted on-premises or on another cloud provider (see Figure 13.7).

FIGURE 13.7   VM Insights

VM Insights delivers health monitoring for the guest Azure VMs when you're monitoring Windows and Linux virtual machines. It evaluates the health of major operating system components to determine the current health state. When it determines the guest VM is experiencing an issue, it will generate an alert.

In addition to monitoring data, Azure Monitor allows you to perform other functions to meet your needs:

- *Alerts* inform you of critical conditions and can attempt to take corrective action. Alert rules (see Figure 13.8) provide near-real-time alerting based on metric numeric values, while rules based on logs allow for complex logic across data from numerous sources. Alert rules use action groups, which contain unique sets of recipients and actions that can be shared across multiple rules.

FIGURE 13.8 Alerts

* Subscription ●	Resource group ●	Time Range ●
Contoso IT - demo ⌄	mms-eus ⌄	Past Hour ⌄

Contoso IT - demo ❯ mms-eus

Total Alerts	Smart Groups ●	Total Alert Rules		Learn More
29	1	15		About Alerts ☑
Since 8/1/2018, 4:38:39 PM	96.55% Reduction	Enabled 13		

SEVERITY	TOTAL ALERTS		NEW	ACKNOWLEDGED	CLOSED
Sev 0	26		26	0	0
Sev 1	0		0	0	0
Sev 2	3		3	0	0
Sev 3	0		0	0	0
Sev 4	0		0	0	0

- *Autoscale* allows you to have just the right amount of resources needed in order to handle application workload. Azure Monitor allows you to create rules that use metrics collected to determine when resources will be added automatically to handle increases in workload and can save money by removing idle resources. You can specify a minimum and maximum number of instances and the logic for when to increase or decrease resources (see Figure 13.9).

FIGURE 13.9 Autoscale

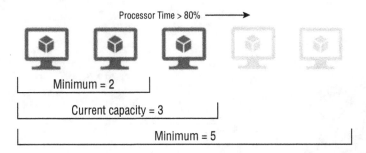

Processor Time > 80% ⟶

Minimum = 2
Current capacity = 3
Minimum = 5

- *Azure dashboards* allow you to join different kinds of data, including metrics and logs, into a single pane in the Azure portal (see Figure 13.10).
- *Workbooks* provide an area for data analysis with the ability to create visual reports (see Figure 13.11). Workbooks can use multiple data sources across Azure and combine them into one unified experience. You can use the workbooks that are provided with Insights, or you can create your own using a template.

FIGURE 13.10 Azure Monitor dashboard

FIGURE 13.11 Workbooks

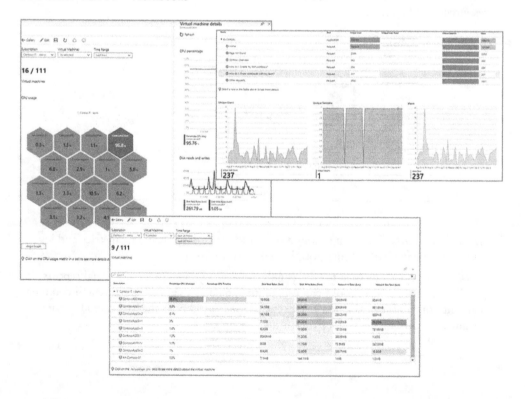

- *Power BI* is a business analytics service that provides interactive visualizations across a wide variety of data sources and makes data available to others either within or outside the organization. You can configure Power BI to import log data automatically from Azure Monitor (see Figure 13.12).

FIGURE 13.12   Power BI

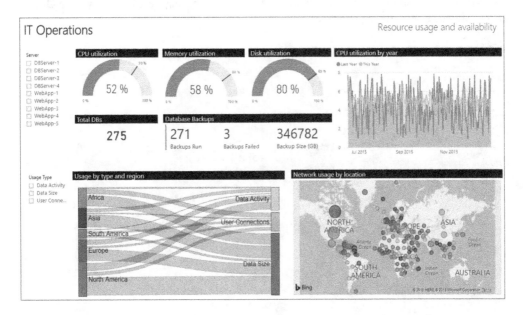

Using Azure Monitor, you can also import and export data to create custom solutions that use your monitoring data to suit your needs:

- *Azure Event Hubs* is a streaming platform and event breakdown service that transforms and stores data using any real-time analytics provider. Use Event Hubs to stream Azure Monitor data to partner SIEM and monitoring tools.

- *Logic Apps* is a service that allows the automation of tasks and processes using workflows that combine different systems and services. Activities are available that read and write metrics and logs in Azure Monitor, which allows you to build workflows integrating with a variety of other systems.

- *Multiple APIs* are available to read and write metrics and logs to and from Azure Monitor, as well as access generated alerts. You can also use them to configure and retrieve alerts.

System Center Operations Manager

Operations Manager is a component of Microsoft System Center. The current version is System Center Operations Manager 2022. This is software that allows you to monitor services, devices, and operations for a number of computers using a single console. The console enables you to check the health, performance, and availability for all monitored objects in the environment and helps you identify and resolve problems. Figure 13.13 shows the Operations Manager Monitoring Console.

FIGURE 13.13   System Center Operations Manager Monitoring Console

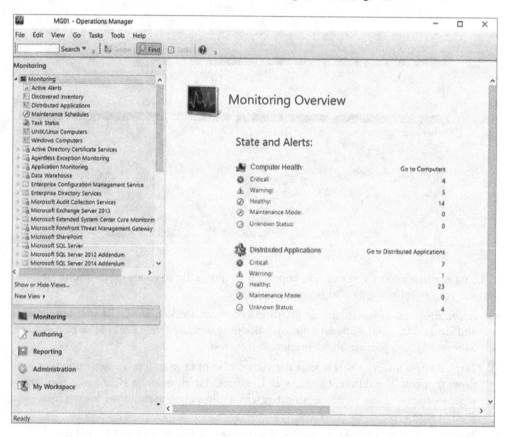

Operations Manager can inform you which objects you are monitoring are not healthy, it can send you alerts if a problem is identified, and it can provide information that will assist you in identifying the issue and possible solutions on how to fix it.

From 2015 until April 2018, Operations Management Suite (OMS) was a bundle of the following Azure management services:

- Azure Automation
- Azure Backup
- Application Insights
- Operational Insights (later called Log Analytics)
- Site Recovery

The functionality of the services that were part of OMS did not change when discontinued; they were realigned under Azure Monitor. In March 2019, Microsoft released System Center 2019 and then in April 2022, Microsoft released System Center 2022.

System Center enables deployment and management at a larger scale to meet data center needs.

System Center 2022 provides the following:

- Tools to monitor and manage data centers
- Support and management capabilities in the most current versions of Windows Server
- Hybrid management and monitoring capabilities with Azure

System Center 2022 is a Long-Term Servicing Channel (LTSC) release and provides five years of standard support and five years of extended support.

Monitor Azure Device Security

Azure IoT Central Applications is an Internet of Things (IoT) application platform that lessens the load and cost of developing, managing, and maintaining enterprise-grade IoT solutions. Azure IoT Central Applications provides you with the ability to focus energy, money, and time working with a business with IoT data rather than simply maintaining and updating an intricate and continually changing IoT infrastructure. Use Microsoft Azure IoT Central Applications to monitor devices and change settings.

Azure IoT Central Applications are hosted by Microsoft, which reduces the administrative overhead of managing applications.

The web user intake allows you to monitor device conditions, create rules, and manage devices and their data through their life cycle. It also enables you to act on device insights by extending IoT intelligence into line-of-business applications.

With Azure IoT Central you can:

- Reduce management burden
- Reduce operational costs and overheads
- Easily customize applications while working with the following:
  - Industry-leading technologies such as Azure IoT Hub and Azure Time Series Insights
  - Enterprise-grade security features such as end-to-end encryption

Azure IoT Central Applications has four personas who interact with an Azure IoT Central Application. They are as follows:

- A *builder* is responsible for defining the types of devices that connect to the application and for customizing the application for the operator.
- An *operator* manages the devices connected to the application.
- An *administrator* is responsible for administrative tasks such as managing users and roles within the application.
- A *device developer* creates the code that runs on a device connected to your application.

After the builder defines the types of devices that can connect to the application, a device developer creates the code to run on the devices. The device developer utilizes Microsoft's open source Azure IoT SDKs to create the device code. These SDKs have broad language, platform, and protocol support to meet your needs to connect the devices to the Azure IoT Central Application. The SDKs can help you implement the following device capabilities:

- Create a secure connection.
- Send telemetry.
- Report status.
- Receive configuration updates.

An operator uses Azure IoT Central Applications to manage the devices. Operators perform tasks such as:

- Monitoring the devices connected to the application
- Troubleshooting and remediating issues with devices
- Provisioning new devices

As a builder, you create custom rules and actions that operate over data streaming from connected devices. An operator can enable or disable these rules at the device level.

An operator can:

- Use the Device Explorer page to view, add, and delete devices connected to the Azure IoT Central Applications.
- Maintain an up-to-date inventory of devices.
- Keep device metadata up-to-date by changing the values stored in the device properties.
- Control the behavior of devices by updating a setting on a specific device from the Settings page.

Viewing an Individual Device

To view an individual device using IoT Central Applications:

1.   On the left navigation menu, choose Devices.

2.   Choose a device template from the Templates list.

3. In the right-hand pane of the Devices page, you will see a list of devices created from that device template. Choose an individual device to see the device details page for that device (see Figure 13.14).

FIGURE 13.14 Devices

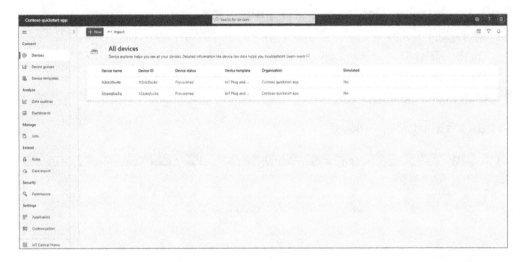

Another way an administrator can view the events collected from a specific computer in Azure is to run a query in Logs Analytics. Run the following query:

```
Event | where Computer = = "ComputerName"
```

Adding a Device to an Azure IoT Central Application

To add a device to an IoT Central Application:

1. On the left navigation menu, choose Devices.
2. Choose the device template to create a device.
3. Choose + New.
4. Enter a device name and ID or accept the default. The maximum length of a device name is 148 characters. The maximum length of a device ID is 128 characters.
5. Choose Real or Simulated. A real device is for a physical device that you connect to your Azure IoT Central Application. A simulated device has sample data generated for you by an Azure IoT Central Application.
6. If your application uses an organization, you can select the organization that the device belongs to. You can set a default organization to appear in the Organization drop-down.
7. Select Create. The device will now appear in the device list for this template.

To connect a large number of devices to an application, you can bulk import devices using a CSV file. The CSV file should have the following columns and headers:

- IOTC_DeviceID (The device ID name should be all lowercase.)
- IOTC_DeviceName (This column is optional.)

Bulk-Registering Devices in an Application

To bulk-register devices:

1. On the left navigation menu, choose Devices.
2. On the left panel, choose the device template to bulk-create the devices.
3. Click Import (see Figure 13.15).

FIGURE 13.15   Import button

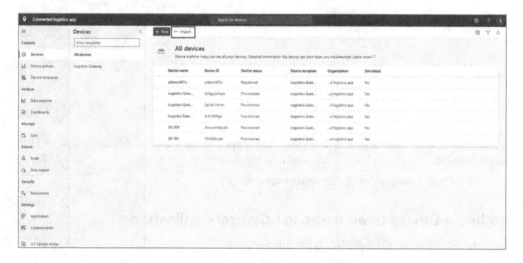

4. Select an organization to assign the devices to. All the devices that you are importing are assigned to the same organization. To assign devices to different organizations, create multiple import files, one for each organization.
5. Select the CSV file that has the list of device IDs to be imported.
6. Device import starts once the file has been uploaded. You can track the import status in the Device Operations panel. This panel appears automatically after the import starts, or you can access it by clicking the bell icon in the top-right corner.
7. Once the import completes, a success message is shown in the Device Operations panel (see Figure 13.16). If the device import operation fails, you see an error message in the Device Operations panel and a log file capturing the errors will be created that you can download.

FIGURE 13.16   Import Complete Success message

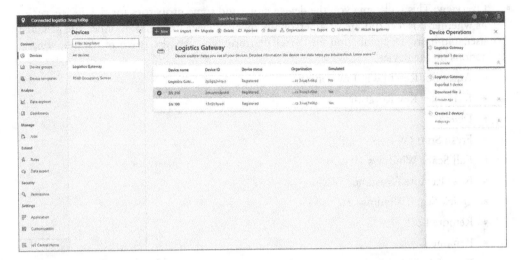

Deleting a Device (Real or Simulated) from an Azure IoT Central Application

To delete either a real or simulated device from your Azure IoT Central application, perform the following:

1. On the left navigation menu, choose Devices.

2. Select the device template of the device to be deleted.

3. Select the box next to the device you want to delete.

4. Click Delete.

Monitor Devices by Using Endpoint Manager Admin Center

Chapter 11 discussed using the Endpoint Manager admin center, but in this section we will delve deeper into how to monitor devices by using this tool. In the Azure portal, you can view all your devices, including their properties. The Devices feature provides additional information regarding the devices you manage, including the hardware and software that is installed.

To view the device details, perform the following:

1. Sign into the Microsoft Endpoint Manager admin center at `https://endpoint .microsoft.com`.

2. Select Devices ➤ All Devices, and then select one of the devices from the list to view its details:

When you select a device, you will see:

- **Overview:** This will show you the device name and some properties for the device, such as whether it is a corporate or a personally owned device, the serial number, the primary user, and more. Depending on the device platform, you can also perform the following actions on the device:

  - Autopilot Reset (Windows only)
  - BitLocker Key Rotation
  - Delete
  - Fresh Start (Windows only)
  - Full Scan (Windows 10 only)
  - New Remote Assistance Session
  - Quick Scan (Windows 10 only)
  - Remote Lock
  - Rename Device
  - Reset Passcode
  - Restart
  - Retire
  - Sync
  - Update Windows Defender Security Intelligence
  - Wipe

- **Properties:** Use this to assign a device category and change ownership of the device to a personal device or a corporate device.

- **Hardware:** This section includes details regarding the hardware of the device, such as the device ID, operating system and version, storage space, and more.

- **Discovered Apps:** This section lists all the apps that Intune found installed on the device, along with the app version.

- **Device compliance:** This section lists all the assigned compliance policies and whether or not the device is compliant.

- **Device Configuration:** This section shows all the device configuration policies that are assigned to the device and whether the policy succeeded or failed.

- **App Configuration:** This section shows how the Apps are configured.

- **Recovery Keys:** This section shows available BitLocker keys that are found for the device.

- **Managed Apps:** This section lists all the managed apps that Intune configured and that have been deployed to the device.

Table 13.1 shows the hardware device details. The information in Table 13.1 was taken directly from Microsoft's website. This is not a complete list; for more information and a complete list, check out Microsoft's website at `https://docs.microsoft.com/en-us/mem/intune/remote-actions/device-inventory`.

TABLE 13.1 Hardware device details

Detail	Description	Platform
Name	The name of the device.	Windows, iOS, Android
UDID	The device's Unique Device identifier.	Windows, iOS
Intune Device ID	A GUID that uniquely identifies the device.	Windows, iOS, Android
Serial number	The device's serial number from the manufacturer.	Windows, iOS, iPadOS, Android
Shared device	If Yes, the device is shared by more than one user.	Windows, iOS
Operating system	The operating system used on the device.	Windows, iOS, Android
Operating system version	The version of the operating system on the device.	Windows, iOS, iPadOS, Android
Total storage space	The total storage space on the device (in gigabytes).	Windows, iOS
Wi-Fi MAC	The device's Media Access Control address.	Windows, iOS/iPadOS, Android
Enrolled date	The date and time that the device was enrolled in Intune.	Windows, iOS/iPadOS, Android
Azure AD registered	If Yes, the device is registered with Azure Directory.	Windows, iOS/iPadOS, Android

The hardware and software inventory are refreshed in Intune every seven days, starting from the date of enrollment.

Monitor Discovered Apps

Intune provides a list of detected apps on the Intune-enrolled devices in your tenant. To see all discovered apps, sign into the Microsoft Endpoint Manager admin center and then select Apps ➤ Monitor ➤ Discovered Apps.

If you want to monitor discovered apps with Intune for an individual device, perform the following:

1. Sign in to the Microsoft Endpoint Manager admin center at `https://endpoint.microsoft.com`.

2. Select Devices ➤ All Devices and then select the desired device.

3. To view detected apps for this device, select Discovered Apps in the Monitor section.

Table 13.2 shows the app platform type, the apps that are monitored for personal devices, the apps that are monitored for company-owned devices, and the refresh cycle. This information was taken directly from Microsoft's website.

TABLE 13.2   Details of discovered apps

Platform	For personally owned devices	For company-owned devices	Refresh cycle from Device Enrollment
Windows 10/11 (Win32 Apps)	N/A	MSI-installed apps on the device	Every 24 hours
Windows 10/11 (Modern Apps)	Only managed modern apps	All modern apps installed on the device	Every 7 days
Windows 8.1	Only managed apps	Only managed apps	Every 7 days
Windows RT	Only managed apps	Only managed apps	Every 7 days
iOS/iPadOS	Only managed apps	All apps installed on the device	Every 7 days
macOS	Only managed apps	All apps installed on the device	Every 7 days
Android	Only managed apps	All apps installed on the device	Every 7 days
Android Enterprise	Only managed apps	Only apps installed on the Android Enterprise work profile device	Every 7 days

Monitoring App Information and Assignments

Intune provides several ways to monitor the properties of apps that you manage and to manage app assignment status. To monitor app information and assignments, perform the following:

1. Sign into the Microsoft Endpoint Manager admin center at `https://endpoint.microsoft.com`.

2. Select Apps ➤ All Apps.

3. In the list of apps, select the app you'd like to monitor. You will see an app pane, which will show you an overview of the device status and the user status.

In the All Apps pane, you will see details on the status of an app in your environment. You will see the following sections: Essentials, Device And User Status Graphs, Device Install Status, and User Install Status.

The Essentials section contains the following information about the app:

- **Publisher:** Who the publisher of the app is

- **Operating system:** The app operating system (Windows, iOS/iPadOS, Android, etc.)

- **Created:** The date and time when this revision was created

- **Assigned:** Indicates whether or not the app has been assigned using Yes or No

The Device And User Status Graphs section shows graphs indicating the number of apps for the following status types:

- **Installed:** The number of apps installed

- **Not Installed:** The number of apps not installed

- **Failed:** The number of failed installations

- **Install Pending:** The number of apps that are in the process of being installed

- **Not Applicable:** The number of apps for which status is not applicable

When you select the Device Install Status section, you will see a list of the device status types. The details table will include the following columns:

- **Device name:** This column shows the name of the device.

- **User name:** This column shows the name of the user.

- **Platform:** This column shows the operating system of the device (Windows, iOS/iPadOS, Android, etc.).

- **Version:** This column shows the version number of the app.

- **Status:** This column shows the status of the app.

- **Status Details:** This column shows the details of the status.

- **Last Check-in:** This column shows the date of the device's last sync with Intune.

When you select the User Install Status section, you will see the user status list, which includes a table that has the following columns:

- **Name:** This column shows the name of the user in Azure Active Directory.

- **User name:** This column shows the unique name of the user.

- **Installations:** This column shows the number of apps installed by the user.

- **Failures:** This column shows the number of failed app installations for the user.

- **Not Installed:** This column shows the number of apps not installed by the user.

Monitoring Devices by Using Endpoint Analytics

Endpoint Analytics is part of the Microsoft Productivity Score. These analytics provide insight for measuring how your company is working and the quality of the experience that you are providing. Endpoint Analytics helps identify policies and hardware problems that could be slowing down your devices. We discussed Endpoint Analytics in Chapter 8, "Deploy Windows Client," but here we'll delve more into monitoring devices by using Endpoint Analytics.

To help you determine what devices may be having issues with the user experience, Endpoint Analytics will show you scores per device. These scores range from 0 to 100. The lower the score, the more improvement is needed. By reviewing the scores per device, you can find and resolve problems and improve the user experience.

To view the device scores, perform the following:

1. Navigate to `https://endpoint.microsoft.com` and sign in to open the Overview page.

2. Select the Device Scores tab to display individual device scores. You can sort by score in order to locate the devices that may need attention, as shown in Figure 13.17.

3. Find the device that may need improvement and select it to open a page that provides you with more information.

Another way you can access per-device scores is by using the device's User Experience page. From this page, you can review the Endpoint Analytics, Startup Performance, and Application Reliability information for the chosen device, as shown in Figure 13.18.

FIGURE 13.17   Devices Scores tab

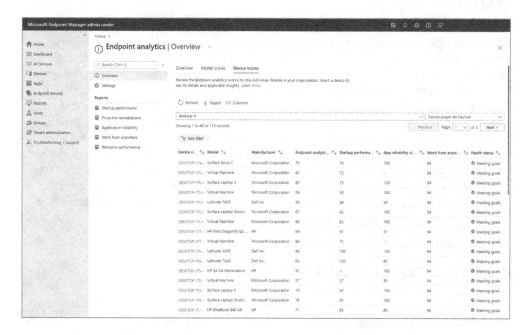

FIGURE 13.18   User Experience page

Summary

This chapter discussed using Azure Monitor cloud-based tools, such as Azure Monitor, System Center Operations Manager (SCOM), Endpoint Manager Admin Center, and Endpoint Analytics. These tools provide monitoring services, which include alerts, service uptime tracking, health monitoring for application and infrastructure, diagnostics, and analytics.

We also discussed how to monitor Azure Device Security. Azure IoT Central is an Internet of Things (IoT) application platform that lessens the load and cost of developing, managing, and maintaining enterprise-grade IoT solutions. Azure IoT Central provides you with the ability to focus energy, money, and time working with a business with IoT data, rather than simply maintaining and updating an intricate and continually changing IoT infrastructure.

Use Microsoft Azure IoT Central Applications to monitor devices and change settings. Azure IoT Central Applications are hosted by Microsoft, which reduces the administrative overhead of managing applications.

Exam Essentials

Be familiar with Azure Monitor cloud-based tools. Microsoft offers two cloud-based tools for monitoring services: Azure Monitor and System Center Operations Manager (SCOM).

Understand Azure IoT Central. Azure IoT Central is an Internet of Things (IoT) application platform that lessens the load and cost of developing, managing, and maintaining enterprise-grade IoT solutions.

Know how to monitor device hardware and software using Endpoint Manager Admin Center. Microsoft Endpoint Manager Admin Center helps you keep your data secure both in the cloud and on-premises. Endpoint Manager includes the services and tools that you will use to manage and monitor mobile devices, desktop computers, virtual machines, embedded devices, and servers.

Understand how to monitor devices by using Endpoint Analytics. Endpoint Analytics is part of the Microsoft Productivity Score. These scores provide a measurement of how your organization is performing and the quality of the experience that you are delivering to your users. Know how to use the Device Scores tab to find and resolve end-user issues.

Video Resources

There are no videos for this chapter.

Review Questions

1. You are the administrator for an organization that uses a hybrid on-site and Azure network. You use Microsoft Azure Log Analytics workspace to collect all the event logs from the computers at your organization. You have a computer named Laptop1. Laptop1 has Windows client loaded on the system. You need to view the events collected from Laptop1. Which query would an administrator run in Log Analytics?

    A. `Eventview | where SourceSystem = = "laptop1"`

    B. `Eventview | where Computer = = "laptop1"`

    C. `Event | where SourceSystem = = "laptop1"`

    D. `Event | where Computer = = " laptop1"`

2. You are the administrator for your company network. You and a colleague are discussing software that runs as a service (SaaS). All of the supporting infrastructure runs in Azure and is handled by Microsoft. What is the name of this program that was created to perform analytics, diagnostics, and monitoring?

    A. Azure Monitor

    B. Event Viewer

    C. Network Monitor

    D. Performance Monitor

3. You are the administrator for your company network. You have about 1,000 Windows client computers that are members of an Active Directory domain. You create a workspace in Microsoft Azure Log Analytics. You plan on capturing the event logs from the computer to Azure. What Azure service should you use?

    A. Azure Cosmos Database

    B. Azure Storage account

    C. Azure SQL Database

    D. Log Analytics

4. You are the administrator for your company network. You and a colleague are discussing reports and how to customize the view to meet your needs. You want to generate a custom device inventory report to show the Device Name, Managed By, and OS Version information. What should you modify to see the needed information?

    A. Columns

    B. Export

    C. Filter

    D. Refresh

5. You are the administrator for your company network. You and a colleague are discussing a service that will recognize compatibility issues and receive mitigation suggestions based on cloud-enabled data insights. What is this service called?

    A. Configuration Associate

    B. Desktop Analytics

    C. Windows Analytics

    D. Windows Services Manager

6. You are the administrator for your company network. You and a colleague are discussing reports and how to customize the view to meet your needs. You want to generate a custom device inventory report that will display only certain requirements that you have selected and only for the requested devices. What should you modify to see the needed information?

    A. Columns

    B. Export

    C. Filter

    D. Refresh

7. You are the administrator for your company network. You and a colleague are discussing Azure Monitor. The data that is collected by Azure Monitor fits into one of two fundamental types. What are these types? (Choose two.)

    A. Logs

    B. Measurement

    C. Metrics

    D. Records

8. You and a colleague are discussing using log queries to help you leverage the value of the data collected in Azure Monitor Logs. There is a tool in the Azure portal that is used for writing log queries. What is this tool called?

    A. Azure Log Creator

    B. Azure Monitor Log Maker

    C. Log Analytics

    D. Log Query Analyzer

9. You are the administrator for a large organization that has started using Azure. You need to use a Microsoft Azure monitoring tool to monitor devices and change settings. Which of the following tools can you use?

    A. Performance Monitor

    B. Microsoft Azure IoT Central

    C. Azure Performance Center

    D. Intune Performance Center

10. You are the administrator for your company network. You and a colleague are discussing reports and how to customize the view to meet your needs. You want to generate and save a custom device inventory report that will show only certain requirements that have been selected. You filter the report to meet your needs. Where should you go next if you want to save the report?

A. Columns

B. Export

C. Filter

D. Refresh

11. You are the administrator for your company network. You and a colleague are discussing Azure Monitor and how it starts collecting data as soon as you create an Azure subscription. What records when resources are created and modified?

A. Activity Log

B. Metrics

C. Azure Resource Graph

D. Autoscale

12. You are the administrator for your company network. You and a colleague are discussing the Microsoft Endpoint Manager admin center. You want to take a look at a device's device ID. Which section should you go to in order to view that information?

A. Device Compliance

B. Hardware

C. Managed Apps

D. Properties

13. You are the administrator for your company network. You and a colleague are discussing Azure Monitor and the tasks that you can use it for. Which of the following allows you to detect and diagnose issues across applications and dependencies?

A. Application Insights

B. Container Insights

C. Log Analytics

D. VM Insights

14. You are the administrator for your company network. You and a colleague are discussing Endpoint Analytics. You fear that a device may be impacting your Endpoint Analytics scores. Which tab do you select if you want to display individual device scores to sort and find a device that may need attention?

A. Device Scores tab

B. Device Performance tab

C. Model Scores tab

D. Overview tab

15. You are the administrator for your company network. You and a colleague are discussing how to import devices in bulk to the Azure IoT Central Application. What file type allows you to bulk-add devices into Azure IoT Central Applications?

    A. A CSV file

    B. An EPS file

    C. A TXT file

    D. An XLS file

16. You are the administrator for your company network. You and a colleague are discussing adding a device to an Azure IoT Central Application. What is the maximum number of characters you can have for a device name?

    A. 40 characters

    B. 56 characters

    C. 128 characters

    D. 148 characters

17. You are the administrator for your company network. You and a colleague are discussing Azure Monitor. Which of the following options allows you to use just the right amount of resources in order to handle an application's load?

    A. Alerts

    B. Autoscale

    C. Dashboards

    D. Visualizations

18. You are the administrator for your company network. You and a colleague are discussing the Azure IoT Central Application personas. Which persona is responsible for defining the types of devices that connect to the application and can customize the application for the operator?

    A. Administrator

    B. Builder

    C. Device Developer

    D. Operator

19. You are the administrator for your company network. You and a colleague are discussing adding a device to an Azure IoT Central Application. What is the maximum number of characters you can have for a device ID?

    A. 40 characters

    B. 56 characters

    C. 128 characters

    D. 148 characters

20. You are the administrator for your company network. You and a colleague are discussing Azure Monitor. Which of the following options will inform you of critical conditions and can attempt to take corrective action?

   A. Alerts

   B. Autoscale

   C. Dashboards

   D. Visualizations

Appendix

Answers to Review Questions

Chapter 1: Windows Client Installation

1. A. The Boot Configuration Data (BCD) store contains boot information parameters that were previously found in `Boot.ini` in older versions of Windows. To edit the boot options in the BCD store, use the bcdedit utility, which can be launched only from a command prompt.

2. B. By modifying the changes on the local Group Policy, you can manually configure your Windows Update settings. You can automatically configure the Windows Update settings by creating a server-issued Group Policy Object (GPO).

3. A. The `/unattend` option can be used with the `setup` command to initiate an unattended installation of Windows 10. You should also specify the location of the answer file to use when using the `Setup.exe` utility.

4. D. You would use the Sysprep utility. The `/generalize` option prevents system-specific information from being included in the image.

5. A. The DISM utility with the `/get-drivers` switch allows you to find out which drivers are installed on the WIM.

6. D. DISM is a command-line utility that can be used to create and manage Windows 10 image (WIM) files. You can configure a reference installation as desired and then use DISM to create an image of the installation that can then be deployed to the remaining computers.

7. B. WDSUTIL is a command-line utility that can be used to configure the WDS server. Several other configuration options need to be specified on the WDS server, and you can set them using WDSUTIL.

8. C. Windows System Image Manager (SIM) is used to create unattended answer files in Windows 10. It uses a GUI-based interface to set up and configure the most common options that are used within an answer file.

9. C. You enable WDS servers to respond to client requests through the Windows Deployment Services (WDS) Microsoft Management Console (MMC) Snap-in. In the PXE Properties dialog box, select the option Respond To Client Computers.

10. B. The `/generalize` option prevents system-specific information from being included in the image. The `Sysprep.exe` utility can be used with a variety of options. You can see a complete list by typing **sysprep/?** at a command-line prompt.

11. A, E. If you are going to implement the Secure Boot feature of Windows 10, then make sure the system firmware is set up as Unified Extensible Firmware Interface (UEFI) and not BIOS. You also need to make sure the disks are converted from Master Boot Record (MBR) disks to a GUID Partition Table (GPT) disk.

12. B. Use Windows Update Delivery Optimization to help get Windows updates and Microsoft Store apps more quickly and reliably. Windows Update Delivery Optimization (WUDO) is a Windows 10 tool that is designed to reduce bandwidth by having computers obtain updates

from other users on the network that have already downloaded the content, thus reducing the amount of traffic generated.

13. B. When installing or upgrading Windows 10, the version of Windows 10 that is installed must match the CPU version. For example, if your system is a 32-bit system, you must use a 32-bit version of Windows 10. If your system is a 64-bit system, you can install either the 32-bit or 64-bit version of Windows 10.

14. A. When Windows 10/11 is installed, the Setup program generates different log files. You can review these logs to check for any installation issues. The log file that you would want to review for this question is the Action log, which is stored as `C:\Windows\setupact.log`. This log includes all of the actions that were executed during the setup process and a description of each action. These actions are listed in chronological order.

15. C. Windows Update allows you to check for new updates and to change settings. To configure Windows Update, do the following:

1. Select Start ➤ Settings ➤ Update And Security.

2. Configure the options that you want to use for Windows Update by clicking the Advanced Options link. You can access the following options from Windows Update:

- Give Me Updates For Other Microsoft Products
- Choose When Updates Are Installed
- Pause Updates
- Delivery Optimization
- Privacy Settings

16. B. Cortana is Microsoft's digital assistant whose task is to help you get things done. Cortana is a powerful search and help utility. If your system has a microphone, you can ask Cortana questions, and it will help find an answer for you. If you don't have a microphone, just type in your question, and Cortana will try to help find an answer. To get started with Cortana, click the Cortana icon in the taskbar or type a command in the search bar. You can also activate the "Hey Cortana" mode.

17. A. Use the `driverquery.exe` command to view the installed devices and drivers. This is a command-line tool that provides a detailed list of all the device drivers installed on a computer. This enables an administrator to display a list of installed device drivers and their properties. If used without parameters, the `driverquery.exe` command will run on the local machine. The syntax for using `driverquery.exe` is as follows:

```
driverquery.exe [/s <system> [/u [<domain>\]<username> [/p
<password>]]] [/fo {table | list | csv}] [/nh] [/v | /si]
```

18. B. When performing a clean install to the same partition as an existing version of Windows, then the contents of the existing `Users` (or `Documents And Settings`), `Program Files`, and `Windows` directories will be placed in a directory called `C:\Windows.old`.

19. B. Microsoft typically releases product updates on Tuesdays. So, this day was given the nickname of Patch Tuesdays. Updates are tested prior to being released to the public.

20. C. The Windows Insider Program allows you to preview builds of Windows 10 (and above) and Windows Server 2019 (and above). It allows you to try new features and provide feedback directly to Microsoft. On the Windows client computer, go to Settings ➤ Update & Security ➤ Windows Insider Program. You will need to have administrator privileges to the computer.

Chapter 2: Configuring Users

1. A. The Group Policy Result Tool is accessed through the GPResult command-line utility. The `gpresult` command displays the resulting set of policies that were enforced on the computer and the specified user during the logon process.

2. A. The administrator should enable Audit Account Logon Events since it determines whether to audit instances of a user logging on to or logging off from a device. It is used to track whenever a user logs on, logs off, or makes a network connection. You can configure auditing for success or failure. The audited events can be viewed using Event Viewer.

3. B, C. Password policies ensure that security requirements are enforced on computers. It is important to know that password policies are set on a per-computer basis; they cannot be configured for specific users. Password Must Meet Complexity Requirements passwords must be six characters or longer and cannot contain the user's account name or any part of the user's full name. Also, passwords must contain three of the following four character types:

- English uppercase characters (A through Z)
- English lowercase characters (a through z)
- Decimal digits (0 through 9)
- Symbols (such as !, @, #, $, and %)

In this case, the password Abcde! meets complexity requirements because it is at least six characters long and contains an uppercase letter, lowercase letters, and a symbol. The password 1247445Np meets complexity requirements because it is at least six characters long and contains an uppercase letter, a lowercase letter, and numbers.

4. B. Folder redirection enables users and administrators to redirect the path of a known folder to a new location, manually or by using Group Policy. Folder redirection has to be configured using a server-based Group Policy object (GPO) and not a Local Group Policy object (LGPO). The new location can be a folder on the local computer or a directory on a file share. So, Windows LGPOs allow you to configure all of the above except for folder redirection.

5. D. Account Lockout Policy, a subset of Account Policies, is used to specify options that prevent a user from attempting multiple failed logon attempts. If the Account Lockout Threshold value is exceeded, the account will be locked. The account can be reset based on a specified amount of time or through administrator intervention. An Account Lockout Policy is a useful method of slowing down online password-guessing attacks.

6. D. The Restore Files and Directories user right allows a user to restore files and directories regardless of file and directory permissions. Assigning this user right is an alternative to making a user a member of the Backup Operators group. So, you will want to grant the new assistant the user right Restore Files and Directories. This setting allows users to bypass permissions when restoring files.

7. B. Password policies ensure that security requirements are enforced on a computer. Password policies are set on a per-computer basis so they cannot be configured for specific users. The Enforce Password History policy allows the system to keep track of a user's password history for up to 24 passwords. This prevents a user from using the same password over and over again.

8. B. Device Guard is a mixture of enterprise-related hardware and software security features that, when organized together, will lock a device down so that it can only run trusted applications. If the application is not trusted, then the application cannot run. It will lock a device so that it can only run trusted applications that are defined in your code integrity policies. The advantage to Device Guard is that it works on two levels: the kernel mode code integrity (KMCI) and user mode code integrity (UMCI). Since Device Guard works at both levels, it protects against hardware- and software-based threats. There are several ways to manage Device Guard: by using Group Policies, Microsoft System Center Configuration Manager (SCCM), Windows PowerShell, and Microsoft Intune.

9. C. To create a new local user account on a Windows client using Windows PowerShell, you will want to use the `New-LocalUser` cmdlet. This will create a local user account or a local user account that is connected to a Microsoft account.

10. A. The `New-LocalUser` cmdlet creates a local user account. This cmdlet creates a local user account or a local user account that is connected to a Microsoft account. The `-Name` parameter specifies the username for the user account. The `-NoPassword` parameter indicates that the user account does not have a password. The `Add-LocalGroupMember` cmdlet adds users or groups to a local security group. All the rights and permissions that are assigned to a group are assigned to all members of that group. The `-Member` parameter specifies an array of users or groups that this cmdlet adds to a security group.

11. B. By default, Windows 10/11 is configured to show the User Account Control (UAC) confirmation box every time a new program is installed or changes are made to the system settings. You can use security policies to configure how UAC works. They can be configured locally by using the Local Security Policy snap-in (`secpol.msc`) or configured for the domain, OU, or specific groups by using the Local Group Policy Editor.

12. C. Device Health Attestation allows you to verify that client systems have the correct BIOS configurations, enabled TPM, and have boot security measures enabled. If you want to use Device Health Attestation on a network or in the cloud, the systems must meet a few minimum requirements, with one being that Internet communication between the Configuration Manager client agent and has.spserv.microsoft.com (port 443) Health Attestation service needs to be established.

13. B. Because this is a service account you will want to set the deny logon locally user right. The deny logon locally is a Group Policy Object (GPO) setting that should be used for all service accounts because it helps keep unwanted users from logging in using an interactive logon. This policy setting controls which users are prevented from logging on directly at the device's console.

14. A, D. You can apply audit policies to individual files and folders on a computer by setting the permission type to record successful or failed access attempts in the security log. So, you would modify the Advance Security settings on the folder. You will also want to configure auditing by configuring the Audit File System setting from a GPO.

15. C. On Windows client computers and devices, the Microsoft Store app offers various apps, games, music, movies and TV, and books that a user can browse through. These can either be purchased or obtained for free to download and install for their Microsoft account. To disable users from being able to access the Microsoft Store app:

   1.   Launch Group Policy Management Console (GPMC).

   2.   Navigate to the Computer Configuration ➤ Administrative Templates ➤ Windows Components ➤ Store.

   3.   Locate Disable All Apps from the Windows Store policy and double-click to open it. Select the radio button next to Enabled, then click OK to enable the policy. This will disable any application(s) installed from the Microsoft Store and will not allow them to run.

16. A. Windows Event Forwarding (WEF) reads any operational or administrative event log on a device in your network and forwards the chosen events to a Windows Event Collector (WEC) server. You should add the account of the computer to the Event Log Readers group, which has access to read the event log on the local computer. There are no default members of the Event Log Readers local group.

17. A. Every time a user logs onto a Windows client computer, the system checks to see if they have a local user profile in the Users folder. The first time a user logs on, they receive a default user profile. A folder that matches the user's logon name is created for the user in the Users folder. The user profile folder that is created holds a file called NTUSER.DAT as well as subfolders that contain directory links to the user's desktop items. A mandatory profile is stored in a file named NTUSER.MAN. To create a mandatory profile, just change the user's profile extension from .DAT to .MAN. In this question, we are changing from a mandatory profile, so we need to change the extension back to .DAT.

18. A. In this question, it states that you want to remotely create and modify the shares on the computers. In that case, because shares are being created remotely, then the group to add the user to would be the Administrators group. The Power Users group can manage shares locally, but to connect to perform these tasks remotely you need to be an administrator.

19. C. The easiest way to handle this transition is to simply rename the old employee's account to the new hire's name. It is important to remember that rights and permissions are associated to a user's Security Identifier (SID) number and not a username. By renaming the old employee's account to the new hire's name, the new hire will automatically obtain all the rights and permissions to any resource that the old employee had. Because every user account obtains a unique SID number, it is a good practice to disable an account rather than delete accounts for users who leave the company or have an extended absence.

20. D. Virtual smart cards use a cryptographic key technology that is stored on the actual Windows client computer. That computer must have a Trusted Platform Module (TPM) installed on the motherboard. Virtual smart card technology from Microsoft uses two-factor authentication. Virtual smart cards imitate the functionality of physical smart cards, but they use the TPM chip, rather than requiring the use of a separate physical smart card and reader.

Chapter 3: Managing Data

1. A, B. Permissions are cumulative among themselves. This means you will obtain the highest level of permissions. But when the two permissions meet the most restrictive set of permissions will apply. In this question, in order to do their job, the Sales group would be Modify on the NTFS side (local permission) and the shared permission (remote permission) should be Change.

2. D. Windows 10/11 comes with a feature called BitLocker Drive Encryption. BitLocker encrypts the drive so that if it's removed or stolen, the data can't be accessed. To configure BitLocker, you must either use a Local Group Policy or use the BitLocker window in Control Panel.

3. A, C, D. BitLocker Drive Encryption is a data protection feature available in Windows Education, Enterprise, and Professional editions of Windows 10/11.

4. D. When both NTFS and share permissions have been applied, the system looks at the effective rights for NTFS and share permissions and then applies the most restrictive of the cumulative permissions. If a resource has been shared and you access it from the local computer where the resource resides, then you will be governed only by the NTFS permissions.

5. A. The easiest way to manage this transition is to simply rename Rick's account to John. It is very important to remember that rights and permissions get associated to a user's SID number and not a username. By renaming Rick's account to John, John will automatically have all of the rights and permissions to any resource that Rick had access to.

6. E. By giving Tom the Modify permission on the NTFS security setting, you're giving him just enough to do his job. You could also give Sales or Finance the Modify permission, but then everyone in those groups would be able to delete, change, and do more than they all need. Also, Tom does not need Full Control to change or delete files.

7. C, E. The Admin group needs Full Control on the NTFS security and shared permission settings in order to do their job. To be able to give other users permissions, you must have the Full Control permission.

8. D. Smart cards are plastic cards (the size of a credit card) that can be used in combination with other methods of authentication. This process of using a smart card along with another authentication method is called two-factor authentication or multifactor authentication.

9. A. Filename extensions for known files are hidden by default. If you want to be able to see the filename extension for all files, you must deselect Hide Extensions For Known File Types. To show file extensions in Windows 11/10 via Folder Options/File Explorer Options, follow these steps:

1. Open Control Panel ➤ Appearance And Personalization.

2. Now, click Folder Options (Windows 10) or File Explorer Option (Windows 11).

3. Select the View tab.

4. Under Advanced Settings, deselect the option Hide Extensions For Known File Types.

5. Click Apply and then click OK.

Windows 11/10 users may also search for "folder options" or "file explorer options" in the Start search box.

10. A. Windows 10/11 comes with a feature called BitLocker Drive Encryption. BitLocker encrypts the drive so that if it's removed or stolen, the data can't be accessed. Any new files added to this drive are encrypted automatically. To configure BitLocker, you must either use a Local Group Policy or use the BitLocker option in Control Panel. However, this question states that it doesn't want the files to be copied or moved to a USB drive. If the files are moved from one drive to another drive, the files will become decrypted automatically. It doesn't prevent the files from being copied.

11. B. The default shared permission for administrators is Full Control. The shared permissions from lowest to highest are Read, Change, Full Control, and Deny. Share permissions can only be applied to folders.

12. D. When a resource has both share and NTFS permissions applied, the system looks at the effective rights for NTFS and share permissions and then will apply the most restrictive of the combined permissions. If a resource has been shared and it is accessed from the local computer where the resource resides, then it will only be governed by the NTFS permission.

13. C. Windows 10/11 has a feature called BitLocker Drive Encryption (BitLocker). It encrypts the drive so that if it's ever removed or stolen, the data cannot be accessed. To configure BitLocker, you must either use a Local Group Policy or use the BitLocker option in Control Panel. BitLocker encrypts the entire system drive. New files added to this drive are encrypted automatically, and files moved from this drive to another drive or computers are decrypted automatically.

14. D. One way to help secure Windows 10/11 is by using smart cards. Smart cards are plastic cards (about the size of a credit card) that can be used in combination with other methods of authentication. The process of using a smart card along with another authentication method is known as two-factor authentication or multifactor authentication. Authentication is the method of using user credentials to log onto either the local Windows client machine or the domain.

15. E. There are many advantages to using NTFS. These include compression, encryption, quotas, and security. NTFS provides the highest level of service and features for Windows 10/11 computers. NTFS partitions can be up to 16 TB with 4 KB clusters or 256 TB with 64 KB clusters. NTFS offers complete folder-level and file-level security.

16. D. There are three types of share permissions:

- **Full Control:** Enables users to read, change, edit permissions, and take ownership of files.

- **Change:** Allows users to change data within a file or to delete files and folders within a share.

- **Read:** Allows a user to view and execute files in the shared folder.

When both NTFS and share permissions are applied to a folder, the system will look at the effective rights for NTFS and share permissions and then applies the most restrictive of the cumulative permissions. If a resource has been shared and you access it from the local computer where the resource resides, then you will be governed only by the NTFS permissions.

17. B. Typically, the directory structure is organized in a hierarchical manner, meaning that there will be subfolders within a folder. By default, in Windows 10/11, the parent folder's permissions get applied to any files or subfolders within that folder as well as any newly created files or folders. These permissions are called inherited permissions. You can assign how permissions are inherited in subfolders and files by clicking the Advanced button on the Security tab of a folder's Properties dialog box. To edit these options, click the Disable Inheritance button. You can edit the following:

- Convert Inherited Permissions Into Explicit Permissions On This Object

- Remove All Inherited Permissions From This Object

So, by disabling inheritance and removing the permissions, this will meet the requirements set out in the new company policy.

18. B. BitLocker requires that you have a hard disk with at least two NTFS partitions. One partition will be utilized as the system partition that will be encrypted, and the other partition will be the active partition that is used to start the computer. This partition will remain unencrypted.

19. B, D. Permissions are cumulative among themselves. This means that you will obtain the highest level of permissions. But when the two permissions meet the most restrictive set of permissions will apply. Shared folder permissions apply only across the network (remotely) and can only be placed on folders. NTFS permissions can apply locally and remotely and can be placed on files or folders.

20. B. Network Unlock allows you to manage desktops and servers that are configured to use BitLocker. Network Unlock allows you to configure BitLocker to unlock an encrypted hard drive automatically during a system reboot when that hard drive is connected to the trusted company network.

Chapter 4: Managing the Windows Client Environment

1. **A.** The Registry is a database used by the operating system to store configuration information. You can edit the Registry in Windows 10/11 by using `regedit.exe` or `regedt32.exe`. However, always use caution when editing the Registry because any misconfigurations can cause the computer to fail to boot. You can use Control Panel or the Settings app if you don't want to open the Registry directly but you still want to perform some Registry changes.

2. **D.** In Windows 10/11, Sleep mode is the preferred power-saving mode. Sleep mode puts a computer into a low-power state and turns off the display when it's not being used. It does not shut down the computer. When you "wake up" from Sleep mode, it resumes where you left off. Sleep mode is a mixture of both Standby mode and Hibernate mode. When in Sleep mode, data is saved to the hard disk. The computer restores faster than if the computer was put into Hibernate mode.

3. **A.** You can configure and manage power settings by using the command-line tool `powercfg.exe`. You can control power settings and configure computers to default to either Hibernate or Standby mode. By default, the `powercfg.exe` tool is installed with Windows 10/11. You can generate a battery report by running the **powercfg / batteryreport** command. The report will be saved under `C:\Windows\System32` as battery report. The report will provide details about the battery such as the name, manufacturer, serial number, chemistry, and cycle count. You can also view a usage report over a period of time.

4. **C.** When a Windows 10/11 computer is configured with the Power Saver power plan, the computer's display and hard disk will be turned off after 20 minutes of inactivity in order to conserve energy. The computer will be put into Sleep mode after one hour of inactivity when using the Power Saver power plan.

5. **A.** There are a number of ways to customize the desktop. However, the easiest way to configure the desktop is by right-clicking an open area of the desktop and choosing Personalize.

6. **C.** The easiest way to recover a deleted file is to restore it from the Recycle Bin. The Recycle Bin holds all of the files and folders that have been deleted as long as there is space on the disk. From this utility, you can retrieve or permanently delete files.

7. **C.** A service is a program, routine, or process that performs a specific function for the Windows client operating system. You can manage services using the Services window. There are several ways to access services. One way to access Services in Window 10 is to go through Control Panel and select Administrative Tools ➤ Services. In Windows 11, Microsoft combined system utilities into a single Windows Tools folder. To access Services in Windows 11, go to Start ➤ All Apps ➤ Windows Tools, then in the new window, scroll down and click Services.

The Recovery tab allows an administrator to determine what action will occur if a service fails to load. Actions include the following:

- Take No Action
- Restart The Service
- Run A Program
- Restart The Computer

You can configure what actions will occur if the service fails to start on the Recovery tab of the service's Properties dialog box. For example, you can configure the service to attempt to restart, or you can configure the computer to reboot.

8. **A, C.** The Registry is a database used by the operating system to store configuration information. You can configure the system by using the Registry Editor (REGEDIT or REGEDT32). Windows 10/11 uses the REGEDIT command; if you type **REGEDT32**, it just opens the REGEDIT command utility. You should always use extreme caution when editing the Registry because improper configurations can cause the computer to fail to boot.

9. **A.** You can configure keyboard and mouse properties by using Control Panel. All of the same configuration settings that you can set in Control Panel can also be set in the Settings section of Windows 10/11. Microsoft has moved options from Control Panel to the Settings section, but you can still use Control Panel in Windows 10/11 while also getting accustomed to the newer Settings section. The Control Panel icons will link to the newer Settings section.

10. **C.** On a laptop computer, Denise can use the battery meter to view the amount of battery power available and to change the power plan configured for the computer. In Windows 10, the battery meter appears in the notification area of the taskbar and indicates the status of the battery, including the percentage of battery charge. By clicking the battery-meter icon, you can select among the preferred power plans available with Windows 10.
    In Windows 11, to check the estimated amount of time remaining, select Start ➤ Settings ➤ System ➤ Power & Battery. At the top of the Power & Battery menu, you'll see Estimated Time Remaining under the percentage figure.

11. **D.** Virtualization creates a virtual computing environment rather than a physical environment. Virtualization can include computer-generated versions of hardware, operating systems, storage devices, and more. Virtualization allows you to partition a single physical computer or server into several virtual machines. Each virtual machine can then interact separately and run different operating systems or applications while sharing the resources of a single host machine. Windows 10/11 Professional and Enterprise come with Hyper-V and all the needed software to run a virtual machine inside Windows. Virtual machines allow you to run an operating system in an app window on a desktop that acts like a full, separate computer. The virtual machine runs as a process in a window on the current operating system.

12. **A.** When setting Sync settings, you can choose to sync the theme, passwords, language preferences, Ease of Access, and other Windows settings. Here are some of the categories and common Sync settings that are included on a Windows client device:

    - **Theme:** Background, system color, system sounds, screen saver, slideshow wallpaper, and taskbar settings
    - **Passwords:** Windows Credential Manager, including Wi-Fi profiles

- **Language Preferences:** Spelling dictionary and system language settings

- **Ease of Access:** Narrator, onscreen keyboard, and magnifier

- **Other Windows Settings:** Device settings for items such as printers and mouse options, File Explorer settings, and notification preferences

To find the Sync settings, select Start ➤ Settings ➤ Accounts ➤ Sync. Using the Ease Of Access ➤ Keyboard settings, a user can do the following:

- Turn on/off onscreen keyboard.

- Turn on sticky keys (off by default).

- Turn on filter keys (off by default).

- Turn on toggle keys (off by default).

13. B. Windows client Task Manager provides a quick overview of important system performance statistics without requiring any configuration. There are several ways to access Task Manager, including the following:

- Right-click the Windows taskbar and then click Task Manager.

- Press Ctrl+Alt+Del and then select Task Manager.

- Press Ctrl+Shift+Esc.

- Type **taskman** in the Windows search box.

The Services tab shows you what services are currently running on the computer. From here, you can stop a service from running by right-clicking the service and choosing Stop. The Open Services link launches the Services MMC.

14. A. You can configure a system to hibernate by using Power Options or by choosing Start and then clicking the arrow and selecting Hibernate from the drop-down menu. This option will appear only if hibernation has been enabled. So, you can minimize the power usage by configuring Hibernate mode. Hibernation means that anything stored in memory is written to the hard disk. This ensures that when the computer shuts down, there will be no data loss of the information stored in memory. When the computer is taken out of hibernation, it will return to its previous state by loading the hibernation reserved area of the hard disk back into memory.

15. B, C. You can configure and manage power settings by using a command-line tool called `powercfg.exe`. This tool allows you to control power settings and configure computers to default to either Hibernate or Standby mode. By default, the `powercfg.exe` tool is installed with Windows 10/11. `powercfg.exe` uses a few switches that provide functionality. The syntax for using `powercfg` is as follows: `powercfg /option [arguments] [/?]`. So, for this question, the /X modifies a setting value in the current power scheme. /export exports a power scheme, represented by a specified globally unique identifier (GUID), to a specified file. /import imports a power scheme from the specified file, and /S makes a power scheme active on the system. For a complete list of switches, go to this page: `http://docs.microsoft.com/en-us/windows-hardware/design/device-experiences/powercfg-command-line-options`

So, for this question, you are using `powercfg /X` on one of the IT computers to modify the power scheme. After configuring the desired settings, the power scheme settings will be exported to a file by using `powercfg /export`. Then the administrator will import the power scheme from the file on each of the remaining computers using `powercfg /import`. Once it's imported, run the `powercfg /S` command to activate the power scheme.

16. A. The Background setting allows a user to pick their desktop background. The background wallpaper can be either a picture or an HTML document. Setting up a desktop background can be as simple as picking a solid color and placing a favorite picture on top of it. To configure the Windows desktop and how it looks, right-click the desktop and select Personalize. When you choose to personalize the desktop, there are several different settings that can be configured. These include Background, Colors, Lock Screen, Themes, Fonts, Start, and Taskbar.

17. B. By default, Windows clients Lock Screen times out and switches off your monitor after one minute. Lock Screen allows you to select a screensaver that will start after the system has been idle for a specified amount of time. When the idle time has been reached and the screensaver is activated, the system will be locked, and you must enter the password of the user who is currently logged in to unlock the computer. To configure the Windows desktop and how it looks, right-click the desktop and select Personalize. When you choose to personalize the desktop, there are several settings that can be configured. These include Background, Colors, Lock Screen, Themes, Fonts, Start, and Taskbar.

18. B. The `New-Service` cmdlet creates a new entry for a Windows service in the Registry and in the service database. `New-Service` allows you to create a new service. The cmdlet syntax is as follows:

```
New-Service
[-Name] <String>
[-BinaryPathName] <String>
[-DisplayName <String>]
[-Description <String>]
[-StartupType <ServiceStartMode>]
[-Credential <PSCredential>]
[-DependsOn <String[]>]
[-WhatIf]
[-Confirm]
[<CommonParameters>]
```

19. B. Offline Files allows network files to be available to users when a network connection to the server is unavailable or slow. The Offline Files feature is enabled by default on Windows 10/11. The best method is to use the Sync Center in Control Panel. To access the Sync Center, click Start ➤ Windows System ➤ Control Panel ➤ Sync Center. The first step to configure offline files is to click the Manage Offline Files link.

20. B. A service is a program, routine, or process that performs a specific function for the Windows client operating system. You can manage services using the Services window. There are several ways to access services. The General tab allows you to view and configure the following:

- The service display name.
- A description of the service.
- The path to the service executable.
- The startup type, which can be automatic, manual, or disabled.
- The current service status.
- Start parameters that can be applied when the service is started.
- Change the service state to Start, Stop, Pause, and Resume.

Chapter 5: Configuring Security and Devices

1. C. Running the `sigverif.exe` program will run a check against all the drivers installed on your machine and then notify you of any drivers that are unsigned.

2. A. The Print Management tool has a utility called Migrate Printers. This utility allows an administrator to migrate the print server queues from one machine and transfer those print settings to another machine.

3. C. If you need to get a stalled computer up and running as quickly as possible, you should start with the Driver Rollback option. This option is used when you've made changes to your computer's hardware drivers and now you have issues.

4. B. The Roll Back Driver option is the easiest way to roll back to a known good driver. You could also use the System Restore utility to roll back your computer to a known restore point if you make harmful changes to your computer, but Roll Back Driver is easier and faster.

5. D. The `Printbrm.exe` command should be run from a command prompt with administrative permission. This command is the command-line version of the Print Management tool.

6. B. When you disable the drivers, the drivers are still installed on the Windows 10/11 system but they are not active. Administrators like to use the disable option so that the user can always reenable the drivers later for use.

7. C. Windows Defender Firewall, which is included with Windows 10/11, helps to prevent unauthorized users or malicious software from accessing your computer. Windows Defender Firewall does not allow unsolicited traffic (traffic that was not sent in response to a request) to pass through the firewall.

8. C. Device Manager is the utility included with Windows 10/11 that allows you to configure and manage your devices and hardware. You can also configure your drivers within Device Manager.

9. A. Driver rollback allows you to replace a newly installed driver with the previous driver. You can perform the driver rollback using the Device Manager utility.

10. B. Windows Security constantly scans for malware, viruses, and security threats. The App & Browser Control section covers the Exploit Protection mitigations. Exploit Protection helps to protect users' devices against malware that uses exploits to sweep through your corporate network. Exploit Protection consists of a number of specific mitigations that must be separately enabled and configured. By default, Exploit Protection already enables several mitigations that apply to the operating system and to specific apps. To access Windows Security and review the Exploit Protection settings, perform the following:

   1. In the search box on the taskbar, type **Windows Security** and then select it from the results.

   2. Select App & Browser Control.

11. D. The Windows Defender Firewall with Advanced Security is a tool that provides detailed control over the rules applied by the Windows Defender Firewall. You can view all the rules used, change properties, create new rules, or disable existing ones. Windows Defender Firewall with Advanced Security allows you to set up inbound and outbound rules by using Windows Firewall.

12. C. To configure your Windows Firewall to allow DNS inbound and outbound traffic, you would set up port 53. Port 20 is for FTP data, port 25 is for SMTP (mail), and port 80 is for HTTP.

13. B. To configure your Windows Defender Firewall to allow SMTP inbound and outbound traffic, you would set up port 25. Port 20 is for FTP data, port 53 is for DNS, and port 80 is for HTTP.

14. A. To configure your Windows Defender Firewall to allow FTP traffic, you would set up ports 20 and 21. Port 25 is for mail and port 53 is for DNS. Port 80 is for HTTP, and port 443 is for HTTPS.

15. B. Windows 10/11 includes Windows Security. Windows Security provides the latest antivirus protection. Devices will be actively protected from the moment the client is started. Windows Security constantly scans for malware, viruses, and security threats. To help keep devices secure, Windows Security will monitor devices for security issues and provides a health report. This health report appears on the Device Performance & Health page. The report alerts an administrator to common issues with the system and offers recommendations on how to fix them. To view the health report for a device in Windows Security, perform the following:

   1. In the search box on the taskbar, type **Windows Security** and then select it from the results.

   2. Select Device Performance & Health. What is displayed in the report will vary, depending on the Windows version, device, permissions, and the issues that are found.

16. C. Microsoft Defender Antivirus can help protect devices by actively detecting spyware, malware, and viruses on both operating systems and Windows 10/11 installed on Hyper-V virtual machines. It runs in the background and installs new definitions automatically as they are released. Microsoft Defender Antivirus can manually scan for malware using the Microsoft Defender scan options. The scan options include the following:

- Custom
- Full
- Quick
- Microsoft Defender Offline Scan

In this question, you are discussing a quick scan that will scan the most likely areas on a hard disk that spyware, malware, and viruses are commonly known to infect.

17. A. If you want to convert an existing partition from FAT or FAT32 to NTFS, you must use the convert command-line utility and insert the drive letter to be converted. The syntax is as follows: `convert [drive:]/fs:ntfs`.

18. B, C. If a network adapter is not functioning properly, a number of things could be causing the issue. It could be an issue with the hardware, the driver software, or the network protocols. If the network adapter has outdated drivers, make sure you have the most current drivers. Windows 10/11 can check for an updated driver using the Driver tab of the Properties dialog box for the adapter. You just need to click the Update Driver button. If the network adapter is not recognized by Windows, you can use Device Manager to see whether Windows 10/11 recognizes the adapter. If you don't see the adapter, then you can try to install it manually.

19. A, C, D. Windows 10/11 includes quotas that allow you to manage and control how much space users can use to prevent a single user from filling up the entire hard drive. Disk quotas give administrators the ability to limit how much storage space a user can have on a hard drive. You can set up disk quotas based on volume or by users. Here are some guidelines regarding quotas:

- They scan the volume every hour to update the storage usage for each user.
- They are configured per volume, not per computer.
- They are available only on volumes formatted using NTFS.
- They can be set per individual user or everyone, but you cannot set limits on groups of users.
- Users who have files already on the drive will have their quota initially disabled, while newly added users will start their quotas as normal.

Follow these steps if you'd like to enable quotas:

1. To start, right-click the partition or drive where you want to create the disk quota and select Properties.

2. In the Properties window, select the Quota tab and click Show Quota Settings.

3. Select Enable Quota Management.

4. Select Deny Disk Space To Users Exceeding Quota Limit.

5. Select Limit Disk Space To and specify the amount of space you want and the size.

6. Set the amount of space before a warning is triggered to the user and specify the size.

7. Click Apply and then click OK.

8. Restart your computer.

20. D. To restrict the amount of disk space used by users on the network, system administrators can establish disk quotas. By default, Windows 10/11 supports disk quota restrictions at the volume level. This allows you to restrict the amount of storage space that a specific user can use on a single disk volume. You can set up disk quotas based on volume or on users.

Chapter 6: Configuring Network Connectivity

1. A, C. The `ipconfig` command displays your IP configuration. Using the `/release` switch will release an IPv4 or IPv6 address that has been assigned through DHCP. Using the `/renew` switch will renew your IP address using DHCP.

2. C. IP addresses are divided into classes, called Class A, Class B, and Class C. Class D and Class E exist as well, but they are not used by end users. You can identify the class of an IP address by looking at the first octet, in this case 192.

   - **Class A:** Uses 1–126 as the first octet.
   - **Class B:** Uses 128–191 as the first octet.
   - **Class C:** Uses 192–223 as the first octet.

   Because the IP address in the question starts with 192, that makes it a Class C address.

3. C. A default gateway allows devices on one subnet to communicate with devices on another subnet. The default gateway is the router's IP address. This question states that you can access computers on one network but not on the remote network. This is an indicator that the issue is with the IP address of the default gateway.

4. D. A Domain Name System (DNS) server has the DNS service running on it. DNS is a name-resolution service that resolves a hostname to a TCP/IP address (called *forward lookup*). DNS can also resolve a TCP/IP address to a name (called *reverse lookup*). If you can connect to a machine by using its TCP/IP address but not the name, then DNS is the issue.

5. D. Computers can communicate only by using a series of numbers. The Domain Name System (DNS) is basically like the phonebook of the Internet. Web browsers use Internet Protocol (IP) addresses, and DNS translates those domain names into IP addresses so that the browsers can load the web pages. The `ipconfig` command displays a computer's IP address

configuration. Using `ipconfig` with the `/registerdns` switch will automatically register the Windows client machine with the DNS server. The registration includes the Windows client machine name and the IP address.

6. **A, B.** You have to use either Class A or Class B. Class C addresses can only handle 254 users. 10.x.x.x and 172.16.x.x are both able to handle the 675 users and they are both internal private address schemes that anyone can use. The IP class assignments are as follows:

Network class	Address range of first octet	Number of unique networks available	Number of unique hosts per network
Class A	1–126	126	16,777,214
Class B	128–191	16,384	65,534
Class C	192–223	2,097,152	254

7. **A.** You should set up a workgroup, also called a peer-to-peer network. All computers on a workgroup are equal. All of the peer-to-peer computers, also referred to as nodes, concurrently act as both clients and servers. Peer-to-peer networks are typically any combination of Windows machines connected by a centralized device such as a router, switch, or hub. You should use this network configuration for smaller environments with 10 users or less. This enables smaller companies to share resources without needing expensive equipment, server software, or an internal IT department. Because they are never going to get any larger, there is no reason to have them use any version of Active Directory or Windows Server.

8. **C, D.** IP addresses are divided into classes, called Class A, Class B, and Class C. Class D and Class E exist as well, but they are not used by end users. You can identify the class of an IP address by looking at the first octet.

    - Class A IP addresses range from 1–126 as the first octet.
    - Class B IP addresses range from 128–191 as the first octet.
    - Class C IP addresses range from 192–223 as the first octet.

    Since both 10.14.100.240 and 65.102.17.9 fall within the range of 1–126 in the first octet, that makes them Class A addresses.

9. **A, B.** IP addresses are divided into classes, called Class A, Class B, and Class C. Class D and Class E exist as well, but they are not used by end users. You can identify the class of an IP address by looking at the first octet.. Class A IP addresses range from 1–126 as the first octet.

    - Class B IP addresses range from 128–191 as the first octet.
    - Class C IP addresses range from 192–223 as the first octet

    Since both 131.107.10.150 and 189.10.14.1 fall within the range of 128–191 in the first octet, that makes them Class B addresses.

10. **A.** Azure is Microsoft's subscription-based Active Directory service. It is a cloud-based Active Directory subscription. This is a great option if the company doesn't want to worry about managing and maintaining a server room. Azure is also ideal for accessing Active Directory from anywhere.

11. A. When you look at an IPv6 address, the first sections tell you the IPv6 address space prefix. `fd00::` `/8` is the unique local unicast prefix, and this allows the server to communicate with all local machines within your intranet.

12. A. A virtual private network (VPN) client is an end device, user, or software that is trying to establish a secure connection between the user and a VPN server. The client is part of the VPN infrastructure, and it is the end recipient of VPN services. A VPN allows you to create secure connections to another network using the Internet. The General tab has a field where you would enter the VPN server address or hostname.

13. C. Classless Inter-Domain Routing (CIDR) is an IP addressing structure that improves the distribution of IP addresses. CIDR is the number of ON bits. So, a subnet mask of 255.255.224.0 equals a CIDR of `/19`. The CIDR representation is the number of bits turned on in the subnet mask. 255.255.224.0 is actually 11111111.11111111.11100000.00000000 (1s are ON bits, and 0s are OFF), which equals 19 bits turned ON, or `/19`.

14. D. Network Discovery is a setting that determines whether a Windows client system can locate other computers and devices on the network and whether other computers on the network can see your computer. To enable or disable Network Discovery, complete the following steps:

1. Open Control Panel.
2. Open Network And Sharing Center.
3. Click Change Advanced Sharing Settings on the left-hand side.
4. Click the arrow to expand your desired profile and then click Turn On/Turn Off Network Discovery.
5. Click Save Changes.

15. C. A Class B address with a default subnet mask of 255.255.0.0 will support up to 65,534 hosts. To increase the number of networks that this network will support, you need to subnet the network by borrowing bits from the host portion of the address. The subnet mask 255.255.252.0 uses 6 bits from the host's area, and it will support 64 subnets, while leaving enough bits to support 1,022 hosts per subnet. The subnet mask 255.255.248.0 uses 5 bits from the hosts and will support 32 subnetworks, while leaving enough bits to support 2,046 hosts per subnet. 255.255.252.0 is the better answer because it leaves quite a bit of room for further growth in the number of networks while still leaving room for more than 1,000 hosts per subnet, which is a fairly large number of devices on one subnet. The subnet mask 255.255.254.0 uses 7 bits from the host's area and will support 126 networks, but it will leave only enough bits to support 500 hosts per subnet. The subnet mask 255.255.240.0 uses 4 bits from the hosts and will support only 16 subnetworks, even though it will leave enough bits to support more than 4,000 hosts per subnet.

16. C. A Domain Name System (DNS) server has the DNS service running on it. DNS is a name-resolution service that resolves a hostname to a TCP/IP address (called *forward lookup*). DNS can also resolve a TCP/IP address to a name (called *reverse lookup*). The `ipconfig` command displays your IP configuration. Using `ipconfig` with the `/flushdns` switch will purge the DNS resolver cache on the machine.

17. A. Classless Inter-Domain Routing (CIDR) is an IP addressing structure that improves the distribution of IP addresses. To determine the subnet mask, you need to count the 1s that are ON. The CIDR /27 tells you that 27 1s are turned ON in the subnet mask. 1s are ON bits, and 0s are OFF bits. /27 equals 27 bits turned ON, or /27. Twenty-seven 1s ON equals 11111111.11111111.11111111.11100000, which is equivalent to 255.255.255.224.

18. B. The loopback address allows you to treat the local machine as if it were a remote machine. The loopback address sends outgoing signals back to the same computer for testing. In a TCP/IP network, the loopback IP address for IPv4 is 127.0.0.1, and pinging this address will return a reply unless there is a firewall preventing it. 127.0.0.1 is the diagnostic loopback address.

19. A. The loopback address allows you to treat the local machine as if it were a remote machine. The loopback address sends outgoing signals back to the same computer for testing. In a TCP/IP network, the loopback IP address for IPv6 is ::1 (or 0:0:0:0:0:0:0:0001), and pinging this address will return a reply unless there is a firewall preventing it. ::1 (or 0:0:0:0:0:0:0:0001) is the diagnostic loopback address.

20. B. Using the ipconfig command displays all of current TCP/IP network configuration values and refreshes Dynamic Host Configuration Protocol (DHCP) and Domain Name System (DNS) settings. Used without parameters, it will display the Internet Protocol version 4 (IPv4) and IPv6 addresses, subnet mask, and default gateway for all adapters. In this case, notice that the DNS server has an IP address that is not in the same network as the rest of the IP addresses. It starts with a 131.107.10 network versus a 192.168.0 network. So, the issue is that the primary DNS server is wrong.

Chapter 7: Configuring Recovery

1. D. Windows Task Manager provides a quick overview of important system performance statistics without requiring any configuration. There are several ways to access Task Manager. All of the applications that are running on the Windows client machine will appear on the Details tab. Using this tab allows you to stop an application from running by right-clicking the application and then choosing Stop to end the process.

2. C. The Windows Performance Monitor is a tool that you can use to examine how programs run on a computer and how those programs affect the computer's performance. The tool can be used in real time, and it can also be used to collect information in a log to analyze the data at a later time. With Performance Monitor, you can set up counter logs and alerts. All performance statistics fall into three main categories that you can measure: performance objects, counters, and instances.

3. C. The Windows 10/11 Backup and Restore utility enables you to create and restore backups. Backups protect data in the event of a system failure by storing the data on another medium. To back up files, follow these steps:
    1. Open the Backup And Restore (Windows 7) utility.
    2. Click the Back Up Now button.

3. Select the location where you want to save the backup and then click Next.

4. When the What Do You Want To Back Up? screen appears, click the Let Me Choose radio button and then click Next.

5. Select the files to back up and click Next.

6. On the Review Your Backup Settings screen, select how often you want a backup to be performed automatically.

7. To start the backup, click the Save Settings And Run Backup button. Windows begins backing up files, and a progress bar indicates how the backup is progressing.

8. When the backup is complete, click Close.

So, for this question, the answer is that the Back Up Now button allows you to start a backup and configure a Windows backup.

4. D. The Windows 10/11 Backup and Restore utility enables you to create and restore backups. The Backup and Restore (Windows 7) utility is used to restore personal files from backup media and to restore a complete image of your computer. Backups protect data in the event of system failure by storing the data on another medium. If the original data is lost due to corruption, deletion, or media failure, you can restore the data by using a backup. If you want to back up and restore a Windows client machine, you will need to use Windows Backup and Restore (Windows 7).

5. C. Windows 10/11 includes a full backup and restore application called Backup and Restore (Windows 7) that allows a user or you to keep a backup copy of any of the Windows client component files and data files that are critical to day-to-day operations. The Backup and Restore utility is used to safeguard your computer. The Backup and Restore (Windows 7) utility is used to restore personal files from backup media and to restore an image of your computer. Images allow you to back up and restore your entire Windows client machine. Using images allows you to back up and restore your entire Windows client machine instead of just certain parts of data.

6. A. If you need to disable previous versions on the D: volume, this needs to be done from the System Protection settings in the computer system properties. System Protection creates and saves information about drivers, programs, system files, and settings. Windows will create restore points automatically. If you need to disable previous versions on the D: volume, this needs to be done from the System Protection settings in the computer system properties.

7. A. Windows 10/11 cannot back up encrypted files. To back up the encrypted files, you will need to copy them manually to an external hard drive or first decrypt the files before performing the backup.

8. C, D. There are several ways to repair system files on Windows 10/11. You can use the installation disc and choose Repair during the installation, or you can boot to the advanced options and select Repair Your Computer. The Last Known Good Configuration is not available in Windows 10/11. When you need to restore an image, you will use the System Image Recovery tool.

9. A, B, C, D. The answer to this question is all of them. Restore points allow you to bring a system back to a previous point in time, and they should be created at all of the times listed. Restore points are snapshots of the Windows client system that can be used to revert to other snapshots. Restore points contain Registry and system information as it existed at a certain point in time. Restore points are created at the following times:

- Before installing applications or drivers
- Before significant system events
- Before System Restore is used to restore files in the event that the changes need to be undone
- Manually upon request
- Weekly

10. A. Safe Mode loads the minimum number of drivers and services needed to boot Windows 10/11. If a computer can be booted into Safe Mode, you can temporarily disable an application or processes, troubleshoot services, or uninstall software. When running a computer in Safe Mode on Windows 10/11, you are streamlining the Windows configuration as much as possible. By starting the computer in Safe Mode, it will load only the basic video drivers and will allow you to fix any video issues, including using the Driver Rollback utility.

11. B. The system creates a user profile the first time that a user logs on to a computer. At successive logins, the system will load the user's profile and other system components to configure the user's environment based on the information in the profile. A user profile consists of the following two elements:

- The Registry hive, which is the file `ntuser.dat`. The hive is loaded by the system at user logon, and it is mapped to the `HKEY_CURRENT_USER` Registry key.
- A set of profile folders stored in the filesystem. User profile files are stored in the `Profiles` directory on a folder per-user basis.

12. C. Boot logging creates a log file that tracks the loading of drivers and services. When you choose the Enable Boot Logging option from the Advanced Boot Options menu, Windows 10/11 loads normally, not in Safe Mode. This allows you to see all of the processes that take place during a normal boot sequence. This log file can be used to troubleshoot the boot process. When logging is enabled, the log file is written to `\Windows\Ntbtlog.txt`. This option won't fix any problems on a device, but it can be used to analyze what might be preventing a Windows client machine from loading property.

13. B. The Startup Repair tool can be used if a computer will not boot into Safe Mode. The Startup Repair tool can be used to replace corrupted system files. This option will not help if there are hardware errors. If a computer won't boot because of missing or corrupted system files, use this tool to fix the issues. Startup Repair cannot be used to recover personal files that have become corrupted, damaged by viruses, or deleted. If the Startup Repair tool is unable to fix the issue, you may have to reinstall Windows 10/11, but this should be a last resort. This is why it's important to perform backups of your Windows client machines.

14. C. Performance Monitor is designed to allow users and system administrators to monitor performance statistics for various operating system parameters. It allows you to collect data from local computers or remote Windows client machines. It also allows for the collection of data from either a single computer or multiple computers concurrently. You can view data as it is being collected in real time or historically from collected data. You have full control over what data can be collected by selecting specific objects and counters.

15. A, B. The Registry is a database used by the operating system to store configuration information. You can edit the Registry in Windows 10/11 by using the `regedit` or the `regedt32` command. Always use caution when editing the Registry because any misconfigurations may cause the computer to fail to boot.

16. D. Using an elevated command prompt, administrators have the ability to configure and manage backups and restores using a utility called WBAdmin. WBAdmin allows you to back up and restore your operating system, volumes, files, folders, and applications. You must be a member of the Administrators group to configure a regularly scheduled backup. To perform other tasks, you must be a member of either the Backup Operators group or the Administrators group or have been given the appropriate permissions.

17. D. One of the easiest ways to restore an accidentally deleted file or folder is to check the Recycle Bin. When you choose the Delete option in Windows, your files are automatically moved to the Recycle Bin. The Recycle Bin has a limited amount of storage, and it will temporarily keep the files there. To restore files from the Recycle Bin, perform the following:

1. Open the Recycle Bin.

2. When the Recycle Bin opens, you'll see all deleted files. If the file is available, right-click it and choose Restore.

18. C. The graphic shown is an example of a Line view output. The three options are Line view, Histogram view, and Report view. The Line view is the default display that is presented when you first access Performance Monitor. The chart displays values using the vertical axis and time using the horizontal axis. This view is useful if you want to display values over a period of time or see the changes in values over a period of time. Each point that is plotted on the graph is based on an average value calculated during the sample interval for the measurement being made.

19. D. The Task Manager allows you to see what applications are running on a Windows system. You can also use the Task Manager to stop applications from running on a system. When open, Task Manager will show all of the programs that are currently running on the system. Click More Details (at the bottom-left corner). To see the startup items, click the Startup tab. Items will be marked as Disabled or Enabled. If disabled, then it is not causing any issues with the startup. If you see an application that you do not want to be part of the startup process, you can disable it. To disable the app from starting at startup, right-click the unwanted app and then select the Disable option from the pop-up menu. Remember to reboot the machine for these changes to take effect.

20. B. Windows 10/11 Performance Monitor is designed to allow users and system administrators to monitor performance statistics for various operating system parameters. You can collect, store, and analyze information about items such as CPU, memory, disk, and network resources. By collecting and analyzing performance values, this allows you to identify potential issues. You should also monitor the Memory counters. If a computer does not have enough memory, this can cause excessive paging, which can be observed as a disk subsystem bottleneck. You should look at a snapshot of current activity for a few important counters. This will allow you to find areas of possible bottlenecks and to monitor the load on the servers at a certain point in time.

Chapter 8: Deploy Windows Client

1. D. Whenever an issue occurs when using Windows Autopilot, you will see a generated error code. When a problem occurs during setup, some error codes will be displayed on the device. Using Windows Autopilot Reset requires that the Windows Recovery Environment (WinRE) be correctly configured and enabled on the device. If it is not enabled or configured, this message will be displayed: error code ERROR_NOT_SUPPORTED (0x80070032). Error 0x80070032 will appear when Windows Autopilot Reset is used to prepare an existing device to become business ready and you need to confirm that the WinRE is correctly configured and enabled on the device.

2. B. Windows Autopilot profiles allow an administrator to choose how the Windows client system will be set up and configured on Azure AD and Intune. Windows Autopilot simplifies enrolling devices. With Windows Autopilot you can give new devices to end users without the need to build, maintain, and apply custom operating system images.

3. B. Endpoint Analytics is a cloud-based service that works in conjunction with Configuration Manager. This service allows you to make informed decisions regarding the update readiness of your Windows clients. Use Endpoint Analytics with Configuration Manager to do the following:

- Assess app compatibility with the latest Windows client feature updates.
- Create an inventory of apps running in an organization.
- Create pilot groups that represent the entire application and driver estate across a minimal set of devices.
- Deploy Windows 10/11 to pilot and production-managed devices.
- Identify compatibility issues and receive mitigation suggestions based on cloud-enabled data insights.

4. B. Windows Autopilot is a way to set up and preconfigure devices. You can use Windows Autopilot to reset, repurpose, and recover devices. Windows Autopilot user-driven mode is designed to enable Windows client devices to be converted from their initial state into a ready-to-use state without an administrator working on the device. The process is designed to be user friendly so that anyone can complete it. The user will do the following:

- Unbox the device, plug it in, and turn it on.

- Choose a language, locale, and keyboard.

- Connect it to a wireless or wired network with Internet access.

- Specify their email address and password for their organization account.

Once they have completed those steps, the rest of the process is automated, with the device being joined to the organization, enrolled in Intune or another Mobile Device Management (MDM) service, and be fully configured as defined by the company.

5.   C. Windows Deployment Services (WDS) is a suite of components that allows an administrator to install Windows 10/11 remotely on client computers. The WDS server must be configured with the Preboot Execution Environment (PXE) boot files, the images to be deployed, and the answer file. A WDS server installs Windows 10/11 onto the client machines. You enable WDS servers to respond to client requests by using the Windows Deployment Services (WDS) Microsoft Management Console (MMC) snap-in. In the PXE Properties dialog box, enable the option Respond To Client Computers.

6.   D. Windows Autopilot profiles allow you to choose how the Windows client system will be set up and configured. Windows Autopilot simplifies enrolling devices. With Windows Autopilot you can give new devices to end users without the need to build, maintain, and apply custom operating system images.

7.   B. Deployment scenarios are assigned to one of three categories. The three categories are as follows:
Modern: Using Modern deployment methods is recommended by Microsoft unless there is a specific need to use a different procedure. Modern deployment scenarios include Windows Autopilot and In-Place Upgrades.
Dynamic: Using Dynamic deployment methods enables you to configure applications and settings for specific use cases. Dynamic deployment scenarios include Subscription Activation, Azure Active Directory Join (Azure AD) with Automatic Mobile Device Management (MDM), and Provisioning Packages.
Traditional: Traditional deployment methods use existing tools to deploy operating system images. Traditional deployment scenarios include Bare-Metal, Refresh, and Replace.
In this question, since you are discussing Subscription Activation, this falls into the Dynamic deployment category.

8.   D. Using Microsoft Intune and Windows Autopilot, you can give devices to your end users without the need to build, maintain, and apply custom operating system images. When you use Intune to manage Autopilot devices, you can manage policies, profiles, applications, and more. For the steps on how to create and configure a Windows Autopilot deployment profile, go to the following Microsoft website: `https://learn.microsoft.com/en-us/mem/autopilot/enrollment-autopilot#create-an-autopilot-deployment-profile`

9. B. Windows Autopilot is a way to set up and preconfigure devices. You can use Windows Autopilot to reset, repurpose, and recover devices. Autopilot Reset removes all of the files, apps, and settings on a device (including the user profile), but it retains the connection to Azure AD, Intune, or third-party Mobile Device Management (MDM). Autopilot Reset will retain the following:

- The region/language and keyboard
- Any applied provisioning packages
- Wi-Fi connections

Autopilot Reset is the best option when reusing a device within your network. So, the Wi-Fi connection and passphrase will be retained by using Autopilot Reset.

10. A. To add a Windows Autopilot device, you will want to import a CSV file with the device's information. To add a device, follow these steps:

1. In the Microsoft Endpoint Manager Admin Center, choose Devices ➢ Windows ➢ Windows Enrollment ➢ Devices (under Windows Autopilot Deployment Program ➢ Import).

2. Under Add Windows Autopilot Devices, browse to a CSV file listing the devices to be added. The CSV file should list the serial numbers, Windows product IDs, hardware hashes, optional group tags, and optional assigned user.

3. Choose Import to start importing the device information. This may take several minutes.

4. After the import is complete, choose Devices ➢ Windows ➢ Windows Enrollment ➢ Devices (under Windows Autopilot Deployment Program ➢ Sync). A message will be displayed stating that the synchronization is in progress. This may take a few minutes to complete, depending on how many devices are being synchronized.

5. Refresh the view to see the new devices.

11. B. Windows Autopilot is a way to set up and preconfigure devices. You can use Windows Autopilot to reset, repurpose, and recover devices. Autopilot Reset removes all of the files, apps, and settings on a device (including the user profile), but it retains the connection to Azure AD, Intune, or a third-party Mobile Device Management (MDM). Autopilot Reset will retain the following:

- The region/language and keyboard
- Any applied provisioning packages
- Wi-Fi connections

Autopilot Reset is the best option when reusing a device within your network. So, the app will be removed by using Autopilot Reset.

12. B. A task sequence identifies a list of tasks that are required to install the OS after the PXE-enabled device boots. In this question, you want to make sure that the computers are configured with the correct product keys. This is done by configuring an MDT task sequence. For the steps on how to create a task sequence with Configuration Manager and MDT, go to the following Microsoft website: `https://learn.microsoft.com/en-us/windows/deployment/deploy-windows-cm/create-a-task-sequence-with-configuration-manager-and-mdt`

13. B. The `shutdown` command is a command-prompt command that powers off, restarts, logs off, or hibernates a computer. If you have access over the network, the `shutdown` command can also remotely shut down or restart a computer. To force an Autopilot profile to be downloaded, you should reboot the device during OOBE to allow the device to retrieve the profile. Press Shift+F10 to open a command prompt at the start of the OOBE and then enter **`shutdown /r /t 0`** to restart the device immediately or enter **`shutdown /s /t 0`** to shut down immediately. In this case, you want to enter into the shutdown process to restart the device immediately, so you use the **`shutdown /s /t 0`** command. This command is used to shut down the local computer immediately. The `/s` switch will shut down the local machine. The `/t` switch is the time, in seconds, between the execution of the `shutdown` command and the actual shutdown or restart.

14. B. By using Windows provisioning, it is easier for an administrator to configure end-user devices without using imaging. By using Windows provisioning, an administrator can specify desired configurations and settings to enroll devices and then apply the configurations to the target device. A provisioning package (`.ppkg`) is a collection of configuration settings. With Windows 10/11, an administrator can create provisioning packages that allows them to configure a device quickly without having to install a new image. A provisioning package can be:

- Installed by using removable media

- Attached to an email

- Downloaded from a network share

- Deployed in NFC tags or barcodes

15. C. Windows Autopilot is a way to set up and preconfigure devices. You can use Windows Autopilot to reset, repurpose, and recover devices. Windows Autopilot user-driven mode is designed to enable Windows client devices to be converted from their initial state into a ready-to-use state without an administrator working on the device. You can add Windows Autopilot devices by importing a CSV file with their information. To import the CSV using the Microsoft Endpoint Manager Admin Center, do the following:

1. Navigate to choose Devices ➤ Windows ➤ Windows Enrollment ➤ Devices (under Windows Autopilot Deployment Program ➤ Import).

2. Under Add Windows Autopilot Devices, browse to a CSV file listing the devices that you want to add.

3. Click Import to start importing the device information. Importing can take several minutes.

4. After import is complete, choose Devices ➤ Windows ➤ Windows Enrollment ➤ Devices (under Windows Autopilot Deployment Program ➤ Sync). A message is displayed to inform you that the synchronization is in progress and may take a few minutes to complete.

5. To see the new devices, refresh the view.

16. C. Windows Autopilot is a way to set up and preconfigure devices. Administrators can use Windows Autopilot to reset, repurpose, and recover devices. Windows Autopilot user-driven mode is designed to enable new Windows client devices to be transformed from their initial state to a ready-to-use state without requiring the IT department to touch the device. Because this is a user-driven deployment, the user needs to enter their Azure AD credentials in order to join the device to Azure AD. When the Windows Autopilot profile is applied to the computer, it will be registered in Azure AD and not joined.

17. C. Windows Autopilot is a collection of technologies used to set up and preconfigure new devices, getting them ready for productive use. It is a zero-touch, self-service Windows deployment platform introduced with Windows 10/11. You can also use Windows Autopilot to reset, repurpose, and recover devices. Windows Autopilot allows you to do the following:

- Auto-enroll devices into MDM services, such as Microsoft Intune.
- Automatically join devices to Azure Active Directory (Azure AD) or Active Directory (via Hybrid Azure AD Join).
- Create and auto-assign devices to configuration groups depending on the device's profile.
- Customize Out of Box Experience (OOBE) content specific to the organization.
- Restrict the Administrator account creation.

18. C. The scanstate command is used with the User State Migration Tool (USMT) to scan the source computer, collect the files and settings, and create a store. The scanstate command's syntax is as follows:.

```
scanstate [StorePath] [/apps]
[/ppkg:FileName] [/i:[Path\]FileName] [/o]
[/v:VerbosityLevel] [/nocompress] [/localonly] [/encrypt
/key:KeyString|/keyfile:[Path\]FileName]
[/l:[Path\]FileName] [/progress:[Path\]FileName]
[/r:TimesToRetry] [/w:SecondsBeforeRetry] [/c] [/p]
[/all] [/ui:[DomainName|ComputerName\]UserName]
[/ue:[DomainName|ComputerName\]UserName]
[/uel:NumberOfDays|YYYY/MM/DD|0]
[/efs:abort|skip|decryptcopy|copyraw]
[/genconfig:[Path\]FileName[/config:[Path\]FileName]
[/?|help]
```

The command that you'd like to run to meet your requirements includes the following:

/i:[Path]FileName: Specifies an .xml file that contains rules that define what user, application, or system state to migrate. This option can be specified multiple times to include all of your .xml files.

/genconfig:[Path]FileName: Generates the optional Config.xml file but does not create a migration store.

/nocompress: Disables compression of data and saves the files to a hidden folder named File at StorePath\USMT. Compression is enabled by default.

/ui:<DomainName>\<UserName> or /ui:<ComputerName>\<LocalUserName>: Migrates the specified users. By default, all users are included in the migration. DomainName and UserName can contain the asterisk (*) wildcard character.

19. C. Windows Autopilot user-driven mode is designed to enable new Windows client devices to be transformed from their initial state to a ready-to-use state without requiring the IT department to touch the device. The end user will do the following:

- Unbox the device, plug it in, and turn it on.

- Choose a language, locale, and keyboard layout.

- Connect it to a network (wireless or wired) with Internet access. If wireless, the user must establish the Wi-Fi connection.

- Specify their organizational account email address and password.

- The user can configure their keyboard layout during the deployment.

20. D. The User State Migration Tool (USMT) uses configurable migration rule (.xml) files to control what user accounts, user files, operating system settings, and application settings are migrated. They can be written to improve efficiency, and it can be customized with settings and rules. USMT migration XML files include the following:

- `MigApp.xml`

- `MigDocs.xml`

- `MigUser.xml`

- Custom XML files that are created

Chapter 9: Managing Identity and Access

1. B. Azure Active Directory (Azure AD) Identity Protection is a tool that allows a company to achieve these three key tasks:

- Automate the detection and remediation of identity-based risks.

- Investigate risks using data in the portal.

- Export risk detection data to third-party utilities for further analysis.

Azure AD Identity Protection identifies risks. The risk signals that can trigger remediation efforts may include requiring users to perform Azure Multi-Factor Authentication, requiring users to reset their password by using self-service password reset, or blocking until an administrator takes action. Azure AD Identity Protection allows an Azure administrator to use the same type of protection that Microsoft uses to protect and secure users' identities.

2. D. Azure AD is Microsoft's cloud-based identity and access management service. It helps users sign in and access resources. Administrators can use the Windows PowerShell command `New-AzureADPolicy` to create a new Azure AD policy. The syntax is as follows:

```
New-AzureADPolicy -Definition <Array of Rules> -DisplayName <Name of
Policy> -IsTenantDefault
```

3. A. Windows PowerShell is a Windows command-line shell designed especially for system administrators. By using the `Get-AzureADPolicy` command, this allows an Azure administrator to view an Azure AD policy.

4. C. The Password Reset section allows an administrator to control if they want to enable self-service password reset (SSPR). If you enable this feature, then users will be able to reset their own passwords or unlock their accounts. An administrator can allow all accounts to use SSPR, or they can just choose certain groups to have the ability to do SSPR.

5. B. Azure AD Connect is a Microsoft utility that allows an administrator to set up a hybrid design between Azure AD and an on-site AD. It allows both versions of Active Directory to connect to each other. Azure AD Connect provides the following features:

- Federation integration
- Health monitoring
- Pass-through authentication
- Password hash synchronization
- Synchronization

6. B. Azure AD simplifies the way that you manage your applications by providing a single identity system for your cloud and on-premises apps. Administrators can use the `Add-AzureADApplicationPolicy` command to add an application policy.

7. D. Azure AD simplifies the management of applications by providing a single identity system for cloud and on-premises apps. Administrators can use the `Set-AzureADPolicy` command to update an Azure AD policy.

8. D. The Custom Domain Names section allows an administrator to add and verify new domain names. When it is first built, the Azure subscription comes with an Azure AD tenant that originates with an initial domain name. Administrators cannot change or delete the initial domain name once it's been created. However, they can add a domain name to the list of supported names.

9. A. Administrators can use the Custom Domain Names section of Azure AD to add an organization's new or existing domain names to the list of supported names. The Custom Domain Names section allows an administrator to add and verify new domain names. When the Azure subscription is first created, it comes with an Azure AD tenant that has an initial domain name. Administrators cannot change or delete the initial domain name once it has been created, but you can add a domain name to the list of supported names. For the steps on how to add a custom domain name to Azure AD, check out the following Microsoft website: `http://docs.microsoft.com/en-us/azure/active-directory/fundamentals/add-custom-domain#add-your-custom-domain-name-to-azure-ad`

10. B. Azure AD simplifies the way that you manage your applications by providing a single identity system for your cloud and on-premises apps. Administrators can use the `Get-AzureADDirectorySetting` command to view their directory settings.

11. B. Azure AD simplifies the way that you manage your applications by providing a single identity system for your cloud and on-premises apps. Administrators can use the `Get-AzureADApplicationPolicy` command to view an Azure AD application policy.

12. A. With Windows 10/11, Azure AD users can synchronize their user settings and application settings data to the cloud. Enterprise State Roaming provides users with a unified experience across their Windows devices. By using Enterprise State Roaming, the desktop background, the Favorites folder, and the browsing history will be available on the new computers.

13. A. Azure AD includes features such as Azure Multifactor Authentication (Azure MFA) and Azure AD Self-Service Password Reset (SSPR). These allow an administrator to protect their organizations and users with secure authentication methods. The use of security questions is available only in Azure AD SSPR. If security questions are used, Microsoft recommends that they be used in conjunction with another security method. Security questions are stored privately and securely on a user object in the directory, and they can only be answered by users during registration. There is no way for an administrator to read or modify a user's questions or answers.

14. C. Azure AD Terms of Use provide a method that you can use to present information to end users. Azure AD Terms of Use are in PDF format. The PDF file can be any content, such as existing contract documents, that allows you to collect end-user agreements during the user sign-in process. To add a Terms of Use document, check out the following Microsoft website: `http://docs.microsoft.com/en-us/azure/active-directory/conditional-access/terms-of-use#add-terms-of-use`

15. C. Windows 10/11 allows devices to be registered in Azure AD and enrolled into Mobile Device Management (MDM) automatically. Automatic enrollment lets users enroll their Windows client devices. To enroll, users add their work account to their personally owned devices or join corporate-owned devices to Azure AD. To configure automatic MDM enrollment, sign into the Azure portal.

16. C. Conditional access policies use conditions and controls that are used to build the rules that will be evaluated by Azure AD when determining access to resources. Assignments are the rules that are checked in accordance with conditional access requirements, such as device encryption or password requirements. Some conditions are based on the following:
   - The client apps that are used to access the data
   - The client browser type
   - The device platform being used
   - The location where the data is being accessed

17. A. Conditional access is the feature used by Azure AD to bring together signals, to make decisions, and to enforce organizational policies. Conditional access policies are basically "if-then" statements; if a user wants to access a resource, then they must complete an action. By using conditional access policies, an administrator can apply the precise access controls needed to keep the organization secure. Conditional access takes into account signals when making a policy decision.

18. B. With Windows 10/11, Azure AD users have the ability to securely synchronize their user settings and application settings data to the cloud using Enterprise State Roaming. Enterprise State Roaming provides users with a unified experience across their Windows devices and diminishes the time required for configuring a new device. When an administrator enables Enterprise State Roaming, their organization is automatically granted a free, limited-use license for Azure Rights Management protection from Azure Information Protection.

19. B. Azure AD Identity Protection is a tool that allows a company to achieve these three key tasks:

- Automate the detection and remediation of identity-based risks.

- Investigate risks using data in the portal.

- Export risk detection data to third-party utilities for further analysis.

Azure AD Identity Protection identifies risks. The risk signals that can trigger remediation efforts may include requiring users to perform Azure Multi-Factor Authentication, requiring users to reset their password by using self-service password reset, or blocking until an administrator takes action.

20. C. Conditional access is a feature used by Azure AD to bring signals together, to make decisions, and to enforce policies. To manage conditional access abilities, you should assign the Conditional Access Administrator role. Users that have the Conditional Access Administrator role have permissions to view, create, modify, and delete conditional access policies. The Conditional Access Administrator can perform the following tasks:

Create: Create conditional access policies.

Read: Read conditional access policies.

Update: Update conditional access policies.

Delete: Delete conditional access policies.

Chapter 10: Planning and Managing Microsoft Intune

1. A. You have the ability to limit and monitor network usage by configuring the network as a metered network. Network metering allows you to watch or meter network downloading so that you can charge users or departments for their network usage. When setting up your company's Internet connection, the ISP has the ability to charge by the amount of data used. That's called a *metered Internet connection*. If you have a metered Internet connection, setting the network connection to metered in Windows can help reduce the amount of data sent and received.

2. D. To review a policy report on the deployment status for the Windows 10 and later update ring, sign into the Endpoint Manager admin center. Then, select Devices ➤ Overview ➤ Software Update Status. To review software updates, select Monitor, and then below Software Updates, select Per Update Ring Deployment State and choose the deployment ring you want to review. In the Monitor section, you can choose from the following reports:

Device Status: Shows the device configuration status

User Status: Shows the username, status, and last report date

End-User Update Status: Shows the Windows device update state

3. C, D. The first thing that you should do is reset the user's password. Then perform a wipe of the user's laptop. By using the Retire or Wipe action, you can remove devices from Intune that are no longer needed, that are being given to another user, or that are stolen or missing. Users can also issue a remote command from the Intune Company portal to devices that are enrolled in Intune. The Wipe action restores a device to its factory default settings. The user data can be kept if you select the Retain Enrollment State And User Account option. Otherwise, all data, apps, and settings will be removed. As long as the sales staff–owned laptop is being managed by the management infrastructure agent, you can use the Remote Wipe feature.

4. D. Mobile Device Management (MDM) enrollment is the first phase of enterprise management. During the enrollment process, devices need to be configured to communicate with the MDM server using security precautions. The enrollment service will verify that only authenticated and authorized devices can be managed. So, in this question, since you want student iOS devices to be able to have access, you will need to obtain an Apple Push Notification service (APNs) certificate. This certificate allows Intune administrators to manage iOS devices.

5. A. Intune includes settings and features that an administrator can enable or disable on different devices. These settings and features are added to a configuration profile. You can create profiles for different devices and different platforms. The Password Reset section allows an administrator to control if they want to enable Self-Service Password Reset (SSPR). If this feature is enabled, then users will be able to reset their own passwords or unlock their accounts.

6. C, D. If using Configuration Manager, Administrators must configure Configuration Manager to manage mobile devices. To do this, it requires administrators to create an Intune subscription and use a connector to synchronize user accounts.

7. A. Before an administrator can configure, assign, protect, or monitor apps, the app must first be added to Intune. You need to determine which apps are needed and then consider the groups of users and the apps they need. After you add an app, you need to assign a group of users who can use the app. First, determine which group should have access to the app. You may need to include or exclude certain types of roles. For steps on how to assign an app, check out the following Microsoft website: `http://docs.microsoft.com/en-us/mem/intune/apps/apps-deploy#assign-an-app`

8. C. By default, licensed users can add up to 15 devices to their accounts. Device administrators have the ability to add devices to Intune, but users can enroll 15 devices on their own.

9. D. When you sideload an application, this means you are loading an application that is already owned, or one that the company has created, into a delivery system such as Intune, Microsoft Store, or images. Benefits of sideloading in Windows 10/11 include the following:

- Devices do not have to be joined to a domain.

- License keys are not required.

- You can unlock a device for sideloading by using an enterprise policy or by using the Settings app.

To turn on sideloading for managed devices, deploy an enterprise policy. To turn on sideloading for unmanaged devices, perform the following steps:

1. Open Settings.

2. Click Update & Security ➤ For Developers.

3. For Use Developer Features, select Sideload Apps.

10. B, C. Intune administrators have the ability to set up different notifications to different emails based on alert type. So, you can send all alerts, critical alerts, warnings, and informational alerts to different IT members.

11. B. App protection policies (APPs) are rules that make sure that corporate data remains safe. A policy can be a rule that enforces or prohibits actions within an app. There are different APPs depending on the type of device. For APP settings for iOS/iPadOS devices, the policy settings can be configured in the Settings pane in the Azure portal. There are three categories of policy settings: Data Relocation, Access Requirements, and Conditional Launch. Configure Conditional Launch settings to set sign-in security requirements.

12. C, D. To meet your corporate requirements, you will want to configure the following:

- User Experience Settings ➤ Automatic Update Behavior ➤ Notify Download

- User Experience Settings ➤ Delivery Optimization Download Mode ➤ Not Configured

User experience settings control the users' capability for device restart and reminders. The Notify Download option will notify the user before downloading the update. Then, the user can choose to download and install updates at that time. With Intune, Delivery Optimization settings are used to reduce bandwidth consumption when those devices are downloading applications and updates. Configure Delivery Optimization as part of a device's configuration profile. The Delivery Optimization Download Mode option should be set to Not Configured since delivery optimization is no longer configured as part of a Windows 10 and later update ring. Delivery optimization is now set through device configuration. Previous configurations are still part of the console. You remove the previous configurations by setting them to Not Configured. For steps on removing Delivery Optimization from Windows 10 and later update rings, check out the following Microsoft website: `http://docs.microsoft.com/en-us/mem/intune/configuration/delivery-optimization-windows#remove-delivery-optimization-from-windows-10-update-rings`

13. A. The Apple Mobile Device Management (MDM) push certificates are valid for one year and must be renewed to maintain iOS and macOS device management. If a certificate expires, enrolled devices cannot be contacted or managed. Apple MDM push certificates, MDM server tokens, and VPP tokens expire 365 days after they are created. If the Apple MDM certificate expires or is deleted, you will need to reset and re-enroll the devices with a new certificate. For the steps on renewing an Apple MDM certificate, go to the following Microsoft website: `http://docs.microsoft.com/en-us/intune-education/renew-ios-certificate-token#renew-apple-mdm--certificate`

14. B. Intune allows an administrator to manage devices and apps and how those devices access company data. To use Mobile Device Management (MDM), the devices must first be enrolled in the Intune service. When a device is enrolled, it's issued an MDM certificate that is used to communicate with the Intune service. By default, devices for all platforms are allowed to enroll in Intune. The method being described in the question is bring your own device (BYOD). BYOD includes personally owned phones, tablets, and computers. Users install and run the Company Portal app to enroll BYODs. This allows users to access company resources such as email.

15. A. Microsoft uses Intune to safeguard proprietary data that users access from their corporate-owned and personal mobile devices. Intune contains device and app configuration policies, software update policies, and installation status to help an administrator secure and monitor data access. App protection policies (APPs) are rules that ensure that corporate data remains safe in a managed app. A policy can be a rule that enforces or prohibits actions within an app. A managed app is an app that has an APP applied to it and that can be maintained using Intune.

16. B. If you install a feature update and it is not as you expected, you can roll back the update. Previously, Windows 10 had a 30-day rollback. Now, however, you have only 10 days to roll back an update.

17. A. Windows 10 and later deployment rings are a method used to separate computers into a deployment timeline. They are a collection of settings that configure when Windows 10 and later updates get installed. You can specify the number of days from 0 to 30 for which quality updates are deferred. This number of days is in addition to any deferral period that is part of the service channel selected. The deferral period initiates when the policy is received by the device. Quality updates are usually fixes and improvements to existing Windows functionality. In this question, Computer1 is a member of Group1, and Ring1 is applied to Group1, so the quality deferral will be 3 days.

18. E. By using the Retire or Wipe action, you can remove devices from Intune that are not needed, that are being repurposed, or that are missing. Using the Wipe action restores a device to its factory default settings. The user data is kept if you select the Retain Enrollment State And User Account option. Otherwise, all data, apps, and settings will be removed. In this question, you can wipe all the operating systems listed.

19. D. There are three types of updates that Windows Update for Business manages for Windows client devices: Quality Updates, Feature Updates, and Non-Deferrable Updates. The update that is being discussed is the Quality Update. Quality Updates are typically released on the second Tuesday of each month and include security, critical, and driver updates. Quality Updates are cumulative in that they supersede all previous updates. Updates for Microsoft products are also categorized as Quality Updates.

20. A, C, E. An administrator can set up Intune to enroll iOS devices automatically, which are purchased through Apple's Automated Device Enrollment (ADE). ADE was formerly called Device Enrollment Program (DEP). ADE allows you to enroll a large number of devices. The administrator gives users access to the Company Portal app on an ADE device. Before a device can be enrolled with ADE, you need to get an ADE token (.p7m) file from Apple. This token lets Intune sync information about the ADE devices, permits Intune to upload enrollment profiles to Apple, and assigns devices to those profiles. Once the token is installed, you then create an enrollment profile for the ADE devices. An Apple enrollment profile defines the settings applied to a group of devices during enrollment. Then you need to assign the enrollment profile to the devices. To see all the steps and how to enroll iOS devices automatically with Apple's ADE, go to the following Microsoft website: `http://docs.microsoft.com/en-us/mem/intune/enrollment/device-enrollment-program-enroll-ios`

Chapter 11: Managing Devices

1. D. You can upgrade your devices by using a device configuration profile. The option that you want to configure is Edition Upgrade. An Edition Upgrade allows you to upgrade Windows 10 (and later) devices to a newer version of Windows.

2. B. One of the options you have in device configuration profiles is the ability to set up custom profiles. Custom profile settings allow an Intune administrator to configure options that are not automatically included with Intune. For example, as an administrator, you can set a custom profile that allows you to create an ADMX-backed policy or even enable self-service password resets.

3. A. Kiosk settings allow an administrator to configure a Windows 10 (and later) device to run a single application or run many applications. Kiosk systems are normally designed in a location where many people can use the same device and that device will only run limited applications.

4. A. Profiles work like policies since they are a way to put rules on Intune devices. Using Intune, along with device configuration profiles, allows you to configure settings and features that can be enabled or disabled on the different devices. One of the options that you can set in device configuration profiles is the ability to set up custom profiles. Custom profile settings allow you to configure options that are not automatically included with Intune, such as the ability to enable self-service password resets.

5. B. The Gramm–Leach–Bliley Act (GLBA) is also known as the Financial Modernization Act of 1999. It is a U.S. federal law that requires financial institutions to explain how they share and protect their customers' private information.

6. B. Device profiles allow an administrator to add and configure settings and then push those settings to devices within the corporate environment. With Intune, use Delivery Optimization settings for Windows client devices to reduce bandwidth consumption when those devices download applications and updates. You configure Delivery Optimization as part of a device configuration profile.

7. B. One advantage of using Azure is the ability to protect corporate data by making sure that users and devices meet certain requirements. When using Intune, this is known as compliance policies. Compliance policies are rules and settings that users and devices must follow to connect and access Intune. Compliance reports allow you to review device compliance and troubleshoot any compliance-related issues. The device compliance shows the compliance states for all Intune-enrolled devices. The device compliance states are kept in two different databases: Intune and Azure Active Directory.

8. C. The Health Insurance Portability and Accountability Act of 1996 (HIPPA) is U.S. legislation that requires data privacy and security provisions for safeguarding medical information. The law has emerged into greater importance recently with the explosion of health data breaches caused by cyberattacks and ransomware attacks on health insurers and providers.

9. D. One of the options that you can set in device configuration profiles is the ability to set up custom profiles. Custom profile settings allow an Intune Administrator to configure options that are not automatically included with Intune. For example, an administrator can set a custom profile that allows you to create an ADMX-backed policy or even enable self-service password resets.

10. C. One of the advantages to using Azure is the ability to protect corporate data by ensuring that users and devices meet certain requirements. When using Intune, this is referred to as compliance policies. Compliance policies are rules and settings that your users and their devices must follow in order to connect and access Intune.

11. D. On Windows client devices, use Intune to run devices as a kiosk. These are also known as dedicated devices. A device in Kiosk mode can run one app or it can run several apps. You can display a customized Start Menu; add different apps, including Win32 apps; add a specific home page to a web browser; and more. Kiosk settings allow an administrator to configure a Windows client device to run a single application or run several applications. Kiosk systems are normally designed to be in a location where many people can use the same device, and that device will only run limited applications. For the steps on how to create a profile using Kiosk, check out the following Microsoft website: `http://docs .microsoft.com/en-us/mem/intune/configuration/kiosk-settings# create-the-profile`.

12. B. A kiosk (also known as Assigned Access) is a feature that allows you to configure a computer or a kiosk device to serve a specific purpose. On Windows devices you can use Intune to run devices as a kiosk. These devices are also known as dedicated devices. When a device is in Kiosk mode it can run one or more apps, you can customize and show a Start Menu, add different apps, specify a specific home page on the web browser, and more.

13. B. There are many Mobile Device Management (MDM) solutions that will help a company protect their data by requiring that users and devices meet certain requirements. In Intune, these are called compliance policies. Compliance policies define the set of rules and settings that users and devices must meet to be compliant. When combined with conditional access, administrators can block users and devices that don't meet the requirements.

14. D. Scope tags are used to assign and filter policies to specific groups. An administrator can also use scope tags to provide just the right amount of access and visibility to objects in Intune. Scope tags can be applied to different objects on Azure and Intune. The tag is basically a unique identifier.

15. A. To access device inventory reports, select the Devices node. You will see an overall summary of enrolled devices. To view additional information regarding enrolled devices, click the All Devices tab. You can also perform the following tasks to customize the view to meet your needs:

- Refresh
- Filter
- Columns
- Export

The option being discussed in this question is the Columns button. You can determine exactly what information is being displayed. Select from the available columns and click Apply. There is a large list of options that allow you to customize the view to what you want to see displayed. In this question, you are looking to see the Device Name, Managed By, and OS Version information. These will be displayed in columns.

16. A. Some issues that may be encountered are issues with the policies and profiles and possible conflicts and Azure AD enrollment. When two profile settings are applied to the same device, the most restrictive value will be applied. Any settings that are identical in each policy will be applied as configured. If a policy has been deployed to a device and is active and then a second policy is deployed, the first policy will take precedence.

17. C. By default, Intune devices check in every 8 hours.

18. C. Device profiles allow you to add and configure settings and then push these settings to devices in your organization. When creating a profile, you can choose from a wide variety of profile types. The profile type being discussed in this question is Kiosk. On Windows client devices, use Intune to run devices as a kiosk, also known as dedicated devices. Kiosk allows an administrator to configure a device to run one or more apps, such as a web browser.

19. B. For this question, the answer that is incorrect is that the configuration profile settings will take priority over compliance policy settings. The actual way that these two policies would interact is that the compliance policy settings will take priority over configuration profile settings. If you have a compliance policy and it includes the same settings that are found in another compliance policy, then the most restrictive setting will be applied. If you have a configuration policy setting that clashes with the setting in another configuration policy, then the issue will be displayed in Intune, and the administrator will need to resolve the issue manually.

20. B. On Windows client devices you can use Intune to run devices as a kiosk. This is also known as dedicated devices. A device in Kiosk mode can run one app or it can run several apps. You can display a customized Start Menu; add different apps, including Win32 apps; add a specific home page to a web browser; and more. Kiosk settings allow an administrator to configure a Windows client device to run a single application or run several applications. Kiosk systems are normally designed to be in a location where many people can use the same device, and that device will run only limited applications.

Chapter 12: Managing Security

1. C. Microsoft Defender Application Guard is designed for Windows 10/11 and Microsoft Edge. Application Guard uses an approach that performs hardware isolation. This allows untrusted site navigation to launch inside a container. Hardware isolation allows companies to protect their network and corporate data just in case a user visits a site that is compromised or is malicious. An administrator can define what sites are trusted, cloud resources, and internal networks. If something is not trusted, it is considered untrusted, and these sites will be isolated from the network and corporate data on the user's device. Administrators can use Microsoft Defender Application Guard to ensure that only applications that you explicitly allow can run on your Windows client computers.

2. A. Microsoft Defender Exploit Guard helps protect systems from common malware attacks that use executable files and scripts that will attack applications. Microsoft Defender Exploit Guard also looks for suspicious scripts or behavior that is not normal on the Windows 10/11 system. It helps protect Windows client systems from malware, ransomware, and other types of attacks by reducing the device attack surface.

3. A. Microsoft Defender Credential Guard is a virtualization-based security tool that helps isolate critical files so that only system software that is privileged can access those critical files. Once it's enabled, a Windows client machine that is part of Active Directory or Azure Active Directory (Azure AD) will have the systems credentials protected by Microsoft Defender Credential Guard. Microsoft Defender Credential Guard can be enabled by using Group Policy, the Registry, or the Hypervisor-Protected Code Integrity (HVCI) and Microsoft Defender Credential Guard hardware readiness tool.

4. A. Microsoft Defender Credential Guard is a virtualization-based security service designed to help isolate critical files so that only system software that is privileged can access those critical files. To enable Microsoft Defender Credential Guard using Intune, perform the following steps:

   1. Sign into Microsoft Intune.

   2. Click Device Configuration.

   3. Select Profiles ➤ Create Profile ➤ Endpoint Protection ➤ Microsoft Defender Credential Guard.

5. C. Microsoft Defender Credential Guard is a Windows 10/11 Enterprise and Windows Server 2016 and newer security feature that uses virtualization-based security to protect credentials. Hyper-V is Microsoft's hardware virtualization product that allows you to create and run a software version of a computer, called a virtual machine. For Microsoft Defender Credential Guard to provide protection, the computers must meet certain hardware, firmware, and software requirements. To provide basic protection, Microsoft Defender Credential Guard uses the following:

   - Secure Boot (required)

   - Support for virtualization-based security (required)

   - TPM 1.2 or 2.0 (preferred)

   - UEFI Lock (preferred)

Virtualization-based security requires the following:

- 64-bit CPU
- CPU virtualization extensions plus extended page tables
- Windows hypervisor (Hyper-V)

So, for this question, you need to ensure that the computers have Hyper-V installed.

6. B. Microsoft Defender Exploit Guard helps protect your system from common malware hacks that use executable files and scripts that attack applications like Microsoft Office. Microsoft Defender Exploit Guard also looks for suspicious scripts or behavior that is not normal on the Windows client system.

7. C. Microsoft Defender Application Guard was designed for Windows 10/11 and Microsoft Edge. It uses a hardware isolation approach. This lets untrusted site navigation launch inside a container, thus safeguarding corporate networks and data. The administrator determines which sites are trusted sites, cloud resources, and internal networks. Anything that is not on the trusted sites list is considered untrusted. If a user goes to an untrusted site through using Microsoft Edge it will open the site in an isolated Hyper-V-enabled container, which is separate from the host operating system. To use Microsoft Defender Application Guard, the environment has a few hardware requirements that must be met. This question is asking what the minimum amount of RAM is to utilize Microsoft Defender Application Guard, and the answer is that Microsoft recommends 8 GB of RAM.

8. A. Microsoft Defender Application Guard is designed for Windows 10/11 and Microsoft Edge. Application Guard uses an approach that performs hardware isolation. This allows untrusted site navigation to launch inside a container. Hardware isolation allows companies to protect their network and corporate data just in case a user visits a site that is compromised or is malicious. You can define what sites are trusted, cloud resources, and internal networks. If something is not trusted, it is considered untrusted, and these sites will be isolated from the network and corporate data on the user's device. Administrators can use Microsoft Defender Application Control to ensure that only applications that you explicitly allow can run on your Windows client computers.

9. D. Microsoft Defender Exploit Guard helps protect systems from common malware attacks that use executable files and scripts that will attack applications. Microsoft Defender Exploit Guard also looks for suspicious scripts or behavior that is not normal on the Windows 10/11 system. It helps protect Windows client systems from malware, ransomware, and other types of attacks by reducing the device attack surface.

10. B. You can onboard the following operating systems using Microsoft Endpoint Configuration Manager:

- Windows 8.1
- Windows 10, version 1709 or later
- Windows 11
- Windows Server 2012 R2
- Windows Server 2016
- Windows Server Semi-Annual Channel (SAC), version 1803 or later

- Windows Server 2019

- Windows Server 2022

Because this question is asking what devices can be onboarded using Microsoft Endpoint Configuration Manager, then the answer would be devices 1, 2, and 3 since they are Windows machines.

11. B. Microsoft Defender for Endpoint is designed to help enterprise networks prevent, detect, investigate, and respond to advanced threats. Microsoft Defender for Endpoint has a number of built-in features and capabilities. These include the following:

- Automated Investigation and Remediation

- Attack Surface Reduction

- Configuration Score

- Endpoint Detection and Response

- Microsoft Threat Experts

- Next Generation Protection

- Threat & Vulnerability Management

Endpoint Detection and Response capabilities are put in place to detect, investigate, and respond to advanced threats.

12. B. Windows 10/11 includes Windows Security. Windows Security provides the latest antivirus protection. Devices will be actively protected from the moment the Windows client is started. Windows Security constantly scans for malware, viruses, and security threats. The App & Browser Control section covers the Microsoft Defender SmartScreen settings and Exploit Protection mitigations.

13. C. Microsoft Defender Application Guard was designed for Windows 10/11 and Microsoft Edge. Application Guard helps protect the corporation while users browse the Internet by segregating untrusted sites. You can configure Microsoft Defender Application Guard in one of two modes:

- **Standalone mode:** In this mode, users can use hardware-isolated browsing sessions without any administrative or management policy configurations.

- **Enterprise mode:** In this mode, you define the company limitations by adding trusted domains and by customizing Application Guard to meet and enforce the needs on the users' devices.

14. C. Microsoft Defender Application Guard functionality is turned off by default. You can quickly install it on a user's device by using the Control Panel, PowerShell, or your Mobile Device Management (MDM) solution. To install Microsoft Defender Application Guard by using the Control Panel, perform the following steps:

1. Open the Control Panel, click Programs and Features, and then click Turn Windows Features On Or Off.

2. Select the checkbox next to Microsoft Defender Application Guard and then click OK.

3. Click OK. You will be prompted to restart the computer.

15. C. In Intune, security baselines are preconfigured groups of settings that are best practice recommendations from the Microsoft security teams for that product. These recommendations protect your users and devices. Intune supports security baselines for Windows 10/11 device settings, Microsoft Edge, Microsoft Defender for Endpoint Protection, and more. Security baselines are supported for devices that run Windows 10 version 1809 and later, and Windows 11. In order to manage security baselines in Intune, you must have an account with the Policy and Profile Manager built-in role.

16. A. Endpoints include desktops, laptops, tablets, mobile devices, servers, IoT devices, virtual machines, and more. Endpoint security helps to protect these endpoints from cyberattacks by using a wide variety of services and solutions. This question is asking about drive-by downloads. This type of attack uses the automated download of software to a device without the user's knowledge or consent.

17. B. Microsoft Defender for Endpoint provides you with near-real-time detection and response capabilities. It collects process information, network activity, user login activity, Registry and filesystem changes, and more. To view threats, you can use the Security Operations dashboard. Here you will see an overview of threats that have been detected and when response actions are required. This question is asking which tile shows you a list of devices that have the most active alerts—that would be the Devices At Risk tile.

18. A. Microsoft Defender Exploit Guard helps protect Windows client devices against malware, ransomware, and other types of attacks. It does this by reducing the attack surface of a device. There are a number of ways that an administrator can turn it on. Microsoft Defender Exploit Guard consists of four components:

- Attack surface reduction rules
- Controlled folder access
- Exploit protection
- Network protection

In this question, attack surface reduction rules are being discussed. Attack surface reduction rules help prevent attack vectors that are applied by scripts, email, and Office-based malware.

19. A. Microsoft Defender Application Guard was designed for Windows 10/11 and Microsoft Edge. It uses a hardware isolation approach. This lets untrusted site navigation launch inside a container, thus safeguarding corporate networks and data. The administrator determines which sites are trusted sites, cloud resources, and internal networks. Anything that is not on the trusted sites list is considered untrusted. If a user goes to an untrusted site through using Microsoft Edge it will open the site in an isolated Hyper-V-enabled container, which is separate from the host operating system. To use Microsoft Defender Application Guard, your environment must meet a few hardware requirements. This question is asking about the minimum amount of free space needed to use Microsoft Defender Application Guard, and the answer is that Microsoft recommends 5 GB of free space.

20. C. Microsoft Defender Credential Guard can be enabled by using Group Policy, the Registry, or the Hypervisor-Protected Code Integrity (HVCI) and the Microsoft Defender Credential Guard hardware readiness tool. You can use Group Policy to enable Microsoft Defender Credential Guard. This will add and enable the virtualization-based security features. This question is asking which setting you need to enable in Group Policy, and the answer is Turn On Virtualization Based Security.

Chapter 13: Monitoring Devices

1. D. Administrator can view the events collected from a specific computer in Azure by running a query in Logs Analytics. All data collected in Azure Monitor Logs is able to obtain and analyze in log queries. The Event query retrieves all records from the Event table. The pipe (|) character separates commands, so the output of the first command is the input of the next command. So, in this question, a way for the administrator to view the events collected from a specific computer in Azure is to run a query in Logs Analytics. Administrators can run the following query:

```
Event | where Computer = = "ComputerName"
```

2. A. Azure Monitor is a software that runs as a service (SaaS). All of the supporting infrastructure runs in Azure and is handled by Microsoft. It was created to perform analytics, diagnostics, and monitoring. It maximizes the availability and performance of applications and services by delivering a complete solution for collecting, analyzing, and acting on telemetry from your cloud and on-premises environments. All data collected by Azure Monitor falls into one of two categories: metrics and logs.

3. D. A Log Analytics workspace is a unique environment for Azure Monitor log data. Each workspace has its own configuration and data repository. A Log Analytics workspace is used for collecting the following data sources:

- Your Azure subscription resources

- On-premises computers monitored by System Center Operations Manager

- Configuration Manager device collections

- Azure storage diagnostics or log data

4. A. To access device inventory reports, select the Devices node. You will see an overall summary of enrolled devices. To view additional information on enrolled devices, click the All Devices tab. You can also perform the following tasks to customize the view to meet your needs:

- Refresh

- Filter

- Columns

- Export

The option being discussed in this question is the Columns button. You can determine exactly what information is being displayed. Select from the available columns and click Apply. There is a large list of options that allow you to customize the view to what you want to see displayed. In this question, you are looking to see the Device Name, Managed By, and OS Version information. These will be displayed in columns.

5. B. The Windows Analytics service was retired on January 31, 2020, and it was replaced with Desktop Analytics. Desktop Analytics is a cloud-based service that integrates with Configuration Manager. The service allows you to make knowledgeable decisions regarding the update readiness of your Windows clients. Use Desktop Analytics with Configuration Manager to do the following:

- Assess application compatibility with the latest Windows 10/11 feature updates.
- Create an inventory of applications running in an organization.
- Create pilot groups that represent the entire application and driver estate across a minimal set of devices.
- Deploy Windows 10/11 to pilot and production-managed devices.
- Identify compatibility issues and receive mitigation suggestions based on cloud-enabled data insights.

6. C. To access device inventory reports, select the Devices node. You will see an overall summary of enrolled devices. To view additional information regarding enrolled devices, click the All Devices tab. You can also perform the following tasks to customize the view to meet your needs:

- Refresh
- Filter
- Columns
- Export

The option being discussed in this question is the Filter option. Using Filter allows you to display only certain devices depending on the options chosen to filter for. There is a large list of options that can be chosen to filter for. Some of the options include filtering for devices that are managed by a specific user, ownership, compliance, operating system, phone number, and so forth. When filtering, only the devices that meet the specified filters will be shown.

7. A, C. All of the data that is collected by Azure Monitor fits into one of two fundamental types:

- *Metrics* are numerical values that express a piece of the system at a specific point in time. They are capable of supporting real-time scenarios.
- *Logs* contain other kinds of data that is arranged into records with different sets of properties for each type.

The data collected by Azure Monitor will appear on the right side on the Overview page in the Azure portal. You may see several charts that display the performance metrics. If you click any of the graphs, it will open the data in Metrics Explorer.

8. C. Log Analytics is the primary tool in the Azure portal for writing log queries and analyzing the results. You can start Log Analytics from several places within the Azure portal. The scope of the data available is determined by how you start Log Analytics. You can do the following:

- Select Logs from the Azure Monitor menu or Log Analytics Workspaces menu.
- Select Logs on the Overview page of an Application Insights application.
- Select Logs from the menu of an Azure resource.

9. B. Use the Microsoft Azure IoT Central applications to monitor devices and change settings. Azure IoT Central applications are hosted by Microsoft, which decreases the administrative overhead of managing applications. Azure IoT Central Applications is an Internet of Things (IoT) application platform that reduces the load and cost of developing, managing, and maintaining IoT solutions.

10. B. To access device inventory reports, select the Devices node. You will see an overall summary of enrolled devices. To view additional information regarding enrolled devices, click the All Devices tab. You can also perform the following tasks to customize the view to meet your needs:

- Refresh

- Filter

- Columns

- Export

The option being discussed in this question is Export. Once you have filtered the devices in the list, click the Export button. When prompted, click Save. This will create a CSV file that can be opened in Microsoft Excel to review the information.

11. A. Azure Monitor begins collecting data as soon as you create an Azure subscription and start adding resources. The Activity Log records when resources were created or modified, and the Metrics will show how the resources are performing and the resources that they're consuming. But this question is asking what records when resources are created and modified, and that would be the Activity Log.

12. B. To view the device details, perform the following:

1. Sign into the Microsoft Endpoint Manager admin center at `https://endpoint.microsoft.com`.

2. Select Devices ➢ All Devices ➢ Hardware.

The Hardware section includes details regarding the hardware of the device, such as the device ID, operating system and version, storage space, and more.

13. A. Azure Monitor helps maximize the availability and performance of applications and services. There are a number of things that you can do with Azure Monitor. This question is asking which feature allows you to detect and diagnose issues across applications and dependencies, and that would be Application Insights.

14. A. Reviewing scores per device may help you find and resolve end-user issues. From the Endpoint Analytics main page, select the Device Scores tab to display individual device scores. You can also sort by scores to help you find a device that may require attention.

15. A. This question is asking how to import devices in bulk to the Azure IoT Central Application. In order to register a large number of devices into your application, you can import devices from a CSV file.

16. D. The device name is a user-friendly name that will be displayed throughout the application. The maximum length is 148 characters.

17. B. In this question, you and your colleague are discussing Autoscale. Autoscale allows you to use just the right amount of running resources in order to handle the load on your application. You will create rules that use metrics collected by Azure Monitor to determine when to automatically add resources when the load increases. You can save money by removing resources that are idle. You can specify a minimum and maximum number of instances and the logic for when to increase or decrease resources.

18. B. Azure IoT Central Applications has four personas who interact with an Azure IoT Central Application. In this question, you and your colleague are discussing the builder. The builder is responsible for defining the types of devices that connect to the application and customizing the application for the operator.

19. C. The device ID is a unique identifier that the device will use to connect. The device ID can contain letters, numbers, and the - character without any spaces. The maximum length is 128 characters.

20. A. In this question, you and your colleague are discussing alerts. Alerts inform you of critical conditions and can attempt to take corrective action. Alert rules provide near-real-time alerting based on metric numeric values, while rules based on logs allow for complex logic across data from numerous sources. Alert rules use action groups, which contain unique sets of recipients and actions that can be shared across multiple rules.

Index

Symbols and Numerics

? command, 71
6to4 technique, 452, 461–462
32-bit processors, 13–14
64-bit processors, 13–14
128-bit address space, 452

A

Access Phase (Microsoft Defender for Identity), 750
accessories, 247–248
account policies
  about, 140
  using, 141–142
account protection, 757
account-lockout policies, setting, 144–147
ACPI (Advanced Configuration and Power Interface), 283
action log, 43
Active Directory (AD)
  about, 97
  administrative tools, 595–597
  Azure Active Directory (Azure AD) compared with, 586–624
  installing, 590–591
  updating schema, 162–163
Active Directory Administrative Center tool, 595–596
Active Directory Certificate Services (AD CS), 587
Active Directory Domain Services (AD DS), 588
Active Directory Domains and Trusts tool, 596

Active Directory Federation Services (AD FS), 625
Active Directory Module for Windows PowerShell tool, 596
Active Directory Rights Management Services (AD RMS), 588
Active Directory Sites and Services tool, 596
Active Directory Users and Computers tool, 596
Active X Filtering, 293
AD (Active Directory)
  about, 97
  administrative tools, 595–597
  Azure Active Directory (Azure AD) compared with, 586–624
  installing, 590–591
  updating schema, 162–163
AD Account Lockout Protection, 598
AD CS (Active Directory Certificate Services), 587
AD DS (Active Directory Domain Services), 588
AD FS (Active Directory Federation Services), 625
ad hoc connections, 439
AD RMS (Active Directory Rights Management Services), 588
add command, 58
Add Counters dialog box, 513, 514
Add Hardware Wizard, 378–379
Add-AzureADAdministrativeUnitMember command, 645
Add-AzureADApplicationOwner command, 710
Add-AzureADApplicationPolicy command, 645, 710

`Add-AzureADScopedRoleMembership`
command, 645
`Add-AzureADServicePrincipalPolicy`
command, 646
`Add-Driver` command, 72
adding
credentials using Credential Manager, 159
devices to Azure IoT central
applications, 811–812
disks, 349
snap-ins, 272
Windows 10/11 to domain, 469–470
`Add-LocalGroupMember` command, 187
address bar, searchability of, 293
Address Resolution Protocol (ARP), 446
address translation, 460
`Add-SignerRule` command, 114
`Add-VMDvdDrive` command, 322
`Add-VMHardDiskDrive` command, 322
`Add-VMMigrationNetwork`
command, 322
`Add-VMNetworkAdapter` command, 323
`Add-VMSwitch` command, 323
ADE (Apple Automated Device
Enrollment), 667
administrative templates, 728
administrative tools
Active Directory, 595–597
Windows 10, 261
administrative units (Azure AD
Dashboard), 609
administrator, defined, 810
Administrator accounts, 95, 96, 665–681
Administrator role, in Windows Admin
Center, 181
Administrators group, 128–129
Adprep, 590
Advanced Audio Policy Configuration,
141
Advanced Configuration and Power Interface
(ACPI), 283
Advanced Power settings, configuring, 286

Advanced Sound settings, 255
Advanced tab
Internet Properties dialog box, 302–303
Printer Properties dialog box, 392–393
Properties dialog box, 429
alerts
Azure Monitor, 804–805
Intune, 686–687
Android
enrolling devices, 675–676
onboarding tool options for, 762
updates for, 703–704
Android app protection policies (APPs),
creating, 707–708
Android Device Administrator, 675
Android Enterprise, 667, 675
Android Open Source Project (AOSP), 675
Anonymous Login group, 130–131
AnonymousAddress, 459
answer files, creating using Windows System
Image Manager, 73–74
anti-hammering, of smart cards, 167
antivirus, 757
anycast addresses, 458
AOSP (Android Open Source Project), 675
APIPA (Automatic Private IP
Addressing), 466–467
APIs, multiple, 807
app configuration policies
about, 708
creating for iOS/iPadOS, 708–710
App History tab (Task Manager), 523
app protection policies (APPs)
about, 706–707
creating, 707–708
Appearance tab (Performance Monitor),
519, 520
Apple Automated Device Enrollment
(ADE), 667
Apple Volume Purchase Apps, 667
application administrator role, 607
Application Control Policies, 141

application developer role, 607
Application Insights, 802–803
application monitoring data, 802
applications (apps)
    bulk-registering devices in, 812–813
    compatibility issues with, 22
    implementing protection for, 706–708
    managing deployment, 571–572
    monitoring
        discovered, 816
        information and assignments,
            817–818
    sideloading using Intune, 688–690
    supporting, 687–698
    Windows 10, 244–247
    Windows 11, 244–247
applications and services logs (Event
    Viewer), 529
applying
    LGPOs, 138–140
    NTFS permissions, 205–207
    provisioning packages, 302–303
approve-autoadddevices command, 59
APPs (Android app protection policies),
    creating, 707–708
architecture, of Windows 10/11, 13–14
ARP (Address Resolution Protocol), 446
assigning
    permissions to groups for password
        access, 163
    static TCP/IP numbers, 463–465
    user rights policies, 151–155
attack surface reduction, 757
audit policies, setting, 148–150
auditSystem, 73
auditUser, 74
Authenticated Users group, 131
authentication, for user accounts, 126–127
Author mode, 271
automatic MDM enrollment,
    configuring, 682

Automatic Private IP Addressing
    (APIPA), 466–467
automation, deployment and, 48–65
Autopilot, 672
AutoPlay option, 261–262
autoscale (Azure Monitor), 805
Azure, 214–215
Azure Active Directory (Azure AD)
    about, 566, 597–599, 667
    Active Directory (AD) compared
        with, 586–624
    audit log, 643
    configuring Enterprise State Roaming
        in, 638–639
    federation with, 627–630
    integration, 598
    managing, 602–616
    pass-through authentication, 626
    password hash synchronization
        with, 625
    questions and answers, 599–602
Azure AD Connect (Azure AD Dashboard)
    about, 610–611, 631
    Azure VPN Gateway, 633–638
    Health Monitoring, 631–632
    installing, 632–633
Azure AD Dashboard, 602–603
Azure AD Identity Protection,
    configuring, 621–624
Azure AD Join, 672
Azure dashboards (Azure Monitor), 805, 806
Azure device security, monitoring, 809–813
Azure Event Hubs, 807
Azure information protection administrator
    role, 607
Azure Monitor, 799–807
Azure resource change data, 802
Azure resource monitoring data, 802
Azure subscription monitoring data, 802
Azure tenant monitoring data, 802
Azure VPN Gateway, 633–638

B

Background setting, 252, 253
backing up
  advanced options for, 503–505
  creating backups, 499–500
  credentials using Credential Manager, 159
  encrypted files, 499
  restoring files from, 500–501
  using home folders for, 125–126
Backup and Restore
  maintaining Windows
    10/11 with, 498–505
  as a recovery technique, 487
  Windows 7, 262
Backup Operators group, 129
BAD (BitLocker Drive Encryption)
  about, 262
  managing using Configuration
    Manager, 228–229
  using, 221–222
Balanced power plan, 284, 285
baselines, 519, 548
basic storage, 337
Batch group, 131
Battery Meter, configuring power
    consumption using, 288
BCD (Boot Configuration Data), 46
bcdedit commands, 46
BDD.log file, 573
behavioral sensors, 750
Better Performance policy, 384–385
bidirectional trusts, 628
Billing Administrator role, 607, 666
biometrics, 111
BIOS, 20
BitLocker
  BitLocker Drive Encryption
    (BAD), 221–222
  encrypting drives with, 165, 230
  features of, 222–224
  Microsoft BitLocker Administration and
    Monitoring (MBAM), 227–228
  provisioning, 222–223
  recovery password/key, 221

BitLocker Drive Encryption (BAD)
  about, 262
  managing using Configuration
    Manager, 228–229
  using, 221–222
boot attacks, using Device Guard for, 112
Boot Configuration Data (BCD), 46
boot images, 568
Boot Logging, enabling, 492–494
Bootstrap.ini file, 572
Bring Your Own Device (BYOD), 672
broadband connectivity, support for,
    694–695
Broadband Tethering, 185–186, 695
broadcast address, 448
builder, 810
built-in accounts, 96–97
built-in groups, 127–131
built-in role permissions (Endpoint
    Analytics), 546
bulk enrollment
  about, 672
  configuring in Intune, 682
bulk-registering devices in
    applications, 812–813
BYOD (Bring Your Own Device), 672

C

CA (certificate authority), 166, 475
Calculator app, 244
certificate authority (CA), 166, 475
certificates
  configuring on client devices, 475–478
  settings for, 728
Certificates Manager Console, 475
Challenge Handshake Authentication
    Protocol (CHAP), 144
Change permission, 214
changing
  computer object permissions, 163
  configuration on virtual
    machines, 311–313
  drive letters, 353–354

paths, 353–354
security baselines, 755–756
user passwords, 110–111
CHAP (Challenge Handshake Authentication
Protocol), 144
checkpoints, configuring, 320–321
Checkpoint-VM command, 323
child domains, 422–423
CHS (Cylinder-Head-Sector), 339
CIDR (Classless Inter-Domain Routing), 450
circular logging, 520–521
Classless Inter-Domain Routing (CIDR), 450
cleaning up restore points, 507–508
Clear-EventLog command, 278
Clearing Their Tracks Phase (Microsoft
Defender for Identity), 751
client machines, 425
client-side extension (CSE), installing in
computers, 163–164
cloud application administrator role, 607
cloud device administrator role, 607
cloud security analytics, 750
cloud-based Azure Active Directory, 424
cloud-based storage, 214–215
cloud-based tools
about, 799
Azure Monitor, 799–807
System Center Operations
Manager, 808–809
CMAK (Connection Manager Administration
Kit), 474–475
Color Management option, 262
Color Management tab (Printer Properties
dialog box), 393
Colors setting, 252, 253
command prompt, 249
command-line integration, 286–287
command-line options, using, 83
commands. *See also specific commands*
PowerShell (*see* PowerShell)
Windows Configuration Designer, 71
common identity scenarios, 630–631
Compact action, 319
Compatibility mode, for Internet
browsers, 294–295

compliance administrator role, 607
compliance policies
about, 721
Conditional Access, 721–723
device configuration profiles, 728–740
migrating to MDM, 727
planning for devices, 723–727
compliance reports (Microsoft Intune), 705
compression, 362
Conditional Access
about, 721–723
planning and implementing
policies, 639–645
troubleshooting, 643–645
conditional access administrator role, 607
Conditional Access section (Azure Ad
Dashboard), 614, 615–616
Configuration Manager
Co-management, 672
managing BitLocker Drive Encryption
(BDE) using, 228–229
configuring
Advanced Power settings, 286
assigned access on public devices, 738
automatic MDM enrollment, 682
Azure AD Identity Protection, 621–624
bulk enrollment in Intune, 682
certificates on client devices, 475–478
checkpoints, 320–321
components through Window System
Image Manager, 73–74
Device Health Attestation, 116–117
device registration for Windows
Autopilot, 557–558
disk storage, 336–340
Enterprise State Roaming in Azure
AD, 638–639
hardware, 365–381
hibernation, 286
Internet browsers, 291–303
Internet options, 297–303
Intune alerts, 686–687
Intune Connector site, 686
Local Computer Policies, 140–141
Microsoft 365 apps, 692–694

Microsoft Intune subscriptions, 658–664
MMC modes, 271–272
mobility options, 279–288
network interface card (NIC) devices, 427–445
network interface cards (NICs), 428–433
NTFS, 361–365
objects, 616–619
Offline Files, 279–281
OneDrive, 215–220
personal preferences, 258–259
personalization, 251–259
policy sets, 682–684
Power button, 285–286
Power Options, 281–288
power plans, 284–285
printers, 390–393
remote management, 167–186
removable storage devices, 381–385
share permissions, 213–214
synchronization, 279–281
user account control, 155–165
user state migration, 573–576
users (*see* user configuration)
VPN clients, 470–478
VPN connections, 182–185
Wi-Fi Direct, 442–444
Windows 10/11 to use DHCP, 465–466
Windows client delivery optimization, 704–705
Windows client on networks, 468–470
Windows Defender Firewall, 401–407
wireless network security, 439–442
wireless network settings, 435
wireless NIC devices, 434–442
conflicts, viewing, 735–736
Connection Manager Administration Kit (CMAK), 474–475
connections
for Remote Desktop, 174–176
security rules for, 407
to VPNs, 473
Connections tab (Internet Properties dialog box), 301–302

Container Insights, 803–804
Content tab (Internet Properties dialog box), 301
Control Panel
about, 249
using, 259–270
controls, for Internet browsers, 293
Convert action, 319
Convert command, 361
ConvertFrom-CIPolicy command, 114
converting filesystems, 361
convert-ripimage command, 58
Convert-VHD command, 323
copy-image command, 59
copying user profiles, 123
Copy-VMFile command, 323
Cortana app
about, 244, 291–292
integration of, 9
cost, of Active Directory models, 423
counter logs, 520
counters, 513
Create Custom View dialog box, 530
createstore command, 46
creating
Android app protection policies (APPs), 707–708
answer files using Windows System Image Manager, 73–74
app configuration policies for iOS/iPadOS, 708–710
backups, 499–500
device compliance policies, 724–725
device configuration profiles, 730–734
disk images using Windows Configuration Designer, 69–71
extended volumes, 356–358
GPOs for LAPS settings, 164
groups, 127–135
Intune policies, 671–672
iOS app protection policies (APPs), 707–708
iPadOS app protection policies (APPs), 707–708

local network gateways, 636–638
local user accounts, 105–106
partitions, 349–351
restore points, 506
shared folders, 211–213
simple volumes, 355–356
spanned volumes, 355–356
striped volumes, 355–356
system images, 503–504
task sequences, 569–571
users
    about, 102–106
    in Microsoft Intune, 668–671
volumes, 349–351
VPN gateways, 634
VPN profiles, 471–473
Creator Owner group, 131
Credential Manager
    managing credentials by using, 157–159
    option for, 262–263
credentials
    managing by using Credential
        Manager, 157–159
    as requirement for Active Directory, 590
Critical alert, 686
critical updates, 701
cross-forest trusts, 628
Cryptographic Operators group, 129
CSE (client-side extension), installing in
    computers, 163–164
Custom Domain Names section (Azure AD
    Dashboard), 611–612
Custom Profile settings, 728
custom views (Event Viewer), 529
customer LockBox access approver role, 607
CustomizationXML command, 71
Customsettings.ini file, 572
Cylinder-Head-Sector (CHS), 339

D

DAC (Dynamic Access Control), 203–204
Data Collector Set, 512
data management
    about, 198
    answers to review questions, 833–835
    exam essentials, 231
    hardware security, 220–230
    managing
        file and folder security, 198–211
        network access, 211–220
    review questions, 232–237
    saving with performance logs/
        alerts, 519–521
    synchronization of data, 695–697
    video resources, 231
Data tab (Performance Monitor), 518
Date And Time option, 263
debugging, enabling, 494
Debug-Process command, 278
Debug-VM command, 323
deep-linking applications using Intune, 694
Default account, 96
Default Apps, 250
default command, 46
Default Programs option, 263
default SID filtering, 628
deferring updates, 79–80
definition updates, 702
delete-autoadddevices command, 59
deletevalue command, 46
deleting
    credentials using Credential
        Manager, 159
    devices from Azure IoT central
        applications, 813
    groups, 135
    partitions, 354–355
    printers, 397–398
    user accounts, 108–109
    virtual machines, 313
    volumes, 354–355
delivery optimization, 81–83, 728
DEM (Device Enrollment Manager),
    666–667, 672
Dependencies tab (Properties dialog
    box), 289–290
deployment
    applications using Intune, 687–694

automated options for, 48–65
Microsoft 365 apps, 691
monitoring, 572–573
options for, 548–549
planning for Microsoft Defender for
    Endpoint, 761–763
software updates using Intune, 699–705
troubleshooting, 572–573
of unattended installations, 66–74
Windows client
    about, 542
    answers to review questions, 850–855
    exam essentials, 576–577
    with Microsoft Deployment Toolkit
        (MDT), 567–576
    planning, 542–551
    review questions, 578–593
    video resources, 577
    with Windows AutoPilot, 551–566
Deployment Image Servicing and
    Management Tool (`DISM.exe`), 71–73
`DeploymentWorkbench_id.log` file, 573
design goals, for access control, 204
Desktop Analytics administrator role, 607
desktop environment, manipulating, 241–251
Desktop folder, 251
Desktop Icon settings, 255
Details tab
    Properties dialog box, 431
    Task Manager, 525
`detectnow`, 83
determining
    effective permissions for NTFS, 208–210
    NTFS permissions for copied or moved
        files, 211
device compliance policies, creating, 724–725
device configuration profiles
    monitoring, 734–735
    troubleshooting, 734–735, 736–737
device developer, 810
device drivers, installing and
    updating, 370–379
Device Enrollment Manager (DEM),
    666–667, 672
Device Guard

about, 9, 112
features of, 112–113
managing, 113–114
Device Health Attestation,
    configuring, 116–117
device loss, 751
device management
    about, 720–721
    answers to review questions, 862–864
    compliance policies, 721–740
    exam essentials, 741
    review questions, 742–745
    video resources, 741
Device Manager
    option for, 263
    using, 366–370
    using applet, 428
Device Settings tab (Printer Properties dialog
    box), 393
Device Specifications section, 272–273
devices
    about, 365–366
    adding to Azure IoT central
        applications, 811–812
    bulk-registering in applications, 812–813
    configuration policies, 728–736
    configuring assigned access on public, 738
    deleting from Azure IoT central
        applications, 813
    enrolling using Intune, 672–681
    enrollment of, 565–566
    features of, 728
    importing, 565–566
    managing
        with Microsoft Intune, 656–687
        security using policies, 756–758
    monitoring
        compliance for, 725–727
        using Endpoint Analysis, 818–819
        using Endpoint Manager Admin
            Center, 813–818
    planning compliance policies for, 723–727
    properties for, 369–370
    restrictions for, 728
    viewing, 810–811

Devices and Printers option, 263
Devices section (Azure AD Dashboard), 610
Devices shortcut, 250
DHCP (Dynamic Host Configuration
   Protocol)
   about, 57
   configuring Windows 10/11 to
     use, 465–466
   server, 426
Diagnose and Solve Problems section (Azure
   AD Dashboard), 603
Dialup group, 131
Direct Memory Access (DMA)-based attacks,
   using Device Guard for, 113
disable command, 59
Disable-LocalUser command, 187
Disable-VMConsoleSupport
   command, 323
Disable-VMMigration command, 323
disabling
   automatic restart after failure, 495
   driver signature enforcement, 494
   early launch anti-malware protection, 494
   user accounts, 107–108
Disconnect-PSSession command, 187
Disk Cleanup utility, 344, 507–508
Disk Defragment utility, 345
disk encryption, 757
disk images
   about, 59–63
   creating using Windows Configuration
     Designer, 69–71
Disk Management utility
   about, 337
   using, 340–355
disk partitioning, 24–25
disk properties, viewing, 342–343
disk space, measurements for, 20
disk storage, configuring, 336–340
Disk Usage tab (Manage Offline Files), 281
disks
   adding, 349
   upgrading to dynamic or GPT
     disks, 351–353
DISM.exe command-line commands, 72–73

Dismount-VHD command, 323
displayorder command, 46
Distributed COM Users group, 129
documents, managing, 393–397
Documents folder, 251
domain controllers
   about, 35, 425, 589
   read-only, 590
domain highlighting, 293
Domain Join, 10
Domain Name Service (DNS) server, 425–426
Domain Name System (DNS)
   about, 57
   as requirement for Active Directory, 590
   support for, 599
domain user accounts, 97–98
domain-based network, 422
domain-join, 597
domains
   about, 422
   adding Windows 10/11 to, 469–470
   setting domain names, 598
Downloads folder, 251
drive-by downloads, 751
driver repository, 569
Driver Rollback, as a recovery technique, 488
driver signature enforcement, disabling, 494
driver signing, 379–381
Driver tab (Properties dialog box), 429–431
drivers
   managing deployment, 571–572
   requirements for, 20
   updates for, 79
drives
   changing letters, 353–354
   encrypting with BitLocker, 165, 230
dual stack, 451, 460–461
dual-booting, 45–46
duplicating policies, 758–759
Dynamic Access Control (DAC), 203–204
dynamic disks, upgrading basic disks
   to, 351–353
Dynamic Host Configuration
   Protocol (DHCP)
   about, 57

configuring Windows 10/11 to
use, 465–466
server, 426
dynamic storage
about, 337–339
managing, 355–358
Dynamics 365
administrator role, 607

E

early launch anti-malware protection,
disabling, 494
Ease of Access Center option, 264
Ease of Access Tools/Accessibility
Settings, 248–249
Easy Connect, 168–173
Edit Disk tool, 318–319
editing credentials using Credential
Manager, 159
Edition Upgrade, 728
EDP (Enterprise Data Protection), 9
EDR (endpoint detection and response),
757, 763–771
EFS (Encrypting File System), 362
elevation-of-privileges attack, 628
Email options, 729
enable command, 59
Enable-LocalUser command, 187
Enable-PSRemoting command, 187
Enable-VMConsoleSupport
command, 323
Enable-VMMigration command, 323
Enable-VMReplication command, 323
Enable-VMResourceMetering
command, 323
enabling
Boot Logging, 492–494
debugging, 494
device encryption, 225
Enterprise State Roaming, 639
Hyper-V role, 304–305
PowerShell remoting, 182
standard BitLocker encryption, 225–226
System Protection, 495
Encrypted command, 71

encrypting
about, 362
backing up files, 499
drives with BitLocker, 165, 230
Encrypting File System (EFS), 362
Encryption tab (Manage Offline Files), 281
Endpoint Analytics
about, 543–545
built-in role permissions, 546
monitoring devices using, 818–819
requirements, 545–546
using, 546–548
endpoint detection and response (EDR),
757, 763–771
Endpoint Manager Admin Center, monitoring
devices using, 813–818
Endpoint Protection
about, 729
implementing, 749–751
planning, 749–751
Endpoint Security
about, 751
best practices, 751–752
managing in Microsoft Intune,
752–756
troubleshooting baselines, 759
Enhanced Security mode, in Microsoft
Edge, 295–296
enrolling devices using Intune, 672–681
Enterprise applications (Azure AD
Dashboard), 609–610
Enterprise Data Protection (EDP), 9
Enterprise State Roaming, configuring in
Azure AD, 638–639
environment, Windows client, 240–334
error log, 43
Error-Checking utility, 345
Event Log Readers group, 129
Event Properties dialog box, 528
Event Viewer
about, 526–530
as a recovery technique, 487
Events tab (Properties dialog box), 432
Everyone group, 131
exam essentials
data management, 231
deployment (Windows client), 576–577

device management, 741
identity and access, 648–649
Microsoft Intune, 711–712
network connectivity, 479
recovery, 533
storage and devices, 412
user configuration, 189
Windows client, 86–87, 329
Windows monitoring, 820
Exchange administrator role, 607
executables, elevated privilege for, 157
exercises
accessing
LGPOs, 140
Local Users and Groups via Computer
Management utility, 100
the Windows client wireless
properties, 440–441
adding
accounts to groups, 134
Azure AD Identity Protection, 622–624
local computer policy snap-in, 139
Local Users and Groups
snap-in, 99–100
users to groups, 119
users to Untune, 668–669
applying user rights policies, 155
assigning home folders, 125
backing up files, 500
booting your Windows 10/11 computer
to Safe Mode from the sign-in
screen, 491–492
changing
computer name on Windows 10/11
computers, 276
system's virtual memory on Windows
10/11 computers, 277
user passwords, 111
configuring
account-lockout policies, 146–147
audit policies, 150
Input/Output devices, 385
locales, 41
MDT, 52–54

network adapter advanced
properties, 370
OneDrive, 502
password policy, 144
Power button for Hibernate mode, 286
power plans, 285
services, 290
a static TCP/IP address in Windows
10, 463–464
Windows 10 desktop options, 258
conforming the Windows
version, 677–678
connecting a Windows client to the
domain, 469–470
converting
basic disks to dynamic disks, 353
basic disks to GPT disks, 352
creating
an Azure AD group account, 618–619
an Azure AD user account, 616–618
differencing hard disks, 318
extended volumes, 356–357
internal virtual networks, 315
local groups, 133
the local network gateway, 636–637
new users via the MMC, 105–106
a new group, 669–671
a new inbound rule, 406
a restore point, 506
the site-to-site VPN
connection, 634–636
a system image, 503–504
virtual machines, 306–311
volumes, 349–351
deleting
partitions, 355
user accounts, 109
disabling
and enabling devices in Device
Manager, 376
user accounts, 107
downloading and installing MDT, 50–51
editing drive letters, 354
enabling

Microsoft Defender Credential Guard
using a GPO, 781–782
Microsoft Defender Exploit Guard
using Intune, 784–786
Remote Desktop on Windows
10, 175–176
enrolling Windows 10 desktop version
1607 or higher, 679–681
installing
Azure AD Connect, 632–633
Microsoft Defender Application
Guard, 772–773
new features, 267
a printer, 389
a shared network print device, 390
logging into OneDrive, 217–218
managing
documents in local queue in Windows
10, 395–396
NTFS permissions, 207
Microsoft Defender Application Guard
Enterprise, 776–780
opening devices, 366
performing clean installations of Windows
10, 27–35
preparing systems for imaging using
System Preparation Tool, 69
removing a printer from Printers &
Scanners in Windows 10, 397–398
renaming user accounts, 110
restoring
files, 501
a restore point, 507
rolling back drivers, 375
seeing how UAC affects accounts, 157
setting up
an Intune account, 660–664
an on-site domain controller, 591–595
self-service password reset, 619–620
user profiles, 120
VPN connections on Windows 10, 184
testing the self-service password reset, 621

troubleshooting failed installations with
setup logs, 44
uninstalling and reinstalling a device
driver, 377
updating drivers, 374
upgrading Windows 8.1 to Windows
10, 37–40
using
BitLocker in Windows 10, 226–227
DHCP in Windows 10/11, 465–466
Microsoft Defender Application
Guard, 775–776
Print Migration tools, 399–401
the Recycle Bin, 511
verifying signed drivers, 381
viewing
the boot log file, 493–494
devices using Device Manager, 367
driver details, 374
the network connection details in
Windows 10, 437
wireless network connection
properties, 438
Exit-PSSession command, 188
Expand action, 319
export command, 46
export-image command, 59
Export-VM command, 323
Export-VMSnapshot command, 323
ExpressRoute, 638
extended volumes, creating, 356–358
extension header, 451
External Identities section (Azure AD
Dashboard), 605–606
external network, 314–315
external trusts, 628

F

F10 button, 495
FAT (File Allocation Table), 359–360

FAT32. *see* filesystems
FDE (full disk encryption), 224
features
    updates for, 79, 80, 702–705
    Windows 10, 9–10
    Windows 11, 9–10
federation
    about, 630
    with Azure AD, 627–630
File Allocation Table (FAT), 359–360
File Explorer app, 250
File Explorer Options, 264
File History option, 264
File Virtualization, 165
files
    managing security for, 198–211
    recovering from OneDrive, 501–502
    restoring from backup, 500–501
filesystems
    about, 358
    capabilities of, 359
    converting, 361
    File Allocation Table (FAT), 359–360
    NTFS, 360
    selecting, 358–359
firewall, 757
Flash Player option, 264
Folder Options/File Explorer Options dialog
    box, 199–203
folders
    managing security for, 198–211
    shared, 211–213
Fonts option, 265
forest-wide authentication, 628–629
Full Control permission, 205, 214
full disk encryption (FDE), 224
full volume encryption (FVE), 224

G

General tab
    Folder Options/File Explorer Options dialog box,
        199, 200
    Internet Properties dialog box, 297–298
    Manage Offline Files, 281

Performance Monitor, 517
Printer Properties dialog box, 391
Properties dialog box, 288–289, 343,
    344, 428–429
generalize, 74
generations, Hyper-V, 321–322
get command, 59
Get-AzureADAdministrativeUnit
    command, 646
Get-AzureADAdministrative
    UnitMember command, 646
Get-AzureADApplication
    command, 710
Get-AzureADApplication
    ExtensionProperty
    command, 710
Get-AzureADApplicationOwner
    command, 710
Get-AzureADApplication
    PasswordCredential command, 710
Get-AzureADApplicationPolicy
    command, 646, 710
Get-AzureADApplication
    ProxyConnectorGroupMembers
    command, 647
Get-AzureADDirectorySetting
    command, 646
Get-AzureADDirectorySetting
    Template command, 646
Get-AzureADObjectSetting
    command, 646
Get-AzureADPolicy command, 646
Get-AzureADPolicyApplied
    Object command, 646
Get-AzureADScopedRole
    Membership command, 646
Get-AzureADServicePrincipal
    Policy command, 646
Get-CIPolicy command, 114
Get-CIPolicyIdInfo command, 114
Get-ComputerInfo command, 278
Get-CurrentEdition command, 72
Get-DriverInfo command, 72
Get-Drivers command, 72
Get-EventLog command, 278
Get-Help /? command, 72

Get-LocalGroup command, 188
Get-LocalGroupMember command, 188
Get-LocalUser command, 188
Get-Service command, 278
Get-SystemDriver command, 114
Get-TargetEditions command, 72
Get-TimeZone command, 278
Get-VHD command, 323
Get-VHDSet command, 323
Get-VHDSnapshot command, 323
Get-VM command, 323
Get-VMDvdDrive command, 323
Get-VMHardDiskDrive command, 323
Get-VMMemory command, 324
Get-VMNetworkAdapter command, 324
Get-VMProcessor command, 324
Get-VMReplication command, 324
Get-VMSwitch command, 324
Global Administrator role, 607, 666
Global Catalog, 426, 590
global unicast address, 458
gMSA (group Managed Service Account), 588
GPOs (Group Policy Objects)
    about, 10, 113, 127
    creating for LAPS settings, 164
    managing security using, 135–155
gpresult command, 137
GPT (GUID Partition Table), 339–340
GPT disks, upgrading basic disks to, 351–353
Graph tab (Performance Monitor), 519
graphics cards, requirements for, 19–20
group Managed Service Account (gMSA), 588
Group Policy Objects (GPOs)
    about, 10, 113, 127
    creating for LAPS settings, 164
    managing security using, 135–155
Group Policy Result Tool, using, 137–138
Group Policy Support, 598
groups
    built-in, 127–131
    creating, 127–135
    deleting, 135
    managing, 127–135
    managing membership for, 133–135

Groups section (Azure AD
    Dashboard), 604–605
Guest account, 96
guest inviter role, 607
guest operating system monitoring data, 802
Guests group, 129
GUID Partition Table (GPT), 339–340

H

hardware
    about, 365
    compatibility issues with, 22
    configuring, 365–381
    devices, 365–366
    driver signing, 379–381
    installing device drivers, 370–379
    requirements for, 18–19, 552
    security for
        about, 220
        smart cards, 229–230
        using BitLocker Administration
            and Monitoring (MBAM)
            utility, 227–228
        using BitLocker drive
            encryption, 221–224
        using Configuration Manager
            to manage BitLocker Drive
            Encryption (BDE), 228–229
        Windows 7 vs. Windows
            10/11, 224–227
    updating device drivers, 370–379
    using Device Manager, 366–370
Hardware tab (Properties dialog
    box), 345–346
Health Monitoring, Azure AD Connect
    (Azure AD Dashboard), 631–632
hexadecimal, 456–457
Hibernate power state, 283
hibernation, configuring, 286
high availability, 599
High Performance power plan,
    284, 285

Histogram view (Performance Monitor),
515, 516
`HKEY_CLASSES_ROOT`, 531–532
`HKEY_CURRENT_CONFIG`, 532
`HKEY_CURRENT_USER`, 532
`HKEY_LOCAL_MACHINE`, 532
`HKEY_USERS`, 532
home folders, setting up, 119–120, 124–126
Hybrid Azure AD Join, 672
hybrid networks
about, 625
Azure Active Directory pass-through
authentication, 626
Azure AD Connect, 631–638
common identity scenarios, 630–631
federation with Azure AD, 627–630
managing, 625–638
password hash synchronization with
Azure AD, 625
Hyper-V
about, 9, 303–304
changing configuration on virtual
machines, 311–313
configuring checkpoints, 320–321
deleting virtual machines, 313
enabling role, 304–305
generations, 321–322
managing
checkpoints, 320–321
virtual hard disks, 318–319
virtual switches, 314–316
on Windows client, 303–322
opening Hyper-V Manager, 305–311
system requirements for, 304
Hyper-V Administrator role, in Windows
Admin Center, 181

I

ICMP (Internet Control Message
Protocol), 446
identifying required updates, 701–702

identity and access
about, 586
Active Directory (AD) *vs.* Azure Active
Directory (Azure AD), 586–624
answers to review questions, 855–858
configuring Enterprise State Roaming in
Azure AD, 638–639
exam essentials, 648–649
implementing Conditional Access
policies, 639–645
managing hybrid networks, 625–638
planning Conditional Access
policies, 639–645
review questions, 650–653
using PowerShell commands, 645–647
video resources, 649
Identity Governance section (Azure AD
Dashboard), 610
Identity Protection, 729
Identity Secure Score (Azure AD
Dashboard), 616
identity sensors, 750
IGMP (Internet Group Management
Protocol), 446
IIS_IUSRS group, 130
IKEv2 (Internet Key Exchange
Version 2), 183
imaging
choosing strategies for, 549–550
preparing installations for, 67–69
implementing
app protection, 706–708
assigned access on public devices, 738
Conditional Access policies, 639–645
Endpoint Protection, 749–751
Microsoft Defender for
Endpoint, 759–761
PXE Boot using Windows Deployment
Services (WDS), 569–573
`import` command, 46
inbound rules, 403–406
Indexing Options, 265
Informational alert, 686

Infrared option, 265
inheritance, managing, 208
Initial User account, 96
`initializer-server` command, 58
InPrivate Browsing, 293, 297
insights, 545, 548
Inspect Disk tool, 318
installing
    Active Directory, 590–591
    Azure AD Connect (Azure AD
        Dashboard), 632–633
    client-side extension (CSE) in
        computers, 163–164
    device drivers, 370–379
    LAPS, 161–162
    Microsoft Store updates, 83–84
    printers, 387–390
    troubleshooting, 43–45
    Windows 10, 25–41
    Windows 11, 41–47
    Windows Client (*see* Windows Client)
    Windows Sandbox, 326–327
    XPS Viewer app, 246–247
instances, 513
Interactive group, 131
internal network, 315
Internet browsers
    about, 291
    Compatibility mode, 294–295
    configuring, 291–303
    configuring Internet options, 297–303
    controls for, 293
    Cortana, 291–292
    Enhanced Security mode in Microsoft
        Edge, 295–296
    InPrivate Browsing, 297
    pinning sites to taskbar, 293
    searchable address bar, 293
    security and privacy
        enhancements, 293
Internet Control Message Protocol
    (ICMP), 446
Internet Explorer 11, 10

Internet Group Management Protocol
    (IGMP), 446
Internet Key Exchange Version 2
    (IKEv2), 183
Internet Options, 265
Internet Properties dialog box, 265, 297–303
Internet Protocol (IP)
    about, 450
    testing configuration, 467–468
Intra-Site Automatic Tunnel Addressing
    Protocol (ISATAP), 451, 461
Intune Administrator role, 607, 666
Investigation Phase (Microsoft Defender for
    Identity), 750
`Invoke-Command` command, 188
I/O devices
    about, 381
    configuring removable storage
        devices, 381–385
    deleting printers, 397–398
    managing
        about, 381–401
        documents, 393–397
        printers, 385–393
    Print Management tools, 398–401
iOS
    configuration policies, 708–710
    creating app protection policies
        (APPs), 707–708
    enrolling, 673–675
    onboarding tool options for, 762
IP (Internet Protocol)
    about, 450
    testing configuration, 467–468
IP addressing, 447–452
IP Security Policies on Local Computer, 141
iPadOS
    configuration policies, 708–710
    creating app protection policies
        (APPs), 707–708
    enrolling, 673–675
`ipconfig` command, 467
IPv4 addresses

about, 448–449
address classes, 449–450
subnet mask, 450–452
IPv6 addresses
about, 450–456
assignment, 457
format, 456–457
information commands for, 462–463
integration/migration, 460–462
shortcuts, 457
types, 458–460
ISATAP (Intra-Site Automatic Tunnel
Addressing Protocol), 451, 461
isolated cryptography, of smart cards, 167
IT Group Properties dialog box, 133–134

K

KCD (Kerberos constrained delegation), 588
Kerberos Authentication
about, 588
support for, 598
Kerberos constrained delegation (KCD), 588
kernel control, using Device Guard for, 112
Keyboard properties, 265
Kiosk settings, 729

L

L2TP (Layer 2 Tunneling Protocol), 183
languages, 25
LAPS (Local Administrator Password
Solutions), 159–164
Layer 2 Tunneling Protocol (L2TP), 183
LBA (Logical Block Addressing), 339–340
LDAP integration, 599
license administrator role, 607
Licenses section (Azure AD Dashboard), 610
Line view (Performance Monitor), 514, 515
linear logging, 521
link-local address, 458–459

Link-Local Multicast Name Resolution
(LLMNR) protocol, 426
Linux Server, onboarding tool options
for, 762
List Folder Contents permission, 206
Lite Touch Installation (LTI), 567
LiteTouch.log file, 573
LLMNR (Link-Local Multicast Name
Resolution) protocol, 426
Local Administrator Password Solutions
(LAPS), 159–164
local disk properties, viewing, 343–349
Local Group Policy Objects (LGPOs)
applying, 138–140
managing
about, 138–140
security using, 135–155
local groups, built-in, 127–130
local policies
about, 141
using, 147–155
Local Security Authority Subsystem Service
(LSASS), 104
local user accounts, 97–98
Local Users and Groups utility, 98–100
Lock Screen setting, 254
Log On tab (Properties dialog box), 289
logging off, 98
Logic Apps, 807
Logical Block Addressing (LBA), 339–340
logon scripts, setting up, 119–120, 123–124
logs, 800
LSASS (Local Security Authority Subsystem
Service), 104
LTI (Lite Touch Installation), 567

M

macOS, onboarding tool options for, 762
Mail properties, 266
Maintaining Access Phase (Microsoft
Defender for Identity), 750

MAK (Multiple Activation Key) license
    management, 550–551
malware, using Device Guard for, 113
malware ads, 751
MAM (Mobile Application Management)
    Azure AD Dashboard, 612
    using, 697–698
Managed Service Accounts, 588
managing
    administrative hard disk tasks, 341–355
    application deployment, 571–572
    Azure Active Directory (Azure
        AD), 602–616
    BitLocker Drive Encryption (BDE) using
        Configuration Manager, 228–229
    certificates on client devices, 475–478
    checkpoints, 320–321
    credentials by using Credential
        Manager, 157–159
    desktop environment, 241–251
    Device Guard, 113–114
    device security using policies, 756–758
    devices with Microsoft Intune, 656–687
    documents, 393–397
    driver deployment, 571–572
    dynamic storage, 355–358
    Endpoint Security in Microsoft
        Intune, 752–756
    file and folder security, 198–211
    group membership, 133–135
    groups, 127–135
    hybrid networks, 625–638
    Hyper-V on Windows client, 303–322
    I/O devices, 381–401
    LGPOs, 138–140
    network access, 211–220
    Performance Monitor options, 517–519
    permission inheritance, 208
    power consumption using Battery
        Meter, 288
    power states, 283–284
    printers, 385–393
    security baselines, 752–755
    security using GPOs and LGPOs, 135–155
    shared folders, 211–213
    storage, 355–358
    user properties, 117–126
    virtual hard disks, 318–319
    virtual switches, 314–316
    Windows, 240–279
    Windows 10/11 services, 288–290
    Windows 10/11 with Backup and
        Restore, 498–505
    Windows client environment, 240–334
    Windows Security, 408–411
mandatory profiles, 121–122
mandatory updates, 702
Maps app, 244, 245
Master Boot Record (MBR), 24
MBAM (Microsoft BitLocker Administration
    and Monitoring), 227–228
*MCSA Windows Server 2016 Complete Study
    Guide: Exam 70-740, Exam 70-741,
    Exam 70-742 and Composite Upgrade
    Exam 70-743, 2nd Edition* (Panek), 77,
    97, 136, 166
MDM (Mobile Device Management)
    about, 10
    Azure AD Dashboard, 612
    device compliance policies and, 723
    migrating policies to, 727
MDM-Only Enrollment, 672
MDOP (Microsoft Desktop Optimization
    Pack), 228
MDT (Microsoft Deployment Toolkit)
    about, 48–54, 567
    configuration options, 568–569
    planning deployments, 567–568
    User State Migration (USMT),
        573–576
    Windows Deployment Services
        (WDS), 569–573
Mechanical Off power state, 283
MEM (Microsoft Endpoint
    Manager), 542–544
member servers, 425, 589

MEMCM (Microsoft Endpoint Manager
    Config Manager), 227
memory, measurements for, 20
Merge action, 319
Merge-CIPolicy command, 114
Merge-VHD command, 324
message center reader role, 608
metering, 694–695
metrics, 544, 800
MFA (multifactor authentication), 165
Microsoft
    Azure (*see Azure entries*)
    product updates, 79
    System Center Configuration
        Manager, 113
    website, 43
Microsoft 365 apps
    configuring, 692–694
    deploying, 691
Microsoft BitLocker Administration and
    Monitoring (MBAM), 227–228
Microsoft Defender Application
    Guard, 771–780
Microsoft Defender Application Guard
    Enterprise Mode, 777–780
Microsoft Defender Application Guard
    Standalone Mode, 772–776
Microsoft Defender Credential
    Guard, 780–783
Microsoft Defender Exploit Guard,
    783–787
Microsoft Defender for Endpoint
    implementing, 759–761
    monitoring, 763
    planning deployment for, 761–763
Microsoft Defender for Identity, 750–751
Microsoft Deployment Toolkit (MDT)
    about, 48–54, 567
    configuration options, 568–569
    planning deployments, 567–568
    User State Migration (USMT),
        573–576
    Windows Deployment Services
        (WDS), 569–573

Microsoft Desktop Optimization Pack
    (MDOP), 228
Microsoft Edge
    about, 10, 245, 247
    Enhanced Security mode in, 295–296
Microsoft Endpoint Manager
    (MEM), 542–544
Microsoft Endpoint Manager Config
    Manager (MEMCM), 227
Microsoft Intune
    about, 656
    answers to review questions, 858–862
    benefits of, 658
    configuring
        alerts, 686–687
        bulk enrollment in, 682
        connector site, 686
    creating
        policies, 671–672
        users in, 668–671
    deploying
        applications using, 687–694
        software updates using, 699–705
    enrolling devices using, 672–681
    exam essentials, 711–712
    managing
        devices with, 656–687
        Endpoint Security in, 752–756
    PowerShell commands, 710–711
    review questions, 713–718
    sideloading applications using, 688–690
    supporting applications, 687–698
    updates, 699–710
    using
        to deep-link applications, 694
        to Restart, Retire, or Wipe
            devices, 684–685
    video resources, 712
Microsoft Management Console (MMC)
    about, 227, 340, 475, 595–596
    adding snap-ins, 272
    configuring modes, 271–272
    using, 270–272
Microsoft Passport, 10

Microsoft Store app, 83–84, 247
Microsoft Store for Business, 10
migrating policies to MDM, 727
Miracast, 9
MLGPOs (Multiple Local Group Policy Objects), 138
MMC (Microsoft Management Console)
  about, 227, 340, 475, 595–596
  adding snap-ins, 272
  configuring modes, 271–272
  using, 270–272
Mobile Application Management (MAM)
  Azure AD Dashboard, 612
  using, 697–698
Mobile Device Management (MDM)
  about, 10
  Azure AD Dashboard, 612
  device compliance policies and, 723
  migrating policies to, 727
mobility options
  about, 279
  configuring
    about, 279–288
    offline files and
      synchronization, 279–281
  configuring Power Options, 281–288
modes (MMC), 271–272
Modify permission, 205–206
monitoring
  app information and
    assignments, 817–818
  Azure device security, 809–813
  deployment, 572–573
  devices
    device compliance, 725–727
    device configuration profiles, 734–735
    using Endpoint Analysis, 818–819
    using Endpoint Manager Admin
      Center, 813–818
  discovered apps, 816
  Event Viewer, 526–530
  Microsoft Defender for Endpoint, 763
  Performance Monitor, 511–521
  Reliability Monitor, 521–522

  Task Manager, 522–526
  Windows, 511–532
  Windows Registry, 531–532
  Windows Update, 81
Monitoring section, 407
Mount-VHD command, 324
Mouse Cursor settings, 255
Mouse properties, 266
Move-VM command, 324
multibooting, 45–46
multicast address, 448–449, 459
multifactor authentication (MFA), 165
Multiple Activation Key (MAK) license
  management, 550–551
Multiple Local Group Policy Objects
  (MLGPOs), 138
Music shortcut, 251

N

NAT (Network Address Translation), 451
NDP (Neighbor Discovery Protocol), 459
Neighbor Discovery Protocol (NDP), 459
neighbor solicitation (NS), 459
netsh command, 462, 468
network access
  about, 211
  cloud-based storage, 214–215
  configuring
    OneDrive, 215–220
    share permissions, 213–214
  creating shared folders, 211–213
  managing
    about, 211–220
    shared folders, 211–213
network adapters. *see* network interface
  cards (NICs)
Network Address Translation (NAT), 451
Network and Sharing Center properties, 266
Network Configuration Operators
  group, 130
network connectivity
  about, 420

answers to review questions, 843–846
basics of, 420–427
configuring
   NIC devices, 427–445
   VPN clients, 470–478
exam essentials, 479
review questions, 480–484
Transmission Control Protocol/Internet
   Protocol (TCP/IP), 445–470
video resources, 479
Network group, 131
network interface card (NIC) devices
about, 427
configuring
   about, 427–445
   NICs, 428–433
   Wi-Fi Direct, 442–445
   wireless, 434–442
troubleshooting NICs, 434
network interface cards (NICs)
configuring, 428–433
troubleshooting, 434
Network List Manager Policies, 141
Network tab (Manage Offline Files), 281
Network Unlock, 223–224
networks
cloud-based Azure Active Directory, 424
configuring Windows client on, 468–470
domain-based, 422
on-site Active Directory, 422–423
peer-to-peer, 420–421
requirements for, 553
new command, 59
New Group dialog box, 132
New User dialog box, 102–103
New-AzureADAdministrativeUnit
   command, 646
New-AzureADApplication
   command, 710
New-AzureADApplication
   ExtensionProperty
   command, 710
New-AzureADApplication
   PasswordCredential
   command, 710

New-AzureADDirectory
   Setting command, 646
New-AzureADObject
   Setting command, 646
New-AzureADPolicy command, 647
New-CIPolicy command, 114
New-CIPolicyIdInfo command, 114
New-CIPolicyRule command, 114
New-EventLog command, 278
New-LocalGroup command, 188
New-LocalUser command, 188
New-PSSession command, 188
New-PSSession
   ConfigurationFile
   command, 188
New-Service command, 278
New-VHD command, 324
New-VM command, 324
New-VMGroup command, 324
New-VMSwitch command, 324
NIC (network interface card) devices
about, 427
configuring
   about, 427–445
   NICs, 428–433
   Wi-Fi Direct, 442–445
   wireless, 434–442
troubleshooting NICs, 434
NICs (network interface cards)
configuring, 428–433
troubleshooting, 434
non-exportability, of smart cards, 166
non-Microsoft updates, 702
Notepad app, 247
NS (neighbor solicitation), 459
NTFS
configuring, 361–365
filesystems, 360
as requirement for Active Directory, 591
NTFS permissions
applying, 205–207
determining
   about, 208–210
   for copied or moved files, 211
viewing, 208–210

O

objects
    changing permissions, 163
    configuring, 616–619
ODT (Office Deployment Toolkit),
    configuring Microsoft 365 apps
    using, 692–694
Office Customization Tool, configuring
    Microsoft 365 apps using, 692–694
Office Deployment Toolkit (ODT),
    configuring Microsoft 365 apps
    using, 692–694
Offline Files, configuring, 279–281
offlineServicing, 74
OMS (Operations Management Suite), 809
onboarding, tool options for, 762
128-bit address space, 452
OneDrive
    configuring, 215–220
    recovering files from, 501–502
OneDrive app, 245
one-way trusts, 628
Online /Enable-Feature /All
    /FeatureName:Microsoft-
    Hyper-V command, 73
on-site Active Directory networks, 422–423
OOBE (out of the box), 566
oobeSystem, 74
Open Systems Interconnection (OSI)
    model, 427
opening Hyper-V Manager, 305–311
operating system (OS), 568
Operations Management Suite
    (OMS), 809
operator, 810
Organizational Units (OUs), 599
OS (operating system), 568
OSI (Open Systems Interconnection)
    model, 427
OUs (Organizational Units), 599
out of the box (OOBE), 566
outbound rules, 403–406

outdated patches, 751
Overview section (Azure AD
    Dashboard), 602–603
Overwrite command, 71
ownership descriptors, 208

P

PackagePath command, 71
packages, 568
Paint app, 247
Panek, William (author)
    *MCSA Windows Server 2016 Complete
    Study Guide: Exam 70-740, Exam
    70-741, Exam 70-742 and Composite
    Upgrade Exam 70-743, 2nd Edition*,
    77, 97, 136, 166
partitions
    creating, 349–351
    deleting, 354–355
pass-through authentication, Azure Active
    Directory (Azure AD), 626
Password Administrator role, 608, 666
password hash synchronization, with
    Azure AD, 625
password policies, setting, 142–144
Password Reset section (Azure AD
    Dashboard), 613–614, 619–621
passwords
    assigning permissions to groups for
        access to, 163
    changing for users, 110–111
PAT (Port Address Translation), 451
Patch Tuesdays, 75
patches, outdated, 751
paths, changing, 353–354
pausing updates, 80
Peer Name Resolution Protocol (PNRP), 168
peer-to-peer networks, 420–421
People app, 245
Performance Log Users group, 130
Performance Monitor, 511–521

Performance Monitor Users group, 130
performance objects, 513
Performance tab (Task Manager), 523
permissions
    assigning to groups for password
        access, 163
    determining for NTFS, 208–210
    Endpoint Analytics built-in role, 546
    managing inheritance, 208
    NTFS, 205–207
    share, 213–214
    viewing for NTFS, 208–210
Personal Identity Verification (PIV) Standard,
    165, 229–230
personal preferences, configuring, 258–259
personalization, configuring, 251–259
per-user device sync status, viewing, 639
phishing, 751
Phone and Modem properties, 266
Pictures app, 251
pinning websites to taskbar, 293
PINs, 111
PIV (Personal Identity Verification) Standard,
    165, 229–230
planning
    Conditional Access policies, 639–645
    deployment for Microsoft Defender for
        Endpoint, 761–763
    device compliance policies, 723–727
    Endpoint Protection, 749–751
    Microsoft Deployment Toolkit (MDT)
        deployments, 567–568
    PXE Boot using Windows Deployment
        Services (WDS), 569–573
    user state migration, 573–576
    Windows client deployment, 542–551
PNRP (Peer Name Resolution
    Protocol), 168
Point-to-Point Tunneling Protocol
    (PPTP), 183
policies
    duplicating, 758–759

managing device security using, 756–758
Microsoft Intune, 671–672
policy sets, configuring, 682–684
pop-up blocker, 300
Port Address Translation (PAT), 451
port numbers, 405, 427
Ports tab (Printer Properties dialog
    box), 391–392
Power BI
    administrator role, 608
    Azure Monitor, 807
Power button, configuring, 285–286
Power Management tab (Properties dialog
    box), 432, 433
Power Options
    about, 266
    configuring, 281–288
power plans, configuring, 284–285
Power Saver power plan, 284, 285
power states, managing, 283–284
Power Users group, 130
powercfg command, 286–287
PowerShell
    Azure AD commands, 645–647
    commands for administrators, 710–711
    commands for Hyper-V, 322–328
    common commands for, 187–188
    enabling remoting, 182
    using, 186–188, 277–279
PPTP (Point-to-Point Tunneling
    Protocol), 183
Preboot Execution Environment
    (PXE), 56–57
prefix notation, 457
preparing, for installation, 14–25
pre-provisioning, 554, 556
prerequisites, for Windows Sandbox, 326
Preview Features section (Azure AD
    Dashboard), 603
Previous Versions tab (Properties dialog box),
    346, 348
Print Management tools, 398–401

Printer Properties dialog box, 391–393
printers
    configuring, 390–393
    deleting, 397–398
    installing, 387–390
    managing, 385–393
Privacy tab (Internet Properties dialog
        box), 298–300
private network, 315
privilege elevation, 156–157
privileged role administrator role, 608
Processes tab (Task Manager), 522–523
processors, 13–14
profiles
    changing security baselines for, 755–756
    VPN, 471–473
    Windows Autopilot, 559–562
Programs and Features, 266
Programs tab (Internet Properties dialog
        box), 302
promotion, 591
properties
    device, 369–370
    of Windows Sandbox, 326
Properties dialog box, 212,
        288–290, 369–370
Properties section (Azure AD
        Dashboard), 614
protection. *see* security and protection
provisioning
    applying packages, 302–303
    BitLocker, 222–223
    user accounts, 665
    Windows devices using
        Autopilot, 563–564
Public Key Policies, 141
PXE (Preboot Execution
        Environment), 56–57
PXE Boot, planning using Windows
        Deployment Services (WDS), 569–573

Q

quality updates, 79, 702
Quick Assist, 176–180

Quick Removal policy, 384–385
quotas, 363–365
Quotas tab (Properties dialog box), 348–349

R

RAID (Redundant Array of Independent
        Disks), 337
ransomware, 751
Read & Execute permission, 206
Read permission, 206, 214
Reader role, in Windows Admin Center, 181
read-only domain controllers (RODC),
        590, 591
realm trusts, 628
recommendations, 548
recommended actions, 545
Reconnect action, 319
recovery
    about, 267–268, 486–488
    answers to review questions, 846–850
    exam essentials, 533
    of files from OneDrive, 501–502
    maintaining Windows 10/11 with Backup
        and Restore, 498–505
    monitoring Windows, 511–532
    review questions, 534–538
    startup/boot options, 488–498
    techniques for, 487–488
    using System Protection, 505–511
    video resources, 533
Recovery tab (Properties dialog box), 289
Recycle Bin, 510–511
Redundant Array of Independent Disks
        (RAID), 337
REGEDIT command, 259
Region tool, 268
regions, 25
Registry, 531–532
Registry virtualization, 165
reject-autoadddevices command, 59
Related Settings section, 273
Reliability Monitor, 521–522
Remote Assistance, 168
Remote Desktop, 168, 173–176

Remote Desktop Connection program, 247
Remote Desktop Users group, 130
remote management
    about, 167–168
    Broadband Tethering, 185–186
    configuring, 167–186
    configuring VPN connections, 182–185
    Easy Connect, 168–173
    enabling PowerShell remoting, 182
    Quick Assist, 176–180
    Remote Assistance, 168
    Remote Desktop, 173–176
    transparent caching, 185
    Windows Admin Center, 180–181
RemoteApp and Desktop Connections, 268
removable storage devices,
        configuring, 381–385
remove command, 58
Remove-AzureADAdministrativeUnit
    command, 647
Remove-AzureADAdministrative
    UnitMember command, 647
Remove-AzureADApplication
    command, 710
Remove-
    AzureADApplicationExtension
    Property command, 711
Remove-AzureADApplicationOwner
    command, 711
Remove-AzureADApplicationPassword
    Credential command, 711
Remove-AzureADDirectorySetting
    command, 647
Remove-AzureADObjectSetting
    command, 647
Remove-AzureADPolicy command, 647
Remove-
    AzureADScopedRoleMembership
    command, 647
Remove-Driver command, 72
Remove-EventLog command, 278
Remove-LocalGroup command, 188
Remove-LocalUser command, 188
Remove-VHDSnapshot command, 324
Remove-VM command, 324

Remove-VMHardDiskDrive
    command, 324
Remove-VMNetworkAdapter
    command, 324
Remove-VMReplication command, 324
Remove-VMSan command, 324
Remove-VMSwitch command, 324
Rename-Computer command, 278
Rename-LocalGroup command, 188
Rename-LocalUser command, 188
Rename-VM command, 325
Rename-VMGroup command, 325
renaming user accounts, 109–110
Replicator group, 130
Report view (Performance Monitor),
        515, 516
reportnow, 83
reports (Microsoft Intune), 705–706
reports reader role, 608
requirements
    Active Directory (AD), 590–591
    Device Health Attestation, 116–117
    Endpoint Analytics, 545–546
    for Enterprise State Roaming, 638
    hardware, 552
    for Hyper-V, 304
    for installing Local Administrator
        Password Solutions (LAPS), 160–161
    for networking, 553
    for software, 553
    Windows Autopilot, 552–557
    for Windows Client, 18–20
resetauthorization, 83
Resize-VHD command, 325
Resources tab (Properties dialog box),
        432, 433
Restart, using Intune to, 684–685
Restart-Computer command, 278
Restart-Service command, 278
Restart-Vm command, 325
restore points
    about, 505–506
    cleaning up, 507–508
    creating, 506
    restoring, 507

restoring
    credentials using Credential Manager, 159
    files from backups, 500–501
    restore points, 507
    system images, 504–505
Resultant Set of Policy (RSoP), 137
`Resume-Service` command, 278
Retire, using Intune to, 684–685
review question answers
    data management, 833–835
    deployment (Windows client), 850–855
    device management, 862–864
    identity and access, 855–858
    Microsoft Intune, 858–862
    network connectivity, 843–846
    recovery, 846–850
    storage and devices, 840–843, 865–868
    user configuration, 830–833
    Windows client, 828–830, 836–840
    Windows monitoring, 869–872
review questions
    data management, 232–237
    deployment (Windows client),
        578–593
    device management, 742–745
    identity and access, 650–653
    Microsoft Intune, 713–718
    network connectivity, 480–484
    recovery, 534–538
    storage and devices, 413–417
    user configuration, 191–195
    Windows client, 88–92, 330–334
    Windows monitoring, 821–825
roaming profiles, 121
RODC (read-only domain controllers),
    590, 591
roles, in Windows Admin Center, 181
Roles and Administrators section (Azure AD
    Dashboard), 606–608
`route` command, 462
RSoP (Resultant Set of Policy), 137
Run box, 250

S

Safe Mode
    as a recovery technique, 487
    starting in, 489–492
`Save-VM` command, 325
saving data with performance logs/
    alerts, 519–521
Scanning Phase (Microsoft Defender for
    Identity), 750
Schannel (Secure Channel), 105
scores, 548
Scriptname`*.log` file, 573
Search tab (Folder Options/File Explorer
    Options dialog box), 202–203
searchable address bar, 293
Secure Boot, 9, 115–116
Secure Channel (Schannel), 105
Secure Socket Tunneling Protocol (SSTP), 183
Secure Sockets Layer (SSL), 293
security administrator role, 608
Security and Maintenance utility, 268
security and protection
    enhancements for Internet browsers,
        293
    hardware (*see* hardware, security)
    managing
        for files and folders, 198–211
        using GPOs and LGPOs, 135–155
    NTFS, 361
    updates for, 702
    Windows 10, 6–8
security audits, 589
security baselines
    changing, 755–756
    managing, 752–755
    troubleshooting, 759
security descriptors, 208
security identifiers (SIDs), 61–62, 104–105
security reader role, 608
Security section (Azure AD Dashboard),
    614, 615

Security tab
    Internet Properties dialog box, 298, 299
    Printer Properties dialog box, 393
    Properties dialog box, 346, 347
Select Users dialog box, 134
selecting
    branch readiness level for feature
        updates, 80
    filesystems, 358–359
    imaging and/or provisioning
        strategies, 549–550
selective authentication, 628–629
Self-Deploying Mode, 554–555
self-service password reset, 619–621
servers
    about, 424, 589
    Domain Name Service (DNS), 425–426
    Dynamic Host Configuration Protocol
        (DHCP), 426
    member, 425, 589
    stand-alone, 425, 589–590
Service group, 131
service packs, 702
Service Support Administrator role, 608, 666
services, managing, 288–290
Services tab (Task Manager), 525–526
set command, 46, 58
Set-AzureADApplication
    command, 711
Set-AzureADDirectorySetting
    command, 647
Set-AzureADObjectSetting
    command, 647
Set-AzureADPolicy command, 647
Set-CIPolicyIdInfo command, 114
Set-CIPolicyVersion command, 114
Set-HVCIOptions command, 114
Set-LocalUser command, 188
Set-ProductKey:<productKey>
    command, 73
Set-RuleOption command, 114
Set-TimeZone command, 278

setting
    account-lockout policies, 144–147
    Administrator accounts, 665–681
    audit policies, 148–150
    domain names, 598
    password policies, 142–144
    quotas by user, 364
    quotas by volume, 363–364
Settings app, 248
Settings window, 273–277
Setup.exe command, 66–67
Set-VHD command, 325
Set-VM command, 325
Set-VMBios command, 325
Set-VMMemory command, 325
Set-VMNetworkAdapter command, 325
Set-VMProcessor command, 325
Set-VMReplicationServer
    command, 325
Set-VMSan command, 325
Set-VMSwitch command, 325
shadow copies, 506
share permissions, configuring, 213–214
Share Permissions dialog box, 213–214
shared multiuser devices, 729
SharePoint administrator role, 608
Sharing tab
    Printer Properties dialog box, 391
    Properties dialog box, 346, 347
shortcut trusts, 629–630
Shut Down or Restart button, 251
sideloading
    about, 676
    applications using Intune, 688–690
SIDs (security identifiers), 61–62, 104–105
sign-in problems, troubleshooting, 644
simple deployment, 597
simple volumes
    about, 338
    creating, 355–356
single-app kiosk, setting up on Windows
    10/11, 738–740

site-to-site VPN connection, 633–634
6to4 technique, 452, 461–462
64-bit processors, 13–14
Skype for Business administrator role, 608
Sleep power state, 283
smart cards
    about, 165–167
    domain login, 230
    using, 229–230
SmartScreen Filter, 293
SMSTS.log file, 573
snap-ins, adding, 272
Snipping Tool, 247
Soft Off power state, 283
software
    deploying updates using Intune, 699–705
    requirements for, 553
Software Restriction Policies, 141
Sound option, 268
Source tab (Performance Monitor), 517–518
spanned volumes
    about, 338–339
    creating, 355–356
special groups, 130–131
Special Permissions, 206–207
specialize, 74
specifying quota entries, 364–365
Speech Recognition tool, 268–269
speed, of processors, 14
SSL (Secure Sockets Layer), 293
SSTP (Secure Socket Tunneling Protocol), 183
stand-alone sensors, 750
stand-alone servers, 425, 589–590
standard user accounts, 95
Standard User PIN and Password
    Change, 223
start command, 59
Start Menu, 10
Start section, for personalization, 256–258
Start-Process command, 278
Start-Service command, 278
Startup Repair tool
    as a recovery technique, 487
    using, 498

Startup tab (Task Manager), 523
startup/boot options
    about, 488–489
    enabling Boot Logging, 492–494
    starting in Safe Mode, 489–492
    Startup Repair tool, 498
    Startup Settings menu, 494–495
    system image recovery, 497–498
    System Restore, 495–496
stateful autoconfiguration, 452–453
stateless autoconfiguration, 452–453
Sticky Notes app, 248
stop command, 59
Stop-Computer command, 279
Stop-Service command, 279
Stop-VM command, 325
storage and devices
    about, 336
    answers to review questions,
        840–843, 865–868
    configuring
        disk storage, 336–340
        hardware, 365–381
        NTFS, 361–365
        Windows Defender Firewall, 401–407
    exam essentials, 412
    filesystems, 358–361
    managing
        about, 355–358
        I/O devices, 381–401
        storage, 355–358
        Windows Security, 408–411
    review questions, 413–417
    using Disk Management utility,
        340–355
    video resources, 412
Storage Sense, 508–510
Storage Spaces, 269
store command, 46
StoreFile command, 71
StormWind Studios, 60
striped volumes
    about, 339
    creating, 355–356

subnet mask, 450
Subscription Activation/MAK license
    management, 550
Subscription Properties dialog box, 530
subscriptions
    Event Viewer, 529
    Microsoft Intune, 658–664
super-mandatory profiles, 123
support
    for applications, 687–698
    for broadband connectivity, 694–695
    for existing devices, 554, 557
Support section, 273
Suspend-VM command, 325
Sync Center, 269, 280–281
synchronizing
    configuring, 279–281
    data, 695–697
Sysprep, switches for, 61
System Center Operations Manager, 808–809
System feature, 269
System group, 131
system images
    creating, 503–504
    recovery of, 497–498
    restoring, 504–505
System Preparation Tool
    about, 59–63
    preparing installations for imaging
        with, 67–69
System Protection
    about, 505–506
    cleaning up old restore points,
        507–508
    creating restore points, 506
    enabling, 495
    Recycle Bin, 510–511
    restoring restore points, 507
    Storage Sense, 508–510
System Restore
    as a recovery technique, 488
    using, 495–496
System Settings, 272–273
System utilities, 249–250

T

Task Manager, 250, 522–526
task sequences
    about, 569
    creating, 569–571
taskbar, pinning websites to, 293
Taskbar and Navigation tool, 269
Teams communications administrator
    role, 608
Teams communications support engineer
    role, 608
Teams communications support specialist
    role, 608
Teams device administrator role, 608
technical flow, 563–564
Tenant Administrators, 666
Teredo Tunneling, 452, 461, 462
Terminal Server User group, 131
Test-Connection command,
    279
testing IP configuration, 467–468
tethering, broadband, 695
themes, personalization, 254–256
32-bit processors, 13–14
This PC shortcut, 250
threat intelligence, 750
timeout command, 46
Tips app, 245, 246
TLS/SSL (Schannel SSP), 589
Tools tab (Properties dialog box), 345
TPM (Trusted Platform Module),
    166, 221–222
tracert command, 468
transitive trusts, 627
Transmission Control Protocol/Internet
    Protocol (TCP/IP)
    about, 445–446
    basic of IP addressing and
        configuration, 447–452
    benefits and features of, 446–447
    configuring on Windows 10, 463–467
    configuring Windows client on
        networks, 468–470

as requirement for Active Directory, 591
testing IP configuration, 467–468
troubleshooting, 468
using IPv6 addresses, 452–463
transparent caching, 185
trees, 422–423
troubleshooting
    about, 269
    Autopilot deployments, 564–566
    Conditional Access, 643–645
    deployment, 572–573
    device configuration profiles,
        734–735, 736–737
    device enrollment, 565–566
    device import, 565–566
    Endpoint Security baselines, 759
    installation, 43–45
    network interface cards (NICs), 434
    sign-in problems, 644
    Transmission Control Protocol/Internet
        Protocol (TCP/IP), 468
    updates, 704
    user account authentication, 126–127
    using What If tool, 644–645
    wireless connectivity, 444–445
Trusted Platform Module (TPM),
    166, 221–222
trusts, 423, 627–630
tunneling, 182, 460, 461–462
two-way trusts, 628

U

UAC (User Accounts Control) Control Panel
    option, 101
UDI (User-Driven Installation), 567
UDP (User Datagram Protocol), 446
UEFI (Unified Extensible Firmware
    Interface), 322
UGMC (Universal Group Membership
    Caching), 586

unassigned code, using Device Guard
    for, 113
unattended installations
    about, 54–56
    deployment of, 66–74
UNC (Universal Naming Convention)
    path, 124
unicast address, 449, 458
Unified Extensible Firmware Interface
    (UEFI), 322
`uninitialized-server` command, 58
unique local address, 459
Universal Group Membership Caching
    (UGMC), 586
Universal Naming Convention (UNC)
    path, 124
`update` command, 59
update rollups, 702
updating
    about, 699
    Active Directory schema, 162–163
    deferring, 79–80
    deploying software updates using
        Intune, 699–705
    device drivers, 370–379
    implementing app protection and app
        configuration policies, 706–710
    Microsoft Store, 83–84
    pausing, 80
    troubleshooting, 704
    using Intune compliance reports, 705
    using Intune reports, 705–706
upgrading
    basic disks to dynamic or GPT
        disks, 351–353
    installing compared with, 20–24
    to Windows 10 from Windows 8.1, 36–41
    to Windows 11 from Windows 10, 43
Used Disk Space-Only Encryption, 223
user accounts
    about, 94–95, 270
    built-in accounts, 96–97

changing user passwords, 110–111
configuring control of, 155–165
creating new users, 101–106
deleting, 108–109
disabling, 107–108
domain, 97–98
local, 97–98
provisioning, 665
renaming, 109–110
types of, 95
using Local Users and Groups
    utility, 98–100
using User Accounts option in Control
    Panel, 100
working with, 98–117
User Accounts Control (UAC) Control Panel
    option, 101
User Administrator role, 608, 666
user configuration
about, 94
answers to review questions, 830–833
configuring
    remote management, 167–186
    user account control, 155–165
exam essentials, 189
managing
    and creating groups, 127–136
    security using GPOs and
        LGPOs, 136–155
    user properties, 117–126
review questions, 191–195
smart cards, 165–167
troubleshooting account
    authentication, 126–127
user accounts, 94–117
using PowerShell, 186–188
video resources, 190
User Datagram Protocol (UDP), 446
user flow, 564
User mode, 271
user profiles, setting up, 119–123
user properties

about, 117
managing, 117–126
managing user group
    membership, 117–119
setting up
    home folders, 119–120, 124–126
    logon scripts, 119–120, 123–124
    user profiles, 119–123
user rights policies, assigning, 151–155
User Settings section (Azure AD
    Dashboard), 614
User State Migration Tool (USMT), 573–576
User-Driven Installation (UDI), 567
User-Driven Mode, 554
usernames, rules and conventions
    for, 103–104
users
    creating in Microsoft Intune, 668–671
    elevated privilege for, 156–157
    setting quotas by, 364
Users group, 130
Users section (Azure AD Dashboard), 604
Users tab (Task Manager), 523
User's tools, 251
USMT (User State Migration Tool), 573–576
utilities, Windows System, 249–250

V

`Variables` command, 71
VHD (virtual hard drive), 25, 41
video resources
    data management, 231
    deployment (Windows client), 577
    device management, 741
    identity and access, 649
    Microsoft Intune, 712
    network connectivity, 479
    recovery, 533
    storage and devices, 412
    user configuration, 190

Windows client, 87, 329
Windows monitoring, 820
Videos shortcut, 251
View tab (Folder Options/File Explorer
    Options dialog box), 199, 202
viewing
    conflicts, 735–736
    devices, 810–811
    disk properties, 342–343
    effective permissions for NTFS, 208–210
    local disk properties, 343–349
    performance information, 514–516
    per-user device sync status, 639
    volume properties, 343–349
    wireless network connection
        details, 437–438
    wireless network connection
        status, 436–437
virtual hard disks, managing, 318–319
virtual hard drive (VHD), 25, 41
virtual LAN (VLAN), 315
virtual machines (VMs)
    about, 303–304
    changing configuration on, 311–313
    deleting, 313
virtual networks, 314–316
virtual private network (VPN) clients
    about, 470
    configuring
        about, 470–478
        certificates on devices, 475–478
    connecting to, 473
    Connection Manager Administration Kit
        (CMAK), 474–475
    creating profiles, 471–473
virtual smart cards, 9
Virtual Switch Manager, 314–316
virtual switches, managing, 314–316
virtualization-based security, 115
VLAN (virtual LAN), 315
VM Insights, 804–807
VMs (virtual machines)

about, 303–304
changing configuration on, 311–313
deleting, 313
volume properties, viewing, 343–349
volumes
    creating, 349–351
    deleting, 354–355
    setting quotas by, 363–364
Volumes tab (Properties dialog box), 343
VPN (virtual private network) clients
    about, 470
    configuring
        about, 470–478
        certificates on devices, 475–478
    connecting to, 473
    Connection Manager Administration Kit
        (CMAK), 474–475
    creating profiles, 471–473
VPN connections, configuring, 182–185

W

Warning alert, 686
wbadmin command, 502–503
WBAdmin utility, 502–503
WCD (Windows Configuration Designer)
    about, 64, 739
    creating disk images using, 69–71
WDAC (Windows Defender Application
    Control), 787–788
WDS (Windows Deployment Services)
    about, 56–59, 589
    planning PXE Boot using, 569–573
WDSUTIL command, 58–59
websites
    Microsoft Azure, 214
    pinning to taskbar, 293
What If tool, troubleshooting using, 644–645
Wi-Fi Direct, configuring, 442–444
Windows
    managing, 240–279

monitoring, 511–532
onboarding tool options for, 762
Windows 7/8/8.1, 22–23, 36–41, 224–225
Windows 10
  accessories, 247–248
  adding to domain, 469–470
  applications, 244–247
  architecture of, 13–14
  configuring
    TCP/IP on, 463–467
    to use DHCP, 465–466
  Control Panel in, 260
  controlling Windows Update Delivery
    Optimization in, 82
  data protection in, 224–227
  feature updates for, 702–705
  features, 9–10
  installing, 25–41
  location of deployment utilities and
    resources for, 65
  maintaining with Backup and
    Restore, 498–505
  managing services, 288–290
  security and protection, 6–8
  setting up single-app kiosk on, 738–740
  unattended deployment options for, 65
  updates, 8
  upgrading
    from Windows 8.1 to, 36–41
    to Windows 11 from, 43
  using Quick Assist in, 177–180
  Windows 11 compared with, 11–12
Windows 10 Education, 15
Windows 10 Enterprise E3/E5, 17–18
Windows 11
  accessories, 247–248
  adding to domain, 469–470
  applications, 244–247
  architecture of, 13–14
  configuring to use DHCP, 465–466
  Control Panel in, 260
  controlling Windows Update Delivery
    Optimization in, 82–83

data protection in, 224–227
feature updates for, 702–705
features, 9–10
installing, 41–47
location of deployment utilities and
  resources for, 65
maintaining with Backup and
  Restore, 498–505
managing services, 288–290
new features in, 12–13
setting up single-app kiosk on, 738–740
unattended deployment options for, 65
upgrading from Windows 10 to, 43
using Quick Assist in, 177–180
Windows 10 compared with, 11–12
Windows 11 Education, 15
Windows Activation, 47
Windows Admin Center, 180–181
Windows Assessment and Deployment Kit
  (Windows ADK), 63–64
Windows Autopilot
  about, 551–552
  configuring device registration
    for, 557–558
  deploying with, 551–566
  Diagnostics page, 566
  profiles, 559–562
  provisioning Windows devices
    using, 563–564
  requirements, 552–557
  troubleshooting deployments, 564–566
Windows Autopilot Reset, 554, 555–556
Windows client
  about, 4–8, 240
  answers to review questions,
    828–830, 836–840
  configuring
    delivery optimization, 704–705
    Internet browsers, 291–303
    mobility options, 279–288
    on networks, 468–470
  deploying (*see* deployment (Windows
    client))

exam essentials, 86–87, 329
managing
    environment, 240–334
    Hyper-V on, 303–322
    Windows, 240–279
    Windows 10/11 services, 288–290
PowerShell commands, 322–328
requirements for, 18–20
review questions, 88–92, 330–334
video resources, 87, 329
Windows Configuration Designer (WCD)
about, 64, 739
creating disk images using, 69–71
Windows Defender Application Control
    (WDAC), 787–788
Windows Defender Credential
    Guard, 114–116
Windows Defender Firewall
about, 270
with advanced security (WFAS), 403–407
configuring, 401–407
Windows Deployment Services (WDS)
about, 56–59, 589
planning PXE Boot using, 569–573
Windows devices, enrolling, 676–677
Windows Ease of Access Tools/Accessibility
    Settings, 248–249
Windows Enterprise, 16–17
Windows Fax and Scan app, 248
Windows Firewall with Advanced
    Security, 141
Windows Hello
about, 10
using, 111
Windows Home, 15
Windows IoT Core Dashboard, 672
Windows Media Player app, 248
Windows Mobility Center, 270
Windows monitoring
about, 798
answers to review questions, 869–872
Azure device security, 809–813
cloud-based tools, 799–809

exam essentials, 820
review questions, 821–825
by using Endpoint Analytics, 818–819
by using Endpoint Manager Admin
    Center, 813–818
video resources, 820
Windows PE, 74
Windows phones, enrolling, 676
Windows PowerShell, 113–114
Windows Pro, 15–16
Windows Recovery Environment
    (WinRE), 489
Windows Registry, 531–532
Windows Sandbox, 325–328
Windows Security
about, 748–749
Endpoint Security, 751–759
implementing
    Endpoint Protection, 749–751
    Microsoft Defender for
        Endpoint, 759–771
managing, 408–411
Microsoft Defender Application
    Guard, 771–780
Microsoft Defender Credential
    Guard, 780–783
Microsoft Defender Exploit
    Guard, 783–787
planning Endpoint Protection,
    749–751
using Windows Defender Application
    Control, 787–788
Windows Server Update Services (WSUS),
    74, 76–77
Windows Specifications section, 273
Windows System Image Manager, creating
    answer files using, 73–74
Windows System utilities, 249–250
Windows Tools (Windows 11), 261
Windows Update
about, 74, 246
Delivery Optimization, 81–83
monitoring, 81

process of, 75–76
using
   about, 76–78
   for business, 78–80
   command-line options, 83
Windows Update Automatic Update Client
   (wuauclt.exe), 83
Windows User's tools, 251
WinRE (Windows Recovery
   Environment), 489
Wipe, using Intune to, 684–685
wireless network connections
configuring
   security, 439–442
   settings, 435
   troubleshooting, 444–445
viewing
   details, 437–438
   status, 436–437
Wireless Network Properties dialog
   box, 441–442
wireless NIC devices, configuring,
   434–442

Wizard.log file, 573
Work Folders, 270
workbooks (Azure Monitor), 805, 806
workgroups, 97, 420
Working power state, 283
Workplace Join, 98
WPEinit.log file, 573
Write permission, 206
Write-EventLog command, 279
WSUS (Windows Server Update Services),
   74, 76–77

X

XML Paper Specification (XPS)
   documents, 166
XPS Viewer app, 246

Z

Zero Touch Installation (ZTI), 567

Online Test Bank

To help you study for your MCA Modern Desktop Administrator certification exams, register to gain one year of FREE access after activation to the online interactive test bank—included with your purchase of this book! All of the practice questions in this book are included in the online test bank so you can study in a timed and graded setting.

Register and Access the Online Test Bank

To register your book and get access to the online test bank, follow these steps:

1. Go to www.wiley.com/go/sybextestprep. You'll see the "How to Register Your Book for Online Access" instructions.
2. Click "here to register" and then select your book from the list.
3. Complete the required registration information, including answering the security verification to prove book ownership. You will be emailed a pin code.
4. Follow the directions in the email or go to www.wiley.com/go/sybextestprep.
5. Find your book on that page and click the "Register or Login" link with it. Then enter the pin code you received and click the "Activate PIN" button.
6. On the Create an Account or Login page, enter your username and password, and click Login or, if you don't have an account already, create a new account.
7. At this point, you should be in the test bank site with your new test bank listed at the top of the page. If you do not see it there, please refresh the page or log out and log back in.